SPORT IN EARLY CALGARY

SPORT IN EARLY CALGARY

William M. McLennan

Best wishes Dave,
Bill McLennan
1985

FORT BRISEBOIS PUBLISHING

Contents

Preface

Sport in Early Calgary may be considered a compilation of recorded sports activity, personalities and sports facilities in Calgary and the surrounding area. This pandest contains much trivia, but hopefully every reader will find some satisfaction in the material. An attempt was made to use the vocabulary, names and phrases of the era and the activity written about. In some instances there will be more than one spelling of a name and some of the statistics may be questionable, but it is not for me to take literary license.

Most of the information found in the following pages has been gleaned from the following newspapers: Fort Benton River Press, Fort Benton Weekly Record, Calgary News-Telegram, Calgary Albertan, Calgary Herald, Fort Macleod Gazette, Medicine Hat News, Lethbridge News, Lethbridge Herald, Edmonton Journal, Edmonton Bulletin, Red Deer Advocate, Banff Crag and Canyon, High River Times, Eye Opener and The Vancouver Sun.

This book is dedicated to those individuals and groups who have given myself and countless youths their time, effort and inspiration to partake in and enjoy sports as they should be played—for the fun and satisfaction of playing and participating.

My thanks to the Glenbow and Provincial Archives and the University of Calgary microfilm department. Special appreciation for the countless hours of typing done for me by Margaret Moffat and Hazel Lenz.

Golf

Golf was introduced to Canada by Scottish officers in General Wolfe's army. The game was reported to have been played on the outskirts of Toronto in the 1860's. In 1873 the Royal Montreal, North America's first golf club, was officially organized.

Golf was reported to have been played at Fort Macleod in 1890. The game was played in Calgary by 1893 on an area north of Notre Dame (17th) Avenue. The course was unofficially known as Buffalo Wallow.

In the fall of 1895 a nine hole golf course was laid out near the police barracks at Fort Macleod. The following year the club was offered a cup by Dr. Hamilton to be awarded monthly to the player who had shot the best round during the month. In the same year the Hudson's Bay Company put up the Chipman Cup for annual competition for the amateur championship of southern Alberta. Later the Macleod course was set aside on Mondays for the exclusive use of the ladies.

In the spring of 1896 a five hole course was laid out in Edmonton by R. Butlan on a site that was later to become Victoria Park links. A course was established in Medicine Hat in 1899.

The Calgary Golf Club was formally organized in 1896. A small club house was constructed near the first hole, located west of the present Fourth Street West, north of Seventeenth Avenue.

In March of 1898 a meeting was held in C.S. Lott's office to reorganize the Calgary Golf Club. The Hon. Justice Scott was elected club president and Horace Harvey served as secretary-treasurer. Membership fees were set up at three dollars for men and a dollar for ladies.

Before the season had ended 33 gentlemen and 15 ladies had paid their fees. Many improvements were made to the course including the completion of a better clubhouse. This was the scene of golf teas on several summer Saturdays.

The 1898 club champion was Mr. Grieve, who shot an 83 for eighteen holes of play. Mrs. Scott and E. Vincent were the ladies' and men's handicap winners, while Miss McCullough and Mr. Wilson's score of 43 for nine holes gave the pair the mixed foursome title. Other events included putting, approach, driving with cleek and driver.

There was a large crowd at the March, 1899 golf meeting in Mr. Lott's office with president Scott occupying the chair. Horace Harvey served as secretary-treasurer for the second term, and W. Toole was elected captain. Cash receipts from the previous year had been $157 and there was an eleven dollar cash balance. A dollar entrance fee was set for new members in view of the improvements made to the course and paid for the previous year. Special country rates for those living beyond a five mile radius of Calgary were two dollars for gentlemen and 50¢ for ladies.

The nine hole course began with a 305 yard first hole, then there were distances of 224, 117, 275, 134, 244, 187, 193, and the ninth hole was 212 yards long.

In June of 1899 the golf season opened with the Harding Tournament and a tea. During the summer button tournaments were held as a lead up to the club championships to be held in October. Jeweller L. Doll donated a cup for the ladies' competition. Other prizes were to be offered by Mr. Scott, M. Mackie, Alderman VanWart and the Herald.

In the three day club championship Justice Scott lost six up with four holes to go in men's championship competition to D. Tobler of the Bank of Montreal staff. The winners' style was unique as he used his lofter in putting and he did not tee up his ball. Mrs. Scott's 63 for nine holes was the low score for the seven lady competitors. W. McKenzie and Miss Cardell were the mixed foursome winners, Mrs. Harris and H. Supple the men's handicap winners.

W. Toole, the putting champion, took the driving competition with a distance of 182 yards, while E. Vincent's 151 yards was tops in driving with a club. Miss McCulloch was the ladies' approach winner, and she also won the ladies' driving competition with a distance of 111 yards.

Christmas Day of 1899 saw several foursomes touring the course in summer-like weather.

Members of the Calgary Golf Club, October 1899. Judge Scott and J. Young are third and ninth from the right.

In April of 1900 it was reported that A.H. Goldfinch, a well known Calgary area rancher had won the Bostock Cup and the championship of British Columbia.

The 1900 annual meeting of the Calgary Golf Club was held in the Herald Block with President Justice Scott in the chair. H. Morgan was elected secretary-treasurer and G. Toller the team captain. Horace Harvey, club secretary for the last two years, had moved to Regina. A five member ladies committee was elected.

The question of moving the links was discussed, but it was decided to retain the present land for a year. There was discussion in respect to the construction of a tennis court beside the clubhouse. Plans were made for weekly button handicaps and monthly tournaments. Mr. Scott planned on presenting buttons for the weekly competition.

Medal play began in early June and continued through the summer. Saturday teas were part of the club's social program.

An expanded program of the club championships was planned for October. Events were to include: men's and ladies' championships, men's and ladies' handicap, foursome, men's and ladies' driving with cleek and driver, putting, approach shots and mixed foursomes. Unfortunately the planned competition was left too late in the season and bad weather caused a cancellation.

Justice Scott was again elected to the Calgary Golf Club presidency at the 1901 annual meeting held in the Herald Block. V.P. Critchley became the club vice-president and O. Toller the secretary-treasurer. Club captain was Major Saunders. The question of an annual tournament for Alberta was discussed. Although the six lots where the clubhouse was situated had been bought for fifteen dollars each, a new site for the course was to be inspected as extensive building and development was taking place south of the railroad tracks and the links would have to be moved sometime in the future. Annual membership for ladies was reduced to 50¢, and the entrance fee for new members also that amount.

In May Mrs. Scott presided over tea at the formal opening of the links. The course had been redesigned to make the layout more difficult, and the nine hole course was now about 3,000 yards in length. Each of the holes had been appropriately named. Judge Scott shot a 41 for low score in opening day competition.

Again the club was unable to complete the club championships.

The 1902 annual golf meeting was held in Molson's Bank, but as club president Scott was moving from the city, little was accomplished. Further improvements were made to the links by groundskeeper Rhodes, but no major golf competition took place in Calgary during the year.

The 1903 Calgary Golf Club organizational meeting, held in Nolan's room of the Herald Block, was well attended. M.L.A. J. Young was moved to the chair, and J. Edgar, manager of the Bay, was the new secretary. The 29 paid-up members set up plans to reorganize the club. It was felt that the commodious clubhouse, now fitted with lockers, could play a greater role in the sport and social life of the city. Late in April the club's official season opening saw Mrs. Sutherland and Mrs. McCulloch preside at the tea table. Many of Calgary's society were reported to have attended the function.

If there was any major golf competition in Calgary during 1903 the results were not made public.

By 1904 Hossacks, a new Calgary store, competed with Alex Martin in selling sporting goods, including golf supplies.

It was obvious at the April golf meeting, chaired by vice-president Hogg, that many members of Calgary's golf fraternity had moved from the city, however there were 15 new members in the club.

Another meeting, held in the stock yards office, saw John Hall elected club president and Mr. Cooke the club captain. There was just $22 in the treasury, but there would be a deficit as the club had purchased lots around the clubhouse, now located west of Fourth Street.

It was decided to prepare the first green with a rolled dirt surface to determine if this would be any improvement over the turf greens which were difficult to keep in good shape. The links were measured and were found to be 2293 yards long. The links extended over that portion of the escarpment that was later to be known as American Hill.

During the season attempts were made to hold inter-city matches with Edmonton players.

Mrs. Hall and Mrs. Sutherland presided over the refreshment table at the official opening of the links in May. The following weekend a handicap tournament was held, and this level of event was the extent of the golf competition held in Calgary during 1904.

By 1905 Calgary newspapers were carrying the results of American and British golf competition.

Jack Dixon opened up a livery stable adjacent to the golf club house. The horses found grazing on the links to their liking, but the golfers were not so happy. The club house of that era was said to be situated in the 500 block of Sixteenth Avenue, however no Sixteenth Avenue exists in that area today.

A small club tournament was held on the links in July. This was the extent of competition during the year.

In late fall the members of the golf club held several important meetings to look into the incorporation of the golf club, and as a result a board of trustees was set up. At that time club membership totalled 34, and the bank balance was reported at $72.57.

Over the winter a new constitution and a set of bylaws were drawn up. By the following summer it was hoped to have an up-to-date clubhouse, good links, tennis court and bowling green. The philosophy behind the Calgary Golf Club was to encourage, not only golf, but other forms of athletics. The club held the deed of sale for four lots where the clubhouse stood, and it was felt that the organization had the potential to develop into a golf and country club.

John Hall was elected club president for 1906. V.P. was H. Hogg and H. Downey was secretary-treasurer. Mr. Downey had once finished seventh out of 154 golfers, including some of the world's best, in a Florida tournament.

The club roster had grown to 57 members, and with increased participation and enthusiasm came more Saturday competitions. The nineteenth hole proved very popular for a cup of tea.

Calgary was in the midst of growth and expansion and the land occupied by the links was within the path of city development. Land for a new course was located in the future Elbow Park area on land formerly occupied by the Owens race track and adjacent to the polo field. A nine hole course was set up on this land north of the Elbow River, with part of the course extending up the hillside, so ideally the course had hills, ravines, and some long straight fairways. Over $600 was spent on improvements to the layout.

The U shaped clubhouse was pleasantly situated beside a grove of trees, and the view from the second hole looked down over the polo field. G. McCullough was hired as manager of the course.

By June the Calgary Golf Club carried 57 members. H. Downey sent a course record of bogey 37 for the nine holes and 77 for a double round. The spring tournament was a success, with C. Hague, formerly of Utica, New York, shooting a 99 to beat out 13 other competitors. Tea was served at the clubhouse every Saturday afternoon. The press, who published a weekly golf column, reported that golf was definitely established as a sport in Calgary.

In August Downey, with a two stroke handicap, beat Hague, a zero handicap player, one up in a 36 hole match. A letter was sent to the Edmonton Golf Club challenging it to send a team of six to ten members to play an 18 hole match, but the Edmonton players did not come to Calgary during the 1906 season.

An enthusiastic assemblage attended the annual golf meeting held in the Herald Block in early May of 1907. O. Severs was elected club president, H. Downey as vice-president and C. Hague as secretary-treasurer. Twenty-seven men and four women were admitted as new members, and because the club did not possess permanent links the initiation fees were eliminated. The old club grounds in Elbow Park were offered for use by owners Ross and Cornwall, and G. McCullough was retained as course manager.

The golf season opened with a sweepstakes handicap and a tea. A. Duffis, shot a 101 minus his 24 stroke handicap to score a net of 77 and beat out 15 other competitors. Handicap sweep competition took place several times during the season. When a last minute cancellation of a visit by a team of Edmonton players took place Mr. Severs team played Mr. Duffis's team instead.

In September C. Hague defeated H. Downey in the finals of the unofficial provincial golf championship. Mrs. W. Clarke, playing from scratch, shot a 70 to capture the ladies' crown. In long drive competition W. Denton hit for 210 yards and first place. Downey's drive was for 206 and Hague hit for 198 yards. More than $300 worth of prizes were presented at the tea, presided over by Mrs. Severs, following the competition.

During the year the Calgary newspapers carried a considerable amount of international golf news. Trophies offered for competition in Calgary during the era included: Watson Brothers for men's handicap, Doll Cup, the Hudson's Bay Company Cup and the Jackson Cup.

In May of 1908 President W. Clark reported that the club had accepted 27 new members. Other club officers were Vice-president Downey and Secretary Govan. The official opening of the links took place May 23.

In a three ball game played at the club in August George Shaw was successful in breaking Hague's course record of 39 with a 37. Miss J. Pinkham, with a 15 stroke handicap captured the ladies' tournament with a net score of 46, while A.

Craddock, whose handicap was 18, shot a 35 to claim the men's handicap tournament. Hague and Shaw each shot a 40, while Miss N. Polkinghorn's score of 53 was low gross for the ladies.

The Calgary Golf Club held the 1908 provincial championships on their links from September 17 to the 21. This tournament was held under the auspicies of the newly formed Alberta Golf Association (A.G.A.) For the event a large marquee was built beside the clubhouse and a large flagpole erected.

Nineteen men, including six players from Edmonton, each played two rounds with their best score for each hole to count towards the sixteen qualifying positions. 36 holes of match play were to follow the qualifying rounds.

F. Wilson's 87 was the low qualifying score, while the highest number of strokes needed by any competitor was 114. In further competition Shaw shot a 76, the best round ever on the course, to earn him the Young Cup. In the men's final Hague, to the surprise of many, defeated Shaw on the 35th hole after a see-saw battle and earned him the provincial title.

The ladies played two 18 hole rounds, and in the finals of this event Miss Brown of Edmonton defeated Mrs. Clarke, the local favourite.

Besides winning the approach competition Shaw's 270 yard drive gave him the honours in the long drive competition. Miss Mathieson's drive of 160 yards proved best in the ladies' competition.

Miss Polkinghorn and Mr. Arison captured the mixed foursome title. Other competition included: ladies' and gentlemen's handicap play against bogeys, and putting competition. Mrs. P. Burns acted as hostess at the tea table.

The Calgary Golf Club selected Mr. Shaw to represent Calgary at the Edmonton golf championships in October. Before a gallery of about 200 people he defeated Bell in the finals two and one. Miss Brown captured the McKay Cup in the ladies competition, and Calgary's Nora Polkinghorn won the ladies' putting and the handicap bogey competition. The Edmonton Club was reported to have so many female members that the links were reserved for the men on Saturdays.

During the season C. Hague won honours in competitions held in Chicago and Seattle.

The Alberta golfing fraternity had hopes of sending a team of six players to the Canadian championships the following year.

In April of 1909 the Calgary Golf Club's executive approved the use of the new rules of the Royal and Ancient Club of St. Andrews. These rules basically dealt with scoring, playing the wrong ball, the order of play, and replaced revisions last made in 1902.

The new club executive consisted of President W. Clark, V.P.D. Young and Secretary Green. It was reported that there was a balance of $2,800 in the club treasury, which helped to give an indication of a successful season. Seven club trustees were elected, and in view of the fact that there would be future development of the land utilized for the club links, they would be inspecting sites for future use of the club.

The spring tournament took place June 12, with men's singles, mixed foursome and putting events. Tea was served by Mrs. Young and Miss Pinkham.

The 1909 Alberta golf championships were held in Edmonton from September

3-7. In the first round Calgarian C. Hague defeated F. Wilson two and one, and G. Shaw overwhelmed J. Reid eight up with seven holes to play, but W. Ross lost his match. In the second round Shaw defeated Bell nine and seven, but Hague lost 3-2 to Sinclair. In the semi-final Shaw continued to show his skills with a 6-5 win over Chattell. His play was just as spectacular in the championship match when he posted an overwhelming 10 up with 9 holes to play win over Dr. C. Cobbett.

Miss Cobbett of Edmonton defeated Miss Lyall of Strome 4-2 to take the Alberta ladies championship and the McKay Cup. In the club match the Calgary team, after a close match, defeated Edmonton by two points.

It was hoped that the Edmonton club would send down a team to compete in Calgary's autumn meet in October, but Edmonton was not represented. During the tournament a motor car supplied transportation from the Alberta Hotel to the links in both the morning and afternoon, returning downtown at 6 p.m. Street cars at this time only travelled as far as Mission Bridge.

The tournament began with 18 holes of medal play, with the eight lowest scores to qualify to compete for a challenge cup and medals. Twelve players entered this competition, with W. Kidd's 82 the low score in the qualifying round. In the semi-finals Shaw won his match, and Downey won on the 22 green from G. Govan. In the final, played on a windy and rainy day, Shaw was five up on Downey by the seventh hole, but Downey came back and by the end of the second round he was one up, with his 39 for the round being the low tally for any nine holes in the tournament. Downey was still one up after 27 holes, but in the last round Downey had a drive ruined when a dog ran in front of him. The ball was topped, the hole lost, and Shaw went on to win the match two up and the Calgary championship.

Mrs. Helm was a surprise winner in the ladies' handicap event, shooting a 65, but her 25 stroke handicap gave her a net of 40. Men's foursome competition was won by W. Ross and G. Romanes, while P. Shaw was the men's driving champion. D. Young and Mrs. Helm were the approaching event winners, and Mrs. Brown was first in the ladies' driving event. W. Ross and A. Mahon each, after handicap, carded 78's in medal sweep competition. C. Hague shot an 80 to beat out P. Shaw by one stroke for the club prize.

In gentlemen's bogey sweep competition G. Romains, with a handicap of nine, shot a net of 38 to take first place. Art Lowes, a newcomer to Calgary and a tremendous athlete, looked good in his first golf competition.

Hostesses during the tournament included Mrs. W.R. Hull, Mrs. Young, Mrs. Jamieson, Miss Winter and Miss Lake. Except for the poor weather conditions the club considered this tournament a success.

On the international scene team matches were played between Canada and the U.S.A.

Meanwhile the club trustees had been looking at various properties in the Calgary area for the future links of the club. In late November at a meeting extraordinary the club decided to purchase 110 acres of land at $100 an acre from the C.P.R. land department, who was reported to have given the club a good price. Several different pieces of land had been considered but this area was ideal, being located in a bend of the river, with enough hills and vegetation to make an ideal golf course.

The management committee of the golf club plus additional members were designated as a finance committee to devise a way of paying for the land. It was expected to locate a country club there, but a golf course was the chief pursuit of the members.

In April of 1910 the members of the golf club met and elected D. Young to the chair, and F. McBeth, A. McMahon and M. Botter as other executives. The club reported a membership of close to 150 persons.

Scenes of the Calgary Golf Club in Elbow Park, 1908.

It was decided not to do anything with the new grounds until the following year, and it was hoped to raise $50,000 by the following spring to complete the course and a new clubhouse. Plans were made to reorganize the club under the name of the Calgary Golf and Country Club. The old links in Elbow Park would be utilized for the 1910 season, so new greens and handicap committees were organized. Initiation fees for 1910 were reduced to $5, while annual dues were left at $10.

The golf club held its formal opening on June 18 with ladies' and gentlemen's nine hole handicap events, and mixed foursome play. G. Shaw proved to be the most skillful among the large number of competitors, winning the men's competition as well as the driving event. Miss Downey took first place in the ladies' putting competition, and H. and Mrs. Steele came out on top in the mixed foursome event.

During the summer Shaw travelled to eastern Canada to compete in the Canadian championships, and Hague went to Winnipeg where he made a good showing in the Manitoba championship competition.

Button competitions were held at the club during the summer weekends. Some of the winners were A. Watson, Art Lowes, and G. Bergson.

In September a group of Calgarians travelled to Edmonton to play in its club tournament, unfortunately much of it taking place in pouring rain. G. Dacre of Calgary, with an 87-14-73 score, won the men's open handicap championship. Miss Cobbett captured the ladies' championship and the McKay Cup. In the finals of the men's championship Mr. Hunter defeated Calgary's Forbes-Wilson for the title. Mr. and Mrs. Heathcote were the mixed foursome winners.

The third annual Alberta Golf Championship was held at the Calgary club's links. Charles Hague was in charge of all entries and the draws. The rules of play were the rules of golf as approved by the Royal and Ancient Golf Club of St. Andrews, except those as modified by the executive committee.

The competition began with a qualifying round of medal play divided into three flights of 18 hole match play; first flight open to all, second open to eight who fail to qualify in first eight of qualifying round, third flight open to all who failed to qualify in the second round.

G. Govan's 89 was four strokes better than Hague's score in the qualifying round, but Hague went on to the finals where he defeated Parker 5 and 4 to capture the provincial title.

The ladies' championship was 18 holes medal play. In the finals of this event, with competition for the Watson Brothers cup, Miss Campbell beat Miss Downey three up. Mrs. Clarke took the honours in the ladies' putting competition.

F. Wilson took first place in both approaching and putting competition, while Hague's 260 yard drive was good for first place in the long distance event. In duffers competition R. Smith beat J. Watson two and one, and G. Bull was the winner of the men's handicap event.

Mrs. P. Nolan and Mrs. Newbolt had served as the hostesses during the final day of the tournament. In the evening more than 200 couples attended a club dance held in the Sherman Hall.

The Calgary newspapers covered the events well and published many pictures of the competition. During this era retailer Alex Martin advertised, "the largest and most complete selection of golf goods in the west". Ladies golf cloaks were in style for daily wear and were being sold by Calgary retailers.

The 1910 club competition saw C. Hague take the Young Cup for the men's championship; Miss Campbell won the ladies' championship and the Hudson Bay Trophy; the Herald Challenge Cup for the men's handicap event went to A. Russel, and Miss Sparrow held the F. Lowes Cup for the ladies' handicap event.

The Calgary Golf and Country Club came into incorporation in December of 1910. The philosophy of the club was, "to promote the physical welfare of its members and encourage the game of golf, tennis, bowling and other games, hunting; or any form of exercise, and for social purposes. . . .". The annual fee for resident shareholders was set at $40, or if the member's residence was more than ten mile from Calgary—$15. An entrance fee of $10 was set for lady associate members and annual dues of $15. Annual fee for juniors was set at $5. Fees for guests, payable in advance, were 50¢ a round or 18 holes, a dollar a day, or $5 a week.

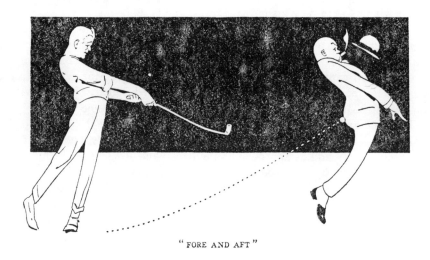

" FORE AND AFT "

In March of 1911 the board of management of the Calgary Golf and Country Club went carefully over the links laying out a nine hole and a possible 18 hole course. "The grounds were considered to be ideal of the umps and oilers, the price of the English golfer in the old country." Plans were made to have a $5,000 club house designed to be constructed in the valley. 2,000 pounds of grass seed were ordered prior to the actual work on the course began.

Tom Bendelow of New York was engaged to lay out the new course. Later he proposed that the city should open a municipal links, and this suggestion was endorsed by the city fathers.

At another spring meeting of the golf club members it was reported that the club roster now numbered over 200, and that almost $30,000 had been subscribed. In April the assets of the old club were transferred to the new club. Plans for the new clubhouse and a set of impressive gates were on the drawing board.

Gordon Downie of Northumberland, England was engaged as groundsman and club professional. Ideal weather had allowed extensive use of the old links since early March by many golfers, but they were anxious to get on the new course. The Herald published a calendar of international golf events.

In the spring golf tournament J. Edgar shot a 99-32 for a net of 67 to take the handicap competition over twenty other players. In match play Art Lowes defeated Dacre on the 18 hole to take first place in that event. The first of the weekly buttom competitions began in July.

Club secretary McMahon travelled to Banff several times in connection of the laying out of the new links at the C.P.R. hotel. Mr. Thompson of Winnipeg had been engaged as its club professional. The Banff course was officially opened July 22 by H. Douglass, National Parks Commissioner. There were many guest players from Calgary, Edmonton and Lethbridge involved in the opening day play.

During the summer newspaper readers in Calgary were able to view a column that gave points on how to play golf.

On October 7, 1911 the official opening of the new links of the Calgary Golf and Country Club took place. The event was reported on the society page rather than in the sports section of the newspapers. Visitors from Granum, Fort McLeod and Edmonton were impressed with the course and the beautiful clubhouse.

The large front doors led into the reception room with its huge fireplace, mission oak chairs, couches and a piano. There was a smoking room, dining room, open and enclosed porches, and dressing rooms and showers in the basement. Plans were for a billiard room to be installed in the dormitory.

Mr. and Mrs. Young were the hosts for the Saturday opening. Many of the players and guests attended the lavish evening dinner. Informal discussion led the way to an intention to again form an Alberta golf association.

Competition at the club opening included: ladies' handicap, mixed foursomes, and gentlemen's competition. There were 14 greens ready for play by this time. The debut of the new course was considered a success.

The club championship was held in October under ideal fall weather conditions. Mrs. Bates captured the ladies' handicap event with a 76-24-52 score to take home the F.C. Lowes Cup. Miss Polkinghorn of Millarville had low gross with a 61 score, but in the championship play Mrs. Downey beat her on the nineteenth hole to take the Hudson's Bay Trophy.

Eight male golfers succeeded in making the course, adjusted to eighteen holes, in less than 100 strokes. C. Hague had the low gross, shooting an 86. In the men's finals for the club championship and the Young Cup he beat Dacre eight up.

Mr. McCallum's score of 220-72-148 for 36 holes gave him the men's handicap title and the Herald Cup. In the mixed foursome final A. Toole and Miss Robertson lost to Dacre and Mrs. Sutherland.

The following week Blue Ribbon events were held at the Country Club. The foursome competition consisted of nine holes of medal play with four teams to qualify, then nine holes and eighteen hole match play. In the finals Dacre and Sutherland defeated Hague and Miss Meyer. The Crawford Trophy, for the Blue Ribbon putting competition, was won by H. Maber.

Calgary's population was growing steadily, and so were the number of people in the city who wanted to golf. In April of 1912 there was a crowded meeting of golf enthusiasts in the offices of Broomfield and Sellar in the Alexander Block, and there and then a new golf club, to be later named the Calgary St. Andrews Golf Club, was created. E. Riley offered to lend this group a piece of land located north-west of Calgary to be utilized for the links. It was planned to limit the club roster, soon up to 120 names, to 250 people.

E. Riley was named honourary president; W.T. White was the club's first president, and W. Sellar served as secretary treasurer. Dues were set at ten dollars for men and five dollars for ladies. Membership tended toward those individuals with a recent British background.

An eighteen hole course was laid out on the bluffs overlooking the Bow River valley, and soon a clubhouse with a veranda on three sides was constructed.

Good weather during the spring of 1912 saw the Country Club's links in constant use. By the May first official season opening of the links the club membership was up by over 50 people from the previous year. The hill had been contoured and electric light and power added to the facilities. Water lines had been laid to each of the greens. Plans were on the drawing board to construct tennis courts, bowling greens and croquet lawns.

Hugh Hamilton, a scratch player of the Royal and Ancient Golf Club of St. Andrews, Scotland was engaged as a professional at the Calgary Golf and Country Club. The club held a spring handicap competition on Victoria Day. M. Butler and H. Mober tied for first in the men's handicap event, but Hague and Downey, playing from scratch, both shot exceptional 67's. Mrs. McMahon's 110-32-78 gave her the ladies' handicap event, and Miss Wheatley had the low gross score. Miss Winter and F. Wilson won the mixed foursome against bogey event.

A letter was received from the Lethbridge golfers inviting Calgarians to play in the southern city in July.

The captain's and vice-captain's teams played to a seven-all draw in Victoria Day competition at the new St. Andrews course, following the official club opening by Captain White. He then went on to shoot an 83, the best round of the day.

In July Mayor Mitchell formally opened the St. Andrews clubhouse. 23 players participated in a club handicap tournament, with W. Gibbon posting a 91-10-81 to capture the Captain's prize and the club gold button that had been put for weekly competition by Mr. Davidson.

During the month an eight man Calgary team, led by Dacre and McMahon, travelled to Lethbridge to defeat its golf team 10-8 in the team match, but tie in the foursome event.

There were many prizes donated to the Calgary Golf and Country Club's July tournament. 57 local entries and fifteen or so from outside the city entered the men's handicap event. There were nine scratch players, while handicaps ranged as high as 60 strokes for the 28 hole event. A. Sclater was the winner of the handicap event, while Hague and Wilson tied for the best gross score for a 14 hole round, each shooting a 64.

The Alberta Golf Association, with representatives from Lethbridge, Fort Macleod, Edmonton and the two local clubs met in Calgary, where it was decided to hold the provincial competition at the Calgary Golf and Country Club in late August. Besides amateur competition there would be a 36 hole open class with first and second prizes of $50 and $25.

From a news point of view the Alberta championships were overshadowed by the Calgary Stampede. There were many close games during the competition with the Hague-Dacre match going to the 21 hole, while two other matches had to be carried to the 19 hole. In the final C. Hague defeated fellow Calgarian F. Wilson to take home the Cross Trophy.

W. Barrett, the Lethbridge golf professional, was the 1912 winner of the Alberta open golf championships, shooting a score of 159 for 36 holes. G. Downie was runner-up, three strokes behind. Hague's 167 was good for sixth place; Dacre and St. Andrew's White each shot an 180.

The Calgary Country Club held its 1912 club championships in October. Many prizes were donated for the various events, but unfortunately the tournament was interrupted by poor weather.

Mrs. Pryce-Jones took 12 shots to sink her three balls to take the ladies' putting event. In men's putting F. Wilson and Hague each needed nine strokes, but Hague won in a playoff. Miss Sparrow hit for 175 yards, and F. Denton's 240 yards was the furthest drive in the distance competition.

In the 36 hole medal play men's handicap event for the Herald Cup M. Fraser shot a 192-50-142 to take first place. Mrs. Sparrow won the Lowes Cup in the ladies' competition, and as well the Hudson Bay Cup and a silver card case. Mrs. McMahon, runner-up in ladies competition, teamed with her husband to take the club mixed foursome title.

Hague was the champion and F. Denton the runnerup in the club championship. A new large silver cup for this event replaced the previous trophy that had been won outright by Mr. Hague.

Following what was considered a successful year the St. Andrews Club held its fall tournament with over 100 competitors taking part. During the tournament S. McCulloch shot a 35-46 for an 81 to lower the course record and capture the club prize. W. Tait White and Mrs. G. Wheatley were winners in the scratch competition and V.P. Searson's Cups. Later J. Walker lowered the course record to 78.

The Davidson Cups for novice play went to Miss Hental and J. Walker, while H. Davis captured the Black Challenge Cup in men's handicap.

Mr. Riley presented the prizes at the tea following the events. Vice-president Searson, dubbed, "Father of the club", was given due credit for his work and effort in getting St. Andrews in operation.

On Christmas Day of 1912 golf competition took place at the St. Andrews Club for prizes presented by G. and A. Macleod.

In May of 1912 Jackson Walton of Edmonton represented Canada at the world amateur championship tournament in St. Andrews, Scotland. He was eliminated in the first round six up with five holes to play.

The St. Andrews Club held its spring competition on Victoria Day, with the new Moffat Trophy up for the handicap competition. Later in the season F. Scholey captured another new trophy, the Black Cup.

The Calgary Golf and Country Club acquired a new professional in the person of H. Turpie of Chicago and New Orleans. His presence was such that many club members got more involved in the game of golf.

In the club's spring tournament Charles Sclater and Janet Sparrow captured the mixed foursome, while the men's foursome event went to George Peet and Mr. Bearisto. Sixty players had entered that event. An equal number of gentlemen entered the handicap event with Norman Weir in good form to be declared the winner. E. Green's 78—two below bogey was the best gross score. In the ladies' handicap event Miss Sparrow and Mrs. Hill tied for the lead, and in a playoff Miss Sparrow was the winner.

In June a team of Country Club golfers travelled across the city to the St. Andrews course to defeat the home team. Later, on their home links, the Country Club again gained a victory over the St. Andrews Club, and then entertained their opponents at dinner.

Entry fees for the Country Club's summer tournament ranged from 25¢ to a dollar per event. Sixteen players qualified for the championship flight towards the club championship. Other competitors were directed into A and B flights. The Golf and Country Club Trophy was offered for this event, and as well gold and silver buttons were added prizes. Forbes Wilson made it to the finals against C. Govan where he won his match with a forty foot put. In the final the pair were even at the 18th hole, but in the afternoon round, before a large gallery, Wilson won 8 and 6.

In ladies' play, for the Hudson Bay Trophy, Miss Johnston beat Miss Sparrow in an extra hole. High winds produced high scores in the ladies' handicap play which saw Mrs. Cyril Hill win the F.C. Lowes Cup. Art Lowes captured the Herald Cup for the men's handicap event. Mrs. Hill teamed with her husband to defeat the Craufords.

The long drive competition took place up a wet hill, which cut down the distances considerably. Janet Sparrow and F. Denton were the winners. Mr. Sclater was the best competitor in the men's approach and putting, while Mrs. Johnson took the ladies event after a playoff.

In August representatives of various clubs in the province met as the Alberta Golf Association. The new executive was: President A. McMahon of Calgary, Vice-president Dr. Cobbett of Edmonton, and Secretary-Treasurer T. Gillespie of Granum. Plans were made to hold the 1912 Alberta golf championships at the newly completed Edmonton Golf Club in late August.

During the month a team of Calgary golfers travelled to Spokane to lose 13-12 to the Spokane golfers in two ball foursomes and singles. McCullough and Dacre were the pick of the Calgary players. It was the intention of the Spokane team to return the visit to Calgary during the fall.

A team of golfers from the St. Andrews Club journeyed to Edmonton to defeat the Edmonton golf team in a weekend tournament.

The Alberta golf championships were held on the magnificent grounds of the Edmonton Country Club. There were many entries and a high standard of play in the ladies' events. However the players were bothered by horses and riders, and at times the course looked as if it were the scene of a polo match. The ladies' golf costume of the era was a long dress and a full hat.

Janet Sparrow defeated Mrs. Simpson two and one in the ladies' finals. It was reported a large gallery watched some spectacular play, with great drives and brassie shots. Miss Martin took the ladies' handicap event and the Brewery Cup. In the ladies' foursome final Nightingale and Martin defeated Sparrow and Johnston.

There were six entries in the Alberta Open Championship play. Walton of Edmonton shot a 167 for the 36 hole competition to take the title. Professional Turpie of Calgary was four strokes behind; Hunter of Edmonton finished third followed by Gillespie of Granum.

In the opening play of the amateur championship J. Hunter of Edmonton made the course in one less than bogey, or a score of 81, to take the men's handicap and the Edmonton Brewery Cup. In the finals he beat clubmate J. Walton five up to become Alberta's 1913 amateur golf champion. Calgarians in the competition were M. Burvey and S. McCullough. The Edmonton club considered this to be the most successful tournament yet held in Alberta.

At the concurrent meeting of the Alberta Golf Association Dr. Cobbett was elected as its incoming president.

In late September the Calgary Golf and Country Club held its annual fall tournament. Mr. Mayber was the winner of a handsome silver trophy and a $50 prize presented by Mr. and Mrs. Crauford. In mixed foursome play the Craufords lost by five holes to Dacre and Sutherland.

In September a kind of marathon golf game was held in Calgary between George Bruce and W. Davis. The course extended from the Elbow Bridge to Mr. Davis's ranch, four miles away. Mr. Davis took 162 strokes and lost three balls, while his opponent shot 212, lost seven balls and broke a club.

The fall tournament at St. Andrews saw W. Scott take home the Hester Cup, while the D. Black Trophy was won by F. Scholey.

There were twenty entries in the ladies' handicap event of the 1914 spring tournament at the Calgary Country Club. Mrs. Bearisto had the best gross score, but Mrs. McMahon's net score was the lowest giving her first place. Mr. J. Burroughs was the winner over 25 other entries in the men's handicap event; while Mr. McMahon and Miss Sparrow took the mixed foursome competition.

C. Hague drove his ball 250 yards, while Nora Johnson hit for 215 yards to earn each of them first place in the long drive event. A golf gymkhana on the miniature course was organized by Freddie Lowes, Chairman of the sports and pastime committee. Ma Traihor's orchestra played at an informal dance held at the club in the evening.

Mrs. Lougheed was Honourary President of the ladies' section of the Country Club; Mrs. Grogan served as president, while the ladies' captains were Miss Sparrow and Mrs. Pryce-Jones. It was said that during this era the bridge games on the clubhouse porch were as popular as the golf games.

The ladies' spring tournament at the St. Andrews Club was reported on the society page rather than in the sports section of the local newspapers. Mrs. C. Stuart won the competition with a score of 105-28 for the 18 hole competition.

The St. Andrews Club held spoon competitions most Saturdays during the season. In August a team of St. Andrews players travelled to Edmonton to lose to the Edmonton club in singles but win in foursomes to take the overall competition. The competition was highlighted by the win of Cruttenden and Tait-White of St. Andrews over the pair of Hunter, the provincial amateur champion, and Walton, the provincial open champion, in foursome play. The Edmonton pair had never before been beaten on their home course. However it is only fair to say that both the Calgary players lost in singles play.

During August the D. Black Trophy was put up for competition at the St. Andrews Club. Many players came to grief on the numerous new bunkers, as a number of hazards had been added and the course lengthened in preparation for the Alberta championship play. Three players had net scores of 78, including scratch player H. Black, 18 handicapper G. Burroughs, and seven handicapper T. Douglass. A playoff was won by Douglass, who was a stroke better than the other two finalists.

The Alberta Golf Association's annual provincial tournament was held on the links of the St. Andrews Club in early September. Mr. Gray was the tournament secretary. In recognition of the event the Herald published a series of golf articles by professional golfer H. Hilton.

Entrance fees ranged from a dollar to ten dollars, depending upon the events, which were: the Alberta open championship—36 medal hole play, amateur championship of Alberta for the Cross Challenge Cup—18 hole match play, men's bogey competition handicap—18 holes, men's foursome handicap—18 hole, team match, ten men per team—18 hole medal play, total aggregate score for a new cup donated by McMahon, Ferris and Peet, ladies' championship of Alberta—18 hole match play for the Dr. W. McKay Trophy, ladies' handicap—nine hole medal play, and ladies' foursome handicap—nine holes.

Forty four men participated in the qualifying round of the men's amateur competition. A Cruttenden was knocked out of further play in the second round. In the final J. Munro of Edmonton defeated J. Gray of St. Andrews. Mr. Gray had a slight advantage up to the tenth hole, then Hunter had the better of the play, and he finished the round up by a margin of five holes. Victory was his on the twelfth hole of the second round, at which time he was seven holes ahead. Both men were excellent putters, but Hunter had good iron play and was the better driver. Calgarian A. McMahon was the second flight winner. A special prize for the low scratch score of 77 was awarded to W. Taite-White, and W. Stevenson took the bogey competition. E. Simpson captured the men's handicap event, and as well teamed with E. Palmer to tie with J. Walker and A. Payne in men's foursome competition.

Another tie occurred in mixed foursome play as Miss Johnston and S. McCullock ended even with Janet Sparrow and A. McMahon.

There were ten entries, including defending champion Miss Sparrow, and many spectators for the ladies' play. In the finals Mrs. Bearisto defeated Mrs.

Simpson. She then teamed with Mrs. McMahon to take the ladies' foursome. The handicap event was won by Janet Sparrow.

St. Andrews, the host club, captured the team event.

The Alberta open event was held in conjunction with the amateur competition. T. Gillespie of Fort Macleod shot rounds of 78 and 79 for a 157 total to prove to be the best golfer among the 20 entries. Calgary's C. Hague had the best first round with a score of 74, but he ballooned to an 84 and a combined total of 158, which gave him a second place tie with Mr. Gee. A. Cruttenden finished fourth, and last year's winner, J. Walter, shot a 163 for fifth place.

The Alberta Golf Association held its annual meeting during the tournament. New officers were: President S. McCulloch of the St. Andrews Club, Vice-president D. Jackson of Fort Macleod, and Secretary-treasurer E. Polve of the Edmonton club. The 1915 Alberta championships were planned for the Edmonton Golf and Country Club, however no competition of this nature took place in Alberta during the duration of the war.

In September the Calgary Golf and Country Club held a club tennis tournament, with Janet Sparrow, the 1913 Alberta ladies' golf champion, taking the ladies' competition. The club also held a billiard tournament in its newly completed billiard room.

Included in the Country Club's fall tournament was the men's handicap for the Sports and Pastime Trophy, ladies' handicap for the Crauford Cup, and a progressive handicap tournament. Mrs. Fred Andrews was the ladies' winner, while Mrs. Crauford and Mr. Hugh captured the mixed foursome competition. Art Lowes was the winner of the men's handicap; his 75 beat bogey by 5 and was one of the lowest scores ever made on the course. L. Smith and J. Duff were the winners of the men's foursome event. Following the competition the clubhouse and verandas were packed for the tea hour.

Twenty members of the St. Andrews Club travelled to the Country Club to earn a 36 to 9 win in singles and foursome competition against the home team. One bright spot for the losers was a win by Hague and Govan over White and Cruttenden of St. Andrews.

The St. Andrews Club invited players from the Lethbridge and Fort Macleod clubs to play in its Thanksgiving Day handicap tournament for the Hester Cup. Unfortunately the weather on that late October Day proved to be very cold. Bill Motherwell was the tournament winner, while Mr. Cruttenden received the Sheriff Graham prize for the low gross score.

In October the Calgary Golf and Country Club held a ladies' day, which was just as important socially as it was a golf event. Nora Johnson took the foursome competition, while Mrs. F Lowes proved superior in the approaching and putting event. The day went so that plans were made to hold similar events every Wednesday while the weather remained nice.

The following week the ladies of the Country Club competed against and then entertained the ladies from the St. Andrews Club. At a reception following the play Mrs. Lougheed presented prizes to Mrs. Fowler of the St. Andrews Club and the winners of the foursome competition, Mrs. Bearisto and Miss Muckleston. A total of 44 women participated in the matches.

The St. Andrews fall special competition was won by Mrs. Lucy, with the prize donated by Mrs. Fowler, captain of the women's team.

In what was probably the largest team competition every played in Alberta a forty player aside match took place at the Country Club, with the home team easily winning to help erase the pain of the previous loss. The quality of participation produced an air of enthusiasm that was not often found around a golf course.

1914 had been a very enthusiastic and competitive year in Calgary's golf circle.

Due to the demands of the war provincial competition did not take place during the period of the hostilities.

The land at Shaganappi Point had originally been given to the city for use as a cemetery. Public pressure for a public course in Calgary had been apparent for quite some time. In 1914 work was commenced on laying out a course at Shagnappi, and by 1915 nine holes were playable. A newspaper article of the era said that, "many poor golfers were now able to play". An 18 hole layout was not completed until the end of the war.

Plans for the Bowness Club were announced by the land developer in 1913, but it was not until 1920 that the course and its pseudo half timbered clubhouse was opened.

By the early twenties the Regal Golf Course was in operation in north-east Calgary, and in 1925 some golf links were opened west of the city by the Hudson's Bay employees' club.

During the 1920's and 30's there were several miniature golf courses operating in Calgary. The Pee Wee course was located on Seventeenth Avenue and Centre Street South, and the Peter Pan was located on Sixteenth Avenue North. In 1930 the La Fonda Golf Garden was established on Centre Street in downtown Calgary.

The Civic Golf Club was established in West Calgary in 1933. During this era rates at the city owned Municipal, otherwise known as Shagnappi Course, were 35¢ a game. 1938 saw the formation of the Parkdale Golf Club in the Parkdale addition.

The Colonel Walker Golf Club was set up in the 1920's, and became the Inglewood Course in the next decade.

The Early Grey Club began as a small community club bordering the settled area of Mount Royal. The club was initiated by Major Duncan Stuart who, along with several of his acquaintances, decided to develop the hilly area where they used to practise their golf shots. A very unique but short eighteen hole links was laid out. Prior to World War II the Earl Grey had been moved to its site beside the reservoir. A driving range, the Skyline, was operating south of the present Glenmore Trail west of Elbow Drive, in the 1950's.

Polo, Gymkhana

Polo was reported to have been introduced into Alberta by Captain Wilmont of the Alberta Ranche Company near Pincher Creek prior to 1886. With the influx of gentleman ranchers and the open prairie, it was natural for polo to be established in southern Alberta.

By 1890 polo was being played in Calgary, Fort Macleod and Pincher Creek areas. In July of that year Mr. Alexander formed a polo club in Calgary. Its eight members first held practises on a field located east of the Elbow River near the store house of the Edmonton and Calgary Railroad.

In 1891 a polo club was established at Fort Macleod. This team defeated a team from Pincher Creek by a 4-2 score in the fall of that year. Four 15-minute quarters and four men on a team were the basis of the rules.

In June of 1892 there was further inter-club competition at Macleod, when Colonel MacLeod donated a trophy and a tournament was held during race week in June. Teams were entered from Pincher Creek, High River, Calgary and Macleod, and the host team won the tournament and the trophy.

During August of 1892 a polo team from Calgary, consisting of Cuppage, Critchley, Critchley and Jamieson travelled to Regina where they played a game against the Qu'Appelle club at the Regina polo grounds. It was a closely contested match, but Calgary had the better team effort. Twice Qu'Appelle players lost the ball right in front of the Calgary goal. In the end Calgary carried off the Hayter Read Cup, and their backers were several hundred dollars richer from the wagers that took place. Mr. Lacelles umpired this game which was watched by a good sized crowd that included many ladies and members of the legislature.

The Calgary Polo Club offered the Calgary Challenge Cup for competition. In the first tournament for this trophy, held in September of 1892, the High River team won the competition with wins over both Macleod and Calgary. In the first game the dash and excellence of the High River players gave them a 10-0 win over the Macleod team. High River then remained undefeated as they beat Calgary 3-2. Calgary goal scorers were H. Alexander and H. Jamieson, while T. Critchely and L. Cuppage completed the lineup. A Browning, N. Baker, H. Davidson and S. Heap played for Macleod, while H. Sampson, D. MacPherson, C. Ross and W. Humphrey formed the winning High River team.

The tournament was held on the Calgary Polo Club grounds situated north of the Bow Marsh Bridge in the area later known as Hillhurst. In conjunction with the polo competition races for the polo ponies belonging to the members of the competing clubs were held.

One evening the Polo Club, assisted by the bachelors of Calgary, entertained the visitors from the south at a dance held in the new sandstone Alexander Block on Stephen Avenue.

A great deal of wagering took place on the outcome of the polo games. It was reported in the local paper that, "Pools on the polo tournament will be paid at the Criterion Restaurant."

A few days after the polo competition the Calgary Polo Club sponsored a gymkhana at the agricultural grounds. Admission to this sports and social event was 25¢. Included in the events were: a postillion race, tent pegging, cigar race, umbrella race, bareback hurdle race, ladies nomination race with side saddle and riding habit, one mile flat and half mile tandem races.

During the summer the Sons of England sponsored a paper chase on horseback.

In the fall some of Calgary's polo players were participating in the game in Victoria. MacPherson from Calgary, earned honours in the gymkhana events at the island competition.

In 1893 James Owen, who in 1887 had established the track and stables besides a bend in the Elbow River south of Calgary, passed away.

Mitford, west of Cochrane, held a polo tournament and gymkhana, with the Mounted Police band in attendance. In its first game Calgary beat High River 4-3, but the next day High River turned the tables with a 4-1 win over the Calgary team. A unique polo match saw the Blackfeet play against the Stoney braves.

In September the annual polo tournament and gymkhana was held in Calgary with competition for both the Calgary Challenge Cup and the Colonel Macleod Cup taking place. The Calgary team won the Colonel Macleod Cup, and High River took home the Calgary Challenge Trophy.

Polo, 1894. Left to right: three Critchley brothers.

A tournament was held in Macleod in 1894 with teams from Pincher Creek, Beaver Creek and Calgary along with the home team participating. Both the host team and Calgary won trophies in this competition. One event was the Balaclava Melee, in which it took the Calgary team five minutes to de-horse their opponents.

In other 1894 tournaments the Beaver Creek team won the competitions at both their own community and at Pincher Creek.

Two polo matches were played at the Elbow Park race track in June of 1895 between the single men and married men teams, with the bachelors winning both contests, much to the surprise of the local polo fraternity. The band of the N.W.M.P. played at the gymkhana, which was held the same week as the polo games. This competition covered 13 events including an Indian race.

O. Critchley, riding Pete, won the quarter mile scurry, then he rode Day to win the bending race, an event comparable to a slalom. Critchley also won the tandem race, and H. Samson was the winner of the bareback hurdles race. The ladies nomination was one of the more popular events. Each competitor was to ride up to his lady, dismount, hand her a needle to be threaded, and when she hands it back the competitor will sew a buttom on his glove, then ride back to the start and give the glove to the judge. Other races included: cigar, umbrella, brandy and soda, and a bicycle race in which Kerr edged Vincent.

The three Critchleys and George Ross travelled to the Territorial Exhibition in Regina where they defeated the Regina Polo Club by 6-2 and 5-2 scores. The Pincher Creek and Moosomin polo teams were also in the competition. Unfortunately the five Calgary polo ponies got out of their pasture and started west. They were last seen north of Moose Jaw. A $25 reward was offered for their return.

In August competition for the Calgary Challenge Cup took place with the High River, Pine Creek, Critchley and Calgary town teams involved in play. The Pine Creek team took a close 5-4 win over the Critchley team, composed of the three Critchleys and J. Holt. O. Browne, J. Rogers, H. Gibb and W. Hooley composed the Pine Creek lineup. The High River quartet of G. Ross, H. Samson, A.E. Cross and A. Pelly then took a 5-1 win over the Calgary town team of McNaughten, T. Lee, C. Ross, and G. Lafferty. In the final of the Calgary Cup High River won over Pine Creek.

At Pine Creek the home team earned a 6-1 win over the Calgary team, then in a return match played in Calgary, where a great deal of money was wagered on the outcome, the Pine Creek team again came out on top by a 4-2 score.

West of Calgary a half mile track was laid out at Wheeler Mickle's place in Springbank. Gopher holes were filled in and here the Springbank polo club practised twice a week and, "were capable of some exciting plays." Sometimes their players came in to practise with the Calgary Polo Club.

The Calgary Polo Club held its annual, social function at the Palace Hotel. However hotel owner T. Skinner was charged for selling liquor to the polo club who had not bothered with the formality of procuring a liquor license.

The Ladies Challenge Cup was offered for polo competition in Calgary in 1896. In this event Samson beat Gardiner's team 6-3, and Critchley's four were edged by Ross 5-4. In the final Ross, sided by A. Eckford, W. Hooley and J. Rogers, beat Samson's team to win the Ladies Challenge Cup. The final game was characterized by the usual good natured earnestness, and all the proceedings were characterized by, "the usual gentlemanly conduct which prevails the world over in sports of this kind". The public was invited at no charge to view these games played at the polo grounds located north of the Bow Marsh Bridge.

In August the Calgary Challenge Cup competition took place, with the Pine Creek, Elbow River and Calgary teams one and two participating. Mr. Milvain did a commendable job of umpiring the matches. In the final the Calgary team of H. and O. Critchley, MacNaughten and Lee earned a close 3-2 win over the Pine Creek foursome of Ross, Hooley, Eckford and Rogers.

A gymkhana, held at the Elbow Park race track, took place the same week as the polo competition. An admission of 25¢ a person was charged. There were 13 entries in the polo quarter mile dash with catch weights over 154 pounds. O. Critchley captured this prime event and later in the program he won the half mile hurdle race. His brother Harry won the postilion race, which involved riding one horse and leading another steed over a set of four hurdles. H. Lott won the bending race and G. Ross was first in the tentpegging competition. Captain Gardiner missed all four balls in the bucket and ball competition, which was won by O. Critchley.

Fourteen couples entered the ladies nomination event in which the rider, carrying a soda pop, travelled over a set of hurdles to his lady partner who opened the soda pop, which was drunk by the rider who then travelled over the hurdles to the start line. This event was won by O. Critchley, who then added to his laurels by coming in first in the Victoria Cross competition. In this event the competitor traversed a hurdle course, picked up a dummy and rode back over the hurdle course. Gymkhanas were greatly enjoyed by both the participants and the spectators, and these sports programs were considered just as much a social function as a sporting event.

Calgary's team of O. Critchley, A.E. Cross, F. MacNaughten and A. Fraser defeated High River 6-4 in the finals of the 1897 Calgary Challenge Cup competition. In a preliminary match Calgary had won over the Sheep Creek foursome of Rogers, the Moseley brothers and Hone.

In the finals of the Ladies Challenge Cup competition, Critchley's team of McNaughten, Cross, and Fraser beat Samson's team by a 6-4 score. The gymkhana, to be held at Brigg's track, formerly Owen's race track, was postponed for the season.

In 1897 the Southern Alberta Polo Association was formed by a group of polo enthusiasts who met in Pincher Creek. The Freebooters were the winners of a tournament held in that community during the summer.

Competition in 1898 for the Ladies Challenge Cup was limited to the White and Blue teams. The Blues, with A.E. Cross, A. Wooley-Dod, and the Critchley brothers defeated the White team 7-3. F. MacNaughten, A. Eckford, T. Lee and H. Samson formed the loser's lineup.

Admission to the gymkhana at the Elbow Park track was now up to 50¢, and it was reported that a large enthusiastic crowd was in attendance. In the tentpegging event A.E. Cross finished first, while Samson won the bucket and ball competition. T. Critchley proved to be the best horseman while directing a polo ball, and the Victoria Cross race went to O. Critchley. The prestige quarter mile dash for polo ponies was won by McNaughten riding his favourite horse, Billy. H. Lott captured the bending race. In the ladies nomination race the rules were changed so that the women handed the men a package of clothes; the men dressed in the costume and rode back to the start, which was now the finish line. Mr. and Mrs. O. Critchley were the winners. In the cigar and umbrella race bedlam occurred when the horses shied away from the open unbrellas. Besides races for the polo ponies there were bicycle races, with W. Riley and Norm Luxton earning prizes.

"The great polo tournament," was advertised as part of the 1889 Inter-provincial Exhibition held in September in Calgary. The fair proved to be a successful three days, and the polo competition was one of the more popular attractions of the Exhibition.

The Qu'Appelle team of Harvey, McCaul, Sargeant and Parker had travelled 600 miles by train to compete, while the North Fork, or Livingston, team of the Gunn brothers, Kennington, Miles and Milvain drove 15 ponies 100 miles over a prairie trail to Calgary. Rogers, Freeman, Hone and Briggs composed the Fish Creek team.

Calgary overwhelmed the North Fork team 9-0 in a game that was in favour of Calgary from the opening whistle. Good team play was evident as Sheep Creek defeated Qu'Appelle 4-1. In the final Calgary earned a narrow 4-3 win over Sheep Creek in what was described as, "one of the best games ever witnessed in Calgary." At the end of the third quarter Sheep Creek led 3-1, but in the final quarter the Calgary ponies outstayed and outgalloped their opponents as Calgary ran their score to four goals to retain the Calgary Challenge Cup. In consolation play North Fork defeated Qu'Appelle.

W. Smith of Livingstone did a good job of umpiring the tournament. Unfortunately Calgary player Samson had two bad falls. However the tournament was a decided success, both in the eyes of the players and the several thousand spectators.

In Ladies Cup competition in 1899 the team of G. Ross, A. Fraser, J. Rodgers and P. Briggs won the trophy.

A July, 1900 polo game saw the 'Irish' team of J. Rogers, A. Hone, J. Freeman and F. MacNaughten defeat the 'Rest of the World' team composed of O. Critchley, G. Ross, P. Briggs and W. Moseley by a 4-1 score. Mr. Welley umpired the match.

Dr. Simard, a member of the Canadian Hunt Club in Montreal, saw and liked the work of the Alberta polo ponies in this game, so he purchased a great number of these ponies at an average cost of fifty dollars each, and then shipped them back to Montreal.

In the finals for the Ladies Challenge Cup, played in August, Ross's team of MacNaughten, P. Briggs and O. Briggs defeated Roger's team by a 2-1 score. It was a good game, but without any goals until the third quarter when Ross scored. A brilliant effort by Freeman tied the score. Finally, in overtime P. Briggs put the ball between the goal posts to give the Ross team the trophy. Other players for the losers were W. Moseley and A. Wooley-Dod.

For the first time in Calgary's history there was an organized polo competition for junior players. George Ross put up a trophy for competition for the youngsters. In the junior final the team of Middleton, Briggs, Anderson and Swann defeated the foursome of N. Williams, H. MacWilliams, G. Sharpe and A. Alexander by a 4-1 score.

Critchley, who had been beaten earlier in the season by Ross in the Ladies competition, challenged the winner in a game advertised as, "for blood."

A gymkhana was held as part of the Inter-Western Pacific Exhibition in 1901. Ross, MacNaughten, Critchley and Newbolt won most of the competitions. The events, and especially the polo ball race, were enjoyed by the crowds. Unfortunately heavy rains cut down on the competition and the number of spectators. The Qu'Appelle Polo Club had travelled a considerable distance for their polo game with Calgary to take place during the Exhibition. The poor weather caused the game to be postponed and postponed, until the Qu'Appelle team had to go home. However the Polo Club dance at the Alexander Hall was a decided success, as 150 people danced until two a.m.

During the summer of 1901 Oswald Critchley purchased and shipped a carload of polo ponies to England.

In August the Irish polo team scored a 4-1 win over the All-comers, or who were described as, "the rest of creation." W. Toole and Freeman joined the old standbys MacNaughten and Hone for the Irish. Ross, Cross W. and D. Moseley played for the All-comers.

Captain Meophon Gardner—Pirmez Creek on polo pony, 1901.

Ladies Cup competition saw the Ross team whitewash the MacNaughten four 6-0, and Freeman's team lost 4-3 to Hone. Hone's team were the favourites over Ross in the finals, however George Ross led his team to a 5-2 win. The winning captain showed his great polo skills when on one occasion he made a great risk on a restart and scored within ten seconds. His winning teammates were: Cross, Wooley-Dod and F. MacWilliams. A. Hones was joined by W. Moseley, Anderson and N. Williams on the losing side.

Mrs. A. Wooley-Dod and Mrs. A.E. Cross received members and visitors at the annual polo ball held in the Alexander Hall.

The Calgary Polo Club defeated the Millarville Polo Club 4-0 in a game for the newly donated Sheep Creek Challenge Cup. It was a game that featured fast play, and it was never one-sided as the score might indicate. Moseley got very sick during the game and was replaced by Willans. Calgary's goals were space out, and the fourth goal came after they were able to sweep the ball down the field after a throw-in. Millarville's lineup was composed of Freeman, Anderson, D. Moseley, Willan and Hone, while Ross, Cross, Wooley-Dod and MacNaughten played for the winners. W. Toole proved to be a capable umpire.

By early May of 1902 club president Wooley-Dod had organized practices for the polo players at the club grounds located west of Colonel Herchmer's place north of the Bow River. Harry Critchley, one of Calgary's better polo players, was back in the city after spending a year being involved in the Boer War in South Africa. Continual rains did a great deal to marr the 1902 polo season in Calgary, and as a result no major competition took place. The only game of any significance occurred in September in which the team of McNaughten, H. Middleton, C. Briggs and P. Shaw scored a 4-3 win over Wooley-Dod's team.

Included in the military sports at the Exhibition held in September was the Victoria Cross race and tilting the rings, but again the rain dampened the competition.

A large crowd watched some good polo played as fourteen different players were involved in a total of seven quarters of play during a June, 1903 weekend of the Calgary Polo Club. Forty polo ponies were tied to the rail ready to be used during the polo play. Mrs. Wooley-Dodd was in charge of the tea table during the two day event.

A gymkhana was part of the 1903 Exhibition, and a new event was the driving competition in which a team of horses hitched to a buggy was to be driven through a figure eight of barrels. In the race for polo ponies George Ross beat Middleton by a neck. MacNaughten finished first in the half mile for polo ponies, while F. Ward of Victoria won the polo pony jumping event. Lord Seymour won the polo pony high jumping competition, and Crooks was first in the mile and eighth hurdle race. In addition, there was saddling, Victoria Cross, nomination, bending, cowboy races and bronco-bucking competition.

In the Ladies Challenge Cup competition W. Toole's team took a 5-1 win over Eckford, while Ross lost to Hone by a 5-4 score. Toole captured the final with an easy 5-1 win from Hone.

The largest meeting of polo people in years took place in the office of W. toole with Mr. Wooley-Dod in the chair. Plans were made to hold a polo tournament in Millarville.

Middleton, who resided in Okotoks, transported forty polo ponies to Toronto where they were exhibited and then sold. When in Toronto Middleton met with polo enthusiasts with whom he discussed the feasibility of a Calgary team playing in a Toronto polo tournament.

When the Calgary Polo Club travelled by train to High River they were met at the station by the High River players and escorted in a regal manner to their hotel. Then in a fast game before a good sized crowd Calgary defeated the High River polo team by a 3-1 score. Playing for Calgary were MacNaughten, G. Noton, A. Wooley-Dod and W. Toole, while the hometown team was composed of Ross, Eckford, Ward and Middleton.

Competition for the Millarville Cup took place in August. A.E. Cross was added to Calgary's lineup for the opening game against Millarville. The city boys led at the half, however Calgary's play deteriorated in the late stages and Millarville won 5-2. A. Hone, G. Noton, J. Dean-Freeman and A. Anderson composed the winning lineup. The next day, in its game against High River, Calgary found itself falling behind, but with McNaughten's tremendous play the team came on strong to win 7-5.

In the last game High River defeated Millarville by a 5-4 score, however the game was marred by an accident as Anderson was hit in the face, and he lost two teeth as a result. Oswald Brown had umpired the games, and R.K. Bennett acted as timekeeper.

Complementing the tournament were two junior games, which in the first the boys of Millarville defeated their High River counterparts by an 8-0 score. The following day there was a complete reversal of form as High River won 5-4. Hone brothers, W. Freeman and Lord Seymour played for Millarville, while W. Christie, H. Robertson, R. Bennett and G. Pemberton played for High River.

In the last game of the tournament the Irish team of MacNaughten, Freeman, Hone and Toole completely outclassed the English as they won 8-1.

During the tournament there was a great deal of discussion about the feasibility of establishing a polo stud farm. The type of mounts needed to be developed were undersized thoroughbreds with speed and endurance. It was felt that the hardy climate of southern Alberta was suitable to raise horses that would have these characteristics.

Polo players Ross, MacNaughten, Middleton and A. Hone represented the Calgary Polo Club, using the nickname 'Freebooters', in a polo tournament held in Toronto in September of 1903 under the sponsorship of the Toronto Hunt Club. Unfortunately it took eleven days by rail to get the horses to Toronto, and they were not even their own mounts, but just some ponies that were being shipped to Ontario to be sold by Middleton.

In their first tournament game with the Rochester, New York team the difference in mounts was obvious, and Calgary came out on the short end of an 8-6 score. The prairie players had fallen behind by four goals, but two quick goals were scored just before the game ended.

Calgary easily won its next game beating the best of eastern Canada, a team that was the pick of the Toronto and Montreal clubs, by a 6-1 score. Unlike play in the west these games were six periods or chukkers long. In their last game

Calgary redeemed itself as they beat Rochester by a 7-4 score. Ross was the star of the game as he gave a display of polo skills that were simply dazzling. Several sports writers in the east wrote that Calgary had had bad luck in the first game against Rochester because of their tired horses. Rochester won the tournament and Canada Cup winners.

The Toronto polo players were interested in listening to Ross tell of his polo pony, Old Grey Johnny, who was 22 years old and had played polo in 1891. Ross claimed the horse knew the game as well as his rider.

On the team's return home, the players reported that they had been treated admirably in the east, and they felt they were capable of beating any team from that area. Middleton said that the eastern players had trouble staying on their mounts. The twenty ponies that he shipped down east were sold at an average price of $170, and Lady Jane fetched $450, the highest price ever paid for a polo pony in Canada.

Hull's Opera House was the scene of one of the most brilliant social functions ever held in Calgary as Mrs. Wooley-Dod and Mrs. Toole received over 200 guests at the 1903 Calgary Polo Club ball. The decorations in the hall gave the impression of a fairy land at this gala event.

Gymkhanas often formed the basis of social functions at ranches and communities in southern Alberta. In June of 1904 a gymkhana, attended by many Calgarians, was held at the Bowness Ranche, owned and operated by the Honourable William and Mrs. Beresford. O. Brown was the star of the day as he won the needle and thread ladies' nomination, bareback race and the fancy dress scramble. The throwing potato in bucket and the whiskey and soda competitions were taken by A.E. Cross. A. Blanco, a new polo player in the Calgary area, captured the Victoria Cross race, and R.K. Bennett was the bending race winner.

Playing in a June game that consisted of three ten minute periods the High River team of A. Eckford, G. Ross, L. Sexsmith and H. Robertson earned a 4-1 win from the Sheep Creek combination of the Hone brothers, Noton and Freeman.

Military sports and gymkhana events were part of the 1904 Calgary Agricultural and Industrial Fair. In the tug-of-war event, with teams of four mounted men, the Mounted Police team defeated two different teams from the ranks of the Canadian Mounted Rifles. Sergeant-Major Page was the winner of the Turk's Head event, and the R.N.W.M.P. team were the champions in the bareback wrestling competition. The large audience was treated to a sham battle taking place between mounted men. There were horse jumping events for men, women and boys. W. Treneven of Bullockville surprised a great many people when he proved superior to the local players in the polo ball event, which consisted of driving three polo balls up and down the track in front of the grandstand.

The High River polo tournament took place in August, and many Calgarians took the train down for this social as well as sporting event. Millarville was defending the High River Challenge Cup that had been put up for competition by Mrs. Eckford in 1903.

Calgary lost to one High River team, and then Pekisko was beaten by a second hometown foursome. Then a High River team of Eckford, Ross, Ward and

Robertson defeated the Millarville team of W., J and A. Hone and Noton 7-3 to win the High River Challenge Cup.

The 1904 Calgary polo tournament for the Calgary Challenge Cup was staged at the polo club grounds located north of the Bow Marsh Bridge. Wooley-Dod, G. Hooley, R.K. Bennett and F. MacNaughten were named to the Calgary lineup. Competition was staged according to the international system of using six periods or chukkers instead of the four period system that had been in use in southern Alberta.

Calgary was shut out 8-0 by the High River team, then High River took an easy 10-4 win over Millarville in the final for the Calgary Cup. The winners opened the scoring early, netting three goals in the first chukker and adding three more in the fourth chukker. In the evening following the final match 150 persons attended the Polo Club dance in the Alexander Hall. The annual Irish versus English polo match completed the tournament.

"Calgary beats High River in an animated polo match amid interesting scenes," read one Calgary newspaper headline in June of 1905. The newspaper gave two full columns of coverage of this game which was viewed by many Calgarians who had travelled to High River by a special train organized especially for the event.

After last year's 8-0 loss to High River the Calgary Polo Club decided that the Honourable C. MacNaughten, A. Hone, J. Deane-Freeman and W. Noton would make the best foursome to turn the tables on High River's team of Ross, Robinson, Ward and Eckford. Although the spectator interest was high the relative strength of the two teams caused very little betting to take place on the outcome.

Ross scored first, but then Calgary went ahead 2-1 and 4-2 at the half; then High river tied the score at 4-4. However Justin Freeman was given a free hit with just 52 seconds left, and when the ball went through the posts Calgary had its winning goal. Many of the spectators thought that this game had supplied the best polo every played in the west. Following the game the High River Polo Club and its friends invited all the Calgary players and visitors to a social function.

Two weeks later the tables were turned as High River, on the strength of Robinson's six goals, trimmed Calgary 12-2. Ross, the High River captain, played his usual spectacular game and added four goals to the winning cause. The lineups of the teams had remained the same as in Calgary's earlier narrow victory.

On Dominion Day a gymkhana military sports and races were held at the Calgary Exhibition Grounds. W. Wooley-Dod rode the winner in the polo pony race, and the Mounted Police were successful in the mounted tug-of-war competition. A unique event during the afternoon was the menagerie race, won by Major Barwiss. Each contestant had a different kind of animal or fowl to direct along the track to the finish line.

In the final game for the Calgary Challenge Cup High River scored five goals in the first ten minutes, and then they went on to take an 8-3 win over the Calgary foursome of A. and J. Hone, Hooley and Blencowe. Wooley-Dod refereed the match. In the evening following the game the annual polo dance at the Alexander Hall was a great success.

In conjunction with this competition the polo players of the district met and formed a polo association for western Canada, and organization secretary Hugh Niven made plans to affiliate with clubs in the east. The group decided that polo ponies used must not be more than 14.2 hands high, and they had to be registered before they would be allowed to be used in a game.

The High River polo team of G. Ross, H. Robertson, M. Sexsmith and T. Noton travelled to Toronto, and, billed as the champions of the North-west, defeated the Toronto team 10-7. Toronto took a 2-0 lead, but the High River players proved to be masters of the game and came back to the fore with their dare-devil riding and Noton's long accurate drives. Several days later the High River foursome defeated the pride of the east, a combined Toronto-Montreal team, by a 6-3 score in a game that was halted by rain at the end of the fourth period. The term chukkers was still not in general use in Canada at this time. Major Ross made some good rushes to lead the western attack in the second win. The success of the High River polo team in the east brought about a front page publication of their team picture in the local Calgary press.

1905 saw the beginning of the Calgary Horse Show, an event that was in future years to grow to be the biggest event of its kind in Canada.

More than 200 Calgarians travelled out to the Fish Creek polo grounds in June of 1906 to see the Millarville team of H. Anderson, A. Landale, Barrett and Noton earn a 9-8 win over the Fish Creek quartet of A. Hone, J. Hone, E. Blencowe and A. Wooley-Dod. McNaughten and Ross umpired, while Reverend Hogbin served as a timekeeper. Fish Creek was away to a fast start and led 2-1, then the Millarville team gathered momentum and went ahead 7-3. Fish Creek fought back, and they tied the score at eight-all when A. Hone made a splendid shot under his horse. Minutes later Barrett scored the winner for Millarville. A tea and social followed the polo competition.

The largest crowd that was reported to have ever witnessed a polo game in Calgary gathered at the old Elbow Park race track to see the Irish beat the Rest of the World team by a 6-3 score. MacNaughten, Freeman and two Hone brothers comprised the winners, while Ross, Barrett, Noton and Eckford played for the losing side. At the social and tea that followed the game the members of the winning team were presented with inscribed pewter mugs.

At the High River military men's sports day, an event that had been postponed from May 24, the Calgary Polo Club defeated the High River team 4-3. The game had been tied 3-3 at full time, then after a change of horses MacNaughten, who proved to be the star of the game, scored the winner. A new face in the Calgary lineups was Hugh Niven. The military sports activities included a musical ride.

Military sports were also part of the recreation program of the summer program of the summer camp of the 15th Light Horse Regiment held in Calgary.

In July competition for the Calgary Challenge Cup took place at the Elbow Park polo field. The old Calgary Polo Club field located north of the Bow River was now part of an area that was subdivided into building lots. Alexander, who had not played for two years, scored two goals as Calgary beat Millarville, 4-2 and Fish Creek won 9-3 over High River. In the cup final Calgary, led by Freeman with six goals, beat Fish Creek 8-3. The game featured end to end play and was not as one-sided as the score would indicate. Other Calgary players were Nevin and Ross. H. and A. Hone, Blencowe and Hooley comprised the Fish Creek lineup.

The competition for the High River Challenge Cup made up what was said to be, "the best polo tournament ever held in the west." In the first match Calgary doubled the Livingstone team by a 10-5 score. Calgary now met the High River team, and at the end of the sixth period the score was 8-3 for Calgary. Mrs. Eckford presented the winning Calgary team of Ross, Freeman, Niven and Alexander with the cup, and it was immediately filled with champagne.

The next day the High River squad beat Fish Creek 7-3 to square accounts for its loss to that team in the game played in Calgary earlier in the season. The competition and festivities ended with a dance at High River's Alberta Hotel.

Ross, Noton, Freeman and Alexander formed the Calgary team that travelled to Montreal in September of 1906 to play in the Canadian Polo Tournament. In their first game they completely outclassed the Montreal team 14-1 in only five periods of polo. Toronto beat Kingston 7-1 in the other preliminary match.

Playing with its continued fine form the Calgary team then beat Kingston 10-1, as Alexander scored seven goals in a match that was too one-sided to excite much interest. Montreal lost its second game by a 3-1 score to Toronto, who would now meet Calgary in a match to decide the tournament championship.

In what was to be a big surprise to many people Toronto beat Calgary 7-2 in a game that saw Freeman as the only western player who played up to form. Toronto, however, had strengthened their lineup, which was contrary to the rules of the tournament, but the protest was not accepted.

Competition for the Ladies Challenge Cup took place in October in Reis's Park, otherwise known as the Elbow Park field. In the first game Blencowe took a 4-3 win over the team of A. Hone. During the competition Wooley-Dod's best pony broke his leg, and it had to be shot, much to the dismay of the many ladies in the crowd. Ross took a close 5-4 win over Justin Freeman's team.

Ross carried home the Ladies Challenge Cup after he beat Blencowe in the final. The score had been tied, then Ross changed his horse, rode in, picked up the ball and carried it straight down to the opposition goal to score! He was indeed a one man team. Blencowe and McHugh also played very well in the tournament.

During this era T.S. Lee the owner of the quarter section which included the polo field in Elbow Park offered to sell the 160 acres to Frank (Bull) McHugh for the grand sum of $5,000, with a thousand dollars down. However the polo players felt that they could use this land for free, so why buy it. Then real estate promoter Freddie Lowes purchased the property and had it surveyed, with the result that survey stakes were erected on the polo playing area. One night the stakes disappeared, and the next day another polo practise took place. Several days later the land developer visited the area. Needless to say that finished polo in that particular location.

The local 1907 polo competition began in May with the Fish Creek tournament. A. Hone donated a new trophy for this competition.

In June play for the Ladies Challenge Cup was held at the new Mewata Park in west Calgary. Six teams, captained by A. Hone, H. Hone, Anderson, Eckford, G. Ross and Blencowe were entered in the competition. In the cup finals Ross scored an 8-2 win over A. Hone's team. McHugh played a brilliant game for the winners as he scored four goals, while team captain Ross thrilled the spectators with some great runs through the opposition.

The Millarville polo tournament was held in July with the Fish Creek, High River, Calgary and Millarville teams in contention. In the finals the Millarville team of Noton, Barrett, Anderson and Douglass beat the Fish Creek foursome of three Hones and Blencowe by one goal. The score was six-all at the end of the sixth period, then Millarville got the winning goal that went in off of a Fish Creek pony.

In further play at Fish Creek the home team of A. and J. Hone, Hooley and Blanco took a 4-3 victory in overtime from Ross, McHugh, Niven and Mac-Naughten representing the Calgary Polo Club. In another game, played at the Fish Creek grounds, the English team won by one goal over the Irish in a close and hotly contested match. It was only the second loss in twelve years for those players of Irish extraction. Playing for the winning side were: Ross, Knowlton, Barrett and Blencowe, while the three Hones and long time player MacNaughten formed the Irish team.

Fish Creek scored six goals in the third quarter as they defeated High River 9-2 at the Fish Creek tournament. In the second preliminary Millarille won 4-3 over Calgary in a game that was a toss-up until the final whistle. Newcomer Gravely scored one of Calgary's goals. In the final the Fish Creek team showed its supremacy with a 10-6 win over the Millarville club. At the social following the games the winners were presented with the tournament cup by Miss Wooley-Dod.

Gravely again demonstrated his polo skills as his quartette from Calgary played Wooley-Dod's Fish Creek team to a draw during an eight period game played in August.

The annual tournament of the Calgary Polo Club took place at Mewata Park in late August of 1907. Prior to each match the city road roller was used to flatten the playing field. Nim Hone proved to be a capable referee for the matches that were played before enthusiastic crowds of spectators. The Hones quintet and Blencowe proved too much for the Calgary club, defeating them 9-4. Using excellent combination play the Fish Creek team then defeated Millarville 7-4 in a match that was considered for the championship of Alberta. Noton's fine work for Millarville helped to stem what would otherwise have been a complete whitewash.

In September the High River team of Sexsmith, Limoges, Holmes and Anderson travelled to Winnipeg where they easily beat an all-Winnipeg team in preliminary play. In another match Pincher Creek lost to Indian Head. In the final for the newly offered Chipman Trophy, High River won over Indian Head by a 10-3 score.

At the meeting of the Western Canada Polo Association, which was held in conjunction with the tournament, J. Court of Indian Head was elected association president, while Fish Creek's A. Hone was elected vice-president. It was decided that no players would be allowed to use a horse over 14½ hands high, except those mounts which were now registered with the association.

Standard English rules, but the American system, or the aggregate number of goals, were used at the Hone tournament at Fish Creek. Games were also shortened to four ten minute periods, and after two teams played for a period they rested and the other two teams went into play.

G. Noton's team of MacNaughten, Blanco and Hett won with 21 goals, followed by A. Hone's total of 20 and Ross with 19. Justin Freeman, who had just returned from coaching the Montreal Polo Club, played for Douglass's team. The Fish Creek Polo Club served lunch following the competition.

Both Lethbridge and Edmonton reported that they hoped to be involved in polo competition by the following year.

Polo was started early in 1908 with the Calgary Polo Club holding practises at Mewata field in April. However inter-club competition did not take place until July and this was as part of the Exhibition.

There were a reported 20,000 people at the grounds as the Calgary team of Dickson, Shaw, McHugh and Amphlett defeated the Pekisko team 2-1 for the American Cup. However, several days later the Pekisko club reversed the score in an exhibition game against Calgary.

Ladies Challenge Cup competition also took place at the Exhibition where Hone's team defeated MacNaughten 9-2, and Ross won over Freeman's quartet by a 5-2 score. Ross captured the Ladies Cup as his team won by one goal over Hone.

The July tournament for the Calgary Challenge Cup was said to be for the polo championship of western Canada. Preliminary play saw Calgary lose 4-2 to Millarville and Fish Creek Whitewash Pekisko 11-0. In the final the Fish Creek quartet of MacNaughten, Freeman, Hume and Ross overwhelmed Millarville 10-0. The tournament showed that Hume and E. Dickson of the Calgary team had developed into two of the better polo players in the area. The scoring power of this Fish Creek aggregation was probably without equal in the west.

The first polo competition of the season at the Fish Creek polo grounds was for the Fortnightly Cup which was then held by Ross and challenged for by Freeman. The score was tied five-all at the end of regular time, then the might Ross scored in overtime to give his team the victory.

At the Millarville tournament the Millarville A team beat Pekisko 14-6, while in B competition, Millarville won by a 6-0 score. That evening the polo club dance was held in the Ranchers Hall, and the next day Millarville again defeated Pekisko.

Jephson, a newcomer to the Calgary area, played very well as the Fish Creek polo team whitewashed the Calgary Polo Club by a 10-1 score. Polo of a different sort took place at Banff where the sport of water polo was introduced.

In September of 1908 the Calgary Polo Club travelled out to Alix to play and win two games from the team of that community. The competition also proved to be a social incentive as dances were held on the two evenings following the games.

The High River Polo Club with players McHugh, Limoges, Carley and Holmes travelled to Winnipeg where in Chipman Cup play they beat High River 4-2 in the final.

There were 32 entries, but only 18 individuals showed up at the High River polo tournament in late September. The American system of team scoring was used in this competition, and a loving cup for the championship was donated by George Lane. Ross beat Freeman, and then Shakerley's Pekisko team won over Millarville. In the last match Ross took a 7-0 win over Shakerley in a great game which saw fierce play from whistle to whistle. After the tournament play two all-star teams played an exhibition match. In addition there was a gymkhana and the polo club dance.

Another equine activity began in Calgary in 1908 with the formation of the Calgary Hunt Club. L. Mewburn was the organization's first president, and M. Carr was appointed master of the hounds. The dogs were a cross between a Russian wolfhound and a greyhound. Five acres of land located along the Elbow River were rented from the golf club and a club house was erected there. Coyote hunts were held along the Elbow River and on the Sarcee Reserve. Mrs. Atkinson and Mrs. Mewburn were the first female members of the club that numbered 23 in its first year of operation.

A good weight carrying polo pony or three-quarter breed was considered the best horse for the hunt. The English or flat saddle was used, as stock saddles were too heavy. Most runs averaged 25 miles, but some were as long as 40 miles. Wire fences were considered a menace by the club members.

One hunt was held on the Burn's pasture, just off Macleod Trail, where two coyotes were secured. The masks and brushes from the animals were presented to Miss Burns and Mrs. Ellis. Both ladies had ridden in the hunt.

The club flourished at least up to the start of the great war.

An early spring in 1909 allowed polo enthusiasts to begin practise in April, and in Millarville ten players were regularly turning out to play. It was reported from Winnipeg that Earl Winterton, proprietor of the London World, had donated a trophy for polo competition in the Dominion of Canada.

The first local tournament of 1909 took place in June at Fish Creek for the Hone Cup. Freeman's team took a 6-1 win over Barrett, and Ross won 9-5 over A. Hone's team. However Ross's ponies were not fit, and in the final Freeman earned an easy 10-2 win from Ross.

Gymkhanas, and their participating events, were no longer part of the Calgary fair, however hurdle races and a half mile polo race for a $400 purse were included in the 1909 program.

The Millarville polo tournament took place in July amidst perfect weather. The Millarville A team had its first two goals called back as the result of penalties, but it still went on to defeat Fish Creek 7-2. The Pekisko B. team defeated Fish Creek B 14-0 and Millarville B 7-1. It was reported that the dance held in the Millarville hall following the competition lasted until the early hours of the morning.

The Millarville quartet of Freeman, Barnett, Molme and Landale proved to be the faster and more skillful team as they defeated Fish Creek 8-3 in a Fish Creek tournament. G. Ross joined the three Hones to make up the Fish Creek team. The Millarville B team beat Glenbow, a new team on the circuit, by an 11-2 score. Playing for the losers were H. and E. Lesuer, Saunders and Inkpen. The Fish Creek B team revenged their 14-0 loss to Pekisko as they earned a 10-4 win from the foothills team.

The lack of a polo field in Calgary had caused a noticeable decline of polo play in the city, and any town players had to join in with the rural clubs if they wanted to play. The Calgary Polo Club received an invitation to participate in Chipman Cup play in Winnipeg, but the locals were unable to muster a team to go to Manitoba.

However, both Pincher Creek and Pekisko did send teams to the Manitoba competition, and both teams were reported to have played excellent polo. Snowden, Holmes, Shakerley and Carley represented Pekisko, who defeated Winnipeg B 6-1 in Winterton Cup play, while Pincher Creek won 6-3 over the Winnipeg A team. Pekisko then captured the Winterton Cup with a 3-1 win over Pincher Creek. In the final of Chipman Cup play Pincher Creek defeated Winnipeg 10 goals to 3.

The community of Cowley formed a polo team in 1909, and in late September held its first tournament. The Cowley team managed to defeat teams from Pincher Creek and North Fork.

In the fall Major George Ross shipped a string of polo ponies to San Diego, California. Besides Ross polo players Justin Deanne-Freeman and H. Robertson travelled to the California community of Coronado Beach to play polo during the winter months. Freeman sold his horse, Bobs, to a California polo player for the very high price of a thousand dollars.

Tragedy struck in March of 1910 as Justin Deanne-Freeman of Millarville, at the age of 29, was killed while playing polo at Coronado Park near San Diego. When another horse and rider collided with him, Freeman's mount reared with the horse's head striking him and knocking him off his saddle, and he suffered a concussion in the fall. Freeman was rushed to the hospital where an operation was performed to relieve the pressure, but he died several hours later. Freeman had been considered as one of the most fearless riders ever seen on a polo field.

In April of 1910 polo enthusiasts of southern Alberta met and set up a tournament schedule for the year that included both A and B class teams. It was decided that an attempt would be made to form a western Canada polo association. A proposal to shorten the ten minute periods to seven and a half minutes was not accepted by the majority.

There was not, however, a great deal of organized polo competition in the Calgary area during the summer of 1910. Practise games were held at the Fish Creek, High River, Millarville and Pekisko polo fields, but arranged competition was somewhat lacking. Hurdle and polo pony races were again part of the annual Calgary exhibition held in July.

Most of Calgary's society was reported to be in attendance at the seventh annual Calgary Horse Show that was held in Sherman's Auditorium in April of 1911. There were over 1,000 entries, coming from many parts of the Dominion, in the competition. Polo ponies were entered in several events, including a heavy weight polo pony class and jumping events. Miss Walsh rode Smokey to a world record of over six feet in the ladies high jumping event. The Shriner's Hall was the scene of the Horse Show Dance following the competition.

Representatives from various polo clubs met in Calgary in April to set up a tournament schedule for the season that included both A and B class competition.

The Hone Cup could be put up for competition or challenged for at the Fish Creek polo grounds every two weeks. The first competition for this trophy took place in June as the Millarville team of G. Milton, M. Fraser, E. Douglass and W. Trevenan beat the Calgary quartet of A. Hone, A. Landale, W. Hooley and J. Jephson by a 5-4 score in a match that showed some excellent polo.

An A team polo tournament was held at Fish Creek in late June. An admission of 50¢ each for spectators was a new high price for local polo competition. Ross scored six goals as Calgary led all the way to defeat Pekisko 12-5. Others on the Calgary lineup were MacNaughten, Captain Amphlett and W. Landale. Shackerley, Snowden, Harper and W. Scort comprised the losing team. The Fish Creek team of three Hones and R. Hett then defeated Millarville in the second preliminary match. In the final Calgary and Fish Creek were tied one-all at the end of the first chukker, but the Fish Creek horses tired, and Landale scored five goals to lead Calgary to an 8-11 win.

In competition for the Millarville Cup played at that community, Calgary defeated the Cochrane team of Kerfoot, Rhodes, Saunders and O. Critchley by a 5-2 score. Pekisko led Millarville 8-0 at the half and won by a 10-2 score. In the cup final Pekisko, behind the fine play of R. Robertson, defeated Calgary 9-4 in what was considered to be a great match. In other competition, the Pekisko B team beat Millarville B 6-5.

Ross displayed superior generalship and stickhandling as Calgary won over Fish Creek by a 7-2 score at the High River polo tournament. The match, in which Millarville edged Pekisko 8-7, was said to be the finest exhibit of polo ever seen in High River.

Gymkhana events formed a good part of the program of the Millarville race meet in 1911, with the Gretna Green race and ladies thread and needle competition two of the favourite events. Included in the longer races were a mile and a half hurdle race over six hurdles and a six furlong polo pony race.

Calgary polo team captain George Ross said that the lack of a local polo field had deferred the Winnipeg Polo Club from playing in Calgary, but an effort would be made to arrange a game on the High River field which he considered to be the best in Alberta.

In October arrangements were completed for a Canadian polo team, consisting of locals A. Hone, J. Noton, A. Landale, G. Ross and K. Snowden, to play polo during the winter at Coronado Beach, California.

The Alberta polo players did well in California, winning their first game by one goal, and then beating a visiting English team. The Canadians then went on to win the California championships, and in the state finals they beat Santa Barbara 15-2 before a cheering crowd that included many Canadians. A Los Angeles paper reported, "Major Ross and his hard driving aggression simply played rings around the Santa Barbara polo team today in the most spectacular game ever seen here." Ross was the shining light of the game, but the long accurate drives of Hone accounted for five goals. Snowden and Norton completed the winners lineup.

The Canadian team then travelled to San Francisco where they lost to two different teams from San Mateo in the Crocker Cup competition. This was a handicap tournament, and the Alberta team's handicap was set at six goals.

Major Ross was injured in the San Mateo game and his place in the lineup was taken by Hobbs.

Snowden scored three goals to lead the Canadians in their win over an English team, then in the Crocker Cup finals they defeated the Slashers 9-8 to take the championship and complete their California competition for the season.

The 1912 Calgary Horse Show ran from April 9-12. It was reported to have opened "with a fanfare of trumpets and a blaze of glory." Lt. Governor Bulyea formally opened the show, which included over 1,000 entries in the many classes.

More than three thousand spectators stayed until after midnight to see Miss Walsh, riding Smokey, the world record holder, capture the ladies amateur high jump title for the second straight year. On the last evening of competition Angus McDonald of Jumping Pound rode Smokey to clear six feet, two inches in the high jump and set a new Alberta record. Polo ponies were entered in various classes in this large and comprehensive show.

In June it was announced that polo pony competition would be a new feature of the Exhibition held in July. This show is not to be confused with Frontier Days, later to be called the Stampede, which took place in October of 1912.

The North Fork polo team defeated High River 11-2 in Winterton Cup competition at Winnipeg in July. North Fork led 4-0 at the end of the first chukker. In the next period High River's Landale had the misfortune of falling off his horse and breaking his shoulder blade. Other High River players were Killam, Nelson, Holmes and Freeman. The North Fork team of Connolly, Gunn, Burns and Evans then beat the Fort Osborne Barracks team 7-1 to take the Winterton Cup and the championship of western Canada. In further competition at Winnipeg the North Fork team went on to capture both the Chipman and the Osler Cups.

There were two Cochrane teams, two teams from Pekisko and representation from both Millarville and the hometown at the August polo tournament in High River. Not long after the first game started so did a continual rain, and the tournament was washed out.

The Canadian team of K. Snowden, O.A. Critchley, H. Robertson and R. Carle opened the winter polo season in California by defeating the Coronado Beach team by four goals in a New Year's Day game. This was followed up by a 9-3 win over Pasadena, with K. Snowden earning individual honours on the strength of his six goals. O. Critchley was the star as the Canadians again defeated Pasadena; this time by an 11-4 score.

In polo pony flat racing Snowden's Jumbo proved to be the fastest polo pony in the competition, and Critchley's Indian horse finished third.

The Canadians had lost only one game until they met up with the All-

Hawaiian team who trounced them by eight goals. Snowden opened the scoring, but from then on the Hawaiians, with their larger horses, took command. The match was refereed by Major Ross who now played for the Coronado Polo Club.

Unfortunately Robertson was injured, and when two other team members had to return to Canada their competition ended. It was reported of the Alberta team that, "the ability of their speedy mounts to take the hard riding made them favourites of the spectators."

The Cochrane Polo Tournament for the Van Wart Cup was held in July of 1913. It was considered that this tournament would serve as the Alberta championship. In the first game the Fish Creek team of F. MacNaughten, R. Brown, A. Hone and H. Hone whitewashed the Cowley team 14-3. Then in the final game Fish Creek defeated the hometown Cochrane team of De la Vergne, O. Critchley, C. Landale and G. Rhodes by a 9-4 score. Fish Creek pressed early in the game, but Rhodes broke away to score two goals and Cochrane led 2-0. However excellent horsemanship and accurate stickhandling soon gave the Fish Creek team the upper hand.

A large crowd of polo enthusiasts had motored out from Calgary for the game. The match, as were all games under the Western Canada Polo Association, was played according to the Hurlingham rules, with the exception of the size limit of the ponies.

There was also competition at the Cochrane tournament for the Ladies Challenge Trophy, with Kennedy's, Trevenan's, Carle's and Proud's teams competing.

There is little evidence of any organized polo being played in Calgary during the 1913 season. However polo ponies were very popular among local riders, and a polo pony dash as well as hurdle races were part of an August equestrian program at Victoria Park.

A tournament for the Osler Cup, emblematic of the polo championship of western Canada, was held at Cowley in September. Many Calgarians travelled to the hamlet to view the competition. North Fork, the 1912 winners of the Osler Cup, defeated the Macleod team by an 11-3 score. The Cochrane and Cowley teams played even for the first three periods, and then Cochrane netted three quick goals in the last quarter to win 6-3.

In the final match North Fork had the initial edge in play, but then Cochrane, behind the great play of Critchley, tied the score at three-all. After thirty minutes of overtime Cochrane scored to capture the Osler Cup and the western Canada championship. Other Cochrane players were Landale, De la Vergne and Rhodes, while North Forks lineup included Connelly, Milvain, Gunn and Burn. Robertson captained the Macleod team. Immediately following the Cowley tournament the four teams boarded the train to go to a polo tournament in Spokane.

The four Alberta teams were joined by the Portland Polo Club in the first international polo tournament at the Interstate Fair. Rule changes in the sport of polo allowed quarter and half point penalties for fouls and safeties.

Portland opened the tournament with a five and a quarter point win over Cochrane, who the next day beat Cowley by four goals. Portland was awarded the tournament championship when they defeated North Fork by one goal. In post tournament exhibition the Macleod team outplayed and outran the Osler

Cup winner Cochrane team to win by three goals. A.C. Landale of Glenbow, and a member of the Cochrane team, said that he was going to move to Spokane to raise polo ponies for the polo enthusiasts of that city.

Coyote hunt near Weasel Head Bridge, 1914.

Alberta did not have a complete polo team playing during the 1913-14 winter season in California as it had for the past two years, but several players did winter and play polo in the San Diego area. In the season opener at Coronado Beach veteran player O.A. Critchley of Calgary played against his son Jack who lived in Winnipeg. Another Calgarian playing at Coronado was George Ross.

1914 competition for the Osler Cup, emblematic of the polo championship of Western Canada, took place at Fish Creek polo field in June between the Fish Creek and Cochrane polo clubs. Prior to the game the trail south from Calgary to the polo grounds was crowded with coaches, democrats, a tally-ho and autos as more than 700 Calgarians travelled to Fish Creek to see the contest.

In the first half the Fish Creek team of A. and J. Hone, R. Brown and F. MacNaughten completely overshadowed their opponents, and when they stopped for refreshments the score was 6-2 in favour of Hone's team. In the second half Cochrane's team play improved and they were able to anticipate the moves of the Fish Creek players much better. However, at the end of the fifth chukker Fish Creek led 11-4, and so they decided to lay back. When Cochrane scored two quick goals the Fish Creek team pressed again and the game ended 13-6.

A. Hone and R. Brown were the outstanding players for the winners, while De La Vergne was the best of the Cochrane team. Other players for the losers were A. Landale, O. Critchley and G. Rhodes. Ross and Trevanen served as referees.

In July an American type tournament, where the results related to goals for and against, was played at Fish Creek. The tournament was a success, and the team of A. Hones came out the winners.

The Alberta teams were again invited to the international polo competition at Spokane. The Americans said that the war would not stop the competition, but this was not the attitude in Canada.

Following the World War polo was played on a field adjacent to the Chinook Jockey Club.

Louis Welsh jumping world record holder "Barra Lad".

Athletics—Track and Field

Although historical details are sparse the walking feats and endurance displayed by many of those individuals who travelled through southern Alberta prior to its settlement are worthy of note.

Impromptu sports days took place at the Metis camps, trading posts and later at the Mounted Police posts. Reverend John McDougall felt that these events provided a good way to make friends. After besting several Indians in a race McDougall said, "That race opened many a lodge and the heart of many a friend in subsequent years."

A track and field program was reported to have taken place at Fort Macleod in 1876, with members of the police, settlers and natives participating for a variety of prizes. Moosewa, a native from Lac St. Anne and one of the best runners in the Territories, won the mile race in a time of five minutes and eight seconds. It was reported that the pole vault event winner cleared nine feet three inches.

With the natural inclination of many men to run, jump and throw the men stationed at the early Calgary police post held foot races among themselves or against the Indians or Metis who frequented the adjacent trading posts. The smooth boulders found in the Bow or Elbow Rivers were ideal for "putting the stone", while a facsimile of cabre tossing probably took place using locally cut logs.

In 1883 foot races were held on the flats adjacent to the Barracks. An interesting and exciting foot race of 150 yards, best two out of three for fifty dollars a side, took place between W. West, formerly of Winnipeg, and Constable Pennyfather. The betting was lively among the spectators. A tie took place in the first race, then West won the next two heats to claim the money.

A five mile race was run between several members of the Mounted Police, a Sarcee, a Stoney and Little Plume—a Blackfoot who emerged victorious. In November Little Plume went to Winnipeg to race J. Irvine, reported to be the fastest runner in Manitoba. The race was to be run on a sawdust track, but it was discovered prior to the race that someone had placed some broken glass in the sawdust. Little Plume wore his moccasins and won the five mile race in a time of 27 minutes and 22 seconds.

An eight hour walking match for a side bet was held in Calgary between Boswell of Calgary and Taylor from Boston. The challenge of competition often brought about such matches.

Footraces were held on the Queen's Birthday in May of 1884. Donahue was the major winner, while other proficient competitors included: Osborne, White,

Smart, Grossick, Critchley, Wright, Little Plume and Big Hawk. A July footrace for $50 a side was run between Constables Draycott and Burnett. Draycott, who carried the mail between Calgary and Medicine Hat, won the race. The competition was repeated the following month.

The 9th Battalion athletics took place on the Queen's Birthday in 1885. An entry fee of 50¢ per event allowed the competitors to compete for prize money from three to ten dollars. J. Patrick was the official starter. French Kid won the 100 yard dash, the 220 in 23.5 seconds, and the hurdles, the 440 and 880 by Saunders, one mile—Critchley, standing long jump—W. Thorburn 10', 7½", running long jump—A. Roselle 15', 10½", standing high jump—Thorpe 4', running high jump—Critchley 4', 10", hop-step and jump—J. Donohue 36', 9", putting 27½ pound stone—Gillies 23', 7"; he also put the 17¼ pound stone 34', 11" and won the hammer throw with a toss of 78', 8". The vaulting with pole winner cleared 8', 6", while Wright won the cricket ball throw with a distance of 339 feet. Other events included, wheelbarrow race with competitors blindfolded, 200 yard sack race, 100 yard three legged race, 50 yard bucket race, smoking race, a greased pig chase with the pig as the prize, tug of war and a Red River jig competition, as well as horse races and a rifle shooting competition. A week later a foot race for a $50 bet was run between Laboucans and French Kid who won the race. A mile race between Stokes and Irwin took place in the fall.

The sports day, held Dominion Day of 1886, was basically the same program as the year before, however several events had been added including a fat man's race, a five mile run with a $100 purse for the winner, as well as events for boys and girls thirteen and under and sixteen and under. A gold medal was offered for the top competitor. Spectators sat in comfort in the new 1,000 seat grandstand that had been built adjacent to the track. Most of the distances and times were not up to the performances of the year previous, but C. Ross ran the 100 yard dash in 11¼ seconds, while O. Critchley raised his high jump mark to 5', 1", and Tom Carney did 16', 6" in the running broad jump. The latter event at one time was known as the wide jump and is commonly known as the long jump today.

The Sons of England sponsored a train excursion to Banff during the summer. Track and field events were held at the mountain town.

In August of 1886 a 50 hour go-as-you-please walking race was held at Claxton's Star Rink. The race was run between set times over a several evening period. The affair was won by Stokes by three miles, however the event was so badly managed that the newspapers would not give a report on it. A five mile race was run in the rink in October for a medal and a $150 side bet between Stokes and Irvine. Irvine gave Stokes a lap headstart but still won in a time of 28 minutes and 20 seconds. A ten mile race included Stokes, Irvine, and two Indians, Deerfoot and Dried Meat. The race was run on the 17 laps to a mile Star rink track. Stokes beat Deerfoot by one lap, but there were many who claimed that the lap counters had erred. Another ten mile race was run between Stokes and Deerfoot, however the race was held up for a lengthy time because the Indian would not run until he got some money. He was paid $12.50 but the race was further held up as he argued for more. Stokes won with a time of 54½ minutes, while Deerfoot took 60 minutes to complete the distance. Besides a 25 mile go-as-you-please race a six hour time limit race was held. Stokes did two laps further than Deerfoot's 32 miles.

Des Brisay, who ran from scratch, defeated three other runners in a mile handicap race at Claxton's in December. Ritchie and Tarrant met in a 100 yard dash, with a great deal of wagering taking place on the outcome.

On May 24 of 1887 G. Irvine defeated Fellow from the Cochrane Ranche in a race that was billed as the Alberta 100 yard championship.

The 1887 Dominion Day sports program was held at Owen's Riverside Track in the present Elbow Park area. J. Irvine won the 100 yard dash; Deerfoot beat Irvine in the 440, and Little Plume won the 880 yard event. There was a tug-of-war competition as well as a hose and reel race. During the summer the bicycle club held several rides and sprints. A twelve hour go-as-you-please running race was held in the Claxton rink in September. The entry fee for the race, which ran for three hours on each of the four evenings, was $10.

During this era the great Indian runner, Deerfoot, did not race, as he was a fugitive from the police.

Nine track and field events as well as a bicycle race were held at the Owen's track on Dominion Day of 1888. The prize moneys for the winners of the half and one mile races were $100 and $125 respectively. More than one 100 yard dash race for $50 a side bet was held during the summer. G. Irvine was the top competitor in the meet. The bicycle championships of the North West Territories were also held on the Riverside Track during the summer. A gold watch went to the winner decided by the winner of two out of three one-mile heats.

A meeting was held by the Calgary Amateur Athletic Association in the Royal Hotel in the spring of 1889. The group, under the executive consisting of J. Thompson, A. Allen, Dr. Lafferty, A. Ellis, and A.D. Braithwaite, formed a joint stock company with 500 shares of $10 par value each to be sold. $1,400 worth of stock was immediately subscribed. Block 78, south of the tracks, was purchased at a price of $30 a lot. A half mile track for running and cycling was laid out as well as a sports field to accommodate cricket, lacrosse and football.

There were 25 events with prize money from $2-25 at the Queen's birthday sports day held at Owen's track in May of 1890. A total of $340 in prize money was given out for the track and field events. Mr. Critchley donated a cup valued at $30 to the top point maker. D. Fraser leaped 18', 10" in the running broad jump event. J. Kerr won the standing broad jump with a distance of 11', 1" and won the 100 yard dash in 11 seconds flat. The times for the 440 and 880 were 58 seconds and 2.24 respectively. The well attended event was considered to be a great succes. During the year some of the members of E. Division, N.W.M.P. formed an amateur athletic association.

Foot races, as well as horse races, were run at Pine Creek on Dominion Day. Deerfoot was the winner of the 100 yard dash. Elsewhere in the Territories Galligher of Lethbridge was reported to have run the 100 yards in 10.7 seconds.

In 1891 the C.A.A.A. had planned to have a Queen's birthday sports day on their field, which was located where the present Victoria school now stands, but this was cancelled in favour of the Firemen's Sports Day to be held at the Agriculture grounds where a half mile track had been laid out. Tarrant won the

100 yard dash in a very good time of 10 1/5 seconds. The value of his win was accented by the fact that the other runners had been given a handicap in the race. C. Marsh won the boy age 13 and under 100 yards in 14 flat, while the winner's time in the under 16 race was 12 1/5 seconds. A. Murphy jumped 10′, 6½″ in the standing broad jump (with weights) event. J. Fraser won the "throwing the hammer" event with a heave of 78′, 7″. Seven competitors ran the 220 yard hurdle race with the winner's time being 30 seconds. The open 440 yard flat race was won by D. Cosgrove in 54 seconds, while McLean ran the N.W.M.P. 440 in 61 3/5 seconds. Deerfoot won the Indian quarter mile race in 57 seconds, and the open mile was won by Henderson with a time of 5 minutes and 38 seconds. The winner's time in the three-legged 100 yard race was 14.8 seconds. Rogers won the running hop, step and jump with a distance of 38′, 7½″. Other events included putting the weight (16 pounds—37′, 7″), cricket ball throw (114 yards, 2″) and the football kick.

A marathon type race took place in the Calgary area in August of 1891. Victor Graham was sure that he could run the 28 miles from Calgary to the Quorn Ranch in five and a half hours. A great deal of betting was done in regards to the outcome of this run, but Graham's backers were the winners as he completed the race against time in four and three-quarter hours.

Wagering also took place the following year when a 220 yard dash competition was held on the agriculture track with G. Baetz and C. Tom as the competitors.

At the Calgary Fair, held June 20-23, there were hose and reel races and ladder climbs against time competition. Bicycle races were held. Even with handicaps up to 75 yards allowed to some Wrigley of Lethbridge won the mile bike handicap in a time of 2.56.6. E. King was second, however he won the two mile in 6.29.

F. Pinkham won a 440 yard foot race in a time of 56.2. F. Fletcher edged Metis J. Hirondelle to take the boys' 12 and under 100 yard dash, while Chester McBride captured the same event for the younger boys. A planned tug-of-war did not materialize.

Torrance of Calgary travelled to Edmonton where he lost in a race to Moo-. sewa of Lac St. Anne, with the winner's backers pocketing the $100 side bet.

On July 3, there were 17 track and field events as well as cycle races held at the C.A.A.A. sponsored sports day. In September the Calgary Bicycle Club held a day of races at the Agriculture Grounds. An entry fee of 25¢ allowed competitors to compete in a quarter mile race, one and two miles distances and a handicap race.

In October Moosewa beat Calgary's Tarrant by three yards, clocking a time of 10.6 seconds, in a 100 yard dash held on Stephen Avenue. The runners were backed at $50 a side, but over $600 changed hands in the wagering.

In 1893 the Fire Brigade held a sports day on May 24, with a gate admission of 25¢. Morris won the 100 yard dash in a time of 10.4; Godenrath took the 440 in 61 seconds flat and the 120 yard hurdles in 17 seconds. Murray led the milers to the tape in a time of 6.09. Bruce's 37′, 6″ was the longest distance in the running hop, step and jump competition, and Nesbit won the football kick with a distance of 158′ 9″. Marshall took the lacrosse ball throw with a distance of 104 yards, and Fraser heaved the hammer 69′ 4″. Nattrass won the pole vault with a leap of 7′

9½", and the Scandinavians beat the All-Comers in the tug-of-war competition. A one mile bicycle race was won in a time of three minutes and 20 seconds.

There was track and field competition as well as bicycle races held at the Calgary Exhibition in July. Wing won the five mile bike race in a time of 16.41.4. There were running races at distances from 100 to 880 yards, a 220 yard hurdle race and a ladder climb.

A 100 mile running race, to be completed over a several day period, was planned to be run in Calgary. However after several postponements it was put off indefinitely.

Track and field, including Indian and squaw races, and bicycle races were part of a Dominion Day sports program held in Calgary in 1894. Dallas, a newcomer to the city cleared 41′ 11″ in the running hop, step and jump. Dallas also won the pole vault with a height of 8′ 2″, and when the bar was raised to 9′ 2″ he almost cleared it. There were over 200 Indians, including many squaws, competing in the obstacle races.

Dr. O'Sullivan, who had arrived in Calgary from Ontario in 1892, set a Territory record of 10.2 seconds in the 100 yard dash and, as well, recorded a time of 23.2 seconds in the 220 yard run. These events were run on election day.

Wrigley won the district one mile bicycle championship with a time of 2.53.4. The Calgary bicycle team competed in meets at Medicine Hat and Macleod. Slow bicycle races were included in the gymkhana held at the Owen's race track located in the future Elbow Park district.

A report from Edmonton claimed that Allen had defeated Moosewa in a 440 yard race in a fast time of 51.8 seconds.

In the spring of 1895, what was billed as the Alberta 220 yard championship, was held in Calgary. Allen beat Indian runner Moosewa to claim the $100 purse. There were claims that wagers placed on the race exceeded $500. The pair met again in September over a 200 yard distance, with the purse being raised to $150. Dr. O'Sullivan served as the starter. Allen led most of the way, but the Indian pulled ahead to win in a time of 20.4.

The Dominion sports meet, for amateurs only, was held at the A.A.U. grounds located south of the railroad tracks. C. Watson won the boys age ten and under 100 yard race in 14 seconds, and E. Fletcher ran the same distance in 12.4 to capture the boys' age 15 and under race. The running high jump was won by C. Marshal with a leap of 5′ 2″. Dr. O'Sullivan won the 100 yard handicap in 11 seconds flat, the 220 in 23.2 and the 440 in 57 seconds flat. Kiss-him-in-the-face bested the tape in 60 seconds to capture the Indian 440 yard dash. A bicycle obstacle race followed a course that went through and under hurdles. Prizes for the competitors were swim tickets to the swim baths.

Calgarian Ernie King left Calgary at 6:45 a.m. one morning and rode his bike to Fort Macleod, arriving there at 6:15 p.m. The next day he rode back to Calgary.

In 1896 the Queen's Birthday was celebrated in Calgary with the Caledonian Games, sponsored by the Sons of Scotland, Camp Robin Adair. The events began with a grand parade, headed by bagpipes and a brass band, with the procession following a route from downtown Calgary to the Agriculture

Grounds. A full slate of track and field and cycle events was held, with prizes ranging from one to ten dollars going to the top finishers. For some events, such as the 440 yard dash and the 120 yard hurdles, but with only five hurdles, the winners received medals as well as cash prizes. Spectators were charged 15¢ for the morning competition and 20¢ for the afternoon events.

Bannister did well by winning the 16 pound stone, throwing the hammer and the running broad jump. The Fraser brothers both captured a good share of place positions. Baird of Canmore won the 440 and the pole vault.

The preliminary tug-of-war competition saw the Scots versus the Irish, town against country, Icelanders pulled against the Germans, and the Fire Brigade matched against the Police. In the finals the Fire Brigade won over a combined team who called themselves the All-Comers for the tug-of-war championship.

Indian tug-of-war saw the Blackfeet outpull the Stonies. As part of the Indian sports program the Blackfeet defeated the Stonies 4-1 in a game of 25 a-side football.

Other events in the Caledonian Games included: catch the greasy pig, climb the greasy pole, Cumberland style wrestling.

Because the planned bicycle races had not been sanctioned, fun races were held instead. Besides a 100 yard slow race, there was a 300 yard run and ride race with two members who changed places after each 100 yards.

There was a matched 10 yard race in which Fred Viney won by five feet over Dr. O'Sullivan. There were also several 100 yard handicap races. Gordon Burndick won the boys ten and under 100, while Sinclair won the event for the older boys.

The C.P.R. offered special rates for those individuals travelling to Calgary for the sports activities.

The North West Territories sports championships were held in Calgary during the summer. The events took place on Stephen Avenue near the Alberta Hotel. The feature event was the ladder, coupling and hose reel race with twelve men to a team.

The Calgary Press Athletic Association held a formation meeting in April of 1897. During the same month the Sheep Creek Amateur Athletic Association sports day was held Dominion Day at the Athletic Grounds. The track and field program included a printer's handicap as well as fun races. The football kick and the cricket ball throw were part of the regular events.

On another day bicycle races were held at the C.A.A.A. grounds; admission 25¢. A fast time of 2.39 was recorded for the mile. The bank clerks held two cycle races out to Fish Creek and back, with B. McIntyre recording the best time of 1.02.36.

The Territorial bicycle meet was held in Calgary in early September. The complete results may be found in the chapter on cycling.

In September track and field was part of the Elbow Park gymkhana. Times of 11 and 24 seconds were recorded by the winner of the 100 and 220 yard sprints.

The Queen's Birthday, 1898, Fire Brigade sports program was said to be the best such a day ever held in Calgary. A grand parade was held following a route from the fire hall to the athletic grounds. Bicycle races were equal to if not predominating in popularity over the track and field events. F. McCarthy took the half mile spring in a time of 1.18.5 and the mile in 2.51.5. J. McLean won the Firemen's Handicap in 2.57.5. There was only one finisher in the slow race as all the other competitors fell off their bikes.

In the track and field competition musician A. Augade put the sixteen pound stone 31' 8", won the 120 yard hurdles in a time of 17.5 and came home first in the 220 in 23.5. M. McNaughlin tossed the cabre 31 feet to win that event, and he also took second place in the hammer throw. E. Riley came home first in the mile, and R. Chipman took first place in the pole vault with a leap of 7' 9". L. Orr again proved the best in the standing broad jump with a leap of 10' 8", and Dio Calihoo of the High River Indian School cleared 37' 8" in the running hop, step and jump.

Ernie King won the boys age 11 and under 200 yards in a good time of 13 seconds. There was a fireman's handicap 100, and the brothers John and Phillip One Spot tied for first place in a time of 11.2 in the Industrial School boys 100 yard dash. Another tie in the open 100 saw Phillip Big Shot and L. Bishop breasting the tape together. L. Orr won the cricket ball throw, while Ed Bush of the High River Indian School was the best athlete in the football kick.

In the catch the greasy pig contest Sam Lloyd was told that, "he could not play the game whole hog and that the game was for the Indian School boys."

In the firemen's sports L. Lloyd won the ladder climb in a time of nine seconds. Comer and Lloyd's time of 1.5.4. was tops in the hose coupling contest. The best time to lay 150 yards of hose was 22.5 seconds.

A team of Calgary's bicycle racers travelled to Edmonton for that town's Dominion Day bicycle races. Although Edmonton won the team race several of Calgary's cyclists won individual events: F. McCarthy won the half and mile events, McLean took the quarter mile, and Ramsay was home first in the five mile event.

The Territorial Wheel Championships were held in Calgary in late summer. Among the events were handicap, pursuit, novice, boys', and a quarter mile fat men's race. W. Riley of Calgary was timed in 35 seconds to win the quarter mile sprint. He also won the half in 1.15.5 and took first place in the mile race for locals. S. Hayward of Winnipeg won the Territorial half and mile championships with times of 1.14 and 2.42 respectively. Five out of the eight riders came to grief in the last lap of the five mile race, which was won by Ramsay in 14.59. Calgary captured the three mile team race.

A 220 yard foot race was an added attraction to the meet. Dr. O'Sullivan was the winner in a time of 24 seconds.

Stewart Mackid of Calgary finished third out of over a hundred runners in a cross country run held at Upper Canada College in Toronto in the spring of 1899.

The Fire Brigade's annual sports day was touted as the greatest day in Calgary's history. Special trains from all directions brought many competitors and spectators to the city, and there was not a spare bed left in the city.

At 9 a.m. a great parade began in the downtown area and was routed to Victoria Park. The Canmore Brass Band led off, followed by the Calgary Fire Brigade Band and the Fire Brigade members in full dress uniform.

There were 42 events including track and field, Indian events and cycle races.

Harold Bannister of Davisburg won the all-round athletic championship, winning the cabre with a 36' 5" heave, tossing the hammer 75' 1", high jumping five feet, and placing second in the shot put, the latter event again won by Augade. The pole vault was the best contested event, which was won by W. Mooney of St. Joseph's Industrial School with a leap of 9' 1". L. Orr again proved his superiority in the standing long jump with a leap of 10' 9". Campbell won the hundred yard dash in 11 flat and the 440 in 59.4. One Spot took the Indian boys 100, and there was a dash just for C.P.R. employees. Two Indian boys from St. Joseph, George Vielle and John English, captured the football kick and the cricket ball throw with distances respectively of 171' 10" and 105.5 yards. There were several bicycle races, with Lou Kerr taking the boys' 14 and under half mile in 1.51.

May 24, 1900 was said to be, "a red letter day in Calgary's history", with a huge program of sports taking place on the Queen's 85th birthday. Many Indians were part of the huge morning parade to Victoria Park.

There were fifteen track events, including a fat man's fifty yard dash for men weighing over 200 pounds, and ten field events included in the day's program. J. Taylor won the open 100 and the 220, while A. Augade won the 120 yard hurdles. The Policemen's 100 ended in a dead heat between brothers L. and M. Seller, and there were dashes for C.P.R. employees, Indian boys, and a Firemen's handicap 100.

H. Riley came home first in the 440. J. MacMillan took first place in the hop, step and jump with a distance of 40' 4", and he won the cricket ball throw with a very good toss of 110½ yards. M. Sherbino recorded a distance of 10' 3" in the standing broad jump, while the cabre and hammer events were won by N. McLaughlin. M. Cardell was a double winner in the running high jump and running long jump. There was keen rivalry in the tug-of-war competition with the Calgary C.P.R. besting Edmonton for the championship.

Included in the six bicycle races was a ladies' quarter mile. Elwin Allan rode home first in the boy's 14 and under half mile bicycle race with a time of 1.38.5. Fred McCarthy won the open half in 1.26 and the mile in 3.02. Woodside captured first place in the three mile cycle with a time of ten minutes, eleven seconds, and G. Bennett was home first in the one mile novice race.

Firemen's sports were held on Stephen Avenue with the Calgary firemen defeating Edmonton's team in the hose and reel competition with a time of 41½ seconds. The Fire Brigade, headed by Cappy Smart, made a brilliant run up Stephen Avenue. In the evening there was music and a brilliant fireworks display.

During the summer the Calgary Wheel Association sponsored a race to Fish Creek. Races were part of the sports program at the Nose Creek picnic, and track and field competition were part of the Baptist Church picnic held on Eau Claire Island.

It was reported that at the May 24, 1900 Olds sports day a member of a work train cleared 13 feet with perfect ease in the standing long jump event.

The May 24, 1901 parade was routed from the Fire Hall, through the streets to end at City Hall. Included in the procession were the Fire Brigade, Medicine Hat, Edmonton, Canmore and Olds bands.

At one p.m. the M.L.A.'s and the South African group travelled to Victoria

Park for the sports program. Cups, medals and cash prizes up to ten dollars were awaiting to be awarded to the various winners. The cycle races were held under the sanction of the Canadian Wheelmen's Association.

Birnie won the 100 yard open in a time of 11¼ seconds, and Fidler was first in the fat man's 50 yard dash. Sherbino was first in the running high jump with a height of 5' 1" and the best running long jumper with a distance of 17' 8". He further displayed his skills by winning the standing high jump with 3' 10", the running hop, step and jump with a 40' 3" distance, and finishing second in the standing broad jump, the latter event won by Orr with an 11¼" leap. H. and E. Riley were first home in the 100 yard three-legged race.

Many proud parents watched their children compete in dashes, both for boys and girls, with classes for those under age 4, 6, 8, 10, 12 and 14. A 200 yard race was held for the squaws. In tug-of-war competition the City team took 2½ minutes to defeat the C.P.R. team.

Chief Smart won the ladder contest with a time of 11.4, and he teamed with Bruce to win the hose coupling contest.

In July a picked group of Calgary baseball players travelled to Medicine Hat for some competition. While in that city some of their members took part in track and field competition. Stagg won the 440 in 54 seconds flat, and Fletcher was first in the 100 in 10.2. Sherbino won the running broad jump with a good leap of 19' 6" and the hop, step and jump with a distance of 41' 6". Orr led in the standing broad jump with a tremendous leap of twelve feet.

During the summer a bicycle gymkhana was held on the grounds of the Pearce Estate. The second "great road race to Fish Creek" saw G. Bennett ride to the finish, the winner, in a time of one hour and two minutes, ten minutes faster than the previous year's time.

In 1902 it was decided to postpone the Firemen's sports from Victoria Day to the planned Coronation Day under the title of Coronation Day Sports. However as the King was sick, this was twice postponed until August. As a result the prizes for the meet, cups, silver medals, field glasses and fancy walking sticks, remained in the display window of Mitchell's Shoe Store for several weeks.

Finally on August 12 the big day arrived, and like previous sports days sponsored by the Fire Department, began with a parade. More so this year, than at similar days in the past, military events played an important role and were keenly contested and enjoyed.

In the track and field competition J. Mitchell of Moose Jaw won the open 100 yard dash and the 120 yard hurdles. J. Taylor took the 220 in 25 seconds as well as finishing second to E. Crasl in the 440. H. Bannister proved to be a top competitor by winning the cabre, hammer throw and putting the shot. A good distance of 318' 2" gave C. Marshall the cricket ball medal, and Boehmer led the football kickers with a distance of 166'. The running high jump as well as the running hop, step and jump went to W. Flint, while L. Orr again won the standing broad jump as well as the running broad jump. A 4' 5" leap gave S. Orr the standing high jump prize. A. Biggins showed versatility as he won the open pole vault and the C.P.R. 100. There was a 100 yard for army men in uniform, firemen's 100, and a bandsman's race. Both boys and girls, from those under four up to age fourteen, had the opportunity to race. The tug-of-war competition was won by the N.W.M.P. team who needed seven minutes to beat a stubborn Canadian Mounted Regiment team.

In cycle competition Orin Adair proved to be the star as he won the mile in a time of 2.46, the three mile in 12 minutes, as well as the novice mile.

Labour Day celebrations were held in Calgary and track and field competition began to play a part in the sports program. A large crowd witnessed a mile relay for the Alberta Cup. Each team consisted of eight men, each of whom were to run 220 yards. The clerk's team won in a time of 3.48, finishing ahead of the leather workers', machinists' and printers' teams. Instead of a baton an envelope was carried to be passed on to the next runner. During the seventh relay position two men on horseback cut into the race and then were well embarrassed. A new cup, the Jackson, was put up for tug-of-war competition.

A wagering 100 yard race took place in September between J. Craske and E. Fletcher; the latter receiving a three yard handicap.

Thousands of Calgarians helped celebrate May 24 of 1903. The Fire Brigade Association again sponsored the sports day which included baseball and football tournaments, a band competition, track and field, and military sports. Festivities began at 10 a.m. with the parade leaving the Fire Hall to march to Victoria Park.

There were 2,400 paid admission and over 1,000 guest passes, not counting a great many who entered free by climbing over the low wooden fence at the grounds for the sports program. The boys' and girls' races, with events ranging for those under four and classes up to age fourteen were first on the program.

Jake Huber proved to be a top competitor by winning the running hop, step and jump and the running long jump as well as placing second in the standing broad jump, the latter event won by Lorne Orr. Vernon Shaw was first in putting shot, throwing the hammer, and as well tied for first in the pole vault. J. Samis tossed the cricket ball further than anyone else. W. McLaren won the 50 yard fat man's race as well as the football kick.

J. Foss edged Augade in the 75 yard bandsmen's race, and H. Niven was the top sprinter by taking the open 100. In the C.P.R. employees 100 M. Cardell finished ahead of Biggins, the 120 yard hurdles winner. Reilly was best in the soldiers 100, while Page had the best time in the tent pegging competition. The V.C. race was won by Sellar. Aron Adair proved to be the top cyclist by winning both the one and three mile cycle events.

The Firemen's sports were not completed during the Victoria Day program, so were held one evening during the summer on Atlantic Avenue. Ross Lyons was the winner of the novelty race. This event consisted of each of the competitors lying on a stretcher placed along the side of the road, and when the bell sounded the firemen had to get up, get dressed and run 50 yards to the finish line. Fletcher won the ladder climb in a time of 8¾ seconds, and the team of Biggins-Beale were the fastest in the three legged race. The coupling contest was won by J. Lloyd and Fred Tarrant. The union men's 100 winner was T. Semper, and the competition ended with the Firemen's handicap 100.

A Dominion Day baseball tournament included competition in base running for time and baseball throwing for accuracy and distance.

Labour Day celebrations were beginning to come into their own in Calgary. Besides a parade and speeches there was a sports program, including track and field, at Victoria Park. There were races for boys and girls, with classes from under age four up to age fourteen. Besides five 100 yard races for the various unions, there was an apprentice 100, fire department 100, and the open 100—won by E. Semper. E. Machon was the winner of the 220, and Miss Fraser edged Miss Morrison in the ladies race. L. Orr won the standing broad jump, and Wallace was best in the pole vault. The Alberta Cup, sponsored by the Albertan Newspaper, went to the Leather Workers followed by the Retail Clerks in the eight man mile relay. Dan Alton's Bridgemen outpulled the Carpenters in the finals of the tug-of-war to take the Jackson Cup.

During the summer the Fire Brigade sponsored Indian sports at the Exhibition Grounds. There was tug-of-war competition between the different tribes.

The C.P.R. ran special trains into Calgary bringing competitors and spectators to the Victoria Day, 1904, celebrations sponsored by the Firemen's Association. The Old's Band as well as 300 people arrived on the train from the north. The baseball tournament was won by Red Deer, and the Caledonians bested Red Deer and then the Brewery team to win the football tournament.

F. Mitchell was a double winner in the 100 and 220. Hornby was second in the 220 but won the 440 in 56.5. There were 100 yard dashes for firemen and one for union men. Vernon Shaw proved to be a tremendous athlete by winning the running high jump, pole vault, putting the shot and second place in the running long jump. Lorne Orr again won the standing high jump and tossing the cricket ball. The cabre toss was taken by H. McClelland, and J. Bartley kicked the football 168' to take first place in that event.

The Bridgemen defeated Trainmen and then the Brewery to take the tug-of-war title. Fletcher was first in the ladder race with a time of 21¼ seconds. In the military sports there were tent pegging, cutting the lemon, and tilting at the ring events. Boys and girls from under age 4 up to fourteen years had their own races.

In the evening the crowds gathered on Stephen Avenue to watch the fireworks. An accident occurred when a rocket went through a window.

Dominion Day festivities were beginning to play a role of importance in Calgary. In tug-of-war competition the Canadian Mounted Rifles team outpulled the men of the N.W.M.P. There was an "in and out" team race as well as military sports during the day.

Running and jumping became part of Calgary school girls' curriculum as provisions were made to include physical culture classes for the female students.

Four teams were entered in the Labour Day tug-of-war competition. However no winner decision was reached as a protest was received from the Waymen who protested that they had been jerked off their feet before they realized the pull had started. There were dashes for each trade group, a married ladie's race as well as children's races. E. Sempel won the open 220, the running high jump, and he was second in the open 100. M. Cardell was the top competitor in the running long jump and pole vault. Although K. White did not win a first prize, he placed second in many of the events. The relay race for the Alberta Cup was won by the leather workers' team.

Calgary homes, stores and schools were gaily decorated with flags in celebration of Victoria Day, 1905. Trains from four directions steamed into Calgary bringing in throngs of people anticipating a festive day in the city. Besides 21 track and field events, there were baseball and football tournaments, firemen's sports and children's races.

There were so many entries for the sprints that heats had to be run. Halward won both the 100 and 220. Vernon Shaw again proved his versatility by winning the putting the shot with a distance of 36' 4", the high jump with a 5' 2' leap, an 84' heave in the 16 pound hammer, first in the hop, step and jump, and a leap of 18' 6" to place second in the running broad jump. Neil McLaughlin, driver of No. 1 hook and ladder truck, won the cabre with a 34' 9" toss, and J. McKenzie of the Leavings placed second in both the cabre and shot put. Lorne Orr cleared 11' 1", with weights, in the standing broad jump, and newcomer J. Wood was first in the running broad jump with a leap of 18' 10". Mr. Alton's boys defeated the Fire Department team to take the tug-of-war title.

Teams from the Strathcona, Red Deer, Calgary and newly organized Brewery fire department competed in the firemen's sports events. The ladder team race as well as the hose race championship were won by the Calgary team. The entire day was deemed a great success, although the runners had found the track in poor shape.

Canada's national birthday celebration was observed in Calgary by sports and festivities. There were foot and fun races at the Baptist picnic held on the Chipman Ranch. A mounted tug-of-war was one of the activities included in the military sports held at the C.M.R. camp. Novelty races and a ladder team race were included in the Firemen's sports program.

On the morning of Labour Day, 1905 a huge parade travelled from Eighth to Ninth to Sixth and finally down Seventh Avenues in downtown Calgary. In the afternoon crowds gathered at Victoria Park to see five classes of both boys' and girls' races, six 100 yard union races, apprentices 100, a 50 yard fat man's race, 220, 440, half mile handicap and a 200 yard polo race. The carpenters won the tug-of-war and the leatherworkers captured the Alberta Cup for the union relay. The football kick went to Caledonian players W. Strang, and the Caledonian team took the three-legged race in some keen competition. Labour Day of 1905 in Calgary proved to be a big success.

During 1905 a ten mile race was held in Calgary. This was the first such long race to be held in the city since those which were held in Claxton's Rink many years before.

There were five starters, but only two runners were left by the time the five mile mark was reached, for three of the competitors had dropped out. Horby crossed the finish line, which was located in front of the grandstand at the Exhibition grounds, in one hour, eleven minutes and 45 seconds. Kibblewaite crossed the finish line in second place four minutes later.

In the fall a 100 yard footrace was held in Calgary between W.W. Smith, champion of B.C., and Russ Graydon, champion of Calgary and Boston. Times of 9.5 to 11 seconds were recorded by the many timers in the large crowd, many of whom had wagered on the outcome, but the official time was listed at 10.2

seconds. Considering the condition of the track the time was very good; possibly the fastest yet recorded in the province of Alberta.

A very heavy rain completely spoiled the 1906 Victoria Day sports program in Calgary. It was decided that the track and field as well as the firemen's sports would be held in August in conjunction with the fire chief's convention to be held in Calgary.

Twenty members of Calgary's Fire Department travelled up to Red Deer for that centre's Dominion Day sports program. Calgary teams won the ladder climb and tug-of-war, and they were second in the hose coupling competition. Two members of the Calgary group carried off a majority of the track and field awards.

Many ex-Americans in Calgary celebrated July 4th by participating in a day of sports. Besides baseball, lacrosse, auto and horse races, there was: climbing the greasy pole, catch the greasy pig, and American versus Canadian tug-of-war competition. Reddie edged Fullerton in a one mile cycle race.

A big parade preceded the Firemen's sports program on August 29, 1906. There were twelve starters in the 100, which was won in a good time of 10.4 by George Paris, a pre-race dark horse. However following his win he was recognized by Dr. O'Sullivan as one of the old greats from the east who he had raced against years before. In the hurdle event Biggins was leading until he fell on the last hurdle; the event won by Dresser in a time of 18.5 seconds. E. McLean's winning time for the 220 dash was 23 flat. He also earned several second place ribbons including one for the 100 yard dash. Hibbs won the 440 yard run as well as the Union Men's dash. V. Shaw won the vault with pole with a height of 7' 11" and Valiant of Winnipeg took the running high jump. E. McLair was first in the standing long jump, and N. Cowan was best in the running hop, step and jump. V. Shaw won the hammer toss with a distance of 78' and was second in putting the shot event. H. Ritchie won the putting the shot event and placed second behind McLaughlin in the cabre toss. E. McLean displayed his versatility by winning the football kick.

The hub and hub hose reel race won by Red Deer in a time of 23 seconds flat, and Innisfail won the open championship hose and reel competition.

Chief Smart finished third in a mile pace horse race. The program also included cowboys' sports, including bucking and roping competition.

There were 22 different union groups in the 1906 Labour Day parade. More than $1,000 in prizes were distributed to the winners in the sports program. There were races for boys and girls, with distances from 50 to 100 yards, depending on the age of the children.

Hibbs, followed by Sinclair, took the open 100, but that order was reversed for the open 220. Hibbs also won the 440, with Sinclair third behind White. Biggins won the main union 100, Milne the firemen's 100, and McKay won the sprint for the 15th Light Horse. McLaughlin was best in the bucking competition and there was a mile pony race.

As it was not possible to complete all the competition that day the program was carried on the next evening. Lexton and Sinclair were the winners in the three-legged race. Anderson, with a leap of 8', won the pole vault, as well as the running long jump. Hibbs came in first in the half mile, and Biery took first place in a one mile cycle race. The tug-of-war competition championship won by the Labourer's team, and the Alberta Cup, sponsored by the morning Albertan, went to the Machinists in the union eight man relay.

In late fall the First Herald Annual Road Race was announced. It was hoped to draw competitors from all over western Canada. Initially a challenge cup, valued at $100, and $160 worth of prizes were offered. The race, for the championship of Alberta, was to be run at 2 p.m. on Christmas Day.

The start was to be at the Herald Building on Centre Street and Seventh Avenue, and the race following a route that went south to Ninth Avenue, east to Third Street East, north to Eighth Avenue, west to First Street, south to Cathedral, a block west and then south across Mission Bridge, up Mission Hill, around the cemetary, north on what was then MacLeod Trail—now Spiller Road, across the Barracks Bridge, following the Barrack's fence to Eighth Avenue and back to the Herald. Where there was a sidewalk the runners were at liberty to run on it, but they must pass to the outside of the judges.

It was stated that the Challenge Cup was to be won three times to be permanently held. The first place medal, valued at $140, consisted of five $20 golden pieces on a gold chain. The second place finisher received a gold medal valued at $50, while third prize was a $20 gold medal, and the medal for fourth place was valued at $15.

One of the pre-race favourites was R. Neilson, a Winnipeg lad who was one of the top runners in Manitoba, and who was sponsored by the Winnipeg Y.M.C.A. Another runner with a great deal of backing was Arthur Burn, who had won the Canadian five mile championship in Ottawa inSeptember of 1905. In the past he had won sixteen other major events including the New England championship in Boston the previous July. Local runners Rimington and Hart were given an outside chance to win, and runners Davis, Brown, Pow and Moodie had registered to run.

The weather was mild on Christmas Day, and at 2 p.m. the runners toed the mark waiting for the sound of Fire Chief "Cappy" Smart's starting pistol. A path had to be kept open through the dense crowd for the runners.

At the gun Nelson set the pace, but it was not long before Burn took the lead, gradually lengthening it as the race ran its course. People in automobiles and boys on horses kept pace with the runners. At the Mission Hill "Big Boy" Davis, who was far behind the leaders, dropped out of the race. Burn gradually increased his lead, and to great applause crossed the finish line in a time of 36.17!

Nelson and Rimington began a sprint from the Queen's Hotel, down Eighth Avenue and around to the finish line, with Nelson being clocked at 40.11, and Rimington one second later. Hart was fourth in 40.22, followed by Brown and Pow. The runners were all treated to baths at the Y.M. club following the race.

The prizes, which had been on display at Doll's and Watson Bros. stores, were presented to the runners at an evening performance at the Lyric Theatre by M.J. Young of the Calgary Herald. The race news was covered on the first page of the evening paper, which considered the race to be the best sporting event in Calgary's history.

An indoor track meet was held on New Year's Day of 1907 in the Y.M. gym. Included in the events were the high jump, broad jump, shot put, 45 yard dash and a four man relay team.

In March Art Burn of Calgary travelled to Seattle to run in its Marathon Race, so named even though its distance was much shorter. Burn added to his growing list of laurels by winning the race, and upon his return to Calgary he received a good reception for his accomplishments.

A track and field day was held in May at Midnapore. A purse of one hundred dollars was offered to the winner of the ten mile race, and the winner was Art Burn! An auto race was held in conjunction with the meet, with the winner Downing travelling the Midnapore-Okotoks route in twenty minutes.

The regular Firemen's sports day was held on May 24. Besides firemen's activities, there was track and field competition, including races for braves and squaws. McLean won the open 100 yard dash in 10.5 seconds and the 220 in 24.5. McLean finished second to Maddock in the hurdles; the latter's time was a respectable 16.8 seconds.

In June there was track and field competition at Western Canada College. In the same month the Bluenose sports day was held at Victoria Park and was attended by a crowd estimated to be in excess of 4,000 people. There were foot and cycle races for all age groups.

The Y.M.C.A. Harriers Club held a track and field meet in July. Art Burn won the 880 in a time of 2.05 and a five mile race with a 29.34 clocking. The best pole vaulter could only achieve a height of 7′ 6″. During the summer the Commercial Travellers held a sports day on the Mission grounds near the bridge.

A Y.M.C.A. track and field day was held August 24. Burn beat ten other competitors to win the 440 yard race in a time of 55.8 seconds. In a four mile race Burn spotted the other runners a quarter of a mile and still won by half a mile in a time of 19.34. He also won the half mile in 2.05. Rice took the 100 yard dash with a clocking of 10.6. Although it was thought that Tom Longboat, the famous Indian runner, would be in Calgary for the meet, he did not show.

A feature of the Labour Day sports meet was a five mile race in which Burn competed against a five mile team, with each of his opponents running a mile relay fashion. Burn won the race by six seconds in a time of 28.22. He also was the winner of the mile race. Many Calgarians enjoyed the obstacle races—either as competitors or spectators.

Burn's reputation as a runner was becoming widespread. Shrubb, the English professional champion, wanted to race him, but Burn would not turn professional.

Plans were made for a ten mile race to be held in New Westminster in October and billed as the championship of the North West Territory. Both Burn and Longboat were invited, but Longboat conceded to the Calgary runner. Burn was then matched with Vancouver's Chandler at fifteen miles. The Calgary runner won in a time of 1.28.54.5, about seven minutes behind the world record. At this time many persons acclaimed Burn as the best runner in North America.

With the added laurel of the coast race the City of Calgary wanted to send Burn to Toronto to run against Longboat. Burn, however, got sick and the tentative trip was called off.

At a benefit soccer game Burn was to race two men, each to run a mile, in an attempt to break the Alberta two mile record of 9.27. Burn won the race, however poor track conditions brought about a slow time.

The Y.M.C.A. held a road race on Thanksgiving Day. The course ran south on First Street, across the Mission Bridge and back to the Y by way of the Elbow Bridge.

In December the Sherman Rink was the setting of Burn's next race. His opponent was Ternway of Claresholm, and there was a great deal of side money bet on the match. The distance was set at five miles, and Ternway was allowed a handicap of one minute. The first mile was run in 5.31, two in 11.40, 17.58 for three miles and 30.40 for the five mile distance. This was a good time considering the race was run on a small indoor track. Burn caught up to Ternway but could not pass him, and in the end the Claresholm runner won the race.

A 40 yard dash on the same program was won by Jenkins in a time of five seconds flat. Another event was a one mile potato relay race.

During December the Sherman Rink was the scene of six continuous nights of roller skating races. There were races from half a mile to two miles in length for both men and ladies. A mile race was held each evening and as an end result Tomlinson was declared the roller champion of Calgary.

Early in December the prizes for the 1907 Christmas Herald Road Race were placed on display in the window of Black's Jewellery Store. The track was measured by E. Princess's auto at six miles, 235 yards. The previous year's route had been six miles, 528 yards in length, however a building was constructed on the race route which caused the change.

By deadline time there were seventeen entries, but when Cappy Smart fired the starting gun a 2 p.m. on Christmas Day there were only sixteen runners starting. The runners were accompanied throughout the race by a quarter mile in length procession of autos, carriages and spectators on horseback.

Burn took the lead from the start with Peter Ternway attempting to stay with him. However the pace was too fast for the Claresholm runner who quit at the end of the first mile unable to breathe properly. As a result those individuals who were backing Ternway lost their money very early in the race.

A warning was shouted to the runners 200 yards from each mile post, and there was a sprint to the judge of that point. The reason for this being that the jeweller and sportsman Mr. Doll had offered a prize to that runner who was in the lead for the most miles. Burn led for the first mile, Meckleburg for the second, Burn forged ahead to capture the third, but Innisfail rancher Meckleburg captured the fourth, fifth and sixth. Stephen Avenue was closely packed with spectators who closed ranks right after the two lead runners passed, making it very difficult for the other runners to complete the race.

With more than 200 yards to go Burn began to sprint and gained a four yard lead before Meckleburg changed gears. As he rounded the corner to Centre Street a dog got in his way, but at the finish line he was only two yards behind the winner—Burn! The first place time was 35.2.5, Meckleburg half a second behind and Western Canada College student McKay third in a good time of 36.40. The next three finishers were Pow, Head and Morren. There were six runners representing the Young Men's Club and three students of Western Canada College.

The prizes were presented that evening in the Sherman Lyric Theatre following the second act of the Summer Stock Company. Two boxes had been reserved for the winners who stepped to the stage when their name was called. One proud member of the audience was James McEwan—Arthur Burn's trainer.

A few days later Mr. Doll hung up a solid gold medal to be given to anyone who could beat Burns' time of 35.25 in a New Year's Day race. Ternway issued a challenge to Meckleburg, and as well issued a challenge to Burn to meet him in a five mile race at Sherman's Rink in January. A brash statement from a man who had not lasted past a mile with Burn the week before. The New Year's Day race did not come off as Ternway developed a cold.

Races were held at Sherman's during the winter, however they were on roller skates. Jim Tomlinson, a Calgary youth who was a newcomer to the sport, outraced the best that Edmonton could send down. There were relays as well as couple races.

In 1908 it was decided to try to run the Herald Road Race every month. The first such race was to be run in February. Plans were made to pace Burn in order to have him run the fastest possible time. However several days prior to the race day Dr. Ings reported that Burn had to be helped to bed and could not run. Instead plans were made to pace Ternway.

In the race J. Caffray set a fast pace for three-quarters of a mile and then dropped out. Ternway set his own pace for the next two miles as two of the pacers did not show up. At the Mission Hill Smith joined in to provide competition to Ternway to the Elbow Bridge. Caffray again set the pace down Eighth Avenue to the finish. Ternway's time was 36.31¼, much slower than Burn's best time.

The St. Patrick's Day road race was cancelled as the roads were covered with too much slush and this condition would have been too much of a handicap to the runners.

New prizes were announced for the April race. First prize was to be a silver cup offered by Jacques and Co.; Watson Bros. gave a solid gold locket for the second place finisher, and sporting goods store owner A. Martin put up cuff links for the third place finisher. H. Kitto offered a prize for the winner of the cycle race, which was to be run over the same route and to preceed the running race. The starter for both races was to be Police Chief English.

On April 28 thousands of Calgarians lined the race route. They were not disappointed as they watched Arthur Burn beat five other runners and lower the time for the course to 34.49¾.

In April a group of interested Calgary sportsmen met together to form the Calgary Amateur Athletic Association. Dr. Mason was elected president of the organization. During this period Burn began training for much longer races. It was decided to hold Olympic trials in Calgary as well as five other cities across Canada. A meeting was held May 9 to determine Calgary's Olympic officials.

The Calgary trials were slated for May 16, but they were postponed until May 27 because of the weather. However it was obvious that there was not enough talent or interest in Calgary to warrant holding the trials.

The Fire Department and the Turf Club co-sponsored the May 24 and 25 sports and racing programs. There was a parade, football tournament, horse races, track and field events, Indian races and highland dancing. Competition was held on the new half mile track at Victoria Park. The Red Deer Fire Dept. beat Calgary in the hose reel race to take home the Herald Challenge Trophy. Sutherland won the quarter mile bike race and the one mile cycle race in 3.02.

Jenkins outran ten other competitors to take the 100 yard dash in 11.5 seconds and the 220 in 25. Rice was second in both events.

On the Victoria Day holiday Burn was at Fort Saskatchewan to run in its 19 mile 234 yard marathon. There were eight starters, and Burn won the race in a credible time of two hours and 45 seconds. Fraser, the second place finisher, was seven minutes behind. This dog-train runner from the north country ws reported to have run 200 miles in two days. Fitzgerald won the nine mile 1224 yard race in 55 minutes, 36½ seconds. In comparison Burn had run ten miles in a New Westminster race in 53 minutes. Shrubb held the world record of 50.40 for that distance.

In May track and field, or athletics as they were called, were part of a sports day held at Western Canada College. During the month sculling and paddling races were held at Banff. Athletics were part of the Cochrane Victoria Day celebrations at Cochrane. The 100 yard dash was won by J. Adlinson, while McCuish won the long jump and throwing the stone events. At Midnapore the Royal Templers of Temperance held a sports day. Miss Stagg won the 50 yard dash, and S. Ward captured the high jump and 880. The Anglican Young People's Athletic Grounds, located on 18th Avenue and 4th Street, were opened.

On may 30 James Knowlton, "the Alberta Longboat", went south to race against Peter Ternway of Claresholm. The Indian runner won the ten mile race in 59 minutes flat, two laps ahead of Ternway.

Another Herald Road Race was planned for the end of May. New prizes were donated by the H.B.C. and Ashdowns. However the sky opened up, and the race was postponed for a week and then till the end of June.

Calgary's Olympic trials were called off as there was just not enough interest. However the Canadian Olympic committee agreed to let Burn go to London to compete for Canada even though he did not participate in any Canadian trials. No other runner who did not take part in the Canadian finals was allowed the same privilege. The commitee said that they would refund his fare if he finished in the first six Canadians in the Marathon race at the Olympics. At the trials the top placers were all easterners except J. Fitzgerald of Edmonton.

A. Fidler, a sports enthusiast, attempted to hold a field day at Victoria Park with the proceeds to help send Burn to London. However the planned meet was postponed and then never did take place. Finally the Provincial Government came up with a grant of $200 to help defray Burn's expenses.

The June running of the Herald Road Race was cancelled, but a race was planned for July 29.

In competition held during the Calgary Fair in July a 440 yard dash was held between Ternway of Claresholm, Jenkins of Calgary and McConnel of Vancouver. McConnel broke away fast to take over a ten yard lead, but Jenkins ran well and ended up only six inches behind McConnel, who had a very good time of 51.2 seconds. On another day there was a 100 yard dash run with four starters at the line. McConnel beat Jenkins by two yards in a race time of ten seconds flat. There were four starters in a three mile cycle race won by Sutherland with a time of 8.25. A quarter mile cycle sprint was taken by G. Beer in 37 1/5 seconds with Sutherland finishing second. It subsequently came to light that McConnel was a professional.

Burn went directly to London from Calgary. Tentative plans had been made for him to run in the 5,000 metre and marathon races. The games committee had decided to cut the Marathon field down and Burn was not entered, however a rescinding of the change put Burn back into the race.

The day of the marathon was very warm, something the Canadian runners had not counted on. Burn was placed in the third row at the start, but right from the gun he lead the field until an English runner passed him at the mile mark. Burn was passed by many runners, but he still finished a respectable 24 out of the 57 finishers in a time of 3.50.17. Canadians Wood, Simpson and Lawson finished sixth, seventh and eighth respectively. Longboat, the great Canadian Indian runner, dropped out at the nineteen mile mark. The Canadian Olympic committee had promised to pay Burn's fare if he had finished in the first six Canadians in the race, however he finished seventh. While he was cheering Canadian Kerr's great 200 metre race an irate American punched Burn in the nose. Burn stopped in Ottawa on his way back to Calgary, and there he reported to the press that wine given to him during the running of the Marathon had affected his performance.

On July 3 the Alberta Amateur Athletic Association met and decided to unite with the C.A.A.A. D. Darroch was the representative for the Calgary district, one of six in the A.A.A.A.

In late July the Herald Road Race was run at 7:30 p.m. on a Saturday evening. The race was held up for ten minutes until the rain lessened. Donald Murphy, a thirteen year old boy, was given a three and a half minute head start. He was well ahead when some spectators, acting in ignorance, steered the rest of the runners up First Street East instead of the usual route on First Street West. However they were rerouted along Twelfth Avenue back to the course. Carmichael, who had a handicap of two minutes and 21 seconds, finished first in a time of 39.50. Albert Murphy, Donald's older brother, finished second and Holliday was third. Although expected to run Indian Knowlton and Ternway did not show up for the race.

During the summer the St. Mary's Club held an athletic meet. Jenkins was the meet's top athlete, winning the 100, 220, 440, running broad jump, and finishing second in the standing broad jump and the hop, step and jump.

The first Alberta Amateur Association athletes meet was held at the Exhibition Grounds in Edmonton in late August. J. Carmichael of Strathcona was the meet grand aggregate winner, being first in the running broad jump, hop, step and jump, kicking the football, and placing third in putting the shot and throwing the baseball. McLean, also from Strathcona, won the 100 in 10.4 and the 220 in 24.2. J. Fitzgerald, Edmonton's Olympic competitor, won the mile in 4.55.6 and the five mile in 29 minutes. R. Sinclair was the only Calgary athlete to place in any event. He won his heat of the 100, did not place in the final of that event, but he earned one point for his third place finish in the 220. A unique event in the competition was the three-legged race.

During August C. King of Montreal passed through Calgary on his 150 day walk from Montreal to Vancouver. Ternway of Claresholm issued a challenge through the newspaper to M. Bick of Calgary to a five mile race.

Another Herald Road Race was run at 2:30 p.m. on August 29. A.A.A.A. cards were necessary to enter the race. Starter Fire Chief Smart sent the five runners on their way, although two of the competitors had a handicap. R. Berry, who started from scratch, was the winner in a time of 37.48.5. May, with a handicap of 1.23, was second in 40.07, third place Morren was time in 41.30 and young W. Murphy, with a three minute handicap, finished in 47 minutes. The youngster was almost run down by a careless driver on Eighth Avenue. Lumley finished last. Following the race one excited spectator gave a special prize to young Murphy.

The Labour Day athletic meet, which was A.A.A.A. sanctioned, contained 16 union and 15 open events. One of the events was a fifty yard skipping race. Jenkins and Sinclair finished one-two in the 100, 220 and 440 yard run. Jenkins also won the 880, beating five other runners in a time of 2.18, and he placed second in the running broad jump. J. Hibbs won the Union men's 100, and Archer and Holme took the wheelbarrow race. Miss Hattie Marwood edged Miss Violet Smart in the Misses' 75 yard dash. Football player Wakelin took the mile in a time of 5.08, but there was a protest on the race because he had been paced for the last 200 yards. However the protest was not upheld, because, as the winner had pointed out, he had not asked for the pace.

Ed Jeffries won the two mile cycle race, and W. Mann was last, to finish first, in the slow bike race. Four teams entered the tug-of-war competition, with the Masons and Bricklayers team coming out on top. If the Machinists again won the eight man relay they would be allowed to keep the Alberta Challenge Cup, however they were upset by the Printers team. A protest was lodged that some of their runners were pressmen.

In September the Brewery tug-of-war team issued a challenge to any other team to a pull. The Labourers took up the challenge and lost.

On September 24 the Banff Fire Brigade held a sports day. L. Crosby was the talk of the day with his tremendous five feet eight inches leap in the running high jump.

The Brewery and the Standard Soap Company offered prizes for the top finishers in the September Herald Road Race. Ralph Perry, with a handicap of 1.15 finished first in a time of 35.42.5 (36.57.5) and 16 year old Doud was second in 36.40. Ternway's time was 37.11, and Bick ran 38.12. Murphy took 44 minutes, and Johnston finished last.

In early October Knox Presbyterian Church held a field day with races from 50 yards to a half mile. J. McNab was the top point winner in the senior class. Ladies' physical exercise classes were begun in the Y gym. Instructor Mrs. Perkins had the ladies running laps. Burns was beaten by a runner in his first major race in an eight mile race held in Ottawa.

The P. Burns Company donated prizes for the October Herald Road Race. The course was run down Seventh Avenue instead of Eighth due to the poor condition of that avenue. In November Ternway and Knowlton issued a challenge through the newspaper to Burn and Meckleburg to compete in a team race.

Ternway moved to Calgary in November. Not long afterward he was suspended by the A.A.A.A. on a charge of professionalism. It had been reported that he ran a 440 yard race for $50 cash at Pincher Creek. Ternway denied this under oath before a Justice of the Peace.

A roller skating race was held at Sherman Rink prior to placing ice on the floor. McLean won the 880 yard race in a time of 1.43.

In early December Burn wired his entry from Ottawa for the Herald Christmas Road Race. Almost every day the newspaper discussed the event as well as publishing a list of those firms or individuals on the prize subscription list. By race time there were 13 entries including teams of runners from the Hillhurst Club, St. Mary's Club, and the Y.M.C.A.

At the start the spectators were so numerous that a path, edged with ropes, had to be cleared so the race could be run. On top of that the roads were very dusty. At the one mile post Meckleburg led, followed by Wakelin. By the time the runners were at the Mission Bridge Indian Knowlton's leg muscles were very tight and his suffering was evident. At the cemetery Art Burn, who appeared to be in poor shape, dropped out on the advice of his trainer, Jim MacEwan. Meckleburg increased his lead and on a downhill section was clocked at a speed of twelve miles an hour.

Meckleburg won in a slow time of 36.38.5. Fitzgerald, who had reached the semi-finals of the five mile race at the London Olympics, was second in a time of 37.07.5. Perry was third—37.22, W.C.C. student Alf McKay—37.42.5, Knowlton—38.01, and Hart 38.14. Dr. O'Sullivan presented the prizes to the winners in between acts of the evening performance at the Lyric.

On Boxing Day the Brewery team defeated the Police for the tug-of-war championship of Calgary.

H. Higgs was the club president and J. Fitzgerald was the captain of the 1909 Y.M.C.A. Harriers Club. The season's first race was a four mile run held in February. In March Calgarian Art Burn won the Oregon Marathon in a time of three hours, four minutes and 42 seconds. He also won the Spokane Marathon in a good time of 2.33.37. It was reported that he had run its fourth mile in an unbelievable four minutes and thirty seconds. Later Burn ran a twelve mile race in San Jose in a time of one hour and eleven minutes.

Jenkins and Merrit were the top competitors in the track and field events held in a Calgary indoor carnival. During the spring the Calgary branch of the Y.M.C.A. held a track meet for its youth members. Jenkins was clocked in six seconds flat for the 50 yard dash, and he ran an indoor 880 in two minutes, ten seconds. The Y held a gym meet in which the boys performed, creating patterns by carrying Japanese lanterns in the dark.

In May the Y Harriers Club held road races on a course laid out utilizing Fifth and Ninth Avenues. Mitchell defeated six other starters to take the boys' age fifteen and under mile in a time of 5.47.4. Cartwright won the 17 and under three mile race in 19 minutes and eight seconds. Fitzgerald took the five mile race in a time of 27.24, which was a good time considering the roads were covered with mud.

Plans were made to construct a 440 yard cinder track on land adjacent to the Y.M.C.A. Other plans were being made for a fenced track to be laid out Mewata Park.

On Queen Victoria's birthday more than 2,500 people attended the Firemen's Sports Day. All senior track and field competitors had to be A.A.A.A. members, membership in which cost 25¢. Included in the track and field events were races for children and a firemen's hose and reel race. The program was complemented by highland dancing competition.

Two days later Western Canada College held a sports day. Geddes won his 100 and 220 yard race, as well as the cricket ball throw.

J. Fitzgerald displayed his distant running capabilities by being clocked in 1.27.20 for a fifteen mile distance. This was accomplished at the new Y track located adjacent to the Y building on Ninth Avenue. In June Fitzgerald broke Burn's Herald Road Race record for the 6.3 mile circuit by running the distance in 34.26, 23 seconds under the existing record.

Shortly after this Fitzgerald turned professional. In a race held in Edmonton he defeated J. Marsh at fifteen miles in a time of 1.22.56.2. At that time the existing world record for that distance was 1.20.04.4.

In June the Y.M. Harriers held races in distance from 50 yards to a mile. A special train ran from Calgary to Shephard for a sports day that included track and field competition. A bicycle race, which was to be two laps of the Herald Road Race, was planned for July first, but it was postponed due to poor road conditions and bad weather.

A joint Dominion Day Athletic Meet and Turf Day was sponsored by the Fire Brigade and Turf Club. There were children's races, Indian and squaw races, dancing competition, and firemen's sports. Jenkins won the 100 and 220, and he was second in the 880.

On July 29 the 5' 4" tall Fitzgerald ran a fifteen mile race on the Victoria Park track against Meadows of Guelph. The diminutive Calgary runner covered the first mile in 5.10, and then he went on to win the race by 225 yards in a time of 1.28.47. Fitzgerald again raced Marsh in Edmonton, covering the first ten miles in 54.48, and winning the fifteen mile race in 1.22.57.

During the summer Fitzgerald, in an exhibition run, completed the Herald Road Race course in a record 34.25.5.

Burn went to Vancouver to race against west coast ace Chandler. The marathon distant race was run on a track, four laps to the mile. Burn quit the race in the nineteenth mile, and Chandler went on to win in a time of 3.22.11.

Jenkins of Calgary was sent to Winnipeg to compete in the Canadian A.A.V. track and field championships, but he did not show for his sprints. Also in Winnipeg—Fitzgerald ran against world champion Shrubbs in a ten mile race, but the Englishman beat Calgary's best by half a mile in a time of 54 minutes. Later the Calgary runner was matched against Indian runner Acouse in a twelve mile race. Fitzgerald was leading the Indian, but he had to retire from the race when he developed stitches in his side.

In August Grace Church held a track and field day with events for both boys and girls. It was a common practise for churches to hold a summer picnic, including running and fun races in the program of activities.

On September 13 the Alberta A.A.A. meet was held at Victoria Park with 56 entries in the track and field events. Dr. O'Sullivan was the official starter for the juvenile, junior and senior events. Fred Jenkins of Calgary was the meet's top athlete by winning the pole vault with a leap of 9' 1", the 100 yard dash in 10.4 and placing third in the 220. Parney of Edmonton set a new Alberta record of 23 flat in the 220, and as well was a member of Edmonton's mile relay team, the winners in 3.51. G. Cundall of Morenville, with a leap of 19' 7", broke Carmichael's record in the running broad jump. Edmonton's Decoteau won the mile in a record time of 4.39.2, and as well won the Cross Cup for his win in the five mile race in a record time of 26.34.4.

A. Halwood set a meet record of 55 seconds in the 440, and Williams ran a two minute, eight second 880. The 220 was won by Hayes in 27.4 seconds, while Pat Lee of Calgary took the one mile walk in seven minutes and 46 seconds. Reidford hurled the 16 pound hammer 116' 5", and the 56 pound weight throwing event was won by Moir with a distance of 26' 8". T. Wallace's 1908 height of 5' 3" was not matched in the high jump, nor was the 38' 8½" shot put of McLean. The Y.M.C.A. team garnered the most points of any team in the meet.

World champion A. Shrubb arrived in Calgary in mid-September and commenced training at the Y track in preparation for a race against Fitzgerald. The next week Shrubb was not ready to run, but Fitzgerald beat Indian runner Acouse by half a mile in a fifteen mile race in a time of 1.28.52. On September 24 Shrubb raced Fitzgerald and defeated him. The winner ran the first mile in a fast 4.47.8. Fitzgerald was handicapped during the race in that he had to run one lap in only one shoe while some repair was being made to the other one. Four days later the two runners met again, and this time Fitzgerald hit the tape the winner.

During September a twelve mile race was held in Blairmore with $500 in prizes going to the first three finishers. Fitzgerald won the race in a time of one hour and 12 minutes.

The Calgary Public School Field Day was held in October with South Ward, Normal Practise, Central, Victoria, Alexandra and Riverside Schools competing. More than 2,500 spectators watched 35 events, including basketball games. There were running events from 100 yards to two miles in length, bicycle races, obstacle races, team races, and a boot and shoe race.

South Ward was the meet winner, followed by Practise and Central. V. Henry won the senior individual championship, and C. Richards was tops in the junior winner.

In October Fitzgerald finished third in the Seattle Marathon, competing against some of the world's best runners. This was followed by a twenty mile race in Spokane where he placed fourth. During the race he was running first at the twelve mile mark, and he came very close to breaking the world record for distance run in one hour. In November Fitzgerald was running in California.

At Vancouver former Calgarian Art Burn lost to Marsh in a five mile race, but Burn won a ten mile race in Victoria. A ten mile race was run in Coleman. During the fall the Baptist Church held a track and field day.

The cup for the Herald Road Race, won last year by rancher Meckleburg, was on display in the window of Doll's Jewellers for several weeks prior to the 1909 race. The race course, beginning at the Herald Building on Centre Street, was marked with red flags, and there was a white flag at every mile point. If the runners were held up by a train at the Elbow Crossing their time difference would be taken and allowed at the finish. Either A.A.A. or C.A.A.A. cards were necessary for a runner to be allowed to compete.

There was a great deal of barbershop and poolroom discussion prior to the race in regards to the skills or accomplishments of the various runners. Jack Saunders was recently out from England; Jarrett of Dog Pound claimed a 4.42 mile and 32 minutes for six miles, while Meckleburg, the Innisfail rancher, had proved his skill by winning the race in 1908. J. Fitzgerald, who had set a course record in June of 34.24.4., was now a professional.

At 2:35 p.m. Christmas Day starter Smart sent the eight runners on their way down a narrow path through the dense crowd at the starting line, but before the competitors were out of the downtown area one runner was out of the race with a twisted ankle. Meckleburg went to the front about the four mile mark and increased his lead from there to the finish line.

Meckleburg's time was 34.42.5, breaking Burn's 1907 time for the Christmas race. McKay was second—a minute behind, followed by Dowd, Jarrett, and Brooke of Didsbury.

Prizes were presented that evening, at a program held before a packed house in the Lyric Theatre, by Teddy Webb, star comedian of the San Francisco Opera Company. Meckleburg was presented with the Challenge Cup to hold for a year, as well as a gold watch from jeweller Doll, who gave a gold watch to any runner breaking the record.

In January of 1910 Art Burn, called "the curly haired Calgary chap", by the Vancouver papers, was at the coast to run against Marsh. The race was to take place on a twelve lap to a mile track in the Imperial Rink. Marsh easily defeated Burn by one lap in a time of 29.18.

Fitzgerald was in San Francisco training for the San Francisco Marathon in which he would run against world champion St. Yves. Fitzgerald's training consisted of sea baths and ten mile runs. Considering many of the world's best runners were in the race Fitzgerald did well, finishing third. He did claim six different Pacific coast records as well as the world's ten mile record, but the latter claim was doubtful.

It was reported that Arthur Shrubb, the great English runner, was going to settle in Calgary. At Victoria Burn ran 56.37 for ten miles to defeat Baylis.

A series of indoor track events, which included: the standing and running high jumps, standing and running broad jumps, fence vault, shot put, sixty and 440 yard potato races. Overall winner was F. Jenkins and C. Merrit was second. S. Murdoe was champion of the employed boys, and C. Lake was the school boy champion.

Forty boys participated in a 50 yard dash for employed boys. Elmer Hudson's time of 7 1/3 seconds was the best. Later a 100 yard dash saw three competitors turn in the best time of 14 seconds. Twenty competitors entered the Y.M. jumping contest, with Chester Davey the winner with a distance of 24' 6".

In March an indoor track meet, as part of the Canadian Y.M.C.A. championships, was held in Calgary. The showings of each competitor was sent to Toronto where the national results were tabulated. Fred Jenkins was the best Calgarian in both the 60 yard and 440 yard potato races, while Bainton was best in the fence vault with a leap of 6' 6". Murray was first in the R.H.J. with 5' 1' and best in the standing broad jump with a 9' 2" leap. Merritt won the twelve pound shot put event with a heave of 34'.

An unofficial jumping distance of 22' 7" was credited to G. Haddock during indoor track competition at the Y during the spring. The Y's second annual gymnasium competition included relays.

Jim MacEwan, Art Burn's trainer, had planned a race in Calgary on Good Friday between some of the world's best distance runners, including world champion St. Yves and Winnipeg's Marsh. However the runners did not show up.

Western Canada College held a sports day in May. Principal Dr. MacRae finished second to a student in the masters versus students race.

Road races were sponsored by the Y on the morning of Victoria Day. Depending upon the event the race courses covered avenues from Fourth through to Fourteenth Avenue. F. Holmes won the senior five mile race. There was a three mile race for those sixteen and under, and a one mile walk for those boys twelve years and under. In the afternoon track events, in distance from a 100 yard dash to the 880 yard run, were held at the Y track.

The Y track club sent a team to the Alberta A.A.A. meet held in Lethbridge on Dominion Day. Edmonton athletes captured the lion's share of top placings, but the Calgary group earned four first places, three second place ribbons and eight thirds.

McLean and Merritt of Calgary were second and third behind Parney of Edmonton who set a new official Alberta record of 10.4 in the 100 yard dash. Parney won the 220 in 24 flat, again followd by McLean and Merritt. The 440 was won by Merritt in a time of 55.8 seconds. Decouteau, Edmonton's Olympic runnner, took the 880 in 2.09.6 and the mile in 5.16. Calgarian Mosher was second in both the 880 and the two mile races. H. Fullerton of Calgary won his heat in the 120 yard hurdles and was third in the final. H. Forward came home first in the mile walk in a time of 7.47, and he won the three mile walk in 26.36. Cundall of Mannville set a new provincial record of 20' 4½" in the running broad jump, and J. Crealock of Edmonton raised the mark to 5' 4¾" in the running high jump. Fullerton of Calgary was third in this event. Calgarian J. Cornfoot set a new provincial record of 9' 9" in the pole vault, and McLean finished third in the shot put competition. Cummings won the discus, a new event that attracted a lot of spectator interest with a throw of 80'. Reidford of Edmonton was voted the meet's outstanding athlete.

The MacLeod Caledonian Association held an athletic day on July first, with the Calgary pipers in attendance. The Hillhurst Amateur Athletic Association was formed, and included in its plans was provision for a track team.

A baseball field day was held, along with a league baseball game, on Labour Day. Included in the events were: accuracy throw, long distance throw, fungo hitting, base running for time, a three legged race, a sack race, and a 100 yard dash. Smith proved to be the fastest of the baseball players.

The Y.M.C.A. and the Trades and Labour Council co-sponsored a planned Labour Day sports meet. There were to be races for different age groups, union and open events. However the meet was postponed following the huge morning parade when rain threatened the day. The meet, rescheduled for September 10th, was rained out again, but a week later the events were held.

McLean, followed by Merritt, won the open 100 yard dash in a time of 10.4 seconds. Merritt took the 220 in 23.5, the 440 yard run in 56 seconds, and leaped 18' 9" to win the running broad jump. Murray, who was second in the 220, won the 56 pound weight with a distance of 16' 4". H. McElyre was first in the running high jump with a leap of 5' 2", and P. McGinnis was the top junior.

The married ladies' race was won by Mrs. Milton, and Miss Tates was the first in the single ladies' race. Pressman Ottaway won the union 100. In the police 100 Orr of the City Police beat out Murison of the Mounted Police. In the tug-of-war final the Brewery workers beat out the electricians. The plumbers won the union relay and the Alberta Cup. G. Sutherland won the five mile cycle race in a time of 16.52.2. There was a girl's skipping race, a baby show and quoits.

A race was held in September at Pincher Creek with Winnipegger Marsh and Indians Knowlton and Deerfoot in the race. Both the Indians dropped out during competition with Marsh being the only finisher. Plans were made to hold the Alberta roller skating championship races at the Auditorium Rink during the fall.

A 100 yard dash, held at a football game for the football players, was won by Houseman in 10.8 seconds. There was track and field competition at the Mitford horse races.

The Sherman Rink was the location of a fifteen mile race between John Marsh of Winnipeg and Deerfoot of Lethbridge. After being pressed for a few laps the Indian collapsed in the arms of his trainer during the fourteenth mile. Marsh hit the tape in a spring to the finish in a remarkable time of 1.21.12.5. Winnipeg papers questioned the actual distance of the race, considering the exceptional time. The first eight miles had been timed in 42.07, ten miles in 52.36, and the last two miles in ten minutes.

In early October the annual school meet was held at Victoria Park before a full grandstand. The classes ranged from A, for those students under seventy pounds, to B, C and D. Robie won the class A 50 yard dash in 7.8, the 100 yard dash in 14 seconds flat, and the standing broad with a leap of 6' 5½". In class B F. McKay won the 50 in 7.2, the 220 in 31.8, and was first in the running broad jump with a leap of 12'7". W. Selbie took the C 100 in 14 flat. W. Sinclair was first in the 440 with a time of 1.11 2/3, and Emery won the junior high jump with a 4' 2" leap. S. McTavish was the first in the D class 100 with a 12.4 clocking, and R. Mathews won the 880 in two minutes, 32 1/3 seconds. McTavish also won the running hop, step and jump with a distance of 33' 9½". Haultain won the 160 and 440 yard, while Victoria School was victorious in the 220 yard relay. Haultain won the shield for the meet championship.

The High School field day was held in October. C. Richards of class six won the junior championship with a standing broad jump of 7' 11¾", a hop, step and jump of 33' 2", putting the shot 27' 10", running high jump of 4' 4½", a 100 yard time of 12.8 and a time of 2.48.2 in the 880.

In the senior events N. Black won the running broad jump with a leap of 16' 6¾", leaped 4' 9¼" in the running high jump and captured the 100 in 11.6. W. Millar's winning pole vault was 7' 8½"; A. McKay ran a 5.16.6 mile. The putting the shot event went to M. Edwards with a distance of 33' 2". The 880 cycle race went to Ross Mills in 1.21 1/3, with N. Black, the senior top point earner, second. Class 8 won the 880 yard relay in 1.53 2/3, and as well, the tug-of-war.

The University of Alberta held a field day for both male and female students. Besides track and field there was a nail driving contest. Over 100 men and boys participated in a gymnasium exhibit at the Y gym.

A list of twelve rules was published to cover the running of the Herald Road Race. Only two attendants were allowed for each runner, and the competitors must run without their attendants from the Elbow Bridge to the finish line. No drugs were allowed to be taken, and only certain sidewalks could be run on. A list of firms and individuals who contributed to the prizes for the race was published daily. Gold medals, in the value of $80, $60 and $30, went to the first three finishers, and there were prizes for the fourth and fifth place competitors. A change in the route saw the race run from the Herald, south on Centre to Ninth, east to Fourth Street, north to Eighth, west to First Street, south to 18th Avenue, west to Fourth Street, and the regular route past the Barracks but west on Seventh Avenue instead of Eighth. The start and finish were well roped off.

Fifteen runners registered for the race including eight entries from the Y.M.C.A. L. Smith, the winner of several major races on the coast, came from Vancouver to run.

The day was ideal and the air a good temperature. Decoteau of Edmonton, followed by Smith, led at the end of the first mile and each succeeding mile. The winner's time, and a new record, was 34.19¼! Smith and Wilson of Calgary ran neck and neck to the finish, with the Vancouver man finishing ahead by 1½ seconds in a time of 34.41.5. Next to finish were Perry and McKay of Calgary, Jarrett of Bottrel and Brooke of Didsbury. Six of the runners did not finish the race. Meckleburg, who had been sick before the race, dropped out at the end of the third mile when he had been running in eighth place.

C. Card of the Edmonton Orpheum Theatre took motion pictures of the race. Camera stations were located at the race start, Mission Hill and the finish line. The films were shown at the Majestic Theatre in January.

J. Fitzgerald was running in Australia and was reported to have run a 25.58 mile and 53.12 for the ten mile distance. On Boxing Day he won the Australian one and five mile championship races.

In January of 1911 Jack Buchanan, the former trainer of Edmonton A.A.A., moved to Calgary.

The Y.M.C.A. held a series of indoor track and field events during the spring. There were five teams of four men each competing for both individual and team honours. The events were a 100 yard dash, 440, potato race, running high jump, running hop, step and jump, and the twelve pound shot put. Merritt won the individual championship, and as well led his team to the team championship. Mosher was the next best individual.

Other meets included classes for school and employed boys. One of the events was 'Snap for height'. A Municipal Athletic Club was formed by the city employers.

A spring gym meet was held at Western Canada College. Harry McKernan was the top competitor, scoring 96½ points out of 100; while second place went to Edgar Lougheed. The College held a field day in June, with Kernan the top senior, Tisdale capturing intermediate honours, and Rich the best of the juniors. McKernan broke the pole vault record with a leap of 9' 2½", and Dubois ran the mile in 5.28. The Old Boy's team bested the Masters in relay competition. There were egg and wheelbarrow races, the hurdles, and the hop, step and jump along with footraces. Paddy Johnson won a prize donated by Jim Sewell for the longest lacrosse ball throw.

R. Mosher was president of the Y.M. Track and Athletic Club. C. Merritt was the captain of the track personnel and S. Phillips was the Harrier captain. The Y.M.C.A. boys held an outing at Midnapore that included track and field competition. A 220 yard foot race for a $95 purse was held at Pincher Creek. Johnson of Hillcrest won the Old Man's Race held at the Bellevue sports day.

There were 85 entries for the track and field competition which was held before a large crowd at Victoria Park during the Calgary Fair in early July. However the track was considered poor for events such as this as it was sandy and soft in some places and as hard as pavement in others.

There were three heats in the 100 yard dash with McLean of Calgary edging Buddo of Edmonton in the final in a time of 10.4. Calgarians made a clean sweep in the 220 with Hepburn winning in 24 seconds, with Merritt and Flint in the next two places. Decoteau, Edmonton's great runner, placed far back in this race.

Hepburn, followed by Merritt, won the 440 in a time of 55.2. He became a triple winner by taking the 880 in 2.14. McIntyre took the 120 yard hurdles in a time of 19.8, and another Calgarian, N. McNeil, was third. Decoteau led Perry to the tape in the mile with a time of 4.58.6. Forward won the one mile walk in 7.47 when Edmonton's Clark was disqualified. In mile relay competition the Y Athletic Club won over teams from the Y soccer and baseball clubs with a time of 4.13.

The running broad jump went to Buddo with a distance of 19' 6". Jenkins was second, 1½" behind. N. McNeil cleared 5' 4½" with ease to set a new provincial record in the running high jump. Jenkins won the pole vault with a leap of nine

feet. Cameron of Edmonton easily won the shot put event with a toss of 39' 1½".
The shot that Cameron was given to use had a hole in it, but when he complained
he was told that it was the type of shot put Calgary athletes used. Before the year
was through Cameron set a new provincial record of 39' 8" in the event. Roberts
set a record of 29' 1" in the 56 pound weight event. He was the Calgary meet
individual champion. The Calgary Y.M.C.A. won the team championship.
Other teams competing were: the Edmonton Y, Lethbridge Y, Edmonton
P.A.A.A., Calgary 103 Regiment, Calgary A.A.A., and Stavely.

On July 12 a Firemen's Sports Day was held in Medicine Hat. Medicine Hat
won the team championship, but Calgary's Cappy Smart won the race for the fire
chiefs.

Organizers of the Herald Road Race were pleased when it was learned that
they would receive a special one hour permit for the route of the race. Drivers of
cars or rigs who followed the runners would be arrested. The route was to be
guarded by Mounted Police.

The provincial track and field championships were rained out in Edmonton in
early July, but the events were staged later in the month by the Police and
Caledonian Amateur Athletic Association. The meet took place at the Exhibition Grounds, but a very muddy track proved to be a hindrance to the runners.

In the 100 dash Parney of Edmonton set a new provincial record of 10.2
seconds. Buddo was second and Hassel of Calgary, third. Parney won the 220 in
23.8 with Merritt of Calgary in second place. George Hepburn of Calgary, who
had been the best in Britain in the 1908 Olympic trials, and who had been credited
with a 50 second 440, won the 440 in 58.6 seconds and the 880 in 2.17. Merritt was
second in the quarter and Decoteau runner-up in the half. O. McNeil of Calgary
won the 120 yard hurdles in 22.2, and the pole vault with a height of 9' 6".

Roberts set a new provincial record of 105' 2" in the discus, and D. Reidford
added six inches to create a provincial record of 37' 6" in the cabre event. Robert's
second record of the day came with a 29' 1" heave in the 56 pound weight, and his
104' 7½" throw gave him a first place ribbon in the 16 pound hammer throw.
Buddo won the running broad jump, with Merritt and McNeil of Calgary second
and third.

The Edmonton Y won over the Calgary Y team in the mile relay in a time of
4.12. The meet was complemented by highland pipe and dancing competition.

Fitzgerald stopped in Honolulu after a successful tour of Australia and New
Zealand in which he won twelve out of fifteen races. In New Zealand he had won
the country's five mile indoor championship with a 26.20 clocking. He was
recognized as the holder of one and ten mile records during a marathon run of
4.52 and 55.52.

While in Honolulu Fitzgerald raced and defeated Soldier King for the Honolulu championship, running the 15 miles in 1.32.57. Later Fitzgerald race a relay
against three runners, but lost the ten mile race by one minute and twelve
seconds.

A full day of athletics was held on Labour Day of 1911 in Calgary. There were
children's age class races, open and union events. Jenkins won the Doll Cup and
$15 for winning the 100 yard dash in a time of eleven flat. Hepburn and Merritt

ran second and third. The Watson Bros. Cup and $10 went to Hepburn for winning the 220; Merritt running second. The 440 resulted in the same finish with the winner receiving the Black Cup and $15. Alex Hepburn was a triple winner by breaking the tape in the five mile race in a time of 28.19. For this he received the Mayor Mitchell Cup, a medal and $85. McLaren and Perry were second and third. The 880 was also won by Hepburn, in 2.25, with Watson second.

Jenkins and Noden each cleared the tremendous height of ten feet in the pole vault, but in six tries neither could clear the bar when it was placed two inches higher.

The Plasterers team won the union relay and the D.E. Black Challenge Cup. There were three different union 100's, and Clark won the apprentice boy's 100 yard dash. Miss Fisher was first in the union men's wives races, and H. Hammond won the fat men's race. Phyllis Tate took home a first place ribbon for the Misses' race, and there was many a laugh from the crowd during the running of the hobble skirt race. The boys boot and shoe race, as usual, produced lots of excitement. A new trophy, the Jones, Blackshire and Littel Perpetual Cup, was offered for tug-of-war competition.

It was felt that interest was lessening in bicycle racing, but there were five entries in the three mile cycle race, won by Sullivan.

In September Fred Parney of Edmonton was sponsored by the Alberta A.A.U. to represent Alberta in the Canadian championships at Montreal. Parney's best effort was in the 100 yard dash where he finished fourth in the finals, just behind Olympic star Kerr.

The third annual school track and field meet was held at Victoria Park in October. There were enough competitors to have heats in the dashes of all four classes. Haultain won the meet with 42 points, Central was next with 32, Mount Royal 31, Victoria 24, Riverside 2, Sunnyside 1, and Alexandra 1. Fred Mathews of Victoria School was the all-round champion, with Fraser second and McKay third. Mount Royal won the class A relay, while Haultain was a double winner in the B and C relays.

F. McKay of Haultain set a record of 4' 4" in the running high jump and 13 seconds flat in the class C 100 yard dash. R. Jenkins lowered the record of 1.10.6 in the class C 440. Central's F. Fraser set a class D standing high jump record of 3' 11", and in the same class Haultain's W. Gardiner lowered the 100 yard time to 12.2, while the 880 record was set at 2.52.2 by R. Mathews of Haultain. M. Robie of Haultain set a new time of 30.8 in the class B 220, and Victoria's R. Differ extended the class A standing broad jump mark to 6' 6½".

The School Athletic Association was formed during the fall. In October the Central Collegiate Institute held a track and field day at Victoria Park. C. Bell set a record by winning the junior 100 in 12.6. In the same class Puller won the shot with a distance of 25' 8½", Fitzgerald's running high jump mark was 4' 8½", and Migh took the standing broad jump with a leap of 7' 4½". Suckley set a record of 2.28.8 for the 80 yard run, and he won the running hop, step and jump with a distance of 30' 5".

The senior 100 went to McLaurin in a time of 11.6. while C. Sinclair won the pole vault with a leap of 8' 4½", a new record! W. Low's time of 30.2 was a new record for the 220 yard hurdles. Sinclair's second record came with a five foot leap in the running high jump. Richards won the running broad jump with a leap of 17′ 5″, and as well won the shot put with a distance of 32′ 6″. F. Cannon's time for the mile was 5.44. Class 12 won the tug-of-war competition and the relay in 1.52. An 880 bicycle race was also part of the program.

Haultain School won the physical training prize, which had been donated by Strathcona Trust for competition in southern Alberta. Gym classes were started in the 103rd Regiment drill hall.

In November Harvey Orr, Manitoba's short distance sprint champion, moved to Calgary. He had been credited with a 10.2 second time for the 100 yard distance.

A new route was established for the Herald Road Race. The runners were to run from the Herald Building on Centre Street down Seventh Avenue to Eighth Street, south to Royal Avenue, west to Cottage Street, south to 25th Avenue, over Mission Bridge, regular route back down McLeod Trail (Spiller Road), across the new Twelfth Avenue Bridge, north on the temporary road to the Barracks, a block on Eighth Avenue, north to Seventh and on to the finish line at the Herald. The course was slightly longer and was measured at 6 1/5 miles.

The first six runners to finish were to receive gold medals, while the next two finishers would receive a year's subscription to the Herald. Running on a side-walk would disqualify a runner.

Included in the list of entrants was Steve Cottrel, who at one time had been a national cross-country champion in England. However he was one of several runners who did not finish the race. Smith came from Bowen Island, near Vancouver, Greenville was from Vancouver, and there were runners from Innisfail and Edmonton. Decoteau was not in good enough condition to compete, nor was Meckleburg in good enough shape to finish with the leaders.

The winner of the race was Alex Hepburn, of the Y.M.C.A. team, in a time of 34.57.5. Runner-up Smith was timed in 36.0.4. McCaghey of Edmonton outraced Clarke for third spot, with the next three positions going to Perry. Greenville and Johnson. Prizes were presented to the winners during the evening show at the Lyric Theatre.

On New Year's Day of 1912 Calgarian Alex Hepburn finished second in a five and three-quarter mile race held in Vancouver. His time of 31.40 was 37 seconds behind Smith, the winner. Early in January Art Burn, a native of Ottawa but a Calgary runner for several years and twice winner of the Herald Road Race, died in Vancouver from tuberculosis. In the 1908 Olympic Marathon he had finished ahead of more than half the field of runners. In April Cameron "Bert" Smith, who had finished second in the 1911 Christmas Herald Road Race, won the Vancouver Harriers Ten Mile Road Race.

A hexathlon, consisting of the running high jump, fence vault, standing broad jump, shot put, and 60 and 180 yard potato races, was held at every large Y in Canada including Calgary's during the spring. Calgary's Addinell did well with a five foot high jump. Another competition held in the Y gymnasium was a double dual athletic meet with intermediates, students, school boys and employed boy's teams participating. One event consisted of the high jump using the springboard as a takeoff. The same four teams competed in another such meet later in the spring. Over 150 boys competed in the Y Circus, competing in such events as the flying rings. A field and sports day, scheduled for the Queen's Birthday, was rained out.

There were four classes, using the weight sytem, at the Western Canada College field day. Among the 27 events were obstacle and three-legged races. Claude "Frenchy" Dubois won three different 880 yard races as well as the mile race, which had been run off the previous Saturday. Later in the season he was timed in 16.47 for the three miles run over a rough prairie track.

Bishop Pinkham College held a successful field day at Hillhurst Park. The events included an egg and spoon race, football kick, and the cricket ball throw. J. Eaton and J. Irwin each picked up five first place ribbons. Gordon Cameron of Lone Butte was the top competitor at the Mount Royal College track and field day at Mewata Park. Included in his wins was the hundred yard dash in eleven seconds flat. The mile race was won by Walker in a time of 5.56.

Alberta's Olympic trials were held at Fort Saskatchewan in late May. Calgarians Fred Parney, who had run the 220 in 23 flat, Harvey Orr—with a flat ten second 100, and high jumper Noden participated in the trials but did not perform well enough to be selected for the Canadian trials in Montreal. Calgarian Alex Hepburn, one of Canada's better distant runners who was generally conceded a place on the Olympic team, had previously declared that he would not be able to take two months off work to travel to Stockholm.

The Alberta trials produced three athletes who were eligible to compete in the national trials: D. Buddo who ran the 100 metres in 11.4 and the 200 metres in 23.4, S. Mansfield, who had run a 400 metre time of 52.6 and 2.04 in the 800 metres, and A. Decoteau. Alex ran a 59.59 ten mile, covering the first five miles in 25 minutes. LeFleur ran the 1500 in 4.20 but was not picked for Montreal. The Alberta Amateur Union asked and received $500 from the Provincial Government to assist in sending these three, all members of the Edmonton Police, to the trials.

Decoteau ran only three miles of the 10,000 metre race, which was won by Indian J. Keeper of Manitoba. In the 5,000 metre trials Decoteau beat the only other runner in a slow time of 16.20.4. However the trials committee decided that he must race Chandler of Vancouver to see which of the two would represent Canada in Stockholm. So two days later Decoteau again ran the 5,000 to beat the west coast runner by 18 yards and set a new Canadian record of 15.27.4. Buddo and Mansfield competed at Montreal but did not place. Eleven Canadian competitors made the trip to Stockholm.

Decoteau entered the 10,000 in Stockholm, led for the first four miles and then dropped out to save himself for the 5,000 metre race. In his heat he finished second, fifteen yards behind the winner in a time of 15.22.4. A packed stadium watched the final. Decoteau was in third place after ten laps, but in the remainder of the race he fell further back and finished as an also-ran. Nevertheless it was an accomplishment for the prairie runner to get to the Olympics and compete against the world's best.

Plans had been made to hold the track and field championships of Alberta under the sponsorship of the Alberta Branch of the A.A.C. at Red Deer on July 17. The A.A.C. sponsored bicycle races in August. Included in the events were green races and matched races. Calgary cyclists journeyed to Medicine Hat for that city's Labour Day races. Dick Corliss captured the half mile sprint and Bob Cunliffe won the five mile race.

Early in September the Department of Natural Resources of the C.P.R. held an athletic meet at Victoria Park. Included in the events was the lady stenographers' race in which the wearers of harem skirts were barred.

There were over 300 entries in the Trades and Labour field day. This athletic meet was under the auspicies of the Trades and Labour Council under the C.A.A.U. rules. Besides foot races ranging in distance from 100 yards to six miles, there were children's races, a union mile relay, baseball throw, union tug-of-war, fifty yard sack, and bicycle races. There were enough entries in the men's 100 yard dash to run heats; the final of this as well as the 220 was won by McIntyre. H. Palmer led five other runners to the tape to take the six mile run in a time of 32.05. B. Conliff captured the half mile cycle race in a time of 1.25. G. Sutherland won the motor paced five mile pursuit in a time of 15.40, however it was claimed by some that the race was fixed. The union men's wives' race was called off due to the lack of entries.

The Calgary Public School track and field meet took place at Victoria Park in early October. 190 competitors from twelve schools participated in the 22 events. There were four competition classes divided according to 70, 85, 100 and 135 pound weights. Points were totalled for the three classes each school decided to count; this was done to allow the smaller school a fair chance. Haultain won the grand aggregate with 28 points, followed by Alexandra with 17, while Central, Riverside and Connaught earned 15 points each. Riverside won the A sections, Alexandra—B, Victoria—C, and Haultain—D. Competitors and starter A. Dawson were bothered by horsemen running their horses in close proximity to the track.

Claude Stewart of Alexandra won a gold medal and the right to hold the Mapson Cup for a year for being the meet's top athlete as well as the class B championship. He won the fifty yard dash, ran a winning 220 in 32.4 seconds and had a best broad jump of 14′ 7½″. Haultain set a record of 31.6 seconds in winning the B 220 relay. Fred Edwards of Riverside won the class A medal and set a record of 8′, 8½″ in the standing broad jump. N. Watts of Riverside ran a 7.2 fifty yard dash to equal the record in that event as well as winning the 100 in 14.2. Haultain won the 160 yard relay in 24.2. Fred Mathews of Victoria won the class C point total, and Banks set a new record of 4′, 4¾″ in the running high jump. D, the senior division, point total was earned by Fred Jenkins of Victoria. His time for the 880 was 2.33.6. Haultain won the senior 880 relay in 2.04.8.

At the High School field day Cameron Sinclair set a record of 19′, 1½″ in the running broad jump, won the 220 hurdles in 32.2 and was first in the pole vault. Clarence Richards was the top point earner in the senior division, and he broke the shot put record with a heave of 34′, 7¼″. MacMillan set a new 100 yard record with an 11.4 clocking. New junior records were set by Ralph Fitzgerald in the standing broad jump and shot put. Rodgers added another record in the standing high jump.

The C.P.R. held a field day which drew 120 entries from its employees. McIntyre, with five first place ribbons captured the Dennis Challenge Trophy valued at $100. He ran the 100 in 11.4, 220 in 26 seconds, 120 yard hurdles in 18.2, 440 in 107.2, and cleared 4', 8" in the running high jump. A. Carter won the 880 in 2.24 and led the milers in 4.47.4. Woods took the two mile walk in a time of 17.34.

The Boys Brigade held a sports day, which included track and field, in November. Meanwhile, south of the border, Fitzgerald, who billed himself as, "the Calgary runner", won a 15 mile marathon in Portland, Oregon.

Entries closed December 23 for the sixth annual Herald Road Race. There were 13 runners entered, six who listed Calgary as their hometown, O. Rindquist listed Sweden, Palmer was from Halifax, and one runner gave Brickburn—west of Calgary as his place of residence.

Ideal conditions prevailed on Christmas Day, and as early as an hour before race time a large crowd was gathered at the starting point. By starting time the crowd had grown so large that the area had to be roped off. Cappy Smart stood in an open auto to fire the starting gun and they were off! Conley of Calgary went to the lead accompanied by a small brown dog.

Several cars, containing officials, spectators, trainers and photographers, followed the runners around the race course. On the backside of Mission Hill photographer Bill Oliver jumped from a moving car and ran with the runners for more than 200 yards in order to get the right picture. Conley and the dog stayed in front until the four mile mark, at which point Palmer charged by the former leader. The little dog appeared bewildered, but then quickly took to Palmer's heel.

An enormous crowd cheered Palmer as he headed down Seventh Avenue and sprinted to the finish line a good hundred yards ahead of Conley. Both Palmer and the dog were timed at 36.14, H. Conley in second spot and A. Carter of Calgary coming in third. The prizes were to have been presented that night, but because of the pressure of Christmas mail, they had not arrived in the city.

A meeting of the C.P.R. Department of National Resources Athletic Association was held in March of 1913, and some of its outstanding athletes were given recognition. Included were A. Carter, who had finished second in the Mayor Mitchell Race, second in the Edmonton five mile race and third in the Herald Road Race; M. McIntyre, the Alberta 120 yard hurdle record holder, and F. McKay, who had won the indoor 50 yard championship in Edmonton in 1912.

There were 27 events in four weight classes at the Western Canada College field day held on its campus in May. The meet all-around, as well as C class champion, was Ivan Maharg of Calgary. He won the running broad jump, leaped 4' 9½" in the running high jump, and won the 440 in 1.06.2. A Bowness of Cranbrook was the A class winner. He was timed in 23.1 in the 150 yard dash. H. McCauley was the class B winner, and H. McCoombs led class D, the larger boys. His hop, step and jump distance was 40' 3", a high jump of 4' 9" and he earned a second place finish in the 100. McKernan won the open 880, and he won the class D pole vault as well as placing second in the high jump. The students and the Masters engaged in a tug-of-war contest to close the meet.

Mount Royal College held their field day late in May. In gym competition at Western Canada College Eric Weir of Strathcona was declared senior champion, while Phil Becker of Pincher Creek was the top junior. There was not any of the usual track and field competition in Calgary on Victoria Day.

The Y.M.C.A. Athletic Club began holding an intensified track and field training program. Alex Hepburn was elected club president, and H. Palmer, the Herald Road Race winner, was the track team captain.

On June 4 the new Hudson Bay Company Athletic Club clubhouse opened. Included in the sports program was track competition. A. McLuckie won the men's 100 yard dash, and Miss Ross won the ladies 50 yard race. There were children's races, three legged and sack races. The single men defeated the married men in tug-of-war competition.

There was military sport competition and foot races, both at Camp Calgary and at the cadet camp during early summer.

There was a great deal of local discussion on what is legally a high jump, but the rule was, "a fair jump is one that shall be made without the assistance of weights, diving, summersaults or hand springs of any kind".

The Alberta provincial track and field championship meet was held at the South-side Track in Edmonton on July 1. R. Jackson of Calgary earned third place ribbons in the 100, 220 and 440 yard races. For the second year in a row M. McIntyre of Calgary won the 120 yard hurdle race, time 19.8 seconds. H. McKernan of Western Canada College won the pole vault with a leap of 8' 4".

W. Pocock of Edmonton set a new provincial record of 2.06.8 in the 880 yard run, and R. Sheppard cut the provincial 440 yard time to 53.6. A unique event was the two man 880 yard relay in the junior competition. A. Carter of Calgary was the last of the runners to finish in the five mile race, run in the mud.

Thousands of Calgarians attended the Retailer's Association picnic, held in July at Lowry Gardens west of Calgary. There was running and jumping competition, as well as sack and potato races. The Welch Club held their picnic and races at Midnapore.

The Calgary Caledonian Games were held August 9 at Victoria Park. Keeping in character with games which are held in Scotland the competition was confined to a small area. The track was seven laps to a half mile and the straightways only 111 feet long, and as a result the running times were slow.

The meet included piping, highland dancing, and wrestling as well as athletics competition. Pipe-major Stephen McKinnon of Edmonton won the piping championship of the Western provinces as well as the Calgary Gaelic Society's silver cup. Miss Jean MacDonald won the three dance competitions that she entered.

Francis Gilbert of Calgary collected 13 points to be named the athletic champion of the games. He won the putting shot, and placed second in both the cabre toss and the hammer throw. Moir and Cameron were runners up in the cabre, Moir second in the shot put, and B. Stewart of Moose Jaw was first in the hammer throw.

Roy Haliburton of Edmonton led T. McLean of Calgary to the tape to take the 100 yard dash in 10.6. The first three finishers in the 220 yard scratch were S.

Pierce of Edmonton, R. Knepper of Calgary, and Halliburton. Moir of Edmonton won the 440 yard scratch in 59 seconds, with R. Jackson of Calgary second. The one mile scratch was won by H. Palmer in a time of 5.09.4, with Calgarians A. Armstrong and W. Lawson second and third respectively. C. Blades of Edmonton out-ran H. Palmer to win the 880 in 2.20.

R. Halliburton set a new provincial record of 43' 8" in the running hop, step and jump. R. Jackson of Calgary was second with a distance of 41' 9". J. Rudolph, A. Little and W. Burns, all of Calgary, tied for first place in the vaulting with pole event with a height of 9' 7½". L. Blades of Edmonton leaped 5' 5" to capture the high jump event, with R. Knapper of Calgary second.

The Edmonton Y defeated the Calgary Y team in a one mile relay. Alex Melville won a 100 yard dash; the event confined to Scotsmen living in Calgary. The obstacle race was won by M. McIntyre, and in the married ladies race Mrs. R. Brown gave Mrs. Fisher her first loss. The boy's race was won by John Hutton, and L. McKay was the winner of the girls' race. The Gaelic Society came out on top in the tug-of-war competition by outpulling both the Calgary Rugby Football Association team and the Brewery team.

Many Calgary boys participated in the twenty track and field events which were run off at the Y.M.C.A. summer camp at Sylvan Lake. One of the events was "three stand jumps". Individual champions were Linton and Staines.

Edmonton athletes outpointed Calgary's team 90 to 35 at the Calgary Labour Day athletic meet. Raymond competitors garnered 19 points and a Carlstadt performer earned four points. Sheppard of Edmonton was the individual champion, and for his accomplishment earned the right to travel to the west coast for a meet. He also earned a suit of clothes from the Scottish Woolen Mills.

The afternoon events were held at the Victoria race track, but the evening events took place in the Horse Show Building. In the evening the amateur boxing championships of Alberta, with 125, 135, and 145 pound categories as well as wrestling matches were held. The afternoon program included two auto and two motorcycle races. A special event, the standing high jump, was added to the program to allow Sheppard to attempt to set a new Dominion record. Admission to the grounds was 25¢.

There were a record number of entries for a Calgary track meet, including 21 entries in the 100 yard dash, 13 runners in the 440 and eight men in the five mile race.

Sheppard, of Edmonton, won the 100 in 10.4, with R. Jackson of Calgary finishing third. The union 100 was taken by McInnes in 10.8, and Edmonton's Halliburton won the 220 in a good time of 22.8. Sheppard was first in the 440 in a time of 55 seconds flat. R. Foster of Edmonton took the 880 in a time of 2.15.4; Glen Hayden of Calgary was third. The mile run was easily won by Edmonton's Decoteau in a time of 4.52. Calgarians A. Mitchell and F. Thompson took the next two spots. Wauttance of Edmonton and Calgary's H. Palmer ran neck and neck for the first four miles of the five mile run, then Wauttance forged ahead to win by 100 yards in a time of 29.23.8.

The putting the shot event went to Edmonton's Roberts with a heavy 37' 10". Second and third places were earned by Calgarians A. Moir and J. Campbell.

Roberts heaved the hammer 111' 7¼", with Moir again second and Gilbert third. The union men's shot put event was taken by Corcoran.

The crowd was thrilled when Edmonton's Ross Sheppard set a new Dominion record of 4' 9¼" in the standing high jump. For his effort he received a solid gold medal. The old record was 4' 8½". Raymond athletes finished 1, 2, and 3 in the 220 hurdles. Miss Edwards won the ladies' 100 yard dash.

The union 440 was taken by C. Jarrett with a time of 1.03.2, and A. McInnes won the 220 in 25 seconds. A team of electricians won the union men's relay in a time of 3.46.

In the evening A.A.U. events, including track and field, wrestling and boxing were held before a good crowd in the Horse Show Building. There were six heats of the 50 yard dash, with Sheppard the winner in a time of 5.6; R. Jackson of Calgary was third. Haliburton of Edmonton leaped 21' 2" to break the old record of 20' 5" in the running broad jump. However officials later said that it would not be accepted as a provincial record because an improper take-off board had been used. Haliburton earned another first with a distance of 43' 2" in the running hop, step and jump. The Skonson brothers of Raymond placed first and third in the 120 yard hurdles, with Rudolph of Calgary in second place; winner's time 23 seconds. In the running high jump Blades cleared 5' 3¼"; Rudolph of Calgary placing second. Rudolph and Cornfoot of Calgary tied for first place in the pole vault with a height of 9' 4". Rudolph captured the union member's running, hop, step and jump and the union running broad jump.

More than 4,000 people attended the Labour Day meet, which was considered the biggest affair of its kind ever held in Alberta.

The Public School games were held in early October in the Horse Show Building at Victoria Park. Thirteen track and field school records were broken during the meet. Riverside School captured both the A and D classes, while Victoria and Haultain took the B and C divisions respectively. H. Saunders was the top athlete in class A, and H. Page of Victoria was the best of class B. Mount Royal's B. Bjornum captured class C honours, and H. Glover of Riverside proved his superiority in D class. Saunders and Page became co-holders of the Davidson Cup and earned fishing outfits for being the meet's top athletes.

The following records were set: In A division A. Poffenroth of Riverside did 6' 11" in the standing broad jump; H. Saunders of Haultain ran the 50 yard dash in seven seconds and the 100 in 13.4; R. Page of Victoria ran the 50 yard dash in 6.8 and the 220 in 30 seconds, and Haultain won the 220 relay in a time of 31 seconds.

The class C running high jump mark was raised to 4' 6½" by B. Bjornum, and C. Johnston of Haultain ran the 440 in 1.05.2. R. Kenney of Haultain set a time of 11.4 seconds in the 100 yard dash, as compared with the old record of 13 seconds. Haultain's team ran the 440 relay in 59 seconds. The D class 100 was run by H. Glover in 11.8 seconds, and his second record was in the running hop, step and jump with a distance of 35' 4½". E.G. Edmunds of Haultain ran the 880 in 2.28.2.

In the fall Olympic sprint champion Bobbie Kerr came to Calgary. However he came not to run, but only as secretary for the Hamilton Football Club which was on tour.

The C.P.R. Department of Natural Resources Athletic Club held a track and field day at Victoria Park in October. M. Benedict won the 100, 220, 440, high jump, hop, step, and jump, and broad jump. As the meet's top point earner he was awarded the J.B. Dennis Cup. Trench was first in the 880, 120 hurdles, second in the hop, step and jump, and third in the 400, broad jump and shot put. McLane won the football place kick, and Reynolds took the two mile walk in a time of 20.30. Schoel was first in the one mile walk, and Reid had the longest time in the 50 yard bicycle slow race. A. Dawson, as he had for many Calgary meets, served as the starter.

The High School held its field day in October. Frank Carscallen won the senior championship, and Wilbur Gillespie was the top competitor in the junior division. Carscallen, Fraser and McLaws were the first three in the 100 yard dash and the 220 hurdles. Carscallen won the pole vault, finished second to McLaws in the shot put and behind Fraser in the broad jump. Fraser set a new school record in the running high jump of 5' 2". Barkley, followed by McLaws and Fraser, won the mile in a time of 5.48.

The best junior sprinters were Gillespie, Miller and Addinell. In the 880 Bass edged Gillespie in a time of 2.34.4. Miller won the standing broad jump and the shot put, while Gillespie was the best in the hop, step and jump. Miller, followed by Shipps and Linton, took the 880 cycle race in a time of 1.25.8.

The 1913 Christmas Herald Road Race was altered slightly to follow a route which was to be used for many years. Instead of running a block on Eighth Avenue after turning the Barracks corner, the runners went directly to Seventh Avenue. The time for the start of the race was moved up to 11 a.m. As Cappy Smart was in Hawaii, ex-mayor Mitchell was given the role as starter.

No attendants were allowed on the course with the runners, and no running on sidewalks was allowed. All competitors had to undergo a medical exam prior to the race, and a runner must drop out of the race if advised to do so by the medical staff.

Three automobiles, containing five judges, timers, a doctor, photographer, and the sports editor of the Herald, followed the progress of the race. The runners had been advised to dress very warmly for the race.

Among the early registrants in the race were R.J. Verne, who had performed in the gymnastics competition of the Stockholm Olympics and who ran under the colours of the Canadian Bank of Commerce Athletic Club, A. Yates of the Bury Athletic Club, J. Fish of the Hillhurst A.A.A., and Johnson of Carlstadt.

By the registration deadline 25 runners had entered the race, however there were only twenty starters at the starting line, which was now located in front of the new Herald Building on First Street West.

There were large crowds along the route, and at the Eighth Street turn and at Seventeenth Avenue the people left the runners only a narrow passage to pass through. Palmer, running under the Y.M.C.A. colours, Warburton of the Broughton Harriers, and H. Conley, running unattached, ran the first two miles together. Warburton led up the Mission Hill, but at the cemetery he developed a side stitch and was forced to walk. Palmer sped by, and Conley caught up to Warburton.

Palmer, the winner, finished the race at a 100 yard clip, however his time was a slow 35.23. Warburton was second, Conley—third, J. Hall of Edmonton—fourth, and Alex Mitchell of the Ranger Football Club and S. Etheridge of the Y.M.C.A. Harriers in the next two positions.

It was estimated that over 10,000 persons watched the running of the race. The prizes were not presented to the winners as they had not yet arrived in the city, and would not be available until after the New Year.

In late February of 1914 the first indoor track meet of the season was held in the Y gym. An open invitation to participate in the meet was extended to all boys over twelve years of age. Over 100 boys participated in either of the A and B weight classes. Events included running, broad jump, hop, step, and jump, and potato races. Timmins clocked the best time in both the 50 and 100 yard races.

Track and field news from such places as England, the U.S.A., and Australia were often published in local Calgary papers.

In the spring the Caledonian Games committee announced that William Sherring, winner of the 1904 Olympic Marathon, would compete in Calgary's Caledonian Games on May 24. Although the marathoner never arrived the games still proved to be a great success. Besides track and field there were bands, dancing, five-a-side soccer, and catch-as-can wrestling. The C.P.R. had offered special rates for those attending the games, and if the day was rainy plans had been made to hold the show in the Horse Show Building. Prize money ran as high as $25 for first place in the 100 yard dash. The J.T. MacDonald Cup valued at $65, was donated for the mile relay.

Edmonton athletes won the major of the events. R. Haliburton of Edmonton won the open 100 in a time of 10.2 and 220 in 23.8 seconds. H. Palmer won the mile run in a time of 5.7.6 and the five mile race in 30.57. W. McRae tossed the cabre a grand distance of 29 feet.

Chief Cuddy and Captain Smart met in a 100 yard foot race. There were 100 yard races for local Scots, policemen in uniform, and firemen. The City Police team won the tug-of-war competition.

The University of Calgary sponsored the Collegiate Track Meet in May, under the auspices of the Cooperated Calgary Interscholastic Athletic Association, at Hillhurst Park. Western Canada College, Mount Royal College, University of Calgary, C.C.I., and the Okotoks High School competed. Invitations had been sent out to all senior schools in southern Alberta. There were 23 events and three divisions according to age, under 16, under 20, and a senior class.

In Junior competition Craig of W.C.C. won the 100 and running high jump; M. Palmer of C.C.I. was first in the shot put, running broad and standing broad jump. S. Miller of C.C.I. won the 220 dash, and C.C.I. beat out Western and Mount Royal in the 440 yard relay.

J. Fraser of C.C.I. ran the 440 in 56 seconds, while his r.h.s.j. distance was 39' 10". W. McLaws of C.C.I. was timed in 11 flat in the 100, while D. McKernan of Mount Royal College cleared ten feet in the pole vault to set a new interscholastic record for Alberta. C.C.I. edged Mount Royal in the 880 yard relay in a time of 1.42.2.

A good time of 53.6 was recorded by T. McLean in the senior 440. P. Smith of Mount Royal put the shot 40' 2½", and Burn, his team mate, cleared 9' 6" in the pole vault. W. MacMillan cleared 5' in the r.h.j., and he won the 100 in 10.8. H. Miller of M.R.C. won the running broad jump, and the University took the senior relay.

Although a sports program, which included baseball and five-a-side soccer, was held Victoria Day, there were not any of the usual track and field events.

Bishop Pinkham College held a field day on the Hillhurst grounds in late May. Gardner won four events in the class A competition, and in B competition Winspear captured first place in four races, with Brown behind him each time. In class C Irwin won the pole vault and high jump, and as well ran second in the 100, 220 and 440. Lane won the 220, 440 and 880, and earned a second in the pole vault. Riley was first in the class D 220, high jump, 440, 880 and 1320 yard run. Irwin took the 100 and was second in four events, while Lane finished second or third in seven events. The program included sack, three-legged, wheelbarrow, an old boy's and a masters' race.

In June Hubert Benedict, one of Calgary's top track and field competitors, died of pneumonia. There was track and field competition at the Calgary Militia Camp in June and at the cadet camp in July.

The Alberta track and field championships were held July first at Medicine Hat. Calgary sent a contingent of athletes to the meet, but as had been the pattern of that era, Edmonton athletes captured the majority of the events. One Dominion and six provincial records were set. R. Shephard of Edmonton broke his own Dominion mark of 5 feet in the standing high jump by clearing the bar at 5' 3/8". He also set a new provincial record of 44' 5¾" in the running hop, step and jump. Edmonton's R. Haliburton provided a new mark of 21' 5¼" in the running broad jump, and as well he won the 220. C. Weir of Medicine Hat established a new record in the 880 yard run with a 2.03.6 clocking. He also won the mile and finished second in the running hop, step and jump.

Calgary's H. Rouse did himself proud by setting a new provincial record of 19 seconds flat in the 120 yard hurdles, and taking first place in the running high jump with a leap of 5' 5¼".

The Orangemen of Calgary held a sports day on July first. Besides track and field there was a motorcycle race. The D.E. Black Trophy and eight medals went to the winning tug-of-war team. More than 3,000 people attended the event, which was held at Victoria Park.

R. Jackson of the Calgary Y track club and R. Pierce of Edmonton both ran and won their heats of the 100 yard dash in 10.1 seconds. After these fast times had been recorded the course was remeasured and found to be inches short. Pierce won the final in 10.1 seconds, and as a result there was little doubt as to his speed. Blades won the 220 in a time of 23.8, with Jack Fraser of C.C.I. in second place. Pierce led Fraser and R. Mayson to the tape in the 440, recording a time of 57 seconds. Blades won the 220 hurdles in a time of 28.4, G. Millar of the Calgary Y was second and Mayson third. Fraser leaped 5' 2½" in the high jump and had a hop, step and jump distance of 41' 5". Long time Calgary track and field competitor Cecil Merrit of the Calgary Y came second to Pierce in the running broad jump. J. Armstrong of the Edmonton Y took the mile in 4.47.6.

In tug-of-war competition Calgary defeated Red Deer and Edmonton outpulled Cochrane. Calgary beat Edmonton in the final after a stiff pull. W. Ansley, carrying a weight of 237 pounds, won the fat man's race. Mrs. A. Jones was home first in the married ladies race. The program included races for children.

By August Calgarians were being influenced by the war in Europe, and some of the Calgary athletes were joining the services.

The street railway employees held their second annual sports day in early August. There were races from 50 to 150 yards in length. W. Splane proved to be the top sprinter. The program included ladies dashes, a costume 100, wheelbarrow and sack races. W. Milligan won the high jump, while noted Calgary athlete J. Cornfoot took the shot put and pole vault events. The Scottish Pipe Band played at the event which was held in the Horse Show Building at Victoria Park.

During August Herb Palmer, a former Herald Road Race winner, moved back east because of his wife's poor health. Throughout the month a supervised children's playground was held in Bowville, otherwise known as Riverside. Several track meets were included in its program.

Motorcycle races were the features of the Labour Day sports program, but a full program of track and field was still included. J. Venimi, followed by J. Fraser, won the 100 in a time of 11.1. The order of finish was reversed in the 220. Fraser led W. Wright and W. Burn to the tape in the 220 hurdle race. G. Haydon won the 880 in a time of 2.22 and the mile in 5.08. J. Thorburn's winning time for the five mile run was 26.23.

J. Fraser was first in the running broad jump with a leap of 18′ 2″, and his hop, step and jump distance of 40′ 1″ was also the best in that event. J. Rudolph high jumped 5′ 2½″, while Wrigh was second or third in each of the jumping events.

McRae's distance of 36′ 4″ was the best in the shot put event, while J. Taylor won the throwing the hammer event with a distance of 92′ 2″.

In the union events A. McInnes and Ethridge were the best sprinters, while Rudolph won the broad jump and hop, step and jump. The musician's 100 yard dash went to Cross, and Dalberg won the fat man's race. Marion McKenzie was the fastest sprinter of the single ladies, and Mrs. Currie won the married ladies race.

The Police team won the open class tug-of-war competition, while the Brewery team were best in the union pull. In the meet final the Police outpulled the Brewery team.

An athletic carnival in aid of the Patriotic Fund was held at Victoria Park in late September. Besides track and field the program included lacrosse, rugby, and a motor race. More than $300 was collected in gate admissions to go to the Patriotic Fund in aid of the war effort. A half holiday had been proclaimed to allow Calgarians to attend this carnival, said to be the greatest event of its kind ever to be held in Canada.

The relays were the highlight of the running events, and the prime event was a two and a half mile race involving 300 boys in teams representing ten Calgary schools. An 880 yard relay for boy scout troops was won by the Church of the Redeemer team, with each boy running 176 yards. Another relay saw the Chinese Y.M.C.A. class compete against each other in a mile relay, with the winning team coming home in a time of 4.18.

The Fire Department was to meet the Police Department in a relay, however Fire Chief Smart was very angry when the ten policemen showed up in running shoes and track suits. Cappy said that was not the agreement, and that his men would not compete, but he would be willing to have all 92 of his men race while in uniform. The ten policemen were divided into two teams for a relay.

A tug-of-war on horseback saw eighteen volunteers compete against the police. Howewer it was discovered during the pull that the rope had been tied to the saddle horn of one of the police horses.

The Separate School's first field day was held at Victoria Park in October. C. McCulloch and J. Trupzak, each with three first place finishes, tied for the gold medal. McCulloch won the 100, running broad jump and the 440, while Trupzak was first in the 50 yard dash, standing broad jump and 120 yard hurdles. The 880 yard relay was the meet's most exciting event with the St. Mary's and Sacred Heart teams finishing in a dead heat. Saint Mary's beat out Sacred Heart and Bridgeland in the 220 yard relay, while St. Mary's edged St. Annes in the 440

Track Team, Connaught School 1914. John Luther, unknown, unknown, Owen Kenney, Jackie Smith.

relay. Sacred heart won the girl's basketball game. A Public School field day had been planned, but it was called off due to inclement weather.

The annual Herald Christmas Road Race was to be run under the sanction of the Alberta Branch of the Athletic Union of Canada. The published rules stated that two attendants would be allowed to use bicycles, but not cars, and must drop out of their duty by the Twelfth Avenue Bridge. All competitors had to take a strict medical exam because, it was stated, "many men coming from lower altitudes find this course very hard on the heart". White flags, bearing the words, "turn here", were placed at any point on the route where there was an alteration of direction. Cappy Smart, after a year's absence, was again the starter of the race. Besides holding the race trophy for a year, the winner received a miniature trophy, while the second through fifth place finishers received gold medals. Seventh Avenue was roped off from Centre Street to the finish line on First Street West.

The weather for the 1914 race was the worst in its history. Several inches of snow covered a very slippery ground.

Sixteen runners started the race, all wearing sweaters and many with gloves and toques. Alex Decoteau, of the Edmonton Police A.A.A. and Alberta's representative to the Stockholm Olympics, led the pack to the one mile mark in a time of 5.01. He gradually increased his lead, running two miles in 11.15 and three in 17.24. By the four mile mark he held a 200 yard lead. Besides being an excellent runner he had the advantage of wearing indoor track shoes which were equipped with short spikes.

Decoteau was the winner in a time of 36.15; slow in comparison to past races but fast considering the terrible conditions the race was run under. Ed Barnes of the 31st Battalion, Calgary, and one of several army runners in the race, finished second in 37.53. James Crerar of the Calgary Y was third, W. McNeely—fourth, A. Mitchell representing the Hillhurst A.C. and B. Rose of the Y finished in that order. Nine others finished the race with only one competitor dropping out. The runners all finished the run with a mantle of snow on their heads and shoulders, while moustaches and sideburns were coated with frost.

By 1915 many of Calgary's athletes were in the armed forces. Calgary did not hold any track and field competition on Victoria Day. In the provincial track and field competition, held in Edmonton, Calgarians G. Sutherland and J. Fraser did very well.

In Labour Day competition the two mile military relay was a feature race, with each of the eight runners going 220 yards. The 66th Regiment from Calgary outran the 63rd from Edmonton. There was an officer's race, married soldiers and soldiers' wives races as well as a military barricade race.

The best performance of the meet was the 11' 3" pole vault by Dr. Bricker of Cornation. The old high jump record of 5' 4½" was broken by Joe Rudolph with a 5' 6" leap and J. Fraser an inch less.

There were eleven army runners out of 24 entries in the Herald Christmas Road Race. Decoteau, the winner, was timed in 37.25. Hall of the 66th Battalion, Edmonton was second and received a special prize of a wrist watch for the first soldier to finish. Miller of the 66th finished third.

Basketball

A game similar to basketball was played by the Mayas many hundreds of years ago. Basketball, as such, was first organized at the Y.M.C.A. training school in 1891. By the following year the game was brought to Canada to be played in some clubs, schools and Y.M.C.A. gyms, including the Winnipeg branch. In the late 1890's basketball was played in the drill hall of the Winnipeg garrison.

The game was generally played in a scramble fashion up until 1897 when the number of players on the floor was decreased and strategy began to enter the game's floor plan.

In 1901 basketball, utilizing a soccer ball, was played in front of the Calgary fire hall, then located on Seventh Avenue East.

In 1902 a basketball club was organized at Anthracite, west of Calgary, but attempts to form a league with Banff and Cochrane proved unsuccessful.

The Mormons introduced basketball into southern Alberta, and in 1904 Raymond played Stirling in the province's first inter-school game. The same year basketball was played between Cardston and Magrath at the Lethbridge race meet. Cardston claimed the ladies' provincial championship and Raymond the men's title in 1904.

In April of 1904 five basketball games were played between the girls in Mr. Porter's and Mrs. Power's rooms of the Central School. A large crowd was in attendance for the deciding and fifth game which saw Mr. Porter's room win after the teams were tied three all at half time.

The local newspaper ran an article on the healthful aspects of basketball for girls. The game costume of the era was a regulation gym suit of bloomers and a loose blouse for indoors and a short skirt and sweater for outdoor play.

In 1905 a team, who called themselves the Uppercrusters, practised on a court set up in the basement of the Methodist Church. The nucleus of this group were: Bill Dingle, Frank Dallas, Lawrence Lambert, Frank Marwood and Hugh Freeman.

Later in the year some competition was organized. Play saw the Olympias defeat the Thistles 15-9, Capitals trounce the Olympias 22-3, and the Thistles take a 16-3 win from the Athletics. Collins, of the Athletics, had his shoulder put out when he received a very hard check. Play during this era tended to be rough, lacking in finesse.

In the fall of 1906 the Young Mens Club League at Central Methodist Church opened its schedule with the Brittanias defending the Celtics 36-11 in a game that was described as a, "good specimen of ball". Hibbs, with nine baskets, and

Connelly, with seven, were the games leading marksmen. Other Brittania players were Whittletown, McCray and Stockdell. The Celtics lineup was composed of: Priestly, G. Page, Robinson, Davidson and S. Page. F. Finlay handled the refereeing, while Lambert served as umpire.

The following Saturday the Argos, before a large crowd, beat the Olympics. The Argos crossed over at half time with a lead of 31-19. After this the Olympics got busy and reduced the lead to two points, but they could not score again to tie the game. Lambert and Patterson scored 30 points between them, while Lindner, Price and bishop completed the winning team's lineup. Captain Bishop, Fairley, Stockdill, H. Eyes and Drummond composed the Olympian team.

The Brittannias defeated Olympians 47-14, and the Argos won over Celtics 30-24. Then in an attempt to get on a winning kick the Olympians changed their team name to the Tigers. However following the new year the local basketball scene consisted only of pickup games.

The Y.M.C. also operated a secondary basketball league in 1906. Clubs in competition included: Tigers, Crescent, Argos and Normalities.

The Argos were the league champions during the 1907-1908 season. Games were still played in the Young Mens Club.

The following season games were mainly played in the new Y.M.C.A. gymnasium. The Crescents, known as the boys in green, won the championship in the final game with a 29-23 win over the Tigers. A good sized crowd witnessed the competition. Members of the winning team were: team captain H. McSpadden, H. Lambert, W. Gouge, H. Clark and R. Vickery.

The Argos still felt that they were the best club, but in a challenge match they lost 25-11 to the Crescents in a fast and cleanly played game. In another challenge match the Eastern Stars, composed of S. Priestly, Charry, A. Wark, Harvey and W. Wark, "had their corners knocked off", as the Crescents beat them 21-9 to retain their city title. In this game, as for most of the competition during the season, the refereeing was handled by H. Eyres.

In May the Crescents travelled to Taber where they were beaten by the hometeam 27-14. The match was played in the open before a crowd of over 500 spectators. However the Calgary boys were enthusiastic over the treatment they received at the hands of the Taber community who treated them to a trip through the mine and an evening dance. Taber's lineup consisted of Evanson, H. Evans, W. Kennedy, H. Van Orman and J. Mitchell.

In early November of 1908 the Lacombe basketball team claimed the championship of central Alberta, with wins over Wetaskwin and Edmonton. The Edmonton Y.M.C.A. challenged Calgary to a game for what they considered the championship of Alberta. Some Calgary players who were interested got together to practise at the Y.M.C.A. gym, then in November Lambert, J. Fowler, Frary, C. Fowler and Donnelly travelled to Edmonton for the Thanksgiving Day game. The Edmonton players completely outclassed the Calgary team as they won 35-15. The southern boys could not mark their men well enough, nor were their shooting skills adequate. It was reported that the Edmonton Y had three leagues in operation during this era.

With its new building and large gymnasium, located on Ninth Avenue and

First Street East, the Y.M.C.A. was the centre for basketball in Calgary. In April of 1909 the Calgary Y team took a narrow 22-21 win over the visiting Edmonton Y.M.C.A. team. The Edmonton players fouled repeatedly, but referee Lambert did not appear to notice. Calgary was behind 19-21 with less than a minute to play, but Woods scored a basket and then a free shot to give Calgary the narrow victory. His 14 points were tops among the players on both teams. Other Calgary players were: Wark, Eyres, Gouge and Clark. Millar, Fyfe, Clark, Dingle and Ray composed Edmonton's lineup.

In August the West Side team from Iowa were in Medicine Hat and attempted to get a game in Calgary, however a contest did not take place.

Basketball was more a sport for girls than boys in Calgary schools during this era. At one field day the Normal School girls defeated the High School girls 11-6. The newspaper reported "Not only these girls, but the public school girsl played very good basketball. They tore up the grounds until they could hardly be seen for dust, and the officials of the game and the spectators were covered with a beautiful grey". In other games Central defeated Alexandria 33-8, Alexander won over Victoria 17-1, and the High School 30-Alexandra 2.

On New Year's Day of 1910 a team from Edmonton, consisting of Cranston, Seymour, Cullen, Dingle and Ash, lost to Calgary 34-23 in, "a very fast and scientific game". Calgary lead 13-8 at the half, at which time the spectators were treated to a display of wrestling. Calgary's lineup was composed of: McCullough, Ironsides, Weir, Ward and Clark. S. Osbourne, the director of the Calgary Y.M.C.A., refereed, while the game umpire was from Edmonton.

In January the Calgary basketball fraternity met in the Y.M.C.A. to form a house league. Four teams, the 4 B's—baseball, basketball, Crescents, Leaders and the Maple Leafs were to play a 12 game schedule on Saturday nights in the Y.M.C.A. gymnasium. L. Hamly was responsible for coaching and organizing much of the basketball at the Y during this period.

McSpadden and Ironsides led the 4 B's to a 35-21 win over the Crescents in the league opener. Other members of the winner's lineup were: Donnelly, Steadman and Jacques. Clark and Gouge were the mainstays of the Crescents. The 4 B's went on to defeat the Leaders 24-19, and then take an easy 42-9 win over the Maple Leafs. Mosher, Hamilton, Pegler, Halbert, Rae and Ayres composed the Leader team, while the Maple Leaf's lineup included: Dickson, Barnes, Smith, Finch and Williams.

In the last league game, at which first place and the league championship were at stake, the 4 B's took a 34-28 decision over the Leaders. At half time the Leaders led 15-13, but in the second half the 4 B's took control with their well delivered and received passes.

A select team was chosen to play against Edmonton. Two of the players, McSpadden and Pegler, had learned their basketball in Calgary, while Clark and Wark had played together in Toronto. Ironsides was the fifth man chosen for the team.

The Edmonton team overwhelmed Calgary 46-26. Calgary claimed their loss was due to referee Jackson who they thought was absolutely useless as a referee. The Calgary five had the best of the combination work, but as soon as they got their hands on the ball they were either floored or tackled in rugby like fashion. Edmonton had little combination, but every chance they got they slammed the ball at the basket, and owing to the smallness of the floor they got quite a few baskets. Clark and Wark each got four baskets to lead the Calgary marksmen. There was talk of a third game to be played on a neutral court, but this never came about.

In post season play the Excelsior Bible class team defeated a Y.M.C.A. team. Basketball was also played in the drill hall on 12th Avenue and Centre Street, St. Mary's Hall and in the gym of the Methodist Church.

Five teams, the 4 B's, All American Stars, Crescents, Dominions and Highlanders, composed the Calgary senior basketball scene during the winter of 1910-11. The Crescents won eight straight games to take the league championship. Their lineup was composed of Clark, Gouge, Priestly, Vickery and Wark.

In March a triple header was held one Saturday evening at the Y gym. In the first two games teams from the Y.M.C.A. met teams from the Young Mens Club. There was no admission charge for this evening of basketball entertainment, and special concern was made to make certain that all the ladies had a good seat.

In the final game the league champion Crescents played an all-star club made up from the rest of the league. The all-stars secured a lead in the first few minutes; the Crescents attempted to stay close, but too many shots were rolling around the rim without dropping through. At half time the score was 16-10, and by the final whistle the Crescents had lost their first game of the season by a 23-18 score.

In April players Sharp, Wilkinson, Priestly, Watt, Wark and Vickery represented Calgary in Edmonton where the Calgary team went down to defeat by a 47-23 score in a hard fought game. Watt held Edmonton star Cormack scoreless with his diligent checking, however Britton, one of the best basketball players ever seen in the province, scored 17 points for the winners. Sharp lead the Calgary marksmen with 14 points, and Wilkinson was given credit for playing an alert game. It was reported that an audience of over 500 people watched this game.

In what was reported to be a surprise a team made up from Calgary's professional baseball nine defeated the Y team 27-25, with Pete Moran accounting for 17 of the winning team's points.

In the fall of 1911 the Calgary basketballers met and elected H. Dingle as league president. Expectations were for a great season. The group considered sending a team east for the Dominion championships. A provincial league, composed of Edmonton, Lethbridge and Calgary, was being mooted.

The Calgary senior basketball schedule was to include: the Crescents, league winners the past two seasons, Tigers, Stars, Maple Leafs, Dominions, Montreals, Giants, Home Plates and the Chateaus, the latter who were to drop out before the league play commenced. A schedule that lasted from December through March gave each team 14 games.

Chan formed the Home Plates, and he got together baseball players Barnstead, Standridge, Wilson, Pritchards, and Christenson. Barnes, Moberly, Ross, Gibson, and Smythe composed the Dominions, while the Steadman brothers were joined by Lunan, Alexander, Witchen, and Atherton on the Giants team.

League vice-president A. Graham organized the Montrealers team, while the Stars, otherwise Americans, had Olsen, Stevens, Long, Rogers, East and Carey in their lineup. The Tigers were made up of rugby players Ross, Vivian, Graam, Blair, Costello, Eakins, Lundner and Priestly. Norden, Clark, Gouge, Wark and Vickery made up the Crescent team, while the Maple Leafs were composed of McSpadden, Ironsides, Snowden, Watt, Dingle and Donnelly.

Maple Leaf basketball team. Back left to right: H. McSpadden, A.M. Snowden, L. Ironside. Front left to right: R. Morrison, W. Dingle, R. Watt, V. Donnelly, F. McNeil.

Dr. MacRae was honourary president and J. Sharpe president of an intermediate league that included teams from Western Canada College, Central Collegiate, the Athletics and the Y.M.C.A. boys clubs. Each team was to play six games in the schedule. Some of the games were played in the gym of St. Andrew's Church. Exhibition play saw a Lethbridge team lose to the Y.M.C.A. 50-32 and 26-20 to the Collegiate.

In senior play there were considerably high scores as the individuals and teams improved their playing and shooting skills. McSpadden and Ironsides each had 21 points as the Maple Leafs beat the Giants. A week later they dropped the Tigers 60-18. The Crescents blasted the Montrealers 62-8, and Carey had 21 points in the Stars 47-24 route of the Tigers.

By January the Home Plates and the Montrealers were just not showing up for games they were going to lose, so they were dropped from the league and a new schedule drawn up. As the league was having trouble meeting expenses a 10¢ spectator charge was initiated. The press expressed little interest in reporting the results of most games played.

With the new admission charge a problem arose in the eyes of the Alberta Amateur Athletic Association as amateurs were not allowed to play with professionals, as Pete Standridge, a professional baseball player, played with the Crescents basketball team.

In February the Crescents, who had been Calgary's best basketball team for several years, were snowed under by the Maple Leafs, now the league power house, by a 52-15 score. Morrison, a product of the intermediate league, and football star Mel Snowden led the Maple Leafs to their win.

The Crescents went on to capture the league title with nine wins and a loss. The Stars were runners-up, followed by the Dominions, Crescents, Giants and the Tigers, who did not win a game.

Bob Watt was chosen as captain, and Doc Watson was to coach a representative team in its quest for the provincial championships. Other players chosen were forwards Stephen and East, centre Mel Snowden, commonly known as Gulliver, Bob Dingle, and McSpadden and Rogers as reserves.

In intermediate play Western Canada College defaulted two games, so the team was suspended for the season. The Y.M.C.A. team took the league title without a loss, followed by Collegiate, Athletics and winless Western Canada.

It was hoped to invite Edmonton and Lethbridge here to stage a provincial tournament. However this did not materialize, and the Calgary Y.M.C.A. select tam was first matched with Lethbridge in a home and home total point series.

Calgary travelled to Lethbridge to win, and then in the return game in Calgary Lethbridge was put out of the running as they went down to defeat 50-32. Prior to this game the senior all-stars defeated the intermediate all-stars 29-10.

As the Alberta championship series continued Calgary travelled to Stirling to lose 26-23. Stirling, who had not been defeated during the season took a lead and never looked back. At half time the score was 10-8 and then the town boys led 20-8 before Calgary found their shooting eye. In the evening the players were hosted at a banquet.

In the return match, played in Calgary, Stirling never had a look in as Calgary defeated them 61-24, in what was said to be the best basketball witnessed locally in a long time. Stirling tried great end to end passes, but generally to no avail. "Every Calgary man was like a dancing spring or a gliding drop of quick silver!"

Calgary's lineup had remained the same as in the Lethbridge series, and D. Steed, A. Steed, Hardy and the Sparkman brothers played for Stirling.

In the provincial finals Calgary defeated Edmonton 30-18, in a game described as "full of ginger". East, with four baskets, was the top marksman for Calgary, while Bob Watt shone on defence.

Provincial senior basketball honours came to Calgary for the first time as Calgary won the second game over Edmonton by a 27-13 score. The Calgary players had speed to burn and with star player Britton out of their lineup Edmonton was swamped.

East had 12 of Calgary's points, and Stevens added six, while Bill scored 12 of Edmonton's 13 points.

In April of 1912 the Public School Basketball League was organized, with J. Sharpe serving as league president. Other offices included an honourary president, honourary vice-president and a long list of patrons. Central, Victoria and Haultain schools each played a four game schedule in the Y gym on Saturday afternoons. One of the league rules was that any team delaying the game would lose a point a minute.

A team from the Calgary Y travelled to Stavely where they lost 26-23, but in a return game, played in Calgary the Y team easily won 61-24. A Calgary college team, composed of Low, Cannon, Clarke, Lindner and Shearer, won 25-20 over a Lethbridge five, and the Mount Royal girl's team, led by Miss Thomas's 13 points, defeated the Y.W.C.A. team 19-13. In church league play the Wesleys beat the Anti-knockers on more than one occasion.

The Calgary Y.M.C.A. intermediates, composed of West, McNeil, Morrison, McFarlane and Lambley, defeated Lethbridge 50-32.

In November of 1912 the Mount Royal College team overwhelmed Central Collegiate 47-17, with Gouge and Burns scoring most of the baskets for the winners.

The Y.M.C.A. senior league began play in early December with the Dominions, Stars, Maple Leafs and Cubs playing a schedule of nine games for each club in a weekly doubleheader.

Uphouse, Hannah, Priestly, Dingle and Donnelly composed the Maple Leafs, while Smythe, Bolin, Sturgeon, Wilkinson and Burns made up the Dominions. The Cubs lineup was composed of McCrystall, Watt, Morrison, West and McNeil; the Stars included the Olson brothers, Rogers, East and Osborne. Rarely were there any substitutes.

Improved individual skills and team play saw scores climb, and there were some lopsided games as Cubs beat the Stars 70-16, and the Maple Leafs humiliated the Dominions 88-15. C. Ollson was handling much of the refereeing during the season. Admission to the double header games was still 10¢.

In early January of 1913 the Brandon basketball team played a Y select team. Brandon played a short passing game, while the Y team had nice team work, but the plays failed to help them to score enough points. When the final bell rang Brandon had won 40-33. The game was a disappointment to the large audience, as they were aware that Edmonton had beaten the Manitoba champions by six points.

The local referee let the Brandon players get away with holding in the first half, and at half time the visitors held a commanding 34-11 lead. A Brandon referee worked the second half and fouls were called on every occasion. Lead by East with 12 points, and Rogers with ten, Calgary rallied towards the close, but Brandon's lead had been too great. Morrison, Watt and Dingle completed the Calgary lineup.

The Cubs were declared the Calgary senior champions at the close of the schedule in February. The Maple Leafs finished second, followed by the Stars and the winless Dominions.

The secretary of the league was in communication with the Lethbridge, Medicine Hat and Raymond teams in an attempt to arrange games. In preparation for such twelve players were chosen for a representative team, and workouts were held three times a week. A new house league was formed for the players who were not picked for the squad. The representative team however was only to play a home and home series against Edmonton for the provincial championship.

Morrison, McSpadden, Robinson, Watt and Dingle were chosen to play in the first game in Edmonton. After 40 minutes of play Edmonton emerged with a slim two point lead. It was not a spectacular game and the crowd had little to cheer about. Calgary lead 3-0, but then the lead see-sawed back and forth. Probably Calgary's loss could be attributed to the fact that Calgary had 19 fouls called on them, and Edmonton players sank 13 shots from the foul line.

Ed Stephens was the best Edmonton player, but McKnight neeted 13 of their points. Hosie, Clark and Cormack completed the winning lineup.

McSpadden led the Calgary combinations, while Watt accounted for 12 of Calgary's points. The Calgary players hoped to turn things around at home on their large floor.

This game, played before a fair sized crowd, proved to be a mediocre exhibit of basketball. Calgary, at times, showed some fast play, and at least two baskets came about through combination play. However behind the consistent play of Morrison Calgary managed to basket 35 points, while Edmonton's final tally was only 28. Thus Calgary took the series, and the provincial 1912-13 championship by a slim margin of points. There was much promiscuous shooting by both teams, but Morrison had eight field goals, while McKnight found the basket 11 times from the foul line.

During the 1912-13 season the Southern Alberta Mutual Improvement Basketball League was formed, with teams from Taber, Raymond, Magrath and Stirling participating.

In the fall of 1913 the hoop fraternity felt that basketball was becoming more popular all over the province. There were almost twice as many players in Calgary as there were the previous season, with fourteen senior A and B teams ready for competition. In the A competition the Leaders, Stars, Tigers, Carneys, Cubs, Maple Leafs, Busmen, Y Men, Robin Hood and Maple Buds would each play a nine game schedule from December through February. Games were to be played on Tuesday and Friday evenings in the Y gym.

Provincial intermediate competition took place in the fall when Edmonton issued a challenge to Calgary's intermediate players to meet in a home and home series. In the first game, played in Calgary, the southern team won by a 37-17 score as they completely outclassed Edmonton. Ralph Fitzgerald, who had played high school basketball the previous year, was a standout on defence. Other Calgary players were: Rich McChrystie, Jim Robertson, Bill McNeil and Fish. In a preliminary game the Tigers defeated the Maple Leafs 31-16.

In the return match, at Edmonton, Calgary led 18-17 at half time, but Edmonton scored many baskets in the last few minutes to win 43-27. However Calgary took the series by four points to claim the provincial intermediate championship. Ed Crozier led the Edmonton scorers with 24 points, while Robertson's 10 was tops among the Calgary players.

When the organizational meeting of the interscholastic league met it was stated, "owing to the short season between rugby and hockey the ball tossers must finish their schedule before Christmas". Western Canada College Collegiate, Mount Royal and the University were to play each other once during the December schedule.

The final game between Mount Royal and the high school ended in a 22-all tie, and as a result the Collegiate was able to claim the championship. Their lineup included: D. McTeer, Johnston, Bryant, G. McTeer and Knight, while Miller, Palmer, Burn, Boucher and Drew played for Mount Royal.

On New Year's Day the Y.M.C.A. held its annual open house. In basketball during the day the Business Men's team beat the Leaders; the Stars won over the Maple Buds, and the Cubs beat the Maple Leafs.

The Y.M.C.A. basketball team was busy practising for its January basketball game against the Moose Jaw Millers, the Saskatchewan champions. Swanson, the Moose Jaw captain, had been the captain of the Toronto Y team when they won the Canadian championship. A record crowd was to be in evidence when every seat in the gallery was bought up three days in advance.

An additional feature of the evening was the preliminary basketball game between the red and blue teams of the Young Women's Christian Association. The blues led 8-4 at half, but in the second half it was red, red, red, and the blues were at the bottom of the 17-11 score. The winning team's lineup was composed of Miss Powell, Miller, Mann, Morton and Rupp, while Henly, Boutilier, Homberg, Brunstead and Burgoine were the girls in the blue uniforms.

The Calgary men's team lineup was composed of team captain Bob Watts, W. McSpadden, F. McNeil, R. Morrison, W. Dingle and Rogers. Calgary took a 13-0 lead, much to the delight of the crowd, but Moose Jaw roared back and the half ended 6-13. In the second half Moose Jaw tied the score several times, but they could not lead, and Calgary ended up the winner. McSpadden with 14 points and McNeil with six baskets were Calgary's top marksmen. After the games the four teams were treated to an oyster supper at the Y.

The Cubs beat the Tigers 31-25 to cinch the city championship. Members of the winning team were: Morrison, W. McNeil, Robertson, McFarlane and F. McNeil. Watt, Wark, Clark, Bryden and Overman played for the Tigers. The Stars, composed of players up from last year's intermediate play, captured the B section. Other teams in competition were the Gophers, Leaders and Business Men.

In March the Calgary Y was again to meet the Edmonton Y for the provincial senior championship. In one of the hardest fought games ever played on a Calgary floor the Calgary team won 35-29. Centre Morrison did the bulk of the work in the first half as Calgary led by six points, but Crozier was all over the floor as Edmonton played even with Calgary in the second half.

Morrison and McNeil led the Calgary point getters with eleven points each, and McSpadden, Watt and Dingle rounded out the Calgary lineup. McKnight scored 22 points for Edmonton, as he was fed up with passes from Stephens, Hammond and Clarke.

In Edmonton there was almost a duplication of the first game as Calgary defeated the Edmonton Y.M.C.A. team 34-28. The loss of Stephens, who had gone to the Peace River country, hurt Edmonton, but Crozier, the star of the series, managed 13 points. McNeil scored five baskets for Calgary and Watt sank 11 foul shots. Each team collected 24 fouls.

Prior to the game in Calgary the University girls defeated the Y.W.C.A. girls by an 18-8 score in what was to be their first annual game. The girl's game was far more rigid than the men's, and was said to be, "a denatured variety of the indoor game".

The Calgary Y had made tentative plans to hold a basketball tournament to include teams from Winnipeg, Brandon, Moose Jaw and Calgary, but the competition did not materialize.

In October of 1914 there was basketball at the Separate School's track and field meet, as Sacred Heart beat St. Mary's 18-8.

The senior men's league included the Cubs, Maple Leafs, Nameless 5, Tigers and the Stars, last year's B champions. The B section was composed of the Leaders, Pros, Black Diamonds, Allies, Busmen, Nova Scotians and Royals.

At the Y.W.C.A., Miss Lewis, the new gym director, was doing an excellent job of organizing and coaching basketball for the members.

Most of Calgary's basketball players were North American born, and did not appear to join the forces in such numbers as did those who played soccer or cricket and had a British background. By 1915 there was basketball competition between the 56 and 89 regiments. During the remainder of hostilities inter-city basketball did not take place as this type of competition was banned by the Alberta Amateur Athletic Union.

In 1916 a Calgary newspaper reported that any challenge to Calgarys basketball team should be directed to the army post office in London, England, and perhaps the Calgary recruiting officer could facilitate their trip.

Girls participation in basketball was on the upswing, and during the 1917-18 season there were 29 teams in the Calgary Public School girl's basketball league.

Swimming

In the year 1864 swimming baths were opened in Toronto. There was a small heated pool for men and another for ladies. The Toronto Swim Club was organized in 1876, and for the next several years held swimming meets. By the 1880's the Montreal Swim Club was the only swim club operating in Canada. A swim race was part of the Queen's birthday regatta at Victoria in 1888. The following year the Montreal Club held what was termed the first Canadian swim championships. Johnson, using the trudgen stroke, won the 100 yard race in one minute and 14 seconds.

An attempt to form a swimming club was made in Medicine Hat in 1889, however this venture met with little success.

In 1896 Mr. Killick of Montreal, professor of swimming and demonstrator of life saving taught swimming to missionaries at Fort Chippewan and Vermillion Forks.

C. Hartly was reported to have swum down the treacherous Bow Falls in Banff in 1901.

Lakes often serve as natural swimming areas, but the early Calgary area was not blessed with any, so as a result the Bow and Elbow Rivers were utilized to a degree. However swimming seasons were short as their waters are cold, and as well the Bow has hazardous currents. On the positive side the water in both rivers is clear and clean. Both rivers have been the haven of Calgary's aquatic youth, with the Elbow especially providing several good swimming holes.

In 1895 a swimming bath was opened in Calgary's Victoria Rink by proprietors Bird and Westlake. During the same summer residents living east of the Elbow River complained of the large number of Mounted Policemen who were bathing in the river, undoubtedly without a swimming costume.

In 1897 an article entitled, "The Art of Swimming", was printed in an edition of a Calgary newspaper.

Mr. H. Snell, a teacher at the Manual Training School, made use of the Elbow River to give swimming instruction to some of the Calgary youngsters. In 1902 Mr. Snell, with the help of some of his students, utilized Brown's Rink on Northcotte Avenue to construct a swimming bath. Snell had solicited and gained the financial backing of Calgary citizens: Hull, Burns, Underwood, Dr. O'Sullivan, Cameron, Allen and MacMillan to help sponsor the venture.

It was reported that 135 boys and girls were taking swimming lessons during the season. A dollar would buy a season pass as a member of the swim association. A 25¢ admission proved to be too high a price for the working boys, so a nominal fee of 10¢ was set for those up to the age of eighteen. The pool was open to the public on Saturday evenings. In the summer Mr. Burnett, a popular singer, took charge of the boys at the swim baths. Kerr proved to be the best Calgary swimmer during 1902.

J. Young was the president of a stock company with a capital stock of $5,000 that canvassed for funds in the spring of 1903 in order to operate a swimming tank in Calgary. Mayor Underwood was the contractor, and the operation opened under the management of Mr. Snell. The pool, located on Northcotte Avenue, measured 24 feet by 60 feet, with a depth of 3½ to 7 feet, with the floor being covered with slate. The water in the pool came from the Bow River and was heated by two boilers to a temperature of 70°; although it was as warm as 74° for special swimming events. The pool structure included four large rooms, 13 private changing and lavatories.

The pool was open from 6:30 a.m. until 9:30 p.m., with a ladies only period set up three times a week. A single bath cost 25¢, six admissions for a dollar, or a season's ticket for five dollars. Children's admission price was 10¢, however if they were the holder of what was known as a privilege ticket the price was only a nickle; a season ticket cost two dollars and swim lessons were 50¢ each. All shareholders in the company received a reduced admission rate. The secretary of the swim association said that profits would allow a 6% dividend to be paid on capital stock.

The highlight of the 1903 season was the October swim carnival. Teams from the public and high schools competed. Besides sprints, team and cork races there was a quarter-mile race. No one was able to swim this distance, but Bellamy completed 18 out of the 22 lengths to be judged the winner. Hunter was considered the top Calgary swimmer during the year.

It was reported by the Calgary Public Swim Association in 1904 that 181 boys had to swim at the Plunge Bath as compared to four Calgary boys who could swim in 1901. The fall carnival included a host of competitors, with 27 alone competing in the 20 yard handicap race. Other events included plunging, high dive, and swimming with hands tied competition. Newton Stirrett won the junior 100 yard race in a time of one minute, 45.6 seconds, and Hunter was the repeat winner in the city 100 yard championship with a one minute, 22.5 clocking. The world record at this time was 1.02.8. Bellamy completed the 440 yard race in a winning time of ten minutes and 25 seconds. Water temperature for the carnival had been raised to a comfortable 80°.

Another 1904 swim meet and exhibition featured races between the men and the boys. Lafferty won the feet first swim race, and W. Harper took first place in the diving contest. He also gave an exhibition of swimming with his hands and feet tied while being in a sack.

During the 1904 season the Public School Swim Association helped to place the sport of swimming on a popular level in Calgary.

The Calgary Amateur Swim Association held a gala and swim contest in July of 1907. The C.A.S.A. team won the 320 yard relay in a time of four minutes, 25 seconds.

An August meet featured events for the ladies. Miss Turner was the winner of the ladies novice race, while Miss Robinson captured the 40 yard race and life saving competition. Kelly was the underwater swim champion. A novelty event was the egg and spoon race.

In July of 1908 water polo was played at the Cave and Basin Pool in Banff between the local team and the C.P.R. boys on the Regina-Moose Jaw run. Dr. Brett refereed as the visitors won by a 6-5 score. In the fall Banff beat Regina 3-2, and then issued a challenge to Calgary swimmers.

The Calgary Swim Club held a gala and swimming contests at the bath in August of 1908. The C.S.C. at that time had 57 members. Merchants donated prizes for competition in the 12 events.

Bush captured the cork competition that included swimming to a cork, securing it in the teeth, and swimming back to the start. Bailey won the finals of the overall race, while Narroway and Douglass captured the men's and boy's tub races respectively. In the straight swim events there was a large field and keen competition. In the finals of the overhand stroke Narroway won over Hurd, while Isaac beat out Stratton in the boy's race. Bailey edged Narroway in the men's breast stroke final, and then won the fun overall event.

Emery was first and Street second in the premier four length open event. Miss Hogg and Miss Marley were first and second respectively in the ladies' race. J. Hotchins was best in both the diving and the obstacle work.

Other events included: swim under water, with a first prize of five dollars, obstacle race, and walking the greasy pole. Dr. O'Sullivan, the master of ceremonies, gave an exhibition of the best method of life saving, and Dr. Mason served as the starter.

In 1909 J. Emerson was president of the Calgary Amateur Swim Association. The Public School Bath was being managed by P. Clarke. However with the opening of the Y.M.C.A. pool the baths played a diminishing role and soon closed.

The Y pool, located in the new Y.M.C.A. building on the south-east corner of Ninth Avenue and First Street East, accelerated local interest in swimming. A Y.M.C.A. swim club was organized by Y director A. Osborne, and R. Mundy was designated team captain. Its fine youthful swimmers included: Woodhouse, L. Hutson, Max Robie, C. Cooper, J. Emery, and W. Dalton.

In a spring swim gala Mundy, in a time of 53.4 seconds outswam Fraser in the 75 yard race in competition towards the Herald Cup; a trophy to be awarded to Calgary's top swimmer. The race provided a handicap event for ladies in the audience who held tickets on the male competitors. A criss-cross race saw competitors swim six times across the pool, so the skill of turning was very important to do well. A sculling, or feet first relay, took place. In the overall race the competitors had to swim a pool length, put on a shirt and overalls without getting out of the water, and swim back to the start.

In June, 1909 the first Alberta swimming championships were held in the Y Pool, and the times attained in the events went into the books as Alberta records. The events were viewed by a capacity crowd of spectators.

E. Weir of Western Canada College won the Juvenile 25 yard race in a time of 19 seconds, while S. Plummers time to win the 50 yard event was 43 seconds. L.

Williams of the Y.M.C.A. team topped the junior swimmers with times of 16.4 and 40.2 seconds in the 25 and 50 yard races, and as well he edged R. West in the 50 yard breast stroke competition in a time of 43.4. Brother G. Williams captured the junior long plunge with a distance of 33′ 6″, and as well he took three second place ribbons.

There were enough competitors to make up three heats in the senior 50 yard race. Mundy, followed by Williams, won the final in a time of 32.4. Mundy was also the 100 yard winner with a time of 1.17.8; Craig was second. In the 100 yard breast stroke final, the result of three heats, A. Hepburn, followed by Jacques, led the way to the finish line with a time of 1.52.6. P. Fell's distance of 47 feet 6 inches in the long plunge earned him a first place ribbon.

The Y.M.C.A. team defeated their opponents from Western Canada in a hundred yard relay, clocking a time of 1.23.8. Each team member in the senior relay swam four lengths, as the Y.M.C.A. team, in a time of 3.46, outswam the Calgary Swimming Association team.

There were five each of midget, juvenile and junior events as well as twelve senior events in the program of a fall 1909 swim gala that attracted 134 competitors. Woodhouse, although only thirteen years old, entered the juvenile class and won the novice and open races, then added to his laurels by swimming the anchor position on the winning team in junior competition.

Mundy won the senior blindfold race and also the handicap race, even though he had to make up a distance almost the length of the tank. A new event to Calgary competition, the backstroke, was won by L. Jacques. Eversfield was first, or last, in the slow race, and Fell again captured the long plunge.

In a second fall swim gala, attended by a large crowd, Mundy again won the handicap race, although he had to start 40 seconds after the other swimmers. Mundy was probably the fastest swimmer in the province. In the senior four styles race, breast, side, back and any, Williams was the winner.

The meet was highlighted by relays, with the Y.M.C.A. seniors touching the finish before the Calgary Swim Club team. The senior employed boys beat the senior school boys by a touch, and as well the junior employed boys were faster than their academic counterparts. Mr. G. Osborne of the Y acted as starter for the events.

In March of 1910 W. Craig was elected the president of the Y.M.C.A. Swim Club, and R. Mundy remained the team captain. The club planned on sponsoring classes and giving free swimming lessons to boys.

The Herald Cup, a trophy for the best swimmer in the city, was up for competition. The city 50 yard championship race took place in May, and Mundy clocked a new provincial record of 31 seconds flat in leading Kelly to the finish line.

City merchants donated many prizes to a Victoria Day swim meet that took on the air of a social function. A special feature of the program was a two length handicap race where every lady in the audience received a number corresponding with the number of a swimmer; the winners to receive prizes.

In the city 75 yard championship race Mundy, followed by Emery and Kelly, won in a time of 54.4 seconds. Craig was the best of eight entries in the senior neat dive, and P. Williams beat out Mundy in a two length breast stroke race. L. Woodhouse was the top junior swimmer, and Mackie won two races and the neat dive in midget competition.

In June Reginald F. Mundy again broke his Alberta record for the 100 yard freestyle with a very good time of one minute and twelve seconds! This time was 6.4 seconds off the existing world record. Mundy's winning time for the one length sprint was nine seconds. Williams, with a time of 45 seconds, edged Barnes in the fifty yard breaststroke, while Hogg's winning time in the one length backstroke was sixteen seconds. Hudson and Emery proved to be the best of the boys in the swimming events. In the neat dive event Hogg was the best midget competitor, Hudson the best junior, while Smyth edged Craig in senior competition. There were plans to send the Y swim team to a meet in Lethbridge.

The 1910 Provincial Amateur Championship swimming events were held at the Calgary Y pool September 29 and 30. The 17 events included those for juvenile, under 14 years, junior, under 16 years, and senior classes. The D.E. Black Cup was offered for competition in the team relay race.

R. Mundy proved his supremacy by winning the 25 yard freestyle in 14.6 seconds, the 50 yard in 36.2, 75 yard in 55.4, and the 100 yard freestyle in a time of 1.12.4 seconds. R. Coffey earned three second place medals, and E. Fraser took second and third places. H. Abbot won the 50 yard back stroke race in a time of 48.4. M. Ekman, H. Abbot and E. Smythe each won a third place medal in different races.

P. Fell's 42′, 6″ was better than runnerups S. Brown and H. Abbot's distance in the long plunge, while W. Emery, E. Smythe, and W. Craig were the top three point earners in the senior neat dive. The Black Trophy for the relay event went to the team of Mundy, Brown, Smythe and Craig.

L. Hutson, with a 15.8 clocking, led Street to the finish in the junior 25 yard race final. A 13.8 time gave J. Emery, followed by C. Cooper, a medal in the junior one length backstroke. Then Emery went on to win the 50 yard freestyle race. R. West and L. Hutson were one-two in the junior meat dive event, and Hutson, West, Robie and Street teamed to win the relay.

M. Robie's winning time in the juvenile 25 yard freestyle was 19.6 seconds; C. Lane finishing second. A. Campbell and G. Jeffries were one-two in the one length backstroke race, time 16.6, and C. Lane took 14 seconds as he edged W. Riley in the one length breaststroke competition.

In march of 1911 Mr. Corsom, the Y swimming instructor reported that 250 boys were receiving swimming lessons and that 50 pupils had received their swim button on their very first lesson. During the month Mr. Corsom gave an exhibition of the various swimming strokes including: three styles of the Australian crawl, trudgeon, English overarm, double overarm, overlapping overarm, broad stroke on back, broadstroke on breast—sailor fashion, steamboat, swimming backward, side underarm, marching, three styles of sculling, racing Indian style, propeller and cartwheel, waltzing, log rolling, crab, feathering and race turn, limitations of a porpoise, swimming with feet tied, and a demonstration of how natives of the Congo swim feet first.

Mr. Dodge was the swim instructor at the new Y.W.C.A. pool on Twelfth

Avenue West. He handled swimming classes for children from age five up as well as adults. An apparatus he used in giving basic swimming lessons consisted of straps, connected to a waist belt, over each shoulder, and a rope fastened to the back of the belt and suspended from a pole held by the instructor, and by means of which the pupil was propelled through the water, meanwhile verbally instructing the student in the techniques of using the arms and legs. During this era the crawl stroke was the technique to be learned.

The Y.W.C.A. pool was 50 by 20 feet with depths from 3½ feet to 6½ feet. Users cost was 25¢ a dip, or three dollars a term. Probably the first published photograph of swimming in Calgary was of the activities at the Y.W. pool.

Girls bathing costumes of this era consisted of long blouse-like suits, knitted from wool, and swimming hats. Boys suits reached to the knee and as well covered the upper torso. Often the tops were decorated with wide horizontal stripes.

During 1911 an aquatic club was in operation at Chestermere lake.

The first major swim gala of the 1911 season took place at the Y.M.C.A. pool in June. In the fifty yard competition towards the Herald Cup Mundy won by a few inches over Californian Phillips in a time of 32.4; Fraser was third. Goudfroy was first in the handicap 50 yard breaststroke, and W. Fraser won the senior tub race. W. Emery edged Phillips in the neat dive competition, and Mundy, with a 4.02 clocking beat Fraser in a 220 yard swim. Mundy, Charlie Lane and Fraser were the members of the winning relay team.

Lane and Addinell were one-two in the 50 yard junior race, then Lane beat out McDougall in the dog race. The junior tub race was taken by Fistroy, while Addinell was the tight rope walking champion.

An August edition of a local paper devoted a whole page to the sport of water polo. Strategy of the sport discussed included the salmon leap and tandem formation.

The same month saw the final competition for the Herald Trophy. A large number of spectators helped to make the evening a great succes. There were only two competitors in the 100 yard freestyle as Mundy, in a time of 1.17.2, defeated his opponent Fraser and thus retained possession of the Herald Cup awarded to Calgary's best swimmer. In the feature overall race Fraser was first and Phillips second. W. Fraser outpointed Bebb in the senior neat dive, while Roberts outlasted the other competitors in the underwater swim with a distance of 128 feet. Phillips edged Emery in a 50 yard handicap race, then the Y.M.C.A. relay team swam for time as there was not any competition.

Swim club secretary Emery was the senior tub race champion and C. Lane the winner of the junior tub race. Lane was also the junior 25 yard freestyle winner.

The 1911 Alberta swim championships were held in the Y.M.C.A. pool in late September. Swimmers from the Edmonton Callies Club and Abbot of Lethbridge were entered. A large audience, including Mayor Mitchell, viewed the events.

Warren, a newcomer from New York, took three-tenths of a second off Mundy's 25 yard record. However Mundy, with a time of 32 flat, edged Warren in the 50, finished second to Edmonton's McAllan in the 75, and won the 100.

Hepburn, with a time of 45.6, lead Warren to the finish in the senior 50 yard breast stroke, while Abbot, from Diamond City, and Phillips were one-two in the back-stroke race, time 42 seconds.

Calgary's team defeated Edmonton in the relay race for the Black Trophy. Competitors used several different swim strokes including the overarm, trudgeon and Mundy's own peculiar style. Fell set a new provincial record of 53′, 11″ in the long plunge, and Emery and Leadbetter finished first and second in the senior neat dive. The event had nine entries.

W. Fraser was the junior 25 yard champion, edging West in a time of 16 seconds, then he won the 50 yard freestyle in 41.4. West, however, won the junior neat dive. Robie was the juvenile 50 yard winner, while second place finisher Lane later nipped Riley at the finish to take the backstroke race. The Calgarian's consensus of the Edmonton swimmers was that, "they were out of it".

Y swimming instructor Hebden was replaced by Mr. Carson and T. Callie in early 1912.

Swim competition in the city was reduced to minor meets. A junior neat dive was held in November. Each of the competitors in the four classes was allowed two dives. The Elliott brothers, Raymer and Kennedy were winners. Across the line many university swim coaches were pushing for recognition of fancy diving in swim competitions.

The Y pool was again the site for the 1912 Alberta swim championships. Two Lethbridge swimmers and many Edmonton entrants helped to improve competition.

In some races there were as many as five heats, and "many neck and neck races produced ties that had to be swum over".

The judges said that Crocket of Edmonton and Calgary's Mundy had tied in the final of the senior 100 yard freestyle, however the Edmonton crowd claimed that Crocket was an easy winner. The judges said that the two would have to race again to break the tie, however the Edmonton swimmer claimed that he was not in fit condition to race again, so Mundy swam by himself to take first place. However by the next event, the relay, Crockett was revived enough to help Edmonton win the race and take home the Black Trophy. Members of the winning team, whose time was 7.52, were McAllan, J. Crockett, G. Crockett and Hartree. Afterwards Calgarians were heard to complain that the relay had been lost because Mundy had been forced to swim the 100 three times.

The first three finishers in the senior 25 were: J. Thom, D. Grossert and Crockett. In the 50 yard backstroke Abbot edged Thom in a time of 43.2, then Abbot won over G. Crockett in the 75 with a 51.4 clocking. R. Luke of Calgary set a new provincial record of 37 flat, four seconds less than the old record, in winning the senior 50 yard breaststroke. A. Oliver of Lethbridge turned in an exceptional fast time of 30.4 seconds in the 50 yard sprint. Mundy, the old record holder placed second in the event. Oliver also won the senior 75 yard freestyle event.

Calgarians Skidmore, Emery and Smythe finished one, two, three in the neat dive, and Peter Fell, winning for the fourth consecutive year, edged H. Abbot by inches in the long plunge.

Cronkite, from Lethbridge, beat Bryant to the finish in both the junior 25 and 50 yard freestyle races in times of 16.2 and 39.9 seconds. G. Potter won the junior breaststroke race and then finished second to Bryant in the backstroke competition. Glover, Kinnear, Addinell and Bryant were members of the winning relay team. M. Elliott gave a beautiful exhibition of grace and east as he won the junior neat dive event; McDougall was the runner-up. Elliott was a double winner as he took the juvenile 25 yard race in a time of 19 seconds, W. Lane won the juvenile breaststroke race.

During the year many Calgarians had journeyed to Banff to try out the Turkish, Russian and plunge baths at the Banff Springs Hotel. F. Owens, the Canadian West Coast champion, set a new world underwater swim record of 73 yards at a swim meet in Spokane.

In November of 1913 the Orpheum Theatre featured the John F. Conroy swimming and diving act, including models and diving girls. Mr. Conroy was billed as the "world's greatest lifesaver", being responsible for saving 137 lives on the Atlantic coast.

During the term H. Flood was the teacher of physical education and swimming in Calgary public schools.

Prior to the Alberta swim championships, again sponsored by the Calgary Swimming Club at the Y.M.C.A. pool, Edmonton swim officials wrote to secretary Horton of the Calgary club asking that an Edmonton official be used in the meet, as they were not happy with the treatment that they had received in Calgary the previous year. Horton replies that unless this slander was retracted all Edmonton entries would be rejected. Edmonton officials then approached J. Ward of the Alberta Amateur Athletic Union, who then appointed R. Pearson, Dr. Dibson and H. Ballantyne to be the officials for the 1913 championships. Edmonton was now satisfied, but Calgary Swim Club officials were swimming. Mr. Dawson remained as referee and starter.

Senior event winners were to receive gold filled, silver and bronze medals, silver medals for the relay winners, and silver and bronze medals for the top junior and juvenile swimmers and divers. The senior events were open to any registered amateur swimmer in Alberta. Entry fees were 50¢, two events for 75¢, or three or more for a dollar; juniors 25¢ or 50¢ for two or more. By the deadline close to 250 entries had been received for the many events.

In the senior 25 yard freestyle Edmonton swimmers Ockendon, with a 14.6 time, Crockett and Abbot garnered the first three places. In the 50 yard race Ockendon equalled Oliver's provincial record of 30.4 seconds; Mundy and Abbot were runners-up. Wraith of Calgary set a new provincial record of 50.4 seconds in the 75 yard race, then won the 100 yard freestyle in a time of 1.13.4, finishing ten feet ahead of Ockendon and Crockett.

Watson and Luke of Calgary finished one-two in the 50 yard breaststroke, but Howe claimed a foul, that was upheld, so he was given first place instead of third. Jones set a new record of 37.4 in winning the senior 50 yard backstroke.

In the 135 yard senior relay race Calgary and Edmonton teams swam to a tie, so the race had to be re-done. In the final lap Wraith pulled even with then passed Ockendon and Calgary won back the Black Trophy, as a partisan crowd cheered!

Fell, with a long plunge of 43', 11½", finished ahead of Watson and Abbot. There were many entries in the neat dive event. Calgarians Watson, McTeer and Emery were the medal winners.

In the junior, under 16 years, 25 yard race Addinel set a new provincial record of 5.2 seconds; Cronkite of Lethbridge and Sinclair were second and third. In the 50 yard race Cronkite beat Addinel by a touch. Addinel outswam the Sinclair brothers in the 50 yard backstroke, however they finished first and second in the breaststroke race. Clark was the top juvenile swimmer.

In April of 1914 the Orpheum Theatre featured swimmer Lady Odiva, Queen of the Samoan pearl divers. Besides her program, that included trained Pacific sea lions, there was to be a swimming and diving competition open to amateur swimmers. The trophy for the winner was displayed in the window of Black's Jewelry Store. A large tank fitted with an open glass front was utilized by this travelling group for the act.

There were fourteen entries, but only eight showed up to display their talents before a packed house and the three judges. Odiva performed each stunt, which included: high dive, march step, imitation of a fish under water, the maiden's prayer, and then the contestants each had a turn. E. Smythe scored 97 points, one more than runner-up G. Phelps, to take home the trophy.

The following evening the swim club of the Y.M.C.A. presented an exhibition of swimming and fancy diving. The latter activity was now becoming popular in North America. Events included exhibition swims for time, boy's and men's handicap races, boy's and men's relay races, and plate dive. At the conclusion of the events medals were presented to the local winners of the 1913 Alberta swimming and diving champions.

In July citizens were requesting a fresh water pool be constructed on the Elbow River, but the city was reluctant to move on this important matter.

During the summer the Elbow River in the vicinity of the Exhibition Grounds was used extensively for swimming and bathing by the troops stationed at the army training camp that was located there. The following year the camp was moved to Sarcee, and it was reported that on some warm evenings the nearby river was literally full of men.

Some of the best diving ever seen in Calgary took place at the Pantages Theatre when Miss Vivian Marshall and her Water Lilies played to full houses for a whole week. Miss Marshall was reported to have given a very creditable performance in the sport of diving.

During the last two evenings, first Calgary's females and then its males, were invited to compete in a diving competition. Lottie Mayer and her diving girls were another troupe that performed at the Pantages.

In 1915 Henry and Andy Baxter, of baseball fame, installed a 36 by 90 foot cement tank on their land on Eighth Street and Seventh Avenue West. This was the first Crystal Swimming Pool. In 1924 a new Crystal Pool was opened on Fourth Avenue West. By the 1920's a swimming pool was operating in part of the lagoon in Bowness Park, and a large wading pool, complete with an island, was operating in Riley Park.

Skating and Hockey

Ice skating dates back to at least the fourteenth century in the Netherlands. A skating club existed in Edinburgh as early as 1642. Animal horns, cornstalks, wooden and iron blades were utilized by early skaters.

Bandy, a forerunner of hockey, was reported as been played in Roxborough, England in the 1830's, and the rules were similar to those of modern hockey. Bandy was played in Ireland, while shinty was the sport in Scotland. Hockey was the name of the game in London.

Ice hockey was reported to have been played in Canada in the eighteenth century by both Indians and the soldiers who were stationed along the St. Lawrence River. Hurley was played by women skaters in New Brunswick by 1833. Ice hockey games were played in Montreal in 1837, and a covered skating rink was used in Quebec in the 1850's. Games were reported to have been played with as many as 28 players aside. Many youths were condemned for participating in the game on the Sabbath. In 1859 the Montreal Skating Club was established.

On Christmas Day of 1855 some members of the military who were stationed at Kingston tied skates to their boots and using field-hockey sticks and a lacrosse ball played hockey on ice.

Probably the first game that was actually called ice hockey took place at the Victoria Skating Rink in Montreal in 1875. The players were students at McGill University who formed nine member teams and played with a round wooden puck. Cricket pads were used by the goalies. The McGill Rules were formulated, and this code of rules was to be used by hockey clubs in other Canadian centres.

A start was made towards forming an amateur hockey association of Canada in 1886, and two years later the Amateur Skating Association of Canada was formed. Upright sticks were used as goals by early hockey teams, and nets made their appearance in 1899.

By 1875 residents of Winnipeg were able to skate on a covered rink that measured 45 by 120 feet.

It is probable that, prior to the arrival of the railroad to the Calgary area, some of the Mounted Police or local traders strapped blades to their boots and skated on the Elbow River. In November of 1883 the new Calgary newspaper reported, "A few police enjoyed a skate on the pond near the barracks."

During the winter of 1883-84 a 140 foot square skating rink was operated on the Elbow River by Barwis and Broderick. The rink was lit by lamps that were hung on fir trees around the cleared ice when it was used for a skating carnival on the first evening of the new year. The facilities included a small changing house

Skating at Mewata Park.

for the ladies. During the fall George Fraser built a covered skating rink on the corner of Osler and Stephen Avenue, near his fruit store. The Fraser Rink, reported to be the first such structure west of Winnipeg, opened December 18, 1884 with 150 skaters in attendance. 52 people attended a costume carnival held at the rink in January. At a following carnival Miss English and Mr. Kevin won prizes for the best skating, while a picolo, flute, tambourine, fiddle and Mr. Munro on bagpipes supplied the music for the occasion. The Bow and Elbow were also used by skaters. In January two citizens skated along the Bow all the way to Padmore and back again.

However the short season gave Mr. Fraser second thoughts, and by March he was busy having a floor installed in the building so that it could be used for roller skating. 100 pairs of roller skates were brought in and skate tickets were sold at six for a dollar. Races as well as carnivals were held at the roller rink. A mile race was won by P. Pugh.

In September of 1885, Mr. F. Claxton, who operated the Star Bakery on Stephen Avenue, hired Jarrat and Cushing to construct a 136 by 60 foot rink on Angus Avenue (Sixth Avenue between Centre and First Street East). Water for the ice came from two wells on the premises. A game of hockey was held here on Christmas day. A carnival was held at the rink the following January 16th. Constable Green won a three mile speed skating race, while J. Brown was awarded first prize for men's fancy skating. There were not any entries in the ladies competition.

Fraser's roller rink was well patronized. A Grand Hat Carnival was held here with top prize going to G.L. Fraser for his eight foot wide hat. 25¢ was the cost of viewing the roller skating races. Four boys entered a two mile race, with the winner finishing in just over eleven minutes. The rink was also the site of Calgary's first agricultural exhibit. In 1886 Mr. Phil Barnes took over the management of the rink, but not long after the rink was leased by Fraser to Smart and Jordan who ran it under the name of the Calgary Roller Rink Company. A roller rink was in operation in Lethbridge the same year.

Skaters on Elbow River near quarry, 1911.

Skating on Elbow River early 1900's.

Besides serving as an ice skating rink Claxton's, which was the largest building in the town, was also used for running races. Often these races were run in stages over a several day period. The track was seventeen laps to the mile. During the winters the only hockey consisted of the odd pick-up game at the rink, or on the river or local sloughs.

A rink was built on the Elbow River by Charles Jackson during the winter of 1888-89. On its opening night free carriages took the people from town out to the torch lit rink complete with band. Other rinks of the era included the Barracks skating rink organized on a slough near the barracks. Ladies were admitted free, while men could purchase an admission ticket for 15¢ from Captain Saunders or at Linton's Book Store. An open air rink operated from 7:30—10:00 p.m. each night at its location on McIntyre (7th) Avenue across from the firehall. Prices were similar to those at Jackson's rink. A well advertised game of shinny was held on the Elbow River by the Sons of Scotia.

The Star Skating Rink was leased by Francis and Sutherland in December of 1888. Music for the skating sessions was often supplied by the E Division Band. In 1889 the Curling Club booked Claxton's rink for the season, but the ice was let for skating twice a week. Eleven new lights of 32 candle-power were added to the six lights already hooked up. During the year Lt. Governor Royal visited the rink.

Fraser's roller rink became George Irvine's gymnasium holding both roller skating and running races. A silver cup was offered for the two out of three winner of mile heats. Competitors of the era included Ross, Holt, Fitzgerald and White. Admission to the rink was 10¢ but for $2.50 a month a pass, which included the use of skates, could be purchased. In 1891 there were quarter, half, and one mile races at the Star Rink with T. Bruce and H. Watson generally finishing first and second. In a 300 yard race skater Tarrant beat runner McDougall.

Baetz and Hutton became owners of the ice rink in 1891. Changing rooms were built where the stage used to be, and the lighting system was improved. One of the skating races held here was a ten mile ordeal in which Johnson Hartley of Medicine Hat defeated T.C. West by three laps. Other events on the program included a half mile backwards skating race and a blind race. In the latter event the contestants were blindfolded and then had to find a huge bag which was suspended from the roof. During the skating season skates were regularly advertised for sale in the Calgary papers of the era. The hospital fund benefited from the proceeds of three successful costume carnivals held at the rink in 1982.

The structure of a hockey team was different than that of modern hockey teams. Besides the goal, there was point, left cover, right cover, as well as the three forward positions. Generally there was only one substitute. There was also ten man hockey, generally played on the larger ice surface of rivers or lakes. When the game was played with a larger number of players it often went under the name of shinny. One such shinny game, played on the Elbow River, ended in a free-for-all. Cappy Smart, the referee, and Eye Opener Bob Edwards both became involved in the mob scuffle.

In January of 1893 the town boys earned a 4—2 win from the Tailors Hockey Club in a game played at the Star Rink. That season the Town defeated the Mounted Police team in three games that were played on the ice of the Bow River. It was reported that large crowds were in attendance at these games.

During the 1893-94 season Lapentiere's and Lloyd's teams met in several hockey games. The Fire Bridge formed a team to provide the main competition for the Town team.

The calibre of hockey in Calgary improved considerably in 1895 with the arrival of several good hockey players. Games were now being played at the Victoria Rink, which was located on the present Fifth Avenue, west of Centre Street. Teams in Calgary included: the Maple Leafs, Fire Brigade, Pica (printers), the Calgary Club, the Y.M.C.A. Juniors and the Fire Brigade Juniors. That season a combined Calgary and Fire Brigade team journeyed to Edmonton to defeat the home team, and as well earn victories over the South Edmonton and Fort Saskatchewan Police teams.

In 1896 skating carnivals, with the Fire Brigade Band in attendance, were held at the Victoria Rink. Events included speed skating, three legged races and football on ice. 10¢ was the admission price to watch the Fire Department play against the Calgary team, or the Mounted Police versus the Calgary Juniors. A

Calgary all-star team was picked to compete in an Edmonton hockey tournament. Those making the trip were Charlie Marshall—goal, Chipman—point, Bruce and T. Douglas—cover, Johnson, Orr, and Henderson—forwards. The trip was a complete success, with the Calgary club thumping the Thistles 8—0, Fort Saskatchewan 9—1 and the Edmonton Shamrocks 12—1.

During the winter many Calgarians took advantage of the good ice on the Elbow River. A 220 yard skating race was held on the river ice between Billy Wier and Jim Hartney for a ten dollar side bet.

In March of 1896 a Calgary hockey club lost at Medicine Hat for what was called the championship of the North West Territories, with the Doll Cup being presented to the winners. The following winter Medicine Hat was the scene of a ladies hockey match; spectators were not allowed.

During this era good hockey clubs were being developed at the Indian schools. In 1898 the Dunbow School Indian team beat the Fire Brigade by a 2—1 score. Other hockey saw the Glenmore team play the Millarville hockey club on neutral ice at Red Deer Lake. The Calgary Juniors found a new competition in A. Creagh's team. Jim McCulloch of Winnipeg gave an exhibition of speed and fancy skating during a Calgary winter carnival.

In 1899 the Calgary Nonpareils were formed to play against the Fire Brigade and the City teams. The Fire Brigade team journeyed to Edmonton where they played games against several clubs from that area. Local games were generally played at the Victoria Rink.

There was more organized minor hockey in 1900 with a C.P.R. juvenile team as well as a club from the public schools. The Bankers were a new men's club, however they did not fare too well against such a powerhouse as the C.P.R. club. J.K. McCoullough, the world's best fancy skater, gave an exhibition in Calgary.

The centre of skating in Calgary during this era was the Open Air Rink, situated on the southwest corner of Seventh Avenue and First Street West, a location now occupied by the Hudson's Bay store. In 1901 the Fire Brigade, Police, C.P.R. and City teams played for the Jackson Trophy on the Open Air Rink. After each team won one playoff game the C.P.R. beat the City in overtime to win the cup. Naturally the goal was contested. Scratch hockey games saw the Bankers being thumped 11-3 by the Mounted Police, while the High School boys played friendly matches against a combination team.

In 1901 the Open Air Rink was used by visiting expert Norvel Baptie who gave an exhibition of fast and fancy skating. One of the most popular social events of the season was the gigantic skating carnival attended by hundreds of people.

On New Years Day of 1902 the C.P.R. hockey team beat the City club by a 3-1 score in a game played on the enclosed rink. Playing for the city were: Edwards—goal, Dodd, Rathbon, Sibbald, Williams, Charles, Miller and Rouleau. The C.P.R. team included: Woodside, Orr, Beal, Coutts, Wilson, Cardell and Walton.

In 1902 new boy's teams included the Herald Boys and the Shamrocks to compete with the Junior clubs of the C.P.R. and Fire Brigade. A new senior club, the Victorias, defeated Smart's Brigade Club 6-5 first time out. However at the season's end the Fire Brigade had won the Jackson Cup with a 6-4 win over the

Y.M.C.A. club. In the Brown Trophy competition the City team defeated the Police club for the cup. During the winter the large amount of snow on the streets made the use of sleighs quite prevalent, however it was against the law to run a sleigh on a main street without bells attached. The speed limit was set at five miles an hour. The big carnival on the Open Air Rink located on Seventh Avenue and First Street West was a huge success, while in a scratch hockey game the Calgary Saddlery defeated the Great West Saddlery team by a 6-3 score. Some hockey games were played at the Victoria Rink.

Calgary Victoria Hockey Club 1901-1902. Back left to right: D. Dodd, A. Edwards, A. Newham, E. Dodds. Front: B. Williams, J. Charles (president), H. O'Sullivan, Charles Rouleau, L. Rathvon.

The 1903 Stephen Trophy competition found the Calgary team journey to Edmonton to win the first game 8-3, lose the second game by an identical score, and before 1,200 hometown spectators drop the third game and the trophy by a 5-3 score.

The Dunbow Indian School team provided keen competition for the Calgary Seniors in February of 1904. The youngsters came to Calgary to defeat the home team 5-2 in the afternoon but lose the evening encounter 6-0. The Calgary team journeyed to Fort Macleod for a game, while the Calgary Junior Maroons lost 6-0 in Medicine Hat. The Juniors split games at Olds. Scratch hockey games included a Herald team versus Western Cartage.

The Calgary Auditorium Rink, located on 17th Avenue and Centre Street South, was opened by George Irish on December 13th, 1904. The structure was reputed to be the most complete building of its kind in the west, with an interior size of 96 by 200 feet and an ice surface 77 by 170 feet. The 48 foot high roof was supported by circle trusses, which did away with posts and obstructions. A balcony ringed the building, with three rows of side seats and end seats adding 1,200 seats to allow for a game viewing capacity of close to 5,000 people. Initially the cost of admission was 25¢ for men, 15¢ for women and children. Eight large electric light fixtures provided for a well lighted surface. There were dressing rooms and waiting areas provided. Later a large cafe provided hot food, while a 50 by 100 foot annex was said to have the largest stage in Canada. The building passed into the hands of Calgary theatre man W.B. Sherman and the rink became known as Sherman's Rink. Besides skating from December through March, the rink accommodated roller skating during the spring and fall, a summer garden, theatre, lecturers, and horse shows. The rink burned to the ground during a fire in 1915.

The Sherman Rink fire. This structure was located on 17 Avenue and Centre St. South. It was opened by George Irish in 1904, and was used for sports, horse shows and meetings until the fire in 1915.

The opening of the Auditorium Rink brought about increased interest and participation in the sport of hockey in Calgary. A city Hockey League was formed consisting of four teams: Bankers, Wholesalers, Victorias, and the C.P.R. A Calgary City team was hard pressed to defeat the Strathmore Tigers by a 2-1 score. A Calgary Junior team journeyed to Okotoks for a game. An informal league was held between the different departments of the C.P.R. Calgary's first Old Timer's team was defeated by the Bankers by a 4-1 score. Pick-up games were being played between the different Banks. An admission of 25¢ got you in to the Fancy Dress Carnival in aid of the Church of the Redeemer building fund, which was held in the Auditorium Rink. The affair began with a grand march. There was public skating to a band at the Auditorium every Tuesday and Thursday evening.

During the year a new 80 x 150 foot covered rink was constructed in Okotoks. the rink contained dressing rooms and was lit by two powerful bulbs.

Sherman's roller rink team. Back left to right: F. Frances, A. Carmichael, C. Rouleau (manager), H. Skipper, W. Fawcett. Centre: G. Wood, W. Sherman (owner of rink), Sam Lee (captain). Front: M. Haig, C. Beale.

A new rink was built in Canmore in 1906. Calgary's hockey club overwhelmed Canmore by a 17-2 score, as well as defeating the touring Rossland club by 6-3 and 6-0 scores. King and Rouleau scored for Calgary when they went down to defeat by Edmonton by a 3-2 count. Other games were played with Fort Macleod and Red Deer. The Calgary team members were Scott, Elliott, Rilance, King, Rouleau, Bates, and McLeod. Besides a Bankers team in the City League, there was a Bankers Hockey League. Their senior club traveled to High River to defeat the home club by a 7-3 score. A Calgary Intermediate team beat Okotoks 3-2. In the skating races held at the Auditorium rink one-armed O.B. Bush of Edmonton won the quarter, half and mile races.

Two new skating rinks were opened in Calgary in 1907 following the conversion of the Auditorium Rink to roller skating. The King Edward Rink was located on Seventeenth Avenue and First Street West. A band provided music for the afternoon and evening skating sessions. Men's admission was 25¢ while women and children were charged 15¢. Captain Bagley's Orchestra played for the skating sessions at the Favorite Rink located on Eleventh Avenue and Second Street West. The City Hockey League games were played at these two new rinks as well as the old Victoria Rink. The downtown open air rink was now a thing of the past. Teams in the league were the C.P.R. Rovers, Bankers, St. Mary's Saints, the Young Men's Club, the Bell Telephone Blue Bells, City, and the Lacrosse-Hockey Club.

The Calgary hockey team consisted of Anderson in goal, McHugh—cover point, Flumerfelt—point, Hemsworth—rover, Rouleau—centre, McLeod—right, and McKenzie—left. The team defeated Medicine Hat 14-4 before a small crowd of 350, beat a combined Lacombe—Olds team 3-2, Red Deer by 17-3, but lost to Strathcona 4-1. The team beat Regina in a two game total goal series by 5 goals to 4. The City League Bankers defeated High River 8 to 5, while the Rovers from the same league beat Canmore 9-7. The Calgary Intermediates defeated the Edmonton Intermediates by an 8 to 3 score to capture the Watson Medal. The station team won the Roy Trophy for the championship of the C.P.R. league. A $200 a side purse game was played between the boarders of the Grand Union and Royal Hotel boarders. A game between Black's Jewelery and the Watchmakers was one of the many scratch hockey games played between commercial firms. North of Calgary the towns of Olds, Didsbury, Crossfield and Red Deer operated a hockey league.

Bush of Edmonton was again the provincial speed skating champion. Roller skating proved to be very popular at the Auditorium. It was reported that a record mile was skated in three minutes. The building was also used for a footrace between Burn and Terway.

Lacrosse-Hockey team and the interior of the Sherman Rink, 1908-1909. Left to right: Dan McLeod, Harry Flummerfelt, Eddie King, unknown, Small, P. Powell, A. Melrose, Charles Rouleau, Baker, Dave McDougall, T. Telfer, Jim Sewell, unknown, B. Collinson, Dr. Hicks.

The 1908 Calgary Hockey League was made up of the Lacrosse-hockey, St. Marys, Y.M.C.A., and Tiger hockey clubs. The Lacross team won the Henning-Hall-Murphy Trophy for the city championship. In exhibition games the St. Mary's club defeated the Dunbow Indian School, the Herald beat the Albertan and also the Hammond Company club, Bankers defeated High River in two games while the Lacrosse team won over Fort Macleod. Other men's hockey teams included the Mills Boarding House, Royal Shield, Has beens, and the Would be's. Ladies hockey was organized in Calgary with the Barrack's and Favorite teams. The Lacrosse-hockey club team members were only allowed to use one hand in an exhibition game against the ladies.

Speed skating races were held at the King Edward rink between N. Baptie and Gib Bellefeulle. Baptie's best times for the 440 was 28 1/5, 1.2 1/5 for the half mile, and 2.08 for the mile on a straightway course. Baptie also gave the crowd an exhibition of stilt and fancy skating. A skating club to encourage fancy skating was organized at the Favorite rink. Both the Favorite and the King Edward rink were the scene of fancy dress carnivals.

Roller skating at the Auditorium rink proved to be very popular. There were four men's teams in roller hockey. The Sherman Eagles team won the championship. Ladies also played, with games between the Wanderers and the Ramblers. Kilpatrick, a one legged man with a wheel attached to the stub, beat three other contestants in a roller speed race. In November of 1908 the Sherman Auditorium Rink became under the ownership of a joint stock company so that it could again be used for ice hockey.

Jim Tomlinson, in a time of 3.11, won the finals of a six heat mile race. Later he defeated 14 year old Edmonton champion H. Vandushkirk to claim the Alberta championship.

The following year the senior hockey clubs in Calgary were: Tigers, Lacrosse-hockey, Y.M.C.A., and St. Mary's clubs. In the intermediate league were Lacrosse-hockey, Tigers 11, Western Canada College, East Calgary, Burns Co., and Dominion Express. St. Mary's 11, Lacrosse-hockey, W.C.C., and Y.M.C.A. made up a junior league which played many of its games on a rink located on the Western Canada College grounds. There were five teams in the C.P.R. league. The hotels sponsored clubs which played against each other as well as with teams from the Miller and the McBride hardware stores.

The final senior league standings found Lacrosse-hockey with a 5-1 record, followed by St. Mary's 4-2, Tigers 3-3, and Y.M.C.A. 0-6. The Lacrosse-hockey club played Strathcona for the provincial amateur championship. The teams were tied 1-1 at the end of the regular two periods, but Strathcona scored three overtime goals to take the championship. The Edmonton professional team, who had defeated the world champion Montreal Wanderers, defeated a picked Calgary squad by a score of 5-0. 25¢ was the usual charge for senior hockey games.

Bush, Edmonton's one armed speed skater, was narrowly defeated by the world's champion at a meet in New York State. N. Baptie, "the World's greatest skater", gave an exhibition at the new East Calgary Skating Rink on Christmas Eve. The rink was open for public skating to a band every Tuesday and Thursday evening during the season. During the winter the Swastika Skating Club was organized in Calgary. It was reported that one roller skating session at Sherman's Rink was attended by in excess of 500 people.

Dr. Gibson of Calgary convened when the Alberta Amateur Hockey Association met in Red Deer on November 23 of 1909. The delegates decided to divide the provinces into five hockey districts, with the Calgary division to include the Tigers, Lacrosse-hockey and the St. Mary's clubs. Later this "three-cornered league" met in Dr. Gibson's office where Joseph Moir was elected its president, with Dr. McGuffin assuming the role of vice-president.

THe Calgary City Amateur Hockey League decided to take intermediate and junior hockey in the city under its jurisdiction. Senior teams were to deposit $50 as a guarantee that they would finish the schedule, while league fees for an intermediate team was $5 and $3 for a junior club.

S. Clancy was the intermediate league president, while Pat Burns was given the position of honorary president. During this era practically every sports team was supported by a slate of honorary positions. The East Calgary Intermediates held their meetings at No. 3 Fire Hall. Other League teams were the Tiger and Burns. The schedule called for each team to play six games at the East Calgary Rink.

Appropriate weather conditions allowed Calgary hockey players to begin practising early in November of 1909. In the season's first hockey game, November 29, the Lacrosse-Hockey intermediates won over Western Canada College, then the teams split the next two games. Sherman's ice was in very poor shape, so the senior clubs used the Western Canada College ice to practise on. The Auditorium ice was still not ready in December, and the start of the senior league had to be postponed.

Norval Baptie, king of the ice skaters, performed at the East Calgary Rink on Christmas night. Baptie had skated a 440 in 28.2, the 880 in 1.00.4, and the mile in 2.08, all on a straightway. An admission of 50¢ allowed the spectators to see his speed, fancy and trick skating, and skating on stilts.

In the first Calgary City Hockey League game of the season, December 27, the Tigers scored a 7-5 win over the Lacrosse-Hockey Club in a hard hitting game. In the early minutes of the contest Doc Gibson, who was given several penalties during the match, hit Grey into the fence breaking two of his ribs. Art Lowes proved to be the offensive star of the game. Lacrosse-Hockey's line-up included: Tansey, MacLeod, Gray, McDonald, Charlie Rouleau, Bates and Dowell. Powell, Glosen, Melrose, White, Pinkham, H. King, Lowes and E. King were the Tiger players. Dick Andrews refereed many of the games, while H. Flummerfelt served as judge of play.

In their next game the Tigers went down to defeat to the St. Mary's club 6-4. The Saint's lineup included Walton, Walpear, A. McHugh, McKenzie, Sparrow and Green. King scored three goals, while Rouleau replied with two markers as the Tigers beat Lacrosse-Hockey 5-2, but L-H earned a win with a 7-6 score of the High River team.

A team composed of D. Machan, Walton, G. Burke, J. Hall, J. Machon, F. Jenkins and G. Blair traveled to Okotoks to earn a 6-3 win. Meanwhile the Bankers League, which included teams from the Bank of Commerce, Union, Imperial and Molsons, began a six game each schedule at the East Calgary Rink.

Forbes handled the refereeing as the St. Mary's club defeated the Edmonton Deacons 4-2. However in the game report a Calgary newspaper declared that it would not report any more hockey from Sherman's rink until the dangerous balcony was made safe for the people using it.

The Saints traveled to Edmonton where they lost 6-1 to the Deacons. However the Edmonton fans were still unhappy because the Calgary judge-of-play gave three more penalties to the Edmonton players than to Calgary.

In a very rough game between Lacrosse-Hockey and the Tigers Don McLeod was hit so hard that he suffered a dislocated shoulder. E. King scored three of the Tigers five goals. Later in the season, during a 14-3 loss to the Saint's team, Guay of L-H knocked referee Burton down after receiving a penalty. Guay again went after him at the end of the game, and for this he was banned from further play by league president Moir. McHugh scored six goals while McKenzie potted five in this one-sided win.

The Tigers went on to win the league, but because they had not joined the A.H.A. in time they were at first prohibited from any further playoffs. However the situation was resolved, and the Tigers went on to beat Didsbury 11-0. In the first of two games for the southern Alberta championship the Tigers lost to Macleod, the Crows Nest League winners, by a 4-3 score. Pinkham scored two goals for the Tigers who led 2-1 at the half. One of the Macleod players was Guay, recently banned from playing in Calgary. The Macleod team was unable to come to Calgary for the second game.

Further inter-league hockey play saw the Tigers nip Stettler 6-5, and a Calgary picked team beat a reinforced Stettler crew 6-4. The Lacrosse-Hockey Club defeated Strathcona 12-7 in what was billed as the amateur hockey championship of Alberta. The Tigers were now to play the Lacrosse-Hockey team but the game never came off.

At the East End Rink, where a season's skating pass cost $4 for men and $3 for women, the Burn's team defeated the East End Club 5-3 in the intermediate title match.

The East Calgary Rink was the scene of several skating carnivals as well as the city skating championship. M. Bick defeated Eric Machon in a time of 16.48 for a three mile race, sixteen laps to the mile. G. Woodhouse took the boys 15 and under with a 4.42 clocking. Miss A. Davis teamed with Machon to win the tandem half mile. The competition also included obstacle races.

The City Junior Hockey League included the St. Mary's, Lacrosse-Hockey, Western Canada College and Ashdown's Hardware teams. A junior pick team consisting of Helmer, Cudig, Dowd, McDonald, King, Kenney, and Brown defeated Okotoks 9-5, while the team split home and home games with the Medicine Hat juniors.

School hockey was played on rinks at Victoria and the Normal Schools. Exhibition games were played by the Banker's team, various banks, Calgary Grain Men, University of Calgary, Lougheed and Bennett, Elevator Men, Commission Men, Wanderers and Pick of the Law Offices team. A Mercantile League included: H.B.C., Campbell's, Neilson & Horne, Great West Saddlery and the Georgeson Co. The Okotoks team traveled in to play W.C.C. on the college rink.

Skating races were held at the Sherman Rink. Crosby of Banff won the 220 in 24.8, while Davidson of Bankhead took the 440 in 57 seconds flat, the 880 in 1.41, the mile in 3.20, and the three mile in 10.43. Bick of Calgary placed second in several races. The meet included competitors from Edmonton and Manitoba, as well as the forementioned skaters.

The Alberta Amateur Hockey Association held an important meeting in Red Deer in November of 1910. Steve Clancy, representing St. Mary's, and Doc Gibson, of the Calgary Hockey Club, were Calgary's delegates. It was announced that 21 clubs, playing in four divisions, would compete for the Herald-Journal Cup. The two Calgary clubs would play in the Central Division along with Stettler, Castor, Lacombe, Red Deer and Didsbury, however Castor dropped out before the league began. The schedule had been planned to run from January 2 through February 20, with each team to play eight games.

A new junior hockey league was formed in Calgary with an age limit for players of eighteen years. H. Ballantyne, the president, stated that teams would pay a dollar to enter and post a two dollar deposit to guarantee that they would finish the schedule. Each of the teams, Y.M.C.A., High School, St. Mary's, West End, Athletics, and Swastikas, were to play eight games each on the Y rink. The East End Club had originally planned on entering a team, but this did not happen.

P. Burns, Central, Y.M.C.A., Dominion Express, and St. Mary's composed the Intermediate League, with most games being played on the Y ice. The Banker's League included The Bank of Commerce, who were league winners the previous year, Royal Bank, Union Bank, and the Imperial team; the latter which was composed of players from several banks in the city.

A City League, under President Forbes, functioned with just two teams—St. Mary's and the Bankers. Games were played at Sherman's Auditorium Rink with the league receiving 40% of the gate collection. The Bible Class League included Grace Church, Excellsior, Y.M.C.A., and the Baraca team; each team playing six games. There were many industrial and commercial teams, such as Comers Hardware and the McBride Company, which just played pick-up games, while the Calgary Wanderers were well enough organized to make out of town trips to Crossfield and Okotoks, defeating both their home town opponents.

Important games were played at Sherman Auditorium Rink on Seventeenth Avenue and Centre Street. Many games, as well as countless practises were held at the Y rink on Ninth Avenue. It was lit with gas arch lamps and had a shack which was used as a changing room. Rinks were flooded on several school yards including one at Western Canada College. Patches were cleaned on sloughs and the Elbow River. Sometimes groups of skaters traveled as far upstream as the Weasel Head Bridge.

Alex Martin was the main supplier of Automobile Skates, which were noted for their steel ankle support, and hockey sticks.

The Calgary Hockey Club opened up its season on January 2 with a 5-2 win over the Didsbury Club in a game played at the Sherman Rink on what was termed "rotten ice". A good crowd saw the Calgary Club outscore St. Mary's 5-4 in a game which included three penalties in the two halfs. Calgary's lineup included: Powell—goal, McLeod—point, Kent—cover, Cain—Rover, McKenzie—centre, Lowes—right, and Wee King on left wing. St. Mary's lineup saw Bell in goal, Teiler—point, Purcell—cover, Redden—rover, Green—centre, Sparrow—right, and Ed King on left wing.

St. Mary's overwhelmed Didsbury 12-3 with Sparrow scoring five goals.

Calgary defeated Stettler 7-2 in their initial encounter. In the second meeting between the two Calgary clubs St. Mary's scored a resounding 14-6 win, with Redden and King each potting four goals.

In City League play St. Mary's defeated the Bankers 12-9 two games in succession.

Complications arose in the A.A.H.A. when several teams resorted to raiding the roster of other teams. When Calgary signed two Strathcona men it was felt that it might cause a breakdown of the entire league. Calgary journeyed up to Lacombe for a game, but it had to be postponed a day because the ice surface was under a foot of snow. The next day the two teams met with Calgary winning 6-2. Its ringers played, but they were treated very viciously by the Lacombe team. Meanwhile St. Mary's had traveled to Didsbury where they lost 3-1.

Doc Gibson, president of the A.A.H.B., called a meeting of its executive, and from this came notice that a residence clause had existed in its constitution even though it was not in print.

At the Sherman Rink St. Mary's lost, but under protest, to the Calgary team by a 9-2 score. Lacombe doubled St. Mary's 8-4 in which there was a high number of four penalties given. Calgary shut out Didsbury 6-0, and then defeated St. Mary's 12-0 with Sutherland and Pritchard each scoring four goals. At the end of the regular seasons play Lowes and Pritchard were the top scorers for Calgary, while Redden and Sparrow were the high marksmen on the St. Mary's team.

Because of the ineligible players on the Calgary team the league declared St. Mary's to be the section champions and said that they would meet the Edmonton Deacons for the provincial championship. The Deacons, meanwhile, traveled to Taber to beat the Taber team, which included five Cook brothers. A combined Deacons-Taber team then lost to the Calgary team by an 8-2 score. The reporter from the Calgary Herald who covered the game was so incensed with the refereeing of Forbes that he referred to him in the game report as the, "High Muckle Muck".

In the first game of a home and home series the St. Mary's Club defeated the Deacons 7-3. The following week the clubs met in Edmonton, this time the Deacons winning 7-5. However St. Mary's won the championship and the Herald-Journal Cup by leading the two game goal total 12-10. St. Mary's foreward line of Green, Sparrow and Powers had been a tower of strength for the Saints during the series.

The Calgary Club had issued a challenge to play for the Allan Cup. However a telegram was received from Northey of Montreal which read, "trustees regret cannot accept Calgary challenge for Allan Cup, owing to some of your players not being eligible according to rule seven". This rule dealt with players jumping from one team to another during the season.

St. Mary's then issued a challenge to the Winnipeg Victorias, the present holders of the Allan Cup, to play for the trophy. The challenge was accepted, but just prior to the teams departure for Winnipeg Sparrow contacted appendicitis. The St. Mary's team did not have a player to substitute for him, so it was decided to cancel the game.

As Calgary's hockey season drew to a close the High School won the city junior championship, and the P. Burns team beat the Centrals 2-0 for the intermediate championship. Western Canada College journeyed to High River to post a 2-1 win, and the Calgary Club earned a 6-2 win over the Taber Club, who played with the five Cook brothers in its lineup. Immediately after the ice was out the Sherman Rink was again used for roller skating and roller hockey.

During the summer of 1911 several of Calgary's star hockey players were offered big money to play hockey in the east during the following season.

In the fall there was talk of a Western Canada professional hockey league composed of teams from Calgary, Edmonton, Brandon, Winnipeg, Vancouver and Victoria. Calgary's entry was to be the Tommy Burn's Calgary All-Stars. The city's hockey crowd was up in arms because the new auditorium at Victoria Park was to be used in the winter exclusively for curling. The curlers had secured the building for a winter fee of $500, while the hockey group felt that they could raise a guarantee of $2000. Jack Aldous, a star Winnipeg hockey player, was transferred to Calgary by the bank who employed him. President Fred Lowes of the Calgary hockey team stated that it was their intention to go after the Allan Cup.

The Alberta Hockey League, with President Reverend Robert Pearson in the chair, met in Calgary in late November. It was decided to divide the league into four sections—Edmonton, Central, Calgary and Southern. The Calgary division was composed of the Calgary A.C., St. Mary's, Central and Tigers. However a residence rule proved to be the basis of dispute among the league members. Within days the Alberta Hockey League had lost many of its members, and Granville turned in his resignation to the A.A.H.A.

As a result the Southern Alberta Hockey League was formed, and Mayor Mitchell donated a trophy for the league championship. The Herald stated that the new league was also eligible to play for the Herald-Journal Cup, emblematic of the provincial championship. League president, Dr. Stanley of High River, said that it was not an outlaw league because it was affiliated with the A.A.A.U. The league would operate under Manitoba hockey rules, among which was one which said that the referee, judge of play and umpires (goal judges) would be chosen by mutual approval of the two teams. A residence rule said that a player must reside in the community for ten days before being allowed to play for its team.

The D.E. Black, Centrals, Y.M.C.A., Hillhurst and Ceepear teams played in the Calgary Senior Hockey League. J. Sharp was the president of minor hockey in the city. Junior competition, composed of players 19 and under, included the Swastikas, Collegiate, Y.M.C.A., and St. Mary's teams. Middle division for players 17 and under, included Y.M.C.A., Western Rangers and Collegiate. Fifteen year olds played in the juvenile section for the Tigers, Iroquois, Collegiate or Y.M.C.A. teams.

A school hockey league was divided into A and B divisions with games being played at the Y.M.C.A. rink. The intercollegiate league was composed of Western Canada College, Garbut's Business College and Mount Royal. Teams from Ashdowns, Pryce-Jones, McBrides, Calgary Paint, and Acme Fruit made up the new Mercantile League.

The Bible Class League, composed of Grace, Wesley, St. Andrews, Excelsior, Anti-Knockers and Olivet Baptist, played their games on the Y rink. West of the city, teams from Canmore, Banff and Bankhead played in the National Park League, while Cochrane played exhibition games against these centres.

The seasons first hockey game, on December 12, saw W.C.C. defeat Mount Royal 5-1. The Calgary A.C. club lost to Bassano 4-3 in one of the first local games played in three periods instead of two halves. The St. Mary's club lost in Edmonton on Christmas Day, with the loss being blamed on the reason that they had not been able to practise. In a return game the A.C.'s traveled to Bassano to lose 5-4.

At this stage of the season a meeting was held with the result that the St. Mary's, Tigers and Centrals hockey clubs decided to form a local branch of the A.A.H.A., and as a result the Calgary section of the Alberta Hockey League was no more. The Calgary A.C.'s were frozen out, being told that they must abide by league rules or go without hockey. The Bassano club was accused of playing three professional players. The A.C.'s and Bassano went on to play each other a series of games in what was called the Southern Alberta Hockey League. The A.C.'s lineup included: Chuck Clark—goal, A. Davidson—point, Bill McCammon—cover, Scottie McKenzie—rover, J. Pritchard—centre, Ab Kent—right, and Art Lowes—left wing.

The Tigers lineup included: Costello, McLeod, Marshall, Dowd, Rouleau, and Pinkham. Pullar, V. Pym, Carruth, Reeves, Irvine, Gillespie, and Grant made up the Centrals, while the St. Mary's Club was composed of Astell, Walton, McHugh, Powers, Green, Merrick and Hurd. Calgary star Eddie King had gone to Ottawa to play professional hockey.

St. Mary's won the Calgary division of the A.A.H.A., and in the first game along the playoff trail defeated Didsbury 7-4. In the next game St. Mary's earned a three-all tie with the Taber team, which included six of the Cook brothers in its lineup. The game was rough, with twelve penalties, and nearly became a free for all. The semi-final of the Alberta championship was again played, however St. Mary's had so many injuries that they forfeited the game, playing an exhibition instead with Taber winning 5-2. Taber went on to whitewash the Edmonton A.C.'s and win the A.H.A. championship.

The Calgary A.C.'s defeated Bassano 5-2 in the final game to take Southern Alberta Hockey League championship, but the A.A.H.A. said that they would not recognize this championship in any way. Never-the-less the Calgary club was determined to prove themselves in order to be accepted for Allan Cup competition, and in their next game defeated High River 13-2.

The A.C.'s travelled to Edmonton for a game against the Maritimers. With the Calgary club trailing by one goal in the dying moments of the game, Ab Kent made a spectacular rush to tie the score. He again scored in overtime and Calgary came away with a 7-5 victory.

In late February the Allan Cup trustees gave the Calgary A.C.'s the first call for Allan Cup competition, but then they ordered Calgary to first play Taber in a home and home series. However only one game was played, with Lowes scoring two goals to give Calgary a 5-3 win. Actually Taber was the better team, but Chuck Clark in the Calgary goal limited the Taber team's scoring punch.

The A.C.'s took Clark, Davidson, McCammon, Reddin, Pritchard, Lowes and Kent to Winnipeg to play against the Winnipeg Victorias for the Allan Cup. Calgary lost the first game 11-0 with the Winnipeg players far the better skaters. In the second game Calgary led for most of the contest, but lost 8-6. The Vics went on to overwhelm the Toronto Eatons by a greater score than they had beaten Calgary, and then they defeated Regina to retain the cup. In other inter-provincial competition the Taber Monarchs tied the Winnipeg Monarchs eight-all.

The Hillhurst rink opened in early February to supply more ice for the City Senior Hockey League. The Centrals won this league and the Harris Trophy. In minor competition St. Mary's won the junior championship, W.C.C. took the middle title, while the Tigers were the age fifteen and under winners. St. Andrews defeated the Anti-Knockers for the bible class championship, but this was under protest that not all their players attended the bible class. Pryce-Jones won the Mercantile League, and after several tie games Garbutt's Business College defeated W.C.C. 10-1 for the inter-collegiate title.

The Payne Shield, for the school championship, was taken by Haultain, who went on to defeat the Okotoks schools twice. C.C.I. won the girl's championship by defeating the Mount Royal girls 2-0 in the deciding game. Bassano beat Strathmore to take the McArthur Cup for the Bow Valley League championship.

In exhibition play the Mount Royal girls defeated the boys, who were only allowed to use one hand on their stick, by a 3-0 score. The St. Mary's juniors beat the Medicine Hat intermediates by 5-2 and 4-3 scores at the Hat. Strathcona Collegiate came down from Edmonton to defeat C.C.I. 6-3 in a game played at Sherman's Rink. The Edmonton girls had challenged the Calgary girls to a hockey game, but it never came off.

During the winter Norval Baptie, perhaps the world's greatest skater, performed at the Sherman Rink. He had held the world record for the ¼, ½, and mile on a straightway since 1898. His program included fancy skating and jumping backwards over six barrels. Baptie spotted local skaters in races and he beat them easily, and in his tag act five people tried to touch him but he evaded them all.

In the new National Hockey Association of Canada rules the rover position was removed. Now the point lined up in front of the goalie and the cover in front of the point.

Calgarians paid tribute to Father Nassens of Sacred Heart for his pioneering of hockey among the Indians of the Calgary area. Although it was hoped for, it appeared that the sought after artificial ice would not be installed in Calgary during the year. Sporting goods retailer Alex Martin reported that Automobile skates were the best selling blades in Calgary.

In the fall of 1912 Calgary hockey players Chuck Clark and Scotty Davidson received offers to try out with the professional Toronto hockey club. Davidson was signed to a contract, and he went on to have a good season in the east. Clark started the season in Calgary but then went on to play with Greenwood of the

B.C. Boundary League. Ivan Reddin, a star in Calgary during the previous season, returned to his eastern home.

The Calgary A.C.'s, last years provincial champions, decided to drop out of hockey due to the lack of enthusiasm on the part of sponsors and players. They had been confident that Calgary would have artificial ice by the 1912-13 season; however this was not the case.

Lloyd Turner was the manager of a new Calgary team sponsored by the Sherman Rink. Along with the Tigers and St. Mary's clubs it would be possible to have a three club division in Calgary and an interlocking schedule with Edmonton. However this did not work out as both the Tigers and the St. Mary's teams dropped out of provincial play.

The annual meeting of the Alberta Amateur Hockey Association was held in November in the Calgary Y. Compared to some of its past gatherings the meeting was quiet. Several revisions were made in the constitution. The Athletics, as the Sherman club, were admitted to the association's membership by its president R. Pearson.

In December the Y.M.C.A. began work on a big rink with a new lighting system. The rink had operated at a loss during the previous season, but the Y felt that the monetary loss was offset by the need and use of the rink by the youth of Calgary.

The Hillhurst A.C. opened a rink, and there were plans to make a rink on the log lagoon which extended from the Bow River to First Avenue West at Fifth Street. More than 200 skaters enjoyed the ice on the opening day of the open air rink located in the sunken gardens by the grandstand in Victoria Park. The Sherman Auditorium rink offered public skating to a band every Tuesday, Thursday and Saturday evenings.

With the loss of the Tigers and St. Mary's teams the Calgary fans were faced with a season of exhibition games by the Sherman team. However the City Senior League was to offer entertaining hockey in its double header games by the Y.M.C.A., Blacks, Centrals, Dominion Express, Revelstoke, Ceepear and Argo teams, each of whom played six games. The Hillhurst club had dropped out just prior to the beginning of the schedule. The Argos were a new club that had been formed due to the split which developed in last year's Central Club.

The Calgary Implement Hockey League included the International Harvester, Canadian Fairbanks, Massey Harris, Cockshott Plow, Ontario Windmill, and Rumley Products teams, while Northern Electric, Wood Vallance, Ashdowns, Pryce Jones, and the Department of Natural Resources teams played in the Mercantile League. In this league all players had to be in the legal employ of the firm for whose team they played.

The City Junior Hockey League teams, Pinkham College, Beavers, and Mission, played at the Y rink. Teams from Olivet, Grace, Central, and Wesley Churches made up the Bible Class League. There were numerous store, company and office teams which played exhibition and pick-up games.

A newly formed body took charge of all interscholastic sports. Public school hockey was divided into three divisions. Collegiate hockey saw Mount Royal College, University, and the Normal School in senior competition; M.R.C.,

W.C.C., and C.C.I. at the intermediate and junior levels. Dan McLeod handled the refereeing of many of the games played in Calgary during that winter.

The Ceepear team was dropped from senior city competition because they had signed only eight players. The league decided to hand a two game suspension to any player using profane language during a game.

Revelstoke and the Y teams made it to the senior finals with Revelstoke coming out on top by a 6-5 score in a hard fought game. The lumber team's lineup included: captain Woods, goalie Helmer, Bevan, Grady, Pritchard, Redman, Deggan and McLean. This club was later to lose to the Sherman club in the provincial playdowns.

Pryce-Jones won the Mercantile League, and then went on to defeat the Hudson Bay Co., champions of the Edmonton Mercantile League, for the provincial mercantile title. Connaught took the school hockey B division title, while Haultain was the winner in both C and D divisions.

A Western Canada College team traveled to Pincher Creek to earn a 3-3 tie with a team composed of the town's senior and intermediate players. The town's businesses closed for the game, upon which a great deal of money was wagered. Banff defeated Cochrane 15-1 in Browning Cup play. Both teams imported players from Calgary for the game. Gleichen beat Bassano for the Bow Valley League championship. Exhibition saw Okotoks overwhelm the Dunbow Indian School team 16-3.

The Shermans opened up their season by losing 8-7 to the Edmonton Dominions in a Christmas Day game in Calgary. The Tigers journeyed to Edmonton to be humiliated by the Deacons by a 13-3 count. Goalie Chuck Clark made countless saves against a much stronger Edmonton club. The following week Sexsmith scored three goals to lead the Shermans to an 8-2 win over the visiting Taber Cooks. Calgary player Hart was badly hurt when a skate blade went through his throat. Clark was again brilliant in goal as the Tigers held the Edmonton Eskimos to a 3-3 tie. The Calgary team lineup included: Clark, Fitzgibbons, Dwyer, McLean, Murphy, Macdonald and Hurd. This was to be the Tiger's last game and the team disbanded.

The Shermans traveled to Edmonton where they were beaten by the Dominions 6-0. However this was to be their last actual loss of the season. In a return game Sexsmith got the hat trick as the Dominions were shaded 7-6. A trip to the pass saw the Shermans trip Blairmore 4-1. Back in Calgary McHugh scored six goals as they whitewashed the Lethbridge squad 14-1. McHugh and Sexsmith again starred as they defeated the Edmonton Capitals 14-2. In their next game a wide-spread chinook had ruined the Sherman Rink ice, but they still overwhelmed the Edmonton Independents 14-3.

Taber tied the score in the last few seconds of a game in Calgary. However after the break they refused to come back out on the Sherman ice to break the 7-7 tie.

The Alberta Hockey Association ordered the Shermans and the Calgary City League champion Revelstoke team to meet for the right to play Taber for the provincial championship. Taber had earned the right to a final berth by defeating the Edmonton champions 6-3. The game was no contest as the Shermans humiliated the Revelstoke team 16-4. Now a two game series was ordered by the A.A.H.A. between the Shermans and Taber.

Meanwhile charges and counter-charges were being hurled at each other by these two clubs regarding registration of players, ringers and professionalism. Taber claimed that Thompson of the Shermans was really Tommy Plette who had played professional hockey with Galt for a few years previous. Leo Cook of the Taber team had his amateur card suspended. As a result Edmonton demanded that their loss to Taber should be forfeited by that club, and that they should be meeting Calgary for the provincial title.

The Taber "Cooks" came to Calgary for the first of the proposed two games. Referee W. Forbes and judge of play Duncan Campbell held a tight reign on the game. Taber went two goals up, then Bishop, Manners and McHugh each scored to give Calgary a one goal lead. Close checking by the Calgary players prevented their opponents from tying the score, and Calgary won 3-2. The Taber team returned home and then decided not to play the second game. Sherman manager Turner announced that if Winnipeg would not accept a challenge for the Allen Cup that the Shermans would disband.

However these plans were only partially to come about, for A.A.H.A. president Pearson said that the Edmonton Eskimos could challenge the Shermans, and if the Calgary team does not play, then Edmonton has the right to challenge for the Allen Cup. The Shermans would not play the Edmonton team, so the Eskimos were awarded the A.A.H.A. championship and the Herald-Journal Cup.

After the Esks had made plans to play in the Manitoba capital Lloyd Turner offered to play them a "saw-off" game in Winnipeg but the offer was refused. The Winnipeg team beat the Eskimos by a total of 18 goals to eight in the two game series, while Calgary had outscored the Eskimos 19-4 in two games.

Although the Shermans were not the official provincial champions they had proved themselves to be the class of the province, winning twelve games, tying one and losing two. Besides playing Edmonton, Calgary and Taber teams, games were played with Canmore, Lethbridge and Coleman. The Shermans scored 147 goals and had only 60 scored against them. Their lineup had included: McCarthy, Allen, McGovern, Sexsmith, Bishop, Thompson and McHugh.

The conditions to maintain natural ice are usually not very predictable in Calgary, but there was still 14" of ice left in the Sherman Rink when April of 1913 rolled around. Many of Calgary's hockey players were still practising or playing shinny. A team of these players traveled up to Edmonton to lose 7-4 to the Dominions.

Calgarians were treated to professional hockey when the New Westminster team defeated Vancouver 10-8 in a game of six man hockey played before a capacity crowd at the Sherman Rink. However the pros felt the ice surface was too small to play their best style of hockey. In another game, played on slushy ice April 2, Quebec edged the Eastern All-Stars 9-8. Former Calgary player Scotty Cameron was one of the All-Stars. A third planned game, between the eastern and western players, never came off. During the season the National Hockey

Association decided to stay with six man hockey, but planned to change to four 15 minute periods instead of three 20 minute periods.

In January Norval Baptie, who at age 34 was in his eleventh year as a world champion skater, appeared in a performance at the Sherman Rink.

In the fall of 1913 Mr. W. Davidson of the Crystal Ice Company announced plans for a proposed artificial ice rink to be constructed on the corner of 11th Street and 14th Avenue S.W. The $250,000 project was designed as a 300 by 130 foot building containing an 85 x 190 foot rink with artificial ice. No one's view from any of the 5,120 seats would be marred by an interior post. Following the public announcement of this project work was commenced on the drilling of wells for its water supply. Soon the members of the curling fraternity met with Davidson, for they too wanted to be a part of such a project. However the venture was not to get off the ground, for a petition against its construction was raised by the people of the area. They pointed out the close proximity of a church, and pointed out the noise problem created by the Sherman rink. Edmonton was fortunate that its new stock pavilion, seating 5,000 people, was to be used as a rink.

During this era the rules of hockey were not consistent across Canada. Both six and seven man hockey was played. A three minute penalty with no substitute allowed was given for an infraction in the west coast professional hockey league. In the east the penalty time was to be for at least ten minutes, but a substitute was allowed. A goalie could be fined for kneeling on the ice.

The Alberta Amateur Hockey Association met in Calgary November 14, with president R. Pearson in the chair. Plans were made for inter-city hockey, and it was hoped to include Redcliffe, Medicine Hat and Lethbridge along with Calgary and Edmonton. An intermediate series for the smaller centres was proposed. Lloyd Cook of the Taber team was reinstated into amateur hockey.

Alberta communities held suppers, smokers or tag days for the purpose of raising money to finance their rinks and hockey teams. If a lake or large slough were nearby, these often served as the town rink, Besides being used for hockey, shinny and skating many lakes were the scene of ice carnivals.

In Calgary Lloyd Turner was preparing the roller skating surface at the Sherman Auditorium for ice by putting down tar paper, tarring the joints, and then covering this surface with four inches of sawdust before the rink was flooded. The 103rd Regiment Band was to again play for public skating. The east Calgary rink was located beside the Royal Crown Soap Company, the Y rink was on Ninth Avenue, and rinks were constructed in every school yard. Skaters travelled up the Elbow River, often as far as the Weasel Head Bridge. Bonfires were built along the way so that skaters could warm their hands and toes. A small stream on Princess Island allowed boys and girls to practise their turning skills as they skated around the bushes sticking up through the ice.

Calgarian Chuck Clark went to play goal for the Vancouver professional club, while Red Sexsmith transferred his hockey talent to Rossland. Manners and McGovern were to line-up with the Edmonton Dominions.

The Edmonton Eskimo and Dominon teams were scheduled in a division with the Calgary Chinooks and the Centrals in the Provincial Senior Hockey League.

Each team was to play six games in a schedule which lasted from January 1 to February 4.

In a Christmas Day exhibition game the Chinooks whitewashed the Centrals 13-3. Art Lowes had four goals and McQuarrie scored three. An innovation in Calgary hockey was the use of numbers on the player's sweaters. Both club's rosters contained a dozen players each, but substitution was rare.

In the teams' first league game, played January 1, Lowes scored six goals as the Chinooks overwhelmed the Centrals 18-2. In their next game the Centrals surprised everyone, themselves included, by beating the strong Edmonton Dominions; Stanley and Baird each scored two goals. The game consisted of three periods, but up in Edmonton the game, won 8-4 by the Eskimos over the Chinooks, was played in two halves. The Calgary team received two penalties, each three minutes in duration. In that era the time registered as to when a goal was scored was timed from the previous goal rather than the start of the game.

The Centrals then turned the table on the Chinooks beating them 5-2. Art Lowes scored his fourth goal of the game in overtime as the Chinooks edged the Dominions 6-5. There were the usual claims that some of the Dominion players were professionals. At Edmonton the Centrals lost 7-2 to the Eskimos, with only the brilliant work of Helmer in goal keeping the score from reaching a double figure.

The Calgary teams got back to their early season form as Chinooks blasted Centrals 13-3, while in Edmonton a huge crowd of 3,500 people saw Dominions edge the Eks 7-6. Further play saw the Eskimos top the Centrals 11-3, and Dominions double Chinooks 6-3. The Dominions took the league title, while in a game for second place the Esks beat Chinooks 8-6. Calgary Centrals ended up in bottom place.

In a game for the provincial title the Dominions defeated Medicine Hat, the southern Alberta champions, 11-5. The Chinooks had beaten Medicine Hat 14-10 in an exhibition game.

In post season exhibition play Bishop, McHugh and McQuarrie each scored a goal to give the Chinooks a 3-1 win over the provincial champion Dominions. Other exhibition play saw Chinooks defeat the Moose Jaw team 5-3 before a crowd of 800 fans at the Sherman Rink. In a second game Loucks of the Department of Natural Resources team played goal for Medicine Hat as they lost to Chinooks 4-3.

During the season the main lineup for the Chinooks included: Maluish, Crooks, McGrath, Bishop, Kerr, McQuarrie, Lowes and B. Gordon. Central players were: Helmer, Hart, Sories, Smith, Scott, Russel and James.

Art Lowes and Archie Bishop of the Chinooks were invited by the Eskimos to play for them in an exhibition game in Winnipeg against the powerful Winnipeg Monarchs. The Dominions, Alberta champions, lost 5-2 to the Regina Vics, who went on to win the Allan Cup.

At one stage, late in the season, Bishop, Helmer and Malvish were temporarily suspended by the A.A.H.A. for playing with the Redcliffe team against Medicine Hat.

The East End Victorias, Chinooks, 103rd and Centrals were competing in the

Calgary section of the Provincial Intermediate Hockey League. Other provincial division were: south, east Wetaskwin, west Wetaskwin, Lacombe and north. The West End Cubs and Trimus clubs dropped out before the Calgary league play began. Each club had to put up a $25 bond that they would finish the season. Double header games were played at Shermans and single games at the East End Rink.

In the previous season the Mayor Sinnot Cup had been offered for local intermediate competition. Now the D.E. Black Cup was provided for the provincial intermediate competition.

The East End Vics beat the Chinooks to gain the intermediate title. Vics then defeated Banff 8-5 in a two game home and home series. In the provincial finals Vics traveled to Lacombe to take the first game 3-2. In the second game, played in Calgary, the water had to be swept off the ice before the periods began. The game ended in a 1-1 tie and the east end seven were the provincal intermediate champions. Their lineup included: Astell, Steele, Riley, Green, Graham, Melton and Ganong. In a mid season charity exhibition game the Vics had dropped a 6-1 decision to the senior Chinooks.

The Iroquois won the city junior championship with a 2-1 win over the Chinooks. Other league teams were the Olympics, Cubs and Excelsiors, with the schedule being played at the Haultain School rink. The Ogden Apprentices had not been able to ice a team. In a provincial junior hockey championship game the Iroquois team traveled to Edmonton where they lost 2-1 to the Edmonton Hustlers. In February W. Plewes was suspended from junior hockey for being over the 18 year six month age level. His age—24 years.

Juvenile league games were played at the Central School rink. League teams were the Iroquois, Tigers and Maple Leafs.

Over 200 games were played in the school hockey leagues with north, east and west sections in the three tier hockey program. The finals were played at the Sherman Auditorium before a packed house of parents and school children. Connaught lost to Central in the D class final. Sacred Heart captured the Separate C class championship while the Public title was shared by Haultain and Practise. Early Grey, the Public School B champions, defeated St. Mary's, the Separate School B titleists. In championship cadet play for the Herald Cup Haultain won over the St. Mary's team.

The University and Mount Royal hockey teams split several games before Mount Royal won the play-off game 13-4 to take the intercollegiate championship. Mount Royal's lineup included: Nixon, Smith, McKernan, O. McHugh, H. McHugh, Palmer and Miller. The Universities' team was Lougheed, McWilliams, C. Mills, T. McCaffrey, Black, Porter, and English. The Winnipeg University had planned to come to Calgary to play against the Calgary University, but reports of warm weather and poor ice halted this. In the Church Hockey League the teams of Wesley, Grace, First Baptist, Knox, and Central Churches played their games at the various school rinks.

Cockshott, the Implement League champions, traveled to Gleichen to lose 7-5. Other implement teams were: John Deere, Ontario Wind and Pump, Runley, and Fairbanks.

The Mercantile League, consisting of Ashdowns, H.B.C., Acme Fruit, Woods-Vallance-Adams, Customs House, and the Department of Natural Resources, played their games at Shermans between 10 and 11 o'clock in the evening. The Department of Natural Resources team captured the league championship and the D.C. Coleman Trophy. During the season the Canmore team, as well as fans, came down to Calgary, with the mountain town defeating D.N.R. 12-5 in an exhibition game.

Ladies hockey drew a great deal of participation and interest in Calgary during 1913-14. The Calgary Crescents ladies hockey team played to a one-all draw with the Okotoks ladies in a game played at that town. The Red Deer ladies team defeated the Crescents 1-0 in a game played before 800 spectators at the Sherman rink. On other occasion they traveled to Medicine Hat to play the ladies team of that city. Included in the Calgary lineup was: Miss MacDonald in goal, Misses McKinnon, Mayott, M. Steele, R. Steele, I. McDonald, and La Marotte.

In February the first mid-winter excursion saw 210 hockey players, fans and families journey by a special train to Canmore and Banff. The Canmore ladies' and Crescents ladies' teams tied one-all, the Vics battled with the Centrals, and in the final game of the evening Canmore dumped the D.N.R. team 9-4. Following the games the group travelled to Banff and their hotel accommodation.

Members of the Ranchmen's Club travelled out to the Calgary Golf and Country Club where they lost a game of hockey 4-0 to the golfing fraternity. The golf club had a rink, but this particular game was played on the Elbow River. Some of the season's games which received the greatest amount of printer's ink involved the boys from the News-Telegram and the Herald. A Western Canada College team played in Taber. The Banff team, who had held the Edmonton Dominions to a 6-4 score, beat the Vics 3-2 and the Calgary University 13-3.

In March plans were announced to add an athletic club to the Sherman Auditorium. This would add proper dresing rooms and showers to the skating complex. Lloyd Turner announced that the Auditorium would have artificial ice by the fall of 1914.

Robert Pearson was again the president of the A.A.H.A. which held its annual meeting in Edmonton in early November. D.E. Black of Calgary received the recognition of being the Association's honorary president. Representatives decided that, in view of world conditions and their effect on Alberta, there would not be any inter-city hockey league, just a final play-off game. It was also decided that officials would attempt to eliminate boarding because of the danger of injury to the players.

During the fall and winter many clubs held farewell dinners or smokers for club members who had joined the forces and were on their way overseas. As their rosters were deleted clubs would combine with another team who found themselves similarly short of playing personnel so that those remaining at home could still play hockey. All Calgary leagues from the previous season were again in operation, but generally with a reduction in the number of teams participating. A. McKinley was to act as the convener for Calgary intermediate and senior hockey.

On December 4th the Candian Amateur Hockey Association was successfully organized at a meeting held in Ottawa. J. Ward was the A.A.H.A. representative at the gathering.

Lloyd Turner gave each of the three city senior clubs, Chinooks, Vics and Monarchs, one of the new dressing rooms at the Sherman Auditorium. Teams were practising on the Sherman annex rink in November. The Sherman Auditorium ice was ready by December 7th, the earliest opening in years. The ice surface was 20 feet longer as the result of the removal of the bleachers from one end of the building. On the opening night of public skating the 103rd Regiment band was in attendance, and each lady received a carnation.

The only city operated rink was located at Mewata. The city would only flood school rinks upon receipt of $20 a rink. During the winter two aspiring parks employees prepared a 200 yard section of the Elbow River in Elbow Park, however their monetary return did not merit the work that they had put into the project. An ice track was constructed at Victoria Park for horse races held five days in late January. The Elbow was put to good use near Victoria Park where curling sheets were laid out on the ice.

Frank McCarthy, who had played his hockey in Calgary during the past two seasons, was now playing with the Montreal Wanderers. He had been the first player to sign a N.H.A. contract.

At noon, on February 20, 1915, Lloyd Turner and his wife were just sitting down to breakfast in their apartment in the Sherman Auditorium complex. They smelled smoke, and when Lloyd opened the connecting door to the rink he was met with a wall of flame. Rigs from the Central Firehall were at the scene within minutes of the 12:03 alarm, and soon there were eight streams of water directed on the flaming structure. One of the walls collapsed crushing the roof next door. By one o'clock all that remained of the big Sherman rink was a blazing heap of charred timbers, red hot galvanized iron and shattered concrete blocks. The loss to the fire was estimated at $50,000. However not everything can be valued in terms of money. Calgary was to have hosted Allan Cup games the following week, and now this could not take place. Calgary's hockey program for the next three years was to suffer.

The Sherman rink had been built in 1904, and a cement addition was added in 1907. The building had housed roller skating, track, wrestling, entertainers such as Madame Melba, politicians, church services, and movies, as well as hockey.

Lawn hockey became part of the Calgary sports scene in 1915, with the Calgary Lawn Hockey Club A and B teams playing games at Victoria Park and the West Mewata field. Freddie Lowes was the club president, while F. Butler was team captain.

In the fall of 1915 the Sherman annex rink became known as the Mercantile rink, and it was here that Calgary's senior hockey was played. The Garrison team, made up of soldiers stationed in Calgary, played in the senior competition. The Crystal Rink, located at 701-8th Street S.W., opened in 1915, as did the roller rink at 209-9th Avenue East.

At the tenth annual meeting of the A.A.H.A., held in November of 1916, intermediate and senior hockey in the province was not sanctioned as, "it was not believed to be in keeping with the times".

Captain Bob Pearson, former A.A.H.A. president was wounded at the Somme, and Captain E. Pinkham, one of Calgary's top hockey and rugby players, was killed in action.

Junior and juvenile hockey was played at Andy Baxter's Crystal Rink. The Academy Skating Rink, located at 12th Avenue and 12th Street S.W., was in the home of the Calgary Art Skating Club, whose aim was to promote figure skating in Calgary. The 211 Regiment Band played at the Central Rink, located on 8th Avenue and 3rd Street S.W. During the following season, 1917-18, the City Hockey League played their games at the Crystal Rink.

Following the termination of hostilities in November 1918 the Horse Show Building was turned back to the Exhibition board by the army. This building had been constructed in 1908 for the Dominion Exhibition. The board announced that the building would be turned into a skating rink with an ice surface 100 by 220 feet. Lloyd Turner was hired as its manager, and he promised to have ice ready for skating by December 20. On New Year's Eve more than 1,200 skaters crowded the ice as their way of bringing in the New Year. The band was not to begin playing until 9 p.m., but by eight there were at least 500 skaters on the ice. At midnight the sounds of twelve buglers brought in the New Year. Calgary hockey crowds were to reach record size in the new rink which served in this capacity until 1949 when the Corral came into operation.

Baseball

Baseball probably had its roots in the ancient English game of stoolball. Later, as the rules changed, the activity went under various names, including: feeder, rounders, peckers and baseball.

In 1839 Abner Doubleday of Cooperstown, New York helped to organize the game in that community. Six years later Doubleday and Alexander Cartwright drew up a crude set of rules for the game, then in 1853 the National Association of Baseball Players adopted a uniform set of rules. There were eleven men on a team, but gloves were not used during this period of baseball history. The pitcher delivered the ball underhand and a batter could wait until he was given the pitch he liked before swinging.

By the 1860's the game was widely played in southern Ontario. The Hamilton Maple Leafs and the Tecumsehs of London were equal in skills to the American clubs.

The game was played in Winnipeg by 1874. Baseball's popularity was spread across the prairies by the Americans working on the railroad.

A game of baseball was organized and played following a cricket contest on May 24, 1875 at Fort Macleod. Richard Nevitt wrote in a letter, "A baseball match was then inaugurated and I was solicited to play. We played against nine "citizens" and beat them badly. At first I was skeptical about nine citizens being around the place but they appeared and were beaten."

A baseball game was reported being played at Fort Macleod in the spring of 1883, with the losing team buying supper for the winners. A baseball team was organized in Edmonton in 1884, and this organization stayed together for several years.

Organized baseball was played in Calgary as early as 1884. In July of that year the Police team defeated the citizens by a score of 31 to 28. Cappy Smart played right field for the town in some of the games, while at other times he served in the capacity of umpire. Pick-up baseball games were played in the town during this early period, however the sport did not play the role that cricket did in the recreation of the local population.

Frank Paupst served as captain of the town team in 1886. In April of 1887 a baseball team was organized at a meeting of interested individuals in the Gerald House. G. Tozen, the proprietor of the Gerald House, was voted team captain, and the "Pilots" was the name given to the team. Practises were held on a borrowed field located south of the tracks.

The following year the baseball club had enough players to form a second 9 who were named the "Colts". In competition for the Ogburn Cup the first nine defeated the second nine by a score of 20-9 in the first game, but the Colts came back to win the next two games and the cup. 200 fans viewed the final game. A Calgary team journeyed to Banff to defeat the hometown team by a score of 25-6 in a seven inning game. The Calgary team was all set to compete in the $300 prize money tournament in Kamloops, but plans fell through in the last minute. A late August tournament was held in Calgary. In the first game Donald beat Calgary by a 12-4 score, then Medicine Hat defeated Donald 21-20 for the championship.

Competition, in 1888, took place between the first and second nines. In late September both clubs took the train to Medicine Hat to play in a tournament.

The 1889 baseball organizational meeting was held in the Palace Hotel. The first nine was composed of Smith, Perry, Watson, Pigeon, McBride, Young, Barlow, Upper and Jordan, while Kerr, Peers, Cowan, Kinnisten, Halliday, Glanville, Davidson, Smart, Pritchard and Clark formed the second nine. 1889 saw a rule change for baseball with a walk being issued for four balls instead of five. The batter was now not declared out for a foul tip. The baseball club played games with the Police and the cricket club, as well as cricket games against the latter club.

The Bowen Tankard was offered for baseball competition in Calgary in 1890. The City and Fire Brigade teams were to play fifteen games with the trophy going to the team winning the most games, however the full fifteen games were never completed. In the following year the same two teams attempted to play a twelve game series for the Jacques Water pitcher, but this series was not completed either.

The Edmonton baseball team travelled to Calgary to play several games with the local club at the Athletic Grounds south of the tracks. Admission to these 1891 contests was 25¢. Saturday afternoon rivalry continued between the City and Brigade teams. The following year Calgary and Edmonton played home and home games at each city's Exhibition. Edmonton won at home by a score of 20 to 17, but Calgary won by seven runs in Calgary to earn the McBride Cup. Those persons making the trip with the teams were given a return railroad ticket for the price of a single fare.

In 1893 the town team defeated the Fire Brigade in a series of games played at the Athletic grounds to capture the Jacques Trophy. Cappy Smart became the manager of the baseball team in 1894. In the following year new competition for the Calgary team was supplied by Canmore, which proved to have a very strong team. Ladies were admitted free to one game at the Athletic grounds where Canmore routed Calgary 15-1.

An Arbor Day game in 1896 saw a new Calgary team, the Innkeepers, play the Calgary nine. In a game played on the Queen's birthday and billed as, "The Championship of the Territories", Canmore defeated Calgary by a score of 15 to 3. Calgary's second nine went down to defeat by the Glenmore farmers.

For the next several years senior baseball was rather lacking in Calgary. However there were many boys and girls playing pick-up games of scrub on the prairie fields. The harness makers were generally the winners in games with the clerks, printers, West enders, and Fire Brigade teams. By 1899 the C.P.R. fielded a team but they proved to be little opposition for the Fire Brigade who beat them by a score of 20-1.

Inter-city baseball returned to the scene in 1900 with a Calgary team defeating Medicine Hat by a score of 26-16 on the Queen's birthday. The following year the Calgary Rangers were organized under President A.E. Cross. The club's colours were red and black. A practise field was leveled on the land behind city hall. Tables were turned as Medicine Hat defeated Calgary in the Victoria Day game. By 1902 baseball in the Territories was gaining momentum. The Calgary nine defeated both the visiting Fort MacLeod and Cranbrook teams. Baseball was the biggest attraction of the fall exhibition. Strathcona, the best team in the north country, beat Calgary 2-0 for the championship.

By 1903 the C.P.R. Bankers, Fire Brigade and the City composed the City League. Calgary beat Fernie, Golden and Red Deer, the latter both at home and in Red Deer. The Bankers Triples team beat the Bankers Dual team in several games played at Victoria Park. The Calgary Brewery Challenge Trophy was put up for competition in 1904 by Mr. A.E. Cross. The Calgary Tigers defeated Nanton, Wetaskwin, High River, Strathcona, Banff, Fernie, Okotoks and the All Comers, as well as splitting games with Red Deer. In late summer the Calgary team went on tour in Saskatchewan and Manitoba and in the first game defeated the Regina team by a score of 12-2. Within the city the All Comers, Wholesalers, Stars and Midnapore provided an opportunity for enthusiastic ball players. Many of the games were played on the new Mission diamond. Calgary's junior team, the Colts, defeated the Medicine Hat Juniors 10 runs to 5. Pick-up games were played between the married and single men. A segment of Calgary's population voiced their complaints to the authorities about the games which were played on Sundays.

In 1905 a Calgary league included the Fire Brigade, Wholesalers, Y.M.C.A., Hotels, Stars, and Victorias ball clubs. Calgary defeated the visiting Wetaskwin team during the Queen's Birthday sports program. Later, in another tournament Calgary again beat Wetaskwin but lost in the final and the $300 prize to Fernie 9-8. There was a cry of "fake" and the tournament, which also included teams from Raymond and Innisfail, was declared to be a scandal. Later in the season Banff defeated Wetaskwin to take home the Brewery Cup and be declared Champions of the West. Other games in the city saw the Victorias playing the Priddis Ranchers and the Calgary Juniors competing with both the Fort MacLeod and Nanton teams.

The baseball season in 1906 opened on January 29 with the Calgary team dropping a 13-1 decision to the hometown Lethbridge. Petrie scored Calgary's only run. The day was as warm as summer and many of the spectators sat in shirt sleeves. A few days later the Lethbridge team visited Calgary to score a 9 to 2 win in 50 degree weather. Not everyone was happy with the mild weather as it ruined the curling ice.

With the advent of spring baseball in Calgary took on a great importance. In an early season encounter Calgary's professional team trounced the amateur Victoria's by a score of 10 to 1. The pros also beat Wetaskwin in two games, Edmonton, Frank, and Didsbury. However on a northern trip Calgary was twice defeated by Wetaskwin. The Edmonton Capitals visited Calgary with the game being played on the diamond located on the Western Canada College grounds. The amateur Victorias played games against High River, Okotoks, Canmore, Didsbury, Banff, Calgary Pros and Calgary Eagles. On a diamond near the C.P.R. roundhouse the boiler makers and the machinists held weekly games. The C.P.R. diamond was also the site of the juvenile ball games. Other spring games saw the Hotels pitted against the Athletics, Millarville versus Fish Creek, and the Americans against the Canadians.

The Juvenile Shamrocks defeated the West End ball team in the first game played at the new West End Park, which was located near the Bow and was surrounded by lots of trees. A short time later it was renamed Mewata; the name which translated from Cree means "be joyous". In the summer the Winnipeg Maroons visited Calgary, however they were able to win only one of three games played against the local pros. Another touring team, from Anacortes, also went down to defeat. Alberta competition proved much stiffer as Calgary lost to Banff 16-15 in Masonic cup competition at the mountain town. During the summer a Calgary junior baseball club was formed. Late in the summer it was decided to send the Calgary baseball team to the East to advertise for settlers.

In early spring of 1907 Calgary's pro backers sent a man and considerable funds to the Boston, Massachusetts area to recruit a team. The team that started from Boston never reached Calgary. The future Bronks were defeated so often by semi-pro clubs that a new manager and club were recruited. The team, known as the Bronks, were part of the Western Canada Baseball League, which also included Edmonton, Medicine Hat and Lethbridge. Medicine Hat finished on top and Calgary finished last in the league but drew 21,021 adults and 257 children to its home games. The W.C.B.L. was unofficially called the Twilight League. The Victorias, Calgary's best amateur team played games with the smaller centres in southern Alberta. The Calgary Juniors played against the White Sox at the Y.M.C.A. diamond on Ninth Avenue. Newsboys from the different Calgary newspapers pitted their baseball skills against each other.

In a New Year's Day baseball game, played on the first day of 1908, the American Irrigated Excessive Adipose Tissue Baseball 9 were defeated 4-2 by the Canadians. The over 1,000 fans were dressed in everything from shirt sleeves to fur coats. Early in the spring the baseball crowd was pressing to have a proper diamond laid out in Victoria Park. Across the Elbow, a baseball field was constructed in the Mission district. During the summer the Calgary team lost to Edmonton 35-15, a pitcher's nightmare, and were defeated by the touring Winnipeg Shamrocks 8-4. New teams in the city included St. Mary's Airdrie, Wholesalers, and Young Liberals. In the Brewery Cup final, played at the Mission diamond the Young Liberals won over the Victorias by a 7-4 score. Other Labor Day activities at the diamond included competition in fungo hitting, accurate throw, bunt and run to first, long distance throwing, circling bases and baseball players 100 yard dash.

Fastball was played in Calgary in 1908. In order to accommodate the smaller school boys Captain Ferguson shortened the base distance to 60 feet and gave the boys smaller bats and a larger ball to play with.

The 1909 Western Canada Baseball League included professional teams from Winnipeg, Brandon, Regina, Moose Jaw, Medicine Hat, Lethbridge, Edmonton and the Calgary Bronks. The season extended from May 12 through September 2 with games being played at the Victoria Park diamond. The Bronco's imported roster included: Duggan—S.S., Carney—2nd B., Clynes—L.F., Smith-or Kellackey—3rd B., Tallant—C.F., Flanagan—R.F., Stanley—C., Gecham and Stanridge—pitchers. In early season exhibition games Calgary's imported pros scored a narrow 5-4 victory over the amateur Colts, but defeated the Y.M.C.A. team by a 13-3 score. However in league play Calgary finished several rungs below Medicine Hat, the pennant winners. A summer exhibition game saw the Druggist's team defeat the Doctors. The Public School Baseball league included teams from South Ward, Central, Victoria, Practise, and Alexandra Schools.

The Calgary Bronks were more successful during the 1910 W.C.B.L. winning both the first and second schedules. League plans were for the two winners to engage in a post-season play off, but with Calgary a double winner this situation did not arise. Included in the 51 games that the Broncos played was a 27-3 win over the Regina Bonepilers, with a record 14 runs in the eighth inning. Attendance averages worked out to 805 paid admissions a game.

The Calgary Junior Baseball league included the Swastikas, Beavers, Y.M.C.A., and Athletics, while the Y.M.C.A., West End Cubs and C.P.R. made up the Intermediate league. Teams in the Mercantile league played their games at Mewata Park. South of Calgary Granum, Claresholm, Stavely and Fort Macleod played in the Alberta Baseball league. In Brewery Cup competition the Victorias were successful over the Red Deer team. At the same Labor Day competition there were contests in individual baseball skills. In the provincial finals for the Brewery Cup the team from Alix took the honors. In November there was indoor baseball at Sherman's Rink with Chandler's Y.M.C.A., Chan's Colts, Giants, and "Moose" Baxter's team participating. Towards the end of the year there was considerable talk in the city about a proposed new league which would include teams from Alberta, Montana, Idaho and Utah.

The 1911 Western Canada Baseball League included Calgary, Moose Jaw, Edmonton, Winnipeg, Saskatoon and Brandon. Calgary finished second to Brandon, winning 62 games and losing 38. O'Brien of Calgary was the league's top hitter, with 100 hits in 255 times at bat for a .392 average. During the season there was discussion among league officials as to whether raising the admission price from 25¢ to 50¢ would be a paying proposition.

The City Hall Municipals, Grain Exchange, C.P.R. and West End Clubs played in the City Baseball league. The Y.M.C.A., Swastikas and Athletics were intermediate teams. Other city teams included Boilermakers, Laborers, Canadian Fairbanks and Customs. East of the city Gleichen, Strathmore, Bassano and Brooks made up the Bow Valley League. Olds, Bowden, Didsbury and Crossfield made up the Rosebud League. There were now three playing fields at Mewata Park. It was hoped that a new ball park seating 6,000 could be built in Victoria Park for the 1912 season. The Athletics and Boys Club held indoor baseball games in October.

Early in 1912 Sam Savage was busy signing ball players for the Bronks, however problems resulted in the passing of the W.C.B.L. Plans were made for an Alberta league with teams from Edmonton, Bassano, Lethbridge and Calgary, but instead of Lethbridge it was Red Deer in the picture. The proposed new diamond could be used for three years. The Bronks and Red Deer opened the secured. New bleachers and showers were installed; Mr. Riley suggested the diamond cold be used for three years. The Bronks and Red Deer opened the season before a good crowd, however trials and tribulations lead to Red Deer and Bassano's decision to quit the league. But the breaches were healed, the league played, and Calgary defeated Red Deer four games to one in the finals. During the schedule Calgary played 45 games, winning 34 and losing 11. Calgary's roster included Roche—catcher, Strieb—F.B., Vavian—2nd B., O'Brien—3rd B., Wells—S.S., Flanigan—R.F., Piper—C.F., Myers—L.F., Barenkamp and Barnstead—pitchers.

The City Intermediate League was composed of the Cashmans, Cubs, Burns, Swastikas and Y.M.C.A. clubs. They played their games on a field in Grandview. The Iroquois, Haultain and Y.M.C.A. Junior teams played at Mewata. Teams from Central Methodist, Grace, the Baptist and Wesley churches composed the Bible Class Baseball League, while eight teams played in the Electrical League. There was also a Bankers League and a Printers League. Twenty baseball teams composed the School League which was divided into four classes depending upon the weight of the boys. Both Irricana and Bieseker had good teams, and in the southern part of the province the towns of Magrath, Warner, Raymond and Cardston had clubs in the Southern Alberta Baseball League.

Before the 1913 season rolled around a new diamond was laid out inside the track and close to the big grandstand in Victoria Park. Previously there had been a smaller grandstand beside the diamond in the infield. Calgary, Medicine Hat, Moose Jaw, Regina and Saskatoon made up the revitalized Western Canada Baseball League. Seat prices were now 25¢ and 50¢. Hollis was the new Calgary short stop, Myers now in left field, and Frink and Wainwright added to the pitching staff. "Cappy" Smart was behind the plate to catch the first pitch which officialy opened Calgary's baseball season. The Broncos were in second place in the league at the mid-point of the season but faded in the stretch to finish fifth with a win-loss record of 22-36. Roche was Calgary's top batter with a .317 average while Piper batted .312. Frink was Calgary's best hurler. The season was not a financial success for Sam Savage, Calgary's perennial baseball backer, who at one point in the summer threatened to pack it up unless the fan support improved.

The Municipal team won the Electrical ball league, which also included North Electric, Canadian General—Cunningham, and Alberta Government Telephones. The Cubs, Moose, Y.M.C.A., Iroquois, Natural Gas, Calgary Furniture, and C.P.R. of the Intermediate League played their games at Mewata and Victoria Park. The six teams of the Church League played their games at Victoria Park. The J.T. McDonald Trophy, emblematic of the Junior Baseball League championship, was won by the Pirates. The four division 30 team Public School League played 120 games. The Herald Sellers played a series of games against the Old Time Kellities. The Central South Alberta League included teams from

Okotoks, High River and Cayley. A freak accident occurred when a pitcher of the Athletic team broke his arm; the accident occurred with a snap when he pitched a fast one.

In the fall of 1913 club owners of the Western Canada Baseball League drew up an agreement with each team posting $1,000 which was to be forfeited if they did not stick in the league for five years, win or lose. James Fleming of Medicine Hat was appointed as the league president at a salary of $1,500 a year. The league set a team salary limit of $1,800 per month.

In the spring of 1914 the Calgary Bronks opened training camp in California. In their first exhibition game they dropped Alameda High School 17-2, however at Salt Lake they lost two games to the Murray team. On the day of the first home game the Calgary stores closed at 4 p.m. so that everyone would have the opportunity to take part in or view the big pre-game parade. Calgary's game line-up was: Piper—C.F., Reynolds—L.F., Croll—S.S., Thompson—R.F., Ryan—C., Devereaux—3 B., Strieb—1 B., Vivian—2 B., Kesselring, Frink and Gage on the pitching staff. Admission to the game was 25¢ but reserved seats were 25¢ extra. The spectators at Savage Field in Victoria Park were eligible for many gate prizes, and Calgary's 7-2 win over Moose Jaw sent the crowd home happy.

Unfortunately the Bronks cold not maintain this winning streak. When the season ended in September Calgary was at the bottom of the Western Canada Baseball League. Out of the 118 games played they only won 37 and lost 81. Saskatoon won the championship. A long associationship was brought to an end as Sam Savage sold the team to a syndicate. However before the next season was to roll around many of the players would be involved in the war effort.

There were many other baseball teams in Calgary in 1914, with games being played on the north and northwest fields at Mewata, Hillhurst Park, and school grounds as well as at Victoria Park. Forty teams played a total of 150 games in the school baseball leagues. Riverside School won the A Division championship, the B going to Normal Practise, and Connaught teams capturing the C and D championships.

The Intermediate League was composed of the North Star, Grain Exchange, Athletics, Iroquois, Y.M.C.A., C.P.R. and Cub teams with the Cubs capturing the championship. Robin Hood had entered a team, but it never got off the ground. The Calgary Senior Amateur Baseball League was composed of the Vics, Y.M.C.A., Athletics, K.C.'s, and Hillhurst Hustlers. Athletics won over the K.C.'s for the league championship. Later the senior Athletics beat the intermediate champions Cubs in two games for the city championship. The Athletics then played the Edmonton City Dairy for the provincial championship. Each team won a game, then the deciding tilt was rained out.

A team, picked from the senior league, defeated the Commercial League pics 2-0. The Western Woodworkers won the Mercantile League, and Trochu defeated Mirror to take home the Brewery Trophy. In July the All-American Girls Baseball team arrived in the city to challenge men's teams, and they were well able to win their share of games. Local baseball came to a close in November when games were played in an athletic carnival held at Victoria Park to raise money for the Patriotic Fund.

Calgarians were very interested in major league baseball even though the war was foremost in the minds of most of the people. The Herald placed a large model of a baseball diamond on its outside wall so that everyone could follow the inning by inning play of the World Series games.

Football, Soccer and Rugby

The games of football have been played for at least as far back as the times of the great Greek and Roman civilizations. Football, otherwise known as soccer, has been a part of the British way of life since at least the Fourteenth Century, although under the rule of some kings it was forbidden. Rugby was developed spontaneously at Rugby School in 1823 when William Ellis caught a kicked ball and ran for the opposition's goal. With the development or rubber vulcanization the animal bladders were replaced by rubber bladders encased in leather. By the 1850's both soccer and rugby teams were being formed. In 1863 the London Football Association was formed, and the game its members played was called association football, later soccer. In 1871 representatives from 20 teams met in London to draw up a code of rules and form the Rugby Union.

Football was prohibited under the Lord's Day Act in the early days of Upper Canada. Organization of soccer in Canada began in 1876 when representatives of various clubs met in Toronto and adopted Association rules. Matches for the Caledonian Cup were first played in 1886.

In the Canadian west there was a report of soccer being played in Edmonton in 1862. Games were played during the winter as well as during the warmer months.

Association football matches were played in Winnipeg as early as 1876, and English rugby was played in Manitoba in the fall of 1880. Interschool matches in soccer were reported to have been played in Manitoba in 1883.

With the nature of most young men to kick and throw a ball it is likely that pickup games were played by the men stationed at Fort Calgary. In the summer of 1883 the Calgary based Mounted Police issued a challenge to any other 15 men to a game of football—rugby rules. The following November the Police, under Corporal James, played the civilians a football game using Association rules. Neither side was able to score. The Police played pickup games against the townsmen in both Association football and rugby in 1884 and 1885. Generally these games were payed at the barracks field.

Occasionally games of soccer were played on roller skates at the Calgary roller rink.

In July of 1888 a meeting was held in the office of the Calgary Lumber company by those Calgarians who were interested in football. A new football club was formed and J. Shirley was elected club president. The following year the town team defeated the Police team by a 9-7 score in a game of rugby football, following Canadian—not British—rules. The Calgary team, at home, defeated an Edmonton team 5-1, but Calgary lost 5-0 at Edmonton. Association football play saw a Calgary team lose to Lethbridge in the southern town. In Calgary there were local games between the Police, Fire Brigade and town teams, with the Police club generally coming out on top.

During 1889 a country team, with many of the players coming from Millarville, played several games against the Calgary Police team. A three day tournament was held on the E Division pitch, with the country, Edmonton and the Regina Depot teams joining Calgary in the competition. Dr. Sanson handled the refereeing, and the Depot team came out on top in the tournament.

In 1890 the Police, Fire Brigade and town team again competed in Association football, and the Rugby Club and the Police met in a game of rugby. A Calgary football team journeyed to Lethbridge, but it lost to the home team.

E. Cave was president and J. Smart was vice-president of the Calgary Association Football Club in 1891. During that and the following year both football and rugby were played at both the Barracks and the C.A.A.A. grounds, which was located south of the railroad tracks. The Calgary Police had plans to send an English rugby team to a tournament in Regina, but this did not come about.

The Manitoba and North-West Territories Rugby Union was formed in 1891, and the Hamilton Cup was offered for competition within this organization. William Toole, later to become a resident and sportsman in Calgary, was a member of the Winnipeg club who were the first recipients of this trophy.

In October of 1892 a Calgary rugby football team composed of: Tom Lafferty, W. Boone, Randell, J. Wilson, Houghton, N. Wallinger, W. Aldwell, Sewell, Lord Douglass, who was the son of the Marquis of Queensbury, and A. Wooleydod lost to an Edmonton team. Calgary was a man short, so an Edmonton player was added to its lineup. This game was played at the C.A.A.A. grounds.

A return match was played in Edmonton on the old Hudson Bay section. the Calgary team picked up some Innisfail players on the trip north, while many on the Edmonton team were actually from Fort Saskatchewan.

The Calgary Football club was organized in 1893. It had hoped to play a game against Lethbridge. There were numerous pick-up games played at the Barracks field. In 1894 it was reported that there were four rugby teams in Calgary. 10¢ was the admission to games at the Athletic grounds.

A rugby football tournament was held in the city in April of 1895 between the teams of the Regina and Calgary Mounted Police. Each team won a game, and then Regina won the third and deciding game by one try to zero. Players on the Calgary Police team were: Fraser—back, Andrews, Bayer—half backs, McNair, Elkins, Oliver, Douglass—three quarter backs, Wooley-Dod, Edroup, Jenkins, Wilson, Cree, Devitt, Dewbolt, Bulloch—forwards. The N.W.M.P. band was in attendance at the games which were well attended by the local population.

In Association football, played at the C.A.A.A. grounds, the Fire Brigade, Y.M.C.A., City, Police, and Calgary Football Club teams played for the Doll Cup. Edmonton defeated the Calgary Rugby Football Club twice in a home and home series played in the fall of 1895.

D. McLean was president and J. Mitchell acted as captain for the new association football club, the Maple Leafs. G. McCarter and K. Johnston served in the same positions respectively for the City Football Club. L. Doll served in the capacity of president of the Calgary Association Football League. Lt. Cochrane donated the Cochrane Cup for local competition between the Maple Leafs, City, Fire Brigade, Mounted Police and Press teams—the Fire Brigade being the winner. Cappy Smart was one of the Brigade's top scorers Some scratch games were played at the old practise grounds near the Baptist Church. The Calgary Rugby Football Club and Police Club amalgamated under president J. Morris and captain Cpl. Morgan. The team dressed in blue jerseys with a white monogram; practises were held at the Athletic grounds. On Arbor Day the city Rugby Football Club beat the Country team 3-0 and later defeated the same team by a 2-0 score.

The Stonies and Blackfeet played a soccer football match at Calgary's Caledonian games. The Fire Brigade beat the Industrial School 2-0 in a game of soccer played at the Athletic grounds on Dominion Day,

In 1897 the Calgary City Association Football Club was reorganized under new club president, Chief of Police English. K.D. Kid was chosen team captain. The Fire Brigade soccer club played games at Innisfail and High River where they defeated the Industrial School 4-0. A Dominion Day game saw Red Deer Lake and Fish Creek play to a tie. Later the Red Deer lake team defeated the Industrial School 3-1.

An Easter Monday, 1898 game saw the Calgary Football Club play against Millarville. A May 24 tournament brought together teams from Golden, Calgary and the two Indian Schools. The day's activities began with a grand parade to the Athletic grounds. Dunbow defeated the Calgary Industrial School and Golden beat Calgary 2-0. In the final game Golden shut out the High River Indian boys 1-0. The Orangemen held a football game at their July celebration. The Mounted Police played the Indian Schools, tying one and winning the other. An Association Football tournament was held in Calgary in August with the Fire Brigade, Mounted police and two Indian Schools competing—the Police won the tournament. The local press of the day reported, "The Indian boys should remember that it is not allowable to collar the goal keeper and throw him through the goal if he has the ball in his hands."

A.E. Cross and R.B. Bennett were the patrons of the reorganized Calgary Association Football Club in 1899. The club, under president J.B. Smith, held practises on the field to the west of G. Lesson's. Their outfits consisted of blue jerseys and white pants. The Fire Brigade Club was reorganized under the leadership of J. Smart. The C.P.R. team defeated the Police, the district's best team the previous year, by a 3-0 score at the Barracks field. There were many pick-up games between the employees or members of different companies and organizations.

In 1900 the Press and Y.M.C.A. teams provided additional top calibre competition to the Calgary soccer scene. The Press beat the City team but lost to the Fire Brigade in a very rough game. The Y.M.C.A. were defeated 6-1 by the City team in its initial outing but improved as the season wore on. The Fire Brigade lost 4-1 to the Dunbow Indian boys.

The Calgary Association Football League began play in April of 1901 with the Y.M.C.A., N.W.M.P., C.P.R., Bow River, Indian School, City and Fire Brigade teams in the competition. Smart, Rev. Hogbin and Brankley were the referees. Most games were played at the Agriculture grounds at 7 p.m. or on weekends; cost of admission to a game was 10¢. Dr. Ings was president and R. Ferguson was captain of the City team. J. Wilson was the president of the Fire Brigade Club, while Smart served as captain-manager and G. Henderson as the team's field captain. In the league semi-final the Police defeated the City team 2-1, and in the finals the Police won the Merchants Trophy with a 3-1 win over the Indian boys. Other teams in the city included Great West Saddlery and the Eau Claire; the latter team had their own field at the mill. The junior Work and Win club lost to the junior Victorias in a game played on the field behind the old court house. In further play the Police beat the Indian School in seven matches by 12 goals to 2. The Police also beat the City 14 goals to 3 in six matches. Calgary beat Lacombe 1-0. At a game played at the Calgary Exhibition the Calgary Industrial School defeated the Red Deer Lake team. The hayseeds and the cowpunchers played a game of football at Bennett's Bush. In October the High School team defeated the Junior Fourth team 2-0 in a game played on a vacant lot on Stephen Avenue. During the season a Calgary junior football team journeyed to Edmonton for a match.

In May there was a meeting of all the rugby players in the office of Dr. Sullivan where the Calgary Rugby Club was formed. N.D. Jackson presented the resolution, ". . . That a club be formed to be called the Calgary Rugby Football Club and that games be played under Rugby Union rules." Colonel Herchmer became the honorary president and Dr. Sullivan was elected president. Club membership fee was a dollar a person. The club's colors were a blue jersey and maroon stockings. Colonel Herchmer offered ten dollars towards a cup for competition. Rugby matches were played at the newly named Victoria Park. One game saw the

Football game at Hillhurst Park. The Calgary Tigers—1909 era.

Irish-Canadians playing everyone else. In another game Great Britian played Greater Britain.

The Fire Brigade decided not to field a team in 1902, so some of their players threw their lot in with the N.W.M.P. team, which was under the direction of Corporal Brankley. The West End United and the Brewery were new teams on the Calgary scene. The Territorial Football League included the N.W.M.P., C.P.R., Y.M.C.A., and Indian School teams. The Police took the league trophy with two wins and a loss, followed by the C.P.R., Y.M.C.A., and Indian teams. In a Coronation Day football tournament the Brewery beat the C.P.R. team and Didsbury beat the Y.M.C.A.; in the final Didsbury defeated the Brewery 5-0. On Labour Day Strathcona bested the Y.M.C.A. 2-0.

Rev. Langford was president of the 1903 Y.M.C.A. Football Club. The Pat Burns Association Football Club was organized, and in their first game they defeated the Brewery club 2-0, but lost 0-3 in a return match. In a Victoria Day tournament held in Calgary Didsbury defeated Olds 3-0. Fort Macleod lost to the Y.M.C.A. team by a 3-0 score, and the C.P.R. team won over Red Deer 2-0. The C.P.R. won the championship with a 1-0 win over Didsbury. Another tournament was held in the city in June. A Didsbury loss to the C.P.R. team was protested and accepted, and they were in the final against the Y.M.C.A team. In October the Public School team travelled to Western Canada College to earn a 0-0 tie in a well contested game. Greer captained the College squad, while Snell led the city school team.

An April 30, 1904 meeting of Calgary's football society was held in the fire hall under the chairmanship of 1903 league president Cappy Smart. Representatives of thé Excelsior, Albion, Caledonian, Industrial School, Dunbow, Maple Leaf and Brewery clubs attended the meeting.

A Victoria Day soccer tournament was held in Calgary with teams competing for the Fireman's Trophy. In play the Maple Leafs were 2-1 over the Caledonians, who in turn beat the Brewery team 3-0, and the Maple Leafs bested the Red Deer team 1-0. In the final match Caledonians upset the Maple Leafs 2-0.

The Merchants Cup was up for competition in a Dominion Day tournament at Victoria Park. The Caledonians beat the Albions 6-0, and in the final Logan led the Scotchmen to a 4-0 win over the Brewery Club.

A Calgary Club journeyed to Red Deer to lose a game, however they defeated the Red Deer Club in a home game. The Victoria Intermediates and the C.P.R. Juniors engaged in friendly soccer matches, and a football game was played at the Salvation Army picnic held at Shagnappi Point.

In Labour Day football the Caledonians and Brewery played for a $75 purse. At the Western Canada College grounds Principal Dr. MacRae played for the schools football team in a game against the Indian School.

The Caledonians, Brewery, C.P.R. and Adelaides were the senior clubs in Calgary in 1905. The Brewery Club showed its strength with an early season 4-0 win over the Caledonian Club. In the Victoria Day tournament C.P.R. shut out the brewery team 1-0, Caledonians humiliated the Adelaides 5-0, and Edmonton put the railroad boys out of the competition with a 2-1 victory. In the finals the Caledonians defeated the visitors from the north by a 3-0 score. Most of the 1905 football games were played at Victoria Park. The Caledonian team included Carr, Drysdale, Newell, Mills, Langford, Logan, McLennan, McDonald, McEwen, Towle and Logan. Brewery players were Royal, Sinclair, Wright, McKay, Morgan, Ross, Park, Andy, Williams, Walshaw and Lloyd.

About this time the People's Newspaper in London, England decided to sponsor a trophy, known as the People's Shield, to be sent to Canada with a touring club. The trophy was won in 1906 by the Toronto Thistles, although it can be said that they had no outside competition.

Local competition began early in 1906 with the Adelaides defeating Western Canada College 3-0 in a February 25th game. The college team was not without scoring punch for before the year was out they were able to beat both the High School and the Normal School teams.

Early in the spring there was a great deal of talk about forming an Alberta Football (soccer) League, however this never came about. On the Calgary soccer scene league secretary Mr. Bennett had his hands full attempting to schedule games to decide who best could represent the city in the quest for the People's Cup. In the first game on the playoff trail the Caledonians beat the Y.M.C.A. team by a 2-0 score. The Scot's lineup included: Ross, W. Strang, Smith, McEwan, A. Strang, Carr, Towill, Cruickshanks, McLean, Mills and Simpson, while the Y.M. players were Royal—borrowed from the Brewery team— Jacques, Woodman, Bright, Ellis, Page, Oxley, Gallacher, Rush, and Jacques.

A playoff games was set between the Caledonians and the Brewery team, however the Brewery boys claimed they could not play because they had arranged a game in Banff for that date. When the Caledonians discovered that no such games was played they claimed a victory by default, and the arguments raged back and forth. Finally a game was arranged for August 3 and before 600 spectators the Caledonians bested a reinforced Brewery team 2-1, with Strang supplying the scoring punch for the Scots and Stewart relying for the losers. Included in the Brewery line-up of Royal, McKechnie, Kent, McEwen, Parks, Armstrong, McCaine, T. Stewart, W. Stewart, Cox, and a Gleichen Indian— Haten, were two imports from Pincher Creek.

Next the Caledonians journeyed to Pincher Creek to defeat its team by a one to zero score in the first game of a home and home series. More than 500 people as well as the local pipers were in attendance at Victoria Park to see McLean score two goals to allow the Caledonians to earn a 2-2 tie with the Pincher team but take the series 3 goals to 2. On August 18 the Caledonians played the Minnedosa team in Manitoba winning the game 2-0 and the Western Canada Championship. There was not any score at half time, but in the second half McLean and Cruickshanks booted home goals for the winners. This was followed by a 1-0 exhibition win over the Winnipeg Celtics; the Callies share of this game's gate receipts—$17. Upon their return to Calgary the team received a large welcome and a reception held in the Eagles Hall where Caledonians captain Strang and trainer Jas. MacEwan told the crowd some of the highlights of the trip. A short time later the Caledonians defeated a local All-Star team.

Not everyone in the province was happy with the praise given to the Calendonians. A letter written to the local paper said that the Callies were not Alberta champions but only the champions of the Calgary Association, known technically as the Territorial Football League. During the season the Caledonians won 16 games, tied one, and lost one game—a 2-1 loss to the Brewery. The Scots scored 46 goals and had ten scored against them.

The Adelaides were another senior team in Calgary during 1906. The team personnel included: Ritchie, Walshaw, Oxland, Hayward, Hutchinson, Oxley, Baird, Millet, Jackson, Fairbrother, and Morice. A team from Okotoks was capable of playing Calgary's senior clubs even. Other soccer clubs on the Calgary scene were the Shackers and the Boarders. Bankhead, Banff and Exshaw had clubs, as well as Lethbridge, Pincher Creek and Taber and the Crows Nest Football League.

Over the years the football kick was a very popular event at various sports and athletic days. Competition of this nature took place in 1906 in conjunction with a five-a-side soccer tournament played at Victoria Park. It was also part of the Labor Day sports program which saw the Stonecutters and Masons play a game against the other trades.

In the fall the College Football League found teams from the High School, Western Canada College and the Normal School engaged in a series of games. The November 17 final game between the College and the Normal School was not played due to poor grounds, and the Normal School claimed victory by default. Other fall games saw a Bankers team defeat the College two to one and draw at Crossfield.

There were pick-up rugby games and one spirited game saw the Bankers play against a picked Calgary team. The Young Mens Club formed a rugby team which held weekly practises.

In February of 1907 Captain Smart announced the formation of the Calgary Fire Brigade Association Football Team. Over the winter it was evident in the city that not all the players of the Brewery and Caledonian teams were happy with these two clubs and thus the formation of the new club came into being.

The exhibition season began March 30 with the Caledonians earning a 2-0 win over the City Team. City team was formerly the Adelaides, and three years previous went under the name of the Albions. Their line-up for the game was: Royale, Edward, Denham, Millet, Oxley—captain, Beacroft, Morris, Jackson, Kemp, Connor and Walshaw.

A meeting of Calgary's Central Alberta Association Football League was held with Dr. McRae in the chair and S. Jackson acting as secretary. Representatives from Hillhurst, Caledonians, City, Fire Department, Bankers and the Builders Labour Union (Labourers) teams attended the meeting. A schedule was drawn up to run from May 7-August 20 with each team to play ten games, however the Fire Department team folded before the league play began. An intermediate league included Caledonians, City, Hillhurst, Western Canada College, Young Mens Club, and Grace Church, but they too could not sustain a team. Over the season there were many arguments in this league as some teams used players from their senior team and there were no league regulations to prevent this. The Macleod Brothers Trophy was the award for the winner of this league.

The Bankers senior club played many exhibition games as well as league games. In May they lost 2-1 to Western Canada College. Included in their roster were: Daintree, Williams, Woodman, Plummer, McLeod, Harris, Grey, Walters, Mason, Johnstone, Cocklane, Drury, Walker and Bennett. Another club, the Stonecutters, played exhibition games only and had not lost a game over the last two seasons and was to go undefeated in 1907 also. Their lineup included Mills, Ross, Lang, Douglass, McLean, Cunningham, Towell, Simpson, McFarlane, Mason and Ferguson.

The name of the team sponsored by the Builders Labour Union was the Labourers. Included in their roster was Ross, Minns, Crisp, G. Brown, Rackham, C. Brown, Attwood, Alten, Little, Grant and McGinnis. The Labourers opened their own season with a 1-0 win over Western Canada College. During the remainder of the season they did not always come out on top but neither were they ever soundly thrashed.

In 1907 the new formed Hillhurst Club provided easy competition for other Calgary clubs. In their initial game the City team defeated them 5-0 on the Victoria pitch. A. Wakelyn handled the goal position, while brother G. Wakelyn played on the forward line. Other players included Orrick, Milton, Hazelwood, Page, E. Riley, Scott, White, Watson and Carslake. Hillhurst did improve and by next season provided good opposition.

Early in the year there was some talk of High River joining the Calgary soccer scene, however the High River Football League was created and included teams from Okotoks, High River, Lineham, Claresholm and the Leavings. In Calgary a Mercantile Football league was formed to provide competition for the various company and store teams not capable of playing in the Intermediate League. The Calgary Junior Football Club played scratch games against the Callies Juniors or Western Canada College.

In northern Alberta the Alberta Football Association was, "calling itself the whole thing", and as a result clubs in Calgary and southern Alberta were reluctant to associate with it. On June eight representatives of 24 southern Alberta Football clubs met in High River to form the Alberta Provincial Association Football Union. This included teams from the Calgary League, Alberta Crow's Nest Pass Football League, B.C. Crow's Nest Pass Football League, High River District League, Crossfield League, and the Banff and District League. It was hoped that the Red Deer, Edmonton and Vermillion leagues would join the new organization. Dr. Ings was chosen to head the new association.

Strang was again captain of the powerful Caledonian team. Other players were Ross, McCusker, Wells, Carr, McLean, Thompson, McEwan, Simpson, Morgan, McKechnie, McFarlane, Towoll, Stewart and Cruickshank. During the season, Petrie, a newcomer to Calgary, proved a valuable addition to the team. The Caledonians proved early in the season that they were still the pick of the local elevens, although in May they were held to a two-all draw by the Okotoks team. A tentative playoff game was in the making with the Old's team, but then they conceded the right of the Callies to travel to Winnipeg to play for the People's Shield, emblematic of soccer supremacy in Canada. Upon their arrival in Winnipeg the Caledonians trained with short fast walks. Calgary's opponents in the first game were the highly touted Toronto Thistles, however Calgary outplayed the eastern team and came out of it with a 2-0 victory on goals by Thompson and Carr. Toronto protested their loss however, criticizing the Manitoba rules that they had had to play under.

In the finals the Callies defeated the home town Brittanias 1-0 in a hard fought game. Andy McLean scored with a header on a neat corner kick from Stewart, and Calgary was the winner of the People's Shield. Upon their return to Calgary a parade, led by the Piper's Band, was held in their honour, and later they were fetted with a banquet and smoker. Requests came from both Edmonton and the west coast for the Callies to play exhibition games. However they still had their own league to contend with. Going into the final league game the Callies and City teams were even on points. In the deciding game the City was leading the Caledonians one to nothing when referee Dalgetty called the game off on account of darkness, thus necessitating a future replay. In this game, played September first, McLean and Johnston scored for the Callies whose 2-0 win allowed them to retain the city championship. The team exploits were such that even the British Press gave them write ups.

A new trophy was put up for Provincial competition. In August A. Bennett returned from England and brought back a magnificent shield, similiar to the People's Trophy. The inscription on it read, "The Bennett Trophy, Presented by Mr. And Mrs. A. Bennett of the City of Calgary, for annual competition for the amateur championship of the Province of Alberta". About this time letters were received in Calgary from the Ponoka Football Club who claimed that they were the Alberta champions, but not much local attention was paid to this claim.

The Crowsnest League was won by Coal Creek, followed by Coleman, Fernie and Michel. In the fall there were several benefit games played. In October the Stonecutters defeated Hillhurst 4-1 and completed their third season of undefeated football. An innovation in Calgary was the running of football coaches from Centre Street to Hillhurst Park at a 25¢ per person cost by the local motor bus line. In late November the Western Canada College team twice defeated the Wigwams on the soccer pitch. The soccer season was over, and a great deal of its success was due to the good refereeing of Dalgetty.

In September Calgary's rugby enthusiasts held their first practise at the Barracks. The number of players out was up over the thirty that had been out the previous year. However as the Police did not get off work until 6:30 p.m. it was decided to use either Victoria Park or the College grounds. On Saturday, October second the players were divided into two teams and a game played at the Barracks. The following week a game was played between players representing the City and the Bankers. On October 14 a meeting of the rugby players was held in the Elks Hall in the Norman Block on Eighth Avenue under the chairmanship of President Dr. Mason. Dr. Ings suggested that the club play international rules, however the group voted to use English rules. Several days later a meeting of the seven man executive was held in the office of team captain Hamber, and he and Bedington were given the task of drawing up a constitution and set of bylaws for the "Calgary Rugby Football Club." Practises were to be held tri-weekly— Tuesday, Thursday and Saturday afternoon. Because many of the players desired to play Canadian rules it was decided to have a branch of the club for this purpose.

On October 19 enough rugby players for three full teams gathered at the Barracks grounds; sides were chosen, and under the coaching of Dr. Mason a vigorous game was played. The following week Gray and Dobbie led the Canadians to a 15-0 win over the English in a rugby game. Other Canadian players were White, Sawyer, MacLeod, Whittaker, Weissman, Jephson, Harris, Bruce, Kemp, Fraser, and Dewitt. On the English side were Dumpy, Allan, Robinson, Everson, Ruckley, Alkinson, Wilson, Dawson, Evans, Kerr, Elliott, Thompson and Hurler.

A game between Calgary's team and Strathcona was planned to be played on the Western Canada College field, however this fell through. Instead a Calgary team was picked to travel to Edmonton for a November 10 game billed as the championship of Alberta. The following players made the trip: Jamieson—back; Sawyer, Dobbie, Drury, Gray—three-quarters; Wiessman, Mason—halves; Millar, Harris, Whittaker, Hazelden, Haig, Ritchie, Jephson, Kemp—forwards. Calgary got more than they could handle, ending up on the bottom of a 23-5 score. Basically the Calgarians could offer no excuse for their loss, although they were rather unhappy when the half time whistle brought a goal line running play to a halt right in the middle of the play.

Edmonton was guaranteed $100 for a return game, and Calgary set about to strengthen its team. Stewart, of soccer fame, Bruce, Daintree, Remington and former Hamilton Tiger Cat player Guay were added to the Calgary line-up. More than 800 spectators saw the game, billed as the best exhibition of English rugby ever seen in western Canada; unfortunately Calgary were outscored 10-5 by a superior Edmonton team. However this series had opened up a new era of rugby—soon to be called football in the province.

A rugby club was organized at Western Canada College and plans were made to play the city intermediate team. However the game was postponed several times either because of the weather or poor field conditions. Another club was organized by the Y.M.C.A., however only inter-squad games were held.

Football began early in 1908 with a January game between the City and the Stonecutters played at the Western Canada College grounds.

In the spring a senior league schedule was drawn up with the City, Hillhurst, Caledonian, and United teams included. An intermediate league included Hillhurst, Western Canada College, Riverside, City, United, Callies, Post Office, and the Normal School. The City Juniors, Rosebuds, Albions, College, Grace Church, Riverside and St. Mary's were junior clubs. The Great West Liquor Challenge Cup was put up for juvenile soccer for such clubs as the College, city, St. Mary's and Albion clubs. Many of the juvenile games were played at western Canada College grounds. Most mens football games were played at Mewata, Hillhurst or Victoria Parks.

There were many other mens soccer clubs in the city including the Fire Brigade, Ironsides, Bankview, Skinshifters, and Riverside. East of the city the Strathmore Football Club was organized. The Alberta Pass Football League included Hillcrest, Coleman, Blairmore, Lillie, Burmis. Several five-a-side tournaments were held during the year in Calgary. the first International game took place April 13 with the Caledonians taking a 2-0 win over the local English team. Later the English and Scottish teams tangled again at the Western Canada College grounds.

The Caledonians defeated the City team in the finals of the Sons of Scotland Cup. In what was billed as the Central Alberta League championship the Callies defeated their Edmonton counterparts 1-0. Further along the playoff trail it was Callies 6 and Stettler, the northern champs, 0 in a game played on the College grounds.

The people's Cup was to be played for in Vancouver by three coast clubs and the Calgary Caledonians. In the finals the Callies and Vancouver Thistles tied one-one, but in a second game the Calgary team defeated the coast squad 7-0 to win the coveted trophy. Following the competition the Callies had a game against a strong team from Ladysmith. More than $5,000 was won in side bets on this trip by the Caledonians and their supporters. Upon their return to Calgary they were fetted with a parade and reception. Over the 1908 season the Calgary Caledonians won 34 games, tied 4 and lost not one, scoring 76 goals with only 6 scored against them.

Calgary Caledonians—champions of Canada 1908. Back left to right: Jim McEwan (trainer), Andy MacLean, Arthur Park, Jock Ross, Dr. Ings, Sandy Strang, D. McKechnie, James Petrie (trainer). Front: J. Towell, Geordie Johnston, W.W. Stewart (captain), Tom Stewart, - Walker.

In 1908 the Calgary Rugby Club was renamed the Tigers. It had been in existence for several years, but had played under the English style, however with the creation of the Tigers came the acceptance of the Canadian style of play. The Tigers were joined in league play by the Hillhurst and Y.M.C.A. teams. In November the Y.M.C.A. and Tigers were equal in standings, however because the Tigers had beaten the Y.M. by a try and a convert it was decided that the Tigers would go to Edmonton to play their best. On November 8th, a game was played in Edmonton before 1,200 spectators. Calgary led 2-0 but lost the game 12-2; however the $100 received in gate money helped to soften the loss. In a return game Edmonton defeated the Tigers 7-1. Calgarys lineup included: Full—W. Dobbie, halves—A. Warke, W. Ross, and E. Pinkham; quarter and captain—A. Quay, Scrimage—E. Bradshaw, G. Johnston, J. Woods, right wings—P. Wood, C. Jackson, G. Patterson, left wings—O. Sawers, W. Gouge, R. Priestley, spares—Whitaker, E. Cundal. The team played a total of seven games.

The City Soccer Club held a meeting in Mr. Dickinson's office in February of 1909. Dr. Sullivan was in the chair and most of the discussion related to building a team that was capable of beating the Callies. Early in the year a new football club, the Maple Leafs, were formed, with D. Gillies as their president and H. Hazelwood appointed team captain. In the first Calgary area football game of the season, played in March, Okotoks defeated Sandstone 3-2. The annual meeting of the Central Alberta Football League was held on March 24; the treasurer reported a balance of $54.88. At that time it was reported that the Senior League would consist of the Caledonian, City, National, Y.M.C.A., and Hillhurst soccer clubs. President Dr. Ing said that Okotoks, Post Office, Hillhurst, Y.M.C.A., Caledonian, City, National, W.C.C., Maple Leafs, and Riverside would field teams in the Intermediate League. Another league meeting was held April 5 and the main topic of discussion was intermediate and senior league player eligibility. It was decided that intermediate players could participate in two senior games without losing their intermediate status.

In the Juvenile League were the Y.M.C.A., W.C.C., Hillhurst, Riverside and St. Mary's teams. Two other elevens, the East End and West End clubs, got no further than the organizational stage.

The Y.M.C.A. club began early season practises at their field on First Street East, while the City club held practises in Riverside. An organizational meeting of the Hearts, a new intermediate club, was held. Good Friday saw the Callies and the City teams meet at Mewata in Calgary's first soccer game of the season.

On April 30 representatives of various football groups met in Red Deer to discuss a provincial organization, and as a result the Alberta Football League was formed with J. Ward of Edmonton being voted the league president. As a result the Calgary senior schedule, originally planned to run from May 10 through September 3 was altered. Calgary league officials were very concerned about the state of the city's playing fields, for Mewata did not have a dressing room and the Victoria field conditions were very poor.

In late May the Callies travelled to Okotoks for a 2-0 win and then on to Lethbridge for a 1-0 victory. On May 26 the football kick was one of the popular events at the W.C.C. sports day. The National Club decided that they could not maintain a club in the Senior League; most of their better players threw their lot in with the City Club. About the same time the Hearts withdrew from the Intermediate division. An exhibition game saw the Calgary Printers take a 3-2 verdict from McLeans Rovers. Western Canada College won the Juvenile League championship with a 2-0 win over the St. Mary's team. The Crowsnest Pass Football League began play with teams from Michel, Fernie, Coal Creek,

Frank, Bellevue, Coleman, and Hosmer involved. North of the city the teams from Carstairs, Didsbury, Innisfail and Crossfield were matched against each other. Okotoks visited Calgary and with only nine men held the powerful Callies to two goals. In the Callies' next match they suffered their first loss in years as the bottom place City team upset them 3-2.

In spite of this loss the Callies did win the city championship and were ready to tackle the provincial playoff trail as well as defend the People's Trophy. In Bennett Shield competition the Callies shut out Lethbridge 5-0. Sometime later in the season they beat the Edmonton Callies 2-0 to win the Provincial Championship and the Bennett Shield. Towill and Sellars provided the goals.

However this win had been anti-climatical to the People's Trophy competition which had been held in Calgary in August. In the first game of this four team competition a crowd of more than one thousand people at Victoria Park watched Vancouver Celtics drop United Weston of Winnipeg 3-2. The following evening the Calgary Caledonians overwhelmed the Victorias of Regina by a 4-0 score. In the final game a crowd of over 1,200 were present to see the Callies and Celtics play to a scoreless draw. However the Celtics could not stay in Calgary to play off the tie, so the Caledonians retained the Peoples Trophy—emblematic of the championship of Canada. The Callies line-up included: Captain J. Petrie, Stirrett, Veitch, J. Ross, J. Haig, W. Strang, Sellars, G. Johnston, W. Stewart, D. McKechnie, Towill, T. Stewart, and A. Strang.

The Callies also won the intermediate championship of Calgary. During the fall there were several exhibition soccer games in the city. The Junior Maple Leafs of the Normal Practise School beat the West Calgary Whirlwinds— formerly Sprucevale School by a 4-0 score, and the Bankers defeated the Normal School 3-0. On Christmas Day the unbeaten team, the Stonecutters, were beaten 5-0 by a picked team consisting mainly of Caledonians.

The Y.M.C.A. and Tigers rugby teams began practising in early August. Both Hillhurst and St. Mary's held organizational meetings, but later the Saints Club dropped out of the planned schedule. J. Leake became the club president of the Hillhurst Hornets, McLean was appointed coach, and Lewis was voted the team captain. The majority of the team players were English who had played English rugby in Calgary the year previous but were now adopting the Canadian system. Dr. Sullivan was the president of the Y.M. team and A. Wark its team captain. The league schedule called for four games for each team between October 2 and November 4. Plans were made to offer medals for place and drop kicking in competition to be held in conjunction with one of the games.

In the league opener the Tigers defeated the Y.M.C.A. by a score of 23-5 with Woods scoring three trys for fifteen points. The Y.M. team came back in the second game to beat the new Hillhurst entry by a 13-5 score. In intermediate play the Tiger Cubs overcame the Western Canada College team 14-0. Tigers picked up their second win with an 11-0 shut-out of the Hillhurst Hornets. The Western Canada Juniors bested the Convent team 18-6 in an exhibition game.

The Belanger Cup had been donated for provincial senior rugby competition by Mr. Belanger of Calgary. Mr. Belanger had played on three Canadian rugby championship teams in the east during his playing career, but now limited his involvement to refereeing rugby matches. In October the Calgary Tigers journeyed to Edmonton to overpower the Edmonton team 25-1. In a return game Calgary again demonstrated their superiority by posting a 21-6 win. Tiger players were: backs—Ross, Gorman, Sawers, Dobbie, Pinkham, Wood; quarters—Johnstone, Barnes; Scrimage—McMaster; Forwards—Beal, Gouge, Gibson, White, Gorman, and Fitzgibbon. In the last senior game of the season the Tigers defeated the Y.M.C.A. 21-0. Trys were scored by Dobbie, Gouge, and Pinkham.

With the Tigers superiority over the other teams so obvious it was suggested that the Y.M.C.A. and Hillhurst teams unite to play against them. An all-star team from the city was chosen, but the Tigers said they would not be able to play them. Hillhurst announced that they were dropping out of city competition but would still challenge for the Belanger Cup. The intermediate season closed with the College losing to the Cubs by 21-0 score. In the final minor game of the year St. Mary's shaded Western Canada College 6-5.

The Caledonians began organizing for the 1910 season with an early February meeting chaired by club president Dr. Ings. The members gave recognition to J. Haag as the team captain. In the same month the clubs annual smoker was held and the guests were treated to several boxing matches. It was announced that the Corinthian Soccer Club from England would meet the Callies during the English team's North American tour. Parker, the People's Newspaper representative, arrived in Calgary to say that there was a protest by the Vancouver Thistles over last year's People's cup final game, and that the game should have been played in the afternoon instead of the evening so that another game could have been played as a result of the tie. The Callies were ordered to pay off the tie in Vancouver on May 24 or forfeit the trophy, however this game was of little interest to them.

Dr. Ings presided over the annual meeting of the Calgary City Football Association. It was decided to raise the team entrance fee to $3 for junior clubs, $5 for intermediate elevens, and $10 for senior clubs. The Senior League was to be made up of the Callies, Hillhurst, City and Glenbow teams. Maple Leafs, Y.M.C.A., City II, Hillhurst II and Callies II were in the Intermediate division, and Western Canada College, Y.M.C.A., St. Mary's and the High School were tentatively scheduled for the Junior League. The Alberta Football Association met in the Y.M.C.A. on Good Friday with President A. Ward of Edmonton in the chair. Dr. McRae of Western Canada College was the Association Vice-President.

Soccer games were played in Calgary in early March of 1910, even before the conclusion of the hockey season. In the first exhibition match Hillhurst doubled the Stonecutters 4-2. Victoria Day competition saw a game at Morley between the Indians and the All-comers. Soccer was a part of the sports and recreation programs at the various Indian Schools in the Calgary area. The Glenbow Club, from west of the city, thumped the City Club by a 5-1 score. In the first game of the Sons of Scotland Charity Cup the Callies defeated City 4-1. Proceeds from the games in this series went to the hospital benefit fund. Soccer was part of the recreation at the Militia camp held in the city during July.

During the same month the City Soccer Football Club, who were at the bottom of the Senior League, dropped out of further play. The Callies won the city senior championship and the Merchants Cup for the sixth time. They were followed in the standings by Hillhurst and Glenbow. In the finals of the Intermediate League Maple Leafs and Hillhurst II played to a scoreless tie, however in a replay Maple Leafs won 1-0.

The Callies were invited, as league champions and trophy holders, to go to Toronto for the People's Cup competition, however they felt it was not worth the cost, and as well they were unhappy with the sponsors of the competition after the problems related to their previous year's win. Hillhurst defeated the Callies in the finals of the Sons of Scotland Charity Cup. Callies protested that the game was six minutes short of regulation time, however the protest was not upheld. As a result of this victory the Hillhurst Club applied to take part in the People's Cup competition, and their entry was accepted. The city fathers authorized $200 to help finance the trip, and a benefit game between Scotland and England, which resulted in a 2-2 tie, helped to raise further funds. The rugby crowd decided to help, however the benefit rugby football match between the Tigers and Y.M.C.A. teams was rained out.

A large crowd was at the railroad station to see the Hillhurst Club and its President E. Riley off to Toronto in their own private railroad car. The playing personnel included: captain A. Stewart. A. Ward, McKechnie, F. Oliver, C. Boss, Baldwin, J. Johnston, A. Wakelyn, F. McEwen, W. Nuttal, H. Haig, J. Ross, and S. Wakelyn.

In Toronto, 2,000 spectators watched McEwen, Nuttal and Johnston each score as the Hillhurst squad defeated the hometown Thistles 3-0. In the semi-finals A. Stewart scored twice to lead his team to a 2-0 win over a Fort William team. The Lakehead group were so taken with the play of the Calgary team that they cheered for them in the final match, and even invited them to stop over in Fort William on the way home for a game.

In the final match for the People's Trophy the Hillhurst team earned a one-one tie with Hamilton in a hard fought game, which meant that another game had to be played. In the second game the teams were scoreless at the end of regulation time. With three minutes to go in the extra time Hamilton led two goals to one—then Archie Stewart scored with just two minutes left and the game was tied! Hillhurst continued to press and a minute later Baldwin booted home the winning goal to give Hillhurst a come from behind 3-2 victory and the People's Cup! The press described the contest as the best soccer game ever seen in Canada. However the Hillhurst management received a let-down after the game for, inspite of good crowds, they received only $35 from the organizers of the tournament. While the tournament was on in Toronto soccer officials of the various clubs met to form Canada's National Soccer Football Association. Hillhurst arrived back in Calgary to a great welcome, and then there was considerable discussion of sending the team on a tour of Britain the next year.

Meanwhile the Callies were still on the playoff trail for the Bennett Cup. The Scots journeyed to Lethbridge to defeat the hometown squad 2-1. Unfortunately some of the Callie players were too boisterous in the post-game celebrations and one of them was shot in the leg by a policeman. Next the Caledonians went to Red Deer to whitewash the area champions 4-0. The provincial final between the

Callies and northern champions Lloydminster was played in Edmonton, however inspite of a 2-0 win it was a frustrating experience for the Callies. Upon arriving in the city they were unable to get a hotel room to change in; the playing field was in poor condition, and the old ball they had to play with burst in the first half. However Fred Williams scored two goals; the opposition was held scoreless, and the Callies were the provincial champions.

In the fall the cricket club members and the tennis club members met on the pitch for a game of soccer. The Plumbers and Printers meet in another game. Thanksgiving Day saw the Callies defeat the Intermediate League champion Maple Leafs 1-0 and the Dominion champion Hillhurst squad played even with a picked team. The Alberta college team from Edmonton came down to defeat the Normal School 3-0 in soccer. Later the Normal School lost 5-0 to their northern opponents in Edmonton.

T. McLean (Wing)   N. V. White (Wing)   W. L. Ross, Capt. (Quarter-back)   J. L. Gibson (Wing)   C. B. Clarke (Trainer)
J. Pinkham (Half-back)   S. Beatt (Wing)   J. C. Woods (Scrimmage)   J. C. H. Johnston (Scrimmage)   L. Clark (Wing)   W. M. Dobbie (Half-back)   R. J. Priestley (Wing)   G. E. H. Johnston (Scrimmage)
C. R. Linduer (Scrimmage)   R. White (Treas.)   J. C. Madden (Half-back)   Dr. Mason (Pres.)   P. R. Barton (Full-back)   G. S. Whittaker (Sec.)   J. FitzGibbons (Wing)

Calgary Tigers Rugby Football Club, 1910.

During the winter there was an indoor soccer league in the Y.M.C.A. gym. In the finals the Giants defeated the Youngsters for the championship. Other teams in the league were Hillhurst, Midgets, Business Men, Bankers and Scots.

The Tigers and Y.M.C.A. rugby football teams began practise in mid-August of 1910. Lethbridge had invited the Tigers to play against their team on Labour Day, however the southern city had to default because they could not put together a full team. Calgary rugby football players were not in favour of a schedule with any teams outside of the city and only wanted to meet them in playoffs. More than forty men turned out at Mewata to play Rugby Union Rules (English) rugby with a team called the Calgary City Rugby Club. The Tiger

Clubs, Y.M.C.A. and Western Canada College entered teams in the Intermediate League.

The Y.M. team, who in the past two years had won only one game against five losses to the Tigers, were hopeful that the addition of former Chicago all-star Clarence Clark to their lineup would strengthen the squad to a contending position. However in the season opener the Tigers took a slim 11-10 win. In the second game the two teams tied five all with all the points coming on touches or rouges. In the game for the city championship the Tigers again proved their superiority with a 13 to 6 win with five point trys by Gibson and Fitzgibbons. McMaster scored a try for the Y. team.

About this time Edmonton rugby people became very emphatic that a final game be played, and so the next Saturday the Eskimos were in Calgary for the first of a home and home series. For these games the Tiger lineup included: back—Barton; halves—Madden, Dobbie, Pinkham; quarter—Ross; scrimmage —Woods, P. Johnston, J. Johnston; the inside middle and outside wings were Priestly, Fitzgibbons, McLean, White, Beat and Gibson. Paul Barton led Calgary to a lopsided 26-6 win over an outplayed Edmonton team. Over 2,500 spectators were at the game but it was reported that less than 2,000 paid the admission. The Tigers then journeyed to Edmonton to well outplay their hosts but only win by a 14 to 12 score, and thus bring home the Belanger Trophy, emblematic of the rugby football championship of the province. Tentative plans had been made for the Alberta Champions to play the Moose Jaw team, however this called off due to the "frosty weather".

The Alberta University team traveled to Calgary for a rugby football game against Western Canada College. The Calgary team had a brilliant kicker named Paddy Johnston who led his team to a 27 to 13 win over the University team. However on their home ground the University was able to reverse the outcome by a 16 to 2 score. During the fall the College also lost to the Tiger Cubs. The Red Deer School defeated an Edmonton school in rugby to capture the Rutherford Cup. On Thanksgiving Day the Vice-captain's team of the Calgary City Rugby Club defeated the Captain's team in a game under union rules. The Tiger Cubs played an exhibition game against the men of the Fire Brigade.

Indoor soccer had been played at least as early as 1867, in various army buildings in England. However the credit for the creation of the modified indoor rule goes to A.B. Dawson of the Montreal Y.M.C.A. An indoor soccer League was played in the Calgary Y. gymnasium during the winter of 1910-11. The teams playing were the Giants, Business Men, Bankers, Scots, Youngsters, and Hillhurst who were the league champions. In a post-season game Hillhurst defeated an all-star team from the rest of the league by a 16-8 score.

Dr. McRae, the outgoing league president, early in 1911 announced that soccer spectators would be seated in a grandstand and that admissions would be charged for senior and other major games during the coming season. In Winnipeg Archie McDougall donated a trophy to be given to the champion soccer football club of Western Canada. Following the annual meeting of the Calgary and District Football League President J. Childs stated that because Hillhurst and Callies were so strong the league would like to limit team signing to twenty players a club. Hillhurst Park was handed over to the Hillhurst Athletic Club, and plans were announced for a 300 seat covered grandstand as well as bleachers seating 1,500 people.

Many of the soccer clubs in the city were hard at practise by early March. The season's exhibition opener saw the Y.M. team defeat the boys from Western Canada College 4-1. The college team became part of a new school league along with teams from the Normal School and C.C.I. A revised City Junior Soccer League of the Callie Thistles, W.C.C., and Hillhurst imposed an age limit of 18 years, while 16 years was the juvenile limit for the teams from St. Marys, the college, and Crescent Heights. The J. Miquelon Trophy had originally been up for competition for boys under 115 pounds, and had been won by St. Mary's in 1908, the Callies in 1909, not competed for in 1910, but would now be the trophy for the Juvenile League. Teams competing were the Callies, Presbyterian Thistles and W.C.C. and games were played at Western Canada College grounds.

Colonel Herchmer was the honorary president of the Westmounts—a new senior soccer club. The Maple Leafs proved their worth by holding the senior Callies to a 1-1 draw in a practise game. About this time the senior clubs, consisting of the Callies, Hillhurst, City, Maple Leafs, and Westmounts, decided that in order to circumvent the senior-intermediate eligibility rule they would classify themselves as class A intermediates. Later they did, however, rescind their decision. J. Ward, the president of the provincial soccer association, said that his group wanted a new set of rules governing the play for the People's Trophy.

A new Trades and Labour Union Association Football League was formed and included the following teams: Machinists, Carpenters, Bricklayers and Masons, Boilermakers, Brewery, Stonecutters, Tinsmiths, Printers, Plasterers, and Plumbers. Many of this league's games were played on the brewery field. Included in the City Intermediate League were the teams of Pryce-Jones, Y.M.C.A., Post Office, Crescent Heights, and P. Burns, with each team playing eight games in the schedule. A new soccer field was prepared on the west side of Mewata, now giving that park three soccer pitches. During the season the south field was fenced off and it was now possible to charge admissions to certain games. The Shamrocks, Eagles, Maple Leafs, and Tigers made up what was billed as "the youngest football league in the Province",—being the four upstairs rooms in the Practise School. North-east of Calgary the towns of Alix, Castor, Stettler, Gadsby, and Halkirk formed the Eastern Branch of the Provincial Football League.

The Hillhurst squad opened up the season with a 4-0 win over the City team and followed up with a 5-0 shutout over the new Westmount eleven. In their first encounter with the Callies, before 1,500 spectators at Mewata Park, Hillhurst came away with a 3 to 1 win. This was the first loss in a long time for the Caledonians. In June the Callies were in better form and scored a record five goals in a thirty-five minute period against the City squad. In the next game the Callies downed Hillhurst 1-0, but Hillhurst went on to win the league and the Merchants Cup, emblematic of the city championship. Hillhurst also bested Lethbridge 4-1 in a Dominion Day game.

Calgary's soccer fraternity were awaiting with great anticipation the game between Calgary's best and the touring Corinthians—one of England's top amateur clubs. In order to pick an all-star to oppose the English squad two exhibition games were held in order to allow a better evaluation of the players. 2,000 people were at Mewata to see the Scots defeat the English in the first game. In the second match the players were divided into A and B teams, and an equally large crowd turned out for this match.

The Corinthians were outclassing their opponents in eastern Canada but did lose to the Toronto all-stars. Prior to the Calgary game the London, England team had amassed a total of 361 winning games. Meanwhile word was received by Hillhurst from the English soccer association that if any of their players participated against the touring Corinthians it would make them ineligible to play in their forthcoming tour in England. The Alberta Locators, a Calgary Company, got into the act by putting up a trophy for the amateur championship of the world, which they felt could be played by the Calgary team and the Corinthians. It was suggested that the two teams engage in a series of games for the trophy. G. Child, Calgary's soccer association president, felt the Calgary team would win, but he did not feel that the winner could be called world champion as the Corinthians were not necessarily the top team Britain could assemble. However the Corinthians were not really interested in playing for the trophy, and besides this, their constitution would not have allowed them to engage in such contests. Parker, the People's representative, wanted back the People's Shield because several of the Hillhurst players would be playing against the Corinthians, and this was not allowed.

Following the two practise games the following players were picked to represent Calgary: Melville, Cooper, J. Haig, J. Petrie, F. McEwen, Judge Williams, Dyke, McLean, A. Stewart and Richardson. On the day of the game the two teams changed at the Y and were then taken to the Hillhurst field. Many of the huge crowd were at the grounds a good hour before game time. At the beginning of the game the Hillhurst grounds and the 800 seat grandstand were officially opened. Mayor Mitchell kicked off the ball to start the game which was played on a sea of mud. Rumours were that the pitch, already soaked with rain, was given an extra hosing down to help slow down the visitors.

McEwan scored first to give Hillhurst a one goal lead. The Corinthians tied it up and then scored again to go one goal ahead. Dyke and Newans each booted home goals and the locals went ahead 3-2! The score was again tied by the Corinthians, and then with fifteen minutes of play left the visitors scored, and when the game ended Hillhurst was on the low end of a 4-3 score. The crowd was disappointed in the loss, but the game had been a good one. That evening the visitors were entertained at a huge banquet. The Corinthians finished their Canadian tour with thirteen wins, a loss to Toronto and a tie with the Ladysmith, B.C. team, before heading south of the border for further games.

Eight local clubs were entered in the Sons of Scotland competition. Games started at 6:45 p.m. and were of eighty minutes duration as compared with modern matches of ninety minutes. City beat Post Office, the Intermediate League champions, one to zero; Callies topped Pryce-Jones 4-0, and the Y team earned a two-one win over Crescent Heights. Hillhurst beat the City and then went on to defeat the Callies 1-0 in the finals on a goal by Johnson. The Intermediate championship had gone to the Post Office team who had defeated Crescent Heights 3-2 in their final match.

Pick-up games were played between Neilsons Furniture and the C.P.R. freight sheds, and St. Andrew's Young Men's Club travelled out to Delaware to play the local men's club. The City Club returned a game with the Banff club and earned a 4-3 win in the mountain town, while the C.P.R. freight shed team shaded a second Banff team 3-2. An exhibition game saw the Calgary Cricket Club overpower the Calgary Tennis Club by a 7-2 score in a game of soccer. Another fall game saw the Callie Intermediates trip the Normal School team 1-0.

The Callies journeyed to Lethbridge in a provincial playdown game for the Bennett Cup, however their win was protested. Again the Callies travelled to the southern city and again won by scoring five goals in the last twenty minutes of play. In the north the Alix team defaulted to the Edmonton Swifts, and so the stage was set for the provincial soccer final between the Swifts and the Callies. By this time the Hillhurst field had been leased to the Big Four rugby organization, so the game was set for Mewata.

The match started with fast and furious play, but the Callies proved superior and came out with a 4-0 win in spite of the fact that Cooper was hurt in the second period, and the Callies had to play one man short. Williams led the attack with two goals and Stewart and Petrie one each. The lineup for the provincial champions and winners of the Bennett Cup were: Cooper, Cunningham, Grindley, Petrie, Strang, Haig, Bradwood, Deakin, Williams, McLean, and Jewell.

In early September Hillhurst received final word of their planned British tour. This followed weeks of anxiety for the team members as a schedule of games had to be worked out and official permission granted for the games to be played. The games were scheduled on an average of two a week over a three month period, and Hillhurst was guaranteed 50-85% of each gate. Nine of the touring team's players were from the Hillhurst squad, with four from Vancouver and another from Hamilton. Eight out of eleven of these players were native born Canadians, and the team members made the tour without pay, often giving up their jobs for the opportunity of the tour. The team was given a smoker prior to its departure.

The Hillhurst squad landed in Liverpool, and the following day lost a 5-4 decision to the Liverpool Reserves. The Canadians played a satisfactory game, considering they had just got off the boat the day before. In following games Hillhurst lost 4-1 to Nottingham, 5-1 to Crewe, Coventry 1-0, defeated Likeston 1-0 and Bradford 3-2, lost to Stockport 8-4 and tied Bradford 2-2. In the first three games four players were injured, and there were times it appeared they would not be able to finish the tour. However overall the team was considered to have made a good showing against some top British clubs, and Frank Riley felt that the money he had paid out to finance the trip had been justified. Melville, one of the Hillhurst players, was signed by Queens Park of the Scottish League.

Calgarians were now informed of "old country soccer" by George Taylor's weekly newspaper column. Late in the year it was announced that the Peoples Shield would now be known as the Canadian Challenge Shield Trophy as it was now owned by the Canadian Football Association. The trophy had not been played for in 1911 because of the Corinthian tour but would be competed for in Winnipeg in 1912. There was word from Britain that the Oxford, Cambridge and London Camel teams wanted to tour Canada and play in Calgary. The city's soccer season drew to a close with a Christmas morning match between the Callies and City teams.

The season's first game of English rugby was played at Mewata in early August between Calgary's English and Welch rugby teams. Before the season was over these two clubs had played five games, with the English club coming out on top in three of them.

August saw the Tigers begin rugby practise on the Mewata field which had been fenced off. Paddy Johnson worked out enough players to complete two full teams. The Rough Rider Rugby Club was organized by Jake Fullerton, an ex Y.M.C.A. player, and practises were held in Victoria Park. The general word was that there would not be a Y team, then Doc Dawson arrived back in the city to dispel the rumour and began signing players. Later he announced that there would not be a team because most of the good players had been signed by either the Tigers or the Rough Riders.

At a Calgary rugby meeting an innovation was proposed—that being the snapping back of the ball with the hands. This was done in the American game and the consensus was that it was more sensible. The rugby crowd was pleased when it was announced that the proposed 120 acre municipal athletic park in Riverside would include a field for rugby and soccer.

The rugby men wanted to take part in an Alberta Big Four, and there were rumours of inter-provincial play. C.H. Belanger, the retiring president of the Edmonton Rugby Club offered a trophy for provincial rugby competition. Mr. Belanger had formerly played in the east on three Canadian rugby champion teams. A contract was secured to use the Hillhurst playing field for rugby.

On September 18 representatives of the Big Four clubs were to meet in Red Deer, however the Edmonton Eskimos backed down and did not send a delegate; as a result the Calgary delegates were not very happy. When the Eskimos announced their intention of participating another Red Deer meeting was arranged, and the Alberta Rugby Football Union was organized to include the Tigers, Rough Riders, Eskimos and Edmonton Y.M.C.A. teams. The founders of the Big Four were: President C. Belanger, vice-president Robert Pearson of Red Deer, secretary Vivian Graham of Calgary, Campbell Young, John Corn-foot and Paddy Young.

The Belanger Cup would be played for by the province's senior clubs, each playing six games in the schedule. The Alberta Locators Cup, a cast-off from the soccer sport, would be up for intermediate competition. The Graham Cup, for junior competition, was sponsored by Vivian Graham, and the Guy Whitaker and Co. medals were for the team members winning the Alberta junior rugby championship. After the season started the Burns and Sewell Trophy, donated by boxing promoter Tommy Burns and Jim Sewell, was put up for the senior rugby championship of Calgary. Much of the poolroom and barbershop talk of the period revolved around the possibility of pro-football in Calgary in 1912.

A small crowd at Hillhurst watched the Tigers beat the Rough Riders 17-8 as Costello proved to be a top calibre quarterback. The Tiger players were: back—Dobbie; halves—Gibson, Ross, Marx; quarter—Costello; scrimmage—Woods, Lynder, Lyons; right wing—Fitzgibbons, Gauge, McLean; left wing—Beatt, McLeod, Beatty. The Rough Rider lineup included: back—McKee, halves—Dumphy, Ross, Sinclair; quarter—George; scrimmage—Miller, Hutchinson, Foreman; right wing—O'Grady, Marshall, McCaulley; spares—Lamarche, Northrup, Incel, Storer, Braithwaite, Hurd, Fullerton. Dr. Sanson was the referee.

In October the Y.M.C.A. team travelled to Calgary to defeat the Rough Riders 11-1. The Calgary team's front wall was steady, but the backfield could not develop any scoring punch. On the same day at Edmonton the Eskimos and Tigers played two overtime periods, but they still could not break a 5-5 tie in what was considered the hardest fought game in Alberta rugby history. For Calgary Dyke kicked a field goal, while singles were earned by Paddy Johnson—on a kick to the dead ball line, and Beatty's rouge. In following games in the schedule the Tigers defeated the Y. team 9-0, with all the points being scored in the first half. In Calgary the Rough Riders lost 11-9 to the Eskimos, with the final whistle halting a Calgary drive which was close to the Edmonton line. McMaster ran Calgary's lone touchdown.

On October 23 representatives from various rugby clubs in western Canada met in Regina to form the Western Canada Rugby Union, and plans were discussed for a playoff between the champions of Manitoba, Saskatchewan and Alberta. Vivian Graham of Calgary was voted its second vice-president.

At Edmonton the Eskimos trampled the Y team 33-13, and in Calgary Jake Fullerton was suspended for punching Paddy Johnson in the last game, won by Tigers 32-0. On Thanksgiving Day the Tigers whitewashed the Y team 33-0 on touchdowns by Costello, Ross and McLean. Warke drop kicked a field goal, and Dobbie had five kicks to the dead ball line. There was dissension in the Rough Rider camp, and Captain McMasters quit the team. In their next game they were beaten 13-0 by the Eskimos. The last game between the Rough Riders and the Y.M.C.A. was cancelled by mutual agreement.

The Big Four title was at stake in the windup game between the Tigers and the Eskimos at Hillhurst Park. Ritchie scored a touchdown and Dobbie earned four points on his kicks to the dead ball line as the Tigers shut out their opponents 13-0. The other points came on a safety touch and a rouge. The Tigers now held the Burns and Sewell Cup, emblematic of the city championship, and the Belanger Cup for winning the Big Four championship. Tigers line-up for the championship game was: full—Nodin; halves—Wark, Dobbie, Barton; quarter—Ross; scrimmage—Woods, Johnson, Roberts; right wing—Beatty, Priestly, White; left wing—McLean, Gauge, Fitzgibbons; spares—Gibson, Ritchie.

The Tigers were now ready for inter-provincial playdowns. Regina was to meet the Winnipeg Rowing Club in Winnipeg, but a -30 degree temperature halted that game. Winnipeg suggested that Regina had defaulted the game. Plans were made to meet the Tigers in Calgary for the championship of Western Canada and the Ross Cup.

The weather was so cold the Tigers held their evening practises in the Y.M.C.A. gym. Before the game took place the city had sweepers clean the Hillhurst field of its covering of snow.

On the day of the game a long automobile parade took place from the C.P.R. station to Hillhurst Park. By game time the overflowing stands and grounds accommodated 2,500 spectators.

Winnipeg went ahead 1-0 on a rouge, but Dobbie booted two kicks to the dead ball line and Ross another to put the Tigers ahead 3-1. The Rowing Club scored a touchdown to lead 6-3 in the third quarter. A Calgary safety touch narrowed the score to 6-5; Dobbie's kick tied the score before Costello crossed the goal line for a touchdown, converted by Dobbie, to give Calgary a 13-6 win and the Ross Cup! It was agreed that Costello's quarterbacking and Dobbie's kicking were the strongest factors of Calgary's game. Following their victory the Tigers announced that they may challenge for the Canadian rugby title, but this never came about because it was learned that the Big Four League was not recognized in the east. Dr. Mason, Tiger president, announced that the club would organize to participate in other sports in the city. The Big Four's application to the A.A.A.A. had been accepted, and an application made to the Canadian Rugby Football Union would be considered at the 1912 meeting.

The first Calgary soccer of 1912 was played in the Y.M.C.A. gym as part of a New Year's Day sports program. Two new teams in the indoor soccer program were the Bees and Irrigation teams. In February the Callies, under President Dr. MacRae, held their annual meeting. Dr. McRae reported that the Callies 1911 record was 12 wins, 3 ties and 3 losses. During his talk he reminisced that the Callies had played their first games on a field in front of Western Canada College. A new C.P.R. soccer football club was organized and J. Wall was elected as the club president.

In the annual City Soccer Association meeting representatives from the Hillhurst Club, including Mr. Riley, were asked to explain the reasons why the team had made the overseas trip, for it had come out that the players were told that they had to make the trip. There were some in local soccer circles who now felt that the Hillhurst team should be classified as professional.

A letter was received from the English Football Association stating that there was not any Canadian football association which was recognized as such. The local group decided to break away from the C.A.A., and as well refused to have anything to do with the C.A.F.A. Attempts were to be made to form a real Canadian football association. A new constitution was written for the Calgary league.

Parker asked Hillhurst to return the People's Shield, however the Calgary team declined to do this until their guarantee was returned to them. Alex Martin, a local merchandiser, advertised, "football jerseys $10.50—22 a dozen, footballs $1-5.00, and football boots $2.50 to 5.50".

The senior soccer league schedule ran from May 14 through August 27, with the City, Hillhurst, Post Office, Callies and the new Thistle Club each to play twelve games. Most of the games were scheduled for Hillhurst Park, and an admission charge of 15¢ a game was set. A team called the Swifts had earlier indicated their desire to enter the senior division, however this never came about.

The Intermediate division was divided into A and B sections and included the following teams: Y.M.C.A., Pryce-Jones, Crescent Heights, C.P.R., Parkhill, Neilson Furniture, Sons of Erin, Tynesiders, St. Andrews, Young Mens Club, Yorkshire Society, and Church of the Redeemer. Cochrane applied for membership in the Intermediate League but was turned down. Teams in the Juvenile division included: Y.M., Boy's Club, Callies, Bishop Pinkham, C.P.R., Thistles, Crescent Heights, and Boy Scouts.

A Trades and Labour Football League was composed of: Stonecutters, Plumbers and Steamfitters, Bricklayers and Masons, Machinists, Carpenters Brotherhood, and Plasterers. In early summer the Civic Football League, comprised of teams from the Street Railway, Fire Department, Police, City Hall, Parks, and Waterworks came into operation. This gave the city 28 men's teams in league play as well as numerous other teams, such as the Mounted police, Bankview, the Langdon Booster Club, and company teams, which played exhibition games. Western Canada College and the Normal School arranged a series of games for the W.C.C. Shield.

"Doc" Dawson of the Y.M.C.A. was appointed to supervise the Mewata fields. On most any given day during the summer there were games of soccer, baseball, rugby and lacrosse played on these fields by the various 92 boy's and men's teams. Other fields used for soccer were Hillhurst, Victoria Park, Western Canada College, Parkhill, the Brewery flats, and the Police grounds where the City Police and the Mounted Police played to a scoreless tie.

Representatives of the Alberta Amateur Football League met in the Calgary Y.M.C.A. to discuss a Dominion association for soccer. On May 24 a soccer meeting was held in Toronto, and the Dominion of Canada Football Association was formed. This organization met in Winnipeg July 15 where a motion was passed to apply for international federation affiliation.

There were two pre-season benefit soccer games played in Calgary to raise funds for injured players. The first of these saw the newly formed Thistles Club lose 2-1 to the City Club. The Tynesiders and Yorkshire Society teams met in another match. Bankview defeated Parkhill, a league team, 7-0 at the Parkhill pitch, and the Thistles went down to a 7-0 defeat to the Hillhurst squad.

There were 1,200 fans at the first senior league game to see the City and Hillhurst teams play to a 1-1 draw. In the first game between Hillhurst and the Callies a large crowd of 1,500 saw the Hillhurst boys come out on top 1-0. Riley's team again beat the City 2-0 in what developed into the roughest game of soccer ever played in Calgary, with several fist fights developing. A $125 in gate receipts was realized in the first International of the year at Hillhurst with England defeating Scotland 2-1. A special train carried a picked Calgary team and its fans to Edmonton where they lost 2-1 to Edmonton's soccer eleven. Stan Wakelyn scored Calgary's lone goal. The Stonecutters met their first defeat in eight years when they were beaten 3-1 by the Carpenter's team.

There were not any Calgary clubs willing to play in the People's Cup competition in Winnipeg. The Lethbridge Club did go and played well enough to earn a berth in the finals, but they were beaten 3-0 by a strong Fort William team for the championship. Shortly after this a new cup, the Connaught Cup, was offered for soccer competition in the Dominion.

Towards the end of the season the Callies took a 1-0 win over the Hillhurst squad, however the feature of the game was a pugilistic encounter between Callie Archie Stewart and one of the spectators. In their next meeting the Callies earned a 2-1 win when a goal was scored with less than three minutes to go in the game when a penalty kick was awarded for a trip. Right up until the late stages of the schedule the Hillhurst, Callies and City teams were in a position to take the league championship. Post Office was in fourth spot and the newly formed Thistles were deep at the bottom of the league.

A very large crowd watched Hillhurst and the Callies battle to a scoreless draw in the league championship game played on Labour Day. A second game was played a week later before a crowd of over 2,000 people, but even with extra time being played neither of the teams managed a score. A third playoff game was necessary, but this time the Callies came out on top 2-0. The game was marred by a fight between Towill and Ross, and then Ross and one of the spectators.

The Callies, along with Lethbridge, Edmonton and Lloydminster were left in the hunt for the Bennett Cup. Calgary's representatives travelled to Lethbridge but only managed a 2-2 tie with the Overseas team. The Callies were behind 2-0 until late in the game until they managed to score two quick goals. However both teams registered protests against certain players that the other team used. A second game was scheduled for Hillhurst Park, but Lethbridge would not play without the players under protest, and so the Callies qualified for the Alberta finals against Edmonton. The final game was played in mid-October at the Hillhurst pitch with the Callies coming out on top 1-0 on a goal by Wilson. The Callies were again in possession of the Bennett Cup, emblematic of the provincial soccer championship! The Callie lineup included: Gillholey Cooper, McLean, Haig, Strang, Petrie, Towill, Nesbit, Williams, Grinley, McBean, Wilson, Braidwood and Mathewson.

In the Intermediate League finals the Tynesiders won the championship with a victory over the C.P.R. This was followed by the Intermediate League International between the league's English and Scottish players. The Trades and Labour League was won by the Carpenters who defeated the Plumbers 2-0 for the title. Soccer games at the Calgary Military Camp saw the 101 Regiment defeat the 103 Regiment by a 7-1 score, and the Army Medical Corps won over the Army Service Corps 6-2. Lethbridge won the Southern Alberta Soccer League which included teams from Pincher Creek, MacLeod, Grassy Lakes, Medicine Hat and Taber. Hillhurst won the Burn's Cup for the championship of the Southern Alberta Pass Football League. The Calgary C.P.R. Soccer Club lost a return game in Red Deer to break even on a home and home series.

In August a Calgary select eleven travelled to Edmonton to drop a 2-0 game to the Edmonton team. However in a return match, at Hillhurst before 2,000 spectators, Stan Wakelyn, Leader and Foley each scored a goal to give Calgary a 3-0 victory. Other Calgary players were: Sutton, Melville, Dickenson, Haig, A. Wakelyn, Petrie, A. Stewart, Nesbitt and Williams. H. Sheidon handled the refereeing. Following the game the Edmonton team was treated to dinner and entertainment. A fall benefit game saw England and Scotland play to a 1-1 draw. In the season's last game a Lethbridge club came to Calgary for an exhibition game against a combined Sons of Erin-Rangers team.

On February 11 an interested group met to form the Alberta British Rugby Football Union. Union president Alex Hannah was to attempt to arrange an Alberta-Manitoba championship. The provincial association was to include teams from Edmonton, Red Deer, Calgary, Black Diamond, and it was hoped Lethbridge. Calgary teams included the Wanderers, Pirates, Welch, as well as the English. Calgary's schedule ran from May 30 through August 15 with international games as part of the regular schedule.

The first international saw the Scots defeat the Welch 3-0 on a try. On August first the Welch were narrowly defeated by the Wanderers, however they only had ten players to oppose the Wanderers fifteen men. On Labour Day the Calgary British Rugby Team journeyed up to Red Deer for an exhibition game.

In the fall a team known as the Alberta British Rugby Team travelled to the west coast where they played three games. In Vancouver the Alberta team played much of the second half a man short when Shearer had some of his ribs broken. In November the Victoria rugby team was investigated when it was learned that they had recruited several of the Alberta players to play for them.

On January 15, 1912 the executive of the Dominion Rugby Football Union met but decided to only grant an honourary membership to the Western Canada Rugby Union. The western organization would be allowed to send delegates to the meetings, but they would not be allowed to vote on any matters. It would be up to the C.R.F.U. as to whether a western challenge for the Grey Cup would be accepted.

South of the border, the American football people decided to go with four downs instead of three, and the playing field would be shortened from 110 to 100 yards.

Hugo Ross, the donor of the Ross Cup, the trophy for the W.R.F.U. championship, was lost in the sinking of the Titanic, and it was suggested that "Memorial", be engraved on the trophy. The Western Canada Rugby Union decided to hold an executive meeting in Moose Jaw on September 17. League president was M. Damoulin of Moose Jaw. It was decided at that time that the semi as well as league finals would be played in Calgary. However this did not come about.

The "Big Four" met in Red Deer on September 5 to become the "Big Three" with the Edmonton Eskimos, Calgary Tigers and Calgary Y.M.C.A. League president was W. Really. Jake Fullerton applied for reinstatement but was refused and barred from further play until December 31, 1912. The league now favoured the snapback system for putting the ball into play.

The Y.M.C.A. team purchased the Rough Rider uniforms, and many of the disbanded team's players joined the Y team. Included in their lineup were: McLaurin, Scott, Nichols, J. Roughton, Lemarche, Seavey, H. O'Grady, Dixon, L.W. Steadman, W. O'Grady, Kemp, R. Stuart, Besse, and Colville.

The Calgary Tigers opened practise at Mewata Park on August 13 under Captain Ross and president Dr. Mason. Initial drills consisted only of kicking and ball handling.

In the season opener the Tigers walloped the Y.M.C.A. by a 30-3 score in what was considered a poor game. There were many illegal tackles made, and Ross was sent off for five minutes for using his elbow in what was considered an unfair tackle. Trys were scored on kick exchanges by Costello (2), Priestly, and Wood. In the next league game the Y team again went down to defeat by a 21-0 score, this time at the hand of the Edmonton Eskimos. Many unrecovered fumbles led to the Calgary team's loss. An innovation of the game's report was a play-by-play diagram published by a local paper.

A special train was arranged for the Tiger game in Edmonton, and fans could make the round trip for only $4.35. The game was won by Edmonton 7-6. Wark picked up an onside kick to score a try and save a whitewash. Edmonton did not have much of an offense, but the Tiger foreward line proved to be very weak. A controversy rose as to the final score which was reported by an Edmonton paper as 8-6 when Edmontonians decided that one play was a safety touch instead of a rouge. This was later declared to be the official score.

On October 12 the Tigers gained their second win of the season by beating the Y.M.C.A. 23-0. At one point in the game a free-for-all fight developed. The referee had not shown up and a spectator, Brydon, was recruited to handle the whistle. Dr. Mason became the judge of play. A fight between spectator Fullerton and Squib Ross was considered a draw, and Pinkham had his nose broken during the game. The best play of the game was made by Pinkham who, on one play, ran the ball to the 35 yard line and then dropped kicked a field goal for three points.

Another special train carried the Y. team to Edmonton where they went down to an 18-0 defeat to the Eskimos. About this time Squib Ross and Charlie Colville were asked to appear before the executive of the A.R.F.U. in regards to their part in fights during the last Tiger—Y. game. In the last league game of the season the Tigers beat the Eskimos 14 to 8 and captured the Alberta championship by the virtue that in the two games played between the two teams the Tigers out scored the Eskimos 20 points to 16. The Tigers led in the first quarter on a try by Dobbie as well as a touch-in-goal. Conway scored a try and the Esks also scored a touch-in-goal in the second quarter. In the last half the Tigers had eight rouges. When the bugle sounded to end the game Edmonton was in possession of the ball on Calgary's one yard line.

Plans were made for the Tigers to play the Winnipeg Rowing Club team in Winnipeg, but then the Tigers, who wanted to play at home, offered Winnipeg $1,000 to play the game in Calgary, and if the game was to be played in the Manitoba capital—demanded the same amount. At the last moment Mel Snowen, Dobbie and Gibson decided they could not make the trip thus weakening the team. Players who did make the trip included manager and player Squib Ross, captain Arnold Wark, Bull Ritchie, Roberts, Woods, Johnson, Costello, Beatt, Pinkham, Harrison, White, Barton, Lyons, McHugh, Fitzgibbons, Fleming and Watt.

The game was tight with Wark keeping Calgary in contention with his sensational running. On one field goal attempt his kick grazed the outside of the goal post and then rolled to the dead-ball line for a single point. Winnipeg had led 4-1, but Calgary narrowed the gap to 4-3. On the last play of the game Calgary had the ball ten inches from the Winnipeg goal line, but time ran out and the Rowing Club were the winners. In the W.R.C.U. finals Regina outplayed Winnipeg to score a 5-0 victory and win the championship. The Tigers guaranteed the Regina Club $1,000 for a game in Calgary, however the contest never came off.

An all-western team was picked by Winnipeg sports writers. Calgary's Wark and Woods earned berths at left half and left scrimmage respectively. Dobbie and Wood were also given consideration for this team.

At a December meeting of the Alberta Rugby Football Union the delegates were enthused about the snap-back system of putting the ball in play. They were also in favour of reducing the number of playing positions from 14 to 12.

In the opening game of the Senior Intercollegiate Rugby Union Mount Royal defeated Central Collegiate by a 10-2 score as "Blonde" Wood ran two trys. Senior star Art Wark handled the referee's chores. The next game saw W.C.C. defeat the High School. Following his team's 21-7 loss to Mount Royal Dr. McRae said that rugby was far too rough for boys and his school was considering not entering any further competition. A tight defensive game saw Mount Royal edge the High School 2-1, but player eligibility was questioned and a replay was necessary. This time Mount Royal scored an impressive 13-5 victory and were declared the winners of the D.E. Black Trophy.

A home and home series for the Alberta championship was arranged with the University of Alberta. Riley donated the use of Hillhurst Park for the local game, and an inspired Mount Royal team defeated the university boys 10-5! Percy Smith, who had never seen a rugby ball before that year, averaged 45 yards a kick, and "Blondie" Wood provided some good tackles. The following week Mount Royal travelled to Edmonton to win 8-6, take the series 8-11 and win the Alberta junior rugby championship. The Regina Intermediates issued a challenge to the Mount Royal team, but a game was not played. The Intercollegiate Junior chamionship was won by Western Canada college. The Tigers Juniors played exhibition games against the schools.

Soccer started early in 1913 in Calgary with a New Year's day game being played between the Married and Single Men.

The 1913 Calgary City and District Football League was run under the direction of Mr. Robertson. Back from last season in senior play were the Callies, City, Post Office and Hillhurst. The Y.M.C.A., Tynesider, and Lancashire teams moved up to senior competition from the Intermediate League. Hillhurst withdrew from the schedule in April and hatchets began to fly, but Hillhurst agreed to rejoin the league if they were allowed to play their home games in their own park, and this was agreed on. League President Robertson resigned and J. Gow filled the chair for the rest of the season.

In an April benefit game R. Wilson scored two goals to help the Callies defeat the Rest of the League 3-1. In another exhibition Scotland beat England 2-1 before over a thousand spectators at Victoria Park. On May 24 Scotland again defeated England, this time by a 1-0 score.

There were four playing fields at Mewata as well as an adjacent pitch known as "the roadway". Hillhurst and the Victoria Park pitches were also in regular use. A $60,000 money bylaw for the purchase of Hillhurst Park was turned down by the Calgary voters during the year, and it looked like the area might be subdivided into residential lots. Junior and intercollegiate football was played at the college grounds and many of the Intermediate League games were played at the Elboya field. Soccer officials were worried that the proposed armory, to be located at Mewata, would reduce the number of playing fields located there.

New teams, the Fire Fighters, News United, 103rd, Baptist Men's Union, and West of England, joined the C.P.R., Neilsons, Pro-Cathedral, and Parkhill in the Intermediate League. In the league finals the C.P.R. team defeated the 103rd for the intermediate football championship and the McLeod Cup.

The Commercial Football League, which charged $10 a team entry fee, included the Hudson's Bay Co., Ashdowns, Dominion Express, Calgary Furniture, Department of Natural Resources, Metals, Pryce-Jones, city Hall and the Street Railway soccer team. The league championship was won by the Hudson's Bay Company team. The Trades and Labour Football League held another successful year. The Carpenters won the championship and the Calgary Brewing and Malting Trophy. Pat Burns presented this cup at a smoker at which each member of the winning team received a gold medal.

Bishop Pinkham School, Western Canada College, Callies Juniors, First Baptist, C.P.R., Boy Scouts, and the V.C.C. played in the Calgary Junior Football League. Bishop Pinkham took the championship.

A five-a-side soccer tournament was held during the Caledonian Games at Victoria Park. More than thirty teams took part with the winners receiving gold medals. Exhibition games were played at the Barracks grounds between the teams of the Pro-Cathedral and St. John's Church. The Calgary C.P.R. played home and home games with the Edmonton C.P.R. team. A strong Fort William C.P.R. eleven visited the city but were defeated 3-1 by a Calgary pick before a large crowd at Hillhurst Park. Later the Callies drew 0-0 with the Fort William team.

The Edmonton All-Stars edged a Calgary select 2-1 in a game played at Edmonton. Stan Wakelyn booted home Calgary's lone goal. In a return game Pat Allen scored two goals for Calgary but they went down to Edmonton 7-3. The Tregillus Club, from west of the city, played several exhibition games, including a 5-2 loss to the West Calgary Team. A team of Intermediate League all-stars played a game against the Lethbridge team.

During the season the City Club dropped out of the Senior League. Alex Melville's soccer column in a local paper said that there were sixty teams in the Calgary area playing association football with close to 1,200 players.

The Calgary Callies edged out Hillhurst for the city championship and the D.E. Black Cup. Then in Bennett Shield competition the Callies defeated Lethbridge 1-0 with Williams scoring the goal. The Calgary Callies then met the Edmonton Callies in the provincial final and the right to hold the Bennett trophy. However Calgary was weak in goal, short on defense, and the Edmonton team won a 2-0 victory. The Callies closed out their season with a fall benefit game against Hillhurst.

On March 13 of 1913 the New British Rugby Team was organized at a meeting held in the Y.M.C.A. R.B. Bennett was named honorary president. A month later the Alberta-British Rugby Union announced that the Pirates, Canadians, Wanderers, and Harlequins would each play six games at Mewata during the league schedule.

The Alberta University team was admitted to provincial senior rugby ranks to compete in league play with the Calgary Tigers and the Edmonton Eskimos. After a month of practise the Calgary line-up was decided on as: backs—Hickey, Wark, Dobbie, McEnteer; Quarter—Ross; and a front wall of Woods, Gordon, McHugh, Watt, Whitaker, Gibson, O'Dell, White and Fitzgibbons.

In September the Tigers topped the Edmonton Eskimos 16-6. The same month the Hamilton Tiger Cats visited Calgary and defeated the Tigers 19-2 in what was not considered a good game of football. Several fights developed during the encounter.

The provincial championship game was held at Red Deer in November with the Eskimos coming out on top of the Tigers by a 10-7 score. Later Regina defeated Edmonton 19-7 to knock the Esks out of further competition.

In Calgary intercollegiate competition Mount Royal won the senior rugby competition with two wins, the Collegiate was one and one, and the University lost both games. The Junior Tigers had wanted to enter this division but were not allowed to do so. The Collegiate topped the intermediate division with four wins, Mount Royal was two and two, and W.C.C. lost all four games. In junior play the Collegiate twice won over Western Canada College.

The High School rugby team had posted five wins before they went down to defeat to an Edmonton team. In a game played at Red Deer the Edmonton Civics defeated Mount-Royal 8-1 for the provincial intermediate championship, but Miller of Mount Royal proved to be the best player in the game. Calgary defeated a Varsity team 25 to 3 to win the provincial junior championship. Half back Fraser punted for an average of over forty yards to help push the Edmonton team back. Other Calgary players were: Quarter—McTeer; Halves—Scotty McLaws, Miller, Wright, MacMillan; forwards—Covey, Clark, Kilbride, MacMillan, Wright, Noble, Louden, G. Langford, Halliday, and W. Langford.

J. Gow was the president of the Calgary soccer organization for 1914. There was $236 left in the treasury from the 1913 season, a considerable increase from the $6 balance of 1910. Many of the players kept in shape by playing indoor soccer at the Y.M.C.A. during the winter months.

The senior clubs each played twelve games each with the schedule completed by late July. The Callies and Hillhurst had played two ties in their first two encounters. In their final league game the Callies were leading 1-0 when referee Dalgetty lost his head and kicked the ball which was close to the Hillhurst goal. Although the ball would not have gone in if he had not touched it, and the rules stated that a ball was still in play when it touches the referee, Dalgetty awarded a goal to the Callies, then called the game when there was still six minutes of playing time left.

Callies won the league with ten wins and two ties, followed by Hillhurst, C.P.R., Post Office, and Tynesiders. Admission charge for senior game was now 25¢.

The Dominion Football Association said in July that just because a team won the provincial soccer championship it did not give them the right to participate in the Connaught Cup competition. City footballers felt that the D.F.A. was a poorly run organization and as a result no Calgary club would enter into play for the Connaught Cup which now took the place of the People's Shield. The Connaught Cup was won by the Norwood Wanderers of St. Boniface.

There was international competition at the senior level with Scotland and England drawing three-all in a June game at Hillhurst. In the following month the Scottish boys doubled England 4-2 before a crowd of over 1,000 spectators to capture the Lawson Cup. Other games saw the Sons of Ireland and Wales play to a one-all draw, and Scotland defeated Ireland. Friendly matches were played between the P. Burns team and Western Woodworkers, Mountview played the Moose team at the Mountview grounds, and the Mounted Police tangled with the Firemen at the Barracks grounds.

A Calgary select team travelled to Edmonton to earn a one-all draw with a goal by Trevor Williams coming on a penalty kick. Calgary won 3-0 in a return match played at Hillhurst Park. The Calgary selects included: Gillhooley, Haig, MacLean, Feeney, Williams, Nesbit, Adamson—all from the Callies, and Melville, Anderson, Mortimer, and Wakelyn from Hillhurst. President Gow of Calgary and the Edmonton president acted as linesmen for these two games.

The Callies defeated a Calgary picked team 4-0, the game played at Hillhurst where it was possible to charge an admission. Five gold watches were awarded to the winners of the five-a-side soccer tournament at the Caledonian games. A late season saw the Senior League all-stars defeat the Commercial League all-stars 2-0. In September soccer as well as rugby were included in an athletic carnival held in aid of the Patriotic Fund.

Besides the Victoria, Mewata and Hillhurst pitches, soccer was also played at the Barracks, 103rd, Mountview, Brewery and W.C.C. fields. A Calgary and Edmonton City and District Football Referees Association was formed during the year. Referees for the senior and intermediate level games generally received two dollars a match.

In Black Cup competition the Callies beat Shephard 6-0. The country team played well until Watson, their best player, was badly hurt. In the semi-finals the Rangers and Hillhurst played two draw games before the Rangers won 2-1. In the other semi-final Callies won 2-0 over a combined Post Office—C.P.R. team. In the city final the Caledonians scored two goals without a reply from the Rangers.

Lethbridge, who had beaten the Medicine Hat team, were to be the Callies next opponents. However they declined to play the Calgary champions. The Callies were now matched with Red Deer, but the central Alberta team scratched from the match. The Edmonton champions had formerly said they were not interested in the provincial playdowns, but now expressed an on but then off interest. The game did not materialize and the Edmonton Callies were asked to return the Bennett Trophy to the donor.

During the league play the Intermediate League was divided into two sections, with Parkhill, 103rd, Pro-Cathedral, Postal United, Neilsons, West of England, and News United in A section, and Rangers, Moose, West Calgary, Triangle, Trinity, Royals and Sons of England in B Section. In league play the Rangers goalie Robertson was unscored upon. However in the league finals a fired up News United team upset them 6-3 to capture the intermediate title. In September the News United played the Callie team and were actually leading 3-1 at half time, however the Callies scored three unanswered goals in the second half to go ahead 4-3.

The City Junior League was composed of the Bishop Pinkham, Calgary Juniors, Callie Thistles, Newsboys, Grandview, C.P.R., Ogden Aprentices, and the B.F.C. soccer clubs. Early in the season competition was held for the R.F. Richardson Trophy, with the Apprentices defeating the Thistles for this cup. In late fall, after the final game was twice postponed either from mud or snow, the Thistles defeated Bishop Pinkham 1-0 to capture the Alex Martin Shield. L. Irwin of the B.P.C. club was the leading junior scorer with fifteen goals which earned him the McFarlane Cup. Alex Melville was considered the star of the league. In junior exhibition play the Scots and English twice tangled with the Scots coming out on top. In late fall the Junior Soccer League formed a basketball team called the Soccerites.

The 1914 Church Soccer League had a seventy game schedule and included teams from Tuxedo Methodist, Pro-Cathedral, Bankview, St. Paul's Presbyterian, First Baptist, Crescent Heights Baptist, Central Methodist, Trinity Methodist, and All-Saints Churches. The league championship was won by the First Baptist Church. The Commercial League included teams from: Shelley's Bakery, Pryce Jones, Fremans, P. Burns, City Hall, Great West Saddlery, Department of Natural Resources, Hudson Bay Company, Tramways, Western Woodworkers, and Ontario Laundry. A league all-star team was chosen to travel to Lethbridge for a game. On the line south of Calgary the Southwestern Football League included Claresholm, High River, Macleod, Cayley, and Stavely.

There were fifteen teams in the C and D divisions of the school soccer leagues in the fall. Connaught won the C Division championship and Victoria captured the D Division trophy. An intercollegiate game saw the High School trounce the University 7-1.

In terms of attendance the 1914 soccer season was less successful than in recent years. When the outbreak of the war came in 1914 the Calgary Association had 1,034 players registered in its organization. Before the war was over 936 of these men and boys had become part of the Canadian Europe Force or the Imperial Forces.

During the summer a Calgary team became part of the Alberta British Rugby Union, however the influence of the European hostilities kept competition to a local level.

Calgary rugby enthusiasts met in February with President Dr. Mason in the chair. It was decided that a Calgary team would be chosen by a committee. A provincial rugby meeting was held in Red Deer in September. There it was decided that, due to the influence of the war, there would not be a senior rugby schedule for Alberta, but that home and home series be played. It was decided the intermediate and juniors teams would now use the snap-back system for putting the ball into play. Although Calgary had only one senior team, Edmonton had four senior clubs including the Edmonton Canoe Club, South Side Athletic Association, Eskimos, and the University. Bob Pearson's revision of the Dominion rugby rules came off the press.

The Tigers practised every night under coach Downey Gleason. If the weather was unfavourable the team practised in the Y.M.C.A. gym. In October the Tigers played an exhibition game against Mount Royal College, winning only by a 7-2 score. Five of the points came as a result of a Mount Royal fumble late in the game. Up until that point the school boys had played equal to Calgary's seniors.

Calgary senior rugby people attempted to get an Edmonton team to play in Calgary on Thanksgiving Day, but not one of Edmonton's teams was interested. Red Deer was busy molding a team together, but they did not feel yet ready to play. Word was received from W.R.U. officials that unless a champion was decided the province would not be allowed to compete in the Union playoffs. About this time former Calgarian rugby player Frank McHugh, now of Gleichen, came up with a certified cheque for $225 to cover the cost of the championship game if it were played at Gleichen. Some Calgary military personnel were advocating the abolishment of sports contests while the European war was on.

In early November the Tigers travelled to Edmonton and were defeated by the University team 3-0. In the second game, played in Calgary, the University were again the winners, this time by a 17-15 score—winning the series 20-15. Calgary made many mistakes in the second half of their home game, and if it had not been for the excellent running and kicking of halfback Fraser, borrowed from the C.C.I. team for the game, the score would have been much worse for Calgary. Other Calgary players were: flying wing—Hickey; backs—Wark, Overman, McCaig; quarter—Ross; Scrimmage—Watts, Spence, Woods; inside wings— Barrett, Odell; mid-wings—Whitaker, Priestley; out wings—Fitzgerald, Harrison. Officials were Pearson and Hardisty.

School rugby practises began early in September, and it was decided that the students would give the snap-back system of putting the ball into play a try. Two positions on a team were done away with, bringing the number of positions down to twelve. A rugby club was formed at the Alexandra High School. At Bridgeland School, across the Bow River, rugby was introduced into the sports program by coach Nolan.

The first school rugby game of the season was a private exhibition for the benefit of the Board of Governors of the Interscholastic Athletic Association. The High School, coached by Joe Price, led the Varsity team 23-0 at the end of the first half, which had been played using the snap-back system. In the second half the snap-back system was not used and coach Priestly's Varsity crew held the school boys scoreless and earned their only point. Rev. Pearson was the referee for this game which was played on the W.C.C. field. The High School earned another league victory over the Calgary University team as they thrashed them 52-0 in a game played at Hillhurst Park.

A total of fifteen games were scheduled in interscholastic play with Mount Royal, Varsity and the High School in senior play, Alexandra, W.C.C. and the High School fielding teams in the intermediate and junior divisions. The High School, with great kicking by Captain G. McTeer, came from behind in the last three minutes of the final game to defeat Mount Royal 7-5 and take the senior championship. In the junior division—that of 125 pounds or less, the High School beat W.C.C. 35 to 5 to take that championship.

Plans were made for the High School seniors to play the Edmonton Civics at Hillhurst Park using Canadian scrimmage rules, but the game never came off. Instead a game was arranged with the Edmonton University intermediates at Hillhurst Park. The game day was snowy and cold. In the morning prior to game time the field was swept clear of snow, but the wind continued to blow wet snow over the grid. During most of the game the ball was encased in ice. The High School boys were outweighed, but they outplayed the Varsity to come out ahead 7-1.

James MacMillan, star of the 1913 High School rugby team, died of typhoid fever during the fall.

Lacrosse

Lacross originated from the old Indian game of baggataway, although this game was not a pastime among the plains Indians that inhabited the area that was to become Alberta. The French played this game with the Indians in the late 1700's in order to maintain harmony between the two cultures. the French called the game la crosse because the curved web stick used by the Indians was like the bishop's crozier. The activity was first adopted by English settlers in the 1840's.

In 1844 seven members of the Montreal Olympic Club were defeated by five Indians in a game of lacrosse. When the Montreal Lacrosse Club was formed in 1856 its members utilized a wider rectangular net that proved its superiority. By 1860 other clubs had been organized in Ottawa, Quebec and Toronto. Twenty-eight clubs were represented when a meeting took place in 1867 to form the National Lacrosse Association of Canada.

The same year it was to become Canada's national game. The first inter-provincial game, between Ontario and Quebec, was organized. In Montreal a crowd reported in excess of 5,000 people watched the town team lose to an Indian team.

Prior to 1888 matches were declared when a team scored three goals. Games could go on for hours. In 1888 the North American Lacrosse Association set a limit of two hours for a game, and the Canadian Lacrosse Association adopted this rule three years later. During this era the J. Allan Lowe Cup was emblematic of the championship of Canada.

Lacrosse was first reported to have been played in Manitoba in 1871, and shortly after this the Prince Rupert Lacrosse Club was formed at Fort Garry. A lacrosse club was formed at Winnipeg in 1876. In 1882 lacrosse equipment was available in Edmonton, and several pickup games were played there during the summer. The following March the Edmonton Lacrosse Club was organized, however it disbanded in 1885 due to lack of competition.

The Calgary Lacrosse Club was organized in 1884, with Captain Boynton serving as the club's first president. The club's membership swelled to thirty, and practises were held on many evenings on the field behind King's store. Games between the club members were held periodically on weekends, and on several occasions competition took place between the citizens and the police. The game did not appear to play that an important a role in the recreation of Calgarians.

After lagging interest the Calgary Lacrosse Club was re-organized in 1887. Mr. Boag, a teacher who was to be elected the club's president, organized a lacrosse meeting at the school house. A practise ground was secured on the prairie to the south of the railway tracks. Mr. Boag introduced the game to some of the older students in the school. The Calgary club operated in a local manner for several years.

In 1890 the lacrosse club entered into an agreement to rent the grounds of the Calgary Amateur Athletic Union for its use during the season at a cost of twenty-seven dollars. Mr. Welsh handled the club's business.

By 1890 several games of lacrosse had been played on the Lethbridge town square, and in that year a lacrosse club was organized in the southern town. In June the Calgary Lacrosse Club travelled to Lethbridge where they played to a one-all tie with the hometown team. The fact that they did not win came as a surprise to the Calgary players, who then were given great encouragement to practise in order to prove themselves in a rematch that was set for August 21 at the C.A.A.U. grounds.

Although it was a wet and windy day 350 spectators braved the elements to see the lacrosse clubs of Calgary and Lethbridge in action. C. MacMillan, formerly of the Winnipeg 90th Lacrosse club, acted as referee; H. Bently and A. Braithwaite shared the Lethbridge umpire duties, while Calgary's were handled by R. Fletcher. H. McCullouch was Calgary's field captain.

Calgary's starting lineup was: goal—Currier; point—Rankin; coverpoint—P. McNamarra; defense—Field, Hardisty, Baetz, Tarrant; centre—Doyle; home-field—Burges, Asselstine, T. West; outside home—A.E. Swift; inside—A.W. Swift.

Lethbridge won the toss and chose to throw with the wind. They outplayed Calgary and scored at the five minute mark and then again twelve minutes later. Calgary protested that the ball had passed six inches above the flags, but this was of no avail. McNamarra went in goal for Calgary; play resumed, and a scrimmage in front of the Lethbridge goal resulted in a score for Calgary! The home team took charge and A. Swift scored to even the score. The fifth match was interrupted by a rain break, but then went on for 33 minutes before Swift scored again, and Calgary captured the competition three matches to two.

It may be said at this time that a match was won by scoring the first goal, rather than playing for a definite period of time.

Following the clean and splendidly fought game each team gave three cheers for the other club and the same for the referee.

There was a great deal of betting on the game, and it was estimated that $1,500 changed hands; the money staying in Calgary. After the first two goals the Lethbridge backers offered large odds.

The same summer the Calgary crew accepted a challenge to play a combined Vancouver-Victoria team that was planning a trip to play in Toronto, however this trip never came about. The Calgary team considered themselves champions of the North West for the 1890 year.

Thirty five members attended the March, 1891 Calgary Lacrosse Club organizational meeting in Mr. West's room of the Alexander Block. Included in the slate of officers were: Honourary President J. Lougheed, President F. Glanville, and Captain A.E. Swift. The club colours were to be maroon and navy. It was hoped to have three practises a week as soon as the ground was ready.

On the Queen's birthday the lacrosse club, minus several of their best players, travelled to Lethbridge for a game. Plans were made for a return match in Calgary, but this was to become a game of letters and words as a date to play could not be settled. Calgary thought the game was to be June 29th, but Lethbridge said that this was because it was the only time that Calgary would be able to get five import players, and that was the only way they could win. The whole affair provided great fodder for the press.

In June club secretary T. West was knocked unconscious when he ran into a pole adjacent to the field while chasing a ball in play. He was carried to the nearby orphanage building, where it was past midnight that he regained consciousness.

In another practise Mr. Kellog of the H.B.C. had a sliver from another player's stick enter one side of his foot and stick out the other side.

In August the Lethbridge paper reported that a Calgary lacrosse club had travelled to the west coast to lose to both the Vancouver and New Westminster clubs.

J. Morris, who formerly played in Lethbridge, introduced the game to Fort Macleod residents who organized a club in 1892.

The Calgary Lacrosse Club held its 1892 organizational meeting in April at the Royal Hotel with twenty members present. J. Bannerman and W. Grant joined Lougheed in serving as honourary presidents, and J. Glanville became the new club president, with W. Grant also serving as field captain. Practises were set on the field just west of the new Alexander Block. Later they were moved west of the Frontier Stables, with play scheduled for three evenings a week. J. Nattras, a newcomer to Calgary, proved to be an exceptional goalie. Scratch matches were played during the summer months.

The Edmonton lacrosse team came to Calgary for a game during the Fall Exhibition. The Calgary boys were confident of success, but the final result was somewhat of a surprise all round.

Calgary's lineup included: goal—G. Nattrass; Dr. MacDonald, Vincent, Baetz, Creagh, Thom, Kelleg, Short, comer, Southom, Swift, and Meldroum.

After a busy twenty minutes of play Swift succeeded in passing the ball between the flags and Calgary led 1-0. During the next ten minutes Calgary pressed, then Southom scored. Tremendous passing on the part of the Calgary players helped Swift to score his second goal one minute later. During the following scrimmage Meldrum was hurt and left the field, but on his return he secured the ball and scored—time seven minutes. The final tally was Calgary—4, Edmonton—0.

The game was marked by an absence of brutal play, although former Calgarian McNamara, who was a standout for Edmonton, had his shoulder dislocated, but he was not aware of it until after the game. Nattras was a standout in goal for Calgary. The Fire Brigade band was in attendance for this event.

Edmonton challenged the Calgary team to a return match in Edmonton, but the Calgary team did not raise the necessary funds to pay for the trip.

A lacrosse game was played at the Calgary A.A.U. grounds before winter had ended in 1893, as Ed Vincent's team beat Bernie Swift's team by several goals.

In early April members of Calgary's lacrosse fraternity held an organizational meeting in Tarrant's and Kerr's Tailor Shop. Dr. McDonald was elected club president and team captain, while H. McCullough was to serve as field captain. The club was planning to affiliate with the Calgary Athletic Association. Two playing teams, the Town and the Fire Brigade, would be drawn from the club's membership.

New players in Calgary whose lacrosse skills were adding to the quality of the game included: Dr. O'Sullivan, Dr. Wells, T. Tarrant, H. Doll, C. Marshall, F. McNeil, W. Livingstone, G. Robinson, G. Henderson, E. King, and P. Goderath.

On the Queen's birthday the town team, captained by Dr. McDonald, and T. Nattrass's Fire Brigade team played to a one-all tie before a good holiday crowd. Hardisty scored for the town, and Meldrum evened up the score for the Fire Brigade.

A game with the Lethbridge team was scheduled to take place during the Calgary Fair. The Calgary players began practising in earnest each evening on the athletic grounds for this important event.

The contest was said to be the hardest fought game ever witnessed in Calgary, with the actual play lasting two hours. Calgary played a better team game, outmatching Lethbridge and winning on their merits. However too often Calgary's wild shooting mean that possible goals were misses and Lethbridge would take possession of the ball. The final score was Calgary 4, Lethbridge 0, with the goals coming at intervals of 10, 4, 47 and 57 minutes.

Nattras, McDonald, Vincent, Meldrum, Baetz, Watson, Tarrant and Wells were the pick of the Calgary team, while Galligher was the best player on the Lethbridge squad.

The Calgary club and the Medicine Hat club met in a lively match in June. Another game took place in Calgary between the Town team and a team composed of military personnel.

Victoria, the B.C. champions, wired the Calgary team that they would play in Calgary for a guarantee of $200, but club secretary Vincent wired back that this amount was too much. During the summer the club held an entertainment evening, when various members demonstrated skills in tumbling, fencing and other individual athletic skills.

In a game played on Arbour Day, 1894, the Town team took a 4-2 win from the Fire Brigade team. Before the season was over these two clubs met six times, coming out even in the end. However the Calgary team had little success against Lethbridge which took home the Calgary Hardware Trophy. Lethbridge did not lose a game in this era defeating, besides Calgary, Medicine Hat, Fort Macleod and Regina.

The 1895 Calgary lacrosse organizational meeting was held in March in the firehall with Cappy Smart chairing the meeting. G. Leeson was elected president, and E. Vincent was to be the team captain for the following year. The club was in the hole financially, as many of the members had not even paid their dollar membership fee for the year previous. This was to be an indication of the interest and success of the sport of lacrosse in Calgary for the next several years.

During the years 1895 through 1900 the only lacrosse games played in Calgary were pick-up games between local players. During this period lacrosse in the province suffered from lack of interest and competition. The police in Lethbridge formed a club, but this had the effect of weakening the town club. In the north country Strathcona had put together a lacrosse team.

The lacrosse ball throw for distance was part of Calgary athletic competition during this era. In 1895 Dominion Day competition C. Marsh won first place and three dollars with a throw of 255 feet. The following year E. Vincent topped seven entries with a distance of 317 feet. This mark was not eclipsed until 1900 when J. MacMillan got off a tremendous throw of 110½ yards.

By 1901 there was renewed interest in the sport of lacrosse in Alberta. Much of this arose because of the great number of men who had played this sport in the east were now living in Alberta. In early spring Medicine Hat's lacrosse backers proposed an Alberta lacrosse league that could include teams from Calgary, Edmonton, Lethbridge, Medicine Hat and Fort Macleod.

Dr. O'Sullivan earned the position of president of Calgary's lacrosse club for the 1901 season. Practises were shifted to the old athletic grounds south of the tracks.

A lacrosse game between Medicine Hat and Calgary was part of the sports program held at the agriculture grounds on May 24. Calgary's team lacked offense, and Medicine Hat's players were on the attack most of the time. Calgary could only manage one goal to their opponents' five, and each of the Medicine Hat players went home with a medal. R. Rose of Vancouver won the lacrosse ball throw with a distance of 289 feet.

Earlier in the month Calgary's E. Marshall and Dr. O'Sullivan had attended a Territories lacrosse convention in Regina. W. White of Regina became the president of the Territorial Lacrosse league, and Dr. O'Sullivan attaining the position of second vice-president. A trophy, valued at fifty dollars, emblematic of the Territorial Lacrosse Association, was presented to the group by Winnipeg's W. Taaffe.

On May 25 representatives of Albertans interested in lacrosse met in Calgary to form the Western Territorial Lacrosse League. (W.T.L.L.) The Saskatchewan and Manitoba teams made up the eastern division. Mayor Findlay of Medicine Hat received the vote for president, and Calgary's Dr. MacDonald became a member of the council. Plans were for a home and home series, or a six game schedule for each of the teams from Calgary, Medicine Hat and Lethbridge. All players had to be registered with the W.T.L.L. or they would not be allowed to play.

The Taaffe Trophy was brought to Calgary and sat on exhibit in the window of the Calgary Clothing Company store.

Unfortunately much of the effort and planning that went into the W.T.L.L. was for not as travel expenses brought about an incomplete schedule. Medicine Hat claimed the western championship by default, then travelled to British Columbia where they defeated Nelson and then lost to Grand Forks. To earn the Taaffe Trophy, Medicine Hat defeated Wolsely, the eastern champions, by a 9-0 score.

The Calgary Lacrosse Club held its organizational meeting for 1902 in the firehall. Cappy Smart was elected club president and J. McCartney team captain.

Pat Burns had said that he would donate a trophy for city play, and as a result of this became an honourary president. Membership was set at a dollar for actives and 50¢ for honourary. The club colours of garnet and white were retained.

In April the city lacrosse players decided to form the Calgary Athletic Association. This was done in order to allow members of both the City and the newly formed Y.M.C.A. team to compete in the W.T.L.L. The club fee to belong to the association was set at ten dollars. Dr. O'Sullivan became its founding president, and then he was off to Regina to a meeting of the Territories Lacrosse League held in Regina.

A Calgary lacrosse team, early 1900's.

Calgary's first game of the season was an exhibition match between the City and Y.M.C.A. teams, but played at a new location—the Exhibition Grounds. Brown and Davis were field captains, and W. McDavidson refereed the match. The City team scored first, then the Y team came back with three goals to end the first half. The second half got very rough, but there was not any further scoring.

On the Queen's birthday the Y.M.C.A. team, with superior passing, defeated the City team 6-3 in the first match towards the Burn's Cup. The City team's lineup included: Davis, Cardell, E. Dodd, J. Crosse, H. Towle, Jackson, Taylor, B. Towle, A. Marshall, Brown, McRae and King, while those playing for the Y team were: Marshall, Lowers, Willett, Johnson, Stanley, Jacques, Hornerbrook, Hanna, McCulloch, Bick, Watson and Kidney.

The W.T.L.L. schedule was set up so that members Calgary, Lethbridge and Medicine Hat would play four games against each of the other teams. Unfortunately very wet weather was the main factor that played havoc with the schedule.

On June 4 Medicine Hat met Calgary in an evening fixture at the Exhibition Grounds. The visitors had the game down to a science and defeated Calgary 6-2.

The hometown players were good individual players but a lack of combination was their weakness. Calgary's lineup included: E. Dodd, Lowes, Willette, D. Dodd, J. Cardell, Taylor, Hanna, McCullough, Allan, Pentland and M. Cardell; Bryan was the game referee.

During June and July several other scheduled league games were not played. A lacrosse game was planned as part of the August Coronation Day, but this also did not come about, although there was a lacrosse ball throw, won by C. Marshall with a distance of 320 feet. The Nelson Lacrosse Club wanted to play in Calgary during the fall, but Calgary was not organized to handle such a venture.

Lethbridge also played with other centres in what was known as the Crossnest Pass League. In this competition they won the Levasseur Cup in both 1902 and 03. Medicine Hat claimed the Alberta title, and then they defeated Moose Jaw 3-2 to claim the Taaffe Trophy for the second year. Four Medicine Hat players had Peard for a last name.

In September the Nelson Lacrosse Club inquired about playing a match in Calgary, but this never came about. Calgary, Lethbridge and Medicine Hat made up, on paper anyway, the W.T.L.L. in 1903. The Hat claimed the title, and they then defeated Souris 4-1 to retain the Taaffe Trophy.

The Alberta Union Lacrosse league and the Crowsnest Pass League had an interlocking schedule in 1904. Red Deer's club played challenge matches with Edmonton. Play in Calgary was limited to pick up matches played on the Victoria School grounds. Calgarians, during this era, were basically baseball orientated. Lorne Orr won the lacrosse ball throw at Victoria Day sports program with a distance of 306 feet.

In the spring of 1905 members of the lacrosse fraternity held an organizational meeting in the Alberta Hotel. Practises and pick up games were held during the season, but many players were discouraged by the poor turnout, and although several challenges were received, only a visit by Edmonton's team was finalized.

A lacrosse sports day was held by the club on the C.A.A.U. grounds. Dr. O'Sullivan won the 100 yard dash. G. Robinson took top honours in shooting a lacrosse ball at a target competition, and Smith proved that he could throw a lacrosse ball further than any other Calgarian. A much improved Fire Brigade team defeated the City team by four goals to one.

The Lieutenant Governors medal was offered for the Territorial championship.

In September of 1905 the Calgary Lacrosse Club travelled to Revelstoke for a Labour Day game. The Calgary players were humiliated by their 12-2 loss to the hometown team.

The Crowsnest Pass League folded. Many persons blamed its demise on the fact that eastern ringers had been brought in by some teams.

The 1906 Calgary lacrosse organizational meeting was held at the Grand Union Hotel in May. Elected president Alderman Stuart said that practises would be held on the Victoria School grounds, but the club was hoping to utilize Victoria Park. There was talk of an Alberta-Kootenay league, as interest in lacrosse was up considerably in that part of the country.

Group of students playing lacrosse at Western Canada College, 1906.

Plans were made for the Calgary team to play in High River on the Queen's birthday. The team was accompanied by the 15th Lighthorse band, however the rains came, and the game was not played.

In June the Intermediates played a game against the Western Canada College team on the College grounds, and they defeated the college boys ten goals to three. McQueen and McHugh were the pick of the Intermediates, and Fulljames, Rankin and McGuinnes were the best college players.

The High River lacrosse team came to Calgary in July and were defeated by the hometeam by an 8-1 score. Curliss was the star of the winners, who proved to be a fast team and good stick handlers. Other members of the Calgary team were: Powell, Clark, McDonald, McLeod, Thorburn, Ross, Graham, Ready, Dodd, Flummerfelt and Laing. Robie proved to be a capable referee. The High River players acknowledged the skills of the Calgary players, but felt the city was completely lacking in hospitality, as they were provided with neither transportation to the playing field nor board.

Calgary played a return game in High River in August and came away with a 5-1 win in what was considered a good game. The following week the Calgary aggregate travelled to Lethbridge where they lost 5-1. A strange turn of events happened when Ross, who was thought to have travelled down to play for the Calgary team, came out on the playing field in a Lethbridge uniform. The hometown team was reported to have several other ringers in their lineup.

In September the Calgary team travelled to Revelstoke for a Labour Day game, but they were badly outclassed, losing 10-2.

The Board of Trade rooms were utilized by the Calgary lacrosse fraternity for an April, 1907 organizational meeting. Dr. Hicks, who chaired the meeting, reported that ten provincial centres were interested in promoting lacrosse, and it would be feasible to utilize the provincial championship trophy again. Letters were to go out to these centres to try to promote a provincial lacrosse association. The club reported a deficit of eleven dollars from the previous years.

Alf Moodie was elected the club president, and the new Honourary President was M. McCarthy, MP. A. MacDonald was the team captain, while W. Stokes served as manager. The coaching staff was bolstered by new Calgarians Jim Sewell, F. Knight and C. Mitchell; all three with considerable experience with top eastern clubs.

Further to the thought of an Alberta lacrosse Association Senator Deveber of Lethbridge called a May 27 meeting in Calgary of all groups in the province interested in the sport. The meeting proved successful, and the Alberta Amateur Lacrosse League was formed with Senator Deveber as its president. Besides an executive, the group set up a judicial committee to settle disputes, and Calgary's McCarthy served on this group. Membership fees were set at twenty five dollars a club.

The Legislator's Cup, also known as the Deveber and the Alberta Cup, was offered for lacrosse competition in Alberta. The funds to pay for the trophy had been collected by Dr. Deveber who convinced 25 Alberta Legislative members to each contribute five dollars towards the purchase of the trophy.

The Lethbridge, Medicine Hat and High River clubs formed the southern division of the A.A.L.A., while Edmonton, Strathcona and Calgary composed the northern divisions. The Canadian Amateur Lacrosse Association's rules were basically used in Alberta. The schedule called for four games against each of the other two teams in the respective divisions.

Calgary's intermediate team journeyed to Medicine Hat on Victoria Day where they lost to the hometown team by a 13-4 score in a clean, fast game.

Lacrosse was becoming very popular at Western Canada College. A new Calgary club, the West End Lacrosse Club, practised on the field at Eighth Avenue and Eighth Street West.

An all-Canadian team from eastern Canada played exhibition games in western Canada while on their way to a tour of Australia. Several of the Calgary players played with the Medicine Hat team in its game with the all-star club.

In June a crowd of over 600 spectators saw the Calgary team, playing in their new blue and white uniforms, lose to the visiting Edmonton team by a close 7-5 score. The Calgary players started agressively, but they lacked conditioning, and Edmonton scored four goals in the third quarter. Calgary's marksmen were Anderson and Ready, with two goals each, and Sewell. Other players in the Calgary lineup were: Powell, Powers, Reynolds, McLeod, Ross, Harrison, McDonell, Curliss, Lang, McQueen and Bowles. McLennan was the referee.

Calgary travelled north, and with a display of poor passing, lost to Strathcona 6-1; Anderson being the lone Calgary scorer. However the next day in Edmonton they redeemed themselves by beating Edmonton 4-1.

Moir, an addition to Calgary's lineup, starred as Calgary held the visiting Strathcona team to a 0-0 draw. The Strathcona team had six penalties varying from two to five minutes in length.

In one game between Edmonton and Strathcona a fight broke out and the game ended in a free-for-all. Boxer Mullen said that, although he had never played lacrosse in his life he felt that with his skills he would be a good lacrosse player, on the basis of what he had witnessed during the game.

The High River team visited Calgary for an exhibition game, and Calgary defeated them 6-3 in what was termed a poor exhibit of lacrosse, but an easy win for Calgary. Ticket prices for these senior games was 25¢.

On the first weekend in August Calgary's lacrosse team again travelled north, and with strong playing in the fourth quarter McLeod and Dodd scored to tie the Edmonton team 2-2. The following day Calgary's players played a snappy and aggressive game to defeat Strathcona 2-1.

Calgary's lineup was bolstered by the addition of Dodd and "Mac" Dunn for its game with Strathcona at Victoria Park. Many of the stores closed early to allow staff and owners to attend the early evening game. The game was almost cancelled as the teams could not agree on an acceptable referee, but they finally settled on Edmunds from Okotoks.

1,200 fans watched a glorious battle as Calgary won 4-2, with Dodd scoring three goals and Curliss notching the other. The score would have been much higher except for the outstanding work of Strathcona goalie Dummy Malonne.

South of Calgary Nanton beat High River in an exhibiton game.

Edmonton's team did not show up and defaulted in the last league game to Calgary, however this meant a loss of close to $500 in gate receipts to the Calgary club.

The lacrosse council decided that rules must be followed and awarded Calgary the Northern division title. Calgary was now to meet Lethbridge in a home and home series for the Alberta championship. Arranging playing dates was another matter, and it was not until September 23 that the first game would be played.

In this rough but exciting game played at Victoria Park, Calgary, on goals by Anderson (2) and Dunn defeated Lethbridge 3-1. Many players on both sides were penalized for roughness, and Dunn had two of his upper teeth knocked out. The game was front page news.

The return game in Lethbridge was featured by a second quarter brawl, and there were twenty penalties handed out during the game. However Calgary outclassed Lethbridge, taking a 3-0 win on goals by Dodd (2) and Harrison.

The team arrived back in Calgary on a train drawn by a locomotive decorated with blue and white bunting, lacrosse sticks and brooms; the latter to show that the team had swept all opposition before them. A big crowd greeted the team members as they stepped off the train with the Legislative Assembly Cup. MacDonald was carried off the platform on the shoulders of his fellow workers from the Bell Telephone Company. Calgary had completed a successful lacrosse season.

During the winter the Lacrosse-Hockey Club was formed to operate success-fully in Calgary's ice hockey league.

In an April, 1908 Calgary lacrosse meeting in the Empire Hotel the team decided to join the newly formed Calgary Amateur Athletic Association. An offer was read guaranteeing the Calgary team $400 if they would play in Regina on Victoria Day. J. Mosley was elected club president, and B. Collinson was appointed team manager. Practise grounds were secured on C.P.R. lands on Tenth Avenue and Second Street S.E.

There were many rule changes made at the Alberta Lacrosse Association's annual meeting that saw Mr. Mosley assume the position of secretary-treasurer. Mr. Mosley donated a cup for the new provincial intermediate division. New intermediate teams were formed at Nanton and Pincher Creek.

On Victoria Day Calgary, minus six of its key players, played a fast but unlucky game, outshooting Regina four shots to one, but losing by a lopsided 8-1 score; Stewart being the only goal scorer from Calgary. Later the Calgary team blamed their loss on Regina's rough play.

When the summer army camp was being held in Calgary a team from the Canadian Mounted Rifles played the Calgary Lacrosse Club. Lacrosse practises were moved to the St. Mary's grounds at the Mission. Here a field had been prepared and bleachers to seat a thousand people had been constructed.

Mayor Cameron faced the ball off in Calgary's season opener against Lethbridge. Weight, speed and conditioning helped Calgary to earn a 4-2 win. Stewart scored two goals, and Dunn was a star, both on offense and defense.

Calgary might have scored more goals, but Lethbridge had a fat goalie who wore a baseball chest protector and stopped shots as if he were shedding water. Lethbridge later protested Calgary's use of Dunn, and the game was designated to be replayed.

Calgary travelled to Medicine Hat to earn a 4-1 victory on goals by Jim Sewell—2, Stewart and Ready. Other players in the Calgary lineup were: Munro, King, McDonnell, Harrison, Horrobin, Melrose, Ross, Longfellow, Anderson, and Tansey who alternated with Munro in goal.

The Calgary Intermediates lost to Nanton by a 7-1 score in a fight filled game played in Calgary. Adding to the turmoil was an unruly crowd of spectators. As a result manager Collinson had a difficult time filling a team roster for their game at High River.

Medicine Hat's senior team travelled to Calgary and earned a 7-0 win from a lackadaisical Calgary team. About this time Lethbridge's executive announced a decision to drop their team from league play, as they had lost too many players from their team.

In what was considered to be the best game ever viewed in the city the Calgary team defeated Medicine Hat 3-1. A revamped lineup worked well, and Harrison was the top marksman with two goals. Sewell played well, and Eddie King was tremendous on defense. Peard, in the Medicine Hat net, made many fine saves, and without his good work the score would have undoubtedly been higher.

On August 11 the world champion and Minto Cup holders New Westminster team played in Calgary. The train carrying this team arrived late, but within three minutes of their arrival on the playing field the champions were ready to play. A great crowd, each admitted for a high price of 50¢ a person, filled the bleachers at Victoria Park.

Calgary's team fought hard, with Sewell and Harrison playing extremely well, but New Westminster decisively beating Calgary 6-2. The west coast players said that the Calgary team was first class and were better than the former world champion Shamrocks whom they had just defeated in their trip east.

In Calgary's last game they travelled to the Hat to take a 4-1 win on goals by Ready and Sewell. Medicine Hat protested their loss, claiming that Ready was ineligible because he had lived in Edmonton for two weeks, but the claim was disallowed. Calgary had won three out of the four games with Medicine Hat and were awarded the Alberta championship for 1908.

In a game played at the St. Mary's grounds High River defeated Red Deer 14-1 to take the provincial intermediate title. Mr. Mosley, proprietor of the Dominion Hotel, presented High River with the trophy he had donated.

On Labour Day the High River team played against Calgary in an exhibition game, but they were badly trounced 17-1 before a holiday crowd. Sewell scored five goals and Dunn added four more to pace the Calgary team to victory.

Calgary now felt that they were ready to challenge New Westminster for the Minto Cup. Dr. Hicks was sent to the coast to arrange for a title game, but discussions suggested that a game could not be considered until at least the following spring.

The Canadian lacrosse team, that was to compete in Olympic competition in England, invited Calgary to send a player on this squad. Allen McDonnell was chosen, but he could not leave the city, so Dan McLeod, who played the point position, was sent instead. It was reported that he was a standout player for the team.

Baseball was a more popular game in Alberta during this era, and as a result drew most of the spectator crowd. The lacrosse fields were in poor shape; the use of eastern professionals led to confusing turmoil, and as a result of these factors the sport of lacrosse in Alberta was on the decline.

During the winter the lacrosse fraternity in Calgary formed an ice hockey team to compete in the Calgary hockey league.

The Calgary Lacrosse Club members met in the spring of 1909 at the Elks Club room to formulate plans for the coming season. Dr. Hicks assumed the club presidency, and A. McDonnell was chosen as the team captain. Barney Collinson took over the duties of club secretary and team manager, however he became ill and could not fulfill his duties.

In May the Alberta Lacrosse Association met in Y.M.C.A. parlours, with Dr. Stanley of High River being installed as the association's president. Medicine Hat decided not to enter a team in senior competition, and the province was divided into three intermediate districts, with Calgary, High River and Nanton to play in the Central Division.

Calgary lacrosse boosters were talking in terms of the Minto Cup, but when practises began at Victoria Park it was apparent the players were lacking in enthusiasm. A new athlete in the city, Art Lowes, showed he would be a valuable addition to the team. Regina planned on playing here on their home leg after playing at the coast, but after losing to New Westminster they changed their minds about playing in Calgary.

The lacrosse season was slow to begin, and it was June before any Calgary players were involved in an inter-town game. A group of players, mainly juniors, travelled to High River to play. With just over a minute remaining in the game they were ahead by a 4-2 score, but the hometown boys did not quit, and High River tied up the game before the final whistle blew.

In August Calgary's team, consisting of Powell, Francis, Burns, Hetherington, McDonnell, King, Ross, Melrose, Laing, Ritchie, Ready and Sewell defeated the visiting Edmonton Lacrosse Club by a 6-0 score. Calgary had a good defense and clearly outclassed their opponents. Six different Calgary players figured in the scoring. Mayor Jamieson had faced off the team to start the match. Spectator prices were 25¢, bleacher seats 15¢ extra.

Calgary's executive felt their team was capable of meeting New Westminster for the Minto Cup, and correspondence was sent to the coast in this respect. However when New Westminster said they would meet Calgary in September the Calgary team decided they did not have all their key personnel handy and changed their mind about the challenge. A Montreal team attempted to arrange a game in Calgary, but this did not take place.

Although major competition was lacking in Alberta during the 1909 season, smaller centres, including Raymond, Lacombe, Granum, Taber and Fort Macleod, were playing lacrosse.

There were many new faces at the 1910 lacrosse organizational meeting held in the Dominion Hotel. Chairman Dr. Hicks said that there was room for another Calgary team on the playing scene. Barney Collinson, secretary of Alberta Lacrosse Association, said that he would offer a cup for city lacrosse competition if another team was formed. Later he did donate a cup for the City School Lacrosse League. A great deal of discussion at the meeting revolved around the idea of a professional lacrosse club in Calgary. It was announced that D. Mann of the C:P.R. had donated a $500 cup to be competed for by Canadian amateur lacrosse clubs.

The Alberta Lacrosse Association held its 1910 organizational meeting in High River with President Moir in the chair. It was reported that jeweler Black of Calgary had donated a trophy for lacrosse competition, and Mr. Wright had offered a trophy for intermediate competition.

The executive decided that Alberta amateur clubs could play against professionals without hurting their amateur standing. The provincial senior competition would see Calgary, High River and Lethbridge play a double home and home series against each other.

The city's first lacrosse game of the season saw the new East Calgary team defeat the Bankview boys 6-5 in a game played on the grounds of the Bankview School.

The Calgary Lacross Club team travelled to High River to lose a league game by a 4-2 score. However they protested that one of the High River players was not a resident of that town, and this protest was upheld. Calgary's lineup included three Curliss brothers. In their next game, that took place at Lethbridge, Calgary earned a four-four tie.

Calgary again journeyed down to High River where they lost the protested game 2-1. Instead of taking the train with the team Dan Macleod decided to travel to High River by horse and wagon, however he lost his way and missed the game.

Another new community team, West Calgary, lost to the East Calgary team by a 6-5 score.

Prior to the visit of the High river team a Calgary paper published a photo of the Calgary Lacrosse Club and accompanied it with a lengthy article on this sport. The game was preceded by a parade of automobiles led by a band.

Mayor Jamieson faced the teams off. The game started with clean play, but the situation deteriorated and the game ended in a riot. High River's lineup included players who had been stars in Cornwall and Chicago, and when they took a 4-2 lead they began to stall the play. Calgary began to play very physically, and there were "stitches galore".

Calgary goals were scored by Coulson and Dickie. Other members of the Calgary team were: Belcher, McLeod, Laing, Hetherington, Kent, Tip Tyson, King, Bass, McDonell, O. Curliss, J. Curliss, T. Curliss and Melrose.

When Calgary played a return game at High River the two teams were lectured on the morals of lacrosse before the game started. The Calgary players were not in condition for the very hot day and went down to defeat by a 7-3 score; Dunseath scored two of Calgary's markers.

At Lethbridge Calgary tied the home team 4-4, with Curliss scoring two goals. However in Calgary, Lethbridge played rings around the Bow River boys and took the game by a 5-2 score. Laing and T. Curliss gave Calgary a 2-0 lead, but the team wilted. When Jim Sewell was not at Victoria Park for the start of the game a player dressed in his street clothes went into the lineup, and when Sewell arrived Lethbridge would not let him play.

In local play Sewell refereed as the Central team defeated the East End team 7-6 on the Central's grounds. Norm McLeod played well for the winners. On the East End grounds Central won again, 6-2. Bankview lost 7-0 to the East End and 10-3 to the Centrals.

High River's game at Calgary was rained out, then Calgary claimed that they could not get the High River team to set a date for the game to be played, and another battle of words began.

Intermediate lacrosse in Calgary took another step forward as the Central team travelled south to play Nanton. However, as had often been the case, local lacrosse was started with great enthusiasm that soon diminished.

Early in 1911 Joe Lally, one of Canada's top lacrosse referees, a manufacturer of lacrosse sticks, and the father of school lacrosse, visited the west and Calgary in an effort to promote lacrosse in the schools. Smaller lacrosse sticks were being manufactured now for children. Barney Collinson, one of the driving forces behind the Calgary lacrosse scene, donated a trophy for school competition. Real estate promoter Hugh Smith offered a new trophy for provincial competition at either the amateur or professional level. Later this solid silver cup became known as the Middle West Cup and was for the championship of the prairie provinces.

Fred Gravelle occupied the chair for the annual Calgary lacrosse meeting held in a packed room in the Dominion Hotel. Representatives from four Calgary clubs—St. Mary's, Centrals, Sewells and the Y.M.C.A., were at the meeting. Mr. Ballantyne of the Y.M.C.A. was elected president of the association. It was reported that the champion New Westminster Salmonbellies wanted to play in

Calgary, but later the Alberta A.A.U. said they would not allow Calgary's amateurs to play against them.

A Calgary School Lacrosse Association was organized at a meeting held in the Y.M.C.A. parlours, with W. Patterson of Western Canada College installed as its president. Mount Royal, Central Collegiate, Normal Practise, Victoria, St. Mary's and Haultain Schools competed in the junior divisions, while W.C.C., C.C.I., St. Mary's and the Y.M.C.A. formed teams for the older boys.

In late April Dr. Stanley presided over a disorganized Provincial Lacrosse Association meeting. Mr. Collinson said that the previous year's lacrosse season had been a poor one, and that many of the players could not be considered amateurs. He claimed that every team had players who were being paid for playing.

The Association increased the residence rule from ten to thirty days. Lethbridge, Taber and Medicine Hat composed the leagues southern section, and when Edmonton decided not to field a team only Calgary and High River were left in the northern section.

It was reported that Tommy Burns, former world's champion boxer and now Calgary's team manager, was offered $10,000 to play lacrosse in Vancouver.

Early May saw a first in Calgary lacrosse as a game was played in which all the players were under nineteen years of age, as Western Canada College defeated Central Collegiate 6-5. T. Durn was the umpire and Jim Sewell refereed. Tommy Burns helped to officiate at some of the school games.

The new Mewata playing fields were the location of some 1911 lacrosse games, but competition for the use of fields was stiff at this location as the baseball and football clubs had first call. One of the Calgary newspapers published a weekly lacrosse column.

In early season city play Jim Sewell's team, composed of: Jackson, Hetherington, McPhee, Gray, Kent, English, Cunning, Tansell, Anderson, Halworth, Kyle and Sewell, defeated the Centrals 4-3. Playing for the loses were: Small, Glass, McGuire, Holley, Ritchie, Fitzgibbons, McCoy, Kerr, McLeod, Johns, Hunter and H. Curliss.

McLaren, Sharp, Fullerton, Stagg, Dunlop, Kerr, J. Ross, Murray, Hooper, Ronan, Lunan and D. Ross made up the Y.M.C.A. team, which used its hockey rink to practise on. Although not doing very well in city play the Y team defeated Didsbury 10-3 on three goal performances by Dunlop and Kerr. Later some of the Y players were barred from further league play after they attempted to jump to Sewell's team.

The St. Mary's team, that went on to meet the Central's team in the city final had Dunn, Curliss, Howard, Complain, Hassard, Appleton, Fowers, T. Curliss, Coulson, O. Curliss and Jardine in its lineup.

On Coronation Day the Calgary Lacrosse team defeated High River 8-3 in a rough and fast game. Gate admission charge to senior games had now been raised to 50¢.

St. Mary's, who had earlier defeated Centrals 8-1, tied this team one-one in the final game that had to be called on account of darkness before a winner could be decided. St. Mary's forfeited the replay as they could not get a full team out, and the Centrals claimed the city championship.

At the March 1912 Calgary Lacrosse meeting there were representatives from the St. Mary's, Central, Y.M.C.A., Sewells and Western Canada College clubs. However the Sewells and Y.M.C.A. did not get around to fielding senior teams.

Several days later the School Lacrosse Association held an organizational meeting and elected Mr. Patterson of W.C.C. as its president. Senior clubs were entered from W.C.C., C.C.I., St. Mary's and the Y.M.C.A., while junior teams were formed at Mount Royal, Central, Normal Practise, St. Mary's, Victoria and Haultain Schools.

Jas McQueen was elected president of the Central club, and R.B. Bennett was one of the club patrons.

There was a great deal of talk in the city of a Calgary all-star club playing for the Mann Cup, and some of the better players practised together as the all-star team, but this was as far as the idea got. The idea of a semi-provincial league was discussed, as the Saskatchewan teams wanted to play semi and final games against Albertan teams.

The first lacrosse game of the season took place at the Mewata field as Mount Royal College, led by the five goal effort of Timmins, defeated Central Collegiate 9-3. Western Canada College, led by McKernan, won all their games to take the senior school championship. At a banquet, held in their honour, they were presented with the Collinson Cup. Lacrosse was often played at the college as the senior clubs used their field to practise on. The lacrosse ball throw was included as part of the sports day programs in Calgary schools.

After the Sewells and the Y.M.C.A. clubs dropped out of senior competition the High River club joined the C.L.C. and the Centrals in senior play of the Alberta Amateur Lacrosse Association. Other towns outside of Calgary were not eager to play in a provincial league. Each of the three clubs was to play an unorthodox seven game schedule, and this was to go incompleted.

Calgary Lacrosse Club lost a May 24th exhibition game at High River by a 5-3 score in a clean and fast game. In the league opener Miller, C. Anderson, H. Curliss and J. Ross scored goals as the C.L.C. defeated Centrals 4-1. Other C.L.C. players were: O. Curliss, Dan McLeod, D. Hetherington, J. Curliss, Sorrels, and Powers. Kerr scored the Centrals lone marker. His teammates were: Small, Ritchie, Glass, Cook, McMann, McKellar, Kerr, Fitzgibbons, Dunlop, Orten, Murphy, and Perkins.

Intermediate lacrosse was also played in Calgary with the St. Mary's team generally besting the Central Intermediates.

At Victoria Park the C.L.C. defeated High River 6-4, with H. Curliss leading the way. In the next game at that park the High river team overwhelmed the Centrals 9-2. A new innovation used in this game was the use of numbers on the players' uniforms, with the player's names and numbers listed in a program. The Centrals travelled to High River, and with a disasterous first quarter lost 9-4.

Several league games were rained out. Then the grandstand at Victoria was torn down in preparation for building a new one and this spelled the death of lacrosse in Calgary in 1912. The Calgary Athletic club publically complained about the loss of the playing field, but this was of no avail. When the Calgary clubs had to travel to High River and pay their own expenses without the revenue from home games they just defaulted, and so High River claimed the Alberta championship.

1913 proved to be the dawn of a new era of lacrosse in Calgary. Mac McKinley, president of the Chinooks, was also elected to the association presidency. Pat Burns offered a new trophy for local competition. Optimism abounded at the annual meeting.

The Chinooks got themselves a clubhouse on Seventeenth Avenue, handy to the practise field at W.C.C. Dan McLeod was the team captain.

Seniors W. Laing coached the Western Canada College team and Jake Curliss handled the Central Collegiate boys. W.C.C., with McKernan leading the way captured the senior title, while the High School took junior honours.

In June High River, the previous year's provincial winners, defeated the Chinooks 4-3 at Victoria Park before a large crowd of 1400 people, including many ladies. R.B. Bennett was to handle the face-off, but he never showed up. Harry Curliss scored two of Calgary's goals and Armstrong netted the third marker. Other Calgary players were: O. Curliss, D. McLeod, W. Marshall, Reynolds, Chapman, Armstrong, Melrose, T. Curliss, Powers, Hardine, and Laing.

At High River the Centrals, who were behind 7-0 at the half, lost 14-6 to the hometeam.

The Chinooks were surprised by the Central youngsters who ran them off their feet to take a 3-1 win on two goals by McMillan and one by Kerr. Other Central players were Clark, Pearson, P. Glass, McAlister, Fitzgibbons, E. Glass, McCoy, Henderson, McMann, and O'Hara.

A new baseball park, the Sam Savage Field, was constructed at Victoria Park with a seating capacity for 3000 spectators. The park was opened with a lacrosse game in which the Chinooks took a 6-1 win over High River. Bill Laing proved to be a terror as he scored four goals for the winners. Jake Curliss got a stick across his mouth and lost several teeth.

High River received another surprise as they lost a home game 7-6 to the Centrals. The High River team allowed its players to experiment with different positions, and in quick order Calgary scored several goals. Kerr and MacMillan each potted two goals.

The following week High River took a 2-1 win over the Chinooks in a hard fought game. Former eastern lacrosse star Brick Gordon drove down from Calgary in 90 minutes and arrived at the High River playing field in a cloud of dust. He scored to tie the score, but High River netted another to win the game.

At Victoria Park High River led the Centrals 8-5, however McAllister and Kerr scored in the final minute and High River took a close 8-7 win. Several days later the Centrals were playing fairly equal to the Chinooks, but they suffered a collapse in the last quarter, and the Chinooks scored five quick goals to win 9-1. Jake and Henry Curliss netted most of the goals.

Lacrosse at Victoria Park early 1900's.

High River travelled to Calgary and lost 8-2 in a very hard fought game. Two Calgary players were laid out by swinging sticks, but they got up and went back into the play.

A shorthanded and crippled Central team lost in High River by an 11-4 score. The following week a special train, the Chinook Special, carried 200 fans, each for a $1.25 fare, to High River to view a game that would determine the league championship. Harry Reynolds shone on defense for Calgary, but the seesaw game ended with the Chinooks on the short end of a 5-4 score.

The Centrals and Chinooks played an exhibition game as part of the 1913 Labour Day sports program. Central players then decided that they had had enough lacrosse for the season and they defaulted their last game to High River. This left Chinooks and High River in a tie for the league championship.

The High River executive asked for a sudden death game to be played on a neutral field, such as Okotoks, with neutral referees. League President McKinley ordered the final lacrosse game to be played on the Cochrane polo field.

A four coach train carried close to 300 spectators from High River and Calgary to the playing field, which was situated adjacent to the railroad tracks west of Cochrane. The games' first three periods were scoreless due to the very close checking by players of both teams, but in the fourth quarter Brick Gordon, Jake Curliss and Harry Curliss each scored before MacMillan replied for High River.

Just prior to the first goal "Mac" MacKinley had yelled into his megaphone, "a thousand dollars for a goal", just then Gordon scored! The contest ended in a free-for-all, but Calgary was the winner.

A challenge was sent to Vancouver, the Mann Cup holders, for a title game, however the Vancouver executive said no. Joe Lally, as a cup trustee, said that Vancouver must play Calgary on October first and fourth. However Vancouver again said that they had hung up their sticks for the season and would not play against Calgary. Lally then wired McKinley that the trustees had decided not to force Vancouver to defend the cup again in 1913. Vancouver had promised a title game for Victoria Day of 1914 and Calgary's challenge was to have priority.

It may be said of 1913 that Calgary's lacrosse had been the best organized and supported by more spectators than any year since 1907.

In early 1914 a new Calgary lacrosse club, the Adanacs, was organized from the personnel of the Centrals. Dr. Francis was the club's first president and A. Maclean its manager. Club colours were to be green and white.

At a Calgary School Board meeting Trustee Macdonald made a strong plea to ensure the place of lacrosse in the school sports program. While Joe Lally was in the city to discuss Calgary's Mann Cup challenge he talked to the students in the schools, and this appeared to be a big boost for lacrosse interest in the city. R.B. Bennett, a patron of the Chinooks, wrote from Ottawa, that he would do anything he could to assist the club. Retailer Alex Martin advertised the sale of lacrosse sticks.

In early April the Alberta Lacrosse Association discussed the feasibility of changing the length of the playing field from 120 to 100 yards and going to a ten man team rather than twelve players. It was felt that these changes would make for a faster game with less team expenses.

The University of Calgary team was the only team entered in senior school competition, and so it played only exhibition games. Mount Royal, Collegiate and the Collinson Cup winners Western Canada College played their games at the Mewata field. A public school lacrosse league included teams from Victoria, Haultain, Earl Grey, Sacred Heart, W.C.C. and Central schools.

The Chinooks were hard at practise for their May 24 Mann Cup challenge game in Vancouver. Previous team stars Dunn and Fitzgibbons were again out with the team. In an exhibition game played to help raise funds for their Vancouver trip only 100 fans came out to see the Chinooks beat the newly formed Adanacs 12-7. Team members then had to begin a daily canvas to raise the necessary funds for their trip.

The Adanacs were challenged by the Medicine Hat club, but the game was never played.

Aubrey Curliss, McLeod, Hetherington, Reynolds, Miller, McPhee, Melrose, Armstrong, Jake Curliss, Allan Kerr, Andrew Russell, Marshall and Bill Russell of the Chinooks boarded the train for Vancouver. Brick Gordon and Bill Laing could not get away from work. When they arrived at the coast the Vancouver team claimed Marshall, the Chinooks third defense man, was a professional, and he was not allowed to play.

The V.A.C. team then went on to humiliate the Chinooks with a 12-0 rout. Curliss, the Chinook goalkeeper covered himself with glory, holding his opponents scoreless in the first quarter and stopping countless shots during the remainder of the one-sided game. The Calgary players appeared to be in poor condition, and they had no idea as to how to score once they secured the ball. Following the loss the Chinooks filed protests on three different matters, but the Vancouver Amateur Union refused the protests.

In the second game of the challenge the Calgary team played much better, losing by a 5-2 score. It appeared to be another rout when Vancouver scored at the one minute mark, however Curliss tied the game up three minutes later, and before the game was up added a second marker.

At a summer meeting of the Alberta Amateur Athletic Union considerable time was spent discussing the status of Vancouver's Kendall, and the members decision was that he was not an amateur as he had played against professionals in B.C. A protest was registered with the trustees of the Mann Cup, and they decided in favour of Calgary, which theoretically gave Calgary possession of the cup. However the Canadian Lacrosse Association overruled this and Vancouver retained the trophy.

1914 had not been a banner year for lacrosse in Alberta, with the Calgary Interscholastic being the only league actually operating in the province.

During the fall Sunday lacrosse games between Marshall's and Curliss's teams were played with the proceeds going toward the Patriotic fund.

The Calgary Interscholastic league suspended play in 1915 as lessening enrollment caused by the effects of the war thinned the playing ranks.

After the Sarcee Military Camp was established a five team league was operated by the military personnel. In 1917 an oldtimer lacrosse game was played at Mewata.

Boxing and Wrestling

Wrestling was practised by the Indians of the plains long before the coming of the white man. With the arrival of the mounted police and settlers the activity of catch-as-can wrestling took place often when men and boys gathered for leisure or recreation. Although it may be said that brawn often played a greater part than did the application of wrestling techniques.

Early boxing was in the form of fisticuffs or bare knuckles, often to settle a grudge. The Marquis of Queensbury rules, first drawn up in 1867, but not used in North America until at least 1892, set up three minute rounds, the ten second count, classification of boxers by weight, and the wearing of gloves.

In March of 1833 a wrestling match took place at Fort MacLeod between D. Fraser and J. Human. There were probably men in the audience who felt they were capable of handling the winner.

Early issues of the Edmonton Bulletin periodically reported of slugging matches that were held in that settlement. In a match held in Lethbridge in 1886 Hawkins of Winnipeg defeated Austin of Calgary in the seventh round for what was reported to be a $250 purse.

Calgary's first fight to be reported in the press took place in 1887. The White and Evans glove contest to a finish for a $50 side bet was held at Shagnappi Point, west of the town. Contests, such as this, provided an opportunity for a great deal of wagering among the backers of the combatants.

Various sports clubs in the Calgary settlement had their own best fighter. Club matches took place in the spring of 1887, and by July Fitzgerald was determined to be the Calgary champion.

Work bees provided, besides hard work, social gatherings that provided men the opportunity to test their strength and agility against their friends and neighbours in rough and tumble competition.

In May of 1887 George Irvine's gym on Stephen Avenue, that formerly had been the Fraser Rink, was advertised as, "The most complete gym west of Winnipeg." It was reported to have contained a greaty variety of training equipment, including punching bags. In one boxing match held at the gym High River's Ross pounded the smaller Irvine all around the ring, but Irvine had stamina, and Ross grew so tired that the contest more or less evened out to a draw.

In the spring of 1890 a boxing exhibition was part of a sports display held in the Opera House located on Stephen Avenue.

A November, 1980 issue of the local paper contained a special article, "The

Knockout blow—the why and wherefore explained by an expert." The long column also contained pictures of blows to the ear, point of jaw, jugular vein and the heart.

By the following year more than 80 men were attending boxing practises held at the fire hall under the instruction of Mr. Stone.

The Alexander Hall, located in the Alexander Block—a sandstone structure that was torn down to accommodate the building of the Hudson's Bay store, was the location of a boxing match between Austin and White in 1892. The match was declared even after the regular eight rounds, but in an extra round Austin won on points.

The same year, in a boxing match held at Fort MacLeod and billed as the championship of southern Alberta, M. Johnson of England defeated A. Dixon from Ontario with a seventh round technical knockout. During the year an attempt was made at Edmonton to form a club for the practice of boxing, gymnastics and fencing, however the venture was not too successful.

The following year the Edmonton Athletic Association proved to be more successful, and this organization staged its first pro fight in December of 1894.

Austin and White were again matched in a bout held in the Alexander Hall, and the two pugilists again finished the regular rounds in a draw.

During the 1890's the boxing club which operated out of the fire hall was quite active. In 1897 the club champion was challenged to a five round match by the fire brigade champion. In August of 1898 the Lemon Circus arrived in Calgary. Among its performers was Fighting Tom, a boxing kangaroo, who would spar four rounds with any and all comers. It was reported that he was well worth watching in action.

Combative sports were beginning to find their way into the school programs. A boxing ring was in operation in the basement of the old Central School. Wrestling activities took place at the Dunbow and St. Joseph Indian schools.

By 1900 boxing was providing a form of entertainment at various club and organization smokers. These gatherings were generally held at the Opera House or the Alexander Hall. Billy Hawkins, the winner more often than not, was often matched with Holloway.

Touring wrestlers were appearing in the Canadian west, but their entertainment was not always of an honest quality. The Terrible Turk was beaten in his Calgary match in what the audience considered a very poor show.

In June of 1902 Kid Macleod and his manager stepped off the train and immediately issued a challenge to meet anyone in the ring. The challenge was immediately taken up by one Coolgardie Smith, who claimed to be the British Columbia champion, had won the Klondike championship in Dawson in 1898 and the South African title in 1896. He said that he had 65 glove contests and had not lost a decision.

A Grand Boxing Contest was advertised for Hull's Opera House at nine p.m. sharp Friday, June 13. The winner to take 75% of the prize money, and the loser the rest. No draw would be accepted; the winner must be the result of a decision. Front seats in the pit and the first three balcony rows were priced at a dollar each, while general admission was 75¢.

A good crowd was on hand for the bout, but upon its conclusion many of the spectators considered the contest to be the worst fake ever placed before a Calgary audience. The only thing that prevented Smith from being knocked out was that Macleod, a boy half Smith's size, took compassion on him. Macleod contented himself with shoving Smith away and during the eighth round did not strike a blow. The audience voiced their displeasure at the lack of competition.

The drill hall of the Canadian Mounted Rifles Regiment was the scene of boxing in 1903. Sergeant-Major Page offered instruction in the art of boxing. In March the hall was packed with spectators to witness the Hannay-Campbell bout.

An illegal fight was staged in a building on Calgary's outskirts. The affair was raided by the local constabulary with the result that many in the audience made a hurried exit through one of the building's windows. It was reported that one such individual was Calgary fire chief Cappy Smart.

In 1904 a fight between Jack Curley and Tom Sidney was advertised as a twenty round bout for the championship of Western Canada. The match was supposed to start at nine p.m., however the contestants argued over the weight of gloves used and sundry other matters, and as a result the contest did not begin until after midnight.

The 500 fans were then treated to three minutes of wrestling before the bell signaled the end of round one. The remaining competition was a complete miscarriage, with Sidney losing the fight on a foul. The law stepped in and those individuals being involved in this sham were called into court.

In the fall of 1904 the city amateur boxing championships were held in the Hull Opera House.

There was considerable interest and action in boxing and wrestling in Calgary in the fall of 1905. Yankee Rogers, a native of the eastern states, arrived in the city and announced an offer to throw any three local men within one hour.

A boxing tournament, held in the drill hall in November, was patronized by a good crowd. Freddie Lowes ācted as master of ceremonies. Spring was matched with Carr in the first bout, while Bennett and Richards mixed it up in the second match of the evening. Prior to the start of the main bout Scotty Milne jumped into the ring and announced that he would fight either of the opponents for a $500 side bet.

In the main event Jake Fullerton and W. Stewart were to box three rounds, each of two minutes duration, using four ounce gloves. The fight was held up because Stewart claimed that Fullerton said he could bandage his hands, but the judges would not allow this additional padding. Stewart gave Fullerton a few licks below the belt in the first rounds, and many spectators called out for his disqualification. However justice prevailed as Fullerton won the fight by a decision.

Following the matches referee Fidler read a letter from Jack Downes of Red Deer stating that he would like to wrestle Yankee Rogers in a catch-as-can match and would be willing to put up fifty dollars.

As a result Rogers and Downs were to meet in a late November match. The rules were set up that Rogers had to throw Downs 3 out of 5, three points down;

Jake Fullerton—a native of Calgary and Bragg Creek who excelled in boxing and football.

Down to throw Rogers three points out, with two points down.

The match proved to be a good one, and it kindled a great deal of interest in the wrestling sport among Calgarians. A wire was received from George the Greek in Edmonton, offering to take on either wrestler.

In early December wrestling matches took place at the Lyric Theatre. Downs, with a handicap, took a decision from Rogers. When Scotty Milne's opponent, Root, did not show up he was matched with Rogers. Milne managed to stay in the ring the full ten minutes, and then he exclaimed that it was the hardest $25 he had ever earned. Krouse of Red Deer and Spring from Airdrie were matched in another contest. At one point in the bout the large audience was reprimanded for booing, as only clapping was allowed at these contests.

The following week G. Gilbert handled the refereeing as Rogers won over Downs before a small crowd. Rogers then took a turn in being the third man in the ring in a sparring match between Carr and Spring, with the former winning as the result of a foul.

In Roger's next match he scored two falls in eighteen and four minutes over a tough and wiry Jack Curran to take a $500 side bet. Curan had just arrived from Montana where, although outweighed by fifty pounds, he had lost a close decision to world champion Frank Gotch. In the preliminary bout J. Downs defeated Watty Watson in a boxing match.

In another boxing evening Sherman's Lyric Theatre offered the patrons "satisfaction or money back". The main 15 round bout was between Detroit's 154 pound Watty Watson and 148 pound Kid Davis. Freddie Lowes acted as master of ceremonies, going over the Police Gazette rules the fight was held under. Besides receiving a share of the gate the combatants made a hundred dollar side bet. Ticket prices were 50¢, a dollar, or ringside seats $1.50.

Knockdowns were frequent in the fight, with both boxers being saved by the bell. Watson won in the seventh round when he knocked down Davis for the count.

A preliminary bout between Jack McCarthy and Don Wilson produced catcalls and hoots. Following the contests Watson offered to fight any man in the house. The local papers reported this bout to be, "a fine exhibition of the manly art of self defense."

In the fall of 1906 local papers were carrying lots of international boxing and wrestling news. A boxing match took place in the Barber Block with Jim Burrows from Fernie meeting Calgary's George Paris. Fire chief Cappy Smart was drafted to referee the contest. In a preliminary match, arranged spontaneously, Dixon traded punches with Kid Foley.

After a half hour wait a committee was sent to the dressing rooms in order to determine whether the main match was to be staged. Finally the competitors entered the ring, and Alf Fidler was appointed referee. Paris, a former west coast track champion who still ran seven miles a day, was the faster of the two. However Burrows was the stronger, and when he finally caught Paris in the ninth round, knocked him down for the count. Immediately after his arm was raised in victory Burrows was rushed by Paris, who wanted to continue the fight.

In December Bill Burrows, Jim's brother, and Billy Yates of Fernie squared off in a ten round bout that was staged in Eagles Hall. As a preliminary bout Jim Burrows offered to stop any man in the house in four rounds, and he would take on any five men under that condition. The days prior to Christmas the Eagles

Hall was used to accommodate a 15 round bout between Kid Foley and "Young" Dixon; a purse as well as a side bet going to the winner.

During that era the Crowsnest Pass settlements were a hotbed of pugilism.

In February of 1907 Billy Lauder of Winnipeg, former lightweight champion of Scotland and Canadian lightweight champion, issued a challenge through the Calgary newspapers, for opponents in the ring. Lauder had arrived from Scotland the year previous and had defeated Young Austin to claim the lightweight title of Canada.

His offer was accepted by Kid Hoagland, who had at one time been a sparing partner for Young Corbett, a former world champion. The 15 round bout, for the lightweight championship of Canada, was set for March 19 in the hall in the Barber Block.

The evening of competition began at 8:45 p.m., at which time Arthur Boody took six minutes to pin Young Berg in a wrestling match. Next Jim Williams and Dick Roach boxed a good six rounds to a draw.

At 9:55 referee Freddie Lowes gave the 135 pound Lauder and 133 pound Hoagland the rules of the fight, and the bell rang for round one. Hoagland fought defensively through the fight, possibly as a carryover from his days as a sparring partner. Finally in the fifteenth round Lauder put his opponent down, but Hoagland was saved by the bell at the count of nine. Referee Lowes awarded a popular decision to Lauder.

The evening provided a catalyst to the fight game in Calgary. Letters were published in local papers from pugilists in other cities offering to mix it up with Calgary boxers.

Another fight program took place April 16th in the Barber Block hall. In the first preliminary referee Jake Fullerton chaperoned Hill and Larkin through six rounds. Then Kid Holley traded punches with young Dixon, and D. Millet mixed it up with W. Reid for six rounds.

In the main event Lauder gave away seven pounds to his opponent Mark Melson of North Dakota. However the clever little Scot put his opponent away in the fourth round with an uppercut that seemed to lift his opponent off the floor. Freddie Lowes refereed this bout, while Fire Chief Smart and Bart Lowes held the clocks.

A ring and seating for 1,000 fight patrons was installed in Sherman's Auditorium Rink for a May, 1907 boxing exhibition between Lauder and Edmonton's Barney Mullin by promoter Stewart.

The boxing began at 10 p.m. in order to allow those working to attend; such were the business hours of the day. Dixon and Hoagland fought to a draw in the first preliminary, then Carr drew with Big Boy, who went into the ring when Spring did not show up.

At first Mullin refused to weigh in, and then when he did the scale recorded an above the limit 148 pounds. As a result all of the bets were called off, and Mullin forfeited 10% of his purse. Lowe announced that the pair would box at catch weights for a percentage of the house. Lauder gained a decision in the 15 round affair, which was said to be, "the best exhibition of the manly art seen in Calgary for a long time".

The next day Sullivan, Mullin's manager, proposed a re-match of twenty rounds, with a $500 side bet. An agreement was reached for this match to be held in Edmonton, but it never took place. Lauder's next bout was a sparring match with W. Stewart, a former lightweight champion of Scotland, at an Eagle smoker.

Lauder was challenged by Nunzie, an import player on the Lethbridge baseball team. At Banff Mullin went into training, then boxed ten rounds with hometown boy E. Tracey before what was reported to be the largest crowd ever to assemble in the Banff Opera House. Big Boy boxed Burrows, a tough miner, at Coleman on Dominion Day, and bareback wrestling was part of the military sports program at High River.

In early July an amateur boxing tournament was held in sherman's Auditorium. $25 gold medals were to be awarded to the winners of the six different classes. Jim Larkin defeated Ben Markin for the amateur boxing championship of Alberta. Jack Riley of Okotoks won over Jack Porter of Calgary to take the lightweight class medal. Heavyweight H. Ritchie and B. Fullerton were even on points at the end of four rounds, so the referee asked them to go another round. Ritchie would not do this, so Fullerton was awarded the decision.

Some of the bouts were refereed by Lauder, who then boxed eight rounds with Kid Scaler. Plans had been for Lauder to fight Mullin, because this had been called off because the chief of police had been instructed to take action against the principals if the prize fight took place. At that time the criminal code of Canada defined a prize fight being an encounter with fists or hands.

Scaler struck several foul blows, hitting in the clinches, but it was said that this happened because he had not fought in clean break fights before.

The same month a wrestling carnival was held in the Bijou Theatre. In a catch-as-can fight to the finish for a $200 side bet Bert Archer of Red Deer proved stronger than Young Berg, winning with two straight falls. In preliminary matches A. Boode won over A. Archer, who strained his shoulder in the scrap, and Holm beat Cameron.

Wrestling matches were also held in Nolan's Hall. In a match, billed as the championship of Alberta, 155 pound L. Boode of Calgary took two falls while losing one to 155 pound Bert Archer to take home a $200 side bet. A. Boode and C. Hanes won their preliminary matches.

The Lauder-Hughie Long bout in August of 1907 provided a large crowd with ten rounds of fast boxing. Referee Jim Sewell called the bout a draw, which did not go down too well with Jimmy McEwan, Lauder's trainer. The purse had been set at 65% for the winner and 35% for the loser, but now it was divided.

Scaler, a Spokane boxer, fought to a fifteen round draw with Lauder on Labour Day in what was called, "the best mix up seen in Calgary". Before referee Freddie Lowes was to start the main bout Kid Davis climbed into the ring to challenge whoever was the winner.

In the evening's preliminaries coloured Young Dixon won from Williams of Guthrie, and Billy Reid decisioned Jim Powell.

The Vaudette Theatre held a small crowd to witness Holm, the lightweight wrestling champion of Alberta, take two falls in less than eight minutes from

Cameron of Toronto. Boxer turned wrestler Billy Lauder won over Bert Dresser of Winnipeg. In a tough match "Farmer" Archer of Red Deer proved too strong for Young Boode. Following the matches Lauder challenged Holm for the provincial lightweight wrestling championship.

The Vaudette Theatre was the scene of a bout between W. Henderson, otherwise known as Big Boy, and Manitoba's Walter Adams for the heavyweight championship of Alberta. The fight was to be a complete fizzle.

Adams threw a low blow, and as a result Big Boy would not go on with the fight. Adams got mad and went after Big Boy outside the ring, but Big Boy just sat down. Alf Fidler, who had been called on to referee, awarded the decision to Adams, but he called all bets off. It was said that, "neither of the contestants knew enough about boxing to amuse kindergarten kids."

The next day Adams said that he was ashamed of the match, which he referred to as, "rough and tumble". His low blow had landed because Big Boy had pushed his hand down. In the next fight he wanted a real ring, not the 12 x 16 foot Vaudette ring.

The previous evening's bouts saw Dick Merino take only twenty seconds to remove Jimmy Duncan from competition. The referee stopped the Dixon-Collins bout, that later ended in a draw, to explain to the crowd about clinches.

Late in September the Vaudette Theatre was used for wrestling matches refereed by soccer and boxing trainer Jimmy McEwen and boxer Lauder. In the main event 160 pound L. Archer of Red Deer took the third and deciding fall over 152 Louise Boode to take home a $150 side bet. A. Holm won from Bert Dresser. Young Boode offered to throw three middleweights in an hour or pay each one $12. Jim Dowdall of Portage La Prairie climbed into the ring with him, but the Manitoba lad was outweighed and outclassed.

The Y.M.C.A. sponsored a wrestling club. During one practise session Holm took on three individuals, defeating them all.

In November a crowd of 1,500 witnessed the Lauder-Louie Long bout at the Vaudette Theatre. Chief Smart refereed the bout, and the local papers reported that he knew what he was doing. Lauder who won by a decision, twice put Long down for a count of nine, but could not push him out. Fullerton refereed as Dave Max of Bristol defeated Jim Reid of Philadelphia. The crowd was exuberant as Jack Porter of Calgary and Dowdles of Winnipeg flailed and wrestled to a six round draw. Porter would argue with the referee when he was hit. He wanted to quit in the fourth round, but his seconds pushed him back into the ring.

W. Collins of Calgary met George Hendley in a boxing match staged in the High River Opera House. Henderson, Collin's manager, made everyone so miserable that it was decided to ban further boxing matches in High River.

Meanwhile the Calgary City Council was questioning the advisability of allowing boxing matches in the city. Promoter Stewart said that he would give free tickets to council members and clergymen to attend the December bout between Billy Lauder and Kid Howell at the Lyric Theatre in order for them to judge the ethics of his promotions.

The taller Howell proved to be easy hitting for Lauder who won by a decision. Jim Larkin and Billy Arnold met in the first preliminary. In the second bout

Merino and Max met for the featherweight title of Alberta, but, "slam, bang, thud", and Merino was out at the one minute mark of the first round. Between events Lew White entertained the audience with vocal selections.

In February of 1908 Harry Lombard of Chicago set up his training camp at the Imperial Hotel in preparation for his bout with Lauder. In view of pressure by some civic and public figures, who viewed boxing matches as undesirable, the bout was announced as the amateur championship of Alberta, with a $250 cup as the prize. Admission prices were set at two dollars for front row seats and a dollar elsewhere.

Cappy Smart was picked to referee, but at first he would not do this because he had promised certain council members that he would not handle this task, however influential members of the audience got in touch with Mayor Cameron who said it was acceptable for Smart to referee.

The boxing was fast, and the pair fought to a clean draw, although Lombard had staggered Lauder in the last round to almost put the fight away. The Chicago boxer said that Lauder was a clean gentlemanly boxer. Both boxers wanted another bout to settle the draw.

Preliminary matches included a six rounder between Larkin and Yanger. George the Greek took part in two wrestling matches, pinning Tom Atkins in 25 seconds, but then he took over six minutes to put down Globe, who was 40 pounds lighter. Jim Reid, featherweight champion of Alberta, took out J. Towell of Winnipeg in six rounds.

A late February wrestling match, to be held in the Eagles Hall, fell through when Louis Golden, the wrestling Russian Jew, forfeited fifty dollars when he decided it would not be wise to get involved after watching George the Greek master his opponents the previous week. Another evening match saw Captain Ross and Seargent-Major Page grapple.

Lauder and Lombard met again in March before 1,100 spectators at the Lyric Theatre. Lauder came out the winner, however this bout did not prove to be as lively as their initial encounter. The city police, under Seargent Mackie, were there to stop the bout if it degenerated into a grueling prize fight, and a squad of Mounted Police attended to see that the letter of the law was upheld. However referee Smart kept things well under control.

Jake Fullerton traded punches with Dawson in the evening's first bout, and then Max and Cowell mixed it up in the second preliminary. The third match proved to be a great fiasco as Australian Lynn Turcott toyed with Kid Sullivan, who gave the impression that he had never had a glove on before. George the Greek refereed a catch-as-can wrestling match in which Holm put a hammerlock on Globe after four minutes, and Globe quit.

The Crowsnest area was a hotbed of boxing during this era. Local boxer Burrows knocked out Kid Davis in the first round in a bout staged in Frank. Wrestling matches were held in Claresholm. Calgary's St. Mary's Club held boxing competitions, while in a bout held in the Drill Hall MacDonald threw George the Greek. Lombard travelled north to box in Wetaskwin, and Lauder travelled to Vancouver where he took a decision from Driver Miller. While at the coast Lauder tried his hand at wrestling, but he lost his match to Swanson.

High River hometowner James Duncan demonstrated his wrestling skills, and

George the Greek wrestled Mcdonald in Lethbridge. Merino and Kid Sullivan fought at Carstairs, while at Banff the improved Jake Fullerton gave Spring an awful beating in a ten round match.

Two locals were to meet for the championship of Langdon, a small settlement east of Calgary, and a $28 purse. Some Calgary gentlemen who were backing one of the fighters went out to test him. An English fellow in the group put on gloves with him and in the ensuing encounter proceeded to darken the Langdon boy's eye. The champ to be immediately pulled off his gloves and went after the English fellow with his bare knuckles, so the group retired to a barn where the now grudge match was completed bare knuckles style.

Several days before the scheduled Scaler-Lombard match Scaler took the night train south after he was offered a more lucrative fight in Spokane. This left the promoter on the spot, so Vancouver's Driver Miller filled in. Lombard won the fight in the third round when his left hook put Driver to the mat three times.

Preliminaries held at this fight night at the Garden Theatre included a ten round draw between Max and Kid Lewis and a six round lovefest involving Spider Bowditch and Kid Reid.

The most unpopular fight of the year occurred when Jim Burrows of Fernie met Tom McCune from Detroit. Burrows arrived late and climbed into the ring in his street clothes. Here he complained about the size of the ring, then told the audience that his feelings were hurt because the crowd was so small, and that as a result he would only box eight rounds. He said that anyone who did not like it could come into the ring and Burrows would convince him otherwise. The coal miner then told promoter Sherman that if he did not get one hundred dollars he would not fight.

Although Burrows was bigger and stronger than opponent McCune he could not box as well, so the bout ended in a draw. Good boxing was provided by Dancey and Merino and Max versus Kid Lewis in the preliminaries.

Prior to his June fight with Chicago's Joe Galliger Lauder said he expected this to be his hardest fight. Both boxers were putting up tough competition when the police stopped the bout. In the first round referee Smart had stopped the bout and handed each competitor a flash card of the straight rules. However there continued to be hitting in the clinches, and when they did not break clear in the third round Chief English stepped into the ring to stop the fight. Smart declared it a draw, with all bets off.

In a preliminary bout Sandy Carr had to quit at the end of the second of a ten round bout after Truman Spring had knocked the wind out of him. He was so upset about his failure that he threatened a spectator as he was leaving the ring. The second preliminary saw Dave Max and Billy Reid go eight rounds to a draw.

The July 8th fifteen round match between Lauder and Harry Lombard of Chicago staged at Sherman's Auditorium for the lightweight championship of Canada was considered by many to have been the fastest action ever seen in Calgary. The match, which began at 11 p.m. and lasted until after midnight, was held up because the two camps could not settle on a referee; finally Mike Welsh, featherweight champion of the western states was chosen. Lauder retained his title by a decision.

Preliminaries saw Larkin of Calgary and Kid Riddle of San Francisco box to a three round draw, while Jim English and Jack Carr also were even after six rounds.

There were indications that the fight game in Calgary was going sour. Public pressure was being exerted on council to make the promoting of fights that much more difficult. Billy Stewart decided that with the high license costs and expenses it was not worthwhile handling any bouts. Lauder said that he was going to quit boxing and move to B.C. to raise fruit. However, as the fight game often goes, this move was postponed.

An August, 1908 fight at Canmore between coloured Bill Crocker, who claimed the heavyweight championship of Alberta, and Bill Johnson of Calgary ended in an argument. Crocker claimed the heavyweight championship of Canada when his opponent went down for the count in the fourth round. Johnson claimed, and many in the audience agreed, that he was down because he had been kneed, but the referee raised Crocker's arm anyway.

The following month Crocker was matched with Jake Fullerton at Banff. The fight ended in a dispute and an assault on Crocker by Fullerton. In the fourth round the referee had warned Jake about fouling; Crocker assumed he had won and proceeded to take off his gloves. Fullerton followed him out of the ring and then knocked him over some chairs. Later the police said that they would not allow any more fights to be staged in Banff. Everyone who had been at ringside agreed that the fight was not a fake and both contestants were out for blood.

At a September smoker, held by the Eagles Club, Billy Lauder sparred four rounds with Billy Stewart and then Lafferty went three rounds with Eddie Marino, a Pacific coast champion from Seattle. Another evening Marino demonstrated different boxing manoeuvres and punches to the audience who were at the Garden Theatre to view the movies of the Gans-Nelson fight.

The Merino-Lauder fight had the fans on the edge of their seats, as Merino went ahead in the first five rounds on points. However he broke a bone in his right hand, then Lauder began to be the aggressor, finally taking the 15 round bout on points. Merino did very well considering his youthful nineteen years and giving away ten pounds in weight.

The evening's first preliminary saw "darkie" Jim Smith and Larkin fight to a four round draw. In the second bout Jake Fullerton knocked down Bill Johnson of St. Paul to claim the Alberta heavyweight championship.

A November bout for Lauder was scheduled with Jack Kearns, a fighter who was reported to once having knocked a man out in two seconds of the first round. Kearns was five inches taller and had a six inch reach over Lauder, but the Calgary boxer put him away in nine rounds with a right hook, left to the stomach, and a right behind the ear.

Billy Reid and Jim Larkins fought to a draw in the opening preliminary. Joe Reid of Boston spotted Calgarian Jake Fullerton 15 pounds but proceeded to knock him around during the first two rounds, however the American boxer lacked stamina, tiring, so the fight ended in a draw.

Muscular 200 pound Billy Emerson, a newcomer to Calgary, challenged George the Greek for the heavyweight wrestling championship of Alberta, but the champion said that it was not worth wrestling in Alberta as the gate receipts would hardly pay for the license.

Eddie Marino was matched in a December bout with Lauder. Many fight patrons considered this match to be the best ever witnessed in Calgary. Marino was about ten pounds lighter, but he repeatedly hit Lauder, once putting him through the ropes. Referee Fidler gave the match to Marino, although there were many in the audience who felt the Calgary boy should have at least earned a draw.

The first preliminary of this fight evening, held in Sherman's auditorium Rink on Seventeenth Avenue, saw Jim Larkin outbox and outpoint coloured Clarence Smith. Then Digger Nelson and Billy Reid went six fast rounds with honours even.

A special train, with a round trip ticket cost of $3.95, carried many Calgarians to Edmonton in December for the Lauder-Potts fight. In a very good match Lauder proved to be much faster than his Edmonton opponent, who plodded but was able to land stinging blows. Following the match Lauder said he would take six months off to rest.

On January 4th of 1909 125 pound Gerry Cove of Ottawa, who had 64 fights under his belt, was matched with Marino in a 15 round bout held in the 19 foot ring on the stage of Lyric Theatre. Cove punched and banged Marino around until the thirteenth round when Marino's manager wisely stepped into the ring to concede the bout. Cove's followers, who had watched him train at the National Hotel gym, were happy with the result.

Following the Curly Smith-Billy Reid preliminary, Carrol Booth and Clarence Smith went at each other with great zest. The rounds were described as: "round one—fast, two—faster, three—fastest, four—wild, five—wilder and quit". Both threw in the towel!

In February there was wrestling at Medicine Hat. Foss of Swift Current won over McKenzie of Lethbridge, then Foss took three falls in forty minutes over the Russian from Medicine Hat. In a boxing match at Coleman Joe Reid of Calgary lost to strongman Burrows. Jake Fullerton drew with Lethbridge champion Clark in that city. Potts and Bennett met in a boxing match held in Carstairs. Cove and Long fought to a ten round draw in Lethbridge, and Reid travelled to Gleichen to meet a local boy in a boxing match.

Lauder bought a half section of land southwest of Calgary. Besides working at the No. 2 firehall Lauder often ran out to his ranch in the morning.

During the year one of boxing's all-time greats was in the city when John L. Sullivan checked into the Albert Hotel for a short visit to Calgary.

On March first, 1909, Lauder won back his Canadian title from Marino before a capacity audience in the Lyric Theatre. Following the bout, in which both competitors landed many punches, referee Smart raised Lauder's hand in victory. However Marino, who was just one of many who disagreed with the verdict, attempted to get at the referee, but the enraged boxer was led from the ring.

The evening's preliminary was stopped in the fifth round because Calgary's Dick Lafferty was just a punching bag for the winner Gene Parker of Omaha.

A few days later coloured world heavyweight Jack Johnson passed through

Calgary on his way back to Galveston after defeating world champion Tommy Burns in Australia. The white population of his home town did not want him to return there as he was now reported to have a white-skinned wife. A Calgary reporter boarded the train in Banff and interviewed the champion on the journey to Calgary. Johnson appeared to be very impressed with the Canadian Rockies.

Jim Potts of Minneapolis and Maurice Thompson of Butte fought to a draw in a March bout held in the Lyric Theatre. Potts floored Thompson twice in the first round, but he could not put him away. Calgary's Lafferty knocked out Burges of Liverpool in the fourth round, while in the second preliminary Gene Parker knocked George Reid, Billy's brother, down in the first, second, and finally out in the fourth round. This immediately brought brother Billy to ringside to challenge Parker.

The Scaler-Marino bout was called off after Scaler hurt his hand sparring with Jake Fullerton. Jake's head was reported to be harder than Scaler's hand.

Spectators could see 35 rounds of boxing at an April boxing carnival held at Sherman's Rink. Tickets for the events were on sale at the Star Pool Room and the Royal Hotel Cigar Stand. Dick Wylie refereed the matches, while auctioneer McDonald handled the announcing. Gene Parker won over Frank Steele in six rounds, then Curly Smith, who came into the ring in his coon coat, fought to a four round draw with Jack Bergin. In a ten round bout for the middleweight championship of Alberta Jake Fullerton put Joe Reid through the ropes to claim the title. Percy Cove mastered Jim Butler in a fifteen round bout for the featherweight championship of Canada.

Jake Fullerton and Joe Reid had a re-match May 14. Jake was given the match by Márino after Reid fouled him. Joe claimed that he did not hit low, but that Fullerton was willing to quit on the lightest pretense.

Sid Thomas and Clarence Smith fought to a preliminary draw, then Gene Parker knocked down Billy Reid down half a dozen times to win in the third round. George Reid, Billy's brother met his match in Curley Smith. Curley went after him with his Zulu crouch, then his Japanese stoop, before putting him out with the Curley corkscrew.

In May of 1909, after 32 Canadian fights, Billy Lauder was given his second defeat and knocked out for the first time in his career by Jim Potts. It was a hard fast match, but in the sixth round Potts scored a hard blow to the pit of Lauders stomach, and he went down for the count. After the bout Lauder proved to be a good sport saying that, "Potts is a good man, and I would rather lose to him than any man I know". Fullerton refereed the match.

Pror to the main bout Curley Smith knocked out Kid West, and Clarence Smith, idol of Calgary's coloured population, knocked out Jockey Williams in the first round. In a wrestling match Bob Lauder beat George Sotaras two falls to one.

For an important forthcoming fight Harry Lombard of Chicago used the open air boxing ring at the rear of the Owl's poolroom for his training quarters, while Marino worked out at the Imperial Hotel. In June they met in a ring on the stage of the Lyric Theatre in what was to be a slow bout that ended in a draw; although for much of the fight it looked as if Scaler was holding back.

Preliminaries saw Curley Smith matched with an old man, then Clarence Smith given the decision over Young Booth, who kept fouling his opponent. Young Maxwell knocked out Billy Reid in the first round of their bout.

Over 300 people were at the arena in Gleichen to see Kid Scaler and McFaden of San Francisco tangle. However McFaden never showed up, so Curly Smith went into the ring; however Scaler blasted him out again with a barrage of blows.

Later Young Maxwell, who trained at the gym located behind the Windsor Hotel, was to fight Kid Morris in a Gleichen bout, but because the town fathers raised the cost of a boxing match license to $200 the fight site was changed to Banff. Also on the card was a wrestling match between George, "the Greek", Sotaras and Jack Calder.

Lauder travelled to North Vancouver, where on Dominion Day he met Harry Lombard of Chicago before a crowd that was said to number about 5,000 people. The Calgary boxer knocked out his opponent in the seventeenth of the twenty round bout. Two weeks later Lauder fought Australian Rod Standen at Nanaimo, however Standen proved very strong, knocking Lauder out in the seventh round.

Calgary's city council had been under a great deal of pressure by various groups and individuals to rid the city of boxing and wrestling. As a result council decided that in order to keep the combatant sport clean the boxing license would be raised to $500. As a result Calgary's promoters would be put in a financial bind in respect to fight promotions, and professional boxing came to a standstill in Calgary.

Lauder again met Marino, this match taking place on the west coast, and beat him. Another coast bout with Standon, saw Lauder outboxed and outfought, but still come out with a draw.

In an October wrestling match held in Stavely Allan Holm of Calgary beat hometown boy Jack Coleman. Holm took the first fall, then he was awarded the match after he got Coleman in a headlock from which there did not appear to be any escape. Holm came away with the gate money and a $500 side bet.

Meanwhile in Calgary a proposed wrestling match between Harry Hein and Olaf Nelson was called off because the promoter could not pay the now hundred dollar license fee. Followers of wrestling petitioned city council to reduce the license cost to $25. These included members of the newly formed Y.M.C.A. wrestling club. Calgary was not the only city where boxing and wrestling was under civic government pressure, and in Vancouver Marino was arrested as party to a prize fight.

Attorney-General Mitchell said that prize fights were against the law, but that boxing matches were acceptable. Superintendent Deanne of the Mounted Police said that fights would not be stopped if the competitors would fight clean instead of holding.

The lack of local bouts sent Calgary fighters elsewhere. Lauder beat Hoagland, the first man he had fought in Calgary, in a January, 1910 bout in Lethbridge. However Hoagland said his loss was the result of Lauder butting him in the nose. Lauder then fought Maxwell at Moose Jaw, and then travelled to Winnipeg for further bouts. Joe Reid, Alberta heavyweight champion, fought to a draw with

Lethbridge's Jack Clark at a bout held in Taber. Percy Cove, who now called Calgary home, was fighting in California. The only public boxing in Calgary took place at the Caledonian Football Club smoker where Jake Fullerton and Billy Harte traded punches.

Wrestler Holm again defeated Coleman at Stavely, this time for a $100 side bet. Roy Gratias, Saskatchewan wrestling champion defeated Jack Ellison of Cardston. A Y.M.C.A. boxing class was organized under Instructor Ferguson. Plans were made to send competitors to the Y.M.C.A. boxing championships to be held in Winnipeg. In that city Lauder earned draws in bouts with Kid Ashe and Bud Burt.

After efforts were made to be allowed to hold boxing in the city proved unsatisfactory the Fairmount Boxing Club sponsored a March boxing card at their makeshift area located on a site beyond the Hillhurst street car line, and outside the city limits. In the main card Jim Potts was awarded a decision by referee Smart over Morris from Miles, Montana. The loser put up a stall and kept his face covered for the entire 15 rounds. Joe Reid of Boston and Jack Carrolls of St. Paul fought to a 15 round draw in a preliminary. then Frenchy Clairmont and Teddy of the National Poolroom were involved in a burlesque type match. Auctioneer McDonald acted as master of ceremonies.

The Star Athletic Club sponsored a May fight between Billy Lauder and the west coast's Rod Standen. The bout was to be held in an open air arena on a site five minutes walk north of Langevin Bridge. However Lauder's camp kept stalling the fight date as he really was not in shape for the match. His training camp was located at the Hillhurst Fire Hall, while Standen's was located at the East Calgary Fire Hall.

The fight finally took place at 11 a.m. on Victoria Day, however the location was changed to the Star Arena, on a site on the brow of the hill but not as far out as the Potts-Morris fight. The match was a clean break contest with catch weights allowed.

Close to 600 fans were on hand to see Lauder win on points. Standen was down twice in the sixth round, the second time being saved by the bell at the count of nine. Smart, in a newly laundered sweater, refereed the main bout, and Fullerton was the third man in the ring for the preliminary. Young Cecil of California boxed to a four round draw with the dogcatcher Mr. Boxwell.

There was a great deal of interest in the forthcoming Johnson-Jeffries world championship fight to be held in Reno. A local paper published the opinions of many prominent local critics in regards to the fight's outcome. Later the paper published many photos of this famous bout. While at Lethbridge a debate took place in the city council chambers as to whether to allow movies of the fight to be shown in a local theatre.

On the same day as the Johnson-Jeffries bout a fight took place in the Porcupine Hills south of Calgary in which Hunter of Pine Creek knocked out his opponent from Granum in the first round to collect what was reported to be a $500 side bet.

Abe Attrel, world champion of the lightweights, arrived in Calgary to set up training quarters at the National Hotel for an August 20 bout with Marino, the fight to be held at a site in Manchester, on the south side of the city limits. Marino set up his training quarters at the East End Fire Hall. Tickets for the event went on sale at the Home Plate Cigar Store.

Bad weather kept the crowd down, but it did include a contingent who had travelled down from Edmonton to see a world champion in action. Because of the rain the preliminaries did not come off, but the main bout began as scheduled at 7 p.m. Jim Sewell was chosen to referee, and the police were on hand to make certain the fighters broke clean.

Attrel was fast and continually the aggressor. Marino saved himself by continually clinching and clinging, just hanging on and taking punishment through the 15 rounds.

The Swastika Club arranged a 15 round bout for Labour Day between Calgarian Billy Lauder and Attrel. McEwen, Lauder's manager, stated that he felt his boy would give the world champion a good match. Jim Sewell was chosen to referee the match.

Box seats were priced at $5, reserved seats $3, and general admission $2. Attrel was to receive $1,200 and Lauder $500. However final gate receipts were only to total $1,200.

Lauder's style was to hit and then get away from his opponent, but this was difficult with Attrel. The first five rounds went well for the Calgary fighter, but in the sixth round Abe solve Billy's style. The following round Attrel floored Lauder to the count of nine. Lauder, upon getting back on his feet, tried to stall until the bell, but Attrel was continually after him. One good strong right to the solar plexus and Billy was down but not out; however he could not regain his feet before the count was completed. The next day Attrel left for England for further defenses of his title.

In September city council granted special permission to show moving pictures of boxing as entertainment in Calgary. Jim Sewell reported that former world champion Tommy Burns would be in Calgary to narrate on the pictures of the Johnson-Jeffries fight to be shown at the Empire Theatre.

On Burn's arrival he was met at the train station by a brass band and a crowd said to number over 2,000. Burns then refereed a baseball game, and that evening was a guest of honour at a banquet held in Cronn's Restaurant. A local paper made him sports editor for a day and devoted a whole page to boxing. Burns said he would train in Calgary for his London bout with Langford.

The Empire Theatre reserved a section of its seats for ladies and their escorts to view the Johnson-Jeffries fight pictures. Jim Sewell introduced Burns to the audience, and Burns described the fight blow by blow along with what were considered to be very clear pictures. Prior to the screening local promoters had said that most white people would not attend because the film would show how the white champion was so inferior to the black champion.

In the fall of 1910 Calgarian Hoagland took part in a bout staged at Bow Island. A bout was planned at Irricana between Calgarians Spring and Davis for the welterweight championship of Canada. Pressure was being exerted in Edmonton to again allow boxing within the city limits. A boxing and wrestling club was organized at the Calgary Y.M.C.A., with Tommy Burns its honourary

Boxing training camp behind the Elbow View Hotel. Left to right: Unknown, McIntyre, Tommy Burns (Calgary fight promoter and former world white champion), Arthur Pelkey, Griffiths.

president. Jim Potts, in the Minneapolis paper, blasted the village of Calgary, where to save a $200 license the promoters took the match outside of the town limits and held it in a tent-like structure. The Starland Theatre charged adults 25¢ and children 15¢ to see a movie of world championship wrestling between Frank Gotch and challenger Zybysco. Bareback wrestling was part of the sports program at the local military camp.

In December Tommy Burns announced that he was retiring from active boxing, and that he would become a resident of Calgary.

On New Years Day, 1911 the Y.M.C.A. boxing and wrestling clubs sponsored an exhibition for the public. On the same day boxing matches were held out in Airdrie. F. Spring knocked out Newton Davis in the second round, breaking his hand with the blow, to claim the middleweight championship of Alberta. In other matches Dawson and McFadden fought to a draw, as did Brown and McCarthy.

In January Burns moved to Seattle where he set up a boxing school. He wrote to the Calgary papers stating that boxing should be allowed within the city limits. The purpose being that he wanted to promote matches in the foothills city. Local wrestling promoters were also pressuring city fathers to reduce the cost of wrestling licenses. After the Swastika Club withdrew its application to promote matches council spent considerable time discussing new boxing and wrestling regulations as well as license fees.

Lauder displayed his fisticuff skills at the Caledonian Football Club smoker; his opponent being Billy Stewart, another ex-Scottish champion.

In April the Y.M.C.A., under physical director Dawson sponsored a boxing and wrestling tournament that proved to be a great succes. Boxing matches were of three rounds, while wrestling matches were of six minutes duration. If no

206

decision was reached the competitors continued for an extra round. Philips won the lightweight special boxing title, the Covery brothers took the light and welterweight classes, Pae was the champion middleweight and Fullerton the heavyweight boxing champion. Dr. O'Sullivan and W. Stewart served as judges, and each competitor was examined by a physician before his bout. Seargent-Major Ferguson handled the refereeing chores.

Jimmy McEwan refereed the wrestling matches, with all four titles being taken by members of the Y.M.C.A. wrestling club. Martland was the top middleweight, Spawton tops in the welterweight class, A. Benson the best lightweight and J. Barnes came out best in the lightweight special class.

In the Lethbridge court Roy George, a boxer, was charged with leaving Canada and engaging in a fight at Sweetgrass, Montana. He was found guilty, but was given a suspended sentence.

Calgary fight fans were handed a lemon in a main bout that was staged on Good Friday. Kid Ash who attempted to give the impression that he had been knocked out in the fourth round by Decoursey, but as Fullerton counted him out he lay on the mat chewing his gum. Ash was considered a poor boxer but a much poorer actor.

In the first preliminary Larkin won over White in three rounds. Two hundred pound Luck McCarthy, known as Calgary's white hope for the world heavyweight title, proved to be a joke in his bout with 158 pound Joe Grimm.

After the bell had signalled the end of the eighth round McCarthy punched Grimm, giving him a bloody nose. Grimm refused to continue the fight and probably should have won on the foul, but referee Fullerton decided to call the match a draw.

In April Calgary's amateur boxers were invited to Spokane to compete in a tournament. Tommy Burns refereed boxing matches that were part of a Western Canada College sports day. The former world champion also began writing a boxing column for a local paper.

The National Boxing Club held a small card east of Calgary's city limits with Maurice Thompson and Curly Ullrich trading punches.

At Lethbridge Ellison of Lethbridge put Francis out of commission after he put an excruciating toe hold on him. One of the spectators at the match was Fitzsimmons, a cowpuncher from Milk river and brother of the great former world champion. D. MacMillan, a former world wrestling champion touted a Wetaskwin wrestling match between Pacific coast champion Sandow and Carl Muchs for the championship of Canada.

In June, at Lacombe, champion wrestler of Alberta Waklow and Rydman, champion of the Dakotas, wrestled for one hour and fifteen minutes without either touching the mat. The referee then decided on a draw, but the audience demanded that they wrestle to a finish. A Calgary newspaper issued a pink coloured extra edition giving the outcome of the Moran-Welgast fight in San Francisco. Word came from a Winnipeg paper that Calgary's white hope Luke McCarthy could beat world champion Johnson or anyone else both in guff and hot air shooting. Johnson, meanwhile, reported from Chicago that he would give a sparring match in Calgary.

Lauder lost his Canadian-title to Billy Allen, then fought Hayes in Winnipeg.

An October paper's sports headline said, "Frank Gotch coming, world's greatest mat artist". The following month the world champion arrived for a match to be held in Sherman's Rink. A special ladies sections was set up in the bleachers. Calgarian wrestling champion Maitland was given his glory when the newspaper published his and Gotch's picture on the front page. However glory was short lived as in the match Maitland was like a fly in the hands of a giant. He had hoped to stay in the ring at least ten minutes, but right after they shook hands Gotch lifted him aloft, slammed him to the mat, then a hammerlock was applied and Maitland cried aloud. The Calgary champion had lasted one minute and five seconds with the world champion. Other matches on the card saw Turkish Yussif Mahmout defeat Guffin from the west coast for the Police Gazette Belt, and then Gotch toyed with Hilderbrand of Buffalo. The card had been sponsored by the Western Canada Athletic Association.

On Thanksgiving Kid Bailey and Eddie Merino, not to be confused with Marino, boxed at Taber. Boxing and wrestling became part of the sports program at the 103rd Regiment gym. A boxing exhibition in the Y.M.C.A. saw the gym crowded to the doors with spectators.

During this era the newspapers published many articles related to boxing and wrestling. One writer said, "many electors who want clean boxing bouts will vote for candidates who will support them." Shortly after all adermanic candidates in the forthcoming civic election were interviewed in respect to relaxing the restrictions on boxing. Eleven candidates were in agreement of less control while four felt that restrictions should remain severe.

At the end of the year the Herald published the 1911 fight records of over fifty prominent boxers. Most of them averaged a bout a month, while one took part in sixteen bouts.

In January of 1912 Joe Bayley of Victoria put Calgary's Billy Lauder to sleep with a kidney punch in the third round. Lauder's seconds threw water on him as he lay on the mat with the referees count only at six, so this mean an automatic disqualification.

Taber was the site of a twenty round boxing match between Jack Cornell of Cardston and Walness of Australia. At Lethbridge Ellison, who now lived in Kalispell, threw Gilbertson in a wrestling match.

Calgary athlete and boxer Jake Fullerton wrote the article for the local newspaper on the city boxing and wrestling championships. In boxing Young Phillips captured the special weights title, won by his older brother the year before, Jack Machon the welterweight crown, Covery the lightweight title, while Charlie Burns was crowned both middleweight and heavyweight city champion. A packed house saw Dower the winner of the featherweight wrestling final, and Spawton took the welterweight title. The heavyweight final was reminiscent of Mutt and Jeff as 154 pound G. Sutherland took a decision from 190 pound Jackson.

A ten round prize fight for a $100 purse was held in an east Calgary hall between Bob Halliday and Jack Leonard, with Jimmy McEwen refereeing. The bout however was not given public notice until the day after it took place because of Calgary's fight bylaw. As a result some of the aldermen laid complaints at the license department of city hall that boxing and wrestling matches were being held in the city under the guise of benefit smokers, and that these sponsoring organizations shold take out the hundred dollar license to cover such events. Out at Bassano hometown grappler Bill Swanson defeated Bob Lauder in two straight falls to win the match and what was said to be the lightweight championship of Canada.

By March Burns was back in Calgary and began working out at the firehall gym. He sent a challenge to world champion Johnson to fight in Alberta on Labour Day. Local papers published several articles praising Burns for his prowess in boxing.

At Lethbridge the local police stepped in and called the wrestling bout off after Jack Ellison kept running off the mat. Plans were made in Calgary to send two wrestlers to the Canadian championship to be held in Vancouver.

In August the site of the Bayley-Allen fight was changed from a proposed location in the Ceepear subdivision to a new site in Manchester. This came about because the C.P.R. could not promise a train to transport patrons to and from the fight, whereas a Calgary transit line ran close to the Manchester site. Burns claimed he would build an arena large enough to hold 15,000 spectators. He then visualized plans for the structure to be an auditorium.

Bayley arrived in the city and set up his training camp at the Hillhurst Athletic Park. His daily training session attracted throngs of people. An invitation was sent to Canada's Governor General to attend the bout, but this was declined.

The bout was held during the same week as Calgary's famous 1912 Stampede. Tommy Burns was to referee all of the bouts which were to be staged under Marquis of Queensbury rules. Sandwich men and pipe sellers plied their wares, and representatives for the Prevention of Tuberculosis solicited donations from the members of the crowd. A crew of film makers were at ringside ready to take motion pictures of the main fight.

In the first preliminary Jack Tinsley of Edmonton won over Alf Boyd of Los Angeles, then Lucas and coloured Kid Lewis of Seattle fought to a draw.

Both Bayley and Allen weighed in at 133 pounds for the main bout. The fight was clean and fast, but short as Bayley knocked out Allen in the third round!

Dick Hayland trained at the Elbow View Hotel, while Pat Brown's training quarters were at the fire hall for their October 5th bout at Burns' Manchester arena. Hayland was knocked down in the fourteenth rounds, however rose before the count was completed, and in the final round carried the fight to Brown, Brown, however, was awarded the decision.

Preliminaries saw Kid Lucas and Billy Lauder box to a ten round draw, then Al Greenwood won over Charlie Carver in another ten rounder.

Special street cars transported Calgarians from downtown Calgary to the arena. Many of the spectators became wet and cold as a flurry of snow fell on the roofless arena.

By the time the Thanksgiving Day bout between Joe Bayley and Dick Hyland took place the arena had been roofed. However the heat generated caused the snow to melt and drip through the cracks between the boards onto the audience.

Incidently the Canadian Thanksgiving Day of that era occurred in late October. At the end of the bout referee Burns held an arm of each fighter up to signify a draw, however most fans felt that Hyland had been the winner.

Curley Smith and Cyclonne Scott's preliminary showed little of the science of boxing, but lots of action. Bob Albrect entertained the audience with a song, then local Fireman Kid Lucas and Smithers, a last minute replacement for Bassano's Charlie McCarthy traded punches.

A fall wrestling match held in Lethbridge's Majestic Theatre saw John Berg and Jack Taylor wrestle two hours without a fall.

In Calgary Hyland says that Bailey should give him a return bout or that he would claim the title. Burns said that he was going to try a new system of judging, where four ringside judges would decide, and if they could not come to a decision the referee's choice would be used. This system was now in use in many eastern U.S.A. cities. Burns said he would offer $500 to anyone who can prove that any of the matches he promotes were not legitimate.

Tommy Burns applied to the Alberta Amateur Athletic Union for their sanction to hold amateur boxing championship bouts, but at the organization's fall meeting this request was refused as it was contrary to the constitution.

Burns also became a haberdasher when he opened up a clothing store at 130 Eighth Avenue West. Typical clothing prices of the day were suits $15-$35. The establishment also served as a location to sell tickets for his fight promotions.

The roof of the Manchester arena was waterproofed and stoves were placed on the floor so as to make the building more practical during the colder months.

A late November card promised patrons a possible 31 rounds including one bout for a Canadian championship. Ticket prices ranged from two to four dollars, while box seats cost five dollars each. The ring judges were the sports editors of two local newspapers, one from the Edmonton paper, and local sportsman and real estate promoter, Freddie Lowes.

Main bout opponents Maurice Thompson and Butte and "fighting" Dick Hyland had both performed in front of Calgary audiences before. Thompson had the best of the early rounds, but then Hyland came on strong raining blows that had the American boxer groggy. In the thirteenth round most of the record crowd were on their feet as Hyland jabbed and punched his opponent. At the bell the police told Burns to stop the bout. He later said that he had planned on doing so anyway, as he always wanted to keep the bouts clean. Later Burns gave Thompson back the money he had forfeited for entering the ring over the fight weight limit.

In the preliminary Roy Orton of Spokane beat Ben Tobins of San Francisco.

Luther McCarty, a fighter who began his pugilistic career in Calgary, stopped Fireman Flynn in a sixteen round bout staged in Los Angeles.

Many Calgarians were under the impression that Burns was making a mint from his matches. Burns said that his gate receipts had only totalled just over $3,000 with the Hyland-Thompson fight providing three thousand of that. The arena cost over $5,000 to build, so that after paying purses and other expenses he was $900 out of pocket.

Former Calgarian Luther McCarty was often in the news as he was now one of the leading contenders for the white heavyweight championship of the world. Luther had a varied background that included working as a miner, cowboy and roughneck. He now wanted to come to Calgary to box Burns in an exhibition bout sometime in the spring. In a New Year's day bout, staged in California, the 205 pound McCarty won a one-sided match from 227 pound Palzer. Following the match Palzer said that Luther was a better boxer than world champion Johnson.

The local press reported that Bombardier Wells would meet Burns in a local match in March. It was said that a local man would put up a $31,000 purse for the contest. This match would be a semi-final to meet the winner of the Palzer-McCarty match for the white heavyweight championship of the world.

Paul Brown, who had just earned a respectable draw with Scaler in Edmonton, set up training camp at No. 4 Fire Hall for his match with local boy Dick Hyland, whose training camp was at the Elbow View Hotel in Mission.

Burns had optimistically expected an $8,000 gate and had promised 30% of the gate to go to Calgary's poor during this festive season bout. However a small crowd produced gate receipts of only $2,244 of which the main bout participants received $1,346. New ring announcer Trynon's voice was said to be louder than the screech of a siren. Besides three sports editors Fire Chief Cappy Smart acted as a ring judge.

Burns awarded the decision to Brown after 15 rounds of strenuous milling. Hyland lead on points in the early rounds, but Brown's work in the last three rounds proved very effective. Afterwards Burns said that this was the best fight between lightweights that he had ever witnessed.

Preliminaries saw Calgary postman Willie Hacker and Jack Goodman of Manchester, England box to a draw. Young Atkins looked good as he took a decision from Billy Reid.

A New Year's Eve match at Wetaskwin saw Korizm, the great Swedish boxer from Camrose, meet local Bob Patterson. A Carstairs hometown boy Freddie Baldwin boxed Bud Stearn of Acme. Then Tommy Burns refereed the main match, billed as for the middleweight championship of Alberta between F. Corry of Calgary and John Guyn of Carstairs. Kid Sullivan and K. Guyn fought. Joe Uvanni, who had boxed in Calgary, opened up a boxing school in Medicine Hat. Billy Lauder, although outweighed by 25 pounds outpointed him in a ten round bout staged in the gas city. Lauder made a monkey out of the larger boxer, landing three blows to every one he received. Up in Edmonton Dick Hyland lost a decision to Scaler, but gained the approval of the fans. South of the International border many cities and states were again legalizing boxing.

In Calgary the Loyal Order of the Moose held several evenings of boxing and wrestling; the events following the regular club meetings.

Tommy Burns worked out at the Central Firehall in preparation for his comeback. His opponent was to be Arthur Pelkey, formerly from Chatham, and as a boxer had earned a draw with Jess Willard. Enthusiastic crowds attended the Pelkey training camp at the Elbow View Hotel in the Mission District.

Considering that Burns stood only five feet, seven inches tall and weighed less than 170 pounds he was a remarkable fighter. When he lost the world championship to Jack Johnson in Melbourne, Australia he was outweighted by 35 pounds.

Tommy, whose real name was Noah Brusso, had originally come to Calgary because of his good friend Jim Sewell. He grew to like the town and its boxing enthusiasts so much that he bought a lovely home at 319-40th Avenue S.W. on the banks of the Elbow. His Eighth Avenue clothing store was a gathering place for the sporting crowd.

His arena had been built in Manchester, outside of Calgary city limits, on the advice of Charles Goss, Alberta's Attorney General. The land utilized belonged to real estate promoter Freddie Lowes. Unfortunately the structure was located half a mile from the nearest water connection.

Thirty two rounds of boxing were promised for the Good Friday bouts at Burn's Manchester Arena. Prices ranged from a dollar general admission to $5 for a box seat. Unfortunately cold weather delayed the matches for a week.

Meanwhile a new approach to boxing took place in Calgary. Burns became a matinee idol as he held a boxing exhibition in the Lyric Theatre for Calgary's ladies.

Calgary's weather warmed up and the Pelky-Burns fight was re-scheduled. Bob McDonald of Edmonton refereed the evening's bouts before a good crowd. In the first preliminary Buster Brown won over Young Phillips. Then Roy George had the much bigger Robinson flat on his back at 1.40 of the first round. In his last match before returning to his home in France Kid Lucas earned a draw with McKay, then Atkins and Tyldesley fought ten good rounds to a draw.

In the evening's main bout Burns proved to be the aggresor, but Pelky held him off with long jabs. Each boxer suffered two knockdowns in the six round bout that ended without a decision being made.

Meanwhile in Philadelphia Luther McCarty was proving himself a claimant to the white world heavyweight championship as he put Jim Flynn away in the sixth round. Several weeks later he defeated top ranked Moran.

An important card was arranged for early May. Boxers Andy Morris from Boston and Billy Griffiths of Cincinnatti set up their training camp in Manchester, while Mickey McIntyre and Arthur Pelkey trained behind the Elbow View Hotel.

The Manchester street cars were packed full of patrons for the evening's matches. Buster Brown and Tommy Haxton went four rounds to a draw, then featherweight Tommy Rawson and Kid Haynes fought to a no-decision. In the semi-final Mickey McIntyre, a top contender for the world welterweight championship, won from Billy Griffiths. The main match between Pelkey and Morris was stopped by referee Burns in the eighth round as Pelkey landed blow after blow on the staggering Morris.

A second successful boxing exhibition was held for the ladies in the Majestic Theatre with Arthur Pelkey appearing centre stage. What was considered to be good boxing took place at Innisfail between Tug Wilson and Tommy Collins. The pair later fought again at Rocky Mountain House. Dick Hyland was now boxing on the west coast, and in a fight staged in Vancouver he lost to Roy Campbell.

Excitement was building up among Calgary's fight fans following the announcement of a Victoria Day bout between Arthur Pelkey and Luther McCarty. Burns personally supervised Pelkey's training camp.

McCarty, who had been away from Calgary for two years, arrived back in the city with much more respect given to him as a boxer than when he had left. In 1910 McCarty had arrived in Calgary from his cowpunching job in Cuthbertson, Montana. Here in Calgary, in his first ring fight ever, Luther stopped Joe Guinn in four rounds. McCarty gave a boxing exhibition at the Majestic Theatre with all the proceeds going to charity. There were lots of horses pastured in the Ogden area, and McCarty, who had spent a great part of his life in the saddle, took the opportunity to ride. This was probably an unwise pre-fight activity.

Burns leased eight street cars to transport Calgarians at 25¢ a head to the fight, otherwise they could ride the regular Manchester street car for five cents.

Prices for this card ranged from a general admission of $2, reserved seats $3-$4, ringside $5 and box seats $6. The only place tickets could be purchased was at Tommy Burn's Clothing Store, that just happened to have a big sale on during the days prior to the card.

The day of the fight arrived! From early morning the Mission Hill road and MacLeod Trail were thronged with fight patrons, all heading to see what many considered to be the most important bout ever to be staged in Calgary. Swarms of young boys hung around the entrances, hoping for a free ticket or waiting for the ticket taker to turn his back so that they might skip in. By 11:30 the excited crowd numbered over 3,000.

The first preliminary saw Jim Potts, newsboy champion from Los Angeles, meet Young Little from London in a six round catch weights bout. In the following featherweight bout Buster Brown decisioned Calgary's Young Phillips, then Spokane's Zeno Casey defeated Calgary middleweight Roy George.

At 12:45 Arthur Pelkey and Luther McCarty entered the ring; Pelkey appeared very jittery, while McCarty looked full of confidence.

The first round began with long range sparring. During the first infighting Pelkey jabbed lightly, Luther rolled with the light punch, stepped back, reeled to one side and collapsed on the floor! One minute and ten seconds of the first round had elapsed.

Referee Ed Smith, who had been brought in from Chicago especially for this bout, was dumbfounded, and it took him a moment before he began the count over the prostrate body of McCarty. Many in the audience thought that McCarty had been done in by a sleeper punch. Manager McCarney jumped into the ring, and upon realizing that his protege was not breathing, sobbed helplessly as doctors in the audience rushed to the fallen man. McCarty was then carried outside and laid on the grass where the doctors continued to attempt to revive him.

After the bout Pelkey went back to his quarters at the Elbow View Hotel. When the undertaker's van went by Pelkey said in a low voice, "I pray to God it isn't McCarty". He soon found out that it was his opponent when a Royal North West Mounted Police officer came to the hotel to escort him down to Calgary's

Court House to book him on a charge of manslaughter. His bail of $10,000 was put up by Burns and Freddie Lowe. Later Burns was also arrested and released on a similar size bail.

Just prior to midnight Sunday, the day following the fight, the caretaker of the arena reported to the city fire department that a fire had started in the northwest corner of the structure. Captain "Cappy" Smart of the fire department took charge, however the nearest water supply was a half a mile away, and soon the fire, fanned by strong winds, roared through the arena. By Monday morning a great stretch of grey smouldering ashes marked the spot where the stadium had stood. The origin of the fire remained a mystery. The structure, that was said to have cost $7,000 to build, was insured for $5,000.

When Pelkey's case came before the court the courtroom was packed to suffocation. A.L. Smith acted as counsel for the accused, while James Short, K.C., represented the crown.

Twelve witnesses were called to the inquest. When the body went on view at the funeral parlor it was reported that thousands of people viewed the remains. meanwhile many of Calgary's clergy were very upset. One called the situation, "a little less than murder!!"

The doctors could not agree as to the cause of McCarty's death. The autopsy showed a hemorrage; there was a blood clot at the base of the brain, and there was a displacement of the fourth vertebra. The Ogden blacksmith testified that McCarty had been in his shop complaining of back pain following a throw from a horse he was riding.

Chief Justice Harvey told the jury to decide whether the bout was a prize fight, and if so it was illegal and the accused could be guilty of manslaughter. After much deliberation the jury declared that the bout was a prize fight, but that Pelkey was not responsible for the death of McCarty. The jury spokesman stated that, "we strongly urge upon the government authorities the necessity of having legislation to stop further contests of this nature." Upon the verdict the crowd applauded Pelkey.

McCarty's body had been taken back to the states for burial, and McCarney, his manager, said that he was through with boxing. Burns announced a voluntary retirement and closing out sale at his clothing store. He and Pelkey left for the west coast to go on a vaudeville tour.

In the fall Pelkey returned to Calgary and trained at the Union Hall for his New Year's fight in San Francisco with Gunboat Smith. Pelkey was knocked out by his opponent in the fifteenth round.

Although the tragedy of McCarty's death had brought professional boxing to a halt in Calgary it did not deter all the amateur enthusiasts as boxing and wrestling classes continued at the Y.M.C.A. At Medicine Hat Sailor Jones and Jack Rogers wrestled in a match staged in the roller rink. The Y sent city wrestlers Hannan, Mooney, McCubbin and Pattie to the provincial championships held in Lethbridge.

In March of 1914 Calgarians H. McLaren and A. Crow won their weight championships at the Alberta wrestling championships held in Edmonton. Wrestling, Cumberland style, was part of the program of the Caledonian games held in

Calgary in May. Jack Slavin opened a boxing school on Centre Street, and James J. Corbett, pugilist, entertainer and one time world heavyweight boxing champion appeared at the Pantages. The Alberta Theatre, at 210 Ninth Avenue East, held some boxing contests.

More than two years passed, following the Pelkey-McCarty fight before there was another boxing match staged publicly in Calgary; at that time amateur events were staged under the sponsorship of Eddie Brusso, Tommy Burn's brother.

Cricket

Cricket was often played in early Canada wherever there was a military establishment. The game was reported to have been played on ice in Halifax in 1805. A cricket club was formed in St. John's, Newfoundland. The Montreal Cricket Club existed as early as 1829, while the Toronto Cricket Club, in operation as early as 1836, was host to a team from New York in 1840.

At Victoria, the Pioneer Club played cricket against sailors from visiting ships, and the New Westminster club, organized in 1860, played the Victoria club in 1865. In 1869 the Victoria players travelled to San Francisco for some competition.

On the prairies, the Northwest Cricket Club was formed in the Red River settlement in 1864, with Governor McTavish as club president. The Manitoba Cricket Club was established in 1876.

Cricket came to Alberta with the men of the North West Mounted Police. Dr. Nevitt, a member of the force stationed at Fort Macleod in 1874-75, describes in letters that he wrote to his bride, "We managed to play cricket with some very primitive home-made implements." It would appear that this was an almost daily activity at the fort during this period of time. Nevitt claimed, "My underhand bowling was superior to the swift overarm of young Wilson."

In a letter dated May 3, 1875 he wrote, "...a game of cricket with stumps made of an old lodge pole, an India rubber ball covered with leather, and a very primitive bat cut out of a piece of hardwood. If the cricket was not first class, the exercise was good."

On May 24 a, "grand match is advertised between C and F Troops. Much interest is taken in the result of this match and it is expected that some fine play will be exhibited on both sides." May 24 was a perfect day for the Queen's birthday and the cricket match, and by 10 a.m. the wickets were pitched. Superintendent Winder captained the C Troop eleven, while Nevitt led the F team. C went to bat for 27 runs and F garnered 41 by their last wicket. Following dinner C added 33 to total 60, but F troop ended up victorious.

The following week F troop scored 103 runs and in the two innings as compared to C Troop's 33. Other games saw officers and ranks against the sub constables.

In the summer following the force's arrival at the junction of the Bow and Elbow Rivers the men of E Division set up some cricket stumps, and cricket began in Calgary. The pitch was set up to the south of the fort, and a boundary could be achieved by batting the ball into the Elbow. The activity proved to be of great amusement to the onlooking Indians. By 1881 play had been organized to such a level that games were being played.

A cricket club, composed entirely of civilians, was formed in Edmonton in 1881. The first match in Alberta between teams from different communities took place in 1883 at Fort Macleod where the local detachment went down to defeat the visiting Calgary police team.

Other than the play between members of the N.W.M.P. the first cricket game in the Calgary area took place in April of 1884 with the Mounted Police team defeating the village team by a score of 130 to 110. In a return match the Calgary club won with three wickets to spare. Following a dinner, attended by both clubs at the Royal Hotel, Colonel Herchmer offered an area of land opposite the barracks for use of the cricket club. In May the Calgary club travelled to Medicine Hat for a game, and on other occasion journeyed to Fort Macleod to defeat the home team. The Calgary police team also travelled to Medicine Hat for a game against a C.P.R. club.

During the summer the United Calgary Cricket Club over 25's lost by one run to the under 25's. During the summer Frank Hardisty went to Winnipeg where he purchased a complete cricket set for the club.

Colonel Herchmer was elected president of the cricket club in 1885, while other members of the executive were Rev. G. Smith and E. King. A country team defeated Calgary by 81 runs, and the town team beat the Mounted Rifles XI by 40 runs. The Calgary club played two games against an XI from the High River district as well as the local police detachment team.

Cricket was organized in Fort Macleod and Fort Saskatchewan in 1885, and in Lethbridge and Medicine Hat the following year.

In the spring of 1886 the Calgary cricket enthusiasts held an organizational meeting in A. McVittie's room. The English team defeated the All-comers in a well attended contest. The town-country games proved to be very competitive. In the fall Boynton Hall was the scene of a dance sponsored by the cricket club. Trott's Drug Store, located on Stephen Avenue, advertised cricketeer's goods among its stock.

The cricket club was reorganized in 1888 as the Alberta Cricket Club. Dues for members were $5 annually, and $2 for honourary members. The nickname of "Knights of the Willow and Wicket" was given to the players. During '88 and '89 regular games were played against the N.W.M.P. team, with both sides earning victories. In 1889 Mr. Prothero organized his own cricket XI. A game was played betwen his team and the Mounted Police team on a neutral pitch at Pine Creek. The baseball team played a cricket match against the cricket club, who in return played baseball against the baseball club.

In 1890 the Calgary Fire Brigade Cricket Club was formed, adopting red and white as its club colours. A schedule was drawn up to include the Fire Brigade, Calgary and N.W.M.P. teams, and league play commenced on a drizzly July first between the C.C.C. and Police.

Calgary went to bat first, but with bowler McMahon showing great ball control, only knocked in 33 runs. The Police went to bat to earn 99 runs, with Currie, Hunt and Reading accounting for 75 of these. In the second inning the

Calgary team showed more skill to add another 102 runs, with Rogers, Curley and May batting well. The Police then used only four wickets to earn 42 runs and take the match by six wickets.

Other players on the Calgary XI were: Beaufort, Kirkpatrick, Cave, Wade, Prothero, McKenzie, Johnson, Whitmee, MacMahop, and Stockton, while the garrison's lineup also included: Herchmer, Harper, Hynes, Nichols, Shambler and Stockton. Captain Mcillree and Mr. Braithwaite were the umpires.

The Medicine Hat team invited the Calgary C.C., as well as teams from Swift Current and Maple Creek, to a tournament. Making the trip for Calgary were: Cave, Browne, C. MacKenzie, H. Wade, O. Critchley, Constable MacMahon, H. Curley, Inspector Harper, R. Kirkpatrick, A. Goldfinch, E. Shelton, Dr. George, W. Whitmee, A. Johnson, E. Beaufort, and team captain E. Prothero. Calgary led Medicine Hat 66-35 at the end of the first inning, and after lunch went on to win 130 to 84.

In August the Fire Brigade team took a 121-120 win over the N.W.M.P. XI, needing only four wickets in the second inning to make the necessary runs. Members of the F.B.C.C. were: Harley, Wade, Prichard, Marsham, Jordan, Swaffer, Kerr, Rogers, Tarrant, Smart, and Wade, the game's top batsman.

In their second meeting the Calgary C.C. put together innings of 32 and 55 runs to defeat the police team by two runs. Another rainy day saw the Fire Brigade earn a one inning 62-27 victory over the town team. In the last league game, as C.C.C. beat the N.W.M.P. 103-63, Cave's 46 was to be the highest tally by any local batsman during the season. On another occasion the Fire Brigade defeated a team made up of country players. In August the Calgary Cricket Club held a smoker; an ideal evening of entertainment and song.

In September local cricket buffs met in the Park Hotel to decide on a proposed trip by a local cricket XI to the west coast. Sixteen players were picked to make the trip, and in a practise game they beat the next eleven by ten runs. An attempt was made to raise subscriptions to finance the trip, but the fund raising fell short and the trip fell through.

Currier of the N.W.M.P., and one of the better players in Calgary, was transferred to Regina in order to bolster the Regina police cricket team who were going to play in a tournament in Winnipeg.

The 1890 cricket season in Calgary was considered very successful in spite of the rainy weather, and the general consensus was that the three local clubs were generally equal in play.

By this era cricket was being played in Red Deer, Pine Creek, Millarville, Innisfail, Banff, Strathcona and Canmore. A tournament was held in Lethbridge in which its team defeated Maple Creek and Fort Macleod.

Each of the three Calgary clubs—Town, Police, and Fire Brigade, had their own cricket pitch. The Calgary Cricket Club made an agreement with the Amateur Athletic Association for the Saturday use of their grounds, which were located south of the railroad tracks. The C.A.A.A. had asked the sum of $150 for the season, but they finally agreed to take 20% of the gate receipts.

In the league opener, played at the barracks on a very windy May day, the Calgary team, on the strength of Nelson's bowling, defeated the N.W.M.P.

cricket club by 13 runs. Other Calgary players were: O. Critchley, H. Jameson, E. Cave, E. May, W. Perry, W. Cardo, E. Wilkins, A. Nelson, Dr. George, and A. Ives. The N.W.M.P. teams lineup included; Spencer, James, Nicholls, Junt, McMahon, Barfoot, Jenkins, Stockton, Gillespie, Dyson, and Barry.

In the Police teams next game Spencer and Hut were very capable at bat to lead their team to a 75-42 win over the Fire Brigade Cricket Club; the latter's fielding proving their downfall. The C.F.B. C.C. lineup included: Swaffer, Barwis, Harley, Masham, McKenzie, Clovaton, Joseph, Rogers, Whitmer, Ritchback, and Rae.

The Fire Brigade XI, playing on their own field, defeated the C.C.C. 75-42. Cuffling and Cave each performed the "hat trick", that is each bowler took three wickets with three consecutive balls.

Plans were in the making for the Medicine Hat cricket team to play in Calgary on Dominion Day, but this competition never materialized.

Critchley batted for 46 runs, not out, and Cave performed his second hat trick as the C.C.C. easily defeated the N.W.M.P. 108-41. However, a few days later, the town team was held to 52 runs as compared to 83 for the Fire Brigade team, who later celebrated their success at a smoker held in the Windsor Hotel. Pouring rain did not stop play between the Police and Fire Brigade cricketeers, although the one inning score of 49 even did not settle anything.

Ricardo's eleven and the N.W.M.P. played an exhibition game on the A.C.C.C. grounds. The Police were behind, but a good second inning saw them win by three wickets. As was the custom of the era, each team gave three cheers and a tiger for their opponents.

Cave played a fine game as the C.C.C. defeated the Fire Brigade by 40 runs. The league standings, probably the first such sports statistics of a local nature, appeared in the local paper.

In a return match played in August the N.W.M.P. team defeated Ricardo's XI by 82 runs. The play was featured by the fine bowling of Cave and the spectacular catches of Hardisty, son of the Hudson Bay factor. In another game Jephson, captain of the town team, became involved in a problem of rules in respect to a bowler changing ends.

Barfoot bowled well for the Police as they beat the Fire Brigade 39-36 in a low scoring game. In the last game of the season an eleven captained by E. Joseph lost to the N.W.M.P. by five runs in a one inning fixture.

In April of 1892 some of the members of the Fire Brigade team met in the firehall, but it was obvious that there was not enough interest in the brigade to operate a cricket team that season. Likewise the Police team ceased to operate, however players from these two teams got together to form the new Maple Leaf Cricket Club.

The new sandstone Alexander Block's hall was officially opened by the Calgary Cricket Club ball, held on the Queen's birthday.

The first cricket match of the season saw a town XI, captained by Jephson, play a country XI, with O. Critchley at their helm. Both Prothero and Andrews batted double figures for the town team, while Barwis was credited with a spectacular catch for the country. In the middle of the day the members of both teams retired to the Criterion Restaurant for lunch; afterwards the players fed their table scraps to the restaurant's mascot, a brown bear.

The teams went into afternoon play even in runs, but the final outcome saw the Country team come out ahead. Other town players were: Gillespie, Hunt, Rogers, Tourney, Perry, Harley, and Douglass, while Moore, Sugden, Ricardo, Fraser, Cuffling, Brasier, Wilkes, Smith, and Campbell played for the country.

In June the single men took a 122-49 win from the married cricket players. Only one inning was played, as the singles were not disposed of until after six p.m.

A great deal of interest was centered on the first game between the C.C.C. and the new Maple Leaf Cricket Club. Rogers bowled well for the Maple Leafs, and as well was their top batsman, but they went down to defeat 49-36 to the Town team. Other Maple Leaf players were: H. Southon, W. Barwis, J. Hunt, H. Aston, R. O'Sullivan, J. Harley, J. Rae, L. Tarrant, W. Whitmee and J. Smart. Playing for the C.C.C. were: J. Child, W. Perry, W. Ricardo, J. Jephson, E. Prothero, O. Critchley, E. Cave, E. Moore, S. Douglass, Morris, and Deyelll.

In a return match the Maple Leafs turned the tables taking a 49-40 win over the Calgary C.C., who attributed their loss to the absence of team captain Jephson. However the credit for the win went to Cuffling for his fine bowling.

The C.C.C. then formed the President's and vice-president's XI's. In the first of several evening matches the President's team won by ten wickets with Pavey and Pavier the top batsmen.

In August cricketeers O'Sullivan, W. Perry, E. Cave, W. Barwis, E. Cuffling, L. Tarrant, J. Jephson, E. Vincent, E. Prothero, J. Pavey, E. Rogers, W. Whitmee, and Sputhoff travelled to Edmonton to play the Edmonton Cricket Club. The C. and E. Railroad gave the group a round-trip for the price of a one-way fare.

Rogers batted for 25 and Pavey added 19 runs as Calgary outscored Edmonton 106-59. Dr. O'Sullivan proved to be in top form to frustrate the Edmonton batters. After the game the teams attended a sumptuous spread at Jasper House, presided over by Mayor McCauley.

The Town team met an eleven from Sheep Creek and came out with an easy 113-48 win.

In late September the Calgary Cricket Club hosted the Edmonton club in a game played on the C.A.A.A. grounds. A good sized crowd, including many ladies, was present at this contest. Calgary won by nine wickets, with Cufflings 34 runs tops in the batting department. Calgary's E. Moore hit over the fence for an automatic six.

One of the highlights of the social season was the Calgary Cricket Club ball, held in the Opera House.

During the year the Canadian Cricket Association was formed with John Wrought of Toronto as its first president.

Calgary cricket buffs held an organizational meeting in the town hall in late May of 1893. It was the unanimous opinion of those present that the two clubs of the previous year should amalgamate to form one strong club. Judge Rouleau was elected president of the new organization. Major Jarvis was the vice-president, W. Whitmee took on the job of secretary-treasurer, E. Rogers as club captain and Dr. O'Sullivan as vice-captain. Subscription rates were set at three dollars for playing members and two dollars for honourary members. The C.A.A.A. grounds were booked for the season, and club members were placed on either the Captain's or Vice-captain's teams.

In the season's first game Hardisty and Dr. O'Sullivan hit for 21 and 25 runs to lead the V.C.'s to a 71-59 win over the Captain's team; the latter group being stymied by the excellent bowling of Dr. O'Sullivan.

The local N.W.M.P. detachment decided, after a year's abstention, to again field a cricket team, and a Saturday afternoon game was set up with the C.C.C. Activities of a sporting nature rarely took place on a Sabbath during this era.

The Police went to bat first and only earned 24 runs during their side as a result of the effective bowling of Cave and O'Sullivan. However Barfoot and Aston bowled well for the Police and the town's 32 runs could not be considered high. The Police XI added another 35 runs in the second inning, then Cave and Barwis managed enough runs between then to give the C.C.C. the match.

The game was played on cocoa matting, which probably helped attribute to the low scores, but the players felt that this surface was an improvement over the prairie grass.

Besides the aforementioned players, Pavey, Critchley, Clark, Sanson, Vincent, McDonald, Rogers, and Hardisty completed the C.C.C. lineup, while other members of the Police XI were: McNair, Oliver, Fife, Jarvis, Andrews, Storey, Jenkins, Rae, and Clett.

In August an XI composed of players of English descent won by 21 runs over an all-comers team. Newcomer Williams and Cave provided excellent bowling for the winners. Unfortunately Dr. Sanson received a fractured arm while batting against Cave's bowling.

In late May of 1895 a meeting of Calgary's cricket enthusiasts was held in the Royal Hotel. M.L.A. O. Critchley was elected president of the organization, with Superintendent Howe of the N.W.M.P. as V.P., and W. Whitmee the club secretary. L. Clarke was designated as playing captain. The executive was authorized to spend $50 on new bats, balls and gloves. Supplies were purchased from Winnipeg retailers. Club subscription rates remained at $3 and $2.

A Calgary newspaper gave two full column's coverage to the exploits of English cricketeer W. Grace who had just hit for his 100 century.

In the first match of the season for the "Knights of the Willow" between the City and the Police the results were left in doubt as playing time ran out when Calgary, who were far behind in the first inning, caught up to finish within one run of the N.W.M.P. Gregory proved to be a tremendous bowler for the Police, while the C.C.C.'s F. Pellant, a new arrival from Toronto, played a tremendous game.

Other N.W.M.P. players included: Storey, Duggan, Iredell, Dr. Sanson, Mallahue, Oliver, Morris, Stillman, Morgan, and Perry, while on the C.C.C. team were W. Barwis, J. Payer, Williams, F. Exham, Dr. O'Sullivan, K. Johnson, E. Vincent, R.C. Thomas, H. Douglas, and Dr. McDonald.

The Police team also won the second match, but in the third game the City put together innings of 80 and 50, then the Police had time called on them during their second time at bat. Even though they were far behind in runs they felt that they had a chance; and as an afterthought they felt that the time limits in these games should be extended. Wilkins, a new player in the City lineup, hit for 30 runs.

Before a "large crowd of five men, two ladies and the Herald reporter", the single men defeated the married players in their annual cricket match. Gregory hit for 52 runs for the winners.

Cricket interest appeared to be lacking in Calgary during the spring of 1896, although the local newspaper was carrying weekly reports of England's cricket results.

In June a Country XI challenged the city players to a game. After much deliberation the town put together an XI consisting of: R.C. Thomas, R. O'Sullivan, L. Clarke, E. Wilkins, W. Barwis, K. Johnston, Iredell, Mellalue, Stillman, R. Sanson, and E. Vincent to accept the challenge. The Country team won the match by ten runs behind the fine bowling of Gregory. Other country players were: Batho, Cory, Ross, Cuffling, Rogers, Webb, Phillips, Critchley, and Stokes.

The Police team met the Country XI in two matches and came out on top in play. However they were considerate enough to treat the losers to a dinner and smoking concert at the barracks following the second game. This was also the first local game for Rev. Webb-Peploe, who proved to be an accomplished batter and bowler. Members of the Police XI were: Iredell, Storey, Stillman, Perry, Oliver, Gregory, Mallalue, Morris, Edrup, French and Istram.

During the summer the English and Australian national cricket teams were in competition, and Calgary's cricket enthusiasts were able to read the complete results of each match, including individual player statistics in the local paper.

In late summer the Calgary XI journeyed to Sheep Creek to play a return match with the Country team. King batted in 46 runs as the town boys put together innings of 30 and 102, however it was an easy win for the ranchers and farmers who added 70 to their first inning 131. A great number of ladies were present for the competition. Lunch was served at Freeman's house, and that evening 18 visitors were billeted at the Adams Ranche. Later the Calgary team took a 110 to 46 win from a Bankhead team.

In May of 1897 the Innisfail cricket club played a game at Antler Lake against the Horse Shoe Lake team. The cricket season opened late in Calgary when a team made up of bankers and professionals defeated the Town by one inning and 24 runs. Bridges and Iredell bowled well for the winners, while Benson led the batters with 26 runs. Pavey hit for 49 and Barton added 40 runs as a West End XI defeated the East End team 102-88. Other games between local teams saw the Benedicts and Singles come together, as well as the President's and Vice-President's XI's. In a Dominion Day sports program L. Orr won the cricket ball throw with a distance of over 107 yards.

The C.C.C.'s lineup for a home game against Millarville included: R. Thomas, P. Barton, L. Clarke, R. Sanson, D. Fraser, H. Gordon, C. Smith, E. Wilkins, G. Andrews, E. Rogers and Ed Vincent. However Millarville did not show up, so a picked team, captained by Mr. Saunders, was organized. The picked team, consisting of: Dyson, Phillips, Pelatt, Sanders, Passey, Bell, Benson, Hallwell, Owen and Birney, surprised everyone with an upset win. Following the game the ladies served ice cream and cake to the players.

The Millarville team did arrive the following Saturday, and then they defeated the Calgary XI by seven wickets. Millarville's Oliver hit for the first six ever recorded at the Athletic Grounds; King scored 34 runs for Millarville, and Calgary's Barton hit for 32.

In a return encounter the Town defeated the Bankers and Professionals with a come-from-behind second inning. The losers said that the Town would not have won without their import from Millarville. The C.C.C. divided their players into two teams according to the alphabet for a game. Barton showed tremendous skill at bat as he garnered 48 runs.

The Calgary team arranged a game at Innisfail, but the trip did not materialize, much to the dismay of the Innisfail team. The Calgary cricketeers did travel to Millarville, where they lost a game to the home team by three wickets, but in a later game, played in Calgary, the C.C.C. won over the Sheep Creek club.

The local paper published statistics of local cricket players. Barton led the batsmen, averaging 22 runs a game. Dr. O'Sullivan and Fraser were the leading bowlers.

J. Smith was elected president of the Calgary Cricket Club in 1898, and E. Vincent took over the responsibility of club secretary in a spring meeting held in the Alberta Hotel. Club members decided to again lease the athletic grounds south of the tracks. The meeting was attended by representatives from Millarville and Innisfail.

A game was arranged at Innisfail on the Queen's birthday, but the Calgary players decided they were not ready to play so early in the season. L. Orr again won the cricket ball throw at the May 24 sports program.

In June O. Critchley, W. Barwis, Dr. O'Sullivan, H. Noton, Sergt. Aston, Const. Pyre, E. Cuffling, J. Pavey, Blind, W. Concarron, and F. Passey travelled to Innisfail where they lost to the home team by five wickets in a rain swept game. Critchley and Cuffling hit for 25 runs each.

On Dominion Day the Calgary team could only put together innings of 34 and 38 as compared with hometeam Millarville's 32 and 104. Poor catching and fielding on the part of the Calgary fielders helped to contribute to their loss. Millarville players included: King, Church, Brown, Cuffling, Austin, Marsack, Miller, Douglas, Lane, E. Church and Jackson. New faces in Calgary's lineup were: Hesketh, McCarthy and Macleod.

A cricket tournament was held in July at the C.A.A.A., grounds. Admission to the games was 15¢ for men and 10¢ for the ladies, and many ladies did come with the visiting teams from Innisfail and Millarville.

Doughty hit for 40 runs as Calgary beat Millarville 149-54. The combined Innisfail-Pine Lake team then gave Millarville its second loss. That evening a smoking concert was held in the Alberta Music Hall for the visiting cricket players.

The next day Calgary, led by the batting of Barton and Vincent, beat Innisfail by nine wickets. What was billed as the first annual cricket dance was held that evening in the Alexander Hall.

During the tournament there was discussion of the feasibility of forming an Alberta cricket league, and forming a representative team to challenge Manitoba. The local paper reported, "The committee should see that in future the enthusiasm of the home team is restrained during the progress of a game with visitors. Effervescent encouragement is not only in bad taste, but decidedly unsportsmanlike. The lady visitors appreciated the ice cream very much".

In August the Calgary club earned a decisive win over Blind's Country team. Doughty's 26 and Barton's 21, not out, were Calgary's top batsmen, while Critchley hit for 27 for the country. Vincent and Blind were the best bowlers.

In September the local paper gave coverage to the first international cricket matches between England and Canada.

By 1899 cricket interest appeared to be on the upsurge in Calgary. At the April club meeting, held in the Alberta Music Store, E. Cuffling was elected to its presidency, and W. Blind was designated as club secretary. Plans were made to rent the club grounds out to other sports groups.

The Millarville cricketeers were anxious to play against Calgary, but due to wet weather it was June before any competition took place. Team captain P. Barton, C. Smith, W. Blind, W. Barwis, H. Noton, H. Knott, G. Edwards, R. O'Sullivan, W. Napier, O'Kelly and Ketchen travelled to Millarville to win over the home team by 72 runs. This was the first time the country team had lost a game on its home grounds. Calgary's win came as a result of O'Sullivan's effective bowling and the fine batting of Barton and Noton. After the game the players were treated to a smoker by Mr. Freeman and Mr. Phillips.

In June the Calgary C.C. travelled to Innisfail where they lost to the Pine Lake team by 18 runs. On Dominion Day Calgary beat Millarville by 9 wickets, with Noton accounting for 55 of Calgary's runs.

Calgary's July cricket tournament was one of the year's biggest sporting events. Admission to the games was 25¢ for gentlemen and ladies were admitted free.

In the first match Calgary easily won by one inning over Innisfail as Barton and Noton put 74 runs on their partnership. Millarville beat Pine Lake, who in turn easily won over Edmonton. Edmonton, however, turned the tables on Calgary winning by four wickets in an exciting game before a good crowd of spectators. In the evening a cricket ball was held at the Opera House with Mr. Wilkins orchestra in attendance.

On Saturday, at the conclusion of the tournament, a combined Calgary-Millarville eleven, captained by Barton, won over the north district team, composed of players from Edmonton and Pine Lake. Following the game over 100 men attended a smoker and music concert held at the Sons of England Hall.

A summer game saw the married players win over those "who ought to be"; later the Clarence Brook players beat the "rest of the team".

In the first such inter-city competition with the Lethbridge Cricket Club Calgary defeated the visitors by eight runs. Napier was the best batsman for

Calgary. The Calgary club was hosted by the Edmonton club on Labour Day. The N.W.M.P. again put together a team to play a fall game against members of the Calgary Cricket Club on a field near the Baptist Church.

The 1900 cricket season opened with Calgary playing at Millarville, where the pitch was now covered with coconut matting. Calgary's lineup included: Barton, Noton, Blind, Gordon, O'Sullivan, Sanson, Rhodes, Hardy, MacDonald, Critchley, and Wainwright, while playing for Millarville were: King, Phillips, Douglas, Williams, Millar, Cuffling, Oliver, Rogers, Freeman, and Tynwett. Calgary lost the game by an inning and 16 runs. Phillips scored 41 runs for Millarville, while Noton hit for 32 for the losers. After the game the players were treated to supper by Reverend Webb-Peploe.

A unique cricket game took place at Millarville where the ladies put together innings of 72 and 29 to complete a tally higher than the men's 31 and 67. The men, however, were handicapped in that they had to use a broom handle instead of a bat. It was reported that an audience of 75 people watched this interesting encounter.

In June the Calgary C.C. again travelled to Millarville to go down to defeat by a 309 to 118 score. Phillips batted in 115 runs and Outram hit for 74. Additions to Calgary's lineup included: Vincent, S. Mackid, Davidson, Birney, Brae, Barwis, and McDonnell. The 427 runs for 20 wickets was considered incredible, and was the highest known score ever recorded in the N.W. Territories.

In July Millarville's cricket team played in Calgary, winning by an inning and 41 runs. Barton batted well for Calgary, knocking in 92 runs. There were many ladies present among the large crowd of spectators.

The C.C.C. played a team composed of C.P.R. employees, and Calgary won the game on the strength of Noton's 42 runs. It was felt that the C.P.R. team had some skilled players and with practise would offer some good competition.

The Millarville team travelled to Lethbridge, and they beat the home team by an inning and 61 runs. They then went on to Medicine Hat where they won with equal ease. This game did stimulate cricket interest in the Hat, and as a result the players formed a cricket club. Later in the season the Medicine Hat team played at Millarville and recorded a convincing win.

During Fair Week in September the Calgary C.C. defeated the visiting Banff cricket XI 62-59. The win was attributed to the excellent batting of Dr. Sanson who ran up 23 runs before he got tired and went home. The annual married-single men's game was won by the family men.

In April of 1901 the Calgary Cricket Club held its annual organizational meeting and elected Captain Gordon as the club president. H. Adams was appointed secretary-treasurer and G. Noton as the club president. Pat Burns was designated as honourary president. The club was going to attempt to make arrangements with the Agricultural Society to lay out a cricket pitch on their grounds.

In May the club's single players, led by Oaks, defeated the married players 71-46. The ladies served tea at the game, which was followed by a club smoking concert held in the Sons of England Hall.

The City team, although stymied by the fine bowling of Monson, defeated the

N.W.M.P. team 92-58 in a one inning fixture. The police then took a second turn at bat and Captain Davidson amassed a high total of 49 runs. Other police players were: Percy, Thomas, Rubbra, Belcher, McDonnell, Mackid, Bruce, Peters, and Lange. The City's lineup included: Noton, Captain Gordon, O'Sullivan, R. Inglis, R. Oaks, Vincent, and N. MacLeod.

Orr again won the cricket ball throw for distance at the Queen's birthday sports program. A few days later Noton and Knott led the Englishmen to a 60-33 cricket win over the All-comers, otherwise known as the "rest of the universe team".

In June the Calgary Cricket Club travelled to Millarville, then offered many excuses when they lost in a rain covered encounter.

In a third match between the City and Millarville clubs the country team came out ahead 95-74. O'Sullivan's 17 runs included 4 fours. Millarville's lineup included: W. King, W. Phillips, C. Browne, C. Holme, J. Oliver, H. Shand, M. Millar, J. Birney, C. Douglas, J. Freeman, and E. Vincent; the latter borrowed from Calgary.

At Millarville the married players took an overwhelming 148-53 win over the single men during a day that saw many of the cricket players also participate in a tennis tournament. For the remainder of the summer there was little interest in cricket in southern Alberta.

In 1902 the Calgary Cricket Club raised money by sponsoring the play, "A Pair of Spectacles", at the Opera House. However it was June before a team organizational meeting was held in W. Barwis's office. Player's fees of two dollars were payable to secretary Oakes.

Millarville again proved its superiority over Calgary, taking two close games. Millarville's Noton batted in 90 runs in the second encounter. Calgary's lineup included: Barwis, Grogan, O'Sullivan, Worsley, N. MacLeod, S. Mackid, B. Bruce, S. Belcher, F. Timewell, R. Oakes, and S. Williams.

Local C.P.R. employees formed a cricket club. On Coronation Day the Canmore Club defeated an XI from Banff. In late August O'Sullivan and Worsley each knocked in 20 runs as the Military defeated the civilian XI 99-31.

An attempt was made in 1903 to reorganize and vitalize the Calgary Cricket Club. Colonel Saunders was the new club president, while Senator Lougheed became the honorary president. A subscription dance was held at the Barracks to raise money for the club. The $1.50 charge for men and 75¢ for ladies included a midnight dinner. During this period correspondence was carried on with the Vancouver club in respect to a coast XI playing a two day game with an Alberta XI.

In April the Calgary Cricket Club beat a Mounted Police XI 87-57. On the Queen's birthday the Calgary C.C. defeated the Canmore XI 108-37 in a game played at the barracks pitch. The feature player of the game was Carrick who only allowed the Canmore team eight runs in eight wickets. Vincent and N. MacLeod did excellent service with the stick for the local team. Other Calgary players were: team captain O'Sullivan, Worsley, Snell, Barker, Lowes, Dickson, Slatter, and Redington.

A large number of spectators paid 25¢ each to see Calgary on the short end of a 157-131 game with Millarville in a match played at the Exhibition grounds. Calgary hit for 71 in their second inning, but because there was not time for Millarville to bat, only the first inning counted. Noton was the top batsman with 101 runs. O'Sullivan did most of the bowling for Calgary, but four other Calgary players also took a turn at throwing. Millarville went on to defeat Calgary twice more during the season. In a game at Millarville Calgary's loss was disasterous, as they were easily beaten by ten wickets.

In a game played at Moccasin Flats in Calgary's suburb of Rouleauville Captain Bellair's team defeated Richardson's team with ten wickets to spare. This was followed by a single wicket game for twenty dollars a side, with Irish collecting the money from Livingstone. In the evening the players were involved in a pick-up game to complete a full day of cricket.

It was a bowlers day as the Army and Navy, led by Captain Worsley beat the City 61-42. The Old-country, or English, took a 116-45 win from the All-comers, who had only seven players turn out. A good crowd attended the annual married versus single players.

On July first the Calgary team travelled to Canmore to put together innings of 36 and 107, while the home team hit for 46 and 26. Adams and Parez were the top batsmen, while O'Sullivan bowled well. The club members were well satisfied with their trip.

The Calgary Old-timers travelled to Millarville to lose by an inning and 23 runs as Noton hit for 63 for Millarville.

Published statistics showed Worsley averaging 24 runs a game, and he was Calgary's top batsman. Carrick and O'Sullivan were the top bowlers.

The season was brought to a close by the Cricket Club dinner held at the Queen's Hotel. R.B. Bennett was the main speaker at this gala affair. The Millarville players, who had been in attendance, wrote back that it was the most enjoyable social event in the history of their club.

The 1904 organizational meeting of the Calgary cricketeers was held in the Canadian Mounted Rifles drill hall. P. Jephson and A.E. Cross were designated as the club's honourary presidents, while Colonel Saunders was re-elected president and Freddie Lowes as secretary. Bagley's Orchestra provided the music for the Cricket Club Ball which was held in the C.M.R. hall.

In the opening game of the Calgary cricket season, played at the barracks pitch, the N.W.M.P. team took an 89-82 win over the Calgary C.C. Worsley's 25 for the Police and Porter's 21 for the C.C.C. were the high individual runs.

At the May 24 sports day L. Orr again won the cricket ball throw for distance.

A new cricket pitch was laid out at the golf grounds, and before a large crowd the visiting Millarville team took a 175-98 win over the Calgary team. Calgary earned 132 runs in the second inning, but as Millarville had to leave for home this turn at bat did not count. Inspector Worsley's 69 was tops among the batsmen. Other Calgary players were: O'Sullivan, S. Williams, Constable Foster, Corporal Haskins, M. McCarthy, J. Carrick, H. Adams, Porter, Sgt.-Major Belcher, and F. Lowes.

At Millarville Calgary put together innings of 65 and 75, but they were edged by Millarville by one run. Belcher bowled effectively for Calgary, and W. King was the pick of the Millarville team.

The tables were finally turned as Calgary, led by Dr. Mackid's 40 runs, defeated Millarville 138-43 in a home game. In the annual single versus married players game the Mavericks won by two runs.

In April of 1905 the Calgary Cricket Club met in the drill hall to again acknowledge Colonel Saunders as club president and Dr. O'Sullivan as team captain.

In a game between the ladies and men the males had to bat, bowl and play left-handed. Doctors Mackid and O'Sullivan accounted for 31 of the men's 54 runs; but the ladies earned 56 runs, thanks to Miss McCullough's 24 and Miss Toole's 17.

The serious play opened with a well published May game played at the barracks between the C.C.C. and the R.N.W.M.P. XI. The police won the toss and sent the city to bat. Captain Clifford and O'Sullivan batted in 109 runs before they parted company; a record for the territories. The Calgary XI then proceeded to set another Territories record as they hit for 224 runs for the loss of only six wickets. The Police ran up a total of 74 runs against a loss of seven wickets in their allotted one hour and 45 minutes batting time.

Other members of the C.C.C. were: Robinson, Williams, Scanlan, Doughty, Lowes, and Keane. Members of the Police IX included: Inspector Duffis, Hosken, Vine, Belcher, Reddington, Saunders, Brayne, Matheson, Josephs, and Spence.

A different method of choosing teams saw C.C.C. players whose names began with A-H defeat the rest of the alphabet and as well, married men playing the unmarried. At Canmore the visiting Bankhead team defeated the hometown XI in a hotly contested game.

The C.C.C. only used one wicket to defeat the Country team 66-84, thanks to Captain Clifford's 89 and V. Bryant's 57. Thus ending a very short cricket season in Calgary.

In 1906 Dr. O'Sullivan again was chosen team captain of the C.C.C. E. Doughty hit for 75 runs in the season's opener as the single players turned the tables on the family men with a 181-66 win.

Calgary defeated an Okotoks team, including many familiar players from the old Millarville team, by a 151-126 score. The Okotoks players were the better fielders, but the city boys were best with the bat. Calgary's lineup included: H. Adames, T. Bryant, Corporal Hoskins, Constable Higginson, E. Vincent, Corporal Joseph, Sgt.-Major Belcher, N. MacLeod, Dr. Mackid, and Dr. O'Sullivan, while powerhouse batman J. Norton combined with H. Phillips, W. King, W. Pavey, P. Connell, S. Grummond, A. Merrick, M. Millar, F. Austin, A. Fullerton and A. Powell to compose the Okotoks lineup.

An in between innings luncheon was held at the Palmetto Cafe, and following the game the Okotoks club was treated to a smoker at the barracks. A return game at Okotoks between the two clubs was rained out.

In July the Calgary eleven again journeyed to Okotoks to put together innings of 100 and 102 as compared with Okotoks 79 for one inning. O'Sullivan and Belcher bowled well for Calgary, while Doughty was the game's top batter.

At Calgary the home team hit for 124 runs, but Okotoks came back to tally 166 runs and outplay Calgary in a game described as, "bright and breezy". Beard bowled well for Okotoks, with Higginson being the only Calgary batman to earn any significant number of runs. Both O'Sullivan and Belcher had to leave the game with sprained ankles after running into gopher holes. At the train station there were speeches by members of both teams, and the Okotoks players gave a great cheer for Calgary as their train pulled out.

A match was arranged with the Lethbridge team, but the game was never played. Any other cricket played in Calgary that season was only of a pick-up nature. However a unique game did take place on Boxing Day as the Calgary Cricket Club defeated a Police XI in a mid-winter encounter.

Dr. O'Sullivan presided at a late March, 1907 organizational meeting of the C.C.C. The club decided to raise the membership fee from three to five dollars in order to meet increased operational costs. An appreciation was shown to the Mounted Police canteen for its twenty dollars contribution to the club. Club members decided to give individual prizes to those individuals who compiled the best season's records in batting, bowling, and fielding. The player who makes the most catches in six games would receive the Bryant Bat, a bat with an engraved silver plate mounted on its face. There was discussion in respect to forming an Alberta cricket association, and the possibility of a game with a touring English team in August.

The elections saw Captain Deanne voted in as club president and J. Jephson as team captain. Honorary club presidents were Lord Strathcona and L. Vanwart.

Practises began in April at the pitch located on the Police grounds. A tentative game with Edmonton, planned for Arbour Day, did not take place. Daniels and Doughty were the big batsmen as Mr. Adam's team took a 156-111 win over Mr. Gilvert's XI in a scratch match.

On Victoria Day a Calgary XI, composed of A. Daniels, Hoskyn, Vincent, Drysdale, E. Doughty, J. Bruce, G. Ryan, N. MacLeod, H. Joseph, E. Danger-field, and H. Adams travelled to Lethbridge where they lost to the hometeam by a 63-54 score. Hings was a fine bowler as well as hitting for 32 runs for Lethbridge. A. Daniel, Calgary's first batter, and the team's top batsman, was bowled over by a treacherous ball, and he was out of the game. Following the inning Calgary's contingent was well entertained by its Lethbridge hosts.

By this time informal talks and correspondence had let to the formation of a loose cricket organization and a tentative schedule for many of the cricket centres in Alberta.

In June the Okotoks team took an easy 122-53 win over Calgary. In the second inning Okotoks hit for 160 more runs in just five wickets, but play was called on account of rain. Connell's 79 for Okotoks was tops in the batting department. O'Sullivan and Daniel bowled, but not too successfully, for Calgary.

For the first time in several years the Medicine Hat team visited Calgary where they were beaten by an inning and 54 runs. The visitors put together innings of 62 and 51, while Adams ran up 54 of Calgary's one inning total of 177 runs. Dr. O'Sullivan bowled well, allowing only 29 runs in seven wickets.

Competition was picking up in the city as the C.C.C.'s first and second XI's met; then the second XI played a team from Western Canada College at the school grounds.

The C.C.C. took the train to Banff where they met an eager Banff XI, however the home team were not in the class of the Calgary team. E. Pinkham, just home from college in Ontario, was the top Calgary batsman, while Dangerfield was brilliant in the field.

During the summer the Calgary Football Club challenged the C.C.C. second XI to a cricket match, and to the surprise of many took a 91-70 win. Hayward hit for 36 for the winners, while footballer Daintry allowed only nine runs in the five wickets he bowled. Later a scratch match was played between the second XI and the Young Men's Club.

A game at High River was rained out and then a planned game between the C.C.C. and Bankhead did not take place. Calgary travelled to Okotoks to come out with a 14-57 win.

In September a Calgary team took the train to Medicine Hat where they put together innings of 115 and 50, while the home team hit for 114 and 71. O'Sullivan and Stephens bowled well, and Heywood was the best Calgary batter with 44 runs. In the evening the Calgary team was entertained with dinner, music and dancing.

Calgary Cricket Club, 1908. Back left to right: J. Robertson, E. Stevens, R. Wood, F. Davis. Middle: E. Daggerfield, E. Vincent, T. Bryant (captain), H. Adames. Front: W. Reilly, F. Wetherall, T. Heywood.

During this era it was often difficult for both teams to complete two innings while the sun was still high enough in the sky, or before the train left, so often only the first inning was completed as far as was possible.

The local season came to a close as Calgary beat Okotoks 137-81 behind the good bowling of Stephens and Aldrich, with Hayward again the top Calgary batter.

By the spring of 1908 there was an increased interest in cricket in Calgary and Southern Alberta. Representatives from the Calgary Cricket Club, Hillhurst Sheep Creek, St. John's, and the Anglican Young People's Association met to form the Southern Alberta Cricket League. It was a loosely knit organization, but it served its purpose.

The new Hillhurst Club, from northwest Calgary, met the Sheep Creek team in a game played at the barracks pitch to open the local season. Hillhurst's lineup included: Canon, D'Easum, Cook, Thompson, Knott, Lumley, Howarth, Davis, White, Wakelyn, Jordison, and Thompson.

The C.C.C.'s 1908 lineup included team captain Bryant, J. Adams, Bally, Hooley, Wicketkeeper, F. Weatherall, Stephen, A. Daniel, T. Heywood, E. Vincent, R. Woods, Robertson, E. Dangerfield, Aldrich, W. Reilly, and F. Davis. In their first game against Hillhurst they managed a one inning total of 102 runs, while other opponents of the C.C.C. were the Banff Club, the Church of the Redeemer XI, and a team from the Canadian Mounted Rifles.

In June the married and single players held their annual game. The St. John's Club travelled to Okotoks, where they lost 104-90 to the Sheep Creek team. Only seven St. John's players had turned up at the train station for the trip, including Percy Power, who garnered 39 of their 90 runs. So they were not dismayed with their loss.

There were several benefit cricket matches held in Calgary with the teams consisting of picked men. The new Hillhurst pitch was the scene of a match between Canon D'Easum's and Aldrich's XI's. Other such matches were the C.C.C. and Mr. Redgrove's XI, and Hillhurst versus Mr. Cunningham's XI.

The C.C.C. took an overwhelming 208 to 51 win, on the strength of Heywood's 77 runs, from the St. John's club. The east end XI's lineup was composed of J. Attwood, Jones, Hall, Redgrove, Williams, Downing, Anderton, Miller, Gates, Hunt, and Evans.

The St. John's XI did improve as the season progressed, and in September they again travelled to the Okotoks where they put together innings of 46 and 51. Okotoks was held to only 18 runs in the initial wicket, but they came on strong in the second frame to add 86 runs. Their lineup included: Adriel, Knowles, Joseph, McMicking, Reverend Fletcher, Taylor, Maloney, Hill, Austin, Barth, Van Telghen, and Walker.

Daniel scored 155 runs, which was close to a Canadian record, besides which he excelled in bowling, as Calgary outscored Bankhead 254-47. Both clubs attended a dinner at the Victoria Hotel following the game.

The Calgary Cricket Club was considered the undisputed champion of the league, and for this they were awarded the Van Wart Cup. They had not lost a game in the 1908 season, and they had only scored less than 200 runs on two occasions.

North of Calgary Red Deer won 140-89 over Pine Lake to capture the Red Deer Cup. This trophy had been put up for competition by Mr. R. Jackson. Cricket on a different level took place on Mrs. Towner's grounds, south of Calgary, as the Meadowfield Cricket Club held its grand wind up match between the ladies' and gentlemen's team. The ladies were narrowly beaten, but they claimed this only happened because a dog had got in the road of one of the players. Tea was served following the contest.

The Calgary season ended with Hillhurst defeated Cunningham's XI 88-44, the C.C.C. played Redgrove's team, and Cunningham's team meeting the Dalgetty XI on the new Mewata pitch.

The West End Cricket Club, with M. Robertson as its president, was formed in Calgary in the spring of 1909. Club play was to be mainly of an internal nature. The St. John's Cricket Club held its organizational meeting in the National Hotel in east Calgary. Tom Bellow was elected club president for the coming season. The city would allow cricket to be played at the Mewata field, but the teams were not allowed to charge admission to any of the games.

The first important game of the season was to take place on Victoria Day as the Calgary Cricket Club planned to play in Banff. However the game did not take place as the train was unable to get to the mountain town that day due to a bridge washout.

Redgrove was in splendid form as he batted in 77 runs to lead the Calgary C.C. to a 200-63 win over the St. John's Cricket Club in a game played at the barracks pitch. A second XI of the C.C.C. played a practise game against the West End Club on the Mewata field.

Bryant hit for 110, scoring a century, as the C.C.C. XI overwhelmed the Okotoks team 229-47. 180 runs were scored while Bryant was at bat.

In June the second XI of the C.C.C. lost 58-53 to a team from Western Canada College in a game played on the college grounds. The school's lineup included: Weston, Times, Palmer, McDonald, Rees, Green, Williams, Walker, and Cuthbert.

The C.C.C. travelled to Edmonton and put together innings of 65 and 36 runs, however the Edmonton club was much stronger, attaining 105 and 47 runs to earn a victory over Calgary. Stephen and Daniel handled most of the bowling for the C.C.C., while Federal Member of Parliament McCarthy scored 15 runs for the losers. Following the game the Calgary contingent were dined and entertained.

The Calgary team bounced back to defeat the Fort Macleod XI by an inning and 144 runs. Stephen, Johnson and Lucas bowled splendidly for Calgary. At Pincher Creek the touring Pollard Opera Company's team defeated the town team 74-32.

A good crowd came out to see the Calgary men take a narrow 66-63 win over the ladies team. Miss Hobbs hit for 31 runs, while Miss Pearson added 13, and as well she played splendidly in the field.

The C.P.R. XI played its first game, but the St. John's club, led by Williams and Woodman, easily handled the railroad boys 60-21.

The Calgary Cricket Club members practised diligently each evening in preparation for their trip to a tournament on the west coast. Making the trip were: Allan, Adames, Bryant, Daniel, Johnston, Lucas, Martin, Heywood, Heap, Remington, Merrick, Eoll, Redgrove, and Stephen. When the team left on the west bound train a large crowd gathered at the station to see them off and wish them luck.

The Calgary team stopped off at Revelstoke for a game. After winning the toss they went to bat and amassed a substantial 250 runs for five wickets, Heywood's 100, not out, and Allan's 59 were Calgary's principal scores. The Revelstoke team replied with innings of 17 and 56.

Led by Heywood Calgary easily won its game with Vernon by an inning and a 190-55 score.

Teams from Portland, Burrard, Vancouver, Seattle, Victoria, and Calgary entered the coast tournament, which offered the International Cup to the winner.

In their first game of the tournament Calgary won, as they put together innings of 144 and 82, while Seattle, their opponents, hit for 151 and 59. Lucas saved the day for Calgary by bowling seven wickets in the two innings and only allowing 29 runs. G. Allan's 60 runs was tops in Calgary's batting department.

Calgary next met the powerful Burrard team. The prairie boys had innings of 79 and 123, but Burrard ran up 177 runs in the first inning. However time had been called before they were able to take their second turn at bat, so they won the game on the first inning score. Burrard went on to meet Vancouver in the final of this great cricket tournament.

Meanwhile in Alberta the St. John's club travelled to Okotoks to record an easy 93-51 win. Then on their own field, located on Colonel Walker's land, St. John's lost to the C.P.R. XI 123-56. The railroad boys had added several players from the Calgary C.C. to their lineup. In a return match the three Downing brothers led St. John's to a narrow 52-51 win over the C.P.R. Other St. John's players included: Lambert, Williams, Hall, Canon, Attwood, Woodman, Jones, Evans, and Stacey.

A. Williams was elected president of the St. John's Cricket Club at its 1910 organizational meeting. The position of patron was held by Pat Burns, while Colonel Walker, A.E. Cross, and Reverend Ray were honourary presidents. R.B. Bennett and W. Pearce acted in the capacity of honourary vice-preidents— an impressive array of personalities. Practises were to be held on the field east of the brewery. The club made plans to build a tennis court as well as a cricket pitch.

It was reported that the Fort Macleod club had built a concrete pitch on their grounds.

In the first game of the 1910 season the St. John XI won by two wickets from the Calgary Cricket Club. The win was attributed to the long stand maintained by Poile and Downing. Cricket was not receiving much press as baseball was a far greater sports attraction in Calgary during this era, however cricket news from Britain was reported weekly.

The C.C.C. turned the tables in a game played on the St. John's pitch when they won by four wickets and 57 runs over the east end club. Johnson and Stephens were instrumental in leading the Calgary team to their win.

In July the C.C.C. defeated an Okotoks XI 219-67 in a game played on the barracks field. Stephen and Spick did an excellent job of bowling for the Calgary team, while Redgrove's 59 runs was tops in the batting department. Other C.C.C. players were: Downing, Johnson, Hall, Wetherall, Reilly, Plummer, and Birks.

The Calgary club continued their winning streak as they defeated the St. John's club 108-67, using only four wickets in the process. Three Downing brothers were part of the St. John's lineup.

The Calgary club travelled to Red Deer where they defeated the Pine Lake team by nine wickets in a two inning game. Bowlers Spick and Johnson showed little mercy for the Pine Lake batters. The Calgary XI were to have played the Red Deer club also, but the game did not take place.

1910 saw the first tournament played under the auspicious of the Western Canada Cricket Association, with the competition being staged in Winnipeg. P. Johnson, T. Bryant, H. Reynolds, Birks, J. Spick, C. Atter, W. Reilly, G. Poile, G. Risk, Syd Downing, G. Downing, A. Redgrove, C. Hall, E. Stephens, and F. Wetherall made the trip to Manitoba as the Calgary team, but there they were to be called the Alberta team. Other than two Macleod players, the rest of the lineup was from Calgary.

In opening day competition Alberta lost to Winnipeg by six runs after the Calgary players had taken a large first inning lead. Johnson and Spick proved to be both Alberta's top batsmen and bowlers. In the other game Manitoba defeated Saskatchewan.

In their second game Alberta put together innings of 56 and 106 runs, but a powerful Manitoba XI needed only two wickets in their second inning to take the win. G. Poile was the best of the Calgary batters.

A bowler's duel took place as Saskatchewan edged Alberta 57-51. Spick took seven wickets, allowing the Saskatchewan batters only 34 runs. Wetherall's 16 runs was tops among the Alberta batsmen.

In the last game of the tournament the Winnipeg Cricket Association put together innings of 144 and 128 for one wicket, while the Alberta side garnered 134 and 64 runs for five wickets. J. Downing and Hall were the top Alberta batsmen in this game.

The Winnipeg XI did not lose a game in the tournament, and they were awarded the championship and the Dingwall Cup.

J. McIntosh of the W.C.A. was the top batter in the tournament, averaging over 50 runs an inning. G. Poile, with a run average of 14, was tops among the Alberta batters, while J. Spick was their top bowler.

At the meeting of the Western Canada Cricket Association, held in conjunction with the tournament, the Lieutenant-Governors of the prairie provinces were appointed as patrons, and the three premiers became honourary presidents. The Honourable T. Daly was elected president of the association; M.P. Maitland McCarthy of Calgary was elected vice-president, and Calgary player J. Spick assumed the secretarial duties.

In Calgary the C.C.C. met a challenge by the "old timers" and defeated them by 135 runs in six wickets. As a result of the outcome the winners were treated to supper at the Crist Brothers Cafe by the losers. In another game, played at the barrack's pitch, the oldtimers took on the kids.

During the summer the C.C.C. XI defeated a Macleod team 145-101. A cricket XI from Crossfield came into the city to lose to the St. John's club on the east Calgary field. Later the St. John's club travelled to Crossfield for a return match. The Calgary Tennis Club fielded a cricket XI and lost to both the C.C.C. and the St. John's clubs.

P. Johnson of Calgary played with the Canadian team in a game staged in Chicago against an American XI. His lucrative batting produced 52 runs. Statistics showed that J. Spick was the top bowler in the Calgary area during the year, and Johnson the best batsman.

Calgarians, and especially cricket enthusiasts, were happy when Mr. Riley made plans to deed to the city land in Hillhurst, said to be valued at $50,000, for use as a park. One of the conditions was said to be that a cricket pitch would be developed there.

The Calgary cricket crowd considered the 1910 season to be a good one, both from the players' point of view and from that of the spectators.

In the spring of 1911 secretary Morrison of the Western Canada Cricket Association attended a meeting of the Canadian Cricket Association held in Toronto.

The Alberta Cricket Association hosted representatives from the Calgary C.C., St. John's, Red Deer, Pine Lake, and Red Cliff in a spring meeting. Correspondence indicated that teams from Pine Creek, Macleod and Medicine Hat were interested in joining the association.

An important event in Calgary's spring social calendar was the Calgary Cricket Club dance held in the Shriner's Hall.

The C.C.C. opened the season with a 168-88 win over the St. John's club in a game played at the W.C.C. pitch. The C.C.C.'s lineup included: team captain P. Johnson, E. Stephens, J. Spick, H. Richardson, Sgt.-Major Vickery, J. Birks, Sergeant Basson, H. Weatherall, N. Plummer, P. Howland, A. Anstie, And E. McLean, while the St. John's lineup was composed of A. Dowing, C. Hall, A. Redgrove, S. Downing, F. Chapman, W. Ardern, W. Brockernshire, A. Baker, J. Devine, and H. Holderness.

Chapman's XI, composed of Calgary and St. John's players were leading the Pryce-Jones team 151-82, but the inning was not completed as time was called. There were so many cricket players in Calgary now that a committee was set up to attempt to negotiate with the city in order to buy five acres on which to place another cricket pitch. The Hillhurst club felt it would be a year before they would be able to play on their new grounds adjacent to Victoria Avenue.

In May the Macleod XI arrived in the city to play a game against the C.C.C.; however rain spoiled the fixture, so an informal smoker was held instead. Later in the season Calgary defeated the Macleod team 231-77. The C.C.C. closed its rings with seven wickets down. J. Spick, K. Richardson, and P. Johnson did the heavy scoring for the winners. Spick proved to be a very proficient bowler, while Mr. Rutty, one of the oldest active players in the U.S.A., officiated. A return game, planned for Macleod on Coronation Day, was rained out.

In a July game P. Johnson scored 73 runs as the C.C.C. earned 160 runs in seven wickets as compared with the St. John's club 52 runs for eight wickets.

There were more players on the sidelines waiting to get into the game than there were players on the field.

What proved to be the best cricket game of the season saw the Colonials, a group who had played cricket in Africa, Australia, and India meet the Gentlemen, the latter who were the best players from the C.C.C., Pryce-Jones, and the St. John's clubs. Before a large crowd of spectators the Gentlemen easily won on the strength of F. Weatherall's batting.

The 1911 Western Canada Cricket Association's tournament was to be held at Indian Head, Saskatchewan in August. All the Alberta team, with the exception of two Macleod players, were from Calgary. Personnel included: team captain P. Johnson, J. Spick, F. Weatherall, J. Eoll, F. Birks, K. Richardson, J. Hill, George, W. Adhern, G. Downing, Adhern, E. Stephen, A. Downing, F. Chapman, C. Hall, McKay, Mathews, and Napper.

In its first tournament game the Alberta team won in a walkaway, defeating the Winnipeg team without any trouble. Winnipeg was very weak in bowling, and Alberta made 257 runs before being retired in the first innings. A. Downing scored one run more than a century to lead the Alberta batsmen. The Manitoba team lost to Saskatchewan.

Alberta had innings of 71 and 114, while Saskatchewan could only muster 52 runs before time ran out. Spick allowed only 20 runs in six wickets, while Johnson took four wickets for 24 runs as good bowling helped in Alberta's win. In the other game of the day Manitoba gave the Winnipeg Cricket Association XI for its second loss.

Manitoba had built up a big lead over Alberta, but rain prevented the finish of this game. Alberta had hit for only 61 runs in nine wickets, and in order to close out the Alberta side all the Manitoba fielders were standing close to the batsman in their endeavours to pick a catch off the bat and end the game. The W.C.A. went down to their third defeat at the hands of Saskatchewan.

However in their next game the Winnipeg XI turned the tables with a strong 187-83 win over the Alberta side. The Alberta wickets fell quickly, except for the last two batters who attempted to hold out until time was called.

Johnson hit for 54 as Alberta garnered 130 runs, while Saskatchewan compiled 124 in eight wickets. However heavy rain made conditions difficult, and the game was brought to a draw. Manitoba and the Winnipeg XI likewise played to a draw.

The Saskatchewan record of 4-1-1, as compared with Alberta's 3-1-2, gave them the title. Alberta's Gus Downing's 46 runs per game average was the highest in the tournament. Plans were made to hold the next tournament in Calgary.

A picked team of Calgary players, stronger than the team that went to Indian Head, defeated an Edmonton XI 164-156. P. Barnett hit for 80 runs, and E. Stephens, who had scored a century against Edmonton in a game played earlier in the season, added 59. Other Calgary players were: Jones, Wetherall, Spink, Collins, Plummer, Basson, H. Millard, E. McLean, and Kennedy.

During the fall months there were a variety of cricket games played in Calgary. P. Barnett scored a century as the C.C.C. took a 186-64 win over a Calgary Tennis Club XI. The same two clubs met in a game of soccer.

The St. John's club defeated an eleven from the Pro-Cathedral and a team called Walker's XI. Pryce-Jones met Mr. Chapman's team, and the married men beat the single gents.

P. Barnett was the top batter in Calgary during the 1911 season, averaging 57 runs a game and an inning high of 101 runs. P. Johnson averaged over 37 runs a game, and as well, along with Stephens and Spick, was one of the three best bowlers in Calgary.

The Alberta Cricket Association, although in idea the year before, came into reality in 1912.

This came about mainly due to the fact that Calgary was to host the W.C.C.A. tournament that year. At the Alberta association's organizational meeting held in Edmonton it was decided that each club should submit a list of its best players so that they may be considered for the Alberta team.

T. Bryant succeeded B. Vine, who resigned, as president of the Calgary Cricket Club. With so many new club members it was the intention to operate two teams of equal strength. A new club constitution was agreed on by the members. Likewise the St. John's club decided to field two teams. A new cricket club, the Civics, was formed with the backing of Mayor Mitchell. The organizational meeting was held in the city hall. Permission was received to hold team practises at Victoria Park.

The C.C.C. opened the Calgary 1912 season with a game between the Captain's and Sub-Captain's teams, with B. Barnett's XI outscoring captain T. Bryant's side 156-141. Barnett aided in his side's win by knocking in 50 runs. Richardson hit for one 6 and two 4's. The purpose of the game was to rate the players so they could be placed on either the A or B team.

In May the C.C.C. scored 210 runs for seven wickets, while the St. John's club earned only 97 in six wickets in a game played at the Western Canada College pitch. However because of the time limitation on play the game was declared a draw.

In a game played at the barracks P. Barnett hit for 29 to lead the C.C.C. to a 71-51 win over a R.N.W.M.P. XI. The bowlers for both teams bowled excellently in this low scoring game.

The St. John's Cricket Club took a 107-104 win from the Pryce-Jones XI. Redgrove led the St. John's players with 36 runs. Other team members were: G. Jones, W. Adhern, E. Hall, A. Downing, S. Dowing, A. Mason, F. Smith, J. Walker, T. Thompson, and R. Adamson. The Pryce-Jones lineup was composed of: Jones, Buxton, Partridge, Holden, Tooke, the McKearns brothers, Mackie, Hutchins, Rand, Morton and Hampson.

In June the local Bankers XI narrowly lost to the C.C.C. 84-90. McLean, the last batter for the Calgary team, hit a six and two fours to save his team from defeat. Fell hit for 33 for the C.C.C., and Grey, 31—not out, was the Bankers top hitter.

On June 20 representatives of various clubs met together, and out of the meeting came the formation of the City and District Cricket League.

The St. John's Cricket Club scored 199 runs in eight wickets to defeat the Macleod XI by 113 runs. Jones, the St. John's captain, won the toss and elected to bat first, thus the great edge in runs.

The stumps were drawn with the St. John's club in the lead, but time alone robbed the east end club of a victory over the Calgary Cricket Club. The St. John's club, led by Collins and Downing, collected 150 runs in nine wickets, while Calgary could manage only 49 runs in five wickets.

In what was to be a remarkable low scoring game the Pryce-Jones team defeated a soldiers XI 30-10 in a game viewed by more than 100 store employees and several hundred military personnel and played at the militia camp located beside the city reservoir in south west Calgary. Mr. Pryce-Jones, who in his day was a prime cricket player in England, scored five runs for his team. Following the game he inspected the troops. Several weeks later the Pryce-Jones team played a friendly game against an XI from the Hudson Bay Company store. Other teams engaged in friendly competition were the All-Saints Cricket Club, the Civil Servants, and the Bankers.

The St. John's club easily defeated the new Civics team, needing only three wickets to score 227 runs against the Civics 56 runs for a full slate of wickets. E. Hall led in the runs department with 77, while A. Goodrich's 27 runs was tops for the Civics.

In a game that saw some brilliant fielding exhibited the C.C.C., behind the great batting of H. Richardson, defeated the Pryce-Jones XI 181-122. Other Calgary players were: J. Basson, H. Brennon, B. Grey, P. Boston, Small, J. Gow, T. Baker, A. Dunn, and N. Holden.

In July a revamped Hillhurst team entered the Calgary and District Cricket League. Mr. Knott was the club president, E. Riley the honourary president and S. Jackson elected as team captain. The club's colours were black and gold, the same as the Hillhurst soccer club. A new club pitch was located south of Campbell's greenhouses in Hillhurst.

The Calgary Cricket Team scored a one inning 98 as compared with Hillhurst's 33 and 69 runs in two innings. The C.C.C. B team defeated St. John's after the St. John's captain closed their innings leaving, or as he thought, too little time for the Calgary club to win. However the superb hitting of Richardson and Barnett proved decisive.

On the east Calgary pitch the St. John's Benedicts opposed the Bachelors, while on another weekend the St. John's oldtimers met the club newcomers.

Calgary cricketeers held a mass meeting in the police court of city hall to discuss the establishment of a headquarters or clubhouse for those persons active in the sport.

A special meeting of the executive of the Alberta Cricket Association met to choose the Alberta XI for the Western Canada Cricket Association annual tournament. Included in the choices were: P. Hardisty, E. Morris, G. Berkingshaw, and A. Dickens of the Edmonton C.C., P. Johnson and E. Hall of St. John's, Macleod's H. Napper, and E. Sharp of Pine Creek, E. Butterworth of the Edmonton Swifts C.C., and T. Bryant, P. Barnett, F. Elaby, G. Nettleton, H. Richardson, J. Spick, F. Weatherall, J. Bell, and E. Stephens of the Calgary Cricket Club. However as some of these players were to play for the host city of Calgary's team, some additions were necessary.

Led by the fine bowling of J. Spick and G. Nettleton the C.C.C. whitewashed the Civic XI 170-20 in a game played on the new pitch of the Hillhurst C.C. At the barracks pitch the Calgary B team beat Hillhurst 120-36. Five Calgary batters reached double figures, while Reverend Winters batted in most of Hillhurst's runs. H. Richardson bowled six wickets allowing only 31 runs as the C.C.C. B team beat the A team 72-58. The Calgary Cricket Club game with Edmonton did not take place when the northern team could not make the trip.

Prior to the August tournament W.C.C.A. secretary Morrison brought the Dingwall Cup, which was inscribed, "Emblematic of the Championship of the Western Canada Cricket Association", to Calgary. Other awards for the tournament included: a silver cigarette case for the highest batting average, and cricket bats for the highest individual score and the highest individual bowling average.

A team representing the host city of Calgary was to include: team captain T. Bryant, F. Weatherall, S. Downing, F. Chapman, E. Hall, H. Richardson, F. Elaby, G. Nettleton, J. Bell, P. Johnson, E. Vincent, E. Stephens, J. Spick, and P. Barnett.

The tournament opened under poor weather conditions, including rain. In opening day play the Alberta team took a 186 to 165 win over the Saskatchewan XI. P. Johnson scored 96 runs and P. Barnett added 65 as Calgary led Manitoba 215-83. However rain interfered, and when it stopped the field was found to be unplayable. As a result the game was called a draw.

The next day the Manitoba players were in fine form scoring 301 runs in just seven wickets, while all the complete Saskatchewan side could muster was 153. The Alberta side ran up only 133 runs, and with only six men out it looked as if Calgary would go on to win, but one run was all the last four batters could earn and Alberta won 133-90. The Western Canada College pitch was receptive to long hits, and there were 20 sixes hit that day.

At the barracks pitch the Manitoba team collapsed as Alberta beat them 115-68. At the W.C.C. field the Calgary XI needed only one wicket to earn a 270-219 win over Saskatchewan. "The finest exhibit of cricket ever seen in the west, and possibly in the whole of Canada", was given by Messrs Barnett and Johnson carrying the score from 15 to 270 to create a Canadian record." Barnett had a dozen hits over the six line to contribute towards his total 158, while Johnson was close to a century. Saskatchewan used six different bowlers against the pair.

In their game against Manitoba Calgary started very slow, but they increased their strength at bat as Stephens hit for 83 and J. Bell added 60 runs to bring the team's total to 223, while Manitoba could only collect 60 runs in their inning. Alberta won over Saskatchewan 176-66. Umpire Stone was credited with doing a good job, earning the admiration of many of the players and spectators.

On the last day of the tournament Alberta defeated Calgary 269-206, as Berkingshaw piled up 117 runs in the first wicket. With this win Alberta took first place and the Dingwall Cup, while Calgary tied for second place with Manitoba and Saskatchewan finished last. This was the third year in a row that the home province had won the cup.

In the game with Alberta Barnett's 69 was the best of the Calgary batters. The dry ground had given the bowlers a gret deal of work. In the other game Manitoba took just seven wickets to defeat Saskatchewan.

In late August Baker hit for 40 runs as C.C.C. soundly trounced Pryce-Jones 213-56. Johnson bowled eight wickets allowing only 17 runs as the Calgary club held St. John's to only 23 runs. In the annual married versus single players P. Barnett accounted for 93 runs as the family men more than doubled the score of their opponents. Sport of a different vein saw the Calgary Cricket Club defeat the Calgary Tennis Club in soccer.

In December players of the St. John's club met and decided that the club should be revamped including changing the club's name and finding new grounds.

In the spring of 1913 local cricket enthusiasts became excited when it was announced out of New York that the Australian Cornstalkers cricket team would be making a tour of North America and possibly would be playing a game in Calgary.

E. Doughty was elected president of the St. John's Cricket Club. The organization made plans to build a pavilion near the pitch on the W.C.C. grounds. The C.C.C.'s slate of officers included: President J. Gibson, team captain P. Barnett, and as well 15 honourary presidents. P. Downey of Bishop Pinkham College was organizing the Provincial Wanderers Cricket Club, whose membership was to be limited to certain men who must agree on certain conditions before being allowed to join.

Calgary cricketeers eagerly began practising in April in anticipation of their competition against the visiting Australians. St. John's old members, led by P. Timm's 49 runs, easily beat the new members XI. Led by bowlers Johnson and Nettleton the St. John's A team won by nine runs over the C.C.C. in a game played at the barracks pitch. Another St. John's team played the Wanderers team at W.C.C.

The C.C.C. scored a 164-52 win over a visiting Mcleod XI in a Victoria Day game played at the barracks pitch. T. Bryant led the batsmen with 62 runs, while the C.C.C. bowling was effectively handled by Spick and Nettleton. Other Calgary players were: P. Barnett, E. Stephens, H. Richardson, Sergeant Major Vickery, Dr. Gibson, F. Weatherall, and L. Lovell.

A. Downing hit for 68 as St. John's A scored a 141-67 win over St. John's B. The feature of the game was the brilliant fielding of G. Jones. The following week St. John's scored a tremendous 326 to 44 win over the Pryce-Jones XI. Redgrove batted in 104 runs, while Brook was 106, not out. Completing the St. John's lineup were: Jones, Timms, Dover, Walker, Johnson, Lambert, and Day. Mackearn and Mackie garnered most of the Pryce-Jones runs.

In June a C.P.R. Cricket Club was formed, with R. Richardson elected president and Steve Newburn as team captain. The C.P.R. allowed the team to practise on grounds located south of Mewata. In their first game the C.P.R. XI lost to St. John's by a 124-37 score.

During the summer the A and B teams of both the C.C.C. and St. John's, and as well Pryce-Jones, met in a regular weekend competition. Besides being played at the barracks and W.C.C. pitches, some of the games took place at a newly developed pitch at Victoria Park.

There were many so called friendly games played during the 1913 season. Victoria won by three wickets over the Hillhurst Baptist Club. A feature of the C.P.R. married players versus singles was the bowling of Law who took nine wickets for 41 runs. The Calgary C.C. scored 305 runs in five wickets as compared to a 33 run inning by the Edmonton Wanderers. P. Barnett knocked in 101 runs, not out, while Parker hit for 85. Bell and Napper executed some very good bowling for the Calgary Club.

By 1913 the Alberta Cricket Association was not very active, and as a result a makeshift team was sent to the Western Canada Cricket Tournament in Winnipeg. Alberta's lineup was to include: P. Barnett, W. Newton, R. Day, L. Lovell, W. Strachan, A. Murdoch, Napper, Pardee, Mountfield, A. Dickens, and R. Mathews.

In its first tournament game the Alberta XI exhibited both weak bowling and fielding as they lost to Manitoba 239-113. Winnipeg defeated Saskatchewan 222-165. Alberta suffered its second loss with a 184-116 defeat at the hands of Saskatchewan. In the third game they fell victims to the Winnipeg XI, and at the conclusion of the tournament Alberta was in last place.

At the annual meeting of the W. C.C.A. Judge Johnson was elected president of the organization, while H. Mountfield of Edmonton and H. Napper of Macleod were elected to the board of governors.

Cricket at Riley Park. The crowd of spectators numbers several thousand.

There appeared to be great interest mounting in Calgary for the visit of the touring Australian Cornstalkers, who had defeated Edmonton 317-76 and had only lost one game, to Philadelphia, during their three month North American tour. Matches were planned for the Victoria Park pitch, beginning at 11:00 a.m., for three consecutive days. Upon their arrival the Australians were given an auto tour of the city and then dinner at the Calgary Golf and Country Club before they retired to their hotel.

In the first game, played before a disappointingly small crowd, the visitors administered an overwhelming 354-96 defeat to the locals. C. Kelly, J. Walker and F. Burroughs were the only Calgary players to hit in double figures, while Australia had ten players who accomplished this. Australian bowler Down put down ten Calgary batters and only allowed 37 runs, whereas the Australians ran up 89 runs against Timms in just one wicket. To impress upon the severity of the defeat it is only fair to mention that Calgary used not a regular eleven, but twenty two wickets to post their 96 runs. After the game the Australians suggested that Calgary should have played their 22 men in the field as well as at bat.

The next day the "Calgary 15" gave the Cornstalkers a close run scoring 102 runs while holding Australia to 129 runs for the inning. T. Barnett had 15, while W. Napper hit for 17 to lead the Calgary batsmen. Doc Gibson proved to be a very good wicket keeper for the home team boys. Credit was also due to Bell and team captain Parker. The Calgarians displayed good fielding all-around. It almost looked like an upset as Australia had only 89 runs at the end of the ninth wicket, then Collins hit for 32 and Calgary's hopes for a win went down the drain.

"One feature of the game was the array of motors on the grounds". That evening the visitors were hosted to a banquet at the Alexandria Hotel, where the principal speaker was R.B. Bennett, M.P.

On the third day the Australians and Calgarians were placed in mixed teams, with Parker's team winning over Barnett's side by a close score, and thus ended what was probably the most impressive cricket ever played in Calgary.

F. Parker of the Calgary B. team led the batters in the Calgary and District Cricket League averaging over 40 runs a game, while P. Barnett took runner-up honours with his average of 35. P. Johnson of St. John's proved to be the best bowler in the league.

In the spring of 1914 T. Bryant, president of the Calgary and District Cricket Association, announced that Calgary had received an invitation to send an all-star club to play at the west coast. Vancouver also wished to send a team to play in Calgary. The local cricket schedule was drawn up to include St. John's Wanderers, St. John's Zingari, St. Michael's, C.P.R., Hillhurst United, and Calgary A and B teams. However before the season began St. John's was down to one club and the C.P.R. team had dropped out of the league. The schedule now included twelve league games for each club.

The Southern Alberta Cricket Association was formed at a meeting held in Macleod, with teams from Taber, Lethbridge and Macleod included in the schedule.

The new St. Michaels club had developed a pitch on Seventeenth Avenue N.E.

In April they defeated a St. Johns XI 110-95. St. Mike's Parker earned 31 runs for the winners.

G. Jones hit for 48 as St. John's defeated Calgary A 123-74 in the first league game. In spite of the loss King Richardson bowled and fielded brilliantly for the C.C.C.

The Calgary Cricket Club A and B teams met on the pitch at Victoria Park. A team scored 202 runs with the loss of one wicket with Kelly, not out, acounting for 113 of these. B team ran up 104 runs on four wickets before time was called, so the game ended in a draw. Included in the lineup was E. Vincent, now playing cricket for his 22 season in Calgary.

The Calgary C.C. travelled to Macleod where they lost to the home team for the first time in eight years. Calgary put together innings of 73 and 50, but Macleod had knocked in 117 runs in their one inning at bat. Inspector Dan of the R.N.W.M.P. bowled seven wickets for the winners and only allowed 14 runs.

P. Johnson hit for 99 runs, including eleven 4's, as St. John's needed only five wickets to dispose of Hillhurst 178-94. Briggs brought in 41 of the Hillhurst runs. C. Bell bowled six wickets, allowing only 15 runs as Calgary A beat St. Michaels 74-62.

As the season unfurled there were some very low scores recorded, mainly due to the excellence of some of the bowlers. At the end of the schedule St. John's had captured the local cricket honours on the strength of an 8-2-2 record. Calgary B edged Calgary A for second spot; St. Michaels were 4 and 8, while last place Hillhurst won one game, lost eight and drew three. Hillhurst's only win was an 111-63 victory over Calgary B.

P. Timms of St. John's, J. Bell of Calgary A, and Hillhurst's Woodhouse had the best bowling averages in the league, while Allen was considered the finest wicket keeper. Calgary A's C. Kelly averaged 43 runs a game to take the batting honours, while P. Johnson, J. McKay, and E. Stephen averaged over 30 runs a game.

Lethbridge defeated Macleod at Macleod to capture the Southern Alberta League honours. Macleod's J. Mole had an exceptional season, averaging 63 runs a game. An interesting combination was Macleod wicket keeper Napper handling his son's bowling.

So called friendly games between the two leagues saw St. John's travel to Macleod to lose to the home team. Their excuse for the loss was that the current oil boom at Turner Valley was causing players to miss practises and as a result drop catches. At the W.C.C. pitch Macleod scored 201 runs in five wickets as compared to the Calgary C.C.'s 107 in six wickets. W. Moles, Macleod's fine batsman, knocked in 110 runs. Macleod outplayed a Granum XI by a 189-80 score.

At Millarville the Ranchers and Parsons played to an 86-all tie, with old timer Phillips doing all the bowling for the Ranchers. A Hudson's Bay Company XI played the Pryce-Jones store team at the Hudson's Bay pitch.

In June the Alberta Cricket Association held a meeting in Calgary in order to decide on sending a team to the tournament in Regina. However, enthusiasm, that was lacking the previous year, was now evident. The members of the team that were picked included 12 Calgarians, 4 from Macleod, three from Edmonton and one Lethbridge player. However when the team did go its members were either from Macleod or Calgary.

The tournament received very little press coverage locally, in spite of the fact that Alberta won the tournament and brought home the Dingwall Cup on the strength of three wins and three draws. In the tournament batting statistics team captain H. Napper led all the tournament players, while teammates P. Barnett, W. Mole, and R. Day occupied the next three spots. Other Alberta players were: G. Nicholson, R. Mathews, N. Vernon, L. Lovell, J. McKay, and J. Eoll. In the Saskatchewan game Barnett scored 117 runs. Manitoba was runner-up to Alberta, with the two Saskatchewan teams finishing last.

As the war situation in Europe developed the cricket ranks were thinned as 83 Calgary players joined Canada's armed forces. Some joined to take advantage of an opportunity to return to Britain.

There was very little cricket in Calgary during the duration of the war. Some friendly matches were played between the city team and the soldiers stationed at Camp Sarcee. At one time there were five teams involved in competition at the army camp.

"Curling"

Curling dates back to at least the sixteenth century in Scotland, Iceland and Holland. The word "curl" probably comes from the German word—kurzweil, which means an amusement or game, while "rink" is derived from the ancient Saxon—hrink or hrincg.

The Muthil, Perthshire, Scotland Curling Club has records of play as far back as 1716. Curling was reported to have been played in Canada in the late eighteenth century by some Scottish officers stationed in Quebec. Games were played in an organized manner at Beauport, Quebec in 1805. Three years later a curling rink was set up on a dock on Quebec's waterfront.

The Montreal Curling Club, the first such organization in North America, was in operation in 1807. The club lost a game to a team from Quebec in 1836. The Canadian branch of the Royal Caledonian Curling Club was formed in 1852. Covered curling rinks made their appearance in Ontario in the 1860's.

One problem faced by early Canadian curlers was that the stones would often break or split. Some wooden stones, where the bottoms were soaked in water and frozen, were used. Curling irons weighing 45-60 pounds and shaped like tea kettles, were smelted from cast iron and were in use until granite stones were imported from Scotland.

A November, 1883 issue of the fledgling Calgary newspaper said, "The enthusiasts of the roaring game should form a club." This would indicate that an interest in curling was evident in Calgary, and possibly the game was played locally on the frozen sloughs at that time. Perhaps the rink made by Barwis and Broderick on the Elbow River was used, however no written record verifies this.

George Fraser opened the first covered ice covered rink west of Winnipeg in December of 1884. The structure, one of the largest buildings in Calgary at the time, was located on the corner of Stephen Avenue and Osler Street.

In the fall of 1885 Calgary's curling enthusiasts held a meeting in Martin Brother's store, and a curling club was organized. The fifteen charter members each paid a ten dollar membership fee. The club had difficulty securing ice to play on, but some games were played at F. Claxton's new 60 x 136 feet covered rink on Angus Avenue—Sixth Avenue between Centre and First Street East. Play consisted of pick up games, and there did not appear to be any organized competition. The following season the curling club rented ice at Claxton's Star Rink on a more regular basis.

Curling rinks were laid out on the river in Edmonton in the late 1880's, while elsewhere on the prairies streams, lakes and sloughs were utilized. An indoor curling rink measuring 38 x 153 feet was opened in Edmonton in the fall of 1889.

In January of 1888 the President's Medal was offered for competition, and the Joseph Bannerman rink defeated the Smith foursome in the final of this event, emblematic of the Calgary club's championship. Both the Bannerman and Smith rinks travelled to Winnipeg to participate in its bonspiel. Plans were discussed about sending a team of Calgary curlers to Montreal's winter carnival bonspiel.

A curling club had been established in Lethbridge in 1887, while Edmonton's club was formed in 1888, and Macleod, Banff and Anthracite had clubs by 1889.

In the early days of curling in the Territories each club normally had a regular draw, and if the ice was playable weekly competition was held. At the end of the season a prize would go to the team that had earned the most points.

Skips were elected at the start of the season, then each skip chose their third, second, and lead. Often the skip was required to select one green player for his team. Competition included team draws, singles, doubles, point matches, while some games were played over a period of several days. In singles competition each contestant threw three pair of stones per end, and the first player to amass thirteen points was the winner. In doubles competition each partner alternated in delivering a rock. Bonspiels also went under the name of curliana.

In 1889 Mr. Hardisty, the factor of the Hudson Bay Company in Edmonton, offered the Hardisty Cup for curling competition in that community.

During the winter of 1888-89 the Calgary Curling Club had fifty members, who each paid an annual club fee of five dollars. Twelve teams were formed, and with the arrival of new curling stones from Scotland the club was now in possession of sixteen stones. Plans were made for the club to affiliate with the Royal Caledonian Curling Club of Scotland.

A competition was held in December of 1888 in which the money raised went to buy food for Calgary's poor, and on another occasion the losers paid for $16 worth of meat, which was distributed by the police chief to the needy. In other competition a fifty point game was won by I. Freeze.

In March of 1889 two Calgary rinks that included J.B. Smith, W. Perry, I. Freeze, Major Walker, J. Bannerman, F. Dick, A. Shelton and W. Hogg went to curl in the Winnipeg Spiel.

Seventy-two curlers paid the Calgary Curling Club membership fee of seven dollars for the 1889-90 season. The Star Skating Rink, which was now illuminated by electric lights, was leased for the season by the curling club, but two nights of the week were reserved for skating. Four sheets of ice were marked off and the club now owned 37 pair of curling stones. Plans were made to play against the Edmonton curlers for a Royal Caledonian medal that had been donated by the Manitoba curling organization. The Bannerman rink was a repeat winner of the President's Medal.

Other local competition included play for the Tribune Cup, otherwise known as the T. Braden Cup. Games were for thirteen points, singles competition, with each competitor playing three pair of stones. The Braithwaite Cup was offered for competition in 1890, and J. McIlree was its first winner. A Calgary rink was entered in the Winnipeg bonspiel.

A bonspiel was held at Priddis, where the community's first stones were wooden blocks. Prizes at the spiel were quarters of beef. John Turner, who ranched near the present Turner siding, curled at Priddis with iron rocks. Iron rocks were also in use in the Innisfail area.

A meeting took place at Bleecher's and Smith's office in 1889 for the purpose of forming a joint stock company to raise funds for the construction of a $1500 curling rink. Principals behind the scheme were Archie Grant, I. Freeze and F. Dick. Later the company held a formal meeting in the town hall. The executive consisted of President Major Walker, Vice-president George Leeson, Secretary J. Costigan and Treasurer A. Grant. 5000 shares of Alberta Rink Company stock, with a ten dollar par value, were offered for sale, and initially over a thousand dollars was subscribed. Within a few weeks this amount was increased to $4,000.

The company purchased three lots on Northcotte Avenue from G. Bigger of Battleford, and F. Dick designed a building for the site. Fred Harren was given the contract to construct a $2,500 building 75 by 168 feet wide and 24 feet high. The lumber came from Walker's Kananaskis mill. The 12 by 33 foot club room had glass windows overlooking the ice surface, and above the club room was a spectators' gallery. The building also contained a room reserved for the use of the ladies. Two sheets of ice were located in the central section and one in each of the wings. After 42 electric lights, including three 32's over the tees, were installed in the building in December more than one hundred Calgarians sat down to a dinner held in the new rink.

Plans had been made to have the waterworks install a tap, but this was not done in time, so a well was dug and a pump set up. Mr. Davidson was hired as a caretaker at a salary of thirty dollars a month.

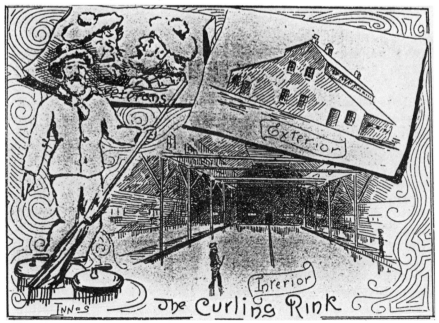

Calgary Curling Club on Northcotte Avenue, sketch by John Innes, December 1890.

The Alberta Rink was rented by the curling club at a cost of $400 for the season, and as well they were responsible for the lights. Club members met at the rink and elected J. Smith, Janes, Perry, Walker, A. Grant, Dick, Freeze, W. Grant and J. Costigan as skips.

Silverware and prizes up for competition now included the Merchants Trophy valued at one hundred dollars, the officers' prizes of four gold medals, Hull Brothers Trophy, and Superintendent Niblock's piano lamp.

The season's first competition took place at the new building in December with five rinks making up the President's side competing against the Vice-president's team. The total points of each side were added up to determine the winner.

There were A and B sections in the Merchant's competition, with the section winners playing a two out of three series to determine the winner. Sectional competition consisted of a round robin series with games being of sixteen ends, and some games took several days to complete.

Twenty-four curlers, including Cappy Smart, competed in knockout games of 13 points, with each player using three pair of stones, in the competition for green curlers. I. Ingram won a pair of curling stones for his first place finish in this event. R.H. Arnold was the winner of the Caledonian medal for the points competition. In the Hull competition Waugh defeated W. Grant 13-10 to win a pair of curling stones that had been donated by H.R. Hull. J.B. Smith took home the lamp for the Niblock competition. The quartette of W. Smith, J. Costigan, Ford and Arnold scored a 13-11 win over Grant's foursome in the playoff for the Officer's medals.

There were many games played during the season in which teams ran up twenty or more points in a game. Not all the games were in competition, for if a sheet of ice was vacant a friendly, or scratch game soon put the ice to good use.

In January of 1891, 24 rinks took part in the Ingham competition. R. Arnold, with 80 points, won the Officer's medal competition, and J.B. Smith placed second. Perry captured the club aggregate. Two Calgary rinks went to the Winnipeg Bonspiel, and J.B. Smith's rink of Maw, Bannerman and Walker won a prize in the Grand Challenge competition. The second Calgary rink was composed of skipp Dick, Smart, Waugh and Munn.

Following the playing season the Calgary Curling Club held a dance at Robertson's Hall.

A gold medal was donated by G. Galt of Winnipeg for the new Galt-Lineham 13 point All Comers competition in the 1891-92 season. Each competitor used three pair of stones. The Hudson's Bay Company silver cup was offered for knockout competition for all club members, and the event had to be won twice before the cup could be kept.

The President's and Vice-president's foursomes met in the Hospital competition, and the bankers beat the lawyers 15-12 in a friendly game.

Twenty-one teams were entered in the Merchant's competition, with A. Grant defeating J. Walker in the A final, then winning 16-10 over B winner Dousett in the final of this prime event. On the same day Grant defeated Walker 16-3 in the Hudson's Bay event final, then in his third game of the day, an encounter that finished long after midnight, Major Walker won over Archie Grant 21-19 in 17 ends to take the Officer's Medals.

Calgary curlers won four games and lost two encounters to take a silver medal at the Winnipeg Bonspiel, possibly the most important curling event in Western Canada during the era.

The Edmonton rinks of McQueen and Raymer played against the Calgary rink of Freeze, Dick, Perry and Walker in March. Calgary won all four games scoring 84 points to Edmonton's 67. The Edmonton curlers were wined and dined at the Alberta Hotel following the competition. In return matches played in Edmonton, the Calgary teams came out ahead 62-34. At the end of the season the second annual curlers' ball was held in April.

In the 1892-93 season the Calgary Curling Club's treasurer reported that the club took in close to a thousand dollars in fees and other income, while the rent for the Alberta Rink amounted to $234. The F. Dick rink won the Calgary Curling Club medal, but the skip suggested that the club could better spend the money that the medals cost.

The Carscallen, Peck and Company Trophy was presented for play in the Merchants' competition in the 1892-93 season. A and B class winners J. Waugh and Dousett met in the final. The game was reported to have included some of the hottest curling ever seen in Calgary, with Dousett coming out the winner 19-14.

Twenty curlers entered the green curlers 13 point competition, with T. Tarrant and W. Kinnisten playing in the finals. In the Hudson's Bay Company final Muirhead scored a 17-13 win over the Cox rink. Costigan and J. Bannerman were winners in the Officers' Medal competition.

Four Calgary rinks skipped by J. Waugh, A. Grant, I. Freeze and F. Claxton travelled to Winnipeg to participate in its spiel. The C.P.R. offered a round trip ticket price of $25 from Calgary to the bonspiel.

W. Grant's foursome of Muirhead, J. Feehan and J. Thompson earned a narrow 14-11 win over a visiting Edmonton curling rink. In another game against the northern quartette, Major Walker's rink was tied, but Edmonton added a single to win the game. The rink of Waugh, Claxton, Freeze and Grant were also tied with their Edmonton opponents, but the home team had a big five ender and won 16-11. Following the games the Edmonton curlers and the Calgarians who had participated in the Winnipeg spiel were guests of the Calgary Curling Club at a banquet held at the Bodega Restaurant.

Calgary curlers travelled to Edmonton where they lost the first game; however, they came back strongly to win the next four games.

A game of this era that created a great deal of interest saw Lord Aberdeen, the Governor General of Canada, play on a team with Cappy Smart against Major Walker's team. On several occasions in the nineties Captain Gately of Golden brought his bagpipes and the Golden curlers would march behind him as he played his way from the Alberta Hotel to the Alberta Rink.

Four hundred persons attended the curlers fancy dress carnival. The two center sheets of ice were used for skating, while curlers in fancy dress costume threw rocks on the outer rinks. The old ladies played the cowboys on one side, while across the building the Africans and young ladies added a great deal of exuberance to their game. The Fire Brigade band was in attendance, and the evening's events included a hockey game. The affair was considered the social highlight of the year in Calgary.

In 1894 the Calgary Curling Club received gold buttons from Galt and Robertson of Winnipeg. The buttons were put up for weekly competition among the club members.

What was considered to be the Calgary Curling Club's first annual bonspiel took place in January. J. Costigan won the District Medal for the second straight year in the open point game competition.

Joseph Bannermann was elected president of the Calgary Curling Club for the 1894-95 season. The club members' annual dues were now set at ten dollars. On Christmas Day the annual President versus Vice-president competition took place. A medal for green curler competition was presented to the club by the Honourable J. Lougheed. Curling interest was high in Calgary, and the local press published a weekly curling column.

The rules of the Calgary bonspiel stated that an individual would not be allowed to play on more than one rink, a practice that had taken place in the past. Among the prizes offered for the bonspiel were bottles of whiskey, and the Calgary Brewery donated a keg of beer for the curlers.

Calgary rinks in the bonspiel were skipped by A. Grant, I. Freeze, J. Walker, J. Smith, W. Grant, H. Johnston, J. Bannerman, and Hastings. Visitor rinks included Rae and McNeish from Golden, Hunter from Fish Creek and Turner's Sheep Creek foursome.

Competition took place for the Merchants, Hudson Bay and the Whyte Trophies, the last named being for the doubles competition. Following the competition the curlers were treated to an oyster supper at the Alberta Hotel.

Curling took place at the Patterson Mine, which was located at the forks of Fish Creek. It was reported that a large number of spectators took in the match. The Fish Creek team of J. Paterson, D. Hunter, W. Edgar and skip J. Hunter won the twenty end game by a 19-13 score over the Sheep Creek quartette of skip J. Aird, J. and R. Turner and W. Paton.

W. Grant's rink travelled to the Winnipeg spiel, where they made it to the quarter finals in the New York Life Grand Challenge event, and as well the quartette won games in the International competition.

During the curling season Lethbridge opened an enclosed rink complete with electric lights.

In December of 1895 Vice-president W. Kinnisten's curlers won a 16-5 win over Calgary Curling Club President J. Walker foursome in the executive's annual competition. The Alberta Hotel curlers challenged but lost to an all-comers team for a barrel of flour, with the prize being donated to the General Hospital.

Thirteen Calgary rinks, and eight visitor rinks, including quartettes from Innisfail, Edmonton, Fish Creek, Golden and Sheep Creek, participated in the 1895 Calgary bonspiel. The Walkerville Trophy, donated by the Hiram Walker Company, was offered for the prime event of the bonspiel, and W. Kinnisten's Calgary rink became the event's first winner. The trophy was to become the possession of the club that won it the most times in the first ten years of competition. Other new competition was for the Bannerman-Critchley Trophy, which was donated by the Calgary members of the Territorial Assembly. A visitor's competition was also included in the 1895 spiel.

In a game that drew a great deal of interest a Calgary Curling Club foursome won a narrow 9-8 win from a team made up of the Presbytery. Two Calgary rinks participated in the spiel at Golden. At the close of the curling season club President James Walker presided over a supper attended by sixty club members.

A curling club was formed at Medicine Hat for the 1895-96 season, and they were able to play in an enclosed rink that had been built by M. Colter. Previous to this the town's curlers had used the ice on the river for their games.

Major Walker served as President and J. Miquelon as Secretary of the Calgary Curling Club for the 1895-96 season. The club paid an annual rent of $250 to the Alberta Rink Company. Membership fees were eight dollars a year, and green curlers under the age of 26 only paid five dollars. Curlers were described in the local press as, "The Knights of the Besom," and competition went under the name of curliana.

In January of 1896 Nels Hoad scored 32 points to take first place in the Royal Caledonian District Medal competition. The runner-up spot was shared by D. Kerr, I. Freeze and Fred Adams. Twelve local rinks were busy competing in round robin play for the Merchants' Cup. When the last rock was thrown W. Kinnisten was the winner.

The Whyte Trophy for doubles competition saw W. Grant and Forbes McNeil as the A winners and J. Irwin teamed with D. Kerr to take the B section. The District Medal went to N. Hoad, while W. Grant and I. Freeze tied for first place in the Points competition. Competition for the Hudson Bay Trophy consisted of a knock out series, and W. Grant was the 1896 winner.

Calgary's third annual bonspiel took place in February rather than January of 1896. Four rinks were entered from Golden, seven rinks from Calgary and single rinks from Sheep Creek, Edmonton, Innisfail and Fish Creek. Unseasonably warm weather turned the ice to a pool of water, which interfered with the timetable and games had to be rescheduled for two, five and eight a.m. draws.

C. Dowsett was the winner of the Galt and Robertson medal, the final of which had to be played in over an inch of water. In the prime Walkerville competition, a knockout event, the J. Johnson rink scored a close 13-12 win over Billy Kinnisten's foursome in the event's final. At the end of the eleventh end, Kinnisten had a 12-6 lead, but Johnson added seven points in the next three ends to capture the solid silver tankard and watch chains for each member of his team.

Kinnisten softened the loss as his rink captured the Bannerman-Critchley competition with a 16-10 win over the Grant rink. Turner of Sheep Creek won over Edmonton's Lauder in the finals of the Visitors' competition. Following the bonspiel the curlers attended an oyster supper at the Queen's Hotel where some "great speeches" were made by various members of the curling fraternity.

The W. Parslow rink entered the Edmonton bonspiel and brought the Frank Oliver Trophy back to Calgary. Two Calgary rinks participated in the spiel at Golden, B.C.

An oyster supper was paid for by members of the President's team who lost by one point to the Vice-president's team in year end competition.

In the fall of the year Curling Club President Kinnisten appointed Major Walker to check into the feasibility of forming a Territorial branch of the Royal Caledonian Curling Club.

Calgary hotels reported a large booking of rooms during the week of the 1897 Calgary bonspiel. There were three rinks from each of Edmonton and Golden, two Millarville rinks, and singles rinks from Innisfail, Davisburg, Didsbury, Lethbridge and Priddis entered in the spiel. Many of the visiting curlers were not happy when it was discovered that local rinks had been broken up and the Calgary rinks entered in the spiel had been packed with skips.

J. Johnson's rink won the Walkerville trophy in the Grand Challenge competition for the second straight year as they bested the W. Parslow quartette 14-7 in the event's final. Parsons of Golden, Aird of Sheep Creek and Taylor from Edmonton took the first three plaes in the visitor's competition. Calgary's McNeil and Walker rinks finished behind Lauder of Edmonton in the Bannerman and Critchley event. The bonspiel was followed by a dinner and entertainment staged at the Queen's Hotel.

When the Innisfail curlers arrived home they said that the reason for their lack of success in Calgary resulted from the fact that they were not used to the granite stones, having only played with metal stones at home.

As the Calgary curling season drew to a close, Cappy Smart's rink, sporting a 12-0 record, was awarded the Merchant's Trophy and Sol Spafford's 11-0 record was tops in the Hudson's Bay Company competition.

A.W. Grant, who had been one of Calgary's better curlers, reported from his new home in Nelson that curling ice was non-existent in that community.

The Semi-annual meeting of the Calgary Curling Club took place at the rink in October. H. McNeil and W.R. Hull were honoured as the club's patrons, and Lord Aberdeen was one of the twelve honourary members appointed. Mr. Kinney was elected president of the club for the 1897-98 season, and J. Johnson was the new Vice-president. However he later left the city and the position was filled by A. Maw. A. Grant was chosen as the club's referee.

The Calgary Curling Club invited the citizens of Calgary to avail themselves of the facilities of the curling rink on Christmas Day of 1897.

Rinks from Golden and Sandon journeyed from British Columbia to join curlers from Lethbridge, Innisfail, Wetaskwin, Lacombe, Sheep Creek, Edmonton and seven Calgary quartettes in the 1898 Calgary bonspiel. With such a large entry an outside sheet of ice had to be pressed into use in order to complete the tournament on schedule. There was a great array of prizes as local merchants contributed goods and merchandise for the top finishers in the various events.

Eleven rinks were in competition for the Visitor's Trophy, and in the event's finals McLeod of Lethbridge scored an easy 16-6 win over McNeish of Golden. W. Kinnisten won a pair of curling stones valued at twenty dollars for his first place finish in the points competition. Runners-up in this event were Cappy Smart and E. Vincent.

Smart won a close 10-9 game over Kinnisten in the finals of the McNeil

Company competition. I. Freeze was declared the winner of the Bannerman and Critchley competition when McNeil defaulted the last game.

The Calgary Brewing and Malting Trophy was newly offered for competition. In the final of this event J. Smith scored a 16-5 win over Edmonton's Lauder rink. In the Grand Challenge event for the Walkerville Trophy, F. McNeil took an early lead and went on to take an 18-8 victory over Major Walker's rink.

F. McNeil's great rink that won 16 games in a row in the 1900 Calgary Bonspiel. Left to right: F. McNeil—skip, Henry Trimble—First, Niven Jackson—Second, J. Hoad—Third.

Following the competition over a hundred persons attended the curler's supper and awards presentation which were held at the Alberta Hotel.

In February Calgary curlers participated in the Golden and Edmonton bonspiels.

The Fish Creek Curling Club was organized in early 1898 with Dr. MacKid as the club patron and W. Hunter as the club president. Annual dues were set at five dollars, and the executive went about raising money so that the club could have a covered rink for the following season. Millarville curlers travelled to Fish Creek to participate in what was to be their first annual game.

At the Alberta Rink the Vice-president's five rinks took a 66-53 series win over the President's rinks to close the Calgary curling season.

Alderman Kinnisten, one of Calgary's better curlers, passed away. His huge funeral procession was led by the Fire Department Band, and one of the many wreaths on his grave came from the Edmonton Curling Club.

Early winter competition during the 1898-99 season saw more games between the President's and Vice-president's sides. W. Parslow and Cappy Smart's rinks went to Millarville where they curled on the river. Millarville's Aird won 12-11 over Parslow and Turner outplayed Smart by a 21-3 score. The Calgary players attributed their losses to the four hour drive to Millarville and the rough and tough ice. In redeeming play the following day Parslow won over Turner 17-8 and Smart took a 10-6 win from Aird.

In early 1899 spectators at the curling rink chuckled as Mayor Reilly and the aldermen were wearing their fur coats while curling. Green curlers were out in force to compete for a new cup donated by club President Cappy Smart.

A group of Calgary curlers travelled to Edmonton and won one of the events at the bonspiel. The Calgarians then travelled to Fort Saskatchewan for some competition against that community's curlers.

Rinks from Macleod, Fish Creek, Lethbridge, Golden, Edmonton, Regina, Priddis, Millarville, Medicine Hat and Innisfail joined Calgary curlers at the 1899 Calgary bonspiel. Kerr and Barslow took first and second places in the points competition. In the team competition of the Burns event the Calgary curlers outscored the visitors 69-44, and in the events rink final J. Smart edged A. McNeil 9-8. Lundy of Innisfail carried home the prize for the Consolation event.

The Dunn rink from Edmonton did themselves proud as they won the Brewery, Visitors and the Bannerman-Critchley events. Sol Spafford won over A. McNeil in the final of the Walkerville, the bonspiel's number one event, McNeil came through on the twelfth end to defeat Spafford. It was reported that a very large crowd of spectators took in this final.

Reverend Herdman, Chaplain of the curling club, welcomed the curling fraternity to his Sunday morning service. The curling banquet was held at the Queen's Hotel, but much to their consternation members of the press were not invited.

A curling game that drew a great deal of interest saw the Queen's Hotel Dubs play and defeat the Alberta Hotel Professionals. The losers donated two sacks of flour to the Calgary General Hospital. Another fun game, but with political overtones, saw six rinks of Liberals score a great 85-57 victory over their Conservative opponents. A startling upset took place when a team made up of junior curlers defeated Major Walker's rink by an 11-10 score in a scratch game. Married curlers played against single men in a ten rink aside competition. M.L.A.'s Bennet and Cross were each backed by six rinks in other competitions.

Major Walker's rink of W. Barwis, J. Mitchell and P. Turner-Bone plus the quartette of skip A. Maw, J. Clarke, T. Braden and J. Miquelon travelled north to Innisfail to meet that community's curlers in competition. Walker earned a 14-8 win over the D. Lundy rink, and Maw took C. McCallum's foursome by a 14-4 count. However the country players received some satisfaction as A. Curry's "Oldman's rink" beat the Walker quartette 12-9. The Calgary curlers were treated to supper and a smoking concert following the game. The following morning the Calgary rinks won over the Smith and Thompson rinks. A large crowd gathered at the Innisfail train station to see the Calgary players off on the south-bound train.

Another curling trip saw a group of Calgary curlers and the Fire Brigade Band travel to Golden. Sol Spafford's rink brought back the Columbia River Trophy.

At the 1899 annual meeting of the Calgary Curling Club, Cameron was elected to the club presidency and P. Turner-Bone as vice-president. Up to this point in the club's history many names of the curling executive and rink's skip have been mentioned. Other individuals who were very active on the Calgary curling scene include J. Winn, A. Lucas, J. Kelley, W. Hoag, H. Douglas, G. Mitchell, J. Reiley, N. McKelvey, A. Morrison, C. Comer, A. McNeil, Dr. G. McDonald, E. Vincent, J. Bangs, L. Doll and many others.

In December of 1899 the Miquelon rink travelled to Priddis where they went down to defeat to the Edgar quartette from that hamlet. The Priddis curlers were in fine form as the community's curling ice had been in use since late October. In the evening following the game the Calgary curlers were entertained at a ball held in the Priddis Hall. During this era the Hunter-MacMillan Cup was offered for competition at Priddis.

The C.P.R. offered a return ticket for the price of a single way to those patrons who were attending the 1900 Calgary curling bonspiel. Besides the Calgary curlers, there were rinks from Fish Creek, Sheep Creek and Golden entered in the spiel. The Edgar rink took home the trophy for the Visitor's competition, and F. McNeil won over James Walker in the Burns competition final. McNeil added to his laurels as he beat S. Spafford 12-8 in the final match of the Calgary Brewery event, with prizes for the winners being gold watches. In NcNeil competition the McNeil rink took a 12-7 win from Edgar Forbes. McNeil then proved beyond a doubt that he had the best rink in the tournament as he beat Cappy Smart in the final of the Walkerville event. In all McNeil, playing a knockout game, won sixteen games in a row in the tournament as he captured the four major competitions. His teammates were: lead Norman Jackson, second H. Trimble and Nelson Hoad at third.

Following the spiel over one hundred persons attended the curling banquet staged at the Queens Hotel. There were many toasts made, songs sung and speeches, including the major address by R.B. Bennett.

In February the Lang rink from Anthracite lost a sixteen end game to A.L. Cameron by a 13-11 score in District Medal competition. Charles Ramsay proved to be the best local in green curler competition. Cappy Smith's Tory rink defeated the Grits, skipped by Forbes McNeil, by a 10-9 score. Several such games with political overtones were played.

The Alberta Curling rink also served as a theatre during this period, and in April of 1900 a motion picture was shown there.

In December the Miquelon quartette travelled to Priddis, which almost always had ice before Calgary did, to lose to the Edgar rink by a 16-7 score. The Calgary curlers were well entertained at the evening ball in the Priddis Hall. On New Year's Day of 1901 competition took place between Calgary Curling Club President P. Turner-Bone and Vice-president Miquelon's sides.

Thirteen rinks competed for $1,400 in prizes at the 1901 Calgary Curling Club bonspiel. Unfortunately unseasonably warm weather left the rinks with as much as an inch of water on the ice at times during the bonspiel.

In the Grand Challenge or Walkerville event Sol Spafford defeated P. Turner-Bone in the events final, with Bruce of Macleod finishing in third place. McNeil won over Ullock of Golden in the final of the McNeil event, however Ullock came back to win the Calgary Brewery Trophy with the Cameron rink second and Vincent in third place. Ullock added further to his laurels by winning the Burns competition. Edgar from Priddis edged out Macleod's McLean in the Visitor's final, but in the Consolation event these positions were reversed.

Romeo Miquelon was elected president of the Calgary Curling Club for the 1901-02 season, while other executive members included S. Spafford, W. Cushing, F. Exham, G. Leeson, J. Smart, A. Maw, L. Doll, H. Hutchings, and H. McLeod. A.E. Cross was honoured as the club patron and Reverend Langford acted as club chaplain.

In December competition at Priddis, club President Miquelon won over the hometown rink of Edgar by one point. In another game, played in the new covered rink, Calgary's Doll foursome crossed brooms with the Patterson quartette.

Fourteen Calgary rinks were involved in a festive season novelty competition. In the event's final Braden defeated Spafford, and his rink members each were the winners of twelve dollar felt boots.

Norm Jackson of the Alberta Hotel put up a new trophy, upon which was a magnificent replica of the Canadian coat of arms, for the Visitor's competition at the 1902 Calgary bonspiel. Another new trophy, the Consolation Cup, was donated by the Honourable W. Wells of Palliser, B.C.

Unseasonably warm weather in January of 1902, in which the temperature rose above freezing in 15 of the first 20 days of the month, brought about considerable frustration among the curlers. However, as the bonspiel approached the temperature dropped and so did the level of anxiety of the curling fraternity.

The Calgary rinks skipped by McNeil, Smart, Cameron, Spafford, Doll and Walker were joined by curlers from Anthracite, Lethbridge, Mcleod, Banff, Fish Creek, Golden and Lethbridge in play. Secretary J. Miquelon scheduled five draws a day in order to finish the competition in the allotted time.

The Dainard rink from Golden made their presence known as they defeated Spafford in the McNeil competition, then they scored a four ender in the twelfth end in their match against Anderson of Anthracite to capture the Visitor's trophy. In Brewery competition Edgar of Fish Creek scored a three in the twelfth end, but he just missed tying the score of event winner F. McNeil.

The Grand Challenge competition for the Hiram Walker cup between the F. McNeil and J. Smart rinks proved indeed to be exciting. In the final end McNeil drew even with his opponents, but with his last stone Smart judged the ice perfectly to end up closest to the tee and win the match. In the points competition F. McNeil led with 42, while Spafford garnered 32, while J. Irwin and J. Miquelon each had 29 points. Over one hundred guests attended the smoker at the Royal Hotel where speeches, story telling and singing took place until 2:30 in the morning.

Following the local bonspiel some of Calgary's curlers travelled to Winnipeg to compete in that city's spiel.

Due to the mild weather there was not the usual interest in curling in Calgary. Competition for only two of the four club trophies was partially completed. J. Miquelon's rink was awarded the Merchant's Trophy, and S. Spafford's rink earned the Hudson's Bay Company Cup. In points competition for the Gault medal N. Hoad was the winner and T. Tarrant placed second. Tarrant's rink went on to win the District Medal.

At the annual meeting of the Calgary Curling Club held in April Secretary-treasurer K. Johnson reported that the club's income for the 1901-02 season as $623 and expenditures of $499. H. McLeod was elected club president for the following term of office, with W. Cushing and J. Douglass as vice-presidents. F. Exham was the new secretary and K. Johnson remained as treasurer. The club patron was R.B. Bennett, M.L.A., and Reverend J. Herdman would serve as the club's chaplain.

In January of 1903 the Calgary rinks of Hoad, Smart, and Johnson played and won a good share of games at Lacombe, Wetaskwin and Edmonton. At Edmonton Cappy Smart's rink won one game by a 20-0 count, and at the end of the spiel were the winners of both the Galligher and Smart events.

The Calgary Palmer rink travelled to Priddis to defeat Hunter 8-7, but then the Calgarians lost to Aird by a close 13-12 score. The Priddis club had sixteen active curlers among its membership.

The Calgary Curling Club held points competition in January, with A. McNeil and J. Miquelon sharing the honours in this event.

The thirteen visitor rinks attending the 1903 Calgary bonspiel included curlers from Macleod, Medicine Hat, Golden, Priddis, Lacombe, Banff, and Moose Jaw. The Calgary rinks entered were skipped by Smith, Smart, Parslow, Walker, McNeil and Spafford. In the initial draws an effort was made to match the Calgary rinks against visitors.

Hunter of Priddis took a 12-4 win over Edwards from Banff in the finals of the Visitor's competition, then in consolation play he captured a second trophy win over the Parsons rink. In Burns' competition eight Calgary rinks played an equal number of visitor's rinks in points competition. The event could not have been closer as the city curlers won by one point.

Smith had a 14-6 win over James Walker in the finals of the Brewery event. Calgary's Spafford quartette easily won by a 19-7 score over Aird of Priddis in the McNeil competition. Sol Spafford also made it to the finals of the Walkerville, the main event, but in a nip and tuck game lost to winner Cappy Smart by an 11-9 count.

All the curlers received free tickets to a hockey game which was played in Calgary during the spiel. The Curlers' Ball was held at the Opera House, and many of those in attendance danced until four a.m. to the music of Captain Bagley's orchestra. A farewell banquet was held at the Royal Hotel, and there President Miquelon and Vice-president McLeod were presented with rings by the Macleod curlers in recognition of a well-run spiel, which many felt was close to rivalling Winnipeg's in prestige. During the bonspiel the wives of the visiting curlers were suitably entertained by the ladies of the Calgary Curling Club.

There were 36 curlers entered in the Calgary Curling Club green curler competition. Club competition also took place for the Hudson's Bay, Doll and Merchant's trophies. Four teams of curlers living in west Calgary played their opponents from the east end of the city, with the losers treating the winners to supper at the Criterion Restaurant. In Liberal-Conservative competition the losers contributed food to the Calgary General Hospital.

In December of 1903 Jack Rae's rink from Edmonton came to Calgary to challenge Cappy Smart who had defeated them at the Edmonton spiel. Cappy was located at the Fire Hall, sitting with his feet up in front of the stove. He accepted the game challenge and went to round up his rink. The results, however, did not change as Smart won 12-6.

Smart was joined by McKillop as their rinks travelled to Priddis to curl against its locals. It was reported that a good trip was had by all.

T. Lee of the T.L. Special Cigar Company of Winnipeg offered a new trophy for competition at the Calgary 1904 bonspiel, its eleventh annual competition of this nature. The local press reported "Ice in excellent shape for lovers of the stane and Bensom." However the spiel organizers had difficulty providing enough ice for the fourteen rinks, including one quartette from Revelstoke, that were entered in the various events. One curler not taking part in the 1904 spiel was Calgary's fire chief Cappy Smart who had not recovered from injuries suffered in a recent fire.

Giles of Edmonton earned a 7-4 win over Edgar of Priddis in the T.L. Lee Trophy finals and Giles was to meet Lauder in the visitor's final that would be played at their home Edmonton rink. The Edgar rink was the winner over Tom of Golden in the finals of the Consolation event.

Giles added to his laurals as he took an easy 15-7 win over Tom in the Brewery Cup final but in the McNeil competition he lost a close 10-8 game to Calgary's Spafford quartette. A large crowd viewed the Grand Challenge final for the Hiram Walker Cup, and the Calgary fans were not disappointed as the hometown Sol Spafford rink earned an 11-5 win over the Lauder quartette from Edmonton.

Calgary's rinks, helped by Major Walker's 21-5 win, had a 37 point advantage over the visitor's rinks to earn the Burns Trophy, while the rink competition in this event went to T. Tarrant. In points competition A. McNeil scored a 42 to win the gold medal. Each of the eighteen competitors in this event received a merchandise prize. A special trophy, donated by Coaville and Company, was awarded to the Spafford rink for their excellent play in the bonspiel.

The closing of the banquet was considered to be one of the most pleasant gatherings ever held in the city. Major Walker spoke to the gathering in respect to the formation of an Alberta branch of the Royal Caledonian Curling Club. The highlight of the evening's entertainment was the highland fling dance contest that was won by J. Ullock from Golden.

James Smart was elected as the first president of the newly formed branch of the Royal Caledonian Curling Club. The Manitoba rules were adopted for play, and any club located in the Territories, Manitoba or British Columbia was eligible to join. The new organization's patrons were Major Walker and R. Secord of Edmonton. J. Morris of Edmonton and J. Ullock of Golden were elected vice-presidents and Calgary's J. Miquelon assumed the position of secretary-treasurer. An executive council, committee on appeals and a committee on annuals were also set up.

The Albertan employees challenged their Herald counterparts to a curling match, and two rinks from each paper met in a "Grand Challenge—A Burns-Brewery-White Horse competition." The final result ws the Herald 25 and the Albertan 18.

The Calgary rinks of Spafford and Smart competed in the Edmonton bonspiel, while Major Walker and J. Palmer skipped rinks in the spiel at Banff. Sam Savage's quartette competed in the Winnipeg bonspiel, and in the Far East-Far West competition Walker lost to a rink from St. John's. Dr. Brett's rink from Banff split games in Calgary with McLeod and Miquelon.

James Walker was elected president of the Calgary Curling Club for the 1904-05 season, and vice-presidents were J. Palmer and P. Turner-Bone. The treasurer reported that the club had broken even financially the previous year.

The executive of the Alberta Branch of the Royal Caledonian Society met in September of 1904 to plan for the first bonspiel to be held under its auspicies. The new Tetley Tea Trophy, donated by the Tetley Tea Company of London, England, was designated to replace the Walkerville Trophy for the bonspiel's main competition. The new trophy was a four foot high silver tankard with four miniature curling stones at its base. Club affiliation to the Alberta Branch of the R.C.C.C. was set at two dollars and member affiliation at 25¢ a person. Secretary Miquelon wrote to the various clubs in eastern British Columbia inviting them to affiliate with the Alberta Branch.

"Greetings to Curlers," read the headlines of a local paper as a prelude to the 1905 Calgary bonspiel. There were 27 rinks, seven more than in the previous year, entered in the spiel that took place at the Alberta Rink and the new Auditorium rink, which was located on Seventeenth Avenue South. This new structure, which offered excellent seating for the spectators, was decorated in a very festive manner for the spiel. The visiting curlers were given the freedom of the city by the mayor.

More than 200 individuals were in attendance at the meeting of the Alberta Branch of the Royal Caledonian Curling Club, which was held in the Y.M.C.A. Secretary-treasurer Miquelon, who was to be re-elected to this position, reported a balance of $395 in the bank. J. Morris of Edmonton was elected as the organization's president for the 1905-06 year, and H. McLeod along with Dr. DeVeber were the new club vice-presidents. Dr. McRae served as the organization's chaplain. J. Palmer, N. Hoad and N. McKelvie, all of Calgary, were members of the six man executive committee.

Competition was keen and there was a great deal of interest in the spiel. Newspapers in several eastern Canadian and American cities requested complete coverage of the events.

Calgary's Sam Savage rink beat Edgar of Priddis by two points in the final of the Grand Challenge event. The Fraser rink from Edmonton placed third and Cappy Smart's quartette finished in fourth spot.

Fraser came back to defeat Savage 15-9 in the Walkerville event, and in the Brewery final Fraser again gained the advantage over Savage in this event's final. Pringle of Medicine Hat finished in third position. J. Palmer, Comer and Morris of Edmonton were the top three finishers in the Consolation event.

Twelve Calgary rinks outcurled an equal number of visitor rinks by a count of 141-114. In the Brewery rink competition the Spafford, Walker and Turner-Bone rinks finished in the prizes. The T. Lee Trophy went to the McLean rink from Macleod, with Stephenson of Red Deer and Lacombe's Pringle in the runner-up spots. MacLean defeated Fraser in the Visitor's final, with Pringle taking third place. Fire Chief Cappy Smart was the winner of the points competition with his high total of 45 points.

G. Lang, T. Tarrant, Cruikshanks, I. Freeze, S. Ramsay and F. Collicut were other Calgary skips who participated in the 1905 Calgary spiel. The bonspiel proved to be successful both as a sports and social event.

During this era the Alberta rink building was also known as the Vaudette Theatre.

By December of 1905 fourteen clubs had affiliated with the Alberta Branch of the Royal Caledonian Curling Club. The area within its jurisdiction was divided into seven regions and regional competition was instituted, with matches to be double team affairs. The executive decided that the rink with the best win-loss record in the four main events in the bonspiel would be the grand aggregate and Alberta champion.

The McNeil competition began early in January at the Alberta Rink, while west of the city the Springback curlers had laid out a sheet of ice, and the farmers and ranchers were gathering together for some competition. District medal competition also began its lengthy playoff.

Eleven rinks, including quartettes from Calgary and Okotoks, competed in the Priddis bonspiel in January of 1906. The Wallace Cup for the Grand Challenge event was captured by the Jack Irwin rink. Four quarters of beef were offered as prizes in the visitor's competition, and the final of this event was later played in Calgary. A week after the Priddis spiel some members of the Calgary Curling fraternity were off to the Golden bonspiel.

Cappy Smart and Jap Palmer skipped Calgary rinks at the Edmonton spiel. In preliminary play Smart defeated McNeil, who had formerly curled in Calgary. Cappy's rink compiled an eleven and one record and won the Galligher Trophy, then Miquelon got sick and the rink lost out on a second trophy. Lacombe's H. Trimble won the Grand Challenge event.

Over $500 in cash subscriptions were collected from business firms and individuals to go towards the operation and prizes of the 1906 bonspiel. The C.P.R. offered reduced fares to Calgary in the area between Revelstoke and Dunmore for persons travelling to the spiel.

The 1906 annual meeting of the Alberta Branch of the R.C.C.C. was held in the Cooperative Hall prior to the bonspiel. The hall was very crowded and there was an air of enthusiasm among its curlers. H. Macleod of Calgary was elected president of the organization for the 1906-07 season, and the new vice-presidents were M. Maclean of Macleod and J. Aird of Priddis. J. Miquelon remained as secretary-treasurer, and Reverend Pearson of Banff became the curler's chaplain. The Maple Creek and High River Curling Clubs were now officially affiliated with the Alberta Branch of the R.C.C.C. Attending members engaged in a great deal of discussion regarding the draw. Finally it was decided to put all the names of the rinks entered in each event in a hat, but an attempt would be made to match town and country rinks, and not match teams from the same centre in the first draw.

Among the 140 curlers in the bonspiel there were twelve Calgary quartettes, and rinks from Golden, Banff, Bankhead, Lethbridge, Macleod, High River, Strathcona, Edmonton, Wetaskwin, Lacombe, Red Deer, Innisfail, Medicine Hat, Priddis and Maple Creek, Saskatchewan, a total of 35 rinks. Nine sheets of ice were now available, with four sheets at the curling rink and five on the skating rink.

Calgary newspaper headlines read, "140 curlers Soop 'er 'up", as Calgary's largest ever and the most important bonspiel west of Winnipeg began.

In opening day play an upset occurred when Calgary's Palmer won over Henry Trimble, the Edmonton Challenge winner. The motto of the Wetaskwin rink was, "draw on your knees and pray." The ice held up for the entire spiel, and keen competition helped to spread the silverware among a good number of rinks.

The Tetley Tea Tankard and four silver tea sets for first place in the Grand Challenge competition went to the Sam Savage rink of McKillop, Hunter and Young, who won over Palmer in an exciting final that was watched by several hundred spectators. The Brown rink from Medicine Hat and Calgary's Smith were semi-finalists in this event.

Eighteen rinks entered the Walkerville competition, with the Mather rink of Banff, but skipped by Pearson, earning a tight 11-10 win over Hunter in the event's final. Calgary's Smith and Savage finished third and fourth.

Innisfail's Wilson rink took home the Burns Trophy, with the Spafford, Palmer and Patterson rink from Priddis all in the semi-finals. In the Brewery Cup competition the Savage rink scored an easy 15-4 win over the Campbell quartette from Edmonton. Ullock of Golden and the Young rink from Mcleod garnered the next two positions.

The Payne Cigar Company of Quebec offered a new trophy for the District competition, and Golden's Ullock rink was its first winner. The N. Jackson Shield for the Visitor's competition went to the Edmonton Campbell rink, with H. Lang of Bankhead, Tom of Golden and Bradshaw of Red Deer taking home prizes. The Consolation Cup, donated by J. Hutchings of Calgary, was won by the Bayne quartette from Bankhead who defeated Macleod's McLean in the event's final.

In February the Sol Spafford rink travelled to Banff to compete in its spiel, and then the Calgarians followed this up with wins over the Edwards and Pearson rinks at Bankhead.

By the spring of 1906 Calgary's population was over 14,000 and the ranks of the curlers had swelled considerably. The members of the Calgary Curling Club discussed both the building of a new rink and the feasibility of forming a new curling club. The executive met with officials of the C.P.R. in regards to the construction of a new rink on the railroad right-of-way at Fourth Street West.

The points competition finished in March and Parslow was the top curler with 38 points, W. Wilson of Innisfail finished second and Miquelon was third. Billy Wilson also earned a prize for the highest score made by an outsider.

A first in Calgary's curling history occurred in March when a spiel was held for juvenile players. Evert Spafford followed in his father's footsteps as he garnered first prize in the competition. Danny Laughlin's rink finished second, while the other school boy rinks were skipped by Harper, Lindsay, McLeod, Harris, Gillis and McKenzie. Competition was keen and there were many close scores.

In May the Alberta Curling Rink on Fifth Avenue East was sold to a group of twelve curlers headed by Colonel Walker, with the purchase price amounting to $3600 and each of the participants paying an equal share.

Southside curlers met in June of 1906 to form the new Victoria Curling Club. Plans were tentatively made to play in a new building to be constructed at Victoria Park. Sam Savage was the first president of the new club, to be called the Victoria, and O. Smith and W. Parslow were elected as vice-presidents. J. Smith assumed the secretarial duties and J. Miquelon accepted the position as club treasurer. Initial admission to the club was one dollar.

Tender for the new $2850 structure, initially known as the Manufacturers Building, was given to Swallow and Garden. Unfortunately after construction commenced in the fall the Eau Clair Lumber Company could not supply the lumber to allow the project to be completed prior to the curling season.

The Victoria Curling Club held its fall meeting in the Number Two Fire Hall. President Savage announced that he would donate a pair of curling stones for green curler competition. Club colours of black and gold were chosen by the members. Eight skips were elected and teams chosen for the following season. Before winter arrived trophies for various competitions had been donated by W. Lee, R. Miquelon, Watson Brothers and O. Smith.

By December it became obvious that the rink building would not be completed in time, so Sam Savage met with J. Irwin, the Calgary Curling Club president, and it was decided to amalgamate the play of the clubs for the 1906-07 season. Members of the Victoria Club would be admitted to the Calgary Club for a ten dollar seasonal fee.

The first draw of the season was for the Whyte Trophy, and long time Calgary curlers Freeze and Tarrant made it to the events finals. Other early season play saw green curler competition for a pair of curling stones donated by club president Irwin.

In December Romeo Miquelon and Sam Savage skipped Calgary rinks in the Lethbridge bonspiel. Both Calgary rinks were knocked out of the Grand Challenge competition, but both quartettes made it to the final of the T.L. competition. The game was later played in Calgary, and Miquelon came out the winner in the high scoring 19-16 game.

Four Banff rinks competed at Bankhead on New Year's Day. Three Calgary

Jacks—Mosley, Irwin, and Douglas travelled to the Priddis spiel, but it was the home ice of Edgar and Hunter who were in the final of the Grand Challenge event. West of Calgary the Springbank curlers were actively playing on their own sheet of ice.

The Alberta Branch of the R.C.C.C. distributed a fifty page booklet on curling to participants in the 1907 Calgary bonspiel. The association's banquet and annual meeting was held in the Palmetto Restaurant. By this time there were seventeen clubs affiliated with the Alberta Branch of the R.C.C.C. R. Miquelon was elected to serve as the organization's president for the 1907-08 season, while D. Bayne of Banff and Calgary's Jas Aird were chosen as vice-presidents. E. Telfer was to serve as secretary-treasurer and G. Fortune of Red Deer as the curler's chaplain.

The bonspiel's games were scheduled at both the Alberta Rink and at the skating rink. A bus carried players and spectators between the two locations for 10¢ a passenger.

There were 27 visitor and 14 local rinks entered in the Grand Challenge event. In a very one-sided game, that was abandoned in the tenth end, Stephenson of Wetaskwin defeated the Calgary Ramsay quartette by a 23-1 count. In another fixture Edmonton's Shepard scored an extraordinary seventh end.

In the luck of the draw Miquelon was drawn against Kremer of Innisfail in three events and Wilson of the same town in the fourth event. Some rinks had to play five or six games in a 24 hour period during the late stages of the spiel, which meant about fifteen hours of hard work. However the ice held up, and upon its conclusion the bonspiel was considered to be the most successful in the history of the west, Winnipeg excepted.

Archie McKillop scored a close 9-8 win over Kearns of Maple Creek in the final of the District Trophy competition. After being behind 7-1 to Wilson, Trimble of Lacombe surged back to win 11-10 in the Walkerville event. The Calgary rinks of Tarrant and Freeze met in the Burns final, and then Tarrant was matched against fellow club member Vincent in the Consolation final. The Bruce rink from Lethbridge won easily over Pringle of Medicine Hat in the Brewery event. Bruce added to his laurels by again defeating Pringle, this time in the Visitor event final.

There was a large crowd out to watch Vincent's kid rink lose out to McKillop in the quarter final of the Grand Challenge event. In this event's final the Wilson rink from Innisfail scored a 12-9 win over the McKillop quartette.

The Bruce rink of Lethbridge was the winner of the Grand Aggregate, Wilson was second and Trimble, who won the Edmonton Grand Challenge the previous year, was third. D. Bayne, F. Pringle and J. Miquelon took the first three prizes in the points competition.

Other Calgary skips whose rinks did not make it to the finals were Walker, Ramsay, O. Smith, Whitacre, Mosley, Lee, Turner-Bone, J. Smith and Savage.

The Wallace competition, limited to local rinks, made its debut in the 1907 competition.

The Sam Savage and Archie McKillop rinks were Calgary's representatives at the Winnipeg spiel, where more than 150 rinks were entered in the various competitions. The Savage foursome was picked as one of the four rinks who competed and won against the U.S.A. teams.

Rinks skipped by Telfer, Miquelon, Walker and Freeze competed in the Golden bonspiel. Later Miquelon won the grand aggregate at the Innisfail spiel, winning all his games except the final of the Grand Challenge event, which he lost to the Palmer rink, also from Calgary. Calgary curlers also participated in the High River bonspiel.

Three man a side curling took place at the Banff spiel, where a Bankhead trio won the Walker Cup.

In a local green curler competition Andrews won the final match over Freeze. The Whyte competition was won by T. Tarrant, and A. Cameron's rink captured the Brewery competition. The O.C. Smith quartette were the winners of both the McNeil and Doll Trophies.

In friendly competition there were many games in which the losers paid for an oyster supper for the winners. In four team a side competition, held at the Alberta Rink, the north scored a 57-34 win over the southside curlers. A most successful 1906-07 Calgary curling season closed with the President's-Vice-president's competition.

A great curling banquet, held in April at the Palmetto Restaurant, was attended by many of Calgary's leading citizens, and guests included the Priddis curlers. J. Irwin was elected president of the Calgary Curling Club for another year. The secretary reported a club income of $1,184 and expenses of $847 for the season.

In October of 1907 the Victoria Curling Club's organizational meeting, held in the Number Two Fire Hall, was well attended.

The Calgary curling season got into gear in early December as the Esquimos, otherwise known as the Calgary Curling Club, challenged the South Sea Islanders, the nickname of the Victoria Curling Club, with the losers to treat the winners to an oyster supper. The new club pulled an upset as rinks skipped by Savage and Smith won over the Calgary Curling Club's Palmer and Irwin quartettes.

On New Year's Day of 1908 inter-club competition again took place with eight rinks from each club involved. The Victoria Club won seven games and tied the eighth, outscoring its opposition 98-63. This rout was considered quite an upset. On the same day Banff curlers defeated Bankhead in Brett Cup competition.

District competition began early in January with the High River, Priddis, C.C.C. and Victoria clubs competing. The Calgary Club rinks of McKelvie and Irwin defeated the Victoria Club rinks of Savage and Smith by a 27-15 score, while the Priddis curlers earned a similar verdict over High River. In the final Calgary curlers outscored Priddis 32-15.

Ten rinks from the Calgary Curling Club and five quartettes representing the Victoria Curling Club were joined by sixteen visitor rinks at the 1908 Alberta bonspiel.

The Gillis rink from High River earned a 13-8 win over King of Golden in the Visitor's event final. T. Tarrant's rink of D. Lucy, K. Johnston, and F. Tarrant took a decisive 13-3 win over the Fletcher foursome in the Burns event final.

However this was to be one of only two games lost by the Eddie Fletcher rink from the Victoria Club, which won 17 other matches in the bonspiel. In the Brewery final Fletcher beat Henry Trimble by eight points with only ten ends played.

The Tucket competition, which had replaced the Walkerville event, saw Fletcher score a five ender in his 12-7 win over the Calgary Georgeson rink. In the consolation final Bayne of Bankhead won over Lapointe of Calgary.

Henry Trimble of Lacombe scored a 14-7 win, on the strength of seven points in the last three ends, over McLaughlin of the Victoria Club in the final of the Grand Challenge event. O.C. Smith's rink placed third and Warren of Golden was fourth in this event. The Fletcher rink, composed of J. Smith, A. Fidler and Dr. Scott, compiled 17 wins against two losses to win the grand aggregate and the Alberta championship. Henry Trimble's rink finished in the runner-up position. The T. Lee Cup for points competition was won by Fletcher.

The 1908 meeting of the Alberta Branch of the Royal Caledonian Curling Club was held in the Alexander Hall, located on Eighth Avenue and First Street West. The officers elected for the 1908-09 season were President D. Bayne of Banff, Vice-presidents Sam Savage and Henry Trimble of Lacombe, Secretary-treasurer S. Blair and Reverend Fortune of Red Deer served as chaplain. An executive committee of six and an appeals committee were also chosen. The Elks and the Alberta Club rooms were placed at the disposal of the executive and committees for the duration of the bonspiel.

A Civic Curling League was organized by City of Calgary employees, and ice was rented from the Victoria Curling Club. In the Civic bonspiel a team from the Engineering Department were the winners. The Engineers added to their laurels when they defeated the Ashdown team for the Ashdown trophy.

A four ender ladies' game was played at the Alberta Rink with Miss Parslow, Miss Tarrant and Miss Crowe playing with skip S. Blair, while Miss Sinclair, Mrs. Blair and Miss Fisher curled with skip J. Miquelon. Ladies' curling at Banff saw the Denzinens and the Cliff Dwellers engage in regular competition. Major play in Banff found Dr. Brett's rink win the Brewery Cup competition.

Other bonspiels took place at Innisfail, Lacombe, Priddis and Golden. Colonel Walker's rink won the Columbia Trophy at Golden, while Ockley finished ahead of the Lee and Ford rinks at the Priddis spiel. Henry Trimble, now living in Calgary, and McKillop skipped rinks in the renowned Winnipeg bonspiel.

The Walkerville final at the Victoria Curling Club saw the Sam Savage rink of Austin, Cowan and Hunter earn a 12-10 win over Scott. At the Calgary Curling Club, the Georgeson, Doll and Green Points competitions took place. In four rink a side competition the C.C.C. earned a narrow 54-48 over the Victoria Club. The Liberals scored a great 12-9 victory over the Conservatives, with the losers donating four sacks of flour to the hospital. During this era curling play had to terminate at midnight on Saturday, as the game was not allowed to be played on Sunday.

At the annual fall meeting of the Victoria Curling Club J. Miquelon was elected to the club presidency, and other members of the executive for the 1908-09 season were A. Cushing, W. Lee and J. Smith. The club also had five patrons.

Citizens living east of the Elbow River met in the fall at the Number Three Fire Hall where they organized the East Calgary Curling Club. Its patron was Colonel Walker, President—A.E. Cross, and Vice-presidents—A. Bassett and E. Lewis. The club applied to affiliate with the Alberta Branch of the Royal Caledonian Curling Club. Two sheets of curling ice were flooded on land adjacent to the fire hall.

The Calgary Curling Club members elected J. Tarrant as president and S. Blair as secretary-treasurer for the 1908-09 season. It was decided that the Doll competition would be a knockout series for class A curlers and the Galt Trophy would serve in the same capacity for class B.

In the season's opening play at the Victoria Club the Vice-president's curlers defeated the President's men by 20 points. O.C. Smith won over Dr. McRae to represent the Victoria Club in the District playdowns. At the Calgary Club play began in the Walkerville and Brewery competitions. In January of 1909 five Calgary rinks competed in the High River spiel. First and final year Calgary law students engaged in what was reported to be, "a great curling game." Single men earned a 13-7 win over the married men at the St. George's Rink.

The 1909 Alberta bonspiel, the fifth such annual event, was known as the crystal bonspiel because of the numerous crystal prizes, including over one hundred items of cut glass. With two buildings being used for the bonspiel a rig was hired to transport players and spectators from one building to the other for ten cents a person. In order to make it easier to determine whose rock was whose red or blue colours were attached to the handles. There were eighteen Calgary rinks entered in the spiel as well as quartettes from Strathcona, Edmonton, Wetaskwin, Banff, Golden, Priddis, Macleod, Lethbridge, High River, Innisfail and Red Deer. A church parade was held and members of the curling fraternity marched in a body from the Alberta Rink to Knox Church where the Reverend Fortune delivered the sermon.

Weather conditions were such to make the ice ideal for the bonspiel. A great deal of interest was taken in the competition by Calgarians, and at one icy spot on Ninth Avenue the hack drivers spent their spare time curling with horse weights.

Colonel Walker, one of Calgary's senior curlers, could not compete in the spiel due to a sprained wrist.

Twenty curling clubs were represented at the annual meeting of the Alberta Branch of the R.C.C.C. Sam Savage was elected as the new president while H. Trimble and H. Shephard of Edmonton were to serve as vice-presidents. S. Blair again assumed the responsibilities of secretary-treasurer, and Reverend Pearson of Edmonton would be the curlers' chaplain for the 1909-10 season.

The 1909 Alberta bonspiel was considered hectic as there were 43 rinks entered and there just was not enough ice to plan efficient draws. Some quartettes had to play four games in a day, and as a result got very tired and their play suffered. Caretaker Cowan of the Alberta Rink went home sick after putting in 22 and 23 hour work days. The final games could not be rushed as D. Bayne of Banff was participating in nearly all the events.

The Grand Challenge Trophy remained in Calgary as J. Miquelon's rink of O. Smith, Esch and A. Cushing defeated the Trimble quartette 9-6 in the final. The

Tucket final saw Sam Savage's rink of D. Lucy, W. Parslow and T. Dallison earn a narrow 10-9 win over the Georgeson quartette after a see-saw game. Miquelon earned a second trophy with a 9-6 win over the Victoria Club's Fletcher in Brewery competition. In the Burns event S. Spafford ousted Savage in the semi-final, and then he earned a tight 12-11 win over Miquelon in the event's final. Spafford's rink was composed of A. Morrison, J. Irwin and N. Hoad. The I. Freeze rink of N. Stirret, E. Lapointe and E. Harris won 10-8 over Onsum of Innisfail in the Consolation event.

There were 20 rinks in the Visitor's competition, and a new sterling silver cup for the event had been offered by D. Campbell and Company.

In the District competition M. McLean, who had curled at Macleod since 1892, took a 13-9 win over Ferguson of Stettler. The Miquelon rink, with 16 wins in the four main events, won the Grand Aggregate and the Alberta championships.

Calgary curlers participated in many bonspiels outside of Calgary. At Winnipeg Sam Savage's rink of N. Hoad, O.C. Smith and A. Cushing reached the finals of the Dingwall competition, and they were one of seven rinks picked to play against the U.S.A. teams for the International Trophy. The Spafford quartette finished second at the Banff spiel, and Colonel Walker's rink won the grand aggregate at Golden. Calgary curlers also participated in bonspiels at Innisfail, Cranbrook, Stettler, Edmonton, Priddis and High River. Residents in High River complained about the noise that came from the curling rink late in the evening, and it was suggested that the rink be moved to the nuisance grounds.

The Victoria Club rinks of Parslow and Fletcher combined to score a 26-23 win over the Wilson and Howard quartettes from the East Calgary Curling Club. Teams from the waterworks, public works, executive and fire departments participated in the Civic bonspiel. The Victoria Club offered Walkerville points and green curler competition for its members, and at Banff the Brewery, Walker, Stenton, Brett and the Winn silverware were competed for.

In the fall of 1909 the Victoria Curling Club held its annual meeting at the Plunkett and Savage warehouse, and the 54 members elected O.C. Smith and W. Parslow as the club's president and vice-president. It was decided to have A and B classes in the Brewery competition and each rink had to have one green curler on its roster. The club held a novelty competition in early November, with Eddie Fletcher's rink taking the honours. This event was followed by the annual President—Vice-president's competition, then the Doll and Great West Saddlery events. Dr. Sisley offered a pair of rocks for green curlers who were paired in doubles competition.

The South Sea Savages of the Victoria Club matched nine rinks with the North Pole Experts of the Calgary Curling Club. Each member of the winning Victoria teams, who won on points 103-90, even though they lost six of the games, was given a bottle by the Great West Liquor Company.

The District competition saw the three Calgary clubs, High River and Priddis play off to represent the district at the provincial spiel. The members of the rink winning the medal would play off in points competition to see which individual would hold the medal. The High River rink beat the East Calgary team 15-12 and

Priddis 20-7. The Victoria quartette won over the Calgary Curling Club 12-9 and in the district final the Victoria Club took a 13-9 win over High River.

Christmas Day play at the Calgary Curling Club saw the President—Vice-president competition. The Victoria Club, represented by A. Cushing's and Sam Savage's rinks, beat Wilson and Towers of the East Calgary Club. North-South competition also took place during the festive season.

J. Miquelon, the district umpire, and D. Bayne, both patrons of the Alberta Branch of the R.C.C.C., donated medals for competition at the Alberta bonspiel held in January of 1910.

The annual meeting of the curlers took place at Nolan's Hall, located at 127A Eighth Avenue West. Daysland and Vegreville were two of the 32 clubs who were now affiliated with the Alberta Branch of the R.C.C.C. W. Sheppard of Strathcona became the organization's new president, while E. Telfer and H. MacLean of Macleod were elected as vice-presidents, S. Blair as secretary-treasurer and Reverend Grant of Fernie would serve as the curlers' chaplain. The patrons were S. Savage and Attorney General C.W. Cross, and the executive committee now numbered twelve.

A special prize was to be given for the Alberta championship, earned by that rink that won the most games, with defaults not to count, in the four major events of the competition. Although Macleod also wanted to be considered as a site, it was decided that the organization's annual bonspiel would be alternated between Calgary and Edmonton. Complaints were voiced that Calgary should have more rinks in the spiel, and it was suggested that the powerhouse rinks be split up so as to accommodate more Calgary curlers in the spiel. Bagley's Orchestra entertained the group following the business meeting. On the following Sunday Reverend Pearson preached a curler's sermon at Central Methodist Church.

Newspaper headlines that read, "Bonspiel off to a good start," and, "Fair ice and good curling today," announed the Alberta bonspiel for 1910. A daily newspaper column entitled, "Outside the Hog Line", gave anecdotes about the curlers in the spiel. Many Calgary merchants got into the spirit of the bonspiel by decorating their premises.

Seventeen local and sixteen visitor rinks were entered in the sixth Annual Alberta bonspiel. Sheets 1-4 were at the Alberta Rink and sheets 5-9 were located at Victoria Park. The ice was very wet as the spiel got underway, but the weather turned cold and the ice was ideal.

When the competition had ended Henry Trimble, with teammates W. Parslow, E. Farncombe, and Clarke had compiled 15 wins to capture the Grand Aggregate. S. Savage and O.C. Smith each had ten wins, but because Savage had beaten Smith he was given second place in the Alberta championships. Trimble won the Brewery Trophy with a 10-9 win over Smith in a contest that was anyone's game until the last rock. In the Burns event final Trimble took a 12-10 win over the John Benson rink from Medicine Hat. Benson's rink did very well considering that there were two green curlers on the team.

The Tucket final saw the team of skip J. Duff, G. Mason, G. Lamont, and McKelvie earn a narrow 10-9 win over the Trimble rink.

For this first five games in the Grand Challenge competition Savage's rink scored 81 points while only allowing 39 against them. Savage, assisted by A. McKillop, E. Fletcher and Esch overwhelmed H. Johnson of Fernie 26-2, and in the event's final Savage played his last rock perfectly to take a 9-7 win over A. Cushing's Calgary rink. The District competition also went to Savage who defeated MacLean of Macleod 13-4 in the event's final.

The Visitor's competition, with the Mother's Favourite Trophy being offered for the first time, went to the Bowen rink from Strathcona, who defeated Bayne of Banff 11-6 in the event's final. Consolation play saw R. Welliver's rink of W. Payne, L. Gaetz and W. Hosking defeat Blundell 11-7 in the event's final to take the Golden West Trophy.

At the Priddis spiel held in March Lee won the Grand Challenge and Black Trophies as he defeated Ockley in the finals of both events. Hunter beat Standish in the final of the Priddis Cup, with the DeMille rink taking the Consolation event and Hugh McLeod winning the points competition. Sixty persons sat down at the Priddis curling banquet. The entertainment featured highland dancing as well as boxing and wrestling in which Billy and Bob Lauder were matched against locals.

In April the Victoria Club members elected W. Parslow as the club's new president, with Dr. McRae and A. McKillop assuming the vice-president positions. Plans were unveiled for a huge rink to be owned jointly by the Victoria and Calgary Curling Clubs. The structure would serve as a horse show building the rest of the year.

The Alberta Rink building ended its days as a curling rink when the structure was sold. Its immediate future was to serve as a livery stable. In 1934 the building was torn down.

The East End Curling Club had to limit its membership as there were just too many applicants for the 1910-11 season. East Calgary merchants offered the club a new trophy for competition. President—Vice-president, Walkerville and District competition began at the Victoria Club in early December, but warm weather near Christmas caused the ice to all but disappear. Lethbridge, with a new four sheet curling building, found itself without any ice at all.

District competition between the Priddis, High River, East Calgary and Victoria rinks continued in January of 1911. The Victoria rink of McKillop, Duff, Savage and Hoad defeated Pinkham's East Calgary rink, and the Campbell rink from High River won over the Priddis foursome. In the District final the score was Victoria 9—High River 7.

Thirteen sheets of ice, located at three Edmonton clubs, were available for the 1911 Alberta bonspiel. Seventy-nine rinks were entered and seventy-eight rinks competed for $3,000 in prizes at the seventh annual bonspiel of the Alberta branch of the R.C.C.C.

Calgary's Archie McKillop earned the Tetley Tea Tankard in the Grand Challenge event as he won 12-3 over Strathcona's Shephard, who conceded in the tenth end. Later a controversy arose as T. Tarrant claimed that his rink should have been in the event's final, and he challenged McKillop to play in Calgary for the trophy. The curling executive said that McKillop was rightfully the winner. However the two rinks did meet later, and Tarrant came out the winner.

The Tucket final saw another abbreviated game as McKillop won over Massie of Edmonton in four ends. Hutson's Provost rink topped McLean of Strathcona 15-6 in the Brewery final, and Dickens, Fraser and Smith were the top three rinks in the Burns event. District competition saw Edmonton's Fraser beat McKillop 13-3.

Forty-two rinks were involved in the Visitor's event, and in the final McKillop added to his laurals with an 11-8 win over Calgary's E. Fletcher. In the Consolation final Ross met R. Forbes of Calgary. The first three places in the Grand Aggregate and Alberta championship went to McKillop, Campbell and Fletcher rinks.

Other Calgary skips and their rinks taking part in the bonspiel were: W. Gardiner, I. Freeze, H. McLeod, O. Smith and G. Bryan. Sam Savage had a death in his family and he did not participate, while Henry Trimble, one of the better curlers in the province was very sick, so his rink did not play in the spiel.

Alberta's newly elected curling executive for the 1911-12 season included President E. Telfer of Calgary, Vice-presidents W. Mould of Edmonton and W. Alexander of Banff and S. Blair retained his secretary-treasurer position. Calgarians O.C. Smith, J. Irwin and H. McLeod were on the executive committee and Sam Savage was part of the appeals and complaints committee.

In February a charity bonspiel was held at the Victoria Curling Club. Most of the rinks involved had two or three ladies in their lineup. In the closing games of the spiel ladies quartettes were matched against the men. The ladies won, but many of the spectators felt that this only took place with the help of the losers. The Calgary ladies who took part in the bonspiel included: Mrs. Blair, Dunlop, McLaren, Campbell, Glass, Cotton, Brocklebank, Stirrett, McLellan, Irwin, Miquelon, Louden, Orr and Miss Parslow, Morten, Scales, Pinkham, McLeod, Tarrant and Jones. Other players in the spiel included a boys' rink and a left handed doctor's quartette.

Archie McKillop's rink had an excellent 16-1 record at the Winnipeg bonspiel, but then the skip hurt his back and his rink lost six out of their last seven games. Other members of the Calgary quartette were McGuffin, at third, Savage at second and Miquelon playing lead. When McKillop sprained his back Savage skipped and Robinson of High River joined the team.

Calgary rinks skipped by Hoad, Freeze and Palmer curled in the Red Deer spiel, and other Calgary curlers took part in the Lethbridge and Golden spiels.

In the spring Calgary's curlers endorsed plans for the proposed horse show auditorium and curling rink that would be spacious enough for ten sheets of ice.

The East Calgary Curling Club was invited to send curlers to Winnipeg to play against the visiting Scottish curlers during their Canadian tour in the winter of 1911-12. The East end club set up five rinks for the season which were skipped by M. Williams, G. Foster, G. Marr, C. Rouff, and G. Wilson.

Retailer Alex Martin sold Kay Red Hone stones, which were imported from Scotland. He also sold extra handles in ivorine and ebony.

A Calgary newspaper headline stated, "Calgary's gigantic curling rink, the largest in the world, will be open next week." Up until then there had only been five sheets of ice in the old agriculture building; these were now taken over the

Civic Curling Club. The East Calgary Curling Club would now use four sheets in the north-west corner of the new auditorium and the Victoria Club would use the main area of the building. The structure also had lots of room for spectators of the roaring game.

Fifty-three rinks, including 28 quartettes from outside of Calgary, took part in the January, 1912 Alberta bonspiel. Conditions were ideal at the new building which was visited by great crowds of spectators during the competition. ▪

After the completion of a successful spiel the Bayne rink from Banff, which included McGowan, Alexander and Johnston, were the champions of Alberta. Bayne and High River's Poile had each won twelve games in the four major events, so a play off game of six ends duration was staged and Bayne won 6-5. The Banff rink also won the Grand Challenge event with a 12-6 win over Ritchie of Strathcona in the event's final.

The Lee rink from Priddis won an 11-10 thirteen end game from Henry Trimble, who now curled out of the Victoria Club, in the final of the Tucket competition. In the Brewery final Savage won 13-5 over McCauley of Edmonton, and in the Burns event Poile took the cup back to High River after a 12-6 win over I. Freeze of the Victoria Club.

A new trophy for the District competition was donated by D.E. Black, and this silverware went to the Savage rink which defeated McCauley in the event's final. The Taylor Milling Company Trophy for the Visitor's competition was won by the Lee rink with the W. Wilson rink in second place. In the consolation final Forbes won over McKillop to capture the Golden West Trophy. J. Irwin and G. Thompson tied for the lead in the points competition, with Archie McKillop finishing a close third.

The $400 Red Letter Perpetual Challenge Cup was offered by the J.P. Weiser Company of Prescott, Ontario as a two rink challenge event, with the total score of two simultaneous sixteen end games declaring the winner. In the event's initial competition at the 1912 spiel the Edmonton rinks of McCauley and Garrison defeated two Strathcona rinks in the event's final. Future competition allowed the winners to always defend the cup on their home ice.

The 1912 bonspiel had included some exciting curling. Lafferty and McBrine of Castor had to go 14 ends in their game before a winner was declared Dr. McRae conceded at the end of the sixth end when he was down 12-1 to Archie McKillop. Near the close of the spiel play continued all through the night as there was a danger of the warm weather ruining the ice. The Innisfail rink was unique in that they were the only curlers competing in the spiel that did not use granite stones. Local newspapers carried several photos of the competition and the curling banquet.

A large crowd was in attendance at the banquet and the annual meeting of the curlers which was held in the Grosvenor Cafe. Mayor Mitchell was the principal speaker and he made two speeches during the evening. Thirty-five clubs were now affiliated with the Alberta Branch of the R.C.C.C. J. Mould of Edmonton was elected president of the curlers for the 1912-13 season, and A. McKillop and Mayor Davis of Strathcona were to serve as vice-presidents. J. Blair remained as secretary-treasurer, and Reverend Short of Innisfail would serve as the curlers' chaplain.

In late January eleven rinks competed in the City Hall bonspiel. Green curlers competition for the Mayor's Trophy saw each man play three pair of stones, with the winner of the match being the first person to make 13 points.

Calgary rinks skipped by Savage, McTavish and DeMille of Priddis competed in the Vancouver bonspiel, which was played on their new artificial ice. In the Cotton competition Savage lost 11-10 to the Bruce rink, but Savage redeemed himself in the Kelly-Douglas event as he won over Ullock, who was now a resident of Vancouver, in the event's final. DeMille took home a mounted ram's head which was first prize in the Rat Portage Cup final, and, as well DeMille won the Kilmer Consolation event. The Pinkham and Palmer rinks took part in the Lethbridge event where they gave a good account of themselves.

During the year the Crow's Nest Curling Association was formed as a branch of the R.C.C.C. The number of regions in the Alberta Branch were increased from seven to twelve.

Mayor Mitchell's team played in but lost the opening game of the 1912-13 curling season of the Civic Curling Club. Thirty rinks took part in the club's President—Vice-president competition. Walkerville competition began early in the season at the Victoria Club. The East Calgary Curling Club began its season with the Brewery competition. The Calgary Brewing and Malting Company supplied trophies for many bonspiels in the Canadian West.

In District competition play at High River the Victoria Club rinks of Wright and Savage won over Towers and Living of the East Calgary Curling Club. High River earned a bye as the Priddis curlers never showed up. In the final the High River curlers earned the right to represent the district in the provincial competition.

The ninth annual Alberta bonspiel was held in Edmonton where nineteen sheets of ice were made available for the competition. The tournament made a good start, but many games in the late stages of competition were defaulted as some rinks left for home.

The Grand Challenge even was an all Edmonton final as John Rae's rink took an 11-9 win over the Hugh Campbell quartette. High River's Bert Poile and the Edmonton Laird rink were in the finals of the Tucket competition, then Pile lost a close 11-10 game to W. Bray of Medicine Hat in the final of the Burns event. A new trophy was offered in this event as the previously played for trophy was out of circulation.

Sam Savage brought the Brewery Trophy back to Calgary after he defeated finalist Cooper of Vermilion 14-11. In the Consolation final Simpson won over Sheppard. Savage earned his second trophy, the Mother's Favourite, with an 11-7 win over Poile in the Visitors' competition, while fellow Calgarian Dr. Wright took third place. Poile did finish ahead of Savage in the Grand Aggregate, and for this he was awarded a silver cup donated by Gorman, Clancey and Grindley Ltd.

In the points competition A. Farncomb of Strathcona won with 36, one more point than Pringle. Cappy Smart's 41 points in the 1905 competition was still an Alberta record for this event.

Other Calgary skips and their rinks who participated in the spiel at Edmonton were Forbes, Living, Marr, Sellers, Lafferty, Telfer and Moffat.

At the annual meeting of the Alberta Branch of the R.C.C.C. an Edmonton delegate made a motion that the organization's annual bonspiel be held in Edmonton each year. This brought about a heated and lengthy discussion, then Sam Savage brought this to an end with a great rebuttal speech in which he said that the following year in Calgary the bonspiel would be played on artificial ice and could be held in March or April.

The organization admitted the Calgary Civic, Edmonton Royal, Olds and Camrose curling clubs to its fold. Calgary's Dr. McRae's motion that each rink competing in the annual bonspiel must have one green curler was defeated. The Bagnall-Wynd system of making draws would be used in the bonspiel.

The curlers' new executive for the 1913-14 season was President Archie McKillop of Calgary, Vice-presidents A. Davis of Edmonton and A. Living of the East Calgary Club. Calgary's E. Telfer, John Irwin, Dr. Wright, A. Morrison and W. Forbes were part of the executive, while the curler's patrons were the mayors of Calgary and Edmonton.

The Civic Curling Club held its annual bonspiel in January, and Darling beat Wilson in the D.E. Black Cup final. Competition took place at the Victoria Club for the Mountain Spring Brewery Cup. Calgary's Palmer rink won the Grand Challenge event at the Red Deer spiel, while Living, whose losses included a 17-15 game, won the hard luck prize. The Georgeson, Telfer, McKenzie and Davidson's East Calgary rink curled in the Banff bonspiel. A ladies' spiel at Banff saw four rinks play for the Front Cup. Calgary newspapers carried the results of many bonspiels in western Canada and the U.S.A.

At the Vancouver bonspiel Sam Savage's Calgary rink was, for a time, the only undefeated rink, but then he lost two straight games in the semi-finals. However his rink did win the P. Burns event and the Grand Aggregate. Another Alberta winner was H. Poile of High River.

In the fall of 1913 the members of the East Calgary Curling Club decided that because the club's membership was now city-wide a new name would be more appropriate, and so the name "Thistle" was decided upon. The club's executive was approached by representatives of the C.P.R. employees who were considering forming a curling club and presented a proposal to build a new rink.

Shortly after this Mr. W. Davidson of the Crystal Ice Company announced plans for the construction of an artificial ice rink to be built on the corner of Eleventh Streeth and Fourteenth Avenue S.W. Members of the curling fraternity were enthusiastic about the project, but residents of the area were less enchanted. Dr. Egbert, president of the Crystal Ice Company requested a $5,000 bond to guarantee this amount for five months curling, and this was supplied to him by a group of curlers led by Sam Savage. Anticipated cost to each curler would amount to twenty dollars for the season. However the new rink was never built as a petition against its construction was raised was raised by the area's residents on the grounds that it would create too many problems in a residential area.

During the fall Edmonton curlers were touting an annual Edmonton bonspiel.

This was not suggested to be a split with Calgary, but it was felt that it was time to form a northern branch of the R.C.C.C.

Thistle Club President Marr arranged to share the Horse Show Building equally with the Victoria Club. Increased memberships raised the number of Thistle rinks to 24.

Red Deer opened its new rink which contained eight sheets of curling ice. A unique five aside curling game was played there by delegates to the meeting of the Alberta Amateur Hockey Association. The Calgary rink of skip J. Price, Mac McKinley, Bruce, Bill Pearson and Boreham scored a two in the last end to defeat the Edmonton rink by a 10-8 count.

A mild fall caused dismay among the Calgary curling fraternity as it was difficult to make ice. Bill Sherman claimed that his auditorium would have artificial ice by the following winter; however this never came about.

At the 1914 annual meeting of the Alberta Branch of the R.C.C.C., a great part of the agenda dealt with the split between the Edmonton and Calgary curlers. There was discussion as to whether defaults should count towards the grand aggregate, and it was pointed out that Savage had been helped in this respect at the previous year's spiel. New curling clubs affiliated with the organization were from Okotoks, Claresholm, Coronation, Nanton, Cochrane, Highlands of Edmonton and the Windermere District Club. It was reported that the prize list was the best in the history of the bonspiel, and the silverware was displayed in the window of Black's store in the Herald Building.

S. Blair, who had served as the organization's secretary for six years, resigned his position and he was presented with a purse of gold. The new executive for the 1914-15 season included President Archie Davies of Edmonton, Vice-presidents John Irwin and High River's Bert Poile, Secretary Robert Pearson and Reverend F. Roxborough of Edmonton would serve as the curlers' chaplain. It was decided that future bonspiels would alternate between Calgary and Edmonton as, it was felt, there was too much Calgary domination.

The tenth annual Alberta bonspiel was held in Calgary's Horse Show Building and at the Civic Curling Club. The railroads offered half price fares to the event, but only one Edmonton rink was entered, and it did not show up. It appeared that curlers from north of Red Deer were boycotting the Calgary held event.

There were 16 Victoria Club rinks, ten quartettes from the Thistle Club, one foursome from the Civic Curling Club and 12 visitors rink in the bonspiel. The weather had turned colder and the ice was ideal for curling, with five draws being held each day. During the course of the spiel the measuring stick had to be often used to settle an end.

Sam Savage's rink of A. McKillop, C. Bromley and W. Lockhart each took home a silver tea service after they defeated the W. Forbes quartette of the Victoria Club 14-2 in the final of the Grand Challenge event for the Tetley Tea Tankard. In the Brewery final Dr. Brett from Banff won 12-4 over W. Georgeson of the Victoria Club. Savage earned his second trophy with a 16-5 win over Georgeson in the Tucket competition. The R. Welliver rink from Red Deer defeated H. Poile's High River quartette 10-8 in the Burns event final. The Grand Aggregate and the Alberta championship for the rink that won the most games in these four events went to Savage, with Georgeson in second place and E. Vincent of the Victoria Club in third position.

Welliver and Brett met in the Visitors final, with Brett again coming out on top. I. Freeze of the Victoria Club won the Consolation event with a win over R. Pearson of the same club.

The Double Rink competition, a new event for the D.E. Black Trophy, replaced the District event. Each club was allowed to enter one pair of rinks in the event. The silver tankard was won by Marshall and Coutts of the Civic Club who defeated two Banff rinks 19-18 in the final. The Premier Trophy, which had been donated by Wright and Grieg of Glasgow, Scotland, was offered for competition for single rinks who were not involved in the Black competition. T. Tarrant's Victoria rink of N. Jackson, J. Miquelon and E. Tarrant won the trophy with a 13-10 victory over A. Living of the Thistle Club. The top curlers in the Points competition were Alf Booth, Jack Miller and Banff's Jack Thompson.

There were three protests made during the bonspiel, but these were handled by the grievance committee with kid gloves. One game was replayed because a wrong rock had been played.

A gala evening for the curlers was held at the Orpheum theatre, and on the Sabbath the annual curlers church parade was held. Newspaper readers were amused by the caricatures of the curlers printed in the daily papers.

Lloyd Turner's rink won the McKillop Trophy at the 1914 Civic bonspiel. Other silverware offered for the competition included the Clarke, Black, Mineral Water, Tudhope-Anderson and F. Lowes trophies. Billy Gardiner's rink were the winners of the grand aggregate. The 120 club members topped off a very successful season with a banquet at the Hudson's Bay Company store.

Sam Savage and W. Cushing skipped rinks in the Vancouver bonspiel, with Savage making the finals of the Kelly-Douglass event. The Cushing, W. Palmer and Bonneycastle rinks did well in the Red Deer spiel and many Calgary curlers participated in the Banff bonspiel. The C.P.R. curlers held their own competition on the Thistle Club's ice.

Col. West Jones skipped the team composed of Mrs. J. Cairns, Miss Cardell and Miss N. Johnston to a 5-3 eight end game over the quartette of Jeff Lafferty, Mrs. Grogan, Janet Sparrow and Mrs. G. Johnston.

With the advent of the World War many members of the Calgary sporting fraternity joined the military, but curling was less affected than other sporting activities because of its popularity among the older citizens and the interest in it that had developed by many of Calgary's ladies. Unfortunately in the fall of 1914 Victoria Park was utilized by the military and the curlers lost their indoor ice. Instead outdoor ice on the Elbow River and the Garden Pond at Victoria Park, an old ice house and the old C.P.R. round house was pressed into use until the military was able to move out to Sarcee Camp.

Tennis

Tennis, first developed in France in the 13th century, was played by the nobles indoors on a walled and roofed court. The word tennis is probably derived from the French "tenez", which means "take it, play". Tennis is thought to have arrived in North America by way of Bermuda in the 1870's. The first Canadian courts appeared in the yards of private residences in Toronto. In 1876 the Toronto Lawn Tennis Club was formed. A ladies tournament was held in Ottawa in the spring of 1881, and the T.L.T.C. held what was billed as the Canadian championship during the summer of that year.

The Winnipeg Lawn Tennis Club was organized in 1879, and Victoria's club formally came into being in 1885. In Alberta the game was reported to have been played as early as 1883 in Fort Macleod, with a club being formed five years later. A tennis club in Lethbridge was organized in 1887. Four players from Fort Macleod travelled to Lethbridge to play in a tournament organized that year. Tennis was played at lawn parties in Edmonton as early as 1888 and a club with seven members was organized in 1891. A club was formed at Dunmore in 1890 and another in Medicine Hat in 1893.

Tennis rules and regulations went through many changes, but by 1881 the rules were standardized and have changed very little since then. In 1890 the Canadian Lawn Tennis Association was organized. During that era tennis courts were surfaced with lawn, plain dirt, or in some cases cinders from the furnaces.

The game of tennis was first played in Calgary on a court laid out on the N.W.M.P. grounds. The local newspaper reported that tennis was one of the activities played at the C.Y.P.A. picnic which was held on the island, later to be called Prince's Island, during August of 1884. In 1888 a lawn tennis club was formed in the town with a court being laid out on land owned by Mr. Hull on the north-west corner of Seventh Avenue and Centre Street.

During the winter the club sponsored a ball to aid in the operation of the town's hospital. The Calgary Lawn Tennis Club held tennis competition with the Mounted Police players during the summer weekends of 1889. It seemed the police players would win one weekend and the club players the following week. Generally the court was reserved for ladies on Tuesdays and Fridays. During the winter a tennis club ball was held in the Opera House.

By the 1890's there were two courts, and the area served as one of Calgary's social centres, hosting band concerts and parties, many of which were sponsored by Mr. Hull.

The club paid him $22.50 rent in 1891, but considering the club income was $146, operating costs were low. In that era a good quality Sykes and Slazenger racket could be purchased for two dollars, while tennis balls were purchased by the club at $5.70 a dozen. It was reported that there were several mid-winter tennis games played in early 1892.

The Hudson's Bay Cup, for the championship of Manitoba and the North West Territories, was won in 1891 and 1892 by H. Higinbothan, a N.W.M.P. historian, from Lethbridge. In 1891 he also won the Great Falls tournament. Another great Lethbridge player of this era was Godwin. W. Toole, who had won the Hudson's Bay Cup in 1890, moved to Calgary, but he travelled back to Winnipeg to again capture the cup in 1893-4-5.

The Calgary summer fair of 1893 was the scene of some tennis matches. Alfred McKay constructed a tennis court on his farm several miles west of Calgary.

Twenty six players participated in an 1894 August Calgary Lawn Tennis Club tournament. In the finals Mr. Clark and Miss Alexander defeated Dr. Douglas and Miss Gravely 6-2. That year the tennis facilities at the barracks were re-built. During this era Drumheller shale was being used to surface local courts.

By the following year the Calgary club's membership had rise to 45 players. W. Toole, the Calgary Champion, successfully defended his territory's title in Winnipeg. The sports social season was highlighted by a lawn tennis party held on the home court of Mr. J. Bangs.

By 1900 tennis clubs were operating in Lacombe, Strathcona and Millarville. During the next several years there was to be some competition between players from Millarville and Calgary. In 1902, in play held at the court installed behind the Ranchmen's Club, located on Calgary's future Seventh Avenue, the Calgary players came out on top 5-3. Following the completion of Hull's Langmore estate on Twelfth Avenue and Sixth Street S.W., a tennis court was laid out in the vast yard. During the summer afternoons many of Calgary's genteel society would gather there for tennis and tea. By 1904 the West End Tennis Club was in operation in the city.

In the late summer of 1905 a city tournament, which did much to revive tennis in the city, was inaugurated by Dr. Pirie, Mrs. Severs and Captain Clifford. Mrs. Christie defeated Miss Pinkham for the ladies' title, and Mr. Wilson teamed with Miss Alexander to capture the mixed doubles competition.

On July 31, 1906, at a meeting held in the city hall and chaired by Dr. O'Sullivan, the Calgary Lawn Tennis Club was organized. Its first slate of officers was to include: Honourary president Senator Lougheed, President W. Toole, Vice-president A. Sayers, and Sec.-treasurer Dr. O'Sullivan. There was discussion in respect to the club forming a joint stock company to purchase land for new courts from the C.P.R.

The 1906 provincial tennis championships, Alberta's first, were held at the two courts on the grounds of the R.N.W.M.P. The men of the police force who were handling the events were granted leave for the occasion, which was considered as much a social function as a sports event. Tea, served each afternoon, was presided over by Mrs. Lougheed.

There were 106 individual entries in the tournament. Entry fees were a dollar an event for men and 50¢ per event for ladies. On Wednesday, sharp at one o'clock, Beard and Ladner, Doughty and Buchanan had the honour of crossing rackets in Alberta's first provincial tournament.

Local jeweller and sportsman Mr. Doll donated the Doll Challenge Cup for the men's singles competition in which there were 26 entries. Former territorial champion Toole lost in a semi-final to R. Beard, in a match that showed the mettle of both players. Friends of Mr. Toole felt that if he had been in condition the decision would have been reversed. R. Beard then defeated brother B. Beard for the title.

Shortly after the singles final the Beard brothers met Toole and Hannebar in the men's doubles for the Cushing Challenge Cup, donated by the Hon. W. Cushing, Minister of Public works. However a doctor intervened saying that R. Beard was in a state of collapse and the match should not go on. The result was that this competition was postponed for several days, at which time Toole and Hannebar won in straight sets.

The P. Burns Challenge Cup, said to be valued at $90, was offered for the mixed doubles competition. However R. Beard and partner Miss Pinkham defaulted the final to Mr. A. Severs and Miss Toole. There were nine entries in the ladies' singles competition. In the final Miss Thomasen outplayed Miss Toole to take the ladies' championship. The tournament was followed by a tennis dance held at the barracks.

In May of 1907 five 70 foot lots were purchased and plans were drawn up to have the grounds prepared at a nominal cost. A major tournament was scheduled for August.

On July 27, 1907 the new courts of the Calgary Lawn Tennis Club, located south of Seventeenth Avenue, west of Eighth Street S.W., were formally opened. Calgary's tennis experts claimed the two courts were equal to the best in Western Canada. Mr. Toole was the club president at this time, but secretary Dr. O'Sullivan and Rev. Ryall were responsible for most of the work done in establishing the new shale courts, which were later increased to four in number.

The 1907 provincial tennis tournament was held here August 21-23. Competitors came from Medicine Hat, Red Deer, Edmonton, Strathcona as well as Calgary. Admission to the tennis ground was 25¢ a spectator, while transportation to the grounds from the Alberta Hotel was supplied by the Downey Auto Company at a cost of 25¢ per person.

R. Beard defeated clubmate Rev. Ryall in the men's singles, while in the ladies singles Mrs. Clark beat Miss Thomason, the previous year's champion. A large crowd filled the adjoining court for the men's doubles final, which was won by the Beard brothers. Miss Thomason teamed with R. Beard to capture the mixed doubles, and the ladies' doubles went to Mrs. Clark and Miss Thomason. This tournament did, as was the pattern, include a full slate of handicap events. A major problem during the competition were the numerous dogs that found their way on to the courts and proved to be a real nuisance.

Late in August of 1907 the Young Men's Club held a tournament on their courts, which were located just west of the court house. It was reported that large crowds viewed the event, with E. Jones capturing the men's singles title.

The Anglican Young People's Association (A.Y.P.A.) opened their tennis courts on Prince's Island during 1908. The courts sat in the midst of a thicket of trees in the middle of the island between 5th and 6th Streets W. The Y.M.C.A. opened its courts on Ninth Avenue east, where it held a summer tournament. In the village of Crescent Heights, located north of Calgary, the Barracca Tennis Club was formed.

Two more courts were added to the Calgary Lawn Tennis Club. Handicap tournaments were held during the spring and early summer. By the end of May a new clubhouse was completed adjacent to the courts. The 1908 slate of officers were: President W. Toole, V.P. Rev. Ryall, and Sec.-treas. Napier Smith. A club tournament for its 84 members was held in July. Mixed doubles winners were Mason and McCarthy; Smith captured the men's singles, R. Beard the men's open singles and the Beard brothers the Men's open doubles.

The Calgary Tennis Club was again the site of the provincial championships, however wind and rain caused many of the matches to be postponed. The Garrett brothers showed great stamina and skill in defeating the Beard brothers in men's doubles play, while R. Holman and Mrs. Dudley Smith captured the mixed doubles crown. Mrs. Smith teamed with Miss Hobbs to take the ladies' doubles competition. R. Beard lost the men's singles title to H. Garrett. This tournament was actually two tournaments in one, as the city championships for city residents took place at the same time. Following the drawn out competition a dance was held at the barracks. It was reported that tennis costume was suitable attire for the event.

In September a group of Calgary players travelled up to Edmonton for its tournament. H. Garrett won the men's singles, and then he teamed up with R. Holman to capture the men's doubles competition.

A new constitution was drawn up at the annual meeting of the Calgary Lawn Tennis Club held in April of 1909. W. Toole was elevated to an honourary position with Dr. O'Sullivan becoming the new club president. Scarlet and white were designated as the team colours. Freddie Lowes donated a challenge cup for club competition, and steps were taken to secure a piece of land for future development.

In the June club tournament Napier Smith captured the men's singles, while Rev. Ryall and Holman were victorious in men's doubles competition.

The 1909 Alberta provincial championships were unique because, although played at the Calgary club, included the Edmonton city championships. Entries for the ten events and $500 in prizes came from Manitoba, Saskatchewan and British Columbia, as well as Alberta. As the street car track was now laid on Seventeenth Avenue, it was hoped that the street cars would be running during the competition, but this utility did not come about in time.

In provincial men's singles play H. Garrett, now living in Cranbrook, won 3-1 over Holman, while in doubles Holman and Rev. Ryall were three-love over the Garrett brothers. Miss Hobbs and Homan teamed to make the mixed doubles, but Hobbs lost to Miss Sterling of Winnipeg in the ladies' singles. Ladies' doubles went to Miss Sparrow and Miss Thomason. A special umpire prize was awarded to Dr. Mason.

Another 1909 summer competition saw the A.Y.P.A. play against the Young Men's Club members on a court located at 19th Avenue and 4th Street S.W.

In September members of the Calgary Lawn Tennis Club travelled to Edmonton for a tournament, from which they returned home with every major prize.

The West End Tennis Club, organized the previous year, had two courts in operation for the 1910 season. East of the Elbow the St. John's Cricket and Tennis Club was organized. Freddie Lowes new house "Lowescroft" was one of the several in the Elbow Park and Mount Royal areas that had a tennis court in the yard. A court was located on the grounds of the Normal Practise School. Calgarians wishing to purchase tennis supplies could visit Alex Martin's store on Eighth Avenue.

The 1910 Calgary Tennis Club's president's position was filled by H. Allison, and H. Garrett became the new V.P.

The annual provincial tennis tournament was open to all comers, however contined rain forced many matches to be postponed. The wet condition caused very slow play throughout the tournament. However tea was served in a very gracious manner every afternoon, and if there was a lack of tennis play there were social activities to make up for it.

G. Garrett, the men's singles champion, lost 1-3 to L. Northrup of Lloydminster in championship play. In ladies' singles Mrs. Dudley Smith defeated Miss Sparrow in very close play. Smith and Kensitt captured the ladies' doubles, then Smith teamed with Garrett to defeat club secretary Holman and Kensitt in the mixed doubles. H. Haines and L. Northrop were the provincial gentlemen's doubles winners. Following the tournament all the participants and officials were invited to a garden party at Senator Lougheed's.

The Y.M.C.A. Tennis Club was re-organized in June of 1910, and the new courts to the rear of the organization's building on Ninth Avenue were used for competition during the month.

An important tennis tournament was held at the Calgary club during Calgary's exhibition week in early July of 1911. During the summer a great deal of local press was given to the forthcoming provincial championships to be held at the C.L.T.C. courts in mid-August. Club president J. Wilson was touting this tournament to be the best ever to take place in Alberta. This gentleman had played his first tennis in Scotland as early as 1880, and in the 1890's had lost to Toole several times in the North West Territories finals.

As well as being a sports event the tennis competition proved to be one of the social highlights of the year. Every day of the competition there were events, such as dinners, drives in the country, entertainment, theatre parties or teas for the tournament competitors and visitors.

Competition was keen and the 1911 tournament proved to be a great success! Daily draws took place from 10 a.m. through 5:30 p.m. Archie Toole and Napier Smith played in the finals for the H. Doll Challenge Cup in the men's singles competition, while Mrs. Dudley Smith beat Miss Winslow to take the F. Lowes

Challenge Cup as she won the ladies' singles competition for the fourth time in succession. The P. Burns Cup for mixed doubles went to Smith and Miss Sparrow who won over A. Toole and Miss Shaw in the finals. Member of Parliament F. Riley had offered a cup for the ladies' pairs competition. In this event Shaw and Wheatley were victorious in the final matches over Toole and Alllen.

During this era the forerunner of the Elbow Park Tennis Club was started by members of Christ Church. Several private courts were located in the yards of some of the new residences in the areas of Elbow Park and American Hill.

By the 1912 season the Calgary Lawn Tennis Club had moved to new facilities in Sunalta. President H. Savary reported that the shale courts were in excellent shape for the Exhibition Week Tournament, held again after its successful debut the previous year.

Janet Sparrow and a friend at the Calgary Lawn Tennis Club, 1912.

It was said that the six courts and $2,500 clubhouse were one of the best facilities in western Canada. All male members had to be shareholders, at a cost of $75, except bank clerks or militia who paid an extra $5 on their yearly dues. The club had plans for the development of lawn bowling and croquet on the site.

Calgarians interested in buying tennis supplies often went to the sporting goods department of Ashdown Hardware. Tennis rackets ran in price from $2-10 and tenni balls cost 35-50¢. The original pear shaped rackets, although still made of heavy wood, were now flat topped. Tennis nets were priced at from $1.50-2.50 and markers cost two dollars.

The Pryce-Jones Department Store, besides the Hudson Bay Company, Calgary's largest retailer, sold men's white flannels, direct from England. Ladies appearing on the courts during this period wore ankle length long sleeve dresses, ties, and hats.

The Crowsnest Pass was becoming a hot-bed of tennis in southern Alberta. Courts were found in Frank, Blairmore, Coleman and Hillcrest, with inter-club matches on the summer weekends.

The 1912 Alberta provincial tennis championships were held again at the Calgary club. Club secretary Wheatley, who was to play in the tournament as well as supervise its operations, reported a record 300 plus entries from many parts of western Canada. Many social functions, including the daily afternoon tea ritual, complemented the tournament, topped off with the lawn tennis ball held in the Al Azhar Temple. The Calgary press felt that this tournament was important enough to include many photographs of the tennis players on both the sports and society pages. The Herald of the day did not include sports news as part of the regular Saturday paper, but put out a Saturday sports extra edition.

Mrs. Dudley Smith lost the first set, but she came back to win the next two and take the ladies' single championship match from Mrs. Mayne. Mrs. Smith and Mrs. Kensitt took a two-love decision from Sparrow and Campbell in ladies' doubles play, while R. Holman and S. Guillon needed five sets to defeat A. Toole and O'Grady in gentlemen's doubles play. Mrs. Dudley Smith teamed with R. Holman to beat Mr. and Mrs. McLaughlin in mixed doubles finals. In gentleman's singles S. Wheatley shut out Carlyle 3-0 to capture the provincial championship. Besides the open competition the tournament included five handicap events.

During the 1912 tennis season a club was organized at the Pryce-Jones Department store with competition being carried out at the courts at Western Canada College.

In May of 1913 play at the A.Y.P.A. courts on Prince's Island saw the Department of Natural Resources tennis team defeat the hometeam. The D.N.R. club now had its own courts and competition took place on many weekends between the A.Y.P.A., D.N.R., and the Y.M.C.A. tennis clubs. The R.B. Bennett Trophy was offered for competition among the members of the Y.P. club. During this era the Baptist Church Tennis Club operated on Fourteenth Avenue and Fourth Street S.W.

The Calgary Lawn Tennis Club held a club tournament in June, and then held the club championships in August. However cool and damp weather caused the tournament to drag on, and it was not until mid-September that it was completed. A first day surprise was R. Carlyle's loss to Noble, who went on to defeat Toole in the final, losing the first set, but coming back to take the match 2-1. Mrs. Welsh, from the Millarville Club, topped Miss Sparrow in the ladies' final. Carlyle and Noble defeated Toole and Constable in men's doubles.

Many Calgarians travelled up to Edmonton to play in the 1913 provincial championships slated August 18-23. Unlike Calgary's shale courts, the Edmonton courts were surfaced with cinders. J. Kinnear of Edmonton won the men's singles and the right to hold the Doll cup for a year. Mrs. Welsh took the T.W.

Lines Cup, awarded for ladies' singles, home to Millarville. Mrs. Welsh then teamed with Mrs. Bourgue to capture the E.H. Riley Cup for ladies' doubles. Calgarians Seymour and Bloomfield captured the men's double handicap event, and Noble won the men's singles handicap event. The other events were postponed a week due to the rain, and then were won by Edmonton players.

In September the Calgary Golf and Country Club held its first tennis tournament for its members. The Crosbie Cup was again played for at the tennis club's fall tournament, with S. Kidd coming out the winner.

The East End Lawn Tennis Club was established on New Street in May of 1915.

Following W.W.1 the A.Y.P.A. courts on Prince's Island became the Prince's Island Tennis Club.

By 1926 lease problems arose with the Prince's Island Courts, while the Calgary Lawn Tennis Club was having financial problems, so an amalgamation took place with the result that the Calgary Tennis Club was formed.

The Canuck Tennis Club was set up adjacent to St. Hilda's school on Eleventh Avenue and Eighth Street S.W. in 1925. The same year the Community Tennis Club was formed at a location on Ninth Avenue and Twelfth Street East. Two years later the Riley Park Tennis Club began play at their court on Fifth Avenue and 11th Street N.W.

The Elbow Park Tennis Club opened its new courts in 1929. With the construction of Currie Barracks in the 1930's, a shale court was laid out behind the officer's mess. Residents of the Scarboro community set up a court in the ravine north of Seventeenth Avenue, that formerly was a sandstone quarry and later became part of Crowchild Trail. Six shale courts were installed at the Glencoe Club in 1931. Other clubs or courts of the era included: Rideau-Roxboro, C.N.R., Ogden, St. Stephens, St. Mary's and Mount Royal College. It was estimated that over sixty courts were in operation in Calgary in the 1930's.

The Y.M.C.A. Foothills Tennis Club located on 5A Street and Seventeenth Avenue in 1935. The Canuck Club became the Excellsior Tennis Club in 1937, and it continued to operate in the same location up until 1947. The courts on Prince's Island were in use almost up to W.W. II. By 1947 the Seventeenth Avenue Courts were just called the Foothills Club.

The sport of tennis was in a period of doldrums during the 1950's in Calgary. However an upswing in interest was strengthened by the establishing of public courts in Stanley Park in the 1960's.

Bowling

Bowling was first reported to have been played in Calgary in November of 1884. That month a 90 by 25 foot building, located behind the Peterson and Peterson Law Office, was constructed at a cost of $3,000. The alleys, reported to be the only ones west of Winnipeg, were made in sections of Minneapolis Oak. The rules of the premises were posted, and the conduct of frequenters of the building would be enforced. It was hoped to create such an atmosphere the gentlemen could have their pipes and read the papers, and it was hoped to disassociate from the usual saloon characteristics.

Colonel Herchmer and Hayter Reid bowled against Mr. S. Bodson and Mr. Secretan to officially open the alleys. The Sheriff of Calgary and the Deputy Sheriff of Macleod set the pins.

The Calgary Bowling Alleys held a bowling competition on November 21 and December 24, with a 50¢ entry fee being charged. A first prize of $15 and second prize of $10 were presented to the winners on Christmas Day.

During the same year a bowling alley was opened in an Edmonton hotel.

It was not until 1896 that Calgary had another bowling alley. The venture was located on Stephen Avenue near McTavish Street. Max Aiken, who later became Lord Beaverbrook, was in partnership with Roxy Hamilton and Dick Broderick to finance the project. The alley was operated by Gerald Dyson in 1899, but by the following year it appeared to have closed down. Elsewhere in the province a bowling alley was opened in the Assiniboia Hotel in Medicine Hat in 1899.

Charles Traunweiser, who had taken over his brother's barbershop in Calgary in 1893 and subsequently operated the Hub Billiards added a bowling alley to this game establishment, which was located in the basement of the Clarence Block in 1901.

In January of 1904 the Calgary Herald reported that, "Bowling is becoming a popular pastime in the city these days. Manager Cameron of the Hub Alleys has offered some valuable prizes for the highest scores of the month. The high man will get a smoking combination of three pipes valued at ten dollars, while the second and third men will receive five dollar pipes."

The St. Mary's Hall was opened in 1904 as a social centre for the members of St. Mary's Church. A bowling alley was installed in the building's basement, and it was here that some of Calgary's children learned how to bowl.

During the 1905-6 season Calgary and Alberta's first perfect ten pin bowling game was recorded as Kip Carson rolled 13 straight strikes to total a 300.

Bowling was becoming more popular in the Canadian West, and in 1907 a team of High River bowlers were entered in the Canadian Bowling association tournament at Toronto. The same year bowling received a boost in Calgary when Ed Hume opened the King Edward Bowling Alleys. Calgary's first five pin bowling tournament was held at the King Edward lanes in 1908. Five pin bowling had been invented by Tom Ryan in Toronto in 1905 as a game that was less strenuous than ten pins, and it could be played by women and children.

The Calgary Bowling League was organized at a meeting held in the Alberta Rooms on January seventh of 1908. The founding executive included: Honourary President Alf Fidler, President C. Traunweiser, Vice-President Ed Hume and Secretary A. Clarke. The league was to be governed by the rules of the American Congress of Bowling. Teams of five men, including the captain, were entered in the league as the Hub, King Edward, Corrals, St. Mary's, Elks, C.P.R. Telegraphers, P.P. Club, Skidoo 23, Albertan and Harmonias. It was reported that this was the first such ten pin bowling league to be established in Western Canada.

A round robin schedule was set up for the league, with each competition consisting of three games and the winner being that team with the highest total score. Referees were in attendance for all games.

The P.P. Club were the winners of Calgary's first bowling league. During the season statistics were kept and published on the 61 bowlers involved in the league play. Cowan of the King Edward and Scott of the Hub Team each rolled an average of 170 a game, while the three game high went to Scott who had totalled a remarkable 591.

Other bowling competitions in Calgary during the season saw a hotel league set up with teams from the Imperial, Victoria, Grand Central, Grand Union and Yale Hotels entered. Knott and Brown were the winners of the two man competition, during which Ed Vincent rolled up a high average of 183. In a second such competition, which was held at the Hub, W. Hunter and Kirkpatrick were the best of the fourteen teams entered. The King Edward held a knock-out singles competition; and W. Hunter of the Albertan staff defeated Clark in the events final. J. Armstrong was the winner of the green bowlers competition. In inter-city play the Calgary bowlers won over an Edmonton team in a total point home and home series.

Women and children did not participate to any great extent in bowling during this era as the alleys were often in pool halls and the general public did not view either of these pastimes with high esteem. Men almost always wore a white shirt and a tie while bowling, however it was not uncommon to see hats being worn by the bowlers.

By 1909 Claresholm, Red Deer and Lethbridge had been added to the list of bowling centres in Southern Alberta. Alleys in this era were built in a continuous plan as opposed to the alleys constructed years earlier which were built in sections that did not always fit smoothly together.

The Royal Alleys were added to Calgary's bowling facilities by the 1908-9 bowling season. Teams in the city league included the Ramblers, Wanderers, P.P.C., Young Liberals, Wholesalers, Elks, Royals and Hotels. Team captain George Scott led his Ramblers to the league championships. J. Shackleton maintained a 167 average over 60 games to be the league's best bowler. He later teamed with MacDonald to win the King Edward's doubles tournament.

In March of 1909 the first provincial tournament was held at the Royal alleys, with the Medicine Hat Royals coming out on top of the Calgary Fill-ups for the team championships. Jim Mitchell and Medicine Hat captain D. Scott were tied, each with a 32, in individual high scores, but Mitchell came out ahead in a rolloff to win a gold locket donated by D. Black.

The tournament doubles competition went to Henthrowe and Dewitt, while Mitchell beat Bert Bowser in the green bowlers final. In the open singles competition Mitchell was again a winner with Bowser and R. Kit Carson taking the next two positions.

Shortly after the Alberta tournament the team of Jim Mitchell, Bert Bowser, Schulz of Edmonton, Scott from Medicine Hat and team captain G. Scott travelled to Seattle to participate in its bowling tournament.

Further competitions in Calgary in 1909 saw Shackleton and Macdonald capture the King Edward doubles tournament. Calgary bowlers participated in a home and home series with the Claresholm bowlers.

President P. Saunders of the city bowling league postponed the opening games of the 1910 schedule as many of the players had not registered with the association. The King Edward alleys were no longer in operation, so the league used the City Alleys, located at 812-First Street East and the Exchange Alleys, located on Ninth Avenue and First Street West.

The Caledonians, led by Mitchell and Carson, went on to win the league championship. Other teams participating were the Y.M.C.A., Wanderers, Ramblers, Enterprise and C.P.R. teams, however the league was not considered a success as too often teams did not show up for their games.

Calgary's number one team of Jim Mitchell, Bowser, Lief, Carson and Scott won the team championship at the 1910 provincial bowling tournament held at Medicine Hat. Team captain Mitchell had to roll a double strike in the last frame of the last game for the Calgarians to win, and he came through to help whip Medicine Hat 2664-2657. The number two Calgary team of Stewart, Patrick, Henthorne, Gray and Kimba lost by 27 points to another of the three Medicine Hat teams. Lethbridge also had two teams in the competition. A large crowd of Medicine Hat supporters used cowbells, horns and whistles to distract the opposition bowlers.

Mitchell, who had held the provincial singles three game record of 748, teamed with Bowser to total 1144 pins and win the doubles competition. Lief's 585 was he best score of the 26 bowlers entered in the singles competition. In this event Finaly of Medicine Hat placed second and Calgary's Carson finished in third place.

In March a junior bowling league was operated by the Y.M.C.A. Raby's team won over those teams captained by West, Hanna, Louden and Cousins. Other competition in Calgary during the bowling season saw the Daily News team defeat the Albertan bowlers.

P. Saunders was re-elected as president and Dr. Hill elected as secretary of the Calgary bowling organization for the 1910-11 season. Competition opened in

November with a telegraphic meet against the Medicine Hat bowlers. During the festive season another telegraph meet was held against Edmonton and Lethbridge bowlers.

The senior bowling league opened its season with six teams, but a shortage of players caused the Y.M.C.A. and Enterprise teams to drop out and a new schedule had to be made up. The Callies took the league championship, winning 90 games and losing only 24, while the club averaged 855 pins a game. Ramblers, Wanderers and Grain Exchange were the other teams in the senior league. Jim Mitchell's 184 was the high single average, while Lief averaged 179, Christenson had a 174 and McCutcheon and Carson followed with 173's. Mitchell put together games of 225, 233 and 226 to give him the season three game high of 684, while Kit Carson's 257 was the season's high score for one game.

The city team won their last three games against the Telephones to take the commercial league title. The alleys were crowded with spectators for this series, and there was a great deal of cheering for the respective teams. Mitchell had the league's top individual average with a high 194. Statistics for senior bowlers who also bowled in the commercial league were kept separate from the other bowlers. Medals for the league's top bowlers had been donated by Moose Baxter.

Prior to attending the Western Bowling Congress at Spokane the Calgary team of Bowser, Collins, Lief, McCutcheon and Mitchell rolled an excellent score of 2,797 in a practice game. At Spokane Los Angeles, the tournament winners, rolled 2718 pins as compared to the Calgary total of 2540, good for seventeenth place. However the Edmonton team finished in eleventh place and Medicine Hat's entry was one position better than Calgary. Following the regular competition an Alberta team, composed of three Edmonton and two Calgary players, won a sweepstake event. During the tournament Mitchell rolled the highest single game score, and he had the highest string of nine games of any of the Alberta bowlers.

The 1911 Alberta bowling tournament, which was sponsored by the Calgary bowlers and organized by the secretary Hugh McAlphine, was held at the Exchange Alleys in the basement of the Grain Exchange Building. Three teams each from Medicine Hat and Edmonton, a team from Lethbridge and a team from Barons were joined by five Calgary teams in the competition.

Edmonton's number one team rolled a score of 2716 to win the handsome Tuckett Trophy and gold medals for each of the team members. The Calgary Wanderers totalled 2705 pins for second place, and Calgary's number one team finished third.

In singles competition Ben Cool, a Langdom farmer formerly of Chicago, rolled a three game total of 651, thirty-nine pins higher than runner up A. Robertson of Medicine Hat. Bowser and J. Mitchell had a 1110 total to take the doubles competition. Second place went to Cowan and Cool; the latter rolled a low 158 in one game or he could have been a double winner. However Ben Cool did justifiably win the Grand Aggregate with a 1,829 total. This steady and careful bowler averaged better than 204 in the tournament, with his highest single game being 232.

A post-feature of the tournament was a Calgary-Edmonton competition with a fifty dollar side bet and the winners to take 113% of the gate receipts. The Calgary bowlers came through in fine fashion to redeem themselves as they won by close to 300 pins. The bowlers were unanimous that the 1911 tournament had been a success.

During the time of the tournament an enthusiastic meeting of bowlers took place at the office of J. Gunn and Company in the Grain Exchange Building, and the Alberta Bowling Association was formed. E. Scrase of Edmonton, a former president of the Winnipeg City Bowling League, was the Alberta organization's first president. J. Gunn was to serve as vice-president and F. Ross of Lethbridge was the association's first secretary-treasurer. James Mitchell and Edmonton's F. Simminton also served on the five man executive. The rules of the American Bowling Association were adopted for Alberta's bowlers. It was decided to hold the following year's tournament in Lethbridge, which had nine alleys in its three bowling centres.

Association membership was set at one dollar per man per annum, an entry fee of two dollars an event and five dollars for teams. A prize for bowlers from towns with a population under 5,000 was to be offered to help stimulate interest in bowling.

Between 1909 and 1911 bowling in Alberta had been under the auspicies of the Alberta Amateur Athletic Association and this was one of the reasons why the bowlers decided to form their own association.

By the Fall of 1911 bowling alleys were now in operation in Castor, Gleichen, Barons, Bassano, Blairmore, Strathmore, Hardisty, Frank, Pincher Creek, Taber and Macleod. At Edmonton F. Simmington was credited with bowling a perfect game.

The 1911-12 Senior City Bowling League began play in October at the City and Exchange Alleys, with the Wanderers, Callies, Grain Exchange and the Harvies, who were at first called the Maple Leafs, competing. In opening night play Patrick bowled a respectable 247 game, and he averaged 203 for the evening. Crack baseball player Pete Standridge also displayed great skill on the alleys. During the fall the Harvies, led by Bert Bowser, established a new Alberta team record of 2870 pins.

The commercial league began bowling in November, with the Citys, Government Telephones, Gunn Co., Commercials, Victorias and Exchange teams participating. A bowling house league was active during the winter at the Y.M.C.A. alley.

In October Calgary bowlers travelled to Edmonton where they gained a 198 pin lead in the first half of a twelve game home and home series billed as the inter-city championship. At Calgary bowlers Bowser, Stockton, Mitchell, Christenson and Patrick, whose place had been taken in Edmonton by Thompson, won by a remarkable 1563 pins and a total 1761 advantage for the 12 games. In two of the Calgary games the locals exceeded 1000 pins; a new record in Calgary's bowling history. Jim Mitchell had an excellent 210 average for the home six games.

The following month Mitchell rolled 13 straight strikes for a 300 score and a perfect game. He then rolled four strikes in the following game to make a total of

17 strikes in a row, which was thought to be a western Canada record. Twice in the previous week Mitchell had 289 scores; each time he failed to knock down the corner pin in the tenth frame. A few days later Jim Mitchell earned a three game total of 685, which was 40 pins more than had been done by a local bowler prior.

A local mathematician estimated that the pin boy at the Exchange Alleys lifted thirty-five tons of pins and balls every working day. 13,000 pins at three pounds each and 1950 balls of sixteen pounds weight added to a total of over 70,000 pounds. The constant bending over and straightening up was a tremendous builder of stomach muscles.

During this era there was an immense increase in the popularity of five pin bowling in Calgary. The City Alleys five pin league, consisting of the Tigers, Rough Riders, the Bunch and the Bronks bowled every Wednesday and Thursday evenings. Opening evening game scores ranged from 14-74. Following the completion of the first half of the schedule Park of the Rough Riders had the highest average in the league with 42.

Just prior to Christmas, 1911 Grain Exchange bowlers Thompson, Boyle, Schram, Birney and Carson set a new provincial team mark of 2936, which was 12 pins higher than the winning score at the previous year's American Bowling copngress Meet held at St. Louis. There was not a Canadian record to compare against, but many bowlers thought that this was the highest team score ever rolled in Canada.

With the conclusion of the Fall schedule of the Calgary Senior League the Callies defeated the Harvies in the last game to take first place. Mitchell rolled an average of 201, seventeen points higher than Bowser who finished second in the league individual statistics. Ben Cool, who was the Alberta singles champion the previous year, had a 175 average.

Calgary bowlers declared themselves the long distance champions after the telegraph competition in which the locals won 3-0 from Winnipeg and 2-1 over the Edmonton trudlers.

There was great excitement among Calgary's bowling fraternity when three world records were established in one evening at the Exchange Alleys. Ole Christenson and Kit Carson bowled a combined three game total of 1427 pins, which was 42 more than the old world record. Christenson put together games of 246, 229 and 256 to total an amazing 731, which was 50 pins better than the previous record of 681 for three consecutive games by an individual. Christenson's and Carson's 2317, an average of 231.7 pins a game, was thought to be a world record for a five game two man total, but this could not be verified.

A few weeks later two Chicago bowlers toppled 1421 pins in three games and proclaimed a world record, but this total was six pins less than Christenson and Carson's score.

In January of 1912 a new schedule for the ten pin bowling league began. The league requested a grant from the city fathers to send bowlers to the Western Bowling Congress competition in Los Angeles. Finally enough money was raised by public subscription to send a team consisting of Bowser, Patrick Carson, Brown, Cowan, Birney and Ward. The team stopped at Spokane where they lost to the hometown bowlers, however at Los Angeles the Calgarians totalled 3549 pins to finish in a respectable third place in the team competition. It was reported that a great crowd of Canadians cheered the Calgary bowlers during their games. Kit Carson finished in fourth place in the singles competition, Bowser in sixth place, A. Patrick was thirteenth and J. Cowan finished in seventeenth position. This was a tremendous showing on the part of these Calgarians against some tremendous competition. Birney and Carson finished in thirteenth place in the doubles competition.

In Calgary the Bachelors team of Christenson, Bower, McCutcheon, Brown and Carson established a new provincial record of 3,009, with three of the team members each bowling over 600, as they beat the Benedicts in a friendly game. However J. Birney of the Benedict team had the best individual score of the evening with an exceptional 640.

Jim Mitchell and Edmonton's Simmington were joined by three Winnipeg bowlers to bowl together under the team name 'Caledwins' at the National Bowling Congress meet held in St. Paul Minnesota. The Canadians did not win, but they did finish in the money. In the team event Mitchell was high man of his team with a 588, and he finished third among all the Canadian entrants in singles and doubles competition.

Three practice games preceeded a world record performance by Jim Mitchell and Ole Christenson at the Calgary Exchange Alleys in March of 1912. Mitchell totalled 1294 pins and a 259 average for five games, which included 44 strikes, 8 spares and one split. His total added to Christenson's 1077 set a new doubles world record of 2371 pins.

At the City Alleys the Royal Bowling Alley team split the competition with the pin boys, otherwise known as Morrow's Elks team. In practice for the Lethbridge meet the Callies, led by Stockton's three game total of 706, set a new provincial five man three game record of 3106 pins.

During this era a Calgary newspaper carried caricatures and biographies of some of Calgary's better bowlers.

The third annual Alberta Bowling congress, which was held in Lethbridge in March of 1912, offered $600 in prizes to the competitors. In the opening play of the team competition the Lethbridge five appeared to have the series on ice, but the Calgary Callies finished strongly to win 2613 to 2603. After the other teams had finished their bowling the Callies team of Bowser, Stockton, McCutcheon, Mitchell, Stark and substitute Brist were the leaders, which gave them the provincial championship, the Tuckett Trophy, medals and the $300 first place prize. Lethbridge placed second and a Medicine Hat team finished in third place. Edmonton, Raymond and a Barons team were also entered in the team event. The Leblanc Trophy, for the best team from a small town, was won by the Raymond Bowlers.

G. Monroe and Evans of Lethbridge won first prize of one hundred dollars for their first place finish in the doubles competition, as they totalled 1088 pins between them. Moore's total of 594 gave him the singles title; Calgary's J. Mitchell also won a special prize for the highest game score in the singles competition.

The Tigers captured the Calgary five pin bowling league when they defeated the Rough Riders in a playoff after the two teams had tied for first place in league play. J. Hambling of the Tigers had the league's top bowling average with 44, while A. Rowan, S. Grimes and B. Everson were close behind.

The Fall, 1912 schedule of the Calgary Senior Bowling League, involving the Wanderers, Ramblers, Callies and Rangers, operated from November first through to Christmas. There were many new faces in the lineups, but Jim Mitchell was still the top bowler, with a season high score of 277 and 710 for three games. First year senior Bob Kelly rolled a very respectable game 253. Mitchell averaged 205.5 for the season, while Stockton was 185 and Carson 184. The Callies won the Fall schedule, winning 36 games and losing nine, and they averaged 905 pins a game. Their highest score for three games was 2852, which was not far below the A.B.C. record of 2905. The Callies also rolled a game record 1065 pins.

J. Miller was president of the eight team commercial league that included teams from the News-Telegram, Ashdowns, Herald, Church and Kerr, Albertan, Land Department of the C.P.R., City Hall, Westinghouse and Wood, Vallance and Adam Co. The Ashdown store donated a pair of bowling shoes to be given to the player with the highest bowling average.

An attempt was made to hold an international telegraph bowling competition, but in the end only Edmonton, Vancouver and Calgary were involved. Calgary's team of Bowser, Patrick, Carson, Stockton and Mitchell rolled a score of 2827 to win the meet. Kit Carson won a ten game challenge match with Jack Stockton by 122 points. Kit rolled a splendid 1054 in the last five games to overtake Stockton's earlier lead. A five pin tournament, held Christmas Day at the Royal Alleys, was won by Calow with A. Moore in runner-up spot. Carson won a box of cigars for a spare-strike game, in which the player had to open with a spare and end the game with a strike. During Christmas week Patrick teamed with Stockton to capture a doubles competition.

In January of 1913 the Royal Alleys bowlers competed against the Cochrane Ranchers in several weeks of home and home competition. In ten pin competition the Royals won all but one game, however the Cochrane bowlers came out ahead in the five pin events.

Calgary bowlers discussed the feasibility of organizing a western Canada bowling association and holding a meet later in the spring. Vancouver had lost the privilege of holding the Western Congress bowling meet for what its officials considered irregularities, and as a result, the coast bowlers were not happy with the parent body, Vancouver, however, did hold a tournament. Again Calgary bowlers were badly in need of funds to make the trip, but they received some backing when they claimed they would advertise Calgary at the coast. In the competition the Calgary team of Alf Patrick, Jock Stockton, W. Schram, Houghton, Owen and J. Mitchell, the latter whose bowling was far below his normal average, finished in fifth spot; their 5304 total being 421 below that of the winning Vancouver team.

The Maple Leafs and the Moose were new teams in the Calgary senior ten pin competition; while the Chiefs, Neverfails, Stags and Clubs composed the 1913 five pin league. A team from the City Alleys travelled to High River where they lost in competition to that centre's top bowlers. Another bowling match took place at the new Ogden Alleys between the Exchange and City bowlers. At Cochrane the Ranchers won all three games of five pins and two out of three ten pin games against the City Alley bowlers.

Alfred Patrick and Jim Mitchell were the first Calgary bowlers to participate at the International Bowling Congress held at Toledo, Ohio. The competition included over 500 five man teams and 2367 bowlers in the singles competition. It was reported that the Calgary bowlers had come the furthest distance of all the competitors. On the trip to Toledo the Calgary pair lost in competition against Winnipeg's best, even though Mitchell bowled a 206 average. J. Murphy and C. Meyer of Winnipeg travelled with the Calgarians who were joined by Ben Cool at Chicago.

At Toledo the team rolled a score of 2699, which put them in second place, only 79 pins behind the winners. The excellent play of the Canadians was greeted with great applause by the gallery during their games. In the doubles competition Mitchell and Patrick totalled 1163, which put them in fourth place for a time. Post-tournament play saw the Calgary pair defeat the champions of Chicago, then Mitchell played one of the top professional all-star bowlers whom he defeated 4-1. In this series Mitchell bowled a remarkable 680; and he averaged over 600 for each of the five 3 game series. On their way home to Calgary Mitchell and Patrick bowled more successful games at Minneapolis.

The Lethbridge number one bowling team visited Calgary and defeated Calgary's best by 144 pins. However it was only competition such as this that was reported in local papers as the importance of bowling was decreasing in the eyes of the press.

F. Simonton of Edmonton, president of the Alberta Bowling Association, announced that prize money totalling $1050, the greatest amount ever offered in an Alberta bowling competition, would be up for grabs in the fourth annual bowling competition to be held in March of 1913. Rule changes included that anyone who bowls in the singles or doubles competition must first take part in the team event.

Teams from Macleod, Barons, Lethbridge, Medicine Hat, Leduc, Vegreville, Daysland, Lacombe and Calgary joined the hometown Edmonton bowlers in the competitions. There were a total of 19 five man teams, 39 double and 78 individual entries. The large number of competitors caused the tournament to be carried over into the following week.

Edmonton bowlers captured the Tuckett Trophy, the money and the first three places in the team event. Calgary's bowling teams did not fare so well, with the Schram's total of 2531 good for fourth place, and the Callies 2453 pins left them in seventh position. Mitchell dropped to a low score of 495 in the team competition play, but Schram's 235 was the highest one game score in this event. When the defending champion Callies bowled they were greeted by cowbells, whistles and hoots by the large crowd.

Houghton of Schram's Calgary team put together games of 213, 209 and 210 to total 632, which gave him first place in the singles event and the $50 first prize money. Alf Patrick was second with 593 and Robertson of Medicine Hat took third place with a 590 score.

Edmonton's Bioun and Simonton knocked down 1180 pins to take the doubles competition; with hometowners Williscroft and Pratt totalling 1162 and Medicine Hat's Robertson and Young finishing in third position. Barons won the team prize for small towns, with Leduc second and Lacombe third. The small town doubles competitioin was shared by Lacombe's Sage and Henry Trimble, one of the province's better curlers.

Laurals went to Calgary's Houghton whose total of 1703 pins gave him the grand aggregate, for which he was awarded the Kirland Medal and $25. According to the Amateur Athletic Union of Canada rules receiving cash prizes in bowling did not necessarily make you a professional.

Other Calgarians bowling in the tournament included: Owens, Thompson, Carter, Stark, Bowser, Stockton, and Cool.

During the summer new drives were installed in both the City and Exchange Alleys. In the Fall owner Bill Cain opened up his new four lane Royal Bowling Alleys located in the Lineham Block. Five pin bowling had never been as popular as the ten pin variety in Calgary, and these new facilities helped to stimulate interest in the five pin activity.

In the Fall of 1913 the Vics, Websters, Tigers, Naps and Giants composed a new five pin bowling league. At the City Alleys a senior five pin league was formed with teams being named the West Ends, Tigers, Thistles, and Rangers. Bowling scores were improving, and it was not uncommon to see games with scores in the sixties and low seventies bowled.

The City Senior Ten Pin League revamped its teams to include the Maple Leafs, Thistles, Wanderers, Cubs, Shamrocks and Alphas. Carmichael bowled a high 254 during the league's opening game in October. During this era the weekly high bowler at the Exchange Alley was presented with a hat by Tom Campbell the hatter.

In November Patrick and Mitchell lost by three pins to Houghton and Gillis after giving them a 150 pin handicap in a special challenge competition.

When the first half of the Royal's five pin league was completed the Vics were in first place. W. Cain's 48 was the best individual average, and Joe Campbell was runner-up with 46.

The Shamrocks were the champions of the ten pin circuit for the 1913-14 season. Alf Patrick of the bottom place Thistles had the highest individual average at 189.6; this was 13 pins higher than runner-up M. Bowser.

The Alberta Government Telephone team were the champions of the electrical bowling league for the 1913-14 season. Other teams in the circuit were the Calgary Municipal, Northern Electric and Canadian General Electric. W. Bruce led the individual bowlers with an 183 average. A.G.T. then went on to beat the Natural Gas Company, champions of the commercial league, for the mercantile championship. Competition for three man teams was beginning to take place during this era.

Calgary bowlers felt that due to financial stringency it would be better to hold a city tournament rather than be involved in a 1914 provincial meet. The local event was to be known as the first annual city of Calgary bowling tournament. Outside teams would be welcome, but no invitations would be issued. Local officials would attempt to affiliate with the American Bowling Congress in case any records were set. There was to be both senior and junior competitions, with the junior events open to members of the Mercantile and Electrical Leagues and nonmembers of the senior league. The cost of each event would be 35-40¢.

These events were held over a two week period in April, with seven teams entered in the senior competition and six teams in the junior play. The Alphas won the senior championship, while in the junior team event Topleys edged out the Municipals.

S. Birney, with a score of 1130, edged Stewart by three pins and Bowser by 16 in the senior singles competition in which 25 bowlers participated. In junior play A. Crowley totalled 1097 pins, with G. Topley and W. Broome taking the next two positions. The pair of Bowser and Brown toppled 2228 pins, with Stewart and Birney as runners-up in senior doubles. Lockart and Bell were the best of the fourteen pairs in junior doubles.

The Royal Alleys held its annual five pin tournament in April, with the Nopes team, consisting of Smith, Pearson, Rowan, Johnson and Herriott defeating the Vics in a six game playoff, Herriott was the high scorer of the playoff as he rolled a 63. Other teams in the competition were the Websters, Elephants, Tigers and Giants. Muir and Campbell were the top bowlers in individual statistics.

With the advent of World War I five pin bowling became more popular among the young people who prefered to use the smaller ball. Several years later there were many five pin bowling leagues and only one ten pin league in Calgary. Harry Young developed into Calgary's top five pin bowler, and he carried a 73 average.

Other bowling alleys to be operated in Calgary included the Woodbine, two Gibsons, windsor, Olympic and the Gayety.

Horse Racing

in

Early Calgary

Horse racing has been a popular activity of the plains Indians since the arrival of the horse to the Canadian prairies in the eighteenth century.

In 1789 the Quebec Turf Club was formed. Horse racing was well established in eastern Canada and at Victoria by the late 1860's. In the early Canadian racing scene trotting and running races were generally held on the same card. The Queen's Plate race was first held in Toronto in 1860.

The Hudson's Bay and other trading posts were ideal meeting places, and horse racing, which included both trials of endurance and speed, were held there. Near Fort Edmonton was a level area about two miles in length where it was reported that horse races took place by at least the 1850's.

By 1874 horse racing was an established sport in Winnipeg. In that year the most important races took place at a two-day meet that was held at Fullerton's Pleasure Park. In 1875 the Manitoba Turf Club was established.

A letter from R. Nevitt, written at Fort Macleod in May of 1875 stated, "A pony race was gotten up and run but it was only for a short distance and only two ponies entered and did not create much excitement."

The first horse racing on the Bow River Flats following the construction of Fort Calgary was done by members of the N.W.M.P. Undoubtedly the area was used by the Indians as well, but it was known that they often held races in the area adjacent to Nose Creek. It has been said that a turf club was organized in the Pincher Creek area in 1882.

Horse races were included in a sports day that was held on the Edmonton River flats in 1882. The same year some members of the Mounted Police competed against Montana riders and Piegans at horse races held in Macleod. On the Queen's birthday of the following year that settlement held a racing program which included a half mile flat and hurdle race, 600 yards and quarter mile flat races, and a 600 yard scrub race as well as an Indian or as it was called "Kyuse" race.

Match races for side wagers took place at many settlements in the Territories. In September of 1883 Calgary's newspaper reported a "well contested" one and a half mile race between the McLaughlin livery stable's sorrel "Humbolt" and Beaupreu's well known racer "Buckskin", quoted at 3-1 odds, for $200 a side.

Shortey's Humbolt proved to be an easy winner on the prairie track, which was located on about the present Third Avenue South. Several days later Lattimer's "Bummer" and McGuire's "Preacher Dad" met on the same track.

In October, Humbolt and Buckskin were to race again. Close to the finish line Buckskin shot ahead to win and this unexpected move brought about a loud protest by the backers of Humbolt, who felt that their choice had been sold out. A disturbance, which soon led to fisticuffs, caused the police to be called in. Meanwhile the stakeholders were ordered not to pay out any money. It was estimated that as much as three thousand dollars had been wagered on the race.

While a Queen's birthday cricket match was being played at Calgary in 1884, Mr. Lougheed, the C.P.R. solicitor, and Dr. Henderson took it upon themselves to hold a horse race. Stephen Avenue was picked as the race site, and the doctor won by a neck. The following month Draycott's and Burnett's horses met in a mile race for fifty dollars a side. Draycott followed on his opponent's tail for most of the distance, then with 20 yards to go he flashed past to win. Late that summer, Sgt. Major Wattams established a riding school in Calgary. Several hurdle horse races were held on the flats adjacent to the barracks grounds.

During a May, 1885 sports day, held by the Ninth Battalion athletes, an Indian, riding a very small pony, arrived at the playing field and challenged the horsemen there to a race. Several riders took up the challenge, but they were unable to match the speed of the Indian's horse.

A group of Calgarians, including Cummings, Scott, Davis, Barnes and J. Clarke, organized horse races for a meet held on Dominion Day of 1885. Subscriptions were solicited and $300 in prizes were offered for the meet at which J. Patrick acted as the starter. There were six races on the program, with entry fees ranging from $2.50 to $5.00 and prize money from $10.00 to $50.00. The regular races were followed by several impromptu match races.

J. McDonough's Biddy McGee won the opening quarter mile race. In the half mile heats, the prime event, Iroquois, owned by Davis, won four of the five heats. David McDougall of Morely won $40.00 for his first place finish in the half mile cowboy race in which the riders and the horses had to be fully equipped with the usual paraphernalia. A 300 yard dash was held for ponies not over 14 hands in height, and a 600 yard consolation race was open to all horses except the winners of the previous event.

A match race was held in July for $100 a side, with Boswell's "Cripple" winning by half a length over Shorty McLaughlin's "Humbolt".

A race week was planned for High River in September, but the activities were not the success that the organizers had planned. Races wre also to be held at Mosquito Creek in October. Five horses, including two from Calgary, were there to run, but their owners could not come to terms, so the competition did not come off.

During the fall of 1885 a group of Calgarians were laying the groundwork for Calgary's first turf association.

Thoroughbreds made their appearance in Alberta in 1885 when the North West Cattle Company brought in a horse with the name "Terror". Tom Beam's

"Mystery" appears to be the first of this breed in the Calgary area. Soon after the Quorn Ranch was importing mares and stallions from Britain.

A group headed by Amos Rowe, George King and George Marsh sponsored a horse racing program on Dominion and the following day of 1886. The horse races, as well as athletic and cycling events were held in front of Calagary's new 1000 seat grandstand. The equestrian events were governed by the rules of the Manitoba Turf Club. The average number of horses in each race was 6-7, but there were ten wagons entered in the trotting race. Entry fees were set at 10% of each event's first prize money, which was as high as $125 in the one mile, best of three heats, race. This event was won by Cable's Zulu, with McLaughlin's Humbolt second.

T. Burn's black mare Susie B. won the first two heats and $50 in the trotting race. There were three entries in the ladies' half mile race, and Georgie McDougall won on Davis's Sam. Other events on the program included a half mile dash quarter mile heats—best two out of three, a half mile slow race, a 300 yard dash and a Mounted Police hurdle race. Visitors to the races were given reduced rail fares by the C.P.R.

Following his race success "Zulu" was advertised to stand for a few approved females at $25 each, to be conducted at the Bow Park Ranche.

A half mile race was held on the straightaway track located just north of the Calgary settlement between Mr. Cable's "Miss Doubtful" and "Black Princess" for a $50 side bet. A large number of spectators witnessed this race and a great deal of wagering took place.

In September of 1886 a large meeting of sportsmen took place in the St. George's Hall. Chairman Amos Rowe explained to the gathering that the Alberta Turf Association had capital stock of $15,000 issued in $100 shares, and $9,300 of this amount had already been subscribed. Messrs. Lougheed and A. Martin acted as scrutineers as the members elected Rowe as president, G. Murdock as secretary and Chas Watson to the position of treasurer. Further voting placed Mat Dunne, J. Lineham, T. Lynch, J. Barter, J. Reilly, H. Leeson and P. Ford on the board of directors. This group's first responsibility was to attempt to raise additional capital through the sale of the unissued shares. Another matter of importance was of securing a race track for the association.

Soon construction was to begin on a new race track. The site was located on the north west quarter of section 23, township 24, which lay on the bench above Mr. Bame's farm north of the Bow River in the future Mount Pleasant area.

The Alberta Turf Association's first meet was held in October, following on the heels of the Calgary Agriculture Society's exhibition. The five race events included one mile heats—best two out of three races, with prize money of $200, $75 and $25 for the first three finishers, with entry fee free to all; a one mile dash with a total purse of $150, but barred to the winner of the one mile heats; one mile trotting heats with a $150 purse; quarter mile heats—best 3 in 5—open to horses 14.1 hands and under; a two mile steeplechase for horses 15 hands and under for a $100 purse, and this race was won by Miss Doubtful over Lucy B. Entry fees for all races but the mile heats were 10% of the first place prize money.

In April of 1887 Happy Jack and Black Princess opened the local racing scene as they competed in the best out of three quarter mile heats in a race held on the prairie south of the tracks. Each owner backed his horse to the amount of $50, but this was a small amount compared to the numerous side bets.

About this time Jim Owens announced his intention of constructing a race track, club house and stables on his ranch land located in the bend of the Elbow River south of Calgary.

The Queen's birthday sports day program spectators saw "Humbolt" finish first in the novelty race, and "Doubtful" won the half mile heats. The steeplechase was cancelled due to insufficient entries, but there was a mile race and half mile heats on the program.

Mr. Owen's project was soon ready for the horses, and he offered the use of his driving park for the Dominion Day races. A committee was formed to solicit merchants and businessmen for subscriptions to help pay for the proposed $300 in purses. Pools for the races were set up at the Palace Billiard Hall.

McKinnon's "Big Jim" was running third at the quarter, but it took the lead to capture the money for first place at the half, three quarters and finish in the novelty race. McKinnon's "Wanda" won the half mile heats, and J. Roussel's "Big Dick" captured the heats for horses 14 hands and under. A lack of entries cancelled the pony race.

In August McKinnon's "Kitty" and "Happy Jack" were matched on the Owen's track for the grand sum of $250 a side. Later "Happy Jack" was taken by owner A. Smith to the Winnipeg races to run at Prairie Park. Races were held at the agricultural fair held in Medicine Hat.

At their September meeting the Alberta Turf Club decided to relinquish the idea of a fall meet, however races were held in conjunction with the fall fair, and the events included a "cowpuncher and horse at work." $800 was subscribed for the five race program. "Happy Jack" beat the great Kamloops horse "Chuck" in a quarter mile dash and the mile heats. As a result the pair were matched several days later at a 600 yard distance for $300 a side and a $50 forfeit. Both horses later raced at Winnipeg.

Alex Lucas was the chairman of 1888 Dominion Day sports and race meet, which saw the sports events staged in town and a bicycle race, half mile foot race and three days of horse races at the Owen's track. The horse races were run under the National Association rules, and all the horses had to be ridden under the colours that they were registered with. The prize list amounted to $2,000, and the C.P.R. offered half fare rates to those travelling to the Calgary races.

Day one saw "Sentries", ridden by Tom Lynch, win the cowboy heats. "Rosebud" captured the half mile heats, and recorded a best time of 53 seconds, while Beham's "Mystery" won the one mile dash and the Merchant's Purse.

Day two included the Livery Stable's quarter mile heats, Corporation Stakes and the Ladies' Stakes, the latter a half mile dash for gentlemen with owners in the saddle.

On the last day of racing "Rosy Patch", a Calgary horse, won three straight heats in the trotters mile, with pacers not barred. The Ranchers' purse, two miles over 14 hurdles, offered prize money of $100, $50 and $25. The Saloon Keepers stakes, a novelty race with a minimum of five starters, saw the leader at each quarter pick up $50, and the fastest horse at the end of the mile race earn a $100 prize. At the end of the regular races several match races took place.

Entries for the horse races had produced a sum close to $700, and with the admission fees from the large crowds attending the events the citizens' sports committee reported a surplus of over $600.

"The Great Stallion Race", advertised the September, 1888 Calgary Citizens' horse races, held under the direction of John Linehan and George Murdoch. It was reported that prizes and stakes totalled over $2,500 in the three day meet. The running races were under the American Jockey Club rules, and trotting races were under the American Trotting Association rules. A race would not be run unless there were at least four entries and three of them started.

The opening day's program began with a bicycle race, and this was followed by sweepstakes for stallions. In this event each owner paid a hundred dollar entry fee which went towards the purse, and the committee added a $100 gold medal. In the hurdle race "Zulu" would not jump, and finally it just turned and ran toward the stables. "Happy Jack" won the three-quarter mile heats, while other first day events included a green trot that was open to all horses that had never raced for money, a free-for-all trot or pace and a 600 yard dash.

The following day's program included a 1¼ mile dash, gentlemen's riding race, a two year old colt run and a three-quarter mile dash. The concluding day of the meet saw a mile novelty race with a winner at each quarter post, half mile heats, a cowboy race, complete with stocksaddles, chaps and spurs, where the contestants had to ride a half mile, circle a picketed cow, and dash back to the finish line. The race meet, which had been held at the Riverside track, was held in ideal autumn weather.

The Southern Alberta Turf Association held a three day affair at Macleod, with races run under the rules of the Dominion Turf Association. In the program was a seven mile horse race in which a runner beat a trotter.

A race meet was held on the Queen's Birthday in May of 1889. The meet was not considered a success as the gentlemen's driving race did not fill. "Chuck" won the half mile running race, and Mr. Lineham's rig took the native trot.

The following month, "horse racing and betting were indulged in on the plateau north of the Bow near the Langevin bridge. Several hundred native Americans with their native ponies were on the grounds. The racing was witnessed by many dusty maidens of the prairies. After the races were over, some of the prize winners sold to the white boys of Calgary for $20-$50."

Match races at the Riverside track saw Firemen's Horse win by three lengths over "Harkaway" for a $500 side bet. Sproule's and McNaughten's horses met in a trotting race, and on another occasion McNaughten matched his horse against White's mount. Dominion Day races were held at Pine Creek where Maggie Watson cleaned up in the ladies' events.

During the summer of 1889 plans were drawn up for the new race track at the Agricultural Grounds. Up to twelve teams of horses and twenty men were put to work rebuilding the track.

In early August a one mile four hurdle race, held at the Riverside track, saw

Mr. Morgan match his horse "Chinook" against T. Lynch's "Jimmy", with the wager being "Chinook" against a $100. Morgan went home without his horse.

The Alberta Turf Club Association, under President John Lineham, had to postpone its September race meet for several days due to snow. The collection of horses for the meet was said to be the finest ever gathered together in Canada, with entries from Prince Albert, Minneapolis, Winnipeg, Fort Macleod and High River as well as local horses. Trotters in the meet had to be registered with the Secretary of National Horses at Detroit. There were lots of visitors to town for the meet, which was run with, "racing strictly to the rules."

The race program went well, but the new track proved to be very slow. Some $35 in fines were levied on jockeys and owners for either being behind time or not starting on time. One foul was claimed, but it was disallowed. There were ten events on the two day program, including two events just for thoroughbreds. A two mile hurdle race with eight hurdles carried a stipulation of 150 pounds up, while the mile race carried a 160 pound weight stipulation. Two great horses, "Grey Eagle" and "Sangaroo", ran neck and neck in the half mile novelty race, which offered a $250 prize for the leader at each quarter mile post.

A great deal of wagering took place during the meet, with many of the bets of a $10 to $25 variety. Pools totalled over $10,000, and there were $1,350 worth of pools on naming three winners. The contingent up from Macleod proved to be great bettors. The association received 2½% of the pools, and as well made money by selling the refreshment privileges for $235. No subscriptions had been solicited prior to the meet by the directors.

Following the meet the directors of the Alberta Turf Club publicly thanked N.W.M.P. officers and men for their support and aid in making the fall meet a success.

Following the meet several of the local horses were shipped to the west coast to compete in races at Vancouver and New Westminster.

At the Calgary fall fair Leeson's "Royal George" was the best of the five horses entered in the trotting heats, and "Harkaway" defeated "Leadstone" in a mile match race, for a side purse.

Coyote hunting was a popular activity among some of Calgary's horses fraternity, including the ladies. Many of the horses that raced on the local track were used were used for this activity.

Horse racing and trotting were part of the Pine Creek sports program held on Dominion Day of 1890. Many Calgarians travelled to the hamlet to either take part or to spectate the events. Mrs. Winterbottom won the ladies' horse race, and J. Carter's "Dexter" took first place to earn the thirty dollar purse in the trotting heats. Farley's "Chuck" came out ahead in the 600 yard heats, while in the cowboy race all the competitors were part of a false start, then the re-run was won by Hamilton. Pony races were held for both boys and girls. Pools for the meet were run by Mr. Ellis.

During the summer the results of the major race meets held at Winnipeg, Regina and Moose Jaw were reported in the local papers. Many of the local horse breeders and trainers appeared to be more interested in running their horses in

Calgary, and many of the horses that had run on the eastern prairie tracks were in Calgary for its three day August meet.

L. MacIntyre of Winnipeg, Lt. Col. Herchmer and Amos Rowe acted as judges, and Joe Bannerman, F. Armstrong and W. Bain were to serve as starters for the races. There was considerable pool selling at the Elite Restaurant, with the wagering being under the jurisdiction of G. Govin. The Fire Brigade Band entertained at the race meet, and the N.W.M.P. maintained a patrol on the grounds. Admission to the grounds was a dollar for gentlemen, but ladies and vehicles were admitted free. A public holiday was declared one of the days of the meet. Hotel owners reported full houses, and it was reported crowds of up to 400 persons at the races.

The 1¼ mile, won by "Jesse Ranks" in a time of 2.19, was the feature race of the meet. This time compared favourable with the 2.27 recorded in Winnipeg for the event. There were seven entries in the Indian race, which proved to be a race for blood.

"Sleepy Jim" won three heats in the free for all trot to earn the $400 purse for the event. G. Wentworth's "Wild Rose" ran an excellent race to capture the two mile hurdle event. Other races on the card included a trotting sweepstakes for colts, a half mile running race for ponies under 14½ hands and 2.30 trot.

In September a race meet was held in Macleod, and events included the Alberta Plate, the Hudson Bay Cup race and a steeplechase. A string of race horses belonging to Green and Lascelle of Calgary went to race on the Minnesota Circuit.

Horse racing and track and field were part of the Calgary Exhibition held in October of 1890. The half mile heats, for gentlemen drivers with horses 15 hands and over that had never raced for public money, did not come off as there were only two entries.

G. Lineham was elected president and G. Murdoch as secretary of the Alberta Turf Club for the 1891 season. The executive met with the Calgary Horse Breeders Association to plan for colt races during the race season.

The Fire Brigade's sports day, held on the Queen's birthday, included a pony race for boys, a half mile open horse race, a half breed race as well as track and field.

Calgary was rapidly becoming a training centre for race horses. There were many horses from Macleod and other points in southern Alberta billeted at the Owens' track, and at the Proctor Stables there were 14 horses in training. There were horses stabled at the Exhibition grounds, at Gilkinson's opposite the fire hall, and the Beckton brothers string was south of the tracks. A friendly trot for a hundred dollars a side, best two out of three at a half mile distance, took place between Allen Caven and J. Ingram.

The Alberta Turf Club sponsored a race program on Dominion Day, the 24th anniversary of the union of the British provinces. Dogs were a problem in early Calgary, and citizens were requested to keep their canines away from the track during the meet. Following a successful Calgary meet many of the local horses were taken to Regina for its race meet.

In August a six race program was held at High River Crossing in conjunction with the polo meet. Events included ¾ mile heats, a quarter mile dash for two or three year olds that had never raced before, a two-mile steeplechase, a quarter mile cowboy race and a ten dollar polo sweepstakes for members of the High River or Calgary Polo Clubs.

A Calgary race week was held in August. The sponsors let privileges for the meet, and J. Salterio paid $215 for the booth privileges; D. Cameron was charged $175 for the games concession and G. Wentworth paid $80 for the privilege of selling and paying pools, although the association handled much of the betting themselves. Many felt that this was the best showing of horses ever seen in the Territories, and there were horses entered from as far away as Winnipeg.

The meet was considered a success as there were good races, ideal weather and the pools were honestly run. There were some excellent runners, and included in the money winners were Autrino, Grey Eagle, Blair Athol, Daisy L., Patchen, Eclipse, Evergreen and Sister Molly. Parkhill, who was ridden by Mr. Jamieson of the Quorm Ranche, took the hurdle event.

Autrino's owner was fined five dollars for not getting around to the paddock in time, and the jockey of Mayflower was fined a like amount for being late and $10 for being cheeky to the judges. The jockey of Mystery was bucked off his mount prior to the race.

The Lethbridge Turf and Athletic Association, which had been organized the previous year, held a program which offered $2,500 in prize money. A Turf Association was organized in Medicine Hat in 1891. The same year Calgary and Macleod, who had both joined the Northwest Circuit Association in 1890, withdrew becuase they felt that they were too far away from the rest of the members of the circuit.

In July members of the racing fraternity met in Regina to joint the new North West Racing Association, and the following officers were elected: President Lawson of Regina, Vice-presidents Lucas of Calgary and Pocklington of Macleod, and Secretary-treasurer F. Faugier of Maple Creek. Other groups affiliated with the organization were from Medicine Hat, Winnipeg and Pincher Creek. The group met at the Royal Hotel in Calgary during the August race meet to further organize their association and set up a rules committee. At this time there was further discussion in respect to a western Canada racing circuit.

During the race meet there was a great deal of interest in the half mile race between Grey Eagle and Chuck. Grey Eagle proved the better of the two, with a clocking of 50½ seconds. A third horse, which had been entered in order to make it a legitimate race just limped around the track.

The following week the Turf Association offered $100 if a good field of four horses showed up for a special race, however only three mounts were there, so the association had to refund a 25¢ admission fee to the 150 spectators who had showed up to view the race.

Over 400 people were at the High River Turf Association races held at High River Crossing. Following the six race program there were four match races. A two day race meet was held at Macleod in early September.

Horse racing took place in the late afternoon at the Calgary Agricultural Show held in mid-October of 1891. Blackfoot Crooked Nose was first of the eight contestants in the Indian race. Godard was the best of the four entries in the cowboy race, which covered a one-mile distance and included four turns. After the first heat of the gentlemen's driving race, the other contestants would not compete because they objected to the gait of McLellan's horse. Ernie King was the winner of the boys' pony race and Nan Bel won the race event for half breeds.

In 1892 the property known both as Riverside and the Owen's race track was advertised for sale. The real estate included a mile track, grand stand, 18 box stalls, corrals and a dwelling horse.

A spring stallion show was held at the Agricultural Grounds. It was reported that some of the horses exhibited had cost as high as $4,000. During the era there were many ads in the local paper advertisintg the services of breeding stallions.

On the Queen's Birthday of 1892 one of the main activities appeared to be riding parties heading for a day in the country.

Local horse breeders met at the Calgary town hall in the spring of 1892 to form the Alberta Horse Breeders Association. The 34 members chose T. Stone as the organization's president, R. Robinson as vice-president and F. Fitzgerald and T. Christie as secretary and treasurer. The group decided to apply for incorporation, and a committee was set up to draft a program for a spring race meet. It was recommended that the Riverside track be used because most of the horsemen refused to run at the Agriculture Society's track. Mr. Gilmour gave the group permission to use his track for free.

The association held a two day meet in June and offered $2,300 in prizes for the races. The first day of the meet was declared a public holiday in Calgary. The crowd of more than 700 spectators gathered there were entertained by the Fire Brigade band, and the Mounted Police were on the grounds to help maintain order. Many of the horsemen were disappointed that the Montana horses, which had just run at the Macleod meet, were not at the Calgary races. Purses for the Calgary races ranged from $100-300, while the admission fee to the meet was a dollar for gentlemen, but ladies and carriages were free. The trott, pace and running races were governed by the rules of the American Trotting Association.

Fred M won three straight heats of the three minute trot and pacing events, with the best time being 3.41½. The 1¼ mile dash, weight for age open, saw Blair Athol come through in a fine 2.16.2 clocking. The next day this horse, who on a previous occasion had run the distance in 1.47, won the mile dash in a time of 1.50.

Other events on the two day program included a 5/8 mile dash for two year olds, 2.40 class trot and pacing, 3/4 mile dash-weight for age, free for all trot and pace, pony race—14.1 hands and under, quarter mile dash—weight for age, a penalty of 7 pounds for blood horses or 5 pounds for three years olds, half mile heats—weight for age and a two mile steeplechase.

Other good horses in the meet were: Larghetta—bred in California, Twilight—who ran 1.19 for the 3/4 mile, Grey Eagle—range bred, Wild Rose—a steeplechaser, and the Bow River Horse Ranche runners Reciprocity and Lord of the Valley.

The meet was not considered a success financially owing to the liberality of the directors of the meet.

Horse races, including events for Indians, were part of the 1892 Dominion Day sports program. On the same day a race program was held at Cochrane, and Sibbald's "Lord of the Valley" won all four quarter of the mile novelty race, and later in the afternoon his horse, "Coon", won the half mile dash. W. Kerr riding "George" was first in the hurdle event, and Kerfoot rode "Starlight" to first place in the cowboy race.

The Pine Creek Dominion Day race meet offered $350 in prizes for the five events, including a steeplechase race, and an Indian race. Lt. Col. Macleod was one of the judges of the races.

Calgary horses "Grey Eagle", "Larghetto", "Malena" and "Sangaree" were all in the money at the Winnipeg races held in July.

Following the Calgary polo tournament was a gymkhana, and the events included: a nine horse field in the quarter mile flat race, half mile, ladies' nomination, bare back hurdle—150 yards and return, cigar and umbrella race, half mile hurdle and return, and a balaclava melee between the Calgary and High River polo players.

Two rail coaches of Calgarians travelled to High River Crossing for the High River Turf Association races in September. The eight event card included flat, hurdle and Indian races, all of which were run under Ontario Jockey Club rules. Purses totalled over $500, with prize money ranging from five to seventy-five dollars.

"Jamieson Chiquita", the favourite, won the hurdle event, while mounts ridden by F. MacPherson and F. Stimson did well in the flat races.

Lethbridge and Macleod held fall race meets, and match races undoubtedly took place at the Davisburg and Red Deer agricultural shows.

There were 36 different classes, including four for blood horses and 13 classes for roadsters and drivers, in the seventh annual fall exhibition of the Calgary Agricultural Society. However the entry list was small and some classes were without competitors.

In the spring of 1893 "Carghetta", owned by Cavan and McAbee of Calgary, easily won a feature mile race at Philadelphia in a time of 1.52½, while competing against some of the best milers in that area.

The track at the Calgary Agricultural Grounds was top dressed, and new box stalls were constructed prior to the three day June summer fair program of the Calgary Agricultural Society. Over $2,100 in purse and prize money was awarded, ranging from $7.50 for the Indian race to $300 in the free for all trot and pace. Daily admission to the events was 50¢ for men and 25¢ for ladies and carriages.

In their first attempt at rodeo the society presented a cowboy race of 600 yards distance around posts, and Mr. Todd of High River came through in the best time. A roping contest was held in which John Ware roped and threw his steer "in an almost incredible space of 54½ seconds."

Blair Athol was the favourite in the pools which were sold in the Lougheed

Block, and this horse came through, winning both the mile and the mile and a quarter races. Five heats of the three minute trot and pace had to be run before Sutherland's "May Sharper", pulling the only wagon on the course equipped with pneumatic tyres, won the event, with a best heat time of 2.50. There were twenty entries in the Indian pony race, which was won by a Sarcee brave.

"Wild Horse" was again a winner of the two mile hurdle race, and Brigg's "Ethel" was the best of the horses in the polo pony race. A unique 220 yard hurdle race was won by A. Bottere, and a tandem polo pony race went to O. Critchley. During a match race Connacher's horse threw his jockey, crossed the Elbow River and was last seen heading south. Condie, the thoroughbred "Flyer" from the coast, earned a hundred dollars when she broke the track record of 2.30 with a magnificent time of 2.25½. Other events in the four day program included a handicap two mile hurdle race with a leaping contest, a polo game between Stoneys and Blackfeet, and cycle and running races.

Many Calgarians travelled by train to the Dominion Day Fish Creek races which took place at the Winterbottom estate.

In August of 1893 James Owens, who had constructed and operated the Owen's track in Elbow Park, died. At the time of his death he still held a half interest in the race plant. Mr. Owens had served in the N.W.M.P. in 1878, and later he was the town assessor under Mayor King.

Calgary horses "Blair Athol" and "Larghetta" were entered in the races at Regina. Other Calgary horses were entered in the High River Turf Association meet. The Lethbridge Turf Club and Athletic Association held a two day race meet in September, and the program included the cycle championship of the Territories. A variety of horse races was held at the polo gymkhanas staged at Calgary and Mitford during the fall of 1893. Included in the Calgary meet was a quarter mile flat race—catch weight of 154 pounds, postillion—consisting of a quarter mile with four jumps and return, performed while leading another horse, a 150 yard four hurdle race with a return to the start, mile handicap, bun eating—cigar smoking and umbrella race, bending race, half mile ladies' nomination and a polo ball race. The Critchley brothers and H. Samson performed well in the various events.

The local paper reported that "Old Lamb", a Montana horse, had died at the very old age of 44 years.

Calgary's 1894 Queen's Birthday Fire Brigade sports day did not include horse racing, but a group of local racing enthusiasts joined the Calgary Turf Association's G. Tempest in a trip to Edmonton for its holiday horse races. Lethbridge and Fort Saskatchewan also held races on May 24, and a few days later races were sponsored by the Macleod Polo Club. A twelve race program and track and field events were included in the June Mitford and Cochrane race day.

The Calgary mid-summer fair included a program of cycle and stake races. There were just three horse races run each day, and "All Smoke" and "Marguerite" proved to be the best runners in the meet. In the hurdle race "Parkhill" fell and broke its neck. Jamieson, the jockey, was pinned underneath, but fortunately he was not badly hurt.

A gymkhana was held at the end of the fair, and the majority of the ribbons were won by H. Samson, the Critchley brothers, H. Alexander and G. McNaughton.

A two day horse race program was held by the Agricultural Society in September of 1894. Events included: boys' pony race, ranchers' double team, trotting and running race, tandem postilion, bareback hurdles, handicap hurdles and gentlemen's driving race for single drivers to harness were a part of the program.

By 1894 the Edmonton Turf Association had raised over $10,000 capital, with the amount being raised through the sale of $25 shares.

During this era an event that involved fast horses and skillful drivers was a fire, and there were always a great many interested spectators when a Calgary Fire Brigade rig raced to a fire.

On the May 24, 1895 holiday there were many Calgary horses entered in the races at Edmonton. Arbour Day found many Calgarians riding distances up to fifty miles while participating in a coyote hunt, but it was reported that there were not any kills.

The Calgary Agriculture Society's three day spring meet offered $2,700 in purses. Included in the 18 event program was a one mile ladies' race, bronco bucking and a roping contest. The C.P.R. offered reduced rates to this meet for horsemen and spectators alike, but the field was small as were the crowds of spectators, in spite of the fact that some of the best horses in the west were in this meet, including Wentworth's "All Smoke" and the old favourite, "Cyclone"., There was a great deal of betting on a match race—with 175 pounds up, won by Kerfoot's saddle pony by a nose over Critchley's polo pony.

A large crowd attended the gymkhana, staged at the Calgary polo grounds north of the Bow River, following the Calgary race meet. A large field of 12 horses was entered in the half mile hurdle race, and there were nine entries in the ladies' nomination event. A new event in the community was the Oolta Poolta race. The crowd was entertained by the N.W.M.P. band between the running events. A gymkhana was also held in Pine Creek in July.

The Territorial Exhibition in Regina's nineteen race program had such unique events as: fastest walking team to heavy wagon, ladies' trot race, bona fide farmers' trot or pace, and a half mile slow race in which balky or unsound horses were barred.

The Calgary 1895 Dominion Day sports day included track and field and cycle events and a one horse race. This race was only for Indians and began with a standing start. At that point the competitors crowded around the fastest horse and ran as a bunch, keeping the fleetest entry from winning. As a result a second race was run, this time for blood.

About $500 in prize money was offered at the Mitford and Cochrane race and sports program held on Dominion Day of 1895. Many visitors from Calgary travelled by train to this ten event meet that included a mile and a half hurdle race. "All Smoke" won the premier 1¼ mile dash, while other great horses in the meet included "Sharper Goldust" and "Cyclone". Miss McDonald won the ladies' half mile race, and a roping contest went to D. McIntosh of Macleod.

Jonas, from the Stoney Reserve, won every Indian horse and foot race. Alex Martin, who was later to operate a sporting goods store in Calgary, acted as met director.

During this era Indians often staged their own horse races on the flats near the Mission Bridge.

Calgary horses "Sharper Goldust" and "Cyclone" recorded wins at the Grand Forks race meet. At the Winnipeg races, "All Smoke" won two straight heats of the three-quarter mile race.

During the year the Owen's track in Elbow Park was purchased by P. Briggs, who made considerable improvements to the operation. The Calgary Polo Club's gymkhana was held there in August. Several local horses were barred from competing in the quarter mile scurry.

In September the community of Mitford staged a polo tourney and gymkhana. Included in the events was a quarter mile flat race, postillion race—quarter mile and back, over four jumps, bareback hurdles—150 yards and back, tandem, bareback—teams of four, bending race—250 yards around six flags, one mile handicap and a ladies' nomination—with contestants in riding outfit and riding sidesaddle.

During the fall a horse show and match races were held at the Davisburg fair, and match races also took place at the Dewdney and Innisfail fall fairs. A unique horse race, held at the Lacombe fair, was to determine the fastest walking team in harness.

On the May 24 holiday of 1896 a large crowd attended the Springbank community race program held at the new half mile race track located near Wheeler Mickle's place. The program included 13 races run at distances from a quarter to one mile, a polo pony race and hurdle events. The entrance fee for each race was 10% of the purse. The Ladies' Cup was awarded to the winner of the half mile dash, while the cowboy race offered a purse of seven dollars. A horse belonging to Bell-Irving, from west of Cochrane, won its race, but it was disqualified for boring. In the mile hurdle event the hurdles were all knocked down during the first lap of the race, so the last half was run as a flat race. Miss Meade, riding "Grey Tom", won the ladies' race, while S. Hutchison on Captain Gardner's "Ike" came first in the 600 yard cowboy race, which included three turns in its distance.

The Calgary Caledonian sports program was also held on the Queen's birthday, but the only horse racing on the program was for the Indians.

Match races were often held at the Elbow Park track during the spring. During this era the local newspaper carried a weekly column covering the English racing scene.

A race meet was held at the Elbow Park track in early June of 1896, with the events governed by the American racing rules. For a race to be included in the program four horses had to be entered and three of them had to start. Pools for the races were sold at the Alberta Hotel on the evening prior to the program. The events included a two mile steeplechase, a mile hurdle race, for horses 14.1 hands and under with 160 pounds up, but with a seven pound allowance for each inch under 14.1, a half mile green saddle horse race—catch weights, 5/8 and 3/8 mile dashes.

A fair crowd attended the meet, but the rains came and much of the program had to be postponed for two days. However local merchants agreed to close their businesses at one p.m., so a good crowd was in attendance, and the admission was cut to a quarter from the original 50¢.

The first race on the program was a match race for $400 at a mile distance in which "Dixie", in a fast time of 1.52, won from "Irrigation". In the half mile dash Wentworth's "Plummer" beat the great "Cyclone" in a time of 50 seconds. During one race a jockey fell at the pole and broke his collar bone.

The Pine Creek community held horse races on Dominion Day, and the Mitford-Cochrane race meet took place in Mid-July. $250 in prizes was offered for the nine event program, which included a ladies' race and hurdle events. The N.W.M.P. band was in attendance, and in the evening following the race meet a dance was held.

"Cyclone", owned by Murphy of Calgary, and P. Brigg's horse "Alpeni" ran neck and neck in the half mile meets of the $300 sprinters' handicap at the Regina races. The heat times were 50, 50½ and 50, with "Alpeni" winning the last two heats in what was said to be the greatest race ever run in Western Canada. "Fortune", a Calgary horse, finished second in the Regina Derby.

At the Winnipeg races "Cyclone" won the first two heats of the half mile dash hands down. "Alpeni" and "Fortune" captured the first two places in the 1¼ mile dash.

A two mile match race was held at Mitford between Kerfoot's "Dick Turpin" and Mrs. Smith's "Keno". By the start of the race "Keno" had gone lame, and Kerfoot, in a gentlemanly manner wanted to call off the race and bets, but Smith refused, sos the race was a walkover.

A very successful Calgary Polo Club gymkhana was held in August with eleven different horse races and a cycle race on the program. The events were full, with 14 entries in the ladies' nomination and one less in the quarter mile dash. In the nomination event the rider raced to his female partner, who took a cork out of a soda pop, which was drunk by the rider before he dashed back to the finish line. In the tent pegging event the rider had to spear a tent peg during the course of his ride. O. and H. Critchley earned a good share of the prizes in what was considered an excellent program.

The Davisburg race meet and fall exhibition included a half mile farmers' trot, ladies' and cowboy races, a sweepstakes race and track and field. Bertha Rouleau, from the Calgary suburb of Rouleauville, was second in the ladies' horse race. Jas. Hogg supervised the races which offered prize money ranging from one to twelve dollars.

There was a six race program, including a ladies' event, at the September Sheep Creek Agricultural Society fall fair. At the Fish Creek Agricultural Society fair and race meet Miss Irving, who had also won at the Davisburg and Sheep Creek races, was first in the ladies' race, and J. Rogers was a double winner in the men's race.

A new Calgary Turf Association applied to the Territorial government for incorporation in October of 1896. The association's directors included: President O.A. Critchley, Vice-president A.E. Cross, Secretary-treasurer D. McPherson,

T.S. Lee, E. Swann, H. Critchley, W. Hull and T. Stone. The executive decided that the association would hold a $400 purse stake race the following June for foals born in 1895. Nominations had to be filed by the first of the year.

During the winter months jockey Billy Fields rode "Cyclone" in various races in the southern states.

A Diamond Jubilee Celebration, the inaugural meeting of the Calgary Turf Association, was held at the Elbow Park track in June of 1897, with a total of $1500 in purses offered during the two day meet. Admission to the grounds was a dollar per person, with the use of the grandstand at 25¢ extra.

Included in the first day's program was the two year old stakes, five-eighth mile dash and a one mile pony hurdle race. In a mile Indian race at the end of the day the winning horse ran the distance in less than two minutes.

The first race on the following day was the Hotelkeepers' Stakes—a ¾ mile overnight handicap. Other events included a ten dollar sweepstake handicap for the Jubilee Cup and the Rancher's Plate—a $20 sweepstake 2½ mile steeple-chase. Orange Peel won this race after the leading horse bucked off his jockey in the home stretch. The race meet also included a polo match and a bicycle race.

Three Stoneys were entered in the half mile dash at the Mitford races in June, but other contestants objected so the race was run off without the natives or a judge in the stands. The eleven mile program included a half mile dash for local stock horses with 190 pounds up. Brisco's Bingin' won both the two mile hurdle and the mile dash.

Mr. Proctor constructed a half mile track at Dewdney, later to be named Okotoks, and race were held there in July. A half mile track was laid out at Banff on the flats near Cascade Mountain. The Herald published a weekly, "Racing Notes", column.

There was not any horse racing in Calgary on Dominion Day, although athletic events and cycle races were held. Horse races for both ladies and children and a roping contest were part of the sports program at the Fish Creek and Priddis picnics held on Dominion Day.

Lee's Maude and Wentworth's Dixie did very well in the Golden races where total prize money for the program approached a thousand dollars. Many Calgarians attended the Springbank races, which included 18 heats in the 14 races. Lee's Maude was the top horse in the meet, while in the ladies' race Miss Warren edged Miss Mickle for first place.

The annual Polo Club gymkhana, scheduled for the Brigg's Race Track in August, did not take place. Race programs were part of the fall fairs held in Davisburg, Red Deer and Fish Creek, while Sheep Creek, which claimed to have the best half mile track in the west, held a fall race meet.

The ladies of the Jumping Pound district celebrated the Queen's Birthday in 1898 with a picnic and horse races at a site known as Spruce Flats. Innisfail and Nose Creek held race programs in June, and the Springbank races were held on Dominion Day. Indian horse races were held on the flats located north of Langevin Bridge. The C.P.R. offered half fare rates to Calgarians attending the Cochrane-Mitford race meet held in July. A gold broach and silver spurs were two of the prizes awarded to race winners at this meet. Davisburg held a race meet and picnic to celebrate Dominion Day. Kerfoot's Dixie won a $100 novelty race at Virden, Manitoba, and there were several Calgary horses entered in the Winnipeg races.

O. Critchley was re-elected as president and E. Ross elected as secretary of the Calgary Turf Association which held its second annual meet in August of 1898 and offered $600 in prize money. The weather was ideal for the meet and over 500 spectators in attendance were entertained by the Fire Brigade band. The program included a half mile dash, 3/8 mile dash for green ponies, one mile handicap, a steeplechase and several match races. In the evening following the meet the Turf Club sponsored a ball, which was held in the Opera House.

The Lemen Brothers Circus visited Calgary during the summer, and included in its program were racing steers, Roman chariot races and a man who raced against horses and mules.

McNaughten's Billy beat Critchley's Dollinger to the tape in the quarter mile dash at the Polo Club gymkhana. In the ¾ mile handicap Billy, who was carrying 50 pounds more than any other horse in the race, could not be caught. T. Critchley captured the polo ball race, and a bending race was held around a flagged course. The Victoria Cross race, with the competitors each carrying a dummy, caused a great deal of excitement as the riders were met at the Zaraba by a volley of shots. In the evening following the events the Polo Club held a dance in the Alexander Hall.

During the fall season horse races were part of the agricultural fairs held at Davisburg, Sheep Creek, Fish Creek and on the Blackfoot Reserve. Doc Lauder of Innisfail ran his horse Tranby Croft in match races at Red Deer, Lacombe and Wetaśkwin.

In the spring of 1899 there was a great deal of wagering on a match race between, "Parslow's phenomenal black saddle and saddle horse and Field's world beater Slim". A paper chase on horseback was part of the day's activities at the opening of the new Millarville hall. Indian and squaw races were planned as part of the Calgary Fire Brigade sports day, but rain interfered. Horse races were held at Innisfail in June and at Okotoks on July 4. News of the Derby and other English races were published by the Calgary paper.

Members of the Calgary Agriculture Society met at the hall where plans were made to reorganize into a non-dividend joint stock company called the Inter-Western Pacific Exposition company Ltd. A. Wooleydod was elected president after A.E. Cross declined the position.

Horse races were held at Morley on the Queen's Birthday. John McDougall won a race which consisted of the competitor running a 100 yards to his horse, saddling it and riding to the finish line. Stoney Jonas's horse Antelope was an easy winner in the Indian races, and it was reported that the squaw races were hotly contested. A few days later Jonas' horse Cyclone was matched with Field's Slim Jim. The race drew a large crowd, and it created quite a stir among the indians who bet money, blankets and horses on their kin, but Field's horse was just too fast for the Indian pony.

Among the local horses racing at Winnipeg was Critchley's Lee Metford, but unfortunately the stud was involved in an accident which disabled it for the season.

Considering the poor weather a good crowd was in attendance at the third annual two day meet of the Calgary Turf Association held in August of 1899. J. Reilley's Billy Little won the 2.45 trot with a time of 2.34½ in what was considered "the best exhibit of trotting seen in years." Billy, who had been in the service of a livery stable ten days prior to the race, trotted in a high wheel sulky, while the other horses were in bikes.

Glenbow Dick's owner was fined five dollars when the horse was late for its race. Kerfoot's Dixie sold favourite in the pools, and it did not disappoint its backers as it won the six furlong dash in 1.22½. A trend to use furlong measurement rather than miles and fractions was evident in the west. There were 15 starters in the Indian race, but there were only two entries in the polo pony race. A ball was held in the evening following the first day of the meet. The following day rain cancelled the program, however the race meet was completed a week later. At the time Adam Dalgliesh won the cowboy race over four other entries, and Klondike was the winning horse in the steeplechase event. In the one mile hurdle race a foul occurred involving the first two finishers; the judges ordered them to run the race again, but the owners would not allow this, so the bets were declared off.

A large crowd was reported in attendance at the Macleod races, and a race program was part of the fall show of the Strathcona Agriculture Society.

The horse races were the chief attraction at the Inter-Western Pacific Exhibition held in late September of 1899. At that time A. Wooley-dod was the president and J. Sousa was the secretary of the organization which offered $3000 in prizes for the fall show. Purses for the races ranged from five to $200.

Wentworth's Tosti won the 5/8 mile dash, but Tosti lost to Fortuna in the mile dash which was staged the same afternoon. Wentworth had another winner as Loug Derg won the half mile for two year olds in a time of 52½ seconds. Conditions of this race were that those horses bred outside the Territories were to carry five pounds extra weight. Other events on the first day's program were: a three minute trot or pace, a 2.30 trot or pace, boys' pony race—14 hands and under, and boys age 16 and under—owners up race.

Day two's program included a six furlong selling race—ten pounds below scale and horses to be sold for $100, ten pounds extra for each $100 up to $300. Bevan, riding Advocate, won the gentlemen's mile, and Sandy McDonald of Cochrane was home first in the cowboy race. The free for all trot or pace heats were taken by Parslow's Cherry Ripe.

Justin Freeman won the polo pony race, steer roping and he took second place in the open half mile at the Priddis 1900 Queen's Birthday sports program. Other events during the afternoon included a slow race and races for ladies and boys. The Calgary May 24 Fire Brigade sports program included four Indian races, including one for squaws up, while at Macleod the competition was improved with the inclusion of Montana horses in the race program.

A special train carries a host of Calgarians to the nine event Cochrane race meet that offered $300 in prizes. Refreshment booths and gambling tents had been set up on the grounds for the pleasure of the visitors. Brigg's mount was the favourite at the pools in the mile and half mile hurdle races, but his horse balked at the second hurdle.

The following week a great match race took place at Calgary's Agriculture grounds between George Wentworth's Tosti and McRae's Lough Derg. The $1000 stakes were the largest ever wagered in Western Canada at that time. The horses ran neck and neck for the six furlongs on a very heavy track, before Tosti won by a nose in a time of 1.18.

There was $1,350 in purse money offered at the eleven race, two day Calgary Spring Race Meet held in June of 1900. However local interest was lacking and the attendance was poor. The best race of the opening day was Lough Derg defeat Scottish Rose, a Montana mare. A best 3 of 5 heat match race for $500 was won by Hard Case.

On the second day of the meet D. McDonald's Monty, who had placed first at Cochrane, won the cowboy race. In the hurdle event Mr. Houghton broke a stirrup, and he was thrown at the first hurdle. However his horse Ukiah took all the rest of the hurdles as regularly as the other entries. The great horse Tosti finished a surprising last in the 5/8 mile dash.

Another great match race took place at the Brigg's track with Kilmarnock, Ukiah and Peacock meeting in a mile and a half hurdle race, with six flights of four foot hurdles on the course.

The Edmonton Dominion Day program offered $2000 in prize money for the trotting and running races and the sports program. South of Calgary the Sheep River and Davisburg Agriculture Societies amalgamated, and as a result there was one less race program in the area. A match trotting race took place in Okotoks in July.

Calgary based horses were running in the Winnipeg and Morden races. In the Ladies' Plate race at Winnipeg Lough Derg finished in first place, but the horse was disqualified and his rider was suspended for a year. As a result Wentworth's Tosti was declared the winner. A string of Calgary polo ponies were taken to Montreal where they were easily sold.

Commenting on Calgary's fall race program the Strathcona Sun suggested that few of the trotters on the Calgary track are eligible for any race but the free for all. The writer felt that the Strathcona and Leduc horses could clean up at the Calgary fall meet.

Calgary's 1900 Inter-Western Pacific Exhibition was held September 12-15, and it offered $6000 in prize money. The fair was officially opened by the Honourable A.E. Forget, Lt. Governor of the North West Territories. A pass for the four day event sold for a dollar, while daily admission cost 50¢. The Calgary and Edmonton Railway offered excursion rates which helped to bring in many visitors to Calgary from both the north and the south country.

The opening day gymkhana events included a potato race, with potatoes at various distances from the start that had to be picked up by the rider. J. McCaul won the quarter mile scurry, while J. Freeman, O. Critchley and J. McNaughton were frequent winners in the other gymkhana events.

Events in the horse racing program included a tandem race, roping and Indian events, a 5/8 mile dash for Alberta bred horses and a farmers' trot or pace. Unfortunately rain caused the meet to be postponed for two weeks, but then many of the horses were still at the Medicine Hat races, so the program was postponed indefinitely.

Poor weather also caused the cancellation of the Sheep Creek-Davisburg and Lethbridge race meets. Several Calgary horses did well at the Macleod meet in competition against local and Montana horses. In a match race, held in Calgary, Critchley's Bingen won over Cook's Kilmarnock.

During the west's early history many students who attended the small schools that dotted the countryside rode their ponies to school, and with the competitive nature of humans, races often developed during the lunch break of after school. Gopher holes too often proved to be the downfall of many a horse and rider on the prairie fields.

It was reported from the South Africa war theatre that the Canadian horses were the best mounts that were used by the British forces. During 1901 army officers toured the Canadian west purchasing suitable horses at prices ranging from $80-$100, however the sellers were required to shoe the animals. 63 horses were purchased at Cochrane, a hundred from the High River area and over 600 horses were purchased in Calgary by the army.

Many Calgarians attended the Edmonton 1901 spring race meet that included a 21 race program and offered $2000 in prize money.

Calgary's spring race meet took place in mid-May. Races during the two-day program were often held up as there were not enough entries and as a result business was not brisk at the betting pool.

A great commotion arose in a match race for a $500 side bet when a protest was made that Hardcase, the leader, had broken his gait to a gallop before passing the mile wire, but the protest was disallowed. In the Alberta bred five furlong race a tiny boy named Gibson thrilled the crowd as he rode his horse to a second place finish. A Calgary track record of 1.03½ was set in the five furlong open race—10 pounds below scale for a $100 purse. The crowd was surprised as the great Tosti was beaten by Synia, a California bred horse, in the six furlong open race. The Indian bareback race and the cowboy race, with the competitors riding 600 yards and making three turns around barriers held a great deal of interest for the crowd. The program did not include any hurdle or steeplechase events.

The small crowds at the meet had been entertained between races by the Fire Brigade band under the direction of Crispin Smith. Following the race meet there were accusations that the races were "not on the square."

Many Calgarians celebrated the Queen's Birthday by attending a sports day which included horse races for both braves and squaws.

Colona, owned by Robert Begley of Calgary, set several trotting records at the Brandon race meet. Other Calgary horses took part in a meet sponsored by the Cranbrook Turf Association. Cochrane sponsored a ten race program, which included ladies, cowboy and hurdle races. Match races were part of the Sheep River Agricultural Exhibit in July. During this era many lottery tickets on the English Derby were sold in Calgary.

The third annual Inter-Western Pacific Exhibition was held in Calgary July 10-13 and offered $10,000 in prizes. The opening day gymkhana was slow, and the only interesting events on its program were the polo ball race and the squaw race. The second day's events included a boys' pony race, Indian races, bronko busting, a cattle stealing act and the farmers' trot or pace. It was reported of the race that, "The best looking horse was owned by Jas. Reilly, who farms at the Commercial Hotel."

Kimberly won three straight heats of the three minute pace. After the first heat of this race Vic Houde was ordered off his rig on suspicion of having pulled his horse. Fortuna captured the 5/8 mile dash for Alberta bred horses. Following a football game Lee Marshall gave an exhibition of fancy roping and riding wild steers.

On the last day of the meet Ione, a ten year old horse, displayed a remarkable burst of speed in the Free For All mile trot, winning four of the five heats to earn the best part of a $600 purse. Later in the year this horse ran the distance of 2.08½ on the Indianapolis track. Lee Marshall on Kruger won the cowboy race, the last event on the program.

Later in the summer it was reported that the Okotoks races developed into a regular donnybrook which involved horsemen, officials and bettors. During the summer Oswald Critchley shipped a carload of polo ponies to England.

In April of 1902, the Calgary Mounted Rifles held a cavalcade out to the Industrial Indian School, located south east of the city, and although this was certainly not a race the parade of horse flesh created a great deal of interest. During the spring many horses from various breeders in the province were sent to Wentworth Stables at Victoria Park for training. Sheriff King purchased Ramona, a Kentucky bred horse, that was reported to be the finest animal of his class in western Canada.

Bad weather caused the May 24 sports and race program to be postponed until Coronation Day. Heavy rain ruined the racing oval situated west of Cochrane.

There was a great deal of controversy about the role of horse racing and betting as part of the Calgary Exhibition, and initially, as a result, city council would not financially support the exhibition, but finally it approved a grant of $300.

The fourth annual Inter-Western Pacific Exhibition offered $10,000 in prize money with twenty events in the two day race program. A large purse of $400 was to be offered for the free for all trot or pace. Unfortunately the wet and cool weather persisted, which caused the exhibition to be postponed until the fall.

Several Calgary based horses were entered in the Winnipeg race meet, and J. Young's Lough Durg, in a time of 2.12, finished first in a mile and a quarter running race. McLaughlin's Tosti was another Calgary horse that was a race winner. Included in the Winnipeg exhibition race program were road races of several miles in length.

The Calgary Fire Department, with Captain Smart on the timing switch, held trial runs of its rigs, and the chemical unit had the best time.

The Calgary race track was used by the trick rider of Dowker's Wild West Show, who rode by standing on the backs of three horses. This was not a race, but it proved to be a great accomplishment while the horses were circling the track at a great speed.

On Coronation Day a large program of military sports, including a tent pegging event, a half mile race and an officers' quarter mile horse race, were held.

A record crowd attended the opening day of the postponed Calgary Exhibition. However only the start and the finish of the races could be seen from the grandstand, so the crowd was more interested in seeing the military sports program, in which there was keen rivalry between the Canadian Mounted Police Rifles and the N.W.M.P., than in the running events. The crowd's favourite events were the Victoria Cross race and tilting the rings. There were many turf fans who felt that the races were just being run for the owners' benefit.

The great horse Tosti again proved its speed by winning the ¾ mile dash; however it was the Indian race that drew the greatest enthusiasm from the crowd. A girl jockey rode Daisy Blair to a win in the five furlong race.

The second day of the meet saw the half mile dash being marred by a great many false starts. Chic McGregor took the first three heats of the named race, and Man-with-a-hole-in-his-shirt won the Indian race.

On the last day of the meet Tom Reynolds rode home first in the cowboy race, and Chic McGregor earned a win for the second time in two days as the horse won the free for all. Other events on the program included a boys' pony race, a plowing match and bronko busting.

During the fall Calgary horses were raced at the Okotok's and Old's fairs. In the winter of 1902-03 trotting races were held on the ice of the Saskatchewan River at Edmonton.

The Territorial Horse Breeders Association met in Calgary in May of 1903. It was estimated that there were about 90,000 horses in the Alberta Territory at that time. During the previous year 4,300 horses were exported out of the area, mainly to Britain, while almost 19,000 were imported, with many of these arriving with settlers from the U.S.A.

On the May 24th holiday a crowd estimated at 4,000 people packed Victoria Park to view the military sports program between the Mounted Police and the C.M.R. members. It was reported of the horse races staged at Morley the same day for a purse of $200 that "the horses were lashed from start to finish."

The Canadian Mounted Rifles held a grand military tournament at Victoria Park in early July. Included in the events were a Lloyd Lindsay race and a trotting race. Sellars and Freeze proved to be two of the superior riders in the competition. Match races were held at both the Davisburg and Innisfail fairs. News about the English Derby received headline status in one of the Calgary newspapers.

The military sports and the gymkhana proved to be the highlights of the July, 1903 Inter-Western Pacific Exhibition. A saddlery race consisted of the competitors starting bareback, riding over a hurdle, then a dash to their saddle, saddling up and back over the hurdle to the finish line. Other events included bareback hurdle races and bareback wrestling.

Lee Johnston won over four other entries in the driving competition in which the competitors had to race their buggies around a figure eight of barrels. F. McNaughten, one of the Territories' better polo players, rode Badger to a win in the polo pony dash, while the quarter mile dash went to George Ross. One of the two entries in the Named Pace race was Glideway Junior, a blind horse. The first two heats were close, but in the third heat the other entry was disqualified because the driver was accused of disobeying the judge. However in the final outcome Glideway Junior was only given second place money.

There were only three entries in the five furlong race for Alberta bred horses only. However there were far too many entries in the Indian race and the result was considerable jostling, with some riders being thrown from their mounts. In a bareback race two of the three jockeys were off their horses before the track had been circled. The mile and an eighth hurdle race, which was won by jockey Crooks, proved to be one of the crowd's favourite events. Young Frank Sparrow won the boys' pony race in a cantor.

Other events in the four day program included a half mile—owners up, polo pony race and a pony high jump event, squaw and cowboy races and a bucking competition.

More than 2,000 persons attended an Indian sports day held at the Exhibition grounds in late July. There were horse races for the Blackfeet and the Stoneys, and then a final, with Stoney Powderface the winner.

A few days later four coaches carrying 200 Calgarians and the Fire Brigade band, as well as a carload of horses, travelled west to Cochrane for that community's race meet. Following the dash for local ponies only, the winner was weighed and the carried weight was found not to be up to the required 160 pounds, so first place was given to the runner-up. Kerfoot won the cowboy race and Miss Parslow finished first of the five entries in the ladies' races. Houghton's Okiah was the best of the field in the mile and a quarter hurdle race and in a $100 match race Mucklejohn won from Kerfoot.

An evening sports program was held at Victoria Park in August and included in the program were Indian and cowboy horse races as well as rodeo events. During the summer the Charles Urban Trading Company of London showed excellent and exciting motion pictures at the Opera House, and included in the film were scenes of horse racing in Calgary, Indian races and branding of colts at the Bow River Horse Ranche.

Horse racing was not a part of the Calgary 1903 Labour Day sports program, however some short races were held at the Mounted Police camp held during the fall in Calgary. Forty Calgary polo ponies were sold in Toronto at prices that averaged $170, with some mounts fetching as high as $450.

Military sports, including tent pegging, cutting the lemon and tilting the ring, were part of the Fire Brigade May 24, 1904 sports program. The following week an Indian pow-wow was held at Victoria Park, where the squaw and braves' horse races provided lots of excitement for the spectators. Horse racing also occurred at the C.M.R. camp, held adjacent to the track. A nine race program, including a ladies' whistling race, took place at the gymkhana held at the Bowness Ranche. Over 200 thoroughbreds were auctioned off at a Calgary sale, with the average price being over a hundred dollars. A thousand dollar purse, said to be the largest ever offered in the Canadian west, was won by the Calgary horse Tosti at the 22 race program held at the Edmonton rair.

The C.M.R. held a sports program on Dominion Day, and it proved to be an unqualified success. Besides flat races there was a musical ride, cutting off the Turk's head, Indian race, Victoria Cross race, tug of war on horseback and bareback wrestling. A unique event was the menagerie race that included many kinds of fowl and animals.

During the year the North American trotting record was reduced to 2.03¾.

A new double decker grandstand that could seat 2,000 people was completed for the Calgary Inter-Western Pacific Exposition held in early July of 1904. F. McNaughton, an expert polo player, was given the difficult position of starter for the three day race program that offered $5000 in purse money, including a $1000 free for all and a $600 mile dash. Bookmakers were charged a hundred dollars each to set up shop, and there were many complaints that Calgary's exhibition was losing money in that the fee in Edmonton was $400.

The first day of the exhibition saw jumping, driving and riding competition take place. The Citizens' Day races were watched by a large and noisy crowd. There were nine entries in the gentlemen's mile race, the large number of which made for great difficulty on the narrow track at the start of the race. At first race Judge J. Good would not allow all of the horses to compete in one heat, but he finally gave in. The race was won by R. Bevan riding Bishop. There was a failure to fill the free for all, and with only three entries, all from Edmonton, the management feared a procession and called the $1000 race off.

The winner of the polo pony dash was disqualified after the runner-up claimed that the winning horse had never been used in a polo game. In the cowboy race, that was run around a barrel circuit, W. Kerfoot won over Louis Robinson and Lord Seymour. Gymkhana events completed the day's program.

The following day a novelty mile race, with prize money for the leader at each of the quarter posts was held in place of the free for all. In the 2.30 trot or pace for a $400 purse Clearwater won in three straight heats. The afternoon's program included a 5/8 mile hurdle race for polo ponies only and Indian races.

The last day of the meet found a fast track and, "Fast Flyers". There was a great deal of betting on the mile dash, which was won by Gawaine by a length over Tosti. Hilderbrand, the renowned American jockey, was brought in to ride Gawaine, and it was reported the owner of the winner picked up $3,600 in side bets on the race.

The following day Hildebrand, much to the dismay of those who had bet on his mount, did little to enhance his reputation as his horse finished way back in the pack. Following the program, that had been witnessed by a record crowd, Judge Good fined several riders five dollars each for being slow in reporting to the start and one owner $25 for withdrawing a horse without the consent of the race committee. However the next day the Exhibition gave the jockeys back their fines.

Following the Calgary meet many of the horses were taken to Winnipeg for its race program. The Canadian Mounted Rifles' musical ride, under the direction of Sgt. Major Page, also took part in the Winnipeg program. Several Calgary owners and trainers claimed that in Winnipeg their horses were often placed in classes with swifter horses than the class called for. Calgary's J. Young stables was second in total prize money winnings at the Winnipeg meet, with Oraviva accounting for $1310 of the purse money. In the gentlemen's race, run in a sea of mud, Calgarian F. Bevans was in the lead, but an accident occurred and he was thrown in the mud. Oraviva, a Calgary horse, won two races at the Brandon race meet, but the prize money was held back until an investigation was made in respect to her entries.

At the New York track Galligher, owned by George McMillan of High River, won a feature event posting a time of 2.03½, which was the fastest mile paced up to that time in 1904.

The Exhibition board met in September, when it was reported that receipts from the race meet were $1500, up considerably from $326 the previous year, but expenditures had risen from $714 to $3720. It was a general consensus that the public was no longer interested in harness racing because "they were no longer on the square."

Saxon Champion, who had been bred on the Rawlinson brothers' ranch located ten miles west of Calgary, won the championship of the open hackney class at the important St. Louis horse show. The sire of this horse was the great Robin Adair, who had won a first prize at the New York horse show, and was reported to be worth $11,000, a tremendous sum for the era.

In January of 1905 the directors of the Exhibition met and resolved not to put up any purse money for harness races; however; it was decided that if any person or group desired to give harness racing exhibits they were free to do so.

Not long after the Calgary Driving Club was formed in order to promote harness racing in Calgary.

The Territorial Horse Breeders Association's annual meet, held at Victoria Park in April of 1905, contained 120 entries. Many of the breeders affiliated with the association were breeders of race horses. During this period the Alberta Stock Judging School was held in Calgary.

In early May a horse race matinee, with the prizes donated by local merchants, was held at the Victoria Park oval. Events included: a 300 yard dash—100 pounds up, gentlemen's road race—best 3 of 5 three quarter mile heats, gentlemen's quarter mile dash—150 pounds up, boys' pony race ¼ catch weights, and a 5/8 mile match race for a $250 side bet between J. Young's Gawain and R. Bevan's The Bishop.

A special train carried Calgarians, the C.M.R. band and a carload of horses out to the Cochrane races. The grandstand was decorated with flags, and games of chance had been set up adjacent to the track. the names of Sibbald, Goddard, Wilson, Freeman, Bevan, and McDonald were prominent among the winning jockeys.

A military sports program was held at Victoria Park on Dominion Day as part of the C.M.R. summer camp. Included in the ten event program were ¼ and ½ mile dashes, polo pony race, Victoria Cross race, menagerie race, with each competitor herding a different animal and bareback wrestling.

Edmonton's summer fair race meet was highlighted by a $1000 purse in the free for all.

The annual Fire Department May 24 sports day included military sports for the horsemen. There was some very close competition between Sgt. Major Page and Captain Jordison in the tent pegging, Victoria Cross race and the lemon cutting events. Two days later an afternoon of Indian sports took place at Victoria Park, and the meet included horse races for each of the Blood, Stoney, Sarcee and Blackfoot tribe members, with separate races for bucks and squaws. Other events on the program included an open 2¼ mile race, a bucking contest and a Pistarken. There were track and field events, and the Fire Brigade band was out to entertain the large crowd in attendance.

The 1905 Calgary Exhibition featured three days of racing, and with many of the events including from 10 to 13 entries, there were many spectators who claimed that the races were as good as had ever been seen in Calgary. The large enthusiastic crowds were entertained with riding competition between the races.

J. Dean Freeman won the cowboy race on the opening, known as the Ranchers' Day program that also included high jump and hurdle competition. Citizens' Day events included the Merchants' purse and the Citizens' purse running races, a gentlemen's mile dash and a mile and a half pony hurdle race.

The highlight of the last day's program was the inaugural running of the Alberta Derby, a mile and an eighth race for Alberta bred horses only—$400 purse—with all the entries to carry 121 pounds. The Bishop, a seven year old horse owned by Calgarian R. Bevans, took the race with ease from the other entries. The Bishop who had been bred on the outskirts of Calgary, posted a time of 2.03¼.

Other events on the final days' program included a mile race for the hotel keepers' purse, a four furlong race for the Ladies' purse, a 1½ mile hurdle race and a mile selling race.

The people of Langdon, just east of Calgary, held a summer picnic and race program. Included in the events were cowboy heats, pony races, a free for all, and roping a pig from horseback contest.

During 1905 there were 20 agricultural fairs in Alberta, with most of the communities sponsoring a race program.

In the spring of 1906 members of the Calgary Driving Club met at the Empire Hotel to draw up plans for the club's race meets. Several such meets were held in April and May, and included in the programs were races at distances from 3/8 mile to one mile. Prominent among the winners were owners J. Ross and Shorty McLaughlin, whose string of horses had just arrived from the west coast.

Heavy rains brought a halt to the May 24 Fire Brigade sports day, however the military sports program of the 15th Light Horse were carried off. On this holiday many Calgary horses were taking part in the Brandon race program, where Zaza, owned by G. Davis, finished in the money.

The highest bid ever received in Calgary for the privilege of handling the pool and bookmaking was received from a Kentucky man who offered $500 for this privilege. The race committee had changed their philosophy, and they were now more receptive to harness racing.

In June the Alberta Hotel held a Derby draw with over 250 Alberta horses being listed in this sweepstake. 2,600 tickets were sold, with a $1000 prize to go to the winner, $500 to the holder of a ticket on the second place horse, $250 for third place, and the remaining money to be divided among the ticket holders of the other starters in the Alberta Derby.

About this time members of the Exhibition board were discussing the abolishment of the pools, however this was vetoed as it was felt that the racing department and the horse owners would suffer too much. Additional seating was added to the grandstand, and a body of water, known as Hornby's Lake, was constructed at Victoria Park.

Many Calgarians boarded the special train to the Cochrane races. At this meet a bad situation occurred with the bookies when a post entry won a race, and the horse had not been on their books. Some bettors with field tickets had wanted to bet on this horse, but the bookies would not allow this. As a result of the complaints charges were laid, and the bookies were taken to Cochrane by authorities.

There were 250 mounted men at the 15th Light Horse summer camp, and a great number of them participated in the military sports and horse racing program at the camp's sports day. Individual races were held for the officers, N.C.O.'s, cooks and regimentals. The High River military held a sports day that included a Victoria Cross race and bareback wrestling.

The people in the Calgary suburb of Shepherd held a race program in conjunction with the community picnic. A "Grand Union of Ex-Americans" was held July 4 at Victoria Park, and included in the program were sports, two auto races, boys and Indian pony races. Calgary horses won a good share of the money at the Edmonton race program.

A Calgary newspaper headline read, "Greatest races ever held here," in anticipation of the Calgary Exhibition. 122 horses, from many points in western Canada, were entered in the fourteen race program, with fields ranging in size from three in the gentlemen's driving competition, ten in the Derby and 14 in the 2.30 pace. An extra purse was to be offered in the free for all trot, "for the horse making the lowest record beating all previous records for Alberta." However not all was rosy in the dilemma about books and pools, as all gambling had been banned at the Exhibition. The police were requested to watch the bookies and pools very closely.

7,000 people attended the first day of the races. Lady Huron, in winning the Hotel Keepers purse race, posted a time of 1.433 1/3 to break the Alberta mile record by two seconds. Justin Freeman won the polo pony race, an event limited to active members of polo clubs. The gentlemen's race involved the driving of buggies in the heats of this event.

The following day's program saw a Manitoba horse set a track record of 50¼ seconds for four furlongs in the ladies' purse event for two year olds. There were only three starters in the mile and a half hurdle race, and only two of them finished the course. Zaza was left at the post in the Merchants' Cup; a protest was made, but the judges said it was entirely the jockey's fault. Fortuna II was the 1906 winner of the Alberta Derby, but the consensus was that this horse did not equal the performance of The Bishop in the previous year's Derby. Crowds at the Exhibition had made it obvious that harness racing was still popular in Calgary. The bronko busting and steer roping was also viewed with a great deal of interest.

A match race for $1000 a side was arranged for the Saturday following the fair between J. McLaughlin's Figardon and George McMillan's Rosarie. A grudge race, that resulted from an Exhibition race, took place between W. Christie's Winnona and G. Godard's Lady Canada for a $500 side bet.

Horse racing was part of an Indian program held in August at Victoria Park. The Burch and Reiss Show played in Calgary and thrilled its audience with its Royal Roman hyppodrome act which consisted of chariot races. The Lethbridge Exhibition offered $5000 in prizes for its program that included relay, harness and saddle races.

During the Firemen's Convention, which was held in Calgary in August of 1906, a sports and horse race program took place. A unique event was the Fire Chief's mile pace race in which Calgary Fire Chief Cappy Smart finished third behind two American entries. An Indian mile race resulted in a dead heat that had to be rerun. There were class B and C harness heats, and bronko busting also as part of the program.

Ice Matinee on Elbow River. Drivers left to right: J. Twobey, W. Parslow, J. Hamilton, I. Ruttle, H. Sommerville, W. Stewart.

The Calgary Labour Day sports program included an open one mile pony race and a bucking contest. The Calgary Driving Club held a race matinee on Thanksgiving Day, with mile races for class A entries and half mile events for class B and C horses. Included in the meet were many horses that were newly arrived in the Calgary area. Victoria Park took on the appearance of a three ring circus that day as football and baseball games were also taking place there. A week later a 3/8 mile match race for a $500 purse took place at Macleod, and Autress beat the great Cyclonne by half a length.

During the season Dan Patch, who had previously raced on tracks in western Canada, earned the right to be called, "King of the Pacers,", after clocking a 1.55 mile.

In the winter of 1906-07, trotting and pacing races took place on the ice of the Elbow River and at Chestermere Lake.

The seventh annual Calgary horse and cattle show took place at Victoria Park in April of 1907. Dr. Tomlie of Victoria judged the light horses, which included many entries from the various strings of horses that were stabled at the race track.

Jas. Reilly, the secretary of the Turf Club, headed a committee from that organization that met with members of the Calgary Driving Club to discuss amalgamation. A new organization was established and Reilly, Alderman Moodie and G. Leeson were placed on a committee to obtain a charter and set up a stock subscription. The new group was approached by Secretary Richardson of the Exhibition in respect to suggestions for its race program.

A "grand athletic celebration" that included horse racing took place at Midnapore on Arbour Day. A race meet at Olds, with $1150 in prize money offered, included a half mile race for farmer's horses. The Edmonton Exhibition offered $5,000 in prize money for its race program that included eight trotting and ten running races.

It was reported of the Fire Department and Turf Club two day May meet that in some events there were more horses entered than had ever started before in Calgary's race history. Events on the program included a 2.40 pace and 2.35 trot, free for all, 2.18 pace and 2.15 trot, 2.23 pace and 2.19 trot, gentlemen's harness race and gentlemen's race—owners up. One race was delayed a half an hour when a tire burst on one of the rigs. In another instance one horse refused to turn up for the start, and it insisted on making a round of the track before it could be stopped. There were complaints that other wagons and riders on the track interfered with the races.

The second day of the meet was said to have produced some of the best races ever seen in Alberta. E. Davis' old horse Zaza won the 7/8 mile in an excellent time of 1.28, which was close to a world record. Monie Musk, a giant of a stallion, took the free for all in a time of 2.17¼, a quarter second off the track record. Many people in the crowd of 6,000 patronized the two bookies who opened up at the east end of the grandstand and did a good business.

A carload of Calgary horses were shipped to Red Deer to compete in its two day June meet, which was followed by Wetaskwin's race program.

The Cochrane races were well attended by Calgarians who travelled to the hamlet by special train. The 15th Light Horse camp was held just east of the Bow River, and the camp's sports day featured many horse races. Roman chariot races, high jumping and cake walking horses and a ballet company composed of a hundred Shetland ponies were included in the program of the Norris and Rowe Circus that visited Calgary. More than 2,000 people attended the military sports and racing program sponsored in High River by the 15th Light Horse. It was reported that more than 15,000 persons attended the Edmonton Fair and its race program.

The Alberta Derby was open to all horses bred in Alberta, but the Exhibition board barred Golden Plume from this race. The Turf Club went on record as suggesting that the Alberta Derby be made an open race. N. Jackson, who had put up the Gold Challenge Cup for the past two years, announced that the trophy could now become the property of the stable that won it twice. The Exhibition would pay a bonus for any track record that was broken in either the running or trotting events, and a $200 bonus would be given to any entry that broke the Alberta track record of 2.14¼.

The 1908 three day race program would offer 16 events, including a bending race. No entrance money was charged for the events.

A record number of entries, from many points in western Canada and the United States, were received for the fair race program. With entry numbers as high as 13 in one race it was decided that no post entries would be allowed. However the first days' program was not well organized and few in the crowd were aware at the time that the bending race was being run. Mrs. Dog Sun of the Sarcee tribe was badly injured in the squaw race.

There were only four entries in the Alberta Derby, however it proved to be a very good race. Beaver Dam Ld, owned by Ed McAbee of Edmonton, posted a time of 1.45 to win the race. Later Anita set a new track record of 1.03 for the 5/8 mile dash, a time that was lower than the Winnipeg track record for the distance.

The following afternoon Lucy won the half mile pony race, but a protest was lodged against the winner for crowding, so first place money was given to Little Comet. There were ten starters in the mile and an eighth pony hurdle race, which was won by Jerry in a time of 2.22.

"The Turf", a column on horse racing, was published almost daily in a Calgary newspaper. Calgary horses were entered in the raced at the Red Deer fair as well as the Claresholm and and Blairmore race meets. A driving club was organized at Wetaskwin during the summer.

In September the members of the Calgary Turf Club met at the Empire Hotel to begin preparation for the Dominion Fair, which was to be held in Calgary in 1908. The members agreed that a new half mile track should be built at a cost of $3,000 to replace the mile track, which was the only one of this size in the Canadian west. Too often horses who had been trained on Calgary's large track were at a disadvantage when they raced elsewhere. It was felt that a smaller track would be easier to maintain, and it would also give the spectators a better view of the race.

A rodeo program was held in Calgary during the fall, and included in the events was a 200 yard horse race.

In April of 1908 representatives of various turf associations of Alberta, British Columbia and Saskatchewan met in Calgary to arrange the formation of a Western Canada Turf Association circuit. President Moodie was one of the three stewards named to serve for two years, while two others would serve for one year. The organization's constitution was practically a copy of the Pacific Jockey Club rules under which all of the eastern circuits were racing, but the harness events were to be run under the American Trotting Association rules. There were 24 racing centers, including 12 in Alberta, involved in the association.

Freddie Lowes, who later would play an important role among Calgary's horsey set, heard that his father's horse had won a major prize at the prestigious New York horse show.

The Fire Department and the Turf Club held a two day program of track and field, cycling, highland dancing and horse racing, with purses for the races totalling $3,700. Thousands of Calgarians attended the well run program which was enhanced by the many good horses up from the California circuit. The smallest number of entries in any race was five while "14 of the finest gallopers faced starter Moodie in the 5/8 mile dash."

A week later the Fire Department and the Turf Club were joined by the United Commercial Travellers, the latter who were holding a convention in Calgary, in sponsoring a two day race meet which contained trotting and running events, including a polo match. During the month the grandstand was being enlarged to accommodate 4,500 people.

The Turf Club held the first of its many weekly matinees, with races for class A, B, C, and D horses. Plans were made to hold weekly matinee meets throughout the summer season. A new event on the matinee program was a series of running races for gentlemen's saddle horses ridden by owners. One matinee program saw a 5/8 mile selling race as the feature event, with the winner being sold at a public auction held, following the race, in front of the judge's grandstand. Race winner Pelham only fetched the minimum price of $300. Attendance at the matinees averaged about 500 persons. Unique at this time in Calgary's history was the publishing of the betting odds and jockeys' weights.

Millarville held a June race meet that included a two mile open steeplechase. Successful race meets were held at Claresholm, Blairmore, Red Deer, Cochrane and Wetaskwin. However the Lethbridge races were called off by its Turf Club that felt it had been given a raw deal by Alf Moodie, president of the Western Canada Turf Association, who was accused of not sending enough horses to Lethbridge. Moodie said that this was not true—that Lethbridge had postponed and that the horses were to go to Red Deer, but he claimed that he still sent the majority of the horses to Lethbridge. The Indian, owned by Parslow and Haag of Calgary, was a big winner at the Edmonton races, which offered $6,400 in prize money and were attended by over 7,000 people.

Military sports were part of the summer military camp held in Calgary and one of the events was a horse race for troopers in uniform.

Many fine race horses, including a large number of American thoroughbreds, were entered in the race program of the Calgary, 1908 Dominion Fair. All the races, with a weight provision applying, were filled, except the stake races, so the Exhibition board called them off. Pools for each of the following day's races were sold at the Empire Hotel.

More than 6,000 spectators, many of whom arrived in the city on the excursion trains, watched the opening day program that included a race for squaws and travois. The betting ring was well patronized, but the bookies made very little money. The crowd was also treated to a horse show that included a great variety of equestrian events. During the fair the crowds were able to view polo, track and field, bicycle races and a pack horse demonstration.

Unfortunately the fair was marred by several accidents. In one race a horse fell and three other steeds fell in a pile. Jockey Charlie Wright was taken to the emergency tent and then to the hospital. One afternoon a great wind picked up lumber from the roof of a stand and blew it into the grandstand, killing one spectator and injuring several others.

There was great pandemonium at the start of the half mile dash for green ponies, as one horse could not be readied and it had to be withdrawn. The bookies had to make a new set of books, but then the departed horse reappeared on the track. Further chaos resulted, with some horse balking and bucking, while others ran the wrong way on the track.

A tragedy occurred when W. Kerfoot, a former part owner of the Cochrane Ranche, was killed when his horse was spooked and ran into a cow. Mr. Kerfoot, who ranched west of Cochrane, had been a top competitor in the cowboy races for many years.

Estimates placed a record crowd of 10,000 people in or near the grandstand during one afternoon program. Beaver Dam Lad, owned by McAbee of Golden, led all the way in the Alberta Derby to earn the $400 purse for this mile race. There were eleven entries in the quarter mile polo pony dash—140 pounds up, which was won by Justin Freeman of Millarville on Glenbow Dick. There were also eleven entries in the polo pony hurdle race, with four hurdles included in the mile and an eighth distance. Probably the feature race of the meet was a ¾ mile match race between D. Campbell's Gay Boy and winner Breen, a Seattle horse. Photos of both horses made the front page on a local paper.

Evening events at the fair included Indian races and a bucking contest. In the Fire Department's hitching exhibition the number one rig circled the half mile track in a time of 1.44.

The Norris and Rowe Circus came to Calgary, and included in its many equestrian acts were Roman Chariot races. Claresholm held a meet for local horses only, and a two day race meet was held at Medicine Hat. The Lethbridge fair race program included a sweepstake race and an Indian two mile relay race. The Calgary Turf Club held a summer race program under the auspices of the St. Mary's Club, and the events included races for horses in classes from A to E. A low number of only 60 spectators attended one Driving Club matinee in August. The Indian, a Calgary horse, won second place money at the Winnipeg races.

The Calgary 1908 Labour Day sports program included a Turf Club matinee, in which many fast horses were entered and most heats were hotly contested. It had been anticipated that the track record of 1.06½ would be broken, but this did not come about.

Calgary horses won their share of races at the Wetaskwin and Daysland race meets. Haag's and Parslow's string of horses won a fair number of the thirteen races they were entered in on the west coast.

In the spring of 1909 the Millarville Race Association met and elected Mr. Kleran as its president. The association decided to buy some land and construct a race track for their July meet.

The first annual Calgary horse show, held at the Sherman Rink on Seventeenth Avenue, was billed as "The largest indoor show west of Toronto." The attendance was very large for this gala event, and thousands viewed the events which included single pacing driver, military remount, the Calgary Hunt Club special and the high jump competition.

The second "semi-occasional" meet of the Rouleauville Turf Club was held at Victoria Park in late April, and a good sized crowd were treated to three interesting races.

The Calgary Turf Club, under President H. Somerville and Secretary Fred Johnstone, began a series of weekly matinee race programs, with A and B classes for businessmen. On May 24 a crowd in excess of 2,000 watched a full program of races, staged by the Fire Brigade and the Calgary Driving Club, on a slow and muddy track. Following this meet George Haag took a string of Calgary based horses on the western grand circuit in the U.S.A., which offered purses up to $10,000. Other Calgary horses were entered in June race programs at Wetaskwin, Claresholm and Edmonton, where one of the events was for the Calgary Brewing and Malting Cup. Trainers often frequented the Calgary Horse Exchange, located on Eighth Avenue and Third Street East, looking for any animals that might have potential on the track.

616 horses were entered in various equestrian events, for a total of $6,000 in purse and prize money, at the Provincial Exhibition, held in Calgary July 5-10, 1909. All the races were under the rules of the American Trotters Association. Horses bred in Alberta, Saskatchewan, Manitoba or British Columbia were allowed five pounds off scale in races over six furlongs. Previous winners of the Alberta Derby were declared not eligible to run again.

A new event on the fair race program was the Inter-Western relay race, which consisted of riding two miles a day for three days, with each rider to change his horse and saddle every half mile, and only two horses could be used by each entry. Regular western saddles with a minimum weight of 25 pounds had to be used, but bridles did not have to be changed. Thoroughbreds and professional horses were barred from this event.

The opening day program of the Exhibition featured members of the militia competing in military sports involving horses. The Burns Cup was offered for an event that was new locally, and it consisted of a 500 yard sprint; dismount and fire five rounds, and then a gallop back to the start.

It was estimated that a crowd of over 8,000 people watched the running of the seven field Alberta Derby. Land-off passed Irish Lad in the stretch to win in a time of 1.47½. Parslow's General H. was an easy winner of the 2.23 pace and 2.18 trot heats, and this was to be an indication of the great career in store for this Iowa born, but Alberta trained horse. The relay had not proved to be as popular among the horsemen as only four entries turned up.

On the second day of the meet, designated as American Day, there were a total of 16 heats or races, as some events had been postponed from the previous day due to the rain. As a result all owners trainers and jockeys were informed that they would be fined or suspended if they caused any delays. However the full program, that included the Hotelkeepers' and Merchants' purses races, a 1½ mile hurdle race, polo pony dash and jumping competition was run off without a hitch.

Citizens' Day proved to be just as busy in its own way, as there were up to 12 entries in some races.

Problems between the bookies and the race committee were resolved in favour of the Exhibition on the last day of the meet. The Stewart Ranche entry, with Wilson up, won the relay race. Other activities on the program were rough riding, roping and Indian races, but the event that drew the most interest was the horse driving competition for ladies. J. McDonald's Pride won both the hurdle race and the jumping competition, while W. Stokes' Import captured the mile and a quarter event.

Several weeks later Calgarians were able to view what was probably the first motion pictures ever taken of the Exhibition and the horse races when "The Great Calgary Pageant Picture" was shown at the Arcade Theatre.

In July a six race program, including boys and girls pony races, was held by the Okotoks Agriculture Society, and at Carbon a sports program included horse racing. The Macleod race program included a half mile ladies race, which was won by Miss Bremner. Later H. Easham and D. Wilson, both of Macleod, raced their horses for a thousand dollar side bet. Lethbridge held a race program, and the Nanton Agricultural Society held a program of racing, trotting and running races. Horse races were part of the sports program at the cadet camp held near Calgary.

The National Bureau of Breeding was shipping horses to many western Canada points, and a strapping chestnut called Baird, who was bred from top Canadian runners, was placed with C. Riddock of Calgary. Cyclades, who had won over $125,000 in its career, and as well had sired two winners of the English Derby, was now owned by E. Nowers of Calgary. This horse was considered by many experts to have been the most valuable thoroughbred stallion in Canada. During this era many other quality English horses were being imported into Alberta.

The Calgary Driving Club held weekly matinees in late summer and the fall, with trophies, which were held until the next matinee by the A-E class winners, being presented by D. Black, F. Johnston, and L. Doll. In September Don M was in great form to smash the track record for a half mile by 2 3/5 seconds. The new mark of 1.03 4/5 was one second slower than the Canadian record. This demonstration of speed spurred local interest, and as a result the matinee meets were continued through October.

During the fall the Calgary Hunt Club held coyote hunts in the area south of Calgary and on the Sarcee Reserve. The rides were up to 25 miles in length and included some hard runs of two to six miles in length.

During this era there was a great deal of pressure on the Canadian Government to abolish betting on horse races in Canada. However the Miller Bill to this effect was not passed by the House of Commons.

General H, who was owned and trained by W. Parslow and G. Haag of Calgary, was a top winner at several of the tracks in the U.S.A.

Lt. Governor Bulyea officially opened the 1910 Calgary Horse Show, held at the Sherman Rink. The event was considered to be "the greatest horse show ever held in the west." Entries in the show included some from the carload of horses that J. Moodie had just brought in from eastern Canada. Many race horses were arriving in the city to be put into training at the Victoria Park track, while some mounts that had wintered here were sent to the Vancouver race meet.

I. Ruttle was elected president of the newly organized 72 member Calgary Turf and Matinee Club. The group made plans to hold a two day race meet for the Queen's Birthday. However the group was told that local judges would not act in that capacity for the new club unless it affiliated with either the Eastern Jockey Club or the Pacific Coast Association. The philosophy of this is that the judges would have more power to levy fines and keep better control of the races.

Another new organization, the Calgary Driving and Turf Club, under president H. Somerville, began weekly meets in April. Among the events was "a special mile for certain stables" and a Hunt Club running race.

During this period attempts were being made to set up a provincial race circuit. Mostly trainers were pushing to have standing starts for the races replaced by the Walk-up method.

Films of the Grand National Steeplechase and the English Derby could be viewed at Calgary's Starland Theater in May 1910. During this month a local newspaper published a full page, including many pictures, on horse training in Calgary. Horse auctions took place at least every month, and in may 400 horses were put on the block at one sale held at the stockyards.

More than 6,000 people were at the May 24, Calgary race program. After one heat a driver was ordered off his rig because the judges felt he was not trying to win, and then another driver was put in his place. The $200 selling race was a farce as some of the jockeys were not ready for the barrier to lift, and the horses did not get away together. Parslow's General H was driven by Haag to first place in the free for all.

The Morley May 24 sports day included a horse race program. The Millarville races included a two mile race for district horses, Galloway race, hurdle, cowboy, polo pony, selling races and a two mile steeplechase.

There were a reported 25,000 persons on the grounds of Victoria Park during the first day of Alberta's big fair. However the opening day's race program of two harness and three running races was not at all satisfactory. Race entries were few, and several times horses were left at the post. There were two accidents, and on one occasion a jockey pulled down the tape.

Llandoff, owned by R. Exham, posted a time of 1.49½ to win the Alberta Derby over seven other starters. The purse for such a prestigious race amounted to only $250. As was often the case the Indian pony race was the most exciting event on the program, and a photo of this event made the front page of a local newspaper. In between the races was a continual program of horse judging.

Day three of the races included the Ladies' Purse, which was a five furlong race for provincial born horses, or those that had been in the province for a year. The pony hurdle race over four hurdles in a mile distance required 140 pounds to be carried by each entry. Another race on the program was a green pony race.

Day four featured Gentlemen's Galloway and Consolation races, the last heat of the western relay race and the daily driving competition. The best mile time in the harness races was clocked by Sir Chauncey, an Edmonton horse, but his time was three seconds slower than Leland Onward's track record of 2.12½.

Many bettors became very upset when a horse that the bookies were backing crowded the leader into the fence. Many visiting owners and trainers felt that allowing this incident to pass was injurious to the reputation of the track.

During the Exhibition only one person, a young boy, was able to ride a high kicking mule that was part of the circus that was performing on the grounds. In all 76,000 people attended the Exhibition, and about a half of this number viewed the race program. Following the Calgary meet many of the trainers and their stables left for the Winnipeg races.

During this era there were individuals and groups promoting western shows at various cities and town in the U.S.A. and Canada. One such program took place at Victoria Park in late July, and included in its events was an old time cowboy race, a horse relay race, Indian races and a bucking contest.

Race matinees, which had been postponed since spring, began in late August and continued well into October. A matinee was part of the Calgary Labour Day sports program, with races for class B, C and D horses. However entries were low with as few as two horses in some races.

Sam Baird's Indian won races at Saskatoon, Prince Albert and Edmonton. Other Calgary horses placed in the money at the Lethbridge and Medicine Hat meets, Bloody, who won the ¾ mile race at the Calgary Labour Day program, came home first in a major selling race at Vancouver. Mrs. Pat Burns' horse Nevermind won the Ladies' Hunters over four jumps event at the Victoria Horse Show, competing against many of the best from the north west.

General H, owned by G. Haag and Parslow, and driven by Haag, finished first in two straight heats at the Empire Track in New York. The Alberta horse recorded a best time of 2.07¼ in the 2.09 trotting class. New York papers quoted Haag as saying that, "Alberta's winter climate was ideal for training horses." At the Charter Oaks $10,000 stake race at Hartford, General H won three straight heats and the first place money of $5,500. This was followed by a win at Syracuse, and then it was on to Columbus to capture a purse of $4,200. Haag closed the season out by driving this great horse to a 2.05½ win in the McDowell stakes at Lexington. General H started 15 races during the year, winning 12, one second and two fourth place finishes, and earning over $10,000 to finish in the top ten money winners in North America.

By 1911 many horsemen in North America were reported to be in favour of a new system of grading harness horses according to the money they had won. This system worked successfully in Russia, and it was felt it would help clear up the irregularities in classifying horses.

General H was one of a string of ten horses that C. Haag took to the Vancouver race meet. During this era the Russian Government was attempting to buy General H and negotiations continued for many months, but the owners' asking price was very high.

The seventh annual Calgary Horse Show, with over 1000 entries, took place at both the Victoria Park and Sherman's Rink. The Honourable Sifton opened the show, which included 160 different classes of competition and a great many female riders. A special horse show supplement was published by a local newspaper. Eighteen year old Miss Walsh of Beaverdam rode Smoky, a 16 year old horse, to a new Alberta high jump record of six feet. "Naturally she rode astride and manages her horse in a true cowgirl style."

Plans were made by the Exhibition board to move and widen the track, which would allow a greater number of entries in each race. The book privileges for the Exhibition meet were awarded to I. Ruttle.

The Calgary Turf Club planned a program to include five running and three trotting races for the Victoria Day holiday. The Calgary Brewery Company donated a trophy for the gentlemen's driving race. However the rain and snow caused a cancellation of the day's activities.

Calgary real estate promoter Freddie Lowe's horse won 13 prizes including the Grand Championship, at the Winnipeg horse show. At the Cochrane races, Mr. Abel captured the Hutchinson Cup, awarded for the gentlemen ranchers' race. Almost all the hurdles were knocked down in the first lap of the two mile hurdle race. The large crowd in attendance especially seemed to enjoy the Indian and the ladies' races.

The Calgary May 24 race program was rescheduled in June, and at this meet was the first appearance of a pari-mutual betting machine in Calgary. The system appeared to work satisfactorily, but the people working the machine got behind after the first race, and so many of the bettors went back to the bookies. Another first in the Calgary race scene was the publication of race charts.

The Calgary Driving Club began its matinee programs in June, and the Glenbow Athletic Club held a sports day and race meet on Dominion Day. A Coronation Day sports program at the army camp included a Victoria Cross race and bareback wrestling.

The Exhibition board announced that they would not allow the horsemen to cause any delays in the races, and no race scratches would be allowed after 11 a.m. on the morning of the race.

The Honourable Frank Oliver, Minister of the Interior, officially opened The Calgary Exhibition before a grandstand crowd of over 10,000 people. The opening day nine event program included the Alberta Derby, a six furlong open race and the Hotelkeepers Purse race. A heavy rain made for a very slow track. The pari-mutuels proved to be a success, but a problem arose in the harness races as these were run in heats, and there were too few horses in some races, when at least six entries were needed in order to show pay money. These factors, plus the reluctance of many bettors to use the new machines, kept the bookies busy.

The seventh running of the Alberta Derby found a six horse field contesting the mile race for a $500 purse. A feature of this race was the running of a sire, Golden Plume, and its colt, Fortune's Plume.

There was a considerable delay prior to the start of the race, and then when all was ready the trigger on the gate would not function.

Smith Bowman fought off Llandoff to win in the stretch. Llandoff's jockey filed a protest against jockey Cummings for crowding into the fence, but the protest was disallowed. M. McAbee rode Golden Plume to show money.

The following day, jockey N. McAbee, who was the oldest rider on the circuit, having ridden locally for over 20 years, won the Merchants purse race. During the afternoon program, track and field events were staged between the horse races. The third day's races were literally washed out by the rain and mud, but a double program was held the following day with continuous racing from two through six o'clock, and then continuing in the evening with the last event, an Indian race, staged at nine p.m. A track record was broken in the evening program as Miss Alverscott was clocked in 1.03 flat in the five furlong consolation event, although a faster time for the distance had been recorded on Calgary's old mile track. Tom Longboat, owned by Alex Storey, clean up in the free for all harness race, and then this horse was shipped to Winnipeg to race in its meet.

The last day of the Calgary meet proved to be the best program of the week. A new track record was set in the three minute class when Haag drove McDermid's Bess M to a paced mile in 2.13¼. There were so many entries in the cowboy race that four heats had to be run. Sandy McDonald, who weighed close to 200 pounds, rode the great jumper Smoky to victory in the cowboy race, and Clem Gardner finished second.

The pari-mutual, which did more business than the bookies at the Calgary meet, were shipped to Winnipeg. Calgary horses did well at the Manitoba track, and in one card won four of the five races staged. Prince Rupert of Smith and Bowman's Wheat City Stables won the Ladies' Plate, while horses owned by Calgarians I. Ruttle and S. Baird won a fair share of the prize money. Calgary's G. Haag continued to display his great driving skills.

Problems arose at the Brandon races when an owner poisoned Man's race horse. Calgarian A. Storey's Tom Longboat and Smith and Bowman's horses were again successful.

A high jump competition was part of the Macleod race program, while up the line Calgary horses took part in the Claresholm Derby. The Calgary Labour Day sports program included harness and Indian races. A western day, promoted by Fred Maxwell and held at Victoria Park, included cowboy and Indian races. The first Langdon Agricultural Society's fair ran horse races on the community's new half mile track, and included in the race program were events for ladies.

Alberta, a new horse acquired in Winnipeg by G. Haag for the Parslow syndicate, paced a mile in 2.09 with comparative ease. This horse was raced on the grand circuit in the U.S.A., and by the end of the year it had won more money than any other Canadian horse.

Polo pony races were often run in connection with the polo games played in southern California during the winter months, and Alberta polo players often entered in these competitions. At a 1912 New Year's race, Calgarians Snowden and Critchley were ribbon winners.

During this era many horse trainers felt that southern Alberta was the best area for their field of endeavour, and a local paper attempted to substantiate this by publishing a long article entitled, "Alberta's Climate Best in the World for Training Horses." General H, the champion trotter of Canada and one of the greatest horses of his day, was cited as an example.

Members of the Western Canada Racing Circuit met to formulize a list of comprehensive rules for their organization, including coverage of green horses and galloway events. It was also decided that all grooms and attendants must wear white coats. Harness events would be run under the American Trotting Association rules and running races under American rules. Entry money would be 15% to enter and 5% to be deducted from purses. The harness purses would be divided 50, 25, 15 and 10%, while the runner division would be a 60, 25 and 15% split.

$120,000 was offered as stake money throughout the circuit that opened with

Calgary's five day show that offered $16,250 in prize money, then moved on to Moose Jaw, Winnipeg ($28,110), Brandon, Regina, Saskatoon, Edmonton ($21,000) and a three day Lethbridge meet. Edmonton and Calgary's Hotel Keepers' Stakes were each for $3000 purses.

April headlines read, "The Horse is King in Calgary", "Big Wigs Arriving in City", "Glittering Pageant Tomorrow"; and thus the 1912 Calgary Horse Show was announced. A total of 18,000 people, with a one day high of 5,000 spectators, witnessed this spectacular equestrian show. There were still 3,000 people in the stands at one o'clock in the morning as Smoky, owned by P. McDonald of Jumping Pound and ridden by Angus McDonald, set a new Alberta high jump record of six feet two inches.

"On the Track" was the name of a weekly horse race program published in Calgary. Local papers carried a great deal of news and results from races throughout the world. The Epsom Derby results were front page news in Calgary. During the spring an organization known as the Chestermere Jockey Club was formed.

Many Calgarians travelled to the Edmonton May three day race program that offered $5000 in prize money. In June the Calgary Driving Club held several matinee programs, and one meet included a special match race for three horses.

The Cochrane race program proved to be very exciting for those in attendance, but unfortunately many race goers did not get to the meet as the special train from Calgary was derailed near Brickburn. The Dean Cup, donated by Mr. Dean of Cochrane's Alberta Hotel, was won by Goldie. Two riders were injured when they were thrown from their mounts in the hurdle race. At Millarville, where only running races were held, there were twelve entries in Buster's race, and to accommodate this large entry three heats had to be run. Other events in the eleven race program included Galloway, Indian and hurdle races. The following week Irricana held a field day that included one horse race.

The Victoria Park Stables were being taxed to capacity, so more stable space was constructed as there were over 300 horses from many points in the northwest in training in Calgary.

Public pressure brought about the revival of the Indian horse races in the 1912 annual Calgary Exhibition. Unique was the fact that the horses had to share the use of the track with five elephants, that were part of a visiting show, and Ward's Flying Machine.

63 runners, pacers and trotters competed for $5,300 in prize money. On the opening day of the race program the bookies proved to be far more popular than the pari-mutuals. G. Haag, one of the west's old time drivers, proved he had not lost his touch as he reined home a winner. The program saw the introduction of a 2.10 pace or 2.05 trot race to Calgary. Mazda was the winner of the 1912 Alberta Derby, and a five furlong selling race included a high number of 13 entries.

A great second day crowd of 40,0000 people on the grounds filled the grandstand to capacity for both the afternoon and evening race programs. The 2.15 pace, which offered a $3,000 purse, was won by Sirois Pointer, who had begun the heats as a 10-1 longshot. During the program a man ran across the track, and he received a broken collarbone when a horse ran into him.

Over 10,000 people witnessed the 2.25 trott, that included nine American horses among the 15 entries. Melos, who earlier in the day had placed second in a one mile race, won the mile and a half hurdle race while carrying a top weight of 149 pounds. A serious accident occurred in the Galloway hurdle race when a jockey was thrown, and then his mount rolled over him. Driver W. Dyson was suspended for the remainder of the season on the Western Canada circuit for using insulting language to a judge. A policeman was assigned to Dyson to escort him off the grounds. An Indian race and the green pony race were the highlights of the last evening's program.

One of the horses on display at the grounds was Dave Campbell's Gay Boy, who had won $68,000 in stake money in six years of racing in the U.S.A. Following the Exhibition the papers reported, "In Greatest Carnival of Racing Ever Witnessed Here Calgary Exhibition Closed."

Calgary's papers carried the race results from various tracks, but Calgary based horses were not as prominent in the money positions as in previous years. Red Deer combined its horse racing with track and field, and Claresholm held its annual Derby. At Edmonton 25,000 people saw Dotty, from the Reade and Moir Stable of Calgary, set a Western Canada record of 1.01½ for the 5/8 mile distance. Billy D, owned by Calgarian Fred Johnson, captured the Hotel Keepers' Stakes. A new Canadian record was set at Lethbridge when Marcus, owned by J. Ferguson of Monarch, ran six furlongs in 1.16¾.

Horse racing played an important part in Calgary's first Stampede, held in September of 1912. It may be pointed out that rodeo shows such as this were not unique in Calgary, and rodeo events had been part of the Calgary race scene for many years prior. The Stampede race program consisted of Indian, cowgirl and cowboy relay races with professional horses barred, a wild horse race, a cowboy turning race, potato race and the Stampede stage coach race. In the latter event six horse teams pulled a stage coach through a figure eight around barrels, and then each of the two entries raced the opposite way around the track. The program also included such events as burro riding, fancy riding by cowgirls and trick riding by cowboys.

The cowboy relay race was a two mile race in which the rider switched his saddle to a new horse every half mile. Johnny Mitchell of Medicine Hat, whose best time was 5.18, won top money of $750, and Doug Wilson of Claresholm finished in second spot. Bertha Blanchett was the top finisher in the cowgirls relay race. The Friday crowd of 17,000 was probably the largest number of spectators to watch horse racing in Calgary.

As a result of the reform movement many American tracks were being shut down, and as a result the Western Canada circuit took on additional importance as many good horses were brought in to Canada to race.

During the spring the Western Canada Fair and Racing Association announced that prize money of $205,700 for running events and $147,250 in harness purses would be offered for the race programs at 17 centres, including Calgary, Edmonton and Red Deer in Alberta. The Calgary purse money included $11,500 for harness events and $21,550 for the runners.

There were a record number of entries for the 1913 Calgary Horse Show. The open high event brought out the greatest attendance, and Sioux, ridden by S. Carter, cleared six feet, three inches to break the provincial record. Lowe's Paddy jumped one inch higher, however as the bar was held fast this could not be accepted as a record. Clem Gardner and his sister took first place in the Okotoks Trophy pairs jumping competition, as they guided their horses around a stiff course of obstacles.

The Calgary Driving Club opened its matinee events in early May, and the programs included many good horses both from Canada and the U.S.A. Calgary papers carried a great deal of news and results from the American race tracks, and the English Derby results were headlines.

In May of 1913 the Chinook Jockey Club was organized in Calgary. The club's executive consisted of Honourary President Pat Burns, President F.C. Lowes, George Lane and A.E. Cross as Vice-presidents and A.K. Morrison served as Secretary-Treasurer. The club acquired 80 acres south of the Country Club and made plans to construct a race track, clubhouse, stables and a grandstand, and plans were to hold its first meet the following spring. The basic philosophy of the Chinook Jockey Club was to encourage the breeding of thoroughbreds in the province.

During this era runaway horses were causing considerable problems on Calgary streets. "One big bay horse on Seventh Avenue, pulling a buggy, appeared to be a candidate for the Derby."

Many of the horses that had trained in Calgary raced in Edmonton on Victoria Day and then followed the circuit to Prince Alberta, Saskatoon, Regina and Moose Jaw before returning for Calgary's Exhibition meet.

The Cochrane race program contained 70 entries, with the events beginning at noon to accommodate the twelve race programs, which included a 2½ mile special feature steeplechase.

A California track harrow was brought in to grade the track prior to the five day Calgary Exhibition meet which offered $22,550 in prizes. Entry fees had been paid 2% at a time, three times prior to the meet. Many of the judges for the horse classes and races were American. There were 63 classes of horses judged the opening day, with one-fifteen entries in each of the classes.

"Races are the best ever held in Canada, say Horsemen," was front page news following the first day of Exhibition racing which was witnessed by a crowd in excess of 10,000. The pari-mutuels, otherwise known as the "Iron bookies", were popular, but this was helped considerably by the fact that the bookies were not allowed at the track. The seven race program included a total of 13 heats, with the green pony and cowboy races on the evening program. Grand Opera paced true to form, winning each of the three heats in the Hotel Keepers $3,000 2.14 pace or 2.09 trot, and in the process posted a time of 2.13¼.

Day two was known as Farmers and Ranchers Day, and in the race meet Commerce pulled off the upset of the week as its win paid 37 to one odds. Trainer Thomas was ruled off the track for life when he bought a horse in a selling race, and then it was discovered that he did not have the $200 to pay for it. The Galloway and Gentlemen's races brought about as much interest as did the thoroughbred races.

There were six entries in the Alberta Derby, and Ben Ara, owned by J. Bremner of Edmonton and ridden by Tom Cummings, was never headed from the start to the finish of the race. The 2.17 trot Merchants Early Closing Event, for a $2000 purse, was one of several harness races won by Joe McGuire of Denver, Colorado.

Dynamite, the high kicking mule, again remained unridden.

Pari-mutuel receipts increased from an opening day $12,000 to $22,000 on the last day of the meet. Trainer Nibbs found himself on the carpet when it was suspected that Gala Wreath was a ringer. A variety of events saw distances raced from the quarter mile polo pony dash to a 1½ mile hurdle race, consisting of five jumps and a required 155 pounds up.

The free for all trot or pace was the chief attraction on the last day of the meet. Alcfrass, the holder of the world record for a half mile track and who held the Canadian record of 2.04¾, was the favourite. However Fern Hal went on to win the race in four heats. This race saw a first time in Canadian history that three horses had to divide second, third and fourth place money.

The 1913 Exhibition and its race program had no more finished when the track and infield were used by the Oklahoma Wild West Show.

A cowboy race and a horse show, which included many classes for ladies, was part of the summer High River Exhibition. The Claresholm fair featured eleven races, including ladies, welter, handicap, farmers trot, hurdle races and the Claresholm Derby in its three day program. The mile and a quarter Macleod Derby and the ladies' hitching and driving race were two of the favourite events at Macleod's August fair. The Red Deer Exhibitiion reported that 5,000 people were in attendance at its race program, and a new track record of 2.11½ was set at the Medicine Hat races by a Monarch horse.

The pari-mutuels were introduced in Edmonton and proved to be a big success. Bettors were shy to use the machines at first, but after a payout of $45.30 on a two dollar ticket, there was a big rush to the wickets. Billy D, owned by Fred Johnson of Calgary, won the 2.14 pace or 2.09 trot race, and many other Calgary horses placed in the money.

In late August a program of pony and Galloway races was held by the newly organized Pony and Galloway Association. There were up to nine entries in each of the seven races on the program, which included a half mile dash for maidens. Stallions were barred in the gentlemen's race, and most races required a minimum weight of 150 pounds to be carried.

There were 70 entries, including horses from many points in western Canada, entered in the Calgary Turf Club two day September meet, which was presented as a pocket edition of the Calgary Exhibition. An extra race had to be added to the program to accommodate the unexpected large number of entries. Prior to the meet a local newspaper published a list of probable winners. The harness races were three out of five heats, with the winners determined by using the point system. Percy Sawtell, one of Alberta's leading jockeys, was suspended for coming up with a poor ride on his own horse. He claimed that his saddle had slipped, but the judges knew about his escapade before the start of the race. Sawtell's plan was to lose so that he could enter his horse in the consolation race.

Two race track followers were arrested for swindling fellow bettors. One race was a half mile heavyweight handicap, and Eunice, owned by W. Cochrane of Millarville, won, in spite of carrying top weight. Homer Mac captured the free for all in a good time of 2.13¾, just a second off the track record, which was jointy held by Captain Derby and Leeland Onward.

Pari-mutuels were not used for this meet, but it was felt that this would probably be the last time for the bookies in Calgary. They lost a bundle when a 10-1 shot came home a winner in the six furlong dash.

The Calgary Exhibition announced plans to move the track to the south east corner of the grounds and construct a new fireproof grandstand to seat 11,000 people who would be protected from the sun and west wind. Relocation of the track cost $24,000 and Ottawa contributed $87,000 towards the $127,000 cost of the new grandstand. Late in the fall the Edmonton Jockey Club announced that they would build a race plant similar to that planned by the Chinook Jockey club. There was discussion among the horsemen of forming a new race circuit to include Calgary, Edmonton, Vancouver and Victoria.

Statistics compiled showed that by 1913 Alberta's horse population had reached a total of 580,000 as compared to 92,000 in 1901.

In the spring of 1914 the Western Canada Race Association announced purse money of $158,000 for the race programs at its twelve prairie tracks.

Newspaper headlines read, "Calgary Horse Show the biggest and best ever held in the Province of Alberta," following the April, 1914 show. Highlights of the horse show included the 16 member R.N.W.M.P. ride and Sifton's string of great jumping horses. In the Okotoks Hunter event E. Robinson's mount did a complete somersault, but the rider kept the horse under control and carried right on in the competition.

Due to the relocating of the track and the construction taking place on the grounds, there was very little thoroughbred activity in the area. However many Calgary based horses were entered in the Edmonton May three day program. The Millarville races were attended by a large crowd whose number was increased by the many men who arrived from the Turner Valley oil fields.

The reconstruction of the race track was completed in time for the 1914 Calgary Exhibition race meet, that included 194 harness horse entries and 110 thoroughbreds in the running races; these numbers being up by 50% from the previous year. Nine pari-mutuel machines were in operation, with one of the machines being used to take the place of the auction starters pool. American starters were brought in to handle all the races.

There were 24 entries in the 2.30 pace or 2.25 trot, and entries close to this number in several other races, but the largest field that ever faced a starter in western Canada was entered in the Merchants early closing event—the 2.17 trot. One of the horses participating was Gratton Boy, who had set a Canadian record of 2.12 for a half mile track. Merry Direct, a world record holder, who was owned by Frank Smith of Calgary, was another horse entered in this race. Old timer, George Haag, drove in several races, and W. Herron, flush with success in Turner Valley oil fields, entered a hore in the four year old green trotter class.

There were great crowds in attendance at the Exhibition horse race programs. The show rings were well patronized, and the pari-mutuels, although not favoured by all, helped to keep the sport clean and above suspicion. During the week there were evening as well as afternoon races.

The feature event of the opening day race program was the President's handicap with $700 added, and winner Prince Phillip Thorpe was ridden to victory by a 15 year old jockey named Cox. During the week jockey Manders was ruled off the track for fouling, while a pileup in another race brought about a horse being shot when it broke its leg. The Indian races again proved to be the most popular events on the program. During the week the number of wins by Edmonton horses far eclipsed those by local horses. The same trend was obvious by the results at the other race tracks in the west, although at Brandon F. Smith's Merry Direct won the 2.12 pace in straight heats, and Gratton Boy set a Canadian record for a half mile track when it stepped the mile in 2.11½ at the Regina track.

Calgary's G. Ruttle, president of the Western Fair and Racing Circuit, acted as head timekeeper at the Edmonton summer race meet.

During this period the Chinook Jockey Club spent $35,000 on the construction of their new race plant, located south of the city, but the operation was suspended in 1914 as a result of the war. In 1925 the Chinook Jockey Club facilities were completed, including a grandstand to seat several thousand people. At this time the Speers Corporation entered the local racing scene. The first meet at the Chinook Track was held in September of 1925. Plans had been made for a seven day program, but a heavy snow storm changed that.

In 1915 a new set of rules for the western fair circuit combined the rules of the Ontario Jockey Club and the Kentucky State Racing Association. The following year a three heat system replaced the best three in five system for trotting races.

As a result of the war purses dropped by at least 50% and racing declined. Many horses ended up as cavalry mounts. In 1917 the War Measures Act prohibited betting on horse races in Canada. The same year the Alberta Thoroughbred Horse Association was organized.

Shooting

The Rifle was brought to the prairies by the explorers and fur traders. Probably some Indians who had travelled eastward to the trading posts had brought back guns. When the North West Mounted Police established posts they built rifle ranges that could be used for shooting practise.

At Fort Macleod Colonel Macleod organized a rifle club which followed the rules of the Mounted Rifle Association. A rifle association was established by the Calgary detachment in 1884. The following year the Alberta Mounted Rifles, who were in Calgary as a result of the North West rebellion, competed against the Canadian Light Infantry members in a shooting competition. The Edmonton Rifle Association was organized in 1886, and not long after rifle clubs were established in Fort Saskatchewan and Lethbridge.

Rifle competition, open to all comers, was part of the Calgary 1886 Dominion Day sports program. Entries for the two events and their combined scores aggregate were handled by Mr. Freeze. The first event of seven rounds from 200 yards with competitors kneeling had prizes ranging from $15.00 for first down to a dollar for eighth place. Any rifle with open sights could be used by the competitors who had to find their own ammunition.

The 1887 Dominion Day sports program included rifle competition from 200, 500 and 600 yards, with a consolation event from 400 yards for those who were not winners of the first three events. First prizes were a dollar for each event.

The Calgary Gun and Angling Club was established in July of 1887 with E. Hodder as the club president. Two meets were held by the club that season using live snow birds as targets. The club went on record as recommending that Indians be required to observe the game laws.

A telegraph competition was held in July of 1888 between the Macleod and Calgary clubs, who telegraphed the results of their respective shoots to each other. It was reported that 32 Calgary ladies had taken part in shooting competition during the season. During the year all Alberta rifle associations joined the Dominion Rifle Association.

The annual matches of the Alberta Rifle Association took place on the ranges located on the Agricultural Grounds in September of 1888. A total of 21 individuals took part in the competition. Firing took place from the 200, 500 and 600 yard marks, with the total scores added to determine the aggregate. Prizes ranged from riding boots, donated by the I.G. Baker store, a ten dollar cash prize from Judge Rouleau, to a gun valued at $20.00 for the aggregate winner. During this era the McBride Hardware Store sold powder, shot and shells to local sportsmen.

In July of 1889 the Calgary rifle team placed third in the North West Territorial Rifle League competition that was held as a telegraph meet. Prince Albert shooters placed first. The following year the Calgary team defeated the Assiniboine Rifle Association 519-505 in a shooting match. I.S. Freeze was the top marksman for Calgary. W. Pavier, the organizer of the competition, reported that bright light and mirages contributd to the low scores at 600 yards.

In the annual town shooting competition, held in September of 1890, Allelstine won the Mayor's prize as he beat Freeze, who was handicapped two points, in a shootoff. Allestine also took the merchant's prize in this competition.

The Calgary District Rifle Association finished several notches below Edmonton in the 1891 North West Rifle League competition. Teams from twelve centres participated in this telegraph shoot. Competition at Macleod took place between that community's team and the Fort Saskatchewan Rifle Association for the Davis Trophy.

In 1892 the president of the Calgary Rod and Gun Club offered a medal to be competed for at the club pigeon shoot which was held at the Agricultural Grounds. In this event, which included a 25 yard rise and a 30 yard boundary, Hodder proved to be the best shot. Dog trials, for dogs owned by any residence of the Territories, were held by the club.

Pair matches were held on other weekends. Thomas Stone beat Hodder ten birds to nine out of 20 birds each. Hodder killed a tenth bird, but, as it fell out of bounds it did not count.

Local competition was held in the Canadian Rifle League, with shooting at targets located from 200 to 600 yards distance. Rodgers Hardware supplied many of the local marksmen with ammunition.

Stone was the top marksman at the first of several trapshoots held by the Calgary Rod and Gun Club at the Exhibition Grounds in the spring of 1893. There were ten shooters in each of the five bird sweeps, with a 20 yard rise and both barrels allowed.

In the third shoot of the season it was reported that the live snow birds flew erratically because of the cold weather. The second sweep was a miss and drop out event, but the supply of birds ran out before it could be completed. MacKay, Hodder and Stone proved to be the top Calgary marksmen during the spring shoots.

Mr. McCaul, the secretary of the Calgary Rod and Gun Club, received an invitation inviting the club members to compete at a Macleod shoot to be held on Dominion Day with competitors from Lethbridge, Pincher Creek and Macleod.

Nine marksmen averaged 78 out of 100 in a July, 1894 match of the Dominion Rifle League. I. McLaren and Colonel Barwis were the top marksmen in the meet. Other men in the community who had proved to be top shots were I. Freeze, W. Pearce, S. Ramsay and Jas Reilly. During the year a gun club was formed at Medicine Hat.

In 1895 the Alberta Rifle Association team, composed of Ede, Russell, Glassford, Ramsay and Pavier outshot the Mounted Police team of Brooks, Whitehead, Caudie, Story, Days and Woverton by a 293-265 score in a match shot at ranges of 200 and 400 yards. A gun club was formed at Mitford, a hamlet located west of Cochrane. Under a Territories Ordinance the duck hunting season would open August 23. The Bow River Trapshooting Club held a tournament in the fall of the year.

The weekly competition of the Military Rifle League, held in June of 1896, saw each competitor take ten shots from each of the 200, 500 and 600 yard distances. Mirages, created by heat rising from the ground, often proved to be a problem for the competitors.

The Calgary Hardware Store advertized Robin Hood loading cartridges for the countless hunters who ventured out to the many sloughs surrounding Calgary during the duck hunting season.

Calgary's major rifle meet took place in October with competition taking place at distances from 100 to 600 yards, with the Dominion Rifle Association rules to govern the events. The meet was open to all comers, any rifle and any sights, with an entry fee of 50¢ for each range. There was a good attendance of competitors, but constantly changing light hurt scores. The merchants and businessmen of Calgary donated many prizes ranging from a leather hat box to medals. Competition included shooting from standing, kneeling and prone positions.

A. Brooke of Edmonton put together a score of 78 to be named the meet's top marksman. T. Ede had a 77, Alex Martin of Mitford a 75 and Colonel Barwis a 72. All together there were 25 participants in the competition.

In October of 1898 a large crowd of spectators gathered at the pigeon shoot held at Irish's place, later to be called the Blue Rock Hotel, near the Mission Bridge. Host Mellon worked very hard to make the shoot a success. The entry fee for the principal match was a very high twenty-five dollars, and four competitors paid the fee. Hodder hit eight birds; Luxton and Robinson shot 13 birds each, but Critchley killed the last eight birds in succession to run his score to 14 and claim the pot.

During the same month a pigeon shoot was held at Okotoks. Besides sweepstake events there was a miss and drop out competition, with the last shooter to miss a bird being declared the winner.

In 1899 the gun club had a new club house, cages for 2,000 pigeons, and it was holding weekly sweepstake matches. The Critchley-Lesson Cup for the best score had become the top prize for the club tournament.

The Calgary Trap Shooting Club advertised that it would pay ten dollars for every 100 live pigeons delivered in crates to any C.P.R. station, and they would pay $2.50 extra if the birds were delivered to the club grounds in Calgary.

The club's first 1899 meet was held in August and consisted of six sweepstakes with five birds per sweep. A. McDonnell with 25% of his birds hit, was the top marksman. A. McNeil was another skilled shooter.

An electric trap was used at the trap shoot held at the Exhibition Grounds during the Calgary fair. Sixteen competitors were entered in the five sweepstakes competitions and a miss and your out event. Each event cost a dollar to enter, so the sport was generally limited to those with means.

The Calgary Gun Club leased a large block of land from the Catholic Mission in 1900. Mr. Heald, the club's president, offered to buy any quantity of pigeons or snowbirds. However live birds were not in great supply, and the club was using more clay pigeons, buying the Blue Rock clay targets from the Calgary Hardware Company.

The Alberta Rifle Association held fortnightly spoon competitions commencing in May at the Association's ranges on the Exhibition Grounds, with shooting taking place from distances of 200, 500 and 600 yards. In July teams were formed to allow group as well as individual competition. The Canada team won by ten points over the rest of the world team. Ramsay, Bagley, Heald, Barwis, Bell and Smyth proved to be the top shots in Calgary during 1900.

The sport of shooting has always been closely connected to the military in Canada. The militia supplied guns and ammunition to rifle clubs and similar organizations. New rifles and 30,000 rounds of 303 ammunition were received in Calgary from Winnipeg in the spring. However anyone who missed two consecutive weeks practise had to turn their rifles back in. Section 19 of the Militia Act made the people who received guns or ammunition from the government liable to serve in the reserve militia.

Telegraph and mail matches often took place between rifle clubs in Canada. The score was to be confirmed by a justice of the peace. One such match took place in August between the Calgary Rifle Association and the Moose Jaw Club.

The duck hunting season, as established under the Territorial games ordinance of 1899, was reported to have attracted several thousand hunters to the Calgary area. Langdon and Nose Creek were reported to be two of the favourite areas for this sport.

In September, during the Inter-Western Pacific Exhibition, a rifle shoot was held under the auspicious of the Exhibition Company. Mr. Van Wart offered a gold medal for this competition, in which four five man teams, including a team from Moose Jaw, were entered. Seven shots at each of the 200, 500 and 600 yards were to be taken by each competitor.

Bagley's team captured the event, with Ramsey second, the Moose Jaw team third and Tillyard's team fourth. Comer's score of 85 gave him the individual honours as well as the winners cup and a pair of field glasses for first prize.

By 1901 the government had extended the militia to the North West Territories, and as a result was going to give more assistance to rifle clubs in the west. Colonel Barwis was busy recruiting for the Calgary troop of the Canadian Mounted Rifles. Colonel Evans, commander of the military district that Calgary was situated in, said the local range was the finest and safest in the west. The Colonel Evans Trophy, emblematic of the club rifle shooting championship of the N.W.T. and Manitoba, was offered for competition. In 1901 and the following year this trophy was won by the Calgary Rifle Association team.

Shooting of a different nature occurred at Miller's Ranch, located south of Calgary, where nine wolf clubs were shot in one den.

Spoon and button competitions took place on alternate weeks on the rifle range. Mr. Crofton presented three buttons, one gold, one silver and a bronze button for competition. He also offered a silver cup for the first person to record a score of 95 or better.

Another area of competition was for the Lynhurst Cup. This event was for teams of two men, one being a first class marksman and the other person holding a second class rating. F. Bagley and H. Higgs were the winners of the first Lynhurst match.

Four teams, including one from Olds, took part in a Victoria Day shooting competition. A. Smythe took top honours for the highest individual score.

The Calgary Rifle Club affiliated with the Military Rifle Association, and under provision of membership were to be supplied with 200 rounds of ammunition for each member and as well a rifle grant. Military League shoots took place at distances of 200, 500 and 600 yards. P. Kidd was the first winner of the Alexander Cup in this area of competition, and he was allowed to hold the cup until someone else could top his score during the season.

In July A. Carmichael shot a magnificent score of 95, including eight bulleyes at 500 yards, to earn the Crofton gold button.

L. Clark was the best of eleven shooters as he hit 20 out of 25 birds at the Calgary Gun Club clay pigeon shoot. In the ten buttom competitions of this club W. heald was to capture the A class competition with W. Barwis and S. MacKid second and third.

A Canadian Military League shoot, for ten man teams, was held in August, and Dr. Macdonald's score of 94 helped his team to an 836-735 win over their local opposition. Other noteable marksmen in Calgary during the 1901 season were H. Crofton, W. Smith, R. Fox, F. Bagley and W. Armstrong.

Rifle enthusiasts from Fort Saskatchewan, Regina, Medicine Hat, Moose Jaw and the Calgary area met in Calgary's Cooperative Hall in March of 1902 for the purpóse of forming the Territorial Rifle Association. Fred Bagley was elected to the chair by the group, with W. Armstrong as secretary and W. Barwis as the organization's treasurer. The association's aims were to get more help and financing from the government to promote the activity of rifle shooting in the west, and to encourage the establishment of competitions.

The same month the Calgary Gun Club met in the Royal Hotel, where W. Heald was re-elected club president by acclamation. The club made plans to construct a new tower a hundred feet high with four floors 20 feet apart. New traps were to cost an estimated $500.00. The club made additions to the club-house and began to put a ten foot fence around its property. An unwritten law was put on record that winners of the weekly button competition were not expected to treat the crowd.

The annual Priddis shoot was held in April, with competition for gold, silver and leather buttons. H. Kervey won the Robert's Competition, an event which saw the winner determined by whoever could fire and score the most points in sixty seconds.

A gold medal was donated by Lord Strathcona to be awarded to that person who made the highest individual score on the ranges during the season. A marksman's badge was to be given to anyone who shot a score of 90 or over twice during the season. First class was a score of 70 or over, second class under 60.

The Elbow River and the Priddis Rifle Clubs were to shoot in a Calgary competition, but severe floods damaged the butts which were located adjacent to the Elbow River below the cliffs. The club's pontoon bridge across the river was also torn loose from its mooring.

H. Lott, Clem Gardiner and H. Young were winners in the spoon shoot competition at the Elbow River Rifle Association meet. The Cochrane Rifle Association held its first Smith Cup Shot, which consisted of seven shots from 200 yards and five shots from 500 yards. Alex Martin proved to be the meet's best marksman, earning a score of 54 out of 60.

Captain Bagley, one of Calgary's top marksmen, left for South Africa where he was to command a regiment in the Boer War. He handed over his duties as president of the Calgary Rifle Club to Dr. MacDonald.

R. Fox was given the contract of building six targets and a semaphore target house on the new ranges located on Colonel Walker's land east of the city. The range was not ready in time, and so the Territorial shoot was postponed until August. When the range was finally completed the opinion was that it was the finest in the west. The annual tournament of the Calgary Rifle Club was then dropped in order to help accommodate the Territorial Rifle Association.

Close to eighty competitors from several points in the Territories were entered in the various events. Mayor Underwood scored a bullseye on his first shot from 200 yards as he opened the Corporation of the City of Calgary match. Three aldermen entered the competition and their total combined scores did not equal the mayor's. A. Carmichael won the twenty dollar first prize for his score of 92 in this event. Priddis captured the team prize, followed by the Mounted Police, C.M.R., Elbow River, Red Deer, Fort Saskatchewan, Cochrane, Edmonton and Calgary teams. The competitors in the Military match for veterans of the South African war competed for a cup presented by the Earl of Minto, Governor General of Canada.

The Merchant's Cup shoot took place from the 500, 600 and 1,000 yard ranges. Armstrong scored an 81 to take the $20 first place prize, and C. Comer was second with a 79. Calgary's Macdonald was the best of 30 competitors to take home the cup and $20 in the Association's match. The Licensed Victuallers match, shot from 200 and 600 yards, was won by Wooley-Dod from Priddis, who finished two points ahead of Cochrane's Alex Martin. Archie Latimer of the Calgary fort took first place in the Military event, with Colonel Barwis in runner-up spot.

The Lieutenant Governor team match was won by Comer's team, with Fort Saskatchewan second, followed by Fox, Elbow River and Priddis. A. Carmichael's score of 386 gave him the grand aggregate and a $25 cash prize. Runner-up A. Martin's 356 score was one point ahead of Fort Saskatchewan's W. Pierce, with Dr. Macdonald fourth and I. Freeze fifth. The competition was followed by a banquet at the Royal Hotel where the awards and prizes were presented.

The expenses of the meet had totalled $2,350, while receipts had totalled $1,730, including a Dominion grant of $500, Territorial Legislative grant of $200 and one hundred dollars received from the City of Calgary. 8,000 rounds of ammunition, purchased at the cost of $120, was used during the tournament.

The Calgary Rifle Club securd the Evans championship for the second year. In the Canadian Military League competition the Calgary team ended up in third place in the Dominion in the 20 man team event and in tenth place for the ten man team event.

Fox, with a score of 587, had the highest aggregate of the six medal matches, followed by Armstrong with 470, and Dr. Macdonald with 415. Fox shot an individual high of 99 to take the gold button in 1902, and Carmichael won the silver button.

In September competition E. Sales, a newcomer to Calgary, proved to be just about as good a shot as anyone in the area. Calgary's newspapers often contained guns for sale ads.

The Calgary Gun Club used 450 live pigeons in the October club shoot. Captain duBray, the celebrated American pigeon shooter, took part. After the morning sweep lunch was taken at Irish's place. In the afternoon there were four sweepstakes of five birds for each competitor. The top marksmen of the meet were Comer, du Bray, W. Heald, Orr, Barwis and Robinson.

Calgary's rifle team placed fourth in an international competition for the Rupyan Cup in 1902.

There was a large gathering of rifle enthusiasts at the second annual meeting of the Territorial Rifle Association held in the Fire Hall in March of 1903. Captain Bagley handled the chair, and A. Armstrong was elected the association secretary. Council members were elected from several points in the Territories. The executive reported that, "the first year had been an unqualified success".

The Calgary Rifle Club, under club president Dr. Macdonald's direction, held its first shoot in April, but fishtail winds helped to keep the scores down. In June a six man team competed against a combined Elbow River-Priddis team at the Elbow River ranges, shooting from the 200, 500 and 600 yard distances. Comer and Macdonald each shot an 85 to help give Calgary a 469-449 win. Hervey and Wooley-Dod were the top marksmen for the country team. R. Freeze proved to be a capable rifleman as he earned a score of 94 the following week. Sergeant Major Page earned the gold target for the highest score at any distance with a 34 at 500 yards. E. Hervey led the combined Elbow-Priddis team to a 471-444 win over the Calgary team in a return match.

The Elbow River Rifle Club annual shoot was attended by 16 competitors including eight with the name of Young. The events included prone and kneeling at 200 and 300 yards, prone at 500 and 600 yards, and seven shots in one minute. Rex Young beat out George Young by one point in the individual championship.

The Penhold Rifle Club was also holding weekly practises, with an average attendance of 25 shooters. The scores were much lower than those recorded in Calgary, however W. Richards was considered to be an expert rifleman.

Competition was held at the Calgary butts in the Canadian Military Rifle League meet. Competitors took ten shots at each of 200, 500 and 600 yard distances. Heat mirages, changing light and tricky winds proved to be a problem for the shooters. After the second shoot Calgary team was in fifth spot in the Dominion, 45 points behind the leaders, but with improved shooting conditions in the last two meets their score improved and Calgary ended up in third position. Armstrong was the best Calgary shot in this competition, and as well he earned the Jordan target for the highest score at any distance.

In August of 1903 the N.W.M.P. held a shoot at the Territorial rifle ranges, and the teams from Regina, Maple Creek, Lethbridge, Battleford, Prince Albert, Macleod, Fort Saskatchewan and Calgary set up their camps adjacent to the ranges along the Bow River.

The Territorial Rifle Association meet was held at the Calgary range in September. There were 105 competitors entered in the Corporation of Calgary match, with Calgary's H. Carmichael taking top honours as he shot a 95, and W. Pierce of Edmonton in second place with a 92. Private H. Hervey of the C.M.R. and Sergeant Major Page finished one-two in the Military match. Comer's Calgary team won the Walker Cup for teams of four men, then S. MacLeod and H. Hervey finished first and second in the Merchant's Cup competition.

In the important Association match R. Fox shot a 90 to take first place, and C. Comer finished second with an 88. E. May and Constable Hoskins were the top competitors in the Licensed Victuallers event.

R. Kisch of Medicine Hat did not win any events, but his consistency paid off, and his score of 359 paid him the Grand Aggregate Trophy. The next five places were taken by C. Comer, A. Jordan, R. Fox, L. Thorsen and Sergeant MacLeod of Maple Creek. Sergeant Major Belcher, whom the Colonel Belcher Hospital is named after, shot a 319.

H. Crofton, a man familiar to the riflemen of Calgary, entered the renowned Bisley competition and got into its second stage of shooting.

In the fall live pigeon shoots were held by the Calgary Gun Club. Inspector Douglass and Barwis excelled in these events.

During 1903 the Calgary Rifle Club had held 32 practises with an average attendance of 18. The club did not retain the Evans Trophy as the score had not been sent down east in time.

By 1904 a rifle association had been formed at Nose Creek, north of Calgary.

The Calgary Rifle Association held an organizational meeting at the C.M.R. drill hall in March of 1904. Macdonald and Armstrong said that they could not run for office as they were on the executive of the Territorial Rifle Association. C. Comer was elected club president and A.E. Cross was appointed as honourary president.

The annual meeting of the Calgary Gun Club was held in the Royal Hotel in April, with W. Heald re-elected to the chair. The club was $750 in debt, but it was able to liquidate this amount by selling five dollar shares for the ownership of the grounds. The club decided to affiliate with the Dominion of Canada Game Protection and Trap Shooting Association. Norm Jackson presented the club with a new cup for competition.

L. Thorsen, P. Palleson, W. Armstrong and Sergeant d'Egville were the winners of the four spring shoots of the Calgary rifle club. A special match was held between Bisley marksman Crofton and R. Fox, with the latter coming out the winner.

A Calgary resident was fined $15 or 90 days for discharging a firearm within the city limits, when he fired a shotgun at a fence.

In a match staged at the Elbow River ranges the combined Elbow River and Lakeview Rifle Clubs defeated a team from the C.R.C. 494-454. At the annual

Elbow River rifle shoot the winner was F. Young, and R. Hollis, a former Bisley competitor, placed second.

The Fifth Regiment of Canada Trophy and the Transavaal Cup, the latter for those who had served in the South African war, were new trophies up for competition in the 1904 Territorial Rifle meet to be held at the Riverside Rifle range.

Several crack shots from Vancouver, and Bisley contestant Captain Denny of Ottawa, were among the eighty entries in the Territorial Rifle competition held during Fair week. Pre-tournament practise took place from the thousand yard marker. A. Carmichael of the Nose Creek team scored a very good 90 at this distance.

Captain Forest from Vancouver won the Military match, Corporation match, Merchant's competition and the grand aggregate award. Captain McHarg of Vancouver captured the Licensed Victuallers event, and as well he placed second in the grand aggregate. Calgarian C. Comer was the Association competition, and his fourth place in the grand aggregate was the best of the locals. Third place in the aggregate went to N. Dineen of London, England. The Elbow River rifle team of the three Youngs and E. May captured the four man competition, and as well they won the Fifth Regiment Trophy for six man teams. The Calgary Mounted Rifles were second and the Nose Creek team third in the Walker Cup for four man teams. The meet ended with a smoker held at the Canadian Mounted Rifles drill hall.

In team competition of the Canadian Rifle League the Calgary Rifle Club score 3,308 points to finish in thirteenth spot in the Dominion. The Calgary competitors blamed the high winds for their poor showing.

During the winter rifle matches were held in the shed range. A challenge skeet shoot match took place in December when Hunter MacMillan of Calgary defeated R. Robinson of the Chipman Ranch by two birds to win a $500 side bet.

Secretary Armstrong reported that over 70 competitors were registered for the 1905 Alberta Rifle Association competition held at the Riverside Range in July. Close to $2,000.00 in prizes were up for competition. Unfortunately the shoot opened under a downpour.

R. Chamberlain and Alex Martin finished first and second in the Merchant's match, while H. Crofton shot a 92 to take the Military match. The Calgary Brewery team competition went to R. Fox's team, and P. MacNaughten captured the Brewery individual honours. The Fifth Regiment Trophy went to the C.M.R. with E. May's Elbow River team in second spot. J. Carmichael of Edmonton took the Con Leary Cup, while the TWA Freens pair match from 1,000 yards went to an extra shoot off with J. and A. Carmichael.

J. Carmichael continued his excellent shooting as he scored a 96 in the Corporation of the City of Calgary match and won the $25.00 first prize. A. Crofton's 94 was second highest of the 41 entries. In the Corporation team match Comer's men were the best of the six teams entered. R. Chamberlain took home the Jackson Challenge Trophy for the Alberta Challenge match, which consisted of seven rounds each at 200 and 600 yards.

E. May's team captured the newly offered Rogers Cup, donated by Mr. Rogers of Vancouver. This event, shot from 300 yards, consisted of three rounds each standing, kneeling and prone. The Golden Rifle match, consisting of five rounds at 1,000 yards without a sighter, was won by Dr. Macdonald. R. Young of Elbow River took home the $15.00 first prize for the Merchant's Cup competition. In the Association match winner P. MacNaughten shot an 85, with E. May and both coming in with 84's.

The grand aggregate went to R. Young, who received a gold medal and $25.00 for his 435 score. Alex Martin was second with 432 and J. Carmichael next with 420.

A number of ladies and Calgary citizens were present at the concluding smoker held at the R.N.W.M.P. barracks. Mrs. Saunders, wife of Colonel Saunders, presented the prizes to the winners. It was generally felt that the success of the meet was largely due to the assistance of the local Mounted Police.

Mild weather in the spring of 1906 allowed for a very early opening of the rifle season in Calgary. During April and May marksmen R. Fox, A. Carmichael, S. Ramsey, Sergent Major Brankley, A Martin and Sergeant Major Belcher all recorded high scores. S. Ramsay, the club president, announced that the executive would allow the members to use the sliding wind gauge on all Lee-Enfield and Lee-Metford rifles, as it is assumed they would be allowed at the T.R.A. and D.R.A. matches at Ottawa.

In July the Calgary Gun Club moved its buildings and traps from Rouleauville to its new quarters, east of the Mounted Police Barracks, at the junction of the Bow and Elbow Rivers. A new blackbird trap was constructed and the grounds were fenced. Club president Dr. Mason reported that open shoots would be held every Tuesday and Friday evening.

The Calgary and Macleod Gun Clubs met in Brewery Cup competition in August, and the C.G.C. won the competition with a four bird advantage over the visitors. R. Robinson won a flask for attaining the highest score, hitting 22 out of the 25 birds thrown for him. In sweepstake shooting both W. Reilly and A. Morrison hit ten out of ten birds. W. Arbuckle won the sweepstake doubles.

In August Hunter MacMillan shot a record high for the new club range hitting 25 out of 25 birds. The Calgary team travelled to Macleod and successfully defenced the Brewery Cup. Alex Martin's sporting goods store and Ashdown's Hardware were two of Calgary's main gun retailers. Single shotguns were advertised for $6.25 and double barrel models sold for $9.25. An interchangeable gun was listed at $14.25, while the Baker hammerless sold for thirty dollars.

With the Alberta Act of 1905 the Territorial Rifle Association became out-modelled and was replaced in Alberta by the Alberta Rifle Association, which affiliated with the Dominion Rifle Association. From 1906 through 1914 the A.R.A. competition was the most important shoot in the province.

Albertans F. Young, R. Young, Macdonald, Fox, Carmichael, Armstrong, Plumber, Martin, Hervey, Page, Barwis and Crofton participated in the Ontario Rifle Association shoot in Toronto and the Dominion rifle Association competition at Ottawa. Armstrong was the best Alberta man in the Toronto competition scoring a 62 as compared with the winner's 66. At the Rockcliffe Range the Youngs, Fox and Crofton shot well in the Banker's match, which was won by Dr.

Webster of Winnipeg. F. Young of the Elbow River Rifle Club was chosen for Canada's Bisley team, but he was declared ineligible when it was found out that he was not a member of any military organization.

The annual prize meet of the Calgary Rifle Club was held in October. In the first match, with seven shots at each of 200 and 300 yards, Constable R. Tait was the winner with a score of 54. Second place was shared by I. Freeze, Sales and Fox, each of whom had a score of 53. The Challenge Trophy competition consisted of ten shots at each of 500 and 600 yards distance. Alex Martin, with a score of 92, was the winner, and L. Thorson was runner-up.

During the fall rifle training was started in the Calgary Public schools.

A challenge skeet match for $25 a side bet was held at Christmas between J. Mosely and R. Robinson. Robinson won the match and the wager, but the loser felt that Robinson's use of two barrels was not quite fair. The pair met again in February of 1907, but this time Mosely stipulated that only one barrel was allowed per target.

A popular pastime of the era for many Calgarians was the shooting gallery operated in downtown Calgary by J. MacDonald. Patrons could shoot at targets or moving birds or animals. Later in the year a charge of gambling with an airgun was laid by the police against the owner of the gallery.

Brewery Cup competition took place in March as the Calgary Gun Club defeated the visiting High River team 93-85. Ben McLaren was Calgary's top marksman and the unofficial Alberta champion, hitting 22 birds out of 25. Other Calgary shooters were R. Robinson, C. Andrews, L. Orr and J. Mosely.

The two clubs met again in April, and there was considerable pressure on the competitors as the clubs had wagered two hundred dollars on each of the four events. A single bird sweepstake was taken by Calgary's McLaren. In the three man team event of 25 birds per participant the Calgary tem won by 17 birds, and in the four man event Calgary was also the winner. McLaren defeated Andrew of High River 21-17 in the premiere match.

Further competition took place for the Dupont Shield in a handicap event. Ben McLaren shot from scratch, while others had up to a twelve yard handicap.

The Alberta rifle team of R. Young, R. and E. May, A. Martin, S. Ramsay, Lieutenant Hervey, Peard, McInnes and Brown, under the direction of Captain Armstrong, went to the Dominion Rifle Association matches in Ottawa, where there were over 600 shooters in the competition. Dugald McInnes of Strathcona won the Governor General's prize, the Bisley aggregate, and as well he took home $200.00 and six medals. In the Coates match, for six men teams, the Alberta competitors finished sixth out of the 21 teams entered. An eight man Alberta team took a sixth place in the London Merchant's match. Lieutenant May shot in the money in the trio match.

Weekly button shoots, some from the 1,000 yard range, were held at the Calgary Riverside Range during the spring of 1908, with the riflemen entered in either A or B class competition. W. Clarke, A. Martin, R. Fox, E. Sales, I. Freeze, A. Carmichael and Dr. Macdonald recorded high scores. After a day at the ranges the club members would often meet at the club room located on Seventh Avenue.

The C.R.C. entered an eight man team in the London Daily Mail Overseas "Empire Day" rifle competition. The club's eight highest scores, led by Staff Sergeant Brankley's 89, represented Calgary, but poor weather kept the local scores low. The results of this meet were cabled to London. Shortly after Alex Martin left for England to take part in the Bisley shoot, Sergeant Brankley continued to impress as he shot a 98 in a Military League match. Another local club who used the Riverside Range was the Calgary Veteran's Rifle Club.

The Calgary Gun Club, who had been holding weekly shoots since April, reported that the new trap was working very satisfactorily. W. Cook was consistently turning in good scores. At the Red Deer Gun Club meet in July Calgary's Ben McLaren won the Central Alberta Trap Shoot title.

Forty shooters participated in the second annual Calgary Gun Club shoot which was held during Fair Week. McLaren won the prime event, hitting 24 out of 25 targets, and R. Robinson ran a close second. High River again challenged for the Brewery Cup and lost. The same results occurred in July and August.

In June W. Armstrong topped the list of the ten member rifle team entered by the Calgary Rifle Club in the Canadian Rifle League series shoot, shot from 200, 500 and 600 yards. The men of the Calgary militia camp, under the command of Colonel Steele, used the Riverside Range for rifle practise.

The Calgary Gun Club held a tournament, which included the Alberta championship shoot, in August. American rules governed the twelve events. Stewart and Lenn won the double competition, and M. Hagen was first in the miss and out. A mixed team, consisting of men from several places, won the team shoot, Calgary second, then Ponoka and High River.

Ben McLaren hit 44 out of 50 birds to capture the championship of Alberta. Runner-up M. Parrot broke 40 targets.

There were 75 entries in the 1908 annual meet of the Alberta Rifle Association, with every provincial district represented. Any rifle of government issue was allowed to be used. W. Pierce of Edmonton edged out E. Thorsen of Calgary to take the ten dollar first prize for the Alberta match. In the City of Calgary competition, which included the Walker Cup Shoot, D. Spence of Strathcona was first and Calgary's H. Crofton, the runner-up. The Calgary team of Freeze, Bell, Ramsay and Crofton compiled a team score of 344, one more than the Elbow River team of May and three Youngs.

W. Young of Elbow River won the twelve dollar first prize in the Association match, and R. Fox placed second in this important event. The Medicine hat team topped their Calgary and Edmonton opponents in both the Rogers Cup competition and the Fifth Regiment team match. The Elbow River Rifle Club won the Brewery team match, and team members W. Young and R. May finished one-two in the event's individual competition. In the City of Calgary competition the Youngs of Elbow River took first, third and fourth positions, with Edmonton's Spence finishing second. Calgary's S. Brankley won the Rutherford and the T.W.A. Freens matches.

The grand aggregate was earned by W. Clarke of Calgary, with Edmonton's J. Carmichael second, followed by R. Fox, G. Reid, R. Young, A. Macdonald, R. Alloway of Didsbury, Constable Tait of the Mounted Police, E. May and W. Young.

The Dupont Trophy, which was actually a watercolour, was shot for in August by members of the Calgary Gun Club. The handicap 100 bird event was won by Slingby, with Mosely in runner-up position. In September some members of the C.G.C. went to the Ponoka skeet shoot, and they placed well in the money.

Lee-Engield rifles were used by the senior boys of Western Canada College in competition against members of the Calgary Rifle Club in April of 1909. In competition between the school's city and country boys, Cadet Sergeant Powell shot a perfect 35, while Lieutenant Young and Cadet A. Turner-Bone each had a 34.

A most successful shoot of the Calgary Gun Club took place on Victoria Day when over a thousand targets were thrown. Ben McLaren demonstrated excellent shooting by hitting 48 out of 50 targets. Other top marksmen were R. Robinson and A. Huddle. McLaren was a consistent winner at the weekly competitions which were attended by an average of twenty competitors.

In the provincial trap shooting competition McLaren won the individual title for the third straight year, as he hit 48 out of 50 birds in the prime competition of this two day event held by the Calgary Gun Club in July. R. Robinson of Calgary and Ed Meade of Ponoka tied for second each destroying 47 birds. The tournament aggregate winner was Lee Barkley, with Meade second and R. Miller of Seattle third.

At the Bisley meet in England Corporal McInnes of Edmonton proved to be one of the top shots on the Canadian team which competed against the best in the vast British Empire.

Twelve rifle clubs, including a group from Prince Edward Island, competed in the 1909 Alberta provincial rifle meet. A regular tent city was set up along the banks of the Bow River by the competitors.

Brankley's quartet outshot eight other teams in the Walker Cup competition, while the Elbow River club placed second. J. Peard and W. Finlay of Medicine Hat finished one-two in the Calgary Brewery individual competition. L. Brown of Medicine Hat edged Seaman of the P.E.I. team in the Martin extra series, and then he added to his laurels by winning the Rutherford competition. Sergeant Clarke just beat out Crofton to take the City of Calgary competition.

H. Crofton's 300 score gave him the grand aggregate honours. A. Martin's score totalled 294, L. Brown of Medicine Hat and R. Bell of the C.R.C. 290, while the next six places went to C. Brown, M. Fulton, R. Fox, A. Carmichael and W. Clark.

In July members of the Calgary Rifle Club and their wives travelled to Okotoks to attend a shoot at the Panorama Range. Twenty-five competitors participated in the shoot which took place from the 200, 500 and 600 yard ranges. After the shoot there was a football game between the Calgary and Okotoks competitors, and the day ended with a picnic.

Members of the Alberta rifle team placed well in the money at the Ontario Rifle Association shoot held at Toronto in August. E. Sales of Calgary, who was not on the Alberta rifle team finished 35th in the competition. Crofton finished 52, R. Fox 64 and R. Bell in 74th position.

At the Rockcliffe ranges in the Dominion Rifle Association competition

Sergeant Crofton finished third and R. Fox was tenth in the Bankers match. In the MacDougall match Crofton again displayed his skill as he tied for first place. Sergeant McInnes of Edmonton had to score a bullseye on his last shot, which he did, and he was again the winner of the Governor General prize, an honour he had previously won in 1907. Ontario riflemen won the other seventeen principal prizes of the competition.

Back in Calgary R. Tait led the Calgary team to a 512-458 win over an Okotoks team in the new Ramsay Trophy competition for six man teams. In the weekly rifle shoots at the Riverside Range Chamberlain was posting the highest scores.

Some members of the Calgary Gun Club travelled to the Ponoka Gun Club meet, where Ben McLaren finished second, H. Andrews fourth and Tait fifth. Club members also participated in shoots held at Olds, Red Deer, Leduc and Edmonton. R. Robinson travelled to Nelson where he won the B.C. championship. Later he and Ben McLaren competed in shoots at Seattle, Spokane and Butte, Montana.

The Calgary Rifle Club competed at Innisfail where the local rifle club offered a new shield for provincial competition. The Calgary team earned the trophy with a score of 453 compared with Penhold's 407 and Innisfail's 453. Teams from the north were invited, but they did not come to the Innisfail meet.

The Canadian Rifle Association was encouraging the organization of miniature rifle meets to be held in the winter. Local shooters met in the local militia drill hall where such a club was organized. A range was set up in a nearby shed.

The Western Canada college rifle club members utilized the Riverside range, where R. Weir proved to be the school's best marksman. The W.C.C. cadets used Lee-Enfield rifles to fire at one inch bulls at their own indoor rifle range during the winter months.

During the winter of 1909-10 the Calgary Miniature Rifle Club held weekly shoots on their 25 yard range. Four meets were held in Canadian Rifle League competition. A. Storrar, F. Kaye, A. Martin, L. Chamberlain and I. Freeze posted the best scores during the winter season. In a telegraph match the club defeated the 48th Highlanders of Toronto by 27 points.

The 1910 organizational meeting of the Calgary Gun Club was held in March with Dr. Gunn in the chair. A.E. Cross was appointed honourary president. It was reported that 45,000 clay targets, at a cost of one and a half cents each, were used by the club in 1909. In spring competition local teams, such as the Sharks and Ashdowns, met in friendly competition. A. Huddell shot the first possible of the season as he downed 25 straight birds.

E. Sales was the new president of the Calgary Rifle Club which opened its season at the Riverside Range with new rifles. At distances of 800-1,000 yards Alex Martin turned in a respectable 85, which was good considering the wind was so bad that as much as 12 degrees adjustment had to be made on shots.

In the spring of 1910 the Calgary Rifle Club defeated the Okotoks rifle team in Ramsay Shield competition. W. White was the best of the thirty riflemen in the meet, with events that included rapid fire and shooting from a kneeling position.

The local militia camp was held beside the Bow River in June, and the Riverside Ranges were put into daily use by the troops.

The Calgary Gun Club's fourth annual tournament was held in July, with six sweepstakes of 20 targets each. The competitors, who were from many points in Alberta and B.C., paid two dollars to enter each event. Ed Meade, a professional from the Ammunitions Company, shot a fair record of 113 out of 120 birds. Bishop, from Nelson, B.C., hit 61 birds without a miss. In the provincial championship shoot both McLaren and Robinson broke 48 out of 50 birds, then McLaren won his fourth championship in an ensuing shoot off. McLaren also earned the Dr. Gunn's Cup for high average as he broke 249 birds out of 270. Andrews placed second and Robinson third in this category. The team competition, for the Brewery Trophy, was a new event that carried a first place prize of $75.00 in gold. This event was won by Calgary with the Lethbridge team second.

Art Hudel of Calgary won the trap shooting championship of Central Alberta at the competition held in Ponoka. The Calgary competitors were not eligible for the team event which was won by Water Glen. In local Calgary shooting a north team competed against a south team.

R. Bell shot a 95 to lead the Calgary rifle team to a 465 to 447 win over the Elbow River Rifle Club at the latter's range. The score was tied three times before Calgary pulled ahead at the 600 yard butt. Two members of the May family were the best shots for the host club. At the Calgary range S. Ramsay, R. Chamberlain, A. Storrar, A. Martin and R. Fox were weekly spoon winners.

The 1910 Alberta provincial rifle championship matches were held at the Riverside range in August. New targets, which were being brought into use throughout the Dominion, were introduced here. The top half of the six foot targets were painted grey to represent the sky, while the bottom was green to represent the earth. The bullseye contained a khaki coloured shape of a man's head. The bull was twenty inches, inner 32 and the magpie 48 inches; these to count 5, 4, 3, and with any other shot on the target to count two. The tournament started out in good weather, but poor weather set in to make it difficult to shoot as the targets could hardly be seen.

W. Pearce won the first stage of the City of Calgary match as he shot a possible 100. The Calgary Rifle Club team of Pearce, Chamberlain, Martin and Fox was the best of the ten teams entered in the Walker Trophy competition. Lieutenant Young of the Elbow River Club was the winner of the Alberta match. Sergeant Martin won the T.W.A. Freen competition, with Pearce a close second; then Plumbley's team took the Fifth Regiment match. R. Chamberlain topped F. Wright in a shoot off, after they had tied for first place in the City of Calgary competition. In the special D. Black event W. Lundy of Innisfail, shooting under almost impossible conditions, made a possible at 1,000 yards.

The grand aggregate was won by R. Young of the Elbow River Rifle Club. R. Chamberlain finished in second place, followed by C. Krause of Medicine Hat, Corporal Reagan and A. Martin.

At the 1910 Ontario Rifle Association competition in Toronto I. Freeze, who had gone east on his own, and F. Herring of the Alberta team made possibles in the Banker's match. A. Martin had possibles at the first three distances and then, much to his dismay, the wind switched and so did his score.

Martin went on to win a shoot off in the Walker Cup match, earning the trophy and the twenty five dollar first prize. Chamberlain and Wright of Medicine Hat shot in the money in other events. Wright won the Gibson match, running man match and the judging distances competition. Carmichael and Chamberlain were near the top in the grand aggregate. The Alberta team won the City of Toronto and General Lake matches, and they finished in fourth position in the D.R.A. competition. Carmichael finished eighth in individual competition, with his 353 score just five points behind the winner. Martin's 351 put him in seventeenth position, and C. Hodson finished four positions further back. All three Albertans qualified for Canada's Bisley team for the following year.

During the fall the 103rd Regiment held weekly shoots at the Riverside Range. Later the regiment formed a separate rifle club for its members.

Alex Martin won the Watson cup for the grand aggregate at the fall shoot of the Calgary Rifle Club, and as well he took home the Secretary's prize and the Jackson Shield, presented for the rapid fire aggregate. R. Fox won the Strathcona medal and the Club Cup. R. Chamberlain captured the secretary's prize, and R. Bell won the presidents' prize.

During the season the Calgary Rifle Club had successfully defended the Ramsay Cup in competition with the Elbow River, Okotoks, Medicine Hat and Edmonton rifle clubs, and they had won the Innisfail Challenge Cup.

In early 1911 F. Martin, Alex's brother and a former Bisley competitor for Scotland, moved to Calgary. Another new resident of the city was Albert Collard, the 1907-8 Welsh champion marksman.

Mayor Mitchell hit a bullseye on his first shot as he opened the Riverside Rifle Range for the 1911 season. R. Wilson and A. Martin proved to be in top form during the spring shoots. During one May shoot a terrible dust storm took place, and the conditions were so bad that the highest score made during the day was an 80.

On a cold and snowy Victoria Day local marksmen shot in the London Daily Mail Cup competition for eight man teams within the Empire. Ford and Martin both scored centurys as Calgary's team had an average of 95. The previous year the winning Australian team had a 102 average.

There were now A, B, and C classes at the Calgary Gun Club shoots. E. Goodwin, Huddell, Robinson, Dr. Gunn, Andrew and McLaren were spoon winners in the weekly shoots. Unfortunately the fifth annual shoot of the C.G.C. was ruined by rain. Robinson, Andrew and McLaren did well at the Lethbridge skeet shoot, but they were no match for the professionals that had entered the competition. At the All-Canada trapshoot championships held in Winnipeg R. Robinson of Calgary finished second.

At the Bisley competition in England C. Hodson earned a pound for his 99 score in the Duke of Cambridge shoot. Martin scored the highest of the three Calgary competitors in the St. George challenge match.

The 1911 Provincial Rifle Association matches were again held at the Riverside Range. F. Wright, Chamberlain and C. Kraus were individual winners in Sales extra series matches. The Ramsay Cup competition, which saw Calgary outshoot Edmonton 551-548, was held in conjunction with the City of Calgary match. Calgary marksmen Freeze and Chamberlain both made possibles at 200 yards. In the City of Calgary team match Calgary's six man team won by eight points over Edmonton.

Private Francis of the 103rd Regiment shot a score of 186 to take the gold medal and twenty dollar first prize in the prime City of Calgary individual competition. Corporal Reagan of the 101st, was second, followed by Lieutenant Young of the 15th Light Horse and Sergeant Freeze.

At the O.R.A. matches in Toronto Martin, Freeze, Regan and Fox all shot in the money. Private Francis of Calgary won the Duke of Cornwall and York match to take home a silver medallion and $25.00. Carmichael turned in some excellent shooting at the D.R.A. matches at Rockcliffe. Other members of the Alberta Rifle team were: Hodson, A. Chamberlain, L. Thorsen, R. Young, D. McInnes, R. Chamberlain, F. Wright, F. Exham and P. Bowen, with L. Carruthers acting as coach.

Calgary cadets were holding weekly shoots at the Calgary rangs. A. Turner won the Page Medal in a shootout with J. Fraser and J. Schmich. Other cadets who shot high scores were Orley Louden and D. McDougall. Central won the Black Trophy for the team competition, with Haultain second and Riverside School third.

The 103rd Regiment shoot was held in October, and the Ross Rifle was used by all competitors. Private Lumm of C. Company beat Corporal Herrington in a shoot off to win Major Bell's rifle and a silver medal. The Mason Cup competition was for five man teams within the unit. Lieutenant Gilder and Private E. Clarke were newcomers who shot well in the gallery and miniature shoots held during the 1911-12 winter in Calgary.

A large crowd gathered at the Riverside range on Victoria Day to witness the Edmonton rifle team defeat the team of the Calgary Rifle Club in competition. Edmonton's Bisley competitor D. McInnes was the best shot during the meet. In the evening the competitors were entertained at a smoker held in the drill hall.

Alex Martin scored a century in the Canadian Military Rifle League competition held in June. The Calgary ten man team averaged a score of 94 in the competition. Sergeant McRae and Private Smith shot very well in the weekly spoon shoots. The cadets from various Calgary schools were practising weekly at the ranges, which were also in great use during the militia camp in June and the cadet camp in July.

The Armstrong prize, for scores of 100 or over, was won by Martin three times, and W. Pearce, W. Chamberlain, and W. Ford. F. Herring accomplished the feat quite often in practise, but he lacked the concentration in competition.

The Alberta Rifle Association matches were held at the Riverside range in July. Fifteen year old cadet Dalton McWilliams won the nursery, cadet and trio matches, and then he placed sixth in the Alberta match. At the end of the tournament McWilliams was presented with a new rifle which had been subscribed for the by the men in the competition.

Eleven teams were entered in the Walker Trophy competition, with the 19th Dragoons of Edmonton finishing in first place, followed by Medicine Hat, the 103rd Regiment and the Elbow River teams. H. Cavan took the event's individual honours.

In the Alberta match A. Chamberlain of the Didsbury club won first prize and $15.00, followed by W. Simmonds and D. McInnes; the latter also captured the Stokes match. R. Fox, Elliot of Acme and H. Hervey of Elbow were the top marksmen in the City of Edmonton competition. In the prime city of Calgary match, with a first prize of $25.00, F. Martin was first, followed by R. Downie and C. Krauss.

Sergeant Balfour won the grand aggregate with a score of 418, four points ahead of Elbow's F. Young, H. Cavan and Edmonton's McInnes. A. Martin, L. Elliott and R. Martin occupied the next three positions. These men, as well as R. Fox, R. Finlay and A. Carmichael, made up the Alberta rifle team to be entered in the O.R.A. and D.R.A. matches in Ontario.

At Toronto the Calgary cadet rifle team of A. Turner, J. Fraser, O. Louden, D. McWilliams, D. McKenzie and J. Semmick trimmed the crack Toronto shots at the Long Branch rifle meet to win the team match and the Pellant Challenge Trophy. J. Semmick won the O.R.A. individual cadet championships.

In the cadet match at the D.R.A. shoot at Rockcliffe, D. McWilliams earned ten dollars for his third place finish in the grand aggregate, and he also won the secretary's prize for the best shot of any competitor under the age of 15. The Martin brothers were in contention for the Governor General's prize in the senior competition of the D.R.A.

In 1913 the Federal Government gave encouragement to the civilian rifle associations by giving each organization a silver salver to be known as the Dominion of Canada prize, to be shot for in four competitions at 200, 500 and 600 yards with 40% of the club members taking part, and the prize going to that individual with the highest average.

Cadets D. McWilliams and C. Watchorn were two of the five Canadian cadets who represented Canada at the cadet shoot at Bisley, England to compete for the Lord Roberts Trophy. The Calgary cadets had practised throughout the winter on the gallery and miniature ranges. Later in the spring there was a cadet series shoot at the Riverside range with competitors from Collegiate, Hillhurst, Riverside, Connaught, and Haultain schools. Collegiate's D. McKenzie turned in the best score. Riverside won the team competition, and the shield was later presented to them in front of a crowded grandstand at the fair.

In senior shooting D. Spence, A. Martin, E. Sales, I. Freeze, A. McNeil and R. Chamberlain were spoon shot winners. Lieutenant Spence was the top shot in the 103rd rifle competition.

The 103rd Regiment rifle team won the Championship of Canada Cup in the Canadian Rifle League competition, and its B team placed second, Sergeant Jacobs and Lieutenant Spence had scores of 99 in the Canadian Military League competition, while Sergeant Major Ferguson came in with a 95. In the miniature series the regiment won the championship and the Dominion Cartridge Trophy.

The Calgary shooters took 13 special marksmen and seven first class certificates; their total of 20 was three more than any other military group in Canada.

Calgary teams took first and seventh positions in the Canadian Rifle League cadet competition, and in the miniature rifle competition Calgary cadets placed first out of the 16 teams entered. D. McKenzie was the top cadet in the four

Military League matches involving thirty boys, 24 of whom received first class marksman badges. D. McDougall was the individual winner of the Calgary Cadet Canadian Rifle League matches.

The Calgary Gun Club team lost by one point to an Edmonton aggregation in Jackson Cup competition. McLaren, Robinson, Croke, Dowler and Karnupp composed the Calgary team.

The 1913 Calgary gun Club's annual tournament, which included ten events and 45 competitors, was considered to be the most successful skeet shoot ever held in the province. Archie Bishop of Calgary smashed 130 birds to capture the Alberta championship. Tied for second with 129 birds each were F. Morris and B. McLaren. Edmonton won the team competition.

The Alberta Rifle Association provincial competition again took place at the Riverside Range in July. Cadet W. DeMille of Haultain won first place and five dollars in the cadet shoot. Other youths with excellent scores were J. Fraser, J. Comer, J. McKenzie and D. McWilliams.

The Edmonton 19th Dragoon team of Balfour, Regan, McInnes and McDonald won the Walker Challenge Cup. R. Chamberlain of the 103rd Regiment and Balfour both shot a 99 in the D.R.A. silver medal competition. In a shoot out the pair went many extra shots before Chamberlain was a point up and the winner. The Jackson Challenge Shield, competition for which consisted of five shots at 500 yards, was won by R. Downie of the 103rd Regiment. A tricky fishtail wind pulled down scores in this and some of the other events.

Edmontonians E. Francis and R. Downie tied for first place in the Alberta match. In the Playzant match Sergeant Balfour shot a 48, while A. MacNaughten and cadet McWilliams each came in with a 47. F. Herring, S. Ramsay and P. Downey were winners in the Stokes extra series. Balfour finished one point ahead of Chamberlain, with J. Page of Calgary finishing third in the City of Calgary match. C. Young, S. Ramsay and E. Sales finished one-two-three in the Rutherford competition, while Herring took the Martin extra series, and W. Pearce won the Sales extra event.

In the Ramsay Trophy competition the cadet team, led by J. Fraser's 100 score, totalled 553 points to take first place. The Calgary Rifle Club and the Edmonton 19th Dragoons each scored 546 points, and Lethbridge was fourth of the six teams entered in this event.

Sergeant Balfour's score of 449 gave him the grand aggregate. W. Pearce finished three points behind to take the silver, and H. Regan won the bronze. The order of the other top finishers were Brankley, Freeze, McNaughten of Didsbury, Simmond of Medicine Hat, Francis of Edmonton, cadet Louden and Downey.

Cadet D. McWilliams placed first in the cadet shoot in Toronto and sixth of over 500 entries in the All-Comers competition of the O.R.A. at Toronto; and as well posted the highest score of any competitor under the age of 16. The Calgary cadet team won the outdoor series, and they were second in the Pellant competition in Toronto.

At the D.R.A. meet in Ottawa Alberta won the Ottawa Trophy for eight man teams. Alberta 513 total was by far the best of the fifty teams that competed in this event which was shot at 800 and 900 yards. Pearce, Gilker, Martin, Carmichael, Jacobs and Herring were the members of the Alberta team that won the Lansdowne Trophy, given for the highest aggregate scores in five events. Sergeant Martin won a rifle for being the best shooter from Alberta, and in all the team brought eight trophies back to the province.

Sergeant Martin and Corporal McInnes won places on the team that competed against the U.S.A. at Camp Perry for the Palma Trophy. In this event eight of the top twelve places were taken by Canadians. Martin, McInnes and Gilker were chosen for Canada's next Bisley team.

Cadet McWilliams earned a place in the second stage of the Governor General's competition as he shot a 99. He also placed well in both the Ottawa grand aggregate and the Bisley aggregate. Charles Gratz, who was only 14 years old, shot a 98 in the Governor General competition, and he won the secretary's prize for the junior cadet championship of Canada. The Calgary cadets won the Anderson Trophy, and they were only one point out of first place in the Empire Trophy aggregate. All told the cadet team of J. Fraser, J. Schmick, D. McKenzie, O. Louden, W. Baker, D. Asby, C. Gratz, D. McWilliams and J. Comer took home 20 medals and ten trophies from Ontario.

In September a team from the 103rd Regiment went to the Innisfail shoot where Sergeant Richard, who shot a score of 97, led his team to win the meet. The Calgary Rifle Club had won this competition the previous four years. Further militia competition took place on the Riverside range in October.

A gun club was organized at Beiseker during the year.

During the winter of 1913-14 the cadets of Western Canada College used the school's new rifle range for shooting practise. New ranges were also installed at Connaught and Hillhurst Schools. Senior cadets used the Ross 303, while the junior boys fired a Ross 22.

Harvie and Louden finished one-two in individual competition, and the Calgary team finished first in the cadet section of the Canadian Rifle League. Nine of the eleven cadets who were to represent Canada at Bisley were from Calgary, as was Sergeant Major Ferguson, the team coach. Calgary boys W. Baker, O. Louden, C. Henderson, R. Harvie, J. Comer, D. McWilliams, F. Sinclair, W. Cameron and C. Gratz made the trip. Dalton McWilliams shot in championship form at the Bisley meet. Later Alex Martin and D. McInnes travelled to England as part of the Canadian Men's Bisley team.

Freeze won several of the spoon shoots of the Calgary Rifle Club spring shoots. Other high scores were turned in by newcomers E. Gilham, L. Elliott and W. MacKenzie.

In May, "Jacques went crazy", as he hit 49 out of 50 birds in a weekly shoot of the Calgary Gun Club. Other members who turned in high scores were R. Robinson, B. McLaren, Lee Dowler and Alex Martin. The Calgary team travelled out to Gleichen, where they won the team competition with a score of 117 as compared with the home club's 104 and the Cluny team's 102. Ben McLaren hit 179 out of the 200 birds thrown for him. In June veteran shooter Robinson broke 74 out of his first 75 birds and hit 78 straight without a miss. Some of the club members travelled north to Strathcona for its shoot.

4,300 pounds of shells and 36,000 clay birds were used in the 22 events of the 1914 annual shoot of the Calgary Gun Club at their range located near the conjunction of the Bow and Elbow Rivers. Some events allowed for handicaps ranging from 16-21 yards.

Eddie Meade of the Remington Arms Company, was the best of the seven professionals entered in the competition, as he hit 199 out of his 210 birds. H. Pilling of Lethbridge broke 25 straight birds in opening day competition. In Dowley Cup competition, H. Simpson beat out McLaren, who had won this cup the previous year.

H. Crabbs of Edmonton won the provincial championship as he recorded scores of 193 and 195 in the two day event. B. McLaren, R. Robinson, A. Bishop, G. Short of Cornation, P. Bowen and G. Cowderoy of Edmonton all recorded high scores. The F. Lowes, D. Black and H. Motley Cups were new silverware offered in the competition. In a new event Archie Bishop won the Championship of the North West as he hit 96 out of the 100 birds in this competition.

During the cadet camp held in July a cadet was shot in the stomach during a sham battle. Surgery was required to remove the bullet.

There were 150 entries competing for three thousand dollars in prizes in the Provincial Rifle Meet. The range telephones had been overhauled which made for a more efficient meet.

The cadet open event was won by Dalton McWilliams, with D. Campbell a close second. F. Hall, a chinese boy, won the junior championship, but later it was realized that he had used a long rifle, which placed him in the first class, so the junior championship went to D. McGregor of Haultain School. L. Hextal of the C.R.C. won the nursery match.

The Colonel Walker Trophy was won by the Lethbridge quartet, with the 103rd Regiment second and the Calgary Rifle Club third. Corporal P. Lunn of the 103rd took the N. Jackson Challenge Shield and the fifteen dollar first prize for his win in the Alberta match. The 103rd Regiment team outshot Lethbridge and the C.R.C. to win the A.E. Cross Challenge Trophy. Captain Gilker took first place in the Brewery match.

The Sales extra series was won by R. Hutchison, and veteran rifleman Major May of Elbow River and Sergeant Freeze tied for first place in the Stokes match. The Payzant competition went to L. Elliott of the C.R.C., and F. Young of the Elbow River club took first place in the City of Edmonton competition. Tyros matches went to Sergeant Cooper and cadet Louden, while D. Gue of Lethbridge won the Martin extra series. Cadet Dalton MacWilliams won the Rutherford Cup, Major E. May Cup, and he finished fourth in the City of Edmonton match.

Three teams from the 103rd Regiment competed in the four matches of the Canadian Rifle League. Their best ten man team scored 1,009 points to capture the Gooderham Cup and the championship of the Military Rifle League of Canada. Sergeants Jacobs and Chamberlain both shot scores of 103 in the competition.

At the 1914 Bisley shoot Alex Martin tied for the lead in the Stock Exchange competition, but in the shoot off he had to settle for third place. Martin tied with three others for the top Canadian score in the coveted King's prize, and he placed

Group at Gun Club, near the Elbow River, 1890's.

38 in the aggregate of this event as well as tenth in the service rifle aggregate.

The June 28 headline announced that, "Austria declares war". Rifle competition in Calgary soon became less of a sporting event and assumed a more serious military nature. The Canadian School of Musketry was established in Calgary with its base camp first set up at the Exhibition grounds under Colonel R. Helmer. The following year the new Sarcee Camp was the centre of military activities and a rifle range was constructed there.

In the fall of 1914 the Alberta Provincial Trapshooters Association was formed. The Kirkland Trophy, emblematic of the championship of Alberta, was offered for competition. Plans were made to hold the provincial competition in Red Deer the following year.

The cadets of C.C.I. won the Kingston Trophy at the 1914 fall shoot. The following year Calgary cadets took second place in the School of the Empire Shoot, an event entered by thousands of boys in the British Empire. Calgary's 486 score was only one point behind the winning New Zealand team, and again Dalton McWilliams was Calgary's best shot. Sadly though, this fine shooter died two years later from meningitis.

The Alberta trap shooting championships were held in Edmonton in 1916 and 1917, but the event was cancelled in 1918. In 1915 Ben McLaren won the Canadian trapshooting title at Ottawa, where he broke 50 straight birds.

Automobile and Motorcycle Racing

In 1898 many Calgarians got their first sight of an automobile when W. Cochrane, who managed his father's ranch, located west of the city, drove into town in his two seater, steam driven White Steamer. Five years later Billy Cochrane of High River brought in another automobile to the area. In 1904 John Prince, of the Eau Claire Saw Mills, drove his new Rambler on Calgary's streets. During that year motorcycles made their appearance in western Canada.

Automobile races were part of the sports program of the Ex-American celebration, which was held in early July of 1906. Prior to the race day a local paper stated, "A decided novelty will be the automobile race."

In the two mile race for touring cars J. Young led R. White to the tape. The mile race for runabouts was won by J. Hillier, with Stewart Mackid driving home in second place. First and second place money in both events was $10 and $5. The races appeared to attract a great deal of attention.

A few days later Calgary auto owners were indignant at the treatment they had received at the Exhibiton, but the Exhibition Board claimed that the autos frightened the horses. The drivers countered that at Edmonton there was an automobile parade, and auto races were held in front of the grandstand.

The number of automobiles in Calgary did not initially increase at a great rate. In the period 1906-08 only 141 vehicles were registered in Alberta, however registration rose to 275 in 1909 and 423 the following year.

In the fall of 1910 J. Cosgrove of Calgary covered 3,000 miles on the Canadian Reliability route over Western Canada.

During this era Tudhope's Everitt sold in Calgary for $1,450, and the Alberta Garage advertised a Cadillac for $2,450. The McLaughlin-Buick Carriage Company sold models of their automobiles priced from $950-4250, and T. Grasswick sold the 30 horsepower Haynes automobile.

One of the questions asked on a local paper's "Motoring, Local and General" page was concerning why there were not any local tours or races.

Immediately Mr. J. Jackson, who managed the local McLaughlin-Buick agency, and who had previously attempted to establish an auto race track near Calgary, issued an open challenge for an auto race of any distance and on any date. Several days later the challenge was accepted and the thousand dollar deposit was covered by Mr. Hatfield, who selected Mr. Bell to drive for him. The race was to start from the McLaughlin car barns and it covered a 150 mile distance to Lethbridge. The race was scheduled for Christmas Day. Inquiries for a race were also received from Winnipeg. Plans for a free-for-all race to Lethbridge were also under consideration. A race between Jackson and Downey, either over a distance or on the Victoria Park track, was also planned.

However the law was to step in, and Superintendent Deanne said that he would not allow an auto race to be run across the territory within his jurisdiction until the government in Edmonton changed the rules in regards to the speed regulations.

Jackson then claimed that the McLaughlin-Buick was the only car in Calgary that had ever successfully negotiated the Brickman Hill, which he now called the "Buickman Hill." As a result T. Grasswick, who sold the Hayes cars from his garage on Centre Street, challenged Jackson to: a hillclimb, a quarter mile speed race—standing start, quarter mile speed race in intermediate gear, a quarter mile slow race in high gear, and a quarter mile speed race in slow gear. Then to prove he was serious Grasswick drove his Haynes, loaded with passengers, up the steep Brickman Hill, a part of the escarpment north of Riverside.

Calgarians purchased 150 of the 423 automobile permits issued in Alberta in 1910. The following year the ratio was lower as only 243 of the 1,631 permits issued went to Calgary automobile owners. New automobile licenses cost $3.00 each, with renewals at two dollars, while transfer fees were 50¢.

The Diamond Motor Company was selling Maxwell cars, and the Franklin was handled by Calgary's Franklin Car Company. Ads for the Metz Friction Roadster and the Tudhope were run in the local papers. The Russel, Overland, Flanders and the E.M.F. 30 were other makes of automobiles that could be purchased in Calgary in 1910.

By 1911 Calgary's rules of the road were established as: a speed limit of 10 mph. and not more than 5 mph. when approaching an intersection. Bicycles and tricycles had the right-of-way. Automobiles were to pull to the right and allow the bicycle or tricycle to pass. Automobiles were to yield to horse-drawn vehicles at intersections and to those who wished to pass.

In 1911 the Calgary Motor Racing Association, under the mainstay of Don Trotter, held a one mile handicap race on the level boulevard built by the South East Calgary Corporation. The time trials were held against time, rather than racing at the same time as the other entries.

Concerns of the Calgary Automobile Club included the construction of good roads and the creation of a uniform speed limit within the province. Members of the club often held runs to towns or out into the countryside. The trip to Cochrane normally consumed an hour and ten minutes, while a trip to Banff was a major undertaking, which required carrying extra gasoline and oil, spare springs, chain and block, and an axe and lumber to build portable bridges. A newspaper ad of August, 1911 suggests, "Banff by Auto—make up a party, D. Williams phone 2155".

The Calgary Auto Club criticized Mayor Brocklebank for continually breaking the speed limit, but the club executive also complained that Calgary's speed limit was too slow.

A film of the Indianapolis 500 mile auto race was on the program at Calgary's Empress and Lyric Theatres.

At Winnipeg motorcycle races were held in conjunction with a horse race program. Sanquine Brothers were selling Reading Standard and Indian motorcycles in Calgary. Local motorcyclists held runs out into the countryside.

In the summer of 1912 members of the Edmonton Motorcycle Association and the Calgary Motorcycle Club took part in the Edmonton Reliability Test, a run which started from the Edmonton post office, with a route travelling fifty miles up the Athabasca Trail and return. There were seven starters in this competition, which saw Andy West arrive back in eight hours and nineteen minutes. However B. Williams was declared the winner as he had accumulated a greater number of points in the competition. Five and ten mile motorcycle races were held in Edmonton on Dominion Day.

Calgary's automobile enthusiasts became excited when it was announced that Barney Oldfield, one of the world's greatest dirt track drivers and the former world land speed record holder, and his professional driving partners, Lee Heinnemann and 'wild Bill' Fritsch, would race in Calgary. The trio would race on the Victoria Park oval on July 27, at the Edmonton South Side track on July 31, and, as well, race at the Lethbridge Exhibition track.

Barney Oldfield breaking the world's record, August 10, 1912.

Over 10,000 people were in attendance at the speed carnival held at Victoria Park, that included five automobile and three motorcycle heats on the program. The spectators, who were each charged 50¢ admission, were warned to keep away from inside the track fence as that area was considered very dangerous. The drivers were out to break the world record of 1.09 for an unbanked half mile track.

Oldfield drove a 300 horsepower Christie, with a front wheel drive, no transmission or speed gears and a 1-1 ratio. Heinnemann was in a Privee Henry Benz and Fritsch drove a Cino.

The soft track hindered the drivers from going all out. Oldfield won the three mile race in a time of 4.06, finishing a half a car length in front of Heinnemann.

There were three local entries in a five mile challenge race, and Julien, driving a Rocket-Schneider, won in a time of 7.07.5. The third place finisher, who was disqualified for his manner of driving, claimed that he had driven an 1.14 mile on the Exhibition oval a year previous.

Trophies for the motorcycle races were donated by Oldfield and F. Sanguine. Sanguine then proved to be the best of the five entries in a best-of-three heats at a five mile distance, as he posted a best time of 7.01.5.

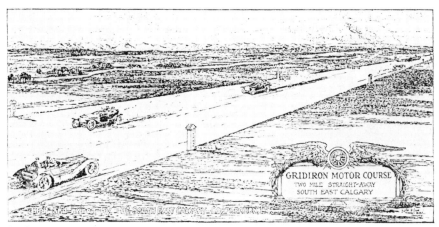

Gridiron Motor Course—southeast of Calgary 1912.

In the evening the Calgary Automobile Club hosted the visiting drivers at a banquet held at the King George Hotel.

The following week Oldfield raced in Regina, where his car went through a mile in 1.08.8.

On the outskirts of Calgary Dan Trotter of the South East Corporation Ltd., a land development firm, spent a reported $15,000 creating an absolutely level two mile straightway on one of their development's boulevards. This stretch of road was named "The Gridiron Speedway". A telegraph signal service, an electrical timing device, was installed in order for the forthcoming races to conform with the rules of the American Automobile Association.

Plans were made for a special train to transport spectators from Calgary out to the race track, but at the last minute the Canadian Pacific Railway cancelled the charter train, using the excuse that the company needed the cars to bring harvesters out from the east. However 4,000 people, many who arrived in the more than 400 automobiles in attendance, still showed up at the Gridiron to see Oldfield break two world speed records and Fritsch a third.

Three time trials were allowed for each event, and times were recorded for the half and mile distances. Cappy Smith, with his megaphone, handled the announcements and informed the crowd of the time recorded.

Oldfield's car went through the mile distance in 41.8 seconds, breaking the old world record of 43.4 seconds, which had been set in Wildwood, New Jersey. A few minutes later Oldfield travelled a half mile in 18.2 seconds, again under the world record, which at that time was a fraction over 19 seconds. Oldfield's time was equal to 99 miles an hour. A third world record, in the class for automobiles with an engine displacement of less than 300 cubic inches, was set by 'Wild Bill' Fritsch, who travelled the posted mile in 48.5 seconds.

The motorcycle races, with events for both single and twin cylinder engines, also provided plenty of excitement. In the auto races for local entries Tom Grasswick came out on top.

The speed trials had exerted an influence on many of the stream of drivers that headed back to Calgary following the meet, and 55 speeders, all of whom had been clocked at travelling at no less than 19 miles an hour, were given a court summons. Oldfield was the slowest driver who had been timed by the police with their stopwatches. The Act at that time set 15 miles per hour as the maximum speed. Later one Calgary man got his $15 fine plus costs back, when it was pointed out that the road used was on the city limits, and as he had been travelling east on the right hand side of the road, he was outside the city limits.

A few days later Calgarians were able to view Oldfield's record breaking performance when films of the race meet were shown at the Empress Theatre. During this era of Calgary's history The Alberta Auto School opened to offer instruction in the repair and maintenance of automobiles.

In 1913 the number of car registrations in Alberta was 3,773, an increase of 1,268 from the previous year. The popularity of motorcycles had risen at an equal rate, and in 1913 both the Calgary and Edmonton Motorcycle Clubs held inaugural race meets. Events covered distances from three to ten miles, tandem races, events for single or twin cylinder machines, or for those with sidecars, competition for private owners or local trade, pursuit and novelty races and a quarter mile slow race.

"In Sparks We Trust" was the slogan of the Calgary Motorcyle Club, which had its own clubroom. George Bain and Charlie Walker, both of whom drove Indian cycles, and Leslie Munro, who owned an Excelsior, went to the races held at the Edmonton Exhibition grounds in October of 1913. Bain earned a first and a second in the seven and ten mile races for twin cylinder-strip stock, open to Alberta entry events. During this era the motorcycle clubs held hill climbs, endurance runs, reliability tests and social runs, with the Calgary club members riding to Red Deer on several occasions.

E. Grandel was returned as president of the Calgary Auto Club in 1913, and Mrs. V. Clarke was elected as the club's secretary. The Calgary Auto Club's first annual race meet took place in 1913, and it included eleven events on the program. Carl Grasswick was the star of the meet, winning the five mile handicap event, a ten mile free-for-all, and the five mile race for the D. Black Cup; the latter event was unofficially recognized as the Alberta championship. Mrs. Carl Grasswick, who took part in the slow race, was the only female participating in the race program.

The same year Bob Burman, who at that time held the world land speed record, set a new world record for one mile on an unbanked half mile track, when he travelled the distance in 1.05.5 on Calgary's Victoria Park track. The crowd in attendance at this record breaking trial were able to witness auto polo, in which the car drivers each used a large mallet in attempting to hit a large ball into their opponent's goal. However the spectators found this sport rather dull when compared to the track races.

E. Clarke was elected president of the Calgary Auto Club at its annual meeting held in March of 1914. The club's vice-president was G. Cavannaugh, and Mrs. V. Clarke remained as secretary.

"News and Views of Auto World" was the name of a weekly special in a local Calgary newspaper. Calgarians read about Barney Oldfield's fifth place finish in the 500 mile Indianapolis race. The Alberta Road Guide, compiled by L. English, was now available to the auto fraternity.

On July 3, over 3,000 people, many who had just arrived in Calgary on special trains, attended the Orangemen's sports day to celebrate the 224th anniversary of the Battle of the Boyne. Included in the sports program were motorcycle races.

A radical change took place in Calgary's Fire Department when its first motorized fire wagon was introduced to the city. Some of the members of the department had fitted a Fiat engine onto a chassis to create the first vehicle that ws legally allowed to race on Calgary's streets.

Mr. Cavannaugh, of the Motor Supply Company, put up a cup for a speed competition involving a run from Calgary to Medicine Hat by way of Lethbridge, and return. Immediately McLeod and Williamson, who handled the Cadillac agency in Calgary, took one of their cars and established a time of 18 hours and 24 minutes for the Calgary-Medicine Hat-Calgary run.

A few days later H. Kerr, driving a Kissel Kar, attempted to beat this time, but near Granum his car hit a culvert and one of his passengers fell to the road, so the rest of the trip was called off.

In late July F. Keeton, of the Keeton Motor Car Company of Brentford, Ontario, arrived in the city and decided to attempt to break the Cavannaugh Cup record. At 3.30 in the morning he and three passengers left Calgary, passing through Lethbridge at 7.45 and arriving in Medicine Hat at 12.49. This was an elapsed time of 9.19 and a running time of seven hours and thirty-three minutes, an average of 33.8 miles per hour. However the car radiator had broke three times during the trip, and Keeton could not make it past Nanton on the return to Calgary. Two blowouts and a puncture also added to his time.

Keeton felt that without the hard luck of the radiator problem he would have broken the record. He quickly got together another car and a crew, with E. Clark doing the majority of the driving. The Keeton 4-35 covered the 518 mile distance in a time of 16 hours and 56 minutes, averaging 21 miles to a gallon, to set a new record and earn the Cavannaugh Cup. At that time the Keeton sold for $1390 f.o.b. Brantford.

The Western Canada All-Star Racing Team, including Miss Lillian Bennett, the only female racing driver in the world, seven fast cars and seven daredevil drivers, appeared in Calgary under the auspicies of the 103rd Calgary Rifles and the Relief Fund of the I.O.D.E., in the summer of 1914. Miss Bennett drove a Regal, while the cars used by the other team members included: an American Underslung, Apperson Jackrabbit, Pope, Russell Rustler, Humber, Stearns Greyhound and a Fantail Special. A dollar admission was perhaps one of the reasons that only a small crowd turned out for the show.

The star of the meet turned out to be local driver George Webber, who drive his small Ford to wins in each of the three events he entered. In one race he won over Miss Bennett, and in the ten mile free-for-all for the Brooks Cup he easily defeated the three American entries. In the five mile, ten lap, event he finished in front of the four other cars in the race.

Motorcycle races were the feature events of the 1914 Labour Day sports program. Leek, driving an Indian, won over four other contestants in a five mile race for twin cylinder seven horsepower machines, and Bert Hill was first in a race for four horsepower single cylinder cycles. Webber drove his Ford in a three mile race against time, finishing the six laps in four minutes and 22 seconds. Following the time trial he issued a challenge to Carl Grasswick, who was the holder of the Black Cup—emblematic of the five mile championship of Alberta. Webber was also aiming at breaking George Bain's track record of 1.04.

The Black Cup competition took place in September, with four competitors entered in the race. Carl Grasswick was driving a McLaughlin, Webber in his Ford, Tom Grasswick with an American Underslung, and Hugh Townsley was behind the wheel of a Ford. Tom Grasswick won the five mile race in a time of 6.52.6, with Townsley in second place and defending champion, Carl, third. Webber, who had put in new pistons prior to the race, finished last. A ten mile free-for-all followed, and Tom and Carl finished one-two. In a five mile race for small cars Townsley energed the winner.

There were three spills in the motorcycle events, which included a slow race. Charlie Walker posted a time of 7.02, the best clocking ever made in Calgary for single cylinder machines over a five mile distance. Leek was the fastest of the seven entries in a race for two cylinder machines.

By 1914 automobile registration in Alberta had increased to 4,728, as compared to 423 in 1910. At least 28 companies were, or had attempted to sell automobiles in Calgary up to that period. At least 84 makes of cars had been seen on Calgary's streets. An attempt had been made to manufacture an automobile in Calgary, when the Toten Motor Car Manufacturing Company was established locally. Gasoline could be purchased at the garages, but many Calgary auto owners maintained their own supply tank on their own property.

Local motorcycle racing received a setback when Scotty Lewis was killed in a race.

Following W.W.I. the professional racing circuits that were held in the province were sanctioned by the International Motor Contest Association.

Billiards and Pool

The game of billiards had its origin in Britain where it was developed as an indoor alternative to lawn bowling.

Following the establishment of Fort Macleod the Fort Macleod Hotel and billiard room was opened by Harry 'old Kanouse' Taylor. Calgary's first billiard table was transported from Fort Benton by oxen, and it was installed in the I.G. Baker post, located near the west bank of the Elbow River.

By 1876 Donald Ross's Edmonton Hotel had three billiard tables. These had been transported across the prairies from Fort Garry at a cost of 10¢ a pound.

These billiard tables often served as beds. An English traveller complained at paying 50¢ a night, but when he was told to pay the billiard rate of 75¢ instead he stopped complaining.

An 1881 Edmonton Hotel advertisement in that community's newspaper read, "... a good game of pool or billiards can be played and a very social evening can be spent in the billiard room."

In 1882 John Ellis took over a building, located west of the Baker post in Calgary, which housed the Benton Saloon. His operation included two billiard tables, a dance hall, restaurant, and as well provided some accommodation. Late in the year the 25 by 68 foot building was refitted with three brass chandeliers and chromo pictures were hung on the walls. Cigar smoke filled the air in the evening, and the men drank their cider or lemonade as they stood around the billiard tables. During the winter Ellis went south in an attempt to cure his sickness, and the establishment was managed by E. Beadois.

The following year Ellis, in partnership with King, purchased the Alberta House—Calgary's first actual hotel, from L. Johnson and ran it in connection with the Far West Billiard Hall. Not long afterwards the bar and billiard operation was sold to Mr. Scott.

In July of 1883 Clark and Beaudwin (Beaduoin) opened up Calgary's second restaurant, saloon and billiard hall located east of the Elbow River. Mr. Clark had served in the Mounted Police for six years, and he served on Calgary's first council.

The Exchange Billiard Hall was opened in 1883 by Keohran and Seabury, on the east side of the Elbow River.

The following February Clark and Beaudwin moved their Castle Mountain Billiard Hall and Saloon to a new 22 by 70 foot building which was located on Stephen Avenue, east of Drinkwater Street. The establishment, which sold cigars, beer and cider, contained two first class billiard tables, while the cabinet organ and wallpaper helped to make it, "the handsomest billiard hall west of Winnipeg."

In March of 1884 McLeod and Ingram opened the Grand Central Hotel, which was located across from the C.P.R. freight warehouse, and included on the premises was a poolroom.

During the summer J. Moulton of the Royal Hotel sponsored a pool and billiard tournament on the hotel's table. The $20 gold piece for the winner of the pool competition went to G. Marsh, while runner up Billy Mitchel took home a revolver. Joe Emmett won the English billiards competition and a $20 gold piece, and finalist Dr. Deveber earned a fishing rod.

During this era Calgary's billiard supplies were ordered from two distributors who were located in Winnipeg.

By 1885 the Exchange Billiard Hall, located on Atlantic Avenue and operated by W. Keohan and G. Seaberry, was catering to Calgary's pool playing fraternity. A bar adjoined the poolroom, and Joe Wyley was the establishment's pianist. Handicaps were established for the frequenters and tournaments were staged. One match that drew a great deal of attention was a $50 a side billiard match between Ed Logan of Banff and E. Conning from New York.

In the fall of 1885 the Athletic Hotel, located on Atlantic Avenue near the train station, was refurnished, and pool and bagatelle tables were added. J. Ingram opened up a three table billiard hall in the building next door to the Lougheed residence.

Another $50 a side game was reported in 1886 when O. Critchley lost to W. Green in a game of English billiards.

By the spring of 1887 T. Peers and W. Fish had established their Turf Billiard Hall in Bannerman's new building located on McTavish Avenue. Pools for the horse races were held at Ogburn's Palace Billiard Hall located on Atlantic Avenue. In 1888 the McNeil Brothers operated the Pullman Hotel and its poolroom. This business, which was located on Stephen Avenue, west of McTavish, was later taken over by J. Cummings. The Alberta Billiard Hall, situated on Stephen Near Osler Street, was run by R. Broderick, and the billiard room at the Royal Hotel was enlarged and more tables were added. Goyette had joined Ingram in the operation of the Pullman Saloon and Billiard Hall.

C.A. Saunders operated the billiard room at the Royal Hotel from 1892 throgh 1898.

Tournaments were held at the various billiard or pool halls, but there was very little mentioin of these activities by the press. The Alberta Hotel held an annual pool handicap tournament. In 1895 there were sixteen entries in this tournament, with Thomas Stone playing from scratch, while some players were allowed up to a 150 point handicap.

The Royal held an English billiard tournament during the summer of 1896, and it was reported that there were 28 entries, with individual handicaps of up to 150 points allowed. Stone and Player were entered at scratch, while low handicaps were given to O. Critchley, McLaws, Nolan and Wing. In the open competition Stone ran up his 300 points, while Ryan, who had a handicap of 150, could manage to sink only 125 points. No further results of this tournament were reported.

By the turn of the century many Alberta towns had a billiard or pool hall. Although this activity was not socially acceptable by many people the pool halls had become a home away from home for many men.

In 1900 Charles Traunweiser, who was later to make a name for himself on Calgary's hotel scene, leased the billiard hall located in the basement of the Alberta hotel, and which operation he ran in conjunction with his shaving parlour. Included on the premises was an American pool table, an American Carom table and an English billiard table.

In 1901 Traunweiser opened up his Hub Cigar Store and Billiard Parlour in the Clarence Block. This business was advertised as, "Calgary's most up to date poolroom." Included on the premises was the new game, Tivoli.

Many Calgarians were entertained by the billiard skills of world champion John Roberts, who appeared at the Opera House in May of 1902.

By 1906, in addition to the Hub and the various billiard rooms located in the hotels, facilities were operated by R. Haskin, G. Hall, E. Hume's King Edward and Alf Fidler's Athletic Poolroom.

The Elks Club held a billiard tournament in 1908, with participants rated from scratch to a 75 handicap. The Empress Poolroom was now open for business in Calgary.

In 1910, besides the Athletic, City, Club, Exchange, Hub, King Edward and Star, poolrooms were operated in Calgary by Ryant and Devrell, Jenkins and Foot, Alma Keyes, Lapointe and Powell, C. Mahaney, Thompson and Soper and Carrie Randall. Two years later there were 21 billiard and poolrooms open in Calgary, and as well there were tables located in social and fraternal clubrooms. The cost of playing pool was generally 10¢ a game or 40-50¢ an hour, depending upon the poolroom. Pool was becoming more acceptable to the general public, and advertisements of the various poolrooms could occasionally be found in the daily newspapers, including an ad which read, "meet me at Casey's Togo Poolroom."

A league at the Waverly Poolroom included five man teams from the Callies, Post Office, City and the Hudson's Bay Company. Ladder and handicap competitions were often held in the city.

Normally Calgary newspapers of that era carried little, if any, news of local billiard or pool games, however this was not the case when American champion Willie Hoppe and English champion Melbourne Inman played a series of games in Calgary as part of a North American tour.

The competition took place in the Paget Hall, located east of the Anglican Church, where a table, borrowed from a nearby billiard hall, had been moved in. The games took place each afternoon and evening over a three day period, and it was reported that, "fair sized crowds were in attendance." Admission to each event was 50¢ or $1.25.

A marvellous exhibition of balkline billiards was given by Hoppe who scored 1000 points compared to Inman's 132. Hoppe, with a best run of 125, won the first block 500-71. Inman took a zero and Hoppe ran up a 92, and so the afternoon competition went. In the evening match Hoppe contributed a break of 137, and then he just took 15 innings to reach 500.

During the following days English billiard competition the tables were turned as Inman scored 1500 points compared to Hoppe's 975. Inman made a sensational break of 159 points off the red ball. After the evening block of 750 points the pair played an exhibition game of snooker.

The same day Jim Corbett, ex-heavyweight champion of the world, defeated Calgarian Tommy Burns, also an ex-world champion, in a hotly contested pool game played at the Commercial Club. Corbett claimed that both Hoppe and Inman were afraid to meet him at the table.

In a 300 balkline game Hoppe won 300 to Inman's 76, however Inman took the English billiards competition 500-136. In the final evening game the English champion had two breaks of 253 and 228, needing only eleven innings to complete the 750 point match.

This competition, which was well covered by the press, provided a great influence for the popularity and acceptance of billiards in Calgary. A daily newspaper of the era reported, "Billiards in this city has even superseded bowling in popularity."

Several months later the Ryle Billiard Parlours, which covered 7,500 square feet of carpeted space, opened in Calgary. The operation included ten English, four American and six pocket billiard tables, all construction of Caucasian walnut and inlaid with ivory. Although most of Calgary's pool and billiard facilities were located in the central part of the city, a pool hall was located in Ogden, where it was frequented by the railroad workers. Pool facilities were also available in Sarcee City, adjacent to the army camp, during World War I.

Badminton

Badminton was played in Calgary as early as 1910 by a few enthusiastic players who organized a club which met to play in the Paget Hall on Saturday afternoons. As only one court could be marked off membership was restricted to 25 players.

S. Wheatley and R. Holman were the pick of the players during that era. Other members of the original group included: H. Savary, Miss Toole, Jack Toole, Mrs. Kensit, Mr. and Mrs. Dudley Smith, Mrs. Wheatley, Mr. Griffin and Mr. L. Gotch.

Following W.W.1 badminton was played at the Ranchmen's Club and at the Armories by the officers of the Lord Strathcona Horse, who organized the Garrison Club. The Garrison Club who also admitted civilians as players, became the largest and strongest badminton group in Alberta. Badminton was also played in church gyms and St. Stephen's Church organized a badminton club. As interest in badminton in the city developed the Calgary Badminton Club was formed, and its membership was successfully able to finance a $15,000 building on Rideau Road. The new club was opened to host the Alberta Badminton Championship in February of 1931.

Fencing

Fencing, using singlesticks and foils, was part of the gym activity at Irvine's Gymnasium in Calgary in 1887. An attempt to form a sports club that was to include fencing in its program occurred in Edmonton in 1892. Two years later fencing exhibits in that city between M. DeRoux and Count Nigrami.

In 1904 the Macleod Amateur Athletic Association held a gymnastics display, and some of its members gave demonstrations in singlestick, foil and quarterstaff combat. In Calgary members of the military, Young Men's Club and the Y.M.C.A. held challenge matches. The master of the Banff Fencing Club in 1909 was reported to have been a world champion in 1897 and 1904.

The sport of fencing in Calgary received a boost in 1911 when Sergeant-Major Page of the Canadian Mounted Rifles travelled to the west coast to take part in fencing competition.

Boating and Canoeing

Boating and canoeing have played an intrigal part in the history of Canada, but this is true only to a lesser extent in southern Alberta.

A canoe, placed on the riverbank by Father Doucette, helped the members of F Troop locate an appropriate place to cross the Bow River near the location of the future Fort Calgary.

Following the location of the Mounted Police at the junction of the Bow and Elbow Rivers John Bunn, who was operating the Hudson's Bay post above the mouth of the Ghost River, decided to move his operation to the area of future Calgary. In September of 1875 he constructed log rafts and floated his building materials and supplies down the Bow River to the new site. Later Mr. Bunn envisaged steamboats carrying supplies up and down the South Saskatchewan River system.

Upon the completion of the railroad line to Calgary trains from the east carried canoes to Calgary, but they were generally shipped to customers in the north country.

One of the first mentions of canoeing in the Calgary newspapers occurred when Mr. Trott of Calgary, Mr. Archibald of Winnipeg and Dave McDougall canoed down the Bow River from Morley, stopping overnight at Cochrane and then arriving at Calgary the next day. What was thought to be a 70 mile trip took the canoeists eleven hours to complete the journey. Later flat bottom boats were used on the Bow River by the log drivers from the Eau Claire Lumber Company.

In the sports field the Victoria Rowing Club was established in 1865, and Winnipeg was a rowing centre by 1895. A rowing machine was part of the equipment placed in George Irvine's Calgary gym in 1887.

On the Queen's Birthday of 1888 single canoe and double scull races were held at Banff. A regatta and trout fly tournament took place at Devils Lake on Dominion Day of 1889.

In 1888 Mr. J. Harper, the proprietory of Half Way House, located near the Mission Bridge south of Calgary, rented boats for use on the Elbow River. The following year a canoe accident on the Elbow caused a death by drowning.

800 people attended a C.P.R. excursion from Calgary to Banff in August of 1900. A canoe race was part of the sports events held for the holidayers.

Elsewhere in Alberta a sailing regatta was held at Buffalo Lake in 1900. In the following years boating clubs were formed at Banff, Wabamum, Seba, Gull Lake and Sylvan Lake. Edmonton had a canoe club, and aquatic clubs were formed at Lethbridge and Chestermere Lake.

In September of 1914 the Edmonton Canoe Club held a regatta at St. Albert that was considered to be emblematic of the championship of Alberta. Included in the events was a ladies' single blade competition. A dozen cups and 40 medals were given out in the competition.

Field Trials

In September of 1891 the Calgary Rod and Gun Club held field trials near Cochrane. Entry fees of a dollar for club members and $2 for non-members were collected by W. Hogg, the club secretary. Judges for the competition were S.W. Trott and H. Lumsden. The meet was considered a success in spite of the fact that the area had been thoroughly shot over by the locals and birds were scarce.

First prize in the all-age stakes, open to all pointers and setters owned in the North West Territories, was $20 and a cup donated by T. Stone. There were 13 entries in the first draw, and by the third draw Ranger was declared the winner. Entered in the competition were the dogs of T. Stone, Hodder, Trott, Arnold, Gouin, McCullough, T. Johnson, Braden, R. Robinson, J. Kelly, W. Hogg, Rickert Elliott, Radcliffe, Fisher and Cowan. The puppy stakes did not fill and the event was called off.

There were further trials in 1892 and 1893, with these events taking place on a hill west of Calgary. In 1893 the prime event of the competition went under the name of the "Alberta Darby". Entry fees were now $5 for club members and ten dollars for non-members.

Mr. Hodder and C. McCaul served in the capacities of club president and secretary.

Game and bird hunting on Sunday was a forbidden practise, and in 1900 several Calgarians were among those charged by the police with this offense.

The Alberta Kennel Club held a bench show as part of the 1906 Inter-Western Fair held in Calgary. There were 46 classes of competition, and the Alex Morriso Medal for the best non-sporting dog in the show went to J. Spooner of Millarville. Competition ws also held at subsequent Calgary fairs.

In February of 1914 the Alberta Kennel Club was promoting field trials for setters, pointers and retrievers. As a result the Calgary Amateur Field Trials Club was formed by Captain E. Clifford, and the organization set up a competition in September.

Events included: puppy stakes, all-age stakes and a shooting dog stake—professional handlers barred. It was hoped that the Lethbridge, Edmonton and Medicine Hat kennel clubs would sponsor meets, and that by the following year a provincial field trial would be held.

Handball

Handball was played in Ireland close to a thousand years ago, and the game was brought to North America by Irish immigrants in the late nineteenth century.

Handball was being played at the Calgary Y.M.C.A. by 1910, when it was reported that there were about twenty players participating in the sport. In the fall of 1910 Tommy Burns, the renowned boxer, played handball against F. Higgs and W. Payne, who were considered Calgary's best players.

The game became in vogue among Calgary's businessmen, and by 1915 more than one hundred players were utilizing the Calgary Y's one outdoor and two indoor courts.

The first local inter-city competition took place at Edmonton in 1918 when C. Peters of that city defeated Calgary's Morton in singles play. In doubles competition G. Robertson teamed with Peters to win from Morton and Richards.

Table Tennis

Table tennis, which also went under the names of ping pong or parlour lawn tennis, became a craze in Calgary during the winter of 1901-02. A ping pong tournament was held in Alexander Hall in January of 1903. Tournaments were also reported to have been held at Macleod, Lethbridge, Edmonton and Fort Saskatchewan during this era. Social and fraternal clubs often incorporated this game into their activities. In 1903 the Calgary Ranchmen's Club reported an income of $84.70 from ping pong.

Horseshoes

Horseshoes were played as early as 150 A.D. by Roman soldiers at their army camps. This game was a natural part of the social and recreational activities of many residents of early Calgary, but the newspapers of that era did not give any reports of competition taking place.

Volleyball

Volleyball was developed as a game by W. Morgan at a Massachusetts Y.M.C.A. in 1895. In 1900 the Physical Directors Society of that organization adopted a standard set of rules for the game.

Volleyball was first reported to have been played in Alberta at the Lethbridge Y.MC.A. in 1912. By the following year there were two volleyball leagues in operation at the Edmonton Y. During the pre-World War One period there was not any mention in the Calgary newspapers of any volleyball being played in that city.

By 1917 the Calgary Y. operated a four team businessmen's volleyball league. In inter-city competition the Calgary Y. won over its Edmonton opponents in a six game home and home series.

Carpetball

Carpetball, an indoor form of lawn bowling, was played in Calgary following the turn of the century. Various fraternal clubs offered play in this activity and on at least one occasion there was an inter-club play. In February of 1905 the A.O.F. team defeated the members of the L.O.L. by eleven points.

The game was played at the I.O.O.F. temple during World War One, and it was reported that an eight team carpetball league operated in Lethbridge during this era.

Lawn Bowling

Lawn bowling became a part of history when in 1588 Sir Francis Drake finished his game of bowls on the Plymouth green before sailing to meet the Spanish Armada.

Lawn bowling was introduced into North America in the Seventeenth Century. A lawn bowling club was formed in Toronto in 1876, and the game was actively played in Winnipeg in 1888. In 1892 the Walker Trophy was offered for lawn bowling competition in Canada. However in spite of the great number of British immigrants who were familiar with this game, lawn bowling was not an activity normally found in Alberta in the nineteenth century, basically because of the lack of suitable grass covered ground.

In the winter of 1792-93 Peter Fidler, the first explorer who made written reports of the Calgary area, wintered in the area of the Livingstone Gap, south-west of the junction of the Bow and Elbow Rivers, that the Indians called "Old Man's bowling green". Here the Indians played simple games which they claimed to have learned long ago from a white man who had come to this area from the south.

Lawn bowling was reported to have been played in Calgary by the year 1904. However in 1906 a local paper reported, "Lawn bowling does not seem to be very popular in Calgary." During this era carpetball, an indoor form of lawn bowling, was played in various halls in Calgary.

Lawn bowling was popular in eastern Canada where competition was held against British bowlers who visited Canada in 1906 and 1910.

In April of 1912 a good number of Calgary citizens attended a meeting, held in the offices of Security Trust, for the purpose of forming a lawn bowling club. On a motion the group agreed to call itself the Calgary Lawn Bowling Club. Dr. F. Smith was elected as the club's first president, with R. Ball and T. Norton as vice-presidents and S. Way as secretary-treasurer. The first task designated by the club members was to find a suitable site for a bowling green.

The club, whose membership now totalled 65 members, reported a good season in 1913. During the summer its bowlers defeated other city teams, including members of the Ranchmen's Club, who now had their own bowling green. Ladies were reported to be part of the local bowling scene during that season. The Calgary Lawn Bowling Club encouraged churches to form teams among their congregates.

It was decided at the club's fall meeting that the temporary greens were unacceptable, so the vegetable garden of Judge Winters, which was located on the corner of Nineteenth Avenue and Fourth Street S.W., was secured for future use. Mr. Major and Judge Winter supervised the construction of the new green.

At the club's annual meeting in April of 1914 T. Heeney was appointed honourary president, Judge Winter was elected club president, vice-president was T. Norton and J. May continued as secretary-treasurer. An executive committee consisting of Waugh, Major, Sinclair, and Postlewaite was appointed from the club's 75 members.

During the 1914 summer lawn bowling was carried out by students at the Normal School, which was located on Fourth Avenue and Sixth Street S.W., and at the Ranchmen's Club. Edmonton had its Highlands Green; the Galt and Empire greens were operating in Lethbridge, and Taber had a bowling green. A challenge was made by Calgary bowlers to meet Edmonton's best in a home and home series for a hundred dollars a game.

The Calgary Lawn Bowling Club held a tournament in August of 1914. The greens were reported to be in excellent shape, but only six of the ten rinks who had entered the tournament did participate. In the finals skip J. May overcame the early lead of J. Norton to capture the silverware. Other skips in the tournament were: J. Smith, J. Macdonald, Judge Winter and W. Waugh.

The war did little to disrupt the growing popularity of law bowling in Calgary as most of the players were over the age of enlistment.

The Calgary Lawn Bowling Club remained at the Mission district location until 1929, and then new greens were established on Sixteenth Avenue South. During the club's early years ladies were allowed to bowl one day a week.

Following W.W.1 the Army and Navy Club operated a bowling green behind their clubhouse, which was located on Seventh Avenue and Second Street West. In 1930 the organization moved its facilities to 328-Fourth Avenue West, where a large bowling green was laid out.

By 1934 the Bowness Valley Bowling Club was in operation on Bowness Road and 17th Street N.W., and the Chinook Lawn Bowling Club operated close to the south bridge of St. George's Island.

Gymnastics

Gymnastics were part of the activities of some of the members of the N.W.M.P. who were stationed at the early Fort Calgary. In 1888 members of the Mounted Police gave a gymnastics display in the Theatre Hall. The same year Sergeant Alfred Taylor, an experienced athlete, fell while practising on the parallel bars and injured his spinal column. He became paralysed as a result and died sometime after as a result of his injury.

The Calgary paper of July 19, 1885 reported that Mr. Symon, ex-deputy sheriff of Edmonton, and Mr. Pagh of Montana intended to open a gym at the Theatre hall. A trapeze, horizontal and parallel bars and dumbells were to be part of the equipment. However the newspapers did not make any further mention of this venture.

In April of 1887 George Irvine, a recent arrival from eastern Canada, leased the roller rink and turned part of it into a gymnasium. A newspaper ad of that era read, "The most complete gym ever opened west of Toronto, including Horizontal Bar, Rowing Machine, Wall Machine, Parallel Bar, Double and Single Trapeze, Double and Single Swinging Rings, Spring Board, Boxing Bag, Hard and Soft Gloves, Indian Clubs and Dumbells, Singlestick, Foils, Running and Walking Shoes, Sparring Boots and all other paraphernalia of a complete athletic institution ... a First Class Bathroom in the building with Hot and Cold Water. Monthly tickets $2.50, Baths Hot and Cold, Tedman's sea salt 50¢. George Irvine manager and proprietor."

The building was also used for roller skating and for boxing matches. It did not take long before Irvine had put together a gym display for the public.

This gymnasium venture was short lived, and the following year the Calgary Theatre Company opened in the "old gymnasium".

A gymnasium display was part of a sports program presented in the Opera House, located on Stephen Avenue, in 1890. The Amateur Athletic Troope's program included barbell routines and exercises on the parallel and long bars.

The Calgary Fire Department's hall, located on McIntyre Avenue (Seventh) soon became the centre of gym activity in Calgary.

In 1891 The Lethbridge Amateur Athletic Club was formed, and many of its members engaged in gymnastics. The following year an attempt was made in Edmonton to form a club for gymnastics, boxing and fencing.

In the Calgary schools gymnastics was carried on in the basement of Central School and at the Dunbow and St. Joseph's Indian Schools. In 1895 the Calgary School Board engaged Sergeant Bagley of the N.W.M.P. to give the boys cadet training, and this was the first organized physical education in Calgary Schools.

In 1899 an article in a Calgary newspaper emphasized the need for a gymnasium in Calgary. The following year the Gym and Merchants Institute was organized. The Eagles and the Nolan Halls saw limited gymnasium use. During this era gym displays were held at Medicine Hat, Edmonton and Macleod.

In 1904 the Calgary schools made provisions to include physical culture classes for female students.

A gymnasium was opened in Central Methodist Church in the summer of 1906. It was reported by the Young Men's Club the following March that over the winter season a hundred gym classes had been held, with a total attendance of 1,792. Individual registration by individuals who used the gym outside of the classes was 2,353. The Y.M.C.A. gave a closing exhibit of apparatus work and basketball drills.

Western Canada College opened its gymnasium in 1907. The 30 by 60 foot structure was fully equipped for gymnastics. During this period R. Barker served in the combined position of drill instructor, truant officer and caretaker at the Central School.

The new Calgary Y.M.C.A. building, located on Ninth Avenue East, opened in June of 1909. Its gymnasium was larger than that of the renowned Montreal Y.M.C.A., and the Calgary gym was said to be one of the best equipped in the Dominion. That fall the Y held a gym meet for the public, and one event that held a great deal of interest for the spectators consisted of boys, carrying Japanese lanterns, creating patterns in the dark.

In 1909 Mr. DeBruyne supervised the St. Mary's Club gymnasium program. A gym located behind the Windsor Hotel was used mainly by the boxing crowd. Gym programs were part of the activities at the Calgary firehalls. The Mirza Golems, an eight member acrobatic team, were part of the program at the Alberta Provincial Exhibition held in Calgary in 1909.

The Y.M.C.A. had become the centre of gymnasium activities in Calgary, and in 1910 more than 100 men and boys participated in a huge gymnasium exhibition held at that institution. Early in the year a death occurred in the Y gymnasium when a man attempted a back flip off the springboard.

In gymastics competition at Western Canada College Harry McKerran scored 96.5 points out of a possible 100 on horizontal and parallel bars, German horse, rope climb and tumbling. Edgar Lougheed, with a score of 90.5, placed second in the competition.

Sergeant Major Ferguson was engaged by the Calgary School Board as a drill and physical education instructor, a position he held until 1944.

In the fall of 1911 the 103rd Regiment held gym classes in their drill hall located on Twelfth Avenue. The hall was well equipped with a ladder, mats, parallel and horizontal bars and a springboard. During the fall the St. Andrew's Church Young Mens Club held a gymnastics display. The church's gym contained ladders, mats and bags. Some gym activity was also carried out at the Paget Hall.

Haultain School won the physical training prize, which had been donated by the Strathcona Trust Company for gym competition in southern Alberta in 1911. Gym classes were held at Mount Royal and Bishop Pinkham Colleges.

In 1912 the springboard at the Y.M.C.A. gym was put to a unique use when it was used as a takeoff of the high jump. Gym classes were now offered at the Y.W.C.A. Eric Weir of Strathcona and Phil Becker from Pincher Creek were the senior and junior gymnastics champions at Western Canada College.

One of the competitors in the 1913 Herald Road Race was R. Verne, who had performed in the gymnastics competition at the Stockholm Olympics in 1912. In Calgary he competed under the colours of the Bank of Commerce Athletic Club. A gym was opened in the barn behind the Elbow View Hotel by members of the boxing fraternity. The 32 members of the Chinese gymnasium class gave a public exhibition. Lloyd Turner announced that the dance hall adjacent to the Sherman Rink would be turned into a gym.

By 1914 it was reported by the local press that the Y.M.C.A. gym was, "taxed beyond capacity."

At the Calgary Industrial Exhibition of 1915, 6,000 soldiers took part in the events that included gymnastics.

Mountain Climbing

The Alpine Club was formed in London, England in 1857, while the American Appalachian Mountain Club was organized in 1878. An alpine club was organized in Canada in 1883, however this group existed only a short time.

Alexander Mackenzie, in 1793, made the first recorded crossing of the Canadian Rockies. David Thompson had travelled in western Alberta in 1787 and 1800, and in 1811 he traversed Athabaska Pass. Ross Cox travelled the same area in 1817 as did George Simpson in 1824. In 1841 Simpson crossed the Rockies by the route which is known today as Simpson Pass.

The first recorded ascent in Canada above the snow line took place in 1827 when Scottish botanist David Douglas climbed Mount Brown. His estimate of 17,000 feet elevation for this peak heightened the mysticism surrounding the Rockies, which at that period of time were called the Stony Mountains.

Reverend Robert Rundle travelled in the Bow Valley in 1841, and Father de Smet crossed over Whiteman's pass in 1845.

The Kananaskis Valley was travelled in 1841 and again in 1854 by James Sinclair, who was guiding settlers bound for the Oregon Territories from Red River. Another group, under the direction of H. Ware and Lieutenant M. Vavasour, crossed Whiteman's Pass on their way to Oregon. Palliser, Hector and Blakiston were others who knew the drugery as well as the grandeur of the Canadian Rockies, and they were responsible for naming some of the mountain peaks. Bourgeau climbed Wind Mountain and Hector led a group up Cascade Mountain.

Much of the early mountaineering in the Canadian west was done by survey crews, either working for the government or the railroad. In 1881 Captain Rogers climbed an unnamed peak above the mountain pass which today bears his name. Castle Mountain, to be later renamed Mount Eisenhower, was scaled in 1884 by A. Coleman, a geologist from the University of Toronto. During this era Dominion botanist John Macoun did considerable scrambling in the Rockies.

With the opening of the Glacier House Hotel by the C.P.R. in 1887 the influx of mountaineers became much greater. In the same year J. McArthur climbed Mount Odaray, the first climb of a Canadian peak with an elevation over 10,000 Feet. Members of the Royal Geographical Society visited the Selkirks in 1888, and two years later representatives of the English and Swiss Alpine Clubs spent some time in the Canadian Rockies. In 1890 Professor Stewart and L. Coleman scaled Mount Brown, then two summers later Walter Wilcox and S. Allen visited various slopes in the Lake Louise area. The year 1895 saw Bill Peyto guide

Robert Barrett and Wilcox to the base of Mount Assiniboine. During this era some of the Calgarians who worked at the Walker or Eau Claire lumber camps in the Kananaskis Valley probably did some exploratory or recreational ridge walking.

The 11,452 foot Mount Athabaska was climbed by J. Norman Collie in 1898. In 1901 Edward Whymper, the conqueror of the Matterhorn, and Sir James Outram visited the Canadian Rockies and completed several first ascents. Among Outram's accomplishments were the initial climbs of Mount Columbia and Mount Assiniboine.

Reverend James Herdman, a native of Nova Scotia, arrived in Alberta in 1885 and for twenty years was the pastor of Knox Church in Calgary. He grew to love the mountains, be it just a walk in the woods or a climb above the timberline. The ice axe he used was made from a pattern furnished to him by a Calgary blacksmith. In 1902 Reverend Herdman and Swiss guide E. Feuz made the first ascent of Mount Macoun. Much of the effort involved in the early years of the Alpine Club of Canada may be credited to this man. Herdman died in 1910, and he was buried in Banff, close to his beloved mountains.

There are many others who have made significant contributions to the Canadian mountaineering scene. Credit is due to botanist Mary Schaffer, surveyor James McEvoy, Hugh Stutfield, Professor Norman Collie, the Vaux family, Professor Charles Fay and Miss Elizabeth Parker. Jim Simpson, C. Thompson, G. Baker, Peter Sarbach, Tom Wilson, Herman Wooley, Christian Bohren are others, each of whom in his own way made a significant contribution to the Canadian Mountaineering scene.

Many Calgarians were treated to the joy and exhilaration of a walk in the mountains when they travelled to Banff or Anthracite on one of the C.P.R. excursion trains that often went to the mountain towns on a statutory or civic holiday.

Professional guides, such as Feuz and Hasler, were brought to Canada by the C.P.R. In 1904 the Banff Springs Hotel advertised, "Swiss guides for mountain climbing and exploration." Shortly after the turn of the century Arthur O. Wheeler, a resident of Calgary and a government surveyor who did most of his work in the mountains, had his article, "Canadians as Mountaineers", published in various Canadian newspapers. His interest in the mountains soon made him a "self appointed public relations man for Canada's mountains".

In 1905 Wheeler and Professor Fay decided to attempt to form a North American alpine club, and an article to push this idea appeared in many Canadian newspapers. By the spring of the following year the proposed club had enlisted 77 interested people. An organizational meeting was held in Winnipeg in March of 1906. The C.P.R. granted a request for 20 railroad passes to assist in the attendance at the meeting.

Arthur Wheeler was elected as the club's first president, with Mrs. Parker as secretary and A. Coleman as vice-president. Calgarians Reverend J. Herdman— of Know Presbyterian Church, the Reverend Dean Paget—of the Pro-Cathedral and Reverend C.W. Gordon, who wrote under the pseudonym of Ralph Connor, were three of the Alpine Club's charter members. The club's primary objective was to, "make Canadians aware of the extent and grandeur of their mountain heritage."

Other original club members from Calgary included: M.P. Bridgland, F.C. Brown, Reverend A. Dunn, T. Hornibrook, Mr. and Mrs. Stan Jones, Reverend A. MacRae—the principal of Western Canada College, H.W. McLean, W. Nicholson, Miss A. Power, C. Rowley, Miss E. Smith and Miss A. Stewart.

Other original members from southern Alberta were: T. Wilson, B. Harmon, S. Baker, E. Barnes, Jim Simpson, Miss I. Griffith and W. Peyto—all from Banff, D. Campbell of Innisfail, L. Coleman of Morley, Reverend Gordon, F. Hyde and G. Harrower from Lethbridge, Mrs. A. Jardine of Stavely, Miss E. Marshall—a resident of Taber, C. Merrill from Stettler and Wetaskwin's G. Neville.

Associate members included Mrs. Pat Burns, Mrs. G. Anderson and Mrs. C. Rowley, all from Calgary.

The club's first annual camp was held in the Yoho Valley in July of 1906. Tents for the camp were borrowed from the Mounted Police units at Calgary and Banff, while the C.P.R. loaned the services of their Swiss guides and provided camp cooks. Representatives of the press were invited to the camp as guests.

Forty-four members, 15 of whom were ladies, made graduate climbs to earn an 'active' status in the club. Successful Calgarians included: Dr. A. Anderson, H. Anderson, A. Ballentine, Miss E. Burnett, A. Crawford, R.E. Edwards, Miss A. Foote, A. Fraser, A. Hart, L. Hoad, J. Lee, Miss E. Leseur, Miss E. Linder, H. Miller, W. Millikan, John McNeil, Miss E. Parslow, Miss M. Patterson, W. Patterson, Miss P. Pearce, J. Percival, C. Reilly, A. Sayre, B. Smith, E. Sutherland, F. Walker, L. Wilson, C. Wright and Mrs. A. Wheeler.

C. Rowley, the manager of the Calgary branch of the Bank of Commerce, joined Wheeler and Swiss guide Peter Kaufman in selecting a campsite in Paradise Valley for the Alpine Club's 1907 camp. The C.P.R. passenger agent in Calgary received instruction to send some of that company's workmen to clear trails and bridge the stream in the valley.

During 1907 A.O. Wheeler and M. Bridgeland served as the club's president and vice-president. Two other Calgarians, S. Mitchell and Stan Jones, held the positions of secretary and advisor.

The 1908 camp was held in the Rogers Pass. A sad tragedy occurred when Miss Helen Hatch from Lethbridge was killed. The accident occurred when Miss Hatch was glissading down a patch of snow with while in the company of a group of Calgarians. Her velocity became too great and she tumbled over a cliff.

Plans for a clubhouse were discussed by the members. Later in the year a letter was received in Calgary, by the club secretary, in which the Department of the Interior offered the water rights at the middle spring in Banff for an annual tax of five dollars.

Mrs. Pat Burns, a keen supporter of the alpine movement, presented the club with a steropticon lantern. During the year Sir Edward Whymper nominated A.O. Wheeler as an honourary member of the English Alpine Club.

By an act of the Alberta Legislative, that was passed in February of 1909, the club was incorporated under the legal name of the Alpine Club of Canada. All the legal work in respect to the passing of this bill was a gift of Stanley Jones of Calgary.

M.P. Bridgeland of Calgary was in charge of the climbs at the club's 1909 summer camp held at Lake O'Hara. A. Wheeler did much of the work in setting up this as well as other camps. Peaks scaled by those attending this camp included: Huber, Stephen, Odaray, Biddle, Hungabee, Ringrose, Glacier, Schaffer and Wiwaxy.

The clubhouse at Banff was now in use. Mrs. Burns contributed a great deal, both in effort and material aid, to help furnish the building.

Calgarians A.O. Wheeler and E. Saunders served as club president and treasurer during the 1910-12 period, during which time S. Jones was the local chairman for Calgary. Wheeler was in charge of climbs at the club's 1910 summer camp, which was held in Consolation Valley.

Mrs. Burns supervised the 1910 camp and Mrs. Wheeler served in a similar capacity at the camp held at Sherbrooke Lake the following year. The 1912 camp was located at Vermillon Pass. During this period the club membership roll contained close to 600 alpine enthusiasts.

Calgary members, under the direction of C. Richardson, established the club's eighth annual camp, which was held at Lake O'Hara. During the same summer another camp ws held at Mount Robson. The 1914 camp ws situated in the upper Yoho Valley.

J. Walker of Calgary served as the club's Honourable Treasurer for the 1914-16 period, and Stanley Jones was the chairman of the Calgary section.

In 1921 Oliver Wheeler was a member of the first Mount Everest expedition. Oliver helped to survey the peak, and he was one of the three climbers who made it to the famous North Col.

Field or Grass Hockey

Various kinds of field hockey have been played for centuries. In Ireland the game was known as hurling, in Wales as banty and in Scotland as shinty or shinny.

R. Nevitt, while stationed at Fort Macleod in 1875, wrote in his diary, "I got up and went out in the bush trying to find a shinny stick, but was unsuccessful."

Field hockey was played in Calgary as early as 1905 under the tutorship of Miss G. Smith, who came to Calgary to open the Bow Valley School. The game was played by the young ladies who were in attendance during the early years of St. Hilda's School.

The first mention of field hockey in Calgary's newspapers occurred in February of 1911, when a letter to the Herald, signed by Bodasko, suggested the local formation of a grass hockey club. However it took some time for this idea to become a reality. In February of 1914 the Calgary Grass Hockey Club was organized. Freddie Lowes served as club president; vice-president was C. Green and G. Hunter was the secretary-treasurer.

The club's first game was described as, "fast and exciting," as Captain Butler's side won 4-0 over Vice-captain F. Lovell's team. Other players in this inaugural game were: Ladler, Melvin, Hunter, C. Ladler, Addis, Francis, Pryce-Jones, Fortescue, Knight, Eccles, Dalrymple, Leach, Herbert, Jones, H. Addis, L. Gotch, Govan, A. Other, Greene and E. Robertson.

The club plans were for games to be played until the warm weather set in. It was hoped that clubs could be formed in Lethbridge, Edmonton and Medicine Hat. By the following year the conditions of war had caused the demise of the club.

Cycling

The walk-a-long, probably the first type of cycle, was invented about 1790. The draisine, which was steered by a bar connected to the front wheel, made its appearance in Germany in 1816. About 1860, Ernest Michaux, a French locksmith attached pedals to the front wheel of his cycle. Cycles that had foot treadles for propulsion became known as velocipedes. The high wheeler, otherwise known as the penny-farthing bicycle had a 50-56 inch front wheel. The safety bicycle made its appearance in 1880, and in 1889 the air-filled rubber bicycle tire was introduced. The first recorded bicycle race occurred in 1883, although it is probable that impromptu races had taken place before that date.

The Montreal Bicycle Club and the Halifax Velocipede Club were formed in 1876. The Canadian Wheelmen held a meet as early as 1882. The Winnipeg Bicycle Club, the first such organization in the Canadian west, was organized in 1883..Safety bicycles with 28 inch wheels equipped with chain drive were being used in Canada by the late 1880's, but they were still not as fast as the high wheel machine. By 1888 the Canadian Wheelmen's was well organized.

A half mile cycle race, with a 50¢ entry fee, was held as part of the Calgary 1886 Dominion Day sports program. J. Harper won the race and the five dollar first prize, with G. Kinnisten in second place. It was reported that the cyclists were slowed by the adverse wind.

Rankin and Allan's dry good store appeared to be the first Calgary firm that sold bicycles.

Bicycle racing competition was held on Dominion Day of 1887, with Harper, W. Clarke and Rankin taking the first three places in the race.

Bicycle races, for what was to be the championships of the North West Territories, were held at Owen's riverside track in Elbow Park in the summer of 1888. A gold watch went to the winner of two out of the three one mile heats.

The following year the Calgary Amateur Athletic Association laid out a track for running and cycling on a plot of land located south of the tracks and east of Drinkwater Street.

In early June of 1892, fourteen local cycle enthusiasts met in the offices of Bourchier and Gouins and formed the Calgary Bicycle Club. E. Rogers was elected club president, and T. Stone was awarded the position of honourary president. R. Arnold was chosen as the team captain, while other club officers included first and second lieutenants, a bearer and a bugle master. Club members wore bicycle uniforms when they made weekly runs. Weekly meets were held on

Tuesday evenings at the Calgary Amateur Athletic Association grounds. Because of the relative high cost of purchasing a bicycle, the club appeared to be exclusive to many Calgarians.

The Calgary Bicycle Club's 1893 organizational meeting ws held in Messrs. Lougheed and McCarter's offices in April, when W. Wing was elected to the club presidency. A race meet was set up for fair week, and invitations to participate in the competition were sent to various points between Winnipeg and the west coast. The club accepted fifteen new members, which now gave the organization a total of 38 active and associate members.

During Fair Week the club cycle races were held in a program that included horse races and track and field. There were six entries in the five mile cycle race, but one competitor did not start as his bicycle had been tampered with before the race. Kerr dropped out at the mile mark, and then Wing went on to beat King by fifty yards in a time of 16.41. Five of the six riders received 30-75 yard advantages in the one mile handicap cycle race, while winner Wrigley of Lethbridge, whose time was 2.56, started from scratch. King, who received a 30 yard handicap, finished second, much to the dismay of his Calgary fans. In an exciting two mile race King, in a time of 6.29, finished just ahead of Wing, Freeman and young. Godenrath, McNamara and O'Brien were the first three finishers in the quarter mile race for green riders.

In 1893 the Lethbridge Chinooks Cycle Club associated with the Canadian Wheelmen's Association. The club held what was called the Territorial cycle championships as part of the Lethbridge Turf Club and Athletic Association meet, but there were not any participants from outside of Lethbridge.

Medicine Hat organized a cycle club in 1894, and the club members constructed a fenced cycle track with a cinder surface. Calgary, Winnipeg, Regina and Lethbridge cyclists participated in the Medicine Hat meet that was reported to have three hundred dollars in prizes. Medicine Hat cyclists participated in races in Calgary and Lethbridge during the season.

Cycle races were part of the Calgary 1894 Dominion Day sports program, and Wingley and Freeman from Lethbridge won all nine of the races in the program. Wrigley won the district one mile championship with a time of 2.53. A slow cycle race, in which Kerr outlasted Vincent, was part of the polo club gymkhana at the Owen's race track in Elbow Park. Some of Calgary's cyclists competed in meets in Medicine Hat and Fort Macleod. In July a group of Calgary wheelers took their bicycles on the train to Banff, where they spent the weekend riding on the roads and trails in the area.

By 1895 the Medicine Hat half mile oval had been banked to include a six foot rise on the turns and a three foot rise on the stretch portions of the thirty foot wide track.

Mr. Allan was elected president of the Calgary Wheel Association, and Mr. Godenrath assumed the secretarial duties of the club. Club membership fees were reduced to a dollar in order to encourage more cyclists to join the club which had been predominantly an organization of men in managerial or professional positions. All lady cyclists in the community were considered honourary members of the Calgary Bicycle Club. In April the Cyclists Ball was held at the Hull Opera

House with 75 couples in attendance at this gala affair. Following a late supper, dancing began at 10:00 p.m. and lasted until 3:00 in the morning.

Club runs, with upwards of twenty members participating, were held weekly with the trips beginning from the Alberta Hotel. Two such favourite routes were up the Edmonton Trail to the Knee Hill Road, or south to Fish Creek and back to Calgary. Mr. Childs laid out a third of a mile cycle track at the Exhibition Grounds.

Members of the C.W.C. entertained Mr. Pope of the Regina Wanderers Cycle Club, who was in town to promote the N.W.T. cycle championships to be held in Regina, at a dinner at the Bodega Restaurant. Club officials were informed that anyone who worked for a firm dealing in cycles or anyone who uses a cycle in his employment must ride in class B rather than class A.

Cycle competition was held at the improved track in Medicine Hat's Bicycle Park on the Queen's birthday. A. Fenton won the half mile handicap from fifty yards in a time of 1.15, and the one mile handicap from scratch in 3.04. The quarter mile handicap from scratch went to E. Chudleigh.

Calgary's 1895 Dominion Day sports included a half mile obstacle cycle race with E. Vincent earning the five dollar first place prize, while C. Carroll collected three dollars for second place. A hundred yard slow race, where the last rider is the winner, was won by H. Brett.

E. Vincent was the Calgary agent for the Centaur Bicycle Company and the American Rambler, with prices ranging between $100-$125. Thompson Brothers sold Raleigh and Quintons, while Linton Brothers represented the Bratford Cycle Company, whose bikes retailed at prices up to $140.

The Molson's Bank offered to supply all their managers and clerks with bicycles at reduced rates.

Calgarian Ernie King left Calgary at 6:45 a.m. to ride his bike to Fort Macleod, where he arrived at 6:15 p.m. The next day he rode back to Calgary.

In 1896 the Queen's birthday was celebrated in Calgary by holding the Caledonian games. There were plans for a number of cycle events, but because of the poor condition of the track, entries were scarce, and as well, the event had not been a sanctioned meet, so fun races were held instead. There were eight starters in the hundred yard slow race, but they all fell off except E. King and Bert McIntyre. In the 300 yard run and ride event there were three pairs entered, and Ellwood and Birnie came out the winners.

B. McIntyre finished first and J. McLean second in a half mile cycle race held as part of a Dominion Day sports program at the C.A.A.A. grounds.

In a cycle event, held as part of the Calgary Polo Club gymkhana, the conditions were to ride around a flag to the judges stand, where each competitor was to take a bite of an apple hanging from a string without the rider taking his hands off the bike handles, then ride back around the flag to the finish.

Another cycle race was held as a hospital benefit event. Ladies were starting to take an active part in local cycle functions. The local club held a run out to Pine Creek south of Calgary.

R. O'Sullivan was elected president of the Calgary Bicycle Club in 1897.

Membership fees were a dollar for men and 50¢ annually for women, and club members were allowed to practice on the C.A.A.A. track. A great effort was made to increase the club's membership in anticipation of holding the territorial cycle championships in Calgary in late summer. The local paper published articles aimed at helping its readers to improve their bike riding skills.

A half mile boy's cycle race was won by McCarthy in a time of one minute and 27 seconds, with Ross second, at the 1897 Dominion Day sports program. McIntyre, in a time of 2.52, edged McCarthy in the one mile lap race. F. McCarthy finished in front of P. McCarthy, who had a 40 yard handicap, in the one mile handicap race. A one mile green cycle race went to M. Ross with F. Higgs placing second.

Smythes Cycle Repair, located across from the English Church, offered wheels for sale or hire. Bike rental varied from 25¢ an hour to 50¢ for a weekend. E. Vincent's Cycle Emporium was offering Centaur, Crescents, Hislop and Cleveland makes. At this period in Calgary's history, there were about 120 bicycles in use in the city. This does not appear to be a great number of machines, but the price of purchasing a bicycle would take several months of the average worker's wages.

The crowd, who had been charged 25¢ a person, were not thrilled by a dull match cycle race in which McIntyre defeated Thompson in a mile event staged at the C.A.A.A. ground. The next week their positions were reversed as Thompson won in a time of 2.36. In a mile race for green riders Norm Luxton won in a time of 2.48.

The North West Territorial bicycle championships, under the auspicies of the Canadian Wheelmen's Association, took place at the Calgary A.A.A. track in early September of 1897. The mayor declared that the two afternoons of cycle competition be civic holidays. The Fire Brigade band entertained a large and gay concourse of spectators, each of whom had paid 50¢ admission to the competition.

There were four local entries and F. Carey of Canmore in the novice mile event. W. Riley won the race in a time of 2.38, but three of the riders were involved in a ground spill, and later they lodged a protest against the winner. Of the six pre-entries in the mile championship race four faced the starter—Fred McCarthy, B. McIntyre, T. Reid of Maple Creek and Fred Pringle of Regina. Reid led for the first three laps, but he folded in the stretch and Pringle won in a time of 2.33, with McIntyre placing second. In the open half mile event McCarthy set the pace, then went on to win the event. There were five starters in the one mile three minute class, and J. McLean, in a time of 2.35, edged out F. Higgs for first place. Seven of the ten entries started the mile handicap race, and McLean, with a 20 yard handicap, finished first with Riley in second place.

There were just two starters in the boys' age 16 and under race, and P. McCarthy led all the way until P. Carey of Canmore passed him just before the finish line. Ramsay and head finished one-two in the club event, in which there were handicaps up to a hundred yards. McLean and Riley, in a time of 2.37 beat out Ramsey and Winn in the mile tandem bike race.

Besides cycle competition the days' program included running races for both whites and Indians. S. McNamara was the chief referee for the program, and E. Vincent and R. O'Sullivan handled the race starts.

There were four entries in the quarter mile with flying start race, the first event on the second day's program. McIntyre got the pole position and he kept it to go on to win the event in 33.6 seconds. In the Territorial half mile championship McNeil of Canmore put on a great spurt near the finish, and he passed the rest of the competitors to win in a time of 1.14. However two of the riders fell, then they lodged a protest, saying he had knocked them down as he passed on the inside. Later the protests were withdrawn. Ramsay was the winner of the lap race in which the first three laps were worth three points each and the final lap four points.

The mile open event resulted in a tie between McCarthy and McNeil. The judges ordered the race to be rerun, but McNeil refused, saying the outcome could be settled by the flip of a coin. The judges refused to award first and second prizes, but the matter was settled amicably between the two riders, which was the normally accepted procedure under the Canadian Wheelmen's Association guidelines. The team race was called off when McNeil, who had been slightly injured, could not participate.

In the five mile championship, the longest race of the program, the event went well until the twelfth lap when McLean and Higgs got tangled in a spill. McIntyre won in a time of 16.48, with Reid a close second and Ramsay third. The two day meet proved to be a fitting way for Calgarians to celebrate the Queen's Diamond Jubilee.

Members of the Calgary Bicycle Club met in Dr. O'Sullivan's office in the spring of 1898 and elected E. Vincent to the office of club president. Norm Luxton took on the new position of statistical secretary, while other club positions included patrons, honourary president and vice president, field captain and bugler.

Neilson's Furniture carried lines of bicycles including: Gendrons, Crescents, Welland Vales and Cleveland, with prices ranging from fifty to ninety dollars. A Vancouver firm advertised Duke and Duchess bicycles in the local paper, and other makes sold locally included Columbia chainless and chain, Victor Ordinary and Road Runner. A cycle wagon, which consisted of a tricycle with an attached wagon, was advertised locally. A.J. Smythe sold the E and D bicycle, "the only winning wheel in the city," and he also advertised, "the largest stock of cycle accessories in the Territories." The Calgary Hardware store advertised ladies' bicycles, including the New Era, for $35, and the $50 Atlas and the Chinook for $60. Ramsay was the local agent for Red Bird bicycles. Thorton's bike repair shop filled a local service need. During the winter a sleigh runner to replace the front wheel on a bike was advertised.

By 1898 the cycle track had been banked at the corners. The city fathers were very concerned about the cyclists who used the sidewalks, and they were considering appointing a "catcher of bicycle sidewalk riders."

Cycle racing was part of the Fire Brigade sports program held on the Queen's birthday in May of 1898. There were many decorated bicycles in the parade that preceded the afternoon events. I. Foss, followed by J. McIntyre, won the novice mile in a time of 3.40. The open half mile event was taken by F. McCarthy in a time of 1.18.5, with W. Blithe in second spot. J. McLean's winning time in the firemen's one mile handicap race was 2.57.5, with Meldrum a close second.

The three mile handicap race was won from scratch by J. McLean, and F. McCarthy, with a 25 yard handicap, finished second. McLean was the winner of the slow race after all of the other competitors fell off their wheels.

More than 250 spectators, who had been charged 15¢ single or 25¢ per couple, were not impressed with the June Cycle Races held at the C.A.A.A. grounds. F. McCarthy and J. McLean finished one-two in the half mile open event. Winn and McLean finished in a dead heat in a very good time of 2.25 in the one mile open event. The potato race, a new event on the local scene, was won by W. Blythe. The club hoped to hold similar races every second Thursday.

Cycle races were part of the Edmonton Dominion Day program. E. Winn won the novice race, while top places in the quarter mile heats went to Winn, McLean and Griesbach. Calgarians McCarthy, McLean and Winn finished one-two-three in the open half mile, and McCarthy, Winn and Ramsay were the top finishers in the open mile. In spite of the many individual Calgary winners, the Edmonton team won over Calgary in the team race.

The Canadian Wheelmen's Association championships were held in Winnipeg in late August, with competition for both amateurs and professionals. Most of the winners were from the Toronto area. The Territorial championships had originally been scheduled for Calgary in late August, but to avoid conflict with the national meet, the local event was postponed until September.

Competitors from Medicine Hat, Winnipeg and Canmore, as well as many Calgarians, were entered in the Territorial cycle championships. There were many entries from Edmonton, but none of them showed up for the competition. Prior to the races, a parade was held from the Alberta Hotel to the C.A.A.A. grounds.

The first race on the program, the one mile novice, was won by E. Douglas of Medicine Hat. Calgary's Joe Elwood had been leading Douglas by fifty yards, but he lost a wheel from his bike. The Territorial half mile championshp was won by W. Reilly in a very good time of 1.15.5, with B. McIntyre finishing in second spot. A 220 yard foot race was included in the afternoon's program, and Dr. O'Sullivan was the winner in a time of 24 seconds flat. S. Hayward of Winnipeg and Ramsay finished one-two in the mile 2.40 class competition. In the two mile handicap race, Ramsay and Foss led the way across the finish line. W. Riley rode a spectacular race in the quarter mile sprint as he rode on the outside right around the curve and went on to win in a good time of 35 seconds. The pursuit race was a new event for the Calgary track. Six miles were covered before all but Ramsay and Foss had been passed, and then another lap was ridden before Ramsay was declared the winner. A novelty event was the quarter mile fat man's race.

On the second day of the competition, Ramsay captured the Territorial mile championship in a time of 2.32. In the mile open event with a 2.40 time limit,

Ramsay again was a winner, but the judges would not allow the validity of the race as his time was too slow. The race was re-run and Hayward, in a time of 2.36, finished ahead of Ramsay.

A pole vault event and a 75 yard dash were included in the second day's program, and Dr. O'Sullivan won the sprint race for the second time. Eight riders started in the Territorial five mile championship race, but on the last quarter Medicine Hat's McIntyre came to grief, and seconds later Elwood followed suit, which caused a pile up of the four following riders. Ramsay and Cavannaugh were left to fight it out and Ramsay, whose time was to be 14.59, won out in the last two hundred yards. In the three mile team race, Calgary won with twelve points to Medicine Hat's nine. The meet's top performer was W. Riley of Calgary who finished first in three races. Following the second day of competition, the Calgary Bicycle Club sponsored an evening of entertainment at the Opera House.

Cycle races were part of the 1898 Calgary Polo Club gymkhana. J. McLean rode home first in the cycle egg and spoon race, and W. Riley and N. Luxton finished one-two in the cycle custom race.

The rains came in the afternoon to ruin what could have been a very successful Fire Brigade sports day on the Queen's birthday in 1899. Postponed races were held later in the month. Lou Kerr and Willie Clarke were the top competitors in the boys under 15 half mile cycle races. J. Foss, in a time of 2.55, edged W. Law in the mile race for novices. In the prime one mile open event F. McCarthy finished first and Ing Foss second. E. Allen rode home first in a quarter mile for boys under 14, and H. Turner edged S. Lee in the boys under 16 mile in a time of 3.22.

Bicycle prices were lower than in the past. The Calgary Furniture Store advertised bargain bicycles as low as $22, and as well the firm sold the Welland and Vale bicycles. About the turn of the century several Canadian bicycle manufacturers joined together to form the Canadian Cycle and Motor Company, commonly called C.C.M.

May 24 of 1900 was a "Red Letter Day," in Calgary's history as the Fire Brigade sports day provided exciting competition in track, field and cycling, including a ladies' quarter mile bicycle race. Elwin Allen, in a time of 1.38.5, finished ahead of B. Wanless in the boys' 14 and under half mile cycle race. G. Bennett and P. McCarthy were the first two finishers in the one mile novice race, then F. McCarthy beat G. Bennett in the half mile open race. In the three mile open cycle race Woodside, in a time of 10.11, finished first and Blanchard placed second. The tandem race proved a novelty for the huge crowd of spectators.

The Calgary Wheelers sponsored a race from the Alberta Hotel to Fish Creek and back to the hotel. G. Bennett was the winner taking one hour and twelve minutes to make the return trip.

At the InterWestern Pacific Exhibition held in Calgary in September of 1900 a bicycle obstacle race was part of the gymkhana events. The contestants had to ride to a table while smoking a lighted cigar, open a bottle of soda pop, pour it into a tumbler and drink it, then ride back to the start. Brae and Allen were the best contestants in this fun event.

In May of 1901 a handsome trophy, donated by the Canadian Cycle Motor

Company, was on display in the front window of Fred Higgs' store. It was to be presented to the rider who earned the most points in six Handicap races. However the trophy was never awarded as local cycle competition was on the wain and not enough races were held to warrant the presentation.

Cycle races were held as part of the Fire Brigade May 24 sports program. Crawford won the one mile novice race in a time of 2.53, with Trueman finishing in second place. E. Allen and B. Wanless finished one-two in the half mile event for boys 14 and under. When Bennett quit half way through the open mile race Large was the only competitor left in the event. However Bennett came back and beat Large in the three mile event in a very good time of nine minutes and four seconds.

Fred Higgs, secretary of the Calgary Bicycle Club, announced that twenty different firms and individuals had donated prize money for the club's second handicap road race to Fish Creek and return. The event's entry fee was 25¢, and a competitor had to be on the role of the Canadian Wheel Association. The race had to be postponed several times due to the muddy condition of the roads from an over-abundance of rain. G. Bennett, who had a five minute handicap, was the winner of the race with a net time of 72 minutes. This gave him a ten dollar first place prize and a ten dollar best time prize. D. Dodd finished second, W. Bates was third and J. Branston, riding from scratch, finished fourth. Seven riders finished the race, while four other competitors had to quit due to punctures or a lost wheel.

During the summer a bicycle gymkhana was held at the Bow Bend residence of William Pearce. Ten couples participated in the various cycle events. Calgary's female cyclists tended to wear long skirts while riding, although in many parts of North America bloomer pants were the rage.

Decorated bicycles were often part of the celebration parades in early Calgary. In the 1902 Coronation Parade, W. Hossack earned the red ribbon for the best decorated cycle in the procession. Cycle races were part of the Coronation Day sports program. J. Crask edged J. Taylor in the open half mile in a time of 1.36.6. Oron Adair won the novice mile, the open mile in 2.46.5, and then he beat the favourite G. Bennett in the open three mile event. A. Allen was second in the other two races. Adair also won the mile cycle race at the Labour Day sports meet.

Adair captured the mile and three mile cycle events at the 1902 Empire Day sports competition before a crowd in excess of 3,000 spectators. No further cycle competition took place at either the Calgary Fair or the Labour Day program until 1906 when G. Biery and Stoodley finished one-two in a mile cycle race that was a minor event on the Labour Day program.

In 1903 City Council members debated a proposed by-law that would require cyclists to carry lanterns at night and for the bikes to have signal bells to be rung before a turn was made.

Bicycles were not appreciated by all early Calgarians, and cyclists were often referred to as "demons on wheels." A September, 1904 local paper reported, "Some wheelmen seem to forget that six mile an hour is the speed limit. Frequently bicyclists are seen on Stephen Avenue going ten to fifteen miles an hour."

During the same month the press reported that a collision occurred when a young girl walked out in front of a cyclist and they both fell to the ground.

Cycle races were part of the Calgary Bluenose sports day held at Victoria Park in June of 1907.

A cycle race, to precede the Herald Road Race and over the same route used by the runners, was to be held in April of 1908. However the race was postponed due to poor road conditions.

Cycle races were part of the May 24, 1908 sports program staged on the new half mile track at the Exhibition Grounds. However the track was very heavy and the mud, combined with the tracks left by the horses did not make for a favourable track for the cyclists. J. Sutherland, followed by E. Jeffries and Berry, won the quarter mile cycle sprint. Sutherland then won the mile in a time of 3.02, with Spence 50 yards back. A five mile race had been planned, but due to the conditions of the track it was called off.

Cycle races were held before crowds of as many as 10,000 spectators at the 1908 Calgary Fair. George Beer, in a time of 37.5 seconds, led George Sutherland and Ed Jeffries to the tape in the quarter mile cycle sprint. There were four starters in the three mile cycle race. Jeffries led until the last lap, then Spence passed him, but Sutherland passed them both to win the race.

A two mile cycle race was held as part of the Labour Day sports program, and Ed Jeffries came out the winner. W. Mann finished last to take first place in the 220 yard slow bike race.

A ten mile cycle race was held in Banff under the auspicies of the Banff Fire Department. The race went from the Alberta Hotel to the Bankhead post office and back to the start. It looked like an easy win for Patreqin, but he took a bad spill as he turned a corner fifty feet from the finish line. Before he could remount, F. Ritchie passed him and rode home the winner. J. Stanley finished third.

Breen and Barnes operated a bicycle repair shop in Calgary in 1908. The Star Cycle Company and Alex Martin's sporting goods store both retailed bicycles.

A twelve mile bicycle race was planned for Dominion Day of 1909. The race was to start and end at Victoria Park and the cyclists would cover the Herald Road Race circuit twice. The event was under the auspicies of the Calgary bicycle dealers, and anyone whose bike was equipped with a new departure coaster brake was qualified to enter. However the race was postponed indefinitely because of the poor condition of Calgary's roads due to the wet weather. There were not any cycle races held as part of the Labour Day A.A.A.A. sports program at St. George's Island. Bicycle races were part of a Public School track and field program in Calgary in the fall of 1909.

George Sutherland, in a time of 16.52, was the winner of a five mile cycle race held in the city in 1910. J. Phillips was first in a one mile race held the same year.

By 1911 local sports organizers had felt that bicycle races had gone out of fashion, but when plans were made for a Labour Day three mile cycle race five entries were received. In this race Sullivan took the lead from the start and maintained it throughout the distance to win the event with little effort. Following the leader were McSpadden, Shaw and Broad.

Dick Corless and Bob Cunliffe, two of Calgary's cyclists, both won honours at the 1912 Medicine Hat Labour Day sports program. Corless won the half mile event in an excellent time of 1.14, and Cuncliffe was the winner of the five mile race. Both riders had won cycling honours in England, and they were quite willing to meet any Canadian cyclists in competition.

During the summer races for green riders and match races were informally held in Calgary.

A cycle race was held at Red Deer on Dominion Day of 1913. In Calgary motorcycle, but not bicycle races, were part of the Labour Day program. A half mile bicycle race was held at Victoria park on October 10. Miller, in a time of 1.26, was the winner, and the next two places went to Shipps and Linton.

New cycle dealers in Calgary included the Calgary Novelty Works, W. Compton's Premier Agency, Winnipeg Cycle Works and Northern Motor Supplies.

Local cyclists helped to publicize the Canadian bike week that was organized in 1916. The same year, and on four occasions after that, Norm Webster of Stavely won the Dunlop Road Race. In 1920 he represented Canada in cycle events at the Olympics.

Ski jump erected on the top of the grandstand at Victoria Park 1922.

Annual
Polo Tournament

25th to 27th August

On the Polo Grounds north of
the Bow River

1897

Gymkhana . .

Saturday, Aug. 28th

On the Elbow Park Race Track

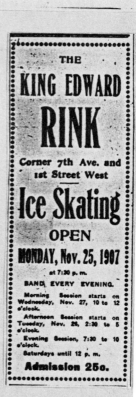

398

Date Due

JUI 2 7 2004		